Richard Edmund Tyrwhitt

Esther and Ahasuerus

An Identification of the Persons so Named, Followed by a History ....

Richard Edmund Tyrwhitt

Esther and Ahasuerus

An Identification of the Persons so Named, Followed by a History ....

ISBN/EAN: 9783337203962

Printed in Europe, USA, Canada, Australia, Japan

Cover: Foto ©ninafisch / pixelio.de

More available books at **www.hansebooks.com**

ESTHER AND AHASUERUS:

AN IDENTIFICATION OF THE PERSONS SO NAMED.

FOLLOWED BY

A HISTORY OF THE THIRTY-FIVE YEARS THAT ENDED AT THEIR MARRIAGE.

WITH NOTES AND AN INDEX TO THE TWO PARTS; ALSO AN APPENDIX.

BY

RICHARD EDMUND TYRWHITT, M.A.,
RETIRED INDIA CHAPLAIN.

IN TWO HALF-VOLUMES.
HALF-VOLUME II.

Oxford and London:
JAMES PARKER AND CO.
1868.

PART II.

CHAPTER III.

I.

RETURN we now to the story of which we have undertaken both to collect the remains, and to set each fragment as near as possible to where its place should be in a complete record. We left Darius in Media, probably at Agbatana, newly seated on a dangerous throne, which the pretended younger brother of Cambyses had occupied for not eight full months. The year was the five hundred and twenty-first before our era, as Ptolemy's Canon attests; but the time of year was some ten months later than at first we supposed; for, interpreted now by the lately-recovered Calendar of Assyrian months, to which it tacitly refers us, Darius's own account shews that the season was about the first month of winter, or the November of the year in which (by slaying the Magian) he ended an usurpation that had lasted since the end of March or the beginning of the preceding hot weather. A little before the usurpation, within the same year, Darius probably had been in Egypt in attendance upon his king and cousin Cambyses, who had been four years absent in that country. Subsequently to the same event, he had witnessed the despair and death of Cambyses; he had accompanied the royal corpse to the old home of the Akhæmenian family in Persis; and now he had punished the presumption that (masked as the next heir, the younger son of Cyrus) had claimed to supersede Cambyses living or to inherit from him after his death. So capable, therefore, and so fortunate, having done so much for his nation and his family, no other Persian, no other Akhæmenian, not even his own father Hystaspes, seemed fit, as Darius, if, indeed, there was any other that would have dared, to sit amid the perils by which the majesty of the throne of Cyrus was surrounded. The new king was about twenty-eight years old. All his vigour of body, all his sagacity, all his force of character, were soon called upon, to procure submission, to anticipate hostility, to crush the open antagonists that threatened him successively or at once in various quarters; in short, to maintain the integrity of the empire.

The news of what had happened in Media produced in an instant commotion in Susiana and Babylonia. In each of these once independent or at least separate kingdoms, arose a man proclaiming himself successor to the former native rulers, and he was recognised as such by the people. But in Susiana (called by the modern Persians Khuzistan) among the various populations, Kissians and Elymæans, besides Mardians and Uxians,[a] there must have been little

---

[a] Strabo xi. 13 §§ 3, 6; quoting Alexander's admiral Nearchus as placing between the Susii (or occupants of the city and proper territory of Susa) to the westward, Persis eastward, Media to the north, and the coast of the Persian gulf to the south, four predatory nations, 1. the Amardi, contiguous to the people of Persis; 2. the Kossæi, who bordered on the Medes; 3. the Elymæi; and 4. the Uxii; the two last lying between the Susii and the Amardi. In the Journal R. A. S. vol. xv. pp. 4 and 97, on the name Afarti, which in the second language of the Behistun inscription is substituted for the Elam (?) or Elumat of the third, the Assyrian language, and for the '*Uwaja* or Khoja of the first, the Aryan language, Mr Norris remarks that the root of the name may have been pronounced Amar, Abar, or Avar, as well as Afar: and referring to Strabo, in the passages above noted, he supposes the cuneiform Afarti to be the Amardi or Mardi of the Greeks. Herodotus makes the Mardi one of the four tribes of Persian nomads, (i. 125); and Arrian's account of their subjugation by Alexander (Exp. Alex. iii. 24) is cited by Rawlinson to shew that they inhabited the range of mountains which divides the valley of Persepolis from the region on the Persian gulf. That the second language of the Behistun inscription was proper to a people seated in Susiana, the country which that language terms Afarti, Mr Norris argues from the fact, that this is the

unanimity. For Darius tells us, with a brevity that defies our curiosity to penetrate into the state and feelings of the province, that he sent thither; that the pretender was arrested and brought before him bound; and that he put him to death. The man who had called himself king and to whom fortune had thus speedily given the lie in Susiana, is named Atrina (or perhaps Athrina) son of Upadarma in the Aryan record; Asina in the only passage of the Assyrian where the name is still legible; and in the Kissian, where he is also described as a native of the country, Assina son of Ukbadarranma.[b] His own name, (whatever may be thought of his father's) seems altered to Assina from the Aryan, rather than to Atrina from the Kissian.

only ethnic appellation peculiar to that version of the inscription; all the rest being similar, if not to the Aryan, at least (as the 19th in the list cited above pp. 417, 418,) to the Assyrian appellations. We have assented to this reasoning, in calling the second language Kissian: for Kissian and Kosseean we take to be Greek forms of the Aryan adjective *Uwajiya i. e. Khojiya*, signifying "who (or which) belongs to 'Uwaja or Khoja." The identity of the monumental articulation *'uwa* with *kho* seems evident from the identity between *'Uwarazmiya* and Χωρασμια, or between *Hara' uwatish* and Αραχωτια. The change by which "Khojiya" would become "Khoziya," is that familiar one by which in India now "Gujarat" becomes "Guzarat." Both this and the greater change which would make it Khosiya, and bring it close to the Greek Κοσσαίος, is parallel to that whereby the Aryan proper name Ka(m)bujiya became in Assyrian (according to Sir H. C. Rawlinson's decipherment) Kambuziya: in Kissian Kanbuchiya and in Greek Καμβυσης. But the change from Khojiya through Khoziya to Κοσσαίος, is well illustrated by the Indo-Mahomedan Lutfullah in his Autobiography; where, p. 139, he speaks of one of the Bilúchí tribes of Khojas "commonly denominated Khossas" which haunted Nagar Parkar, an island in the Ran of Kach.

[b] For this Kissian or Afartian appellation "Assina son of Ukbadarranma," see col. 1. line 56 of the Kissian, in Journal R. A. S. vol. xv. pp. 54, 104; also 28, 181. As the father's name is softened to Upadarma in the Aryan, so the son's name is softened to Assina in the Kissian; for the Aryan *tr* always becomes *ss* in the Kissian. If Assina had not been thought a mispronunciation, would it not have been preserved in the Aryan text? The proper designation of the man appears, therefore, to have been "Atrina son of Ukbadarnma." If so it is remarkable (perhaps a sign of Aryan influence over an inferior race) that to this Afartian or Kissian should have been given by his father an Aryan name. Nor is it yet clear that the harsher as well as the softened form of the father's name was not Aryan.

Darius was at the head of an army, perhaps already in motion and threatening Susiana, when the revolt of the province was thus suppressed. He then proceeded towards Babylonia, where his other adversary, one Naditabel,[c] called himself Nebukhadrezzar son of Nabunita, a name and surname calculated to win the devotion of the nation and to awake its pride. Indeed, since the death of Belshazzar, which had happened seventeen years before, at the capture of Babylon by Cyrus, it is probable the surname " son of Nabunita" contained the most specious claim that a Babylonian could lay to the throne. It recalled the man who, though not of the blood-royal himself, yet (when the son and successor was cut off of an usurper by whom Evil Merodakh son of Nebukhadrezzar had been deprived of crown and life) had been set up, as the present husband of queen Nitokris and step-father of the next heir Belshazzar, to protect the rights of his wife and her son; while (with the titles of king and the king's father) he should exercise the kingly functions. The administration of Nabunita, had lasted for seventeen years, during which time the internal prosperity of the country had been maintained, public buildings had been added or repaired throughout the territory, and, though the Medes and Persians from useful allies had become formidable enemies, the capital had been greatly strengthened and secured. In the end, when Babylon was surprised and Belshazzar slain, Nabunita (after the surrender of Borsippa where he was blockaded) had been sent by Cyrus into an honourable

---

[c] "Naditabil son of Haniri'a" is his designation in the Assyrian version, line 31. For this we have in the Kissian, col. 1 line 59 " Nititpaal son of Ahinahira" and in the Aryan, col. 1 line 77, " Naditabira son of Aina[ira]." Here the *l* of the Assyrian (for which Perso-Median pronunciation had no equivalent; Journal R. A. S. vol. x. p. 145) is replaced by *r*; as in col. 2 line 90 of the Aryan, *Arbira*, and in col. 2, line 60 of the Kissian, *Arpara*, are substitutes for *Arbil* of the Assyrian line 63, the Αρβηλα of Alexander's historians, a city whose site is still called *Arbil*. See Sir H. C. Rawlinson's "Ancient Persian Vocabulary," Journal R. A. S. vol. xi. p. 39. But a more familiar instance is *Babirush*, the name substituted in Aryan for the Babel or Babilu of the Assyrian, for the Bapilu of the Kissian, and for the Βαβυλων of the Greek.

exile in Carmania. And now, he might certainly be thought to have a son fit for the throne at Babylon, as there was a son of Hystaspes become king at Agbatana. But if merely to be son of Nabunita was to have a good claim upon the Babylonians for their allegiance, the name of Nebukhadrezzar gave lustre to the claim, and conveyed to the people the notion that the bearer (no less than Belshazzar formerly) was descended from that great Nebukhadrezzar, under whom Babylon had attained not only her splendour and dimensions as a city but her dignity as queen of the nations of Western Asia. On the whole, since the family of her conqueror Cyrus was now confessedly extinct, whether Smerdis had met his death at the hand of Darius or of Cambyses, it might be hoped that under a new Nebukhadrezzar Babylon would recover her independence and her glory. The revolt, therefore, was universal in favour of the native pretender.

When Darius arrived upon the Tigris, he found a part of the new Nebukhadrezzar's levies at the spot, occupying the passage, which one might suppose was an ordinary and frequented one, having, if not a ford or bridge of boats, some other facility for crossing, of which it was desired to deprive the Persians. Indeed, Darius's record, as in the matter of Gaumâta's religious innovations, gives us unwonted explanation; having a brief statement of the mode in which he was obstructed and of the operation by which he overcame the difficulty. But our translators appear to be unable here as yet to explain the mutilated original texts. The result was, that by the aid of Auramazdà Darius gained the right bank of the river, where the bulk of the Babylonian army was posted in support; and he routed it with great slaughter. This victory he gained about six and forty days after he slew the Magian; for it was on the twenty-sixth of the month Atriyáda, the Assyrian and Jewish Khisleu, in the latter part of December B. C. 521.

From the Tigris, Darius went on towards Babylon. Near this capital, at a town on the Euphrates called Zazána, after five or six days, Naditabel (or, as he was called,

Nebukhadrezzar) met him in person, and gave him battle. The Babylonian army was defeated, driven into the river, and destroyed. This day was the second of Anámaka, the Assyrian and Jewish Tebeth, a month which (for the most part of it at least) corresponded with the January of B. C. 520; though it may have begun before the close of the previous December.

Naditabel himself with a faithful body of horsemen, reached Babylon. Darius followed and obtained possession both of the city and of the person of its new-made king, whom he put to death. If any considerable resistance had been offered to the entrance of the conqueror, it is probable, that the date of this capture of Babylon would have been noted, like the days of the preceding battles. Nor does any very great number of executions appear to have followed the occupation of the city; for if such a punishment had been inflicted immediately, the practice of Darius's record in other places leads one to believe that it would have been commemorated. We may surmise that the Chaldæan capital at this, her second capture by a Persian conqueror, was treated with what (according to the existing usages of war) was considered great tenderness. Indeed, the still critical condition of Darius's enterprise evidently demanded a conciliatory conduct towards the people whose master he was become, as soon as the immediate wants of his army had been supplied.

II.

At Babylon, where Darius's stay was protracted (in the city or the province) for not less than fourteen months, the new king at a moment of the utmost need found a dignity, security, and strength, befitting his pretensions. Scarcely was he master here, at the head of forces well satisfied with their leader and with themselves, when news came that the people in Media had cast him off and taken another for their king. Nevertheless, at Babylon he seemed, and from Babylon to every quarter of the empire, where doubt or indecision prevailed, he was assuredly announced, both king and conqueror. He had won the most famous seat of empire and the best centre of operation, at a time when perhaps he had been like to depend on the territory which for the day he could cover with his cavalry. Had Naditabel declined a decisive engagement in the field; had Babylon been ready or resolved to sustain a siege, as she showed herself three years afterwards, the revolt of Media might at once have placed Darius in a situation, the difficulties of which he perhaps could not have overcome. But, possessed of Babylon, notwithstanding the rising of a Median rival, *his* might well appear to be the same imperial throne to which the Mede whose name he bore had been conducted by the wars of Cyrus. Moreover, in the great capital which Nebukhadrezzar had created, Darius, with his victorious Persians and Medes, occupied the most strongly fortified city in the wealthiest of the kingdoms of Western Asia. He was surrounded with all that sun and water could enable a skilled and industrious population of cultivators to raise from the soil of an extensive country; and for purposes of war or peaceful life and enjoyment, he was abundantly supplied in the work-shops or manufactories of the great city, and the numerous district towns, where all arts anywhere known had been immemorially practised and improved.

But he had more than the power of Media proper to contend against. He has left us a list of provinces that revolted from him, or the news of whose revolt reached him (if we may venture so to modify his expression) while he was at Babylon. They are not enumerated in the order of the seasons at which they severally either rose against Darius, or were reduced to submission. The succession of those revolts with which the recorded leaders were immediately connected, seems to be displayed in the scene sculptured at Behistun; the series of victories is related in the trilingual inscription which accompanies that piece. But a comparison of other lists of provinces evinces that here, as in them, precedence of name is given partly to rank, partly to geographical position; a combination of respects which (according to Herodotus) was in use with the Persians.[a]

Darius tells us; "Whilst I was in Babylon, these are the provinces that rebelled against me, Persis, Kissia, Media, Assyria, Egypt, Parthia, Margia, Sattagydia, Sakia." Of these countries, the only one which we have not seen named in the general catalogue, Aryan, Kissian, and Assyrian, already cited, is Margia, or according to Darius's trilingual nomenclature, *Margush*, *Marcus-pa*, and *Margu'a*. It appears to have been a dependency of the great Baktrian satrapy, and to be unnamed in the general lists of provinces because comprehended under the name of Baktria.[b] At the head of the particular list now before us, we have Persians, Kissians (or people of Susiana) and Medes; the Kissians taking rank before the Medes. Then, we have the western nations that were to be included, being in number only two. Then come the nations that rebelled in the east, four in number, beginning with the Parthians. Now, it is exactly the same method that Darius employs on the south wall of the platform at Persepolis, in a list of the tributary nations that besides the Persians owned him their king. This list forms part of an inscription intended especially for the Persian population of the royal city, being in Aryan only; for the accompanying Kissian and Assyrian inscriptions do not

[a] See Herod. i. 134.

[b] If, then, we number the Margians as Baktrians, the nine revolted provinces here enumerated may be found above in their respective places at pp. 417, 418, in the provinces of the trilingual list there numbered 1, 2, 10, 4, 6, 13, 17, 21, and 20. The name of Egypt (*Mudr'aya*, and *Misir*) has been restored to the defective Aryan and Assyrian lists on the authority of the Kissian, which has in that place *Matsariya-fa*. For *Nammiri*, the true Assyrian name of the Sakas, see Journal R. A. S. vol. xv. p. 236. For the initial character equivalent to *n*, the copies of the Assyrian version of the tomb inscription at Nakhsh-i-Rustam made by Tasker and Westergaard, had led Sir H. C. Rawlinson to substitute in his own copy of the Behistun inscription a character equivalent to *g*, and to suppose that the Assyrians regarded the Sakas as of the race called by the Greeks Κιμμεριοι and often supposed to be represented by the modern *Cymry* and the *Cimbri* of the Roman annals.

contain the list and are not otherwise translations of the Aryan. Now, of these states, tributary to Darius and lying beyond the limits of his ancestral Persian kingdom, the first two are Kissia (or Susiana) and Media. Then come eight western provinces, the last of which is Ionia "both of the mainland and of the sea;" for isles of the Egæan had now been acquired to the obedience of Darius. To these, the remaining nations are subjoined; with this connecting preface, "also the provinces in the East;" which clearly indicates a geographical arrangement. They are thirteen in number; their first and second being *Asagarta* or Sagartia (in other lists not named, because included in a neighbouring province) and Parthia.

The lesson thus given in the list at Persepolis, how to construe the order in which Darius at Behistun enumerates the nations that revolted while he was at Babylon, is a lesson repeated with almost equal clearness in Darius's tomb-inscription, when we examine the order of the enumerated provinces, the number of which is there swelled by a train of conquests made in, or after, the great expedition into Thrace and across the Danube. After the Persians, at the head of the tributary states, we find the Medes and Kissians; the precedence being now given or, perhaps we should say, restored to the Medes.[e] Next to these, we have eleven eastern countries, beginning with the Parthians and ending with Sakas of two descriptions. Then follow eight countries of the west, the first being Babylon and the eighth Ionia. Lastly, subjoined to these, are seven other names, evidently denoting countries conquered beyond, and beginning with certain Sakas, who, if seated (as we understand their description)

---

[e] The Medes were placed next after the Persians and before the Kissians, in the muster-roll referred to by Herodotus, of the nations that composed the great host of Xerxes; see above p. 112. In Darius's list of the nations that composed the empire of Cambyses, he has placed the Medes in the tenth place only, but apparently at the head of the nations which formed the Median empire before the wars in which Cyrus the Persian commanded.

beyond the narrow sea, the Hellespont, Propontis, and Bosporus, should be Thracians.[d]

By thus examining the lists of Darius's provinces, extant at Persepolis and at his tomb, we learn, then, that in the enumeration of nations that revolted while he was at Babylon in the year B. C. 520 and the first two months of B. C. 519, the order of names results from their having been set down as they occurred in running over a complete catalogue of provinces,[e] and that it is not intended to

[d] For the tomb inscription and the list of nations contained therein, see Sir H. C. Rawlinson for the Aryan text, Mr Norris for the Kissian, and Mr H. F. Talbot for the Assyrian, in Journal R. A. S. vols. x. xv. and xix. For the Aryan inscription containing a list of provinces at Persepolis, see Sir H. C. Rawlinson, Journal R. A. S. vol. x. pp. 279-285.

[e] Even the Behistun catalogue which we have given above pp. 417, 418, setting forth the extent of the empire which Darius became possessed of by the death of Gaumâta the Magian, if a list were made of the provinces that revolted while Darius was at Babylon in the order in which they there severally stand—would exhibit them (with the exception of the Medes and Satagydians) in the same order as Darius sets them down here. But the arrangement of the names in that former list is peculiar. It may exhibit chronological indications and not only dignity and geographical position. The Persians and Kissians, who stand first and second, are followed by Babylon and the other western provinces *except Armenia and Cappadocia*. Then comes Media, followed first by these two western provinces, and after them, by Parthia and the rest of the eastern provinces. This arrangement might suggest that Armenia and Cappadocia as well as the eastern provinces appertained more peculiarly to Media, having been acquired before the wars of Cyrus and growth of the Persian horn. That Cappadocia belonged to the Medes before the fall of Sardis B. C. 554, and that the river Halys till then had been the Median boundary towards the west, is asserted in Herodotus's account of the war between the Lydians under their king Crœsus and the Medes commanded by Cyrus; see Herod. i. 72. And Xenophon makes Armenia to be a kingdom in vassalage to the Medes, at the time when the war commenced between the Medes and Assyrians, after the accession of the son of Astyages to the Median throne (B. C. 558). See Cyrop. ii. 1 § 6 ; iii. 1 §§ 1, 10, 33, 34 : ii. 4 § 12 &c. &c. iii. 2 § 24. But if (to speak summarily) the catalogue of states given above at pp. 417, 418 exhibits the empire in two great divisions ; the first composed of Persia and the Persian conquests, the second of Media and the Median conquests, we should suppose not only

convey any chronological information whatever; although such service was designed, as we have said, not only by Darius's verbal account of his achievements, but by the sculptured tablet also, in the order in which the conquered kings are exhibited to all beholders, strung together, one behind another, and forming a file which Auramazdà causes to come before Darius, as the king stands with his left foot on the belly of the prostrate Gaumàta the Magian.

By the testimony of this sculpture, confirmed by the date of the first engagement between the forces of Darius and the revolted Medes, we are assured that Frawartish the Mede (who stands immediately behind Naditabel the Babylonian) led the revolt which in time as well as in importance was the first that ensued; though before he lost his life towards the end of the year B. C. 519, the pretender, who follows him in the sculpture, had finished a much shorter career in like manner, as we learn from the inscription. We are able, then, to say that hardly two months can have elapsed since the Magian's death and that Darius can scarcely have taken possession of Babylon and put Naditabel to death, when he heard (or we perhaps might better say, it became known to his army) that a rival had arisen behind him, whom the Medes had acknowledged as their king. Then, all saw how precious had been the vigour and promptitude with which Darius had crushed the rebellion of Naditabel and won such a basis for future operations as the great and wealthy seat of the late splendid Chaldæan monarchy. But, as we

that the connection of Kissia (Susiana) with the Persians was as intimate as we shall find that of Armenia to have been with the Medes, but (as we have already on other grounds contended) that Kissia or Elam never formed part of the dominions of Astyages. See pp. 25–29. Two other conjectures which we have made elsewhere, might also seem confirmed; first (a matter of which, indeed, we have no doubt) that Assyria proper (as in B. C. 592, Ezek. xxiii. 23) had belonged to Babylon ever since the fall of Nineveh in B. C. 608 : second, that Cyrus's first war, whereof Persis was the theatre, the war for Persian independence, was waged in the latter part of the reign of Astyages, not against the Medes but against the forces of Babylon: Persis having been previously in immediate vassalage to the king of Babylon.

have said, Darius had more than the Medes alone to cope with, in the partisans of Frawartish. Except Susiana where a king of its own was set up, when its second revolt was made; and Egypt, where, to the natives we may suppose a Mede would be not less odious than a Persian; it seems not improbable that all the provinces which abandoned obedience to Darius about the time when the Medes did so, or before the Medes were subdued, supported the Median pretender. At least, it is plain that this was the purpose of the rebels (or, the foes ultimately subdued) the traces of whose proceedings during six and twenty months, both in Armenia to the west and eastward in Parthia, will be chronicled in their turn from the beginning of Thuraváhara or February, the month after that in which Darius took possession of Babylon in B. C. 520, and the beginning of Garmapada or April in the year B. C. 518. Of Darius's Median rival, antecedently to his unsuccessful enterprise, we know only what the conqueror may intimate in the record of its commencement; "There arose among the Medes a man, named Frawartish, who addressed the people saying, I am Khshathrita of the family of (Kh)uwakhshataru. Then the people (or soldiery) of the Medes that were at home went over to Frawartish and he became king in Media." By the legend which describes his figure in the sculpture, it is affirmed that in so saying Frawartish lied. And in like manner, all the pretenders in the sculpture (except the high-capped Saka named Sakuka, whose figure was added at a later date [f]) are called liars.

[f] The rivals of Darius are likewise called liars in the great inscription itself, in a recapitulation of the king's victories, subjoined to the record of the last of them, the capture of Babylon after its second revolt. For an engraving of the rock-sculpture exhibiting Darius and his vanquished competitors; see Journal R. A. S. vol. x. We shall have occasion to refer to it again, as exhibiting the order of time in which those rivals arose and declared themselves; while for the order of the dates of Darius's victories, we refer to the inscription. For Darius's trilingual account of the rising of Frawartish, see Journal R. A. S. vol. x. pp. 216, 241 and (for the legend belonging to his figure in the sculpture) 263; also vol. xv. pp. 108, 125 and (for the legend) 134; also vol. xiv. "Sheets exhibiting the Assyrian text of the great inscription," lines 43

Scanty and fragmentary as is our knowledge of the times and countries, the defection of the Medes on this occasion is not surprising or unaccountable. Such of them as had now survived to the great age of eighty years, were contemporaries of that last king of their nation, Darius, who both when he came into possession of the throne at Babylon, on its capture by the Medes and Persians under Cyrus, and afterwards, in the third year of the reign of Cyrus, is distinguished, by his epithet "the Mede," first from his Chaldæan predecessors and again from his Persian successor. For this king (named more fully "Darius the son of Akhshurush or Khshurush of the seed of the Medes") was sixty-two years old when he took the kingdom of Babylon in B. C. 538; so that his birth happened eighty years before the time of which we now write, when the Medes rejected the son of Hystaspes and accepted for their king Frawartish their countryman, calling himself Khshathrita descendant of (Kh)uwakhshatara.

The wars of the days of Darius the Mede and of the days of his father Khshurush were a time of glory for the name of Medes in which these old warriors and their fathers had played a part. Their fathers had served

and 92; and "Detached Inscriptions" (legends describing the several figures of the sculpture) No. 4. For the later date of composition and engraving of the figure of Sakuka the Saka and of the fifth column of Aryan text, which seems to have no Kissian or Assyrian counterpart, see Journal R. A. S. vol. x. p. 265. Observe, that the revolt of the Medes under Frawartish, who called himself Khshathrita a descendant from Khuwakhshatara, is Herodotus's revolt of the Medes in the reign of Darius (the only Darius of the Akhæmenian family who had yet been king while the historian lived) the mention of which revolt is introduced by Herodotus (i. 130) in connection with his account of the fall of Astyages. By not mentioning this revolt and the suppression of it by force of arms, in his history of Darius's reign (where also he erroneously supposes the pretended Smerdis who dispossessed Cambyses, to have been a Mede because he was a Magian, and his usurpation, therefore, to have been an imposture by which the Medes unawares recovered their pristine superiority) Herodotus indicates very plainly that this passage was introduced into his first book (as the description of the city Babylon may have been likewise) after the third book had been completed, and perhaps after the first draught of all the nine books; see above p.301, 302.

with the prince called by the Greek historians Astyages,
before he succeeded to the throne, when the power of the
domineering Scythian host was broken and when (with
the Persians in their train) the Medes aided the revolt
from Assyria of the ruler of Babylon, Nabopolassar father
of Nebukhadrezzar; and so the great city Nineveh with all
that remained of her supremacy in Asia was overthrown.
Afterwards, whether in quarrels where their own king
was a principal or in others in which he served the cause
of the king of Babylon, these fathers of living Medes had
fought against the chief of the kings of Lesser Asia, the
Lydian Alyattes, whose daughter afterwards became the
wife of Astyages. They had swelled the hosts of Nebukhadrezzar in his wars with successive kings of Egypt,
the Pharaohs Nekho and Hophra. But besides their
fathers' exploits, the aged Medes might with much reason
claim for theirs, as the superior and most numerous
nation, the chief merit in all the successful wars wherein
after the deposition of king Astyages they themselves
had fought for his son under Cyrus the Persian. The
capture of Sardis the Lydian capital, with Crœsus the last
of the Lydian kings, the capture of Babylon, when Belshazzar the last Chaldean king was slain and left his
throne to their own Darius son of Akhshurush, that is,
apparently to the son of Astyages, they must have regarded as Median achievements, though they may have
owned the valour of the Persian bands and the surpassing
merits of the Persian general to whom (as son of Astyages's
daughter Mandanè and nephew of Astyages's successor)
the command of the Medes and Persians had been entrusted
in the field; and who from that post of second in the
kingdom had succeeded to the throne, on the death of
their own Darius son of Akhshurush. But now, the sons
of Cyrus the Persian were both dead, kings who had
received their homage rather for the father's sake than because through their mother they were said to be descended
from the Median line; as Cyrus was descended likewise. No
issue male of either Smerdis or Cambyses was pretended
to exist. Therefore, when a countryman presented him-

self as descended, (through males of course) from the father of Astyages, from (Kh)uwakhshatara (the Kuakhshara or Cyaxares of the Greeks) under whom they had broken the Assyrian yoke and overthrown the seat of Assyrian empire, his claim to be their king was more to their mind than that of the son of Hystaspes; whose act, in slaying the pretended Smerdis son of Cyrus, was odious to all under Magian influence or not convinced that the king thus slain was an impostor. The claim of the son of Hystaspes to be king, was not derived from Cyrus but only from Cyrus's Persian ancestor Akhæmenes. It entitled him at the utmost to the subordinate Persian kingdom; but assuredly not to that of the Medes or to the throne of King Supreme, which with Babylon had been won at first for their own Darius son of Akhshurush. Such must have been some of the reasons why the people in Media, especially those of a past generation who had outlived the age for foreign service, preferred Frawartish or (to use the Greek form) Phraortes[s] to the Persian Darius son of Hystaspes, even though the latter through his mother may have claimed to be a grandson of Darius the Mede, as before this we have offered some reasons for believing. Where polygamy existed, even if females were held capable of inheriting and transmitting the kingly rank, a title to the throne derived from a mother must have been particularly liable to distrust.

III.

NOTWITHSTANDING the revolt in Media, the Persians and Medes of Darius's army at Babylon remained faithful. He even proceeded to detach a part of them against the rebels, under a leader whose name would identify him

[s] This form Φραόρτης occurs in Herodotus's line of Median kings; where one of this name is grandfather of Astyages and father of Kwakshara or Cyaxares, (Κυαξάρης) the (Kh)uwakhshatara of Darius's inscription. Of the latter the historian writes οὗτος λέγεται πολλὴν ἐπὶ γενέσθαι ἀλκιμώτερος τῶν προγόνων. Herod. i. 103. But for his account of the kings Phraortes and Cyaxares, see above pp. 25-27.

with one of the Persian Six that lately at Siktakhotish in the Median district Nisæa, had helped to slay the pretended Smerdis. He is called Vidarna, a name better known to us in the form in which it was written by the Greeks, Hydarnes. When this force was ready to depart, the king addressed it, saying, as he briefly relates; "Go, smite the people of the Medes who are not called mine." Hydarnes then set forth with the people; they arrived in Media, and there, in the district called Ka(m)pada, entirely defeated the rebel forces at a town the name of which (as preserved in the Kissian and Assyrian texts) was Marus or Maru'a. This success was obtained on the twenty-seventh day [a] of a month, corresponding mostly with the Julian January, the Anámaka of the Persians or Thabitu and Tebeth of the Assyrians and Jews, the same month in which Darius by the defeat of Naditabel on the Euphrates had opened his way to the gates of Babylon. From this capital back to the western border of the Median district, within which (but how far within, we cannot say) the town Marus appears to have stood, that is, the district called in Greek geography under the Parthian kings Kampadêné, the distance by the Gate of Media on Mount Zagros must have been about twelve marches of seven hours each, if we suppose the Tigris to have been crossed where afterwards on the right bank stood Seleukeia and on the left its Parthian suburb Ktesiphon.[b] After his victory at Marus, Hydarnes made

[a] So the date is given in the Kissian and Assyrian versions. In the Aryan it appears to be in part obliterated. See Journal R. A. S. vol. xv. p. 109; vol. xiv. Assyrian Inscription, line 46. and Sir H. C. Rawlinson's observation as to the Aryan text, on his second visit to the rock, in the note appended to vol. xii.

[b] The distance from Babylon to Seleukein was 300 stades, according to Strabo xvi. 1 § 5. By this we are to understand ten skhœnes (σχοινοι); for the same author (not to adduce other passages) at xii. 3. § 34 in respect of a piece of ground in Pontic Cappadocia, two skhœnes in compass, added by Pompey to the temple-lands of the goddess of the Pontic Comana, subjoins parenthetically, τοῦτο δ' ἐστὶν ἑξήκοντα στάδιοι. From Seleukeia the road, through Apolloniatis (*i. e.* Sitakéné,) Khalonitis and the Median province Karina, to the border of Kampadéné (Kapada in the Aryan, Kampattas in the Kissian, and *Kammabad* in the Assyrian) is computed by Isidore of Kharax at (33 + 21 + 22=) 76 skhœnes. There-

489

no further advance, but remained stationary in Kampadéné till Darius should enter Media in person, as undoubtedly he proposed to do as soon as possible. Thus, occupying

fore, from Babylon to the border of Ka(m)pada by this road, was a distance of 10 + 76=86 skœnes. See Isidore's *Stathmi Parthici* §§ 2–4, in O. Müller's *Geog. Gr. Minores, tom.* 1. pp. 219, 220. The length of the σχοῖνος used by Isidore, in the measurement of the Parthian stage roads, in an examination of Isidore's account of the road between Seleukeia and Apobatana (*i. e.* Agbatana, now Hamadan) is taken by Mr. C. Masson to be equal to two and a half English miles: so that the whole 129 skhœnes from Seleukeia to Agbatana would be 322½ miles. The accuracy of this result Mr Masson establishes, by comparison of a measurement by perambulator of the road from Baghdad to Hamadan, made by Mr Webb the surveyor attached to the mission of the late Sir John Macdonald. This line of road Mr Webb found to be 323½ English miles in length. See Mr Masson's article in Journal R. A. S. vol. xii. pp. 97–124. Allowing, then, two and a half miles or 4400 yards English to each, the 86 skhœnes from Babylon, by way of Seleukeia and Mount Zagros, to the border of Kampadéné, is 215 miles or twelve marches of about 18 miles apiece. This skhœne of Strabo and Isidore is the parasang of other writers, who reckon the parasang also as equal to thirty Greek stades; see Herod. ii. 6. v. 53; Xenoph. Anab. ii. 2. § 6. *et passim;* Suidas and Hesychius *in voce.* In ii. 6. Herodotus mentions an Egyptian σχοῖνος equal to two (Persian) παρασάγγαι, and therefore (as he supposed) to 60 Greek stades (of 606¾ English feet apiece.) But his own example shews that he has assigned too many stades by about one quarter to this double parasang, and if so, that the parasang was rather 22 than 30 stades long. He reports the distance along the Mediterranean shore from the Plinthinetic bay to the Serbonid Lake that extended along the base of Mount Casius, to be 60 skhœnes of Egypt or 120 Persian parasangs. Reducing this to Greek measure, he makes the Egyptian seaboard 3600 stades long, which (at 606¾ English feet to the 600 Greek feet which made a stade) is equal to 413 miles and 1220 yards English ; whereas the real length of the coast from the bay of Plinthiné even to the eastern end of Lake Serbonis, according to Sir J. G. Wilkinson, is by the shore little more than 300 miles. The day's journey of 150 stades in Herod. v. 55, will be seventeen miles and 417½ yards, that is, nearly seven instead of five parasangs according to Isidore's measurement. We may take the skhœne of Isidore and Strabo or the parasang of Herodotus and Xenophon for an hour's march, and as to our twelve marches each of 7½ hours or 7½ skhœnes measure between Babylon and the border of Kampadéné, note that in Herod. iii. 26 the journey across the sand from Egyptian Thebes to the city Oasis (which is reasonably identified with El-Khargeh, the modern chief town of the Great Oasis) is reckoned one of seven days. But El-Khargeh is said to be distant

the south-west of Media, not only did the force under Darius's lieutenant bar any progress the movement might have made in that quarter in favour of Frawartish, but, moreover, it protected the mountain passes in the northern frontier of Susiana; and, perhaps, kept open a communication with Agbatana in Upper Media, if the fortress at that capital remained still in the possession of Darius.

Having sent Hydarnes into south-western Media, the next step against his Median rival which Darius has recorded, was this. The king despatched into Armenia a man of that country, Dadarshish by name, with a commission exactly like the one given to the troops of Hydarnes, empowering and commanding him to destroy all that did not own Darius for their lord, and were not called his. It is not said that Dadarshish was furnished with troops. But, bearing in mind the custom of the king's record we can only conclude from this, that the Armenian departed without any Persians and Medes in his train. And if by birthright or by office (as it is probable) he was powerful in his own country, he may have needed little more than the authority of Darius to employ the means Armenia itself might furnish against those by whom the country was disturbed.

When Dadarshish reached Armenia, he was assailed, but the forces of Darius which now we find under his command hit the enemy heavily, at a fortress or mansion which the Kissian and Assyrian copies of the king's record name Zuza, and where perhaps Dadarshish had arrived to take up his residence as Darius's representative.[c]

---

by one road 42, by another 52 hours, from ancient Thebes. If so, the seven days of Herodotus are marches of six hours each by one road and seven and three-sevenths by the other. But as the distance now seems to be computed at 6 days only by the shorter and 7½ by the longer road, it appears that each day's march is one of seven hours. Alexander is related to have reached Rhagá on the 11th day from Ekbatana, hoping to overtake Darius in his flight, that is (since the distance is stated by modern authority to be 198 miles) after eleven successive marches of 18 miles apiece; see Arrian, Exp. Alex. iii. 20.

[c] In the Assyrian text prefixed to the name of this place is the ordinary monogram for a city, as Sir H. C. Rawlinson supposes, pronounced *ir* (Heb. עִיר) In the Aryan the name has in apposition to it the pre-

We have assumed that the enemy with whom Dadarshish contended, was a professed friend of Darius's Median rival; and we would point out, that (though for a whole year after this, the scene of an obstinate struggle between two of Darius's lieutenants and his enemies) Armenia is not included by the king among the provinces which became disaffected while he was at Babylon, (or as we may be allowed to understand him) between the dates at which he crossed the Tigris against Naditabel and recrossed that river on his return by way of Susa into Media against Frawartish. In all the three professed lists of the various nations or great provinces of the empire, engraved at different epochs in Darius's reign we find separate mention of Armenia, although this country seems to have been reduced to vassalage by the Medes before the Persians under Cyrus began to take the lead of them. Therefore, if here it is omitted from the list of the provinces that revolted from Darius while he was at Babylon, though during those fourteen months the field of many battles, this cannot be because it was not considered as in itself a province. To understand the omission, we should rather connect it with the fact that the first person who received Darius's commission to act against the enemy in Armenia, was himself an Armenian. Another fact that may help to explain why Armenia is acquitted of rebellion and yet the enemy was five times defeated

dicate *awahanam* (rendered by Sir H. C. Rawlinson "village," but by Mr Norris (Journal R. A. S. vol xv. p. 212) "residence") and in the Kissian it is defined by the term *Yuvanis*, likewise applied to the place where Gaumáta was slain. But Siktakhotish is described by the Aryan term *didá*, rendered "a fort," of which the usual Kissian correspondent is *afvarris* (expressed by the Greek βᾶρις and by the Hebrew and Aramaic בִּירָה) as in the description of the places where Dadarshish had his second and third fight. In the Assyrian, Siktakhotish has the prefix supposed to be sounded *ir*. Just so (to borrow the words of Gesenius) "creberrimè dicitur הַבִּירָה שׁוּשַׁן non tantùm de arce regiá, Nehem. i. 1. Esth. i. 2; ii. 3, 8; iii. 15; Dan. viii. 2, sed etiam de totá urbe adjacente, Esth. 1. 5. ii. 5. viii. 14, ix. 6, 11, 12 (confer Ezra vi. 2.) quæ alibi accuratiùs שׁוּשַׁן הָעִיר vocatur, Esth. iii. 15, viii. 15." The place seems to have been at once a fortress and a palace, having a city adjoining it. So Zuza or Zutza may have had its palace which Dadarshish occupied in his viceregal capacity.

there, is this—that the country claimed by the Armenians and called Armenia (though not by the Assyrians, yet) by the Persians as well as the Greeks, and after the Persians by the Kissians also, was inhabited by several races of men occupying separate districts, and not fused into one people. Those whom the Medes and Persians called Armenians, bordered in one direction, on the Medes, in another, on the Kardukhæan mountaineers, in another, on the Khaldæans of the north. These last appear to have shared the same origin and language with the Khaldæans of Babylonia, though whether as the parent stock, or as transplanted from the south, we cannot say. They are described as the warlike inhabitants of a mountainous country the productive part of which was small, so that armed with a shield of the sort called γερρον by the Greeks and with a couple of darts, they were ready to serve any one for hire in war, and were constantly seeking pillage on the lands of their Armenian neighbours. Before the first campaign in which Cyrus commanded for the successor of Astyages against the empire of Babylon, the story was told that, in order to consolidate the power of the Medes, he reduced the rebellious Armenians to submission, and then seized and fortified certain heights in the Khaldæan territory which commanded the Khaldæan and Armenian confines. Putting here a garrison of Medes to keep the peace, he caused the two nations to come to terms of amity, with interchange of daughters for wives, and of plough-lands and pastures for more convenient occupation. And this treaty still subsisted in the time of Xenophon, between these northern Khaldæans and the king of Persia's lieutenant in Armenia.[d]

Another matter of import to the question, Who were Darius's enemies in Armenia, is the probability, which even what has just been noted suggests, that throughout the territory there were lords of lands, villages, towns, and castles, of Median extraction, whose grants were from the Median kings and who naturally favoured the new

[d] Xenoph. Cyrop. ii. 1. § 6; iii. 1. § 34; iii. 2 §§ 1–15, 24; iii. 3 § 1.

king of their nation, called Khshathrita and said to be descended from the famous king of the Medes Khuwakh-shatara.

That Armenia at this time was in some sense a dependency of Media, appears from this, that the operations of Darius's forces there (like those that ended, as we shall see, in the defeat of the Sagartians by Khamaspâda the Mede) are certainly included by the king, along with those begun by Hydarnes and finished by himself in the proper country of the Medes, when, at the end of the detail, he sums it up with the words, "This I did in Media."

After the victory at Zuza, obtained on the eighth day of Thuravâhara (the month called by the Assyrians and Jews Sabatu and Sebat and answering mostly to the Julian February) Dadarshish was not left unmolested in his proceedings in Armenia. The enemy soon mustered again, and assailed him a second time at a fort named in Aryan, like the famous river, Tigra. But they were again defeated, on the eighteenth of Thuravâhara. Here, as in the record of some subsequent battles in Armenia, Parthia, and Margia, the Assyrian copy of Darius's inscription gives a bill of the slain whether in or after battle. It was not part of the king's plan, ever to commemorate disasters or to note the cost of his victories, but at this second fight the troops of Dadarshish are said to have slain of the king's enemies 546 in action and 520 afterwards.

However, though broken now in two encounters during the first moon of spring, the enemy within three months gathered together again and attacked Dadarshish for the third time. They beat up his quarters, as apparently he was proceeding in the pacification of the province, at a fort named in the Kissian (as deciphered by Mr Norris) Huiyama, and in the Aryan (as Sir H. C. Rawlinson conjectures) Uhyáma. As usual, they are reported to have been heavily smitten; and, perhaps, none but what were regarded as handsome slaughters or hard blows upon the enemy were admitted for remembrance. After inflicting this defeat (probably in May or the first moon of the midsummer quarter; for it is dated the ninth of the month Thaigarchish which the Assyrians and Jews called Airu and Iar B. C. 520) Dadarshish advanced no further in the province, but waited till Darius should himself enter Media. Here we see again, if not the dependence of Armenia on the province properly called Media, yet certainly, that the operations in Armenia were carried on against that enemy whom Darius was to destroy in his strong-hold of Media proper.

Nothing further is related of Dadarshish in Armenia ; and though other battles, fought and won in that country by Darius's people, require to be registered before the forward movement into Media, of the king's main army commanded by himself, yet we find that the space of eight months intervened before the date of the first of them. We will, therefore, not proceed at once to the operations of Vaumisa in Armenia, as does the narrative of Darius; but, during the interval, we turn to other matters which certainly belong to it, or else may conveniently be treated of here.

IV.

AMONG the nations that revolted at this time, particularly those three (if not four) concerning which nothing more than their names is known in the matter, Egypt, the recent conquest of Cambyses is, perhaps, the one which most excites our curiosity. But all that we have been able to find bearing on this revolt, is no more than the fact that (if we believe Herodotus) the same satrap Aryandes, in whose hands Cambyses had left the country, was still invested with the government, so long after as at the date of the expedition which Darius made across the Bosporus into Thrace and across the Danube into the country of the Scythians.[*] His conduct, then, during the

---

[*] For this synchronism, see Herod. iv, 145, 165, 167. The date of the invasion of the Scythians by Darius is doubtful. It is placed by Wesseling (ad Herod. vi. 40, cited by Clinton) at B. C. 508–507, later than the year in which Mordecai succeeded Haman as Darius's prime-minister, which was his 12th regnal year and began with Nisan B. C.

revolt of Egypt recorded in the Behistun inscription, must have been satisfactory: and we can only suppose that the disaffection—whether a rising of the natives or a mutiny in the Perso-Median army—was suppressed by the satrap and his subordinates before Darius (who may have been far from inactive on the occasion) quitted Babylon for the eastward. We might have expected a brief record of the success, like those relating to the two revolts in Susiana. That there is none, may be taken to indicate, either that no one in Egypt, of the natives or of the foreign soldiery, pretended to the throne of the Pharaohs, or else, that the adventurer escaped the hands of those by whom Darius was served in the country. But perhaps the king's satrap was resisted by a portion of the army, in behalf of the man who calling himself Khshathrita, and claiming descent from the ancient kings of the country, was reported to be the king acknowledged in Media.

In Syria at this time, we find Darius served by zealous and active officers on an occasion which now demands our attention.

We have already seen that, having changed his pretended proper name of Smerdis for the regal appellation Artaxerxes, Gaumâta the Magian, on a representation transmitted to him by the Samaritans, had sent a royal letter commanding to stop the rebuilding of the temple at Jerusalem, and forbidding any work there to be resumed without special order from himself. Also, incidentally, we have been led to some particulars connected with a renewal of the building which the people at Jerusalem were induced to undertake without any such license. To this matter we are brought now by the course of events and in the order of time.

510. For the silver coinage of Aryandes, and his being put to death by Darius as meditating revolt, see Herod. iv. 166. On the coins supposed to be of Aryandes, see Sir J. G. Wilkinson's note in G. Rawlinson's Herodotus, vol. 3, p. 145. For the expedition sent by Aryandes from Egypt against Barka, to aid Pheretima mother of king Arcesilaus in taking revenge for the murder of her son, see Herod. iv. 165, 167 and 200–203.

Its date (according to Ezra, Haggai, and Zechariah) is the second regnal year of Darius; and this seems to be that Assyrian no less than Jewish calendar year, which followed immediately after the one wherein Gaumâta was slain and Darius became king in fact.[b] But this next year, to the one marked in the Jewish and ordinary Assyrian calendar by the accession of Darius, had begun with Nisannu or Nisan, the moon before that in which the last victory of Dadarshish was gained for Darius in Armenia. In other words, the second year of Darius spoken of by the fore-mentioned Hebrew writers, was that calendar year of the Jews and Assyrians which began about April B. C. 520. Evidently, it was not the Jewish civil year, or year of contracts, which began with Tasritu or Tisri, the seventh month of the Mosaic and of the Assyrian calendars. Nor yet was it the regnal year of the Khaldæan annalists (used also by Nehemiah) which (as we have seen reason to conclude) began with Markhesvan, the eighth month of the same calendars. For, the series of days noted in the second year of Darius by the fellow prophets Haggai and Zechariah, begins with the sixth month Ululu or Elul, and ends in the eleventh month Sabatu or Shevât;[c] that is, begins before either of those twelvemonths. The same argument also shews, that this year, which Haggai and Zechariah's series of notable days belongs to, is not the year of the Egyptian calendar reckoned for Darius's second regnal year in Ptolemy's Canon; for this is the year E. N. 228, which began a quarter of a day before 1 January B. C. 520, that is, in the course of Thabitu or Tebeth, the tenth Mosaic and Assyrian month. But, if the year called by Haggai

[b] Just so, the second month of the second year of the coming of Zerubbabel's expedition to the house of God at Jerusalem (Ezra iii. 8.) was the next Iar after the seventh month (or Tisri) of the year in which they arrived, Ezra iii. 1.

[c] The series of dates is as follows; the first of the sixth month (Elul,) Haggai i. 1; the 24th of the same month, Hagg. i. 15; the 21st of the 7th month (Tisri,) Hagg. ii. 1; the (beginning of the ?) 8th month (Markhesvan,) Zech. i. 1.; the 24th of the 9th month (Khisleu,) Hagg. ii. 10 and 20; the 24th of the 11th month "which is the month Sebat," Zech. i. 7.

and Zechariah the second of Darius, began in the circle of months, later than the eleventh and earlier than the sixth, what other can it be than the year beginning with Nisannu or Nisan, the first month of both the Assyrian, and the Jewish calendar, which also seems to begin the twelvemonth according to the use of the author of the book Esther? No other year can be proposed.

It was in the autumn, then, of B. C. 520, about September, after the lapse of more than ten months since the death of the Magian king, when the Jews began again to work at the house of God in Jerusalem, on the 24th day of the sixth month, that is, Elul, the sixth month from Nisan.[d]

Previously, on the first day of the month, the word of Jehovah by the hand of Haggai the prophet had come to the captain or governor of Judah, Zerubbabel son of Shealtiel or Salathiel, and to Joshua son of Jozedekh the high priest. It had said; "Thus speaketh Jehovah Sabaoth, saying, This people say, The time is not come, the time that the house of Jehovah should be built." But, answered the Word, "Is it time for you, O ye, to dwell in your cieled houses, and this house to lie waste? Consider your ways. Ye have sown much and bring in little; ye eat, but ye have not enough; ye drink, but ye are not filled with drink; ye clothe you, but there is none warm; and he that earneth wages, earneth them for a bag with holes therein. Consider your ways. Go up to the mountain, and bring wood, and build the house, and I will take pleasure in it, and I will be glorified. Ye looked for much; and lo, it came to little; and when ye brought it home, I did blow upon it. Why? Because of My house that is waste, and ye run every man to his own house. Therefore the heaven over you is stayed from dew, and the earth is stayed from her fruit; and I called for a drought upon the land, and upon the mountains, and upon the corn, and upon the new wine, and upon the oil, and upon that which the ground bringeth forth, and upon men, and upon cattle, and upon all the labour of the hands."[e]

[d] Hagg. i. 15.   [e] Hagg. i. 1-11.

Hearing this message from Jehovah, Zerubbabel and Joshua and all the people testified their submission, and did homage before Jehovah. It would seem, that for their procrastination in the work of the house of God, since the removal of legal hindrance effected by the death of the king who pretended to be Smerdis son of Cyrus, and surnamed himself Artaxerxes, the people of Judah had met with unusual failure in all they had put their hands to on their own account. In particular, they had received but a scant measure of the good gifts of God in the late harvest, the present fruit season, and the year's increase of their flocks and herds. They had also miscarried in the use of that which they had brought home. It was for themselves alone that they had laboured, and their labour had but tended to poverty. But now that they humbly promised obedience to the Word of Jehovah, His messenger Haggai spake again unto the people and said; "I am with you, saith Jehovah."[f]

Then the spirit of Zerubbabel and the spirit of Joshua and the spirit of all the people was stirred by Jehovah, so that on the four-and-twentieth day of the month (as we have already related) they came and worked in the house of Jehovah Sabaoth. Intending to dwell in the midst of them again, this God (Who is our God as well as their's, through His adoption of us) had upbraided them for their slowness in the work of preparing Him the house. Perhaps, the three weeks that elapsed, after the delivery of Haggai's first message from Jehovah, were not spent in the stirring up of their spirit by Jehovah. Perhaps in those weeks they were making all ready for the building which they resumed on the twenty-fourth of the month. The command on the first of the month had been, "Go up to the mountain, and bring wood, and build." Perhaps, before the twenty-fourth they had been to the mountain and brought wood, and on the twenty-fourth they began to lay it on the walls.[g]

Again, in the following month (the seventh of the Assyrian and Mosaic twelvemonth but the first of the

---

[f] Hagg. i. 13.   [g] Comp. Ezra v. 8.

civil year) on the twenty-first day of the month, which was the last and great day of the feast Tabernacles, Haggai was visited by the Word of Jehovah again, and was commanded to speak to the governor, to the high priest, and to the people, and say thus; "Who is left among you that saw this house in its first glory? And how do ye see it now? Is it not in your eyes, in comparison of that, as nothing? Yet now, be strong, O Zerubbabel, saith Jehovah; and be strong, O Joshua son of Josedekh the high priest; and be strong, all ye people of the land, saith Jehovah, and work; for I am with you, saith Jehovah Sabaoth. According to the word that I covenanted with you when ye came out of Egypt, so My Spirit remaineth among you; fear ye not. For thus saith Jehovah Sabaoth; Yet once, it is a little while; and I will shake the heavens and the earth and the sea and the dry land, and I will shake all nations, and the DESIRE OF ALL NATIONS shall come; and I will fill this house with GLORY, saith Jehovah Sabaoth. The silver is Mine, and the gold is Mine, saith Jehovah Sabaoth. The glory of this latter house shall be greater than of the former, saith Jehovah Sabaoth, and in this place I will give PEACE, saith Jehovah Sabaoth." [h]

The promise was fulfilled when our Lord Jesus the Messiah (Who is to come again) came first. Then, before the faithless and perverse generation whom He visited had entirely passed away, the house and the city were destroyed by the people of a second Babylon, the Romans. The city has been rebuilt and there are Jews among its people; but they are not its masters; and they have no temple.

Again, in the eighth month, about November B.C. 520, came the word of Jehovah to Zechariah son of Berechiah son of Iddo, saying, "Jehovah hath been sore displeased with your fathers. Therefore, say thou unto them, Thus saith Jehovah Sabaoth, Turn ye unto Me, saith Jehovah Sabaoth, and I will turn unto you, saith Jehovah Sabaoth. Be ye not as your fathers, unto whom the former prophets

---

[h] Hagg. ii. 1–8.

have cried saying, Thus saith Jehovah Sabaoth, Turn ye now from your evil ways and your evil doings; but they did not hear nor hearken unto Me, saith Jehovah. Your fathers, where are they? And the prophets, do they live for ever? But My words and My statutes which I commanded My servants the prophets, did they not overtake your fathers?"[1]

Again, on the four-and-twentieth day of the ninth month (which fell in December B. C. 520) the word of Jehovah came to Haggai the prophet, commanding him to put this question to the priests upon the law; "If one bear holy flesh in the skirt of his garment, and with his skirt do touch bread or pottage or wine or oil or any meat, shall it be holy?" Accordingly, he asked the question, and they answered; "No." Then he (as he was commanded) asked again; "If one that is unclean by a dead body touch any of these, shall it be unclean?" They answered, "Unclean." Then said the prophet; "So is this people, and so is this nation before Me, saith Jehovah; and so is every work of their hands; and" (consequently) "that which they offer there" (at the altar of burnt-offering) "is unclean." Then the message bade them review the years that had elapsed since the day that the foundation of Jehovah's house was laid,[J] how when one

[1] Zech i. 1–6. The remainder of the sixth verse is, perhaps, no part of the message from Jehovah, but describes its effect with the people. It is, "And they returned and said, Like as Jehovah Sabaoth thought to do unto us, according to our ways and according to our doings, so hath He dealt with us." Here the "they" may perhaps mean Zerubbabel and Joshua and all the people; for this is the meaning of "them" in verse 3, a pronoun which has no expressed antecedent in the previous text. Otherwise, we are to understand God's message as affirming that the fathers of those who heard it had glorified God by confessing that they had deserved their chastisement and that it was no other than that with which God had threatened them when He called on them to repent.

[J] The foundation was laid in the 2nd month (*Iar*) of the second year of their coming to the house of God at Jerusalem, Ezra iii. 8—13, that is, about May B. C. 535. Therefore, the word "even," identifying the day when the foundation of Jehovah's Temple was laid, with the four and twentieth day of the ninth month in Haggai ii. 18, has been erroneously supplied by the Anglican translators. The days there mentioned and also in Hagg. ii. 15. are the two limits of a period

came to a heap of twenty measures, there were but ten; when one came to the press-vat for to draw out fifty vessels, there were but twenty; "I smote you," said Jehovah, "with blasting, and with mildew, and with hail, in all the labours of your hands; yet ye turned not to Me!" But after this retrospect, the message ended with a promise of His favour to them in spite of their ill desert. It asked, "Is the seed yet in the barn? Yea, as yet the vine and the fig-tree and the pomegranate and the olive tree hath not brought forth." The season was December; and man could neither ensure nor foresee the result of his labours, that the next harvest and next fruit season were to bring forth; nor did the remembrance of those past years to which their attention had been turned, encourage hope. But our God gave them notice; "From this day will I bless you." All things were to be made to work together for their good. The years of chastisement were ended, years of prosperity were begun. The civil year (which was now three months old) would be crowned with abundance between Passover and Pentecost at the corn harvest, and again in the fruit season at the end of the twelvemonth; and years of like prosperity should follow.[k]

Before corn-harvest arrived, and while (with the Jews as with the Assyrians) the regnal year was still the second of Darius, the word of Jehovah came to His people again through Haggai's fellow servant Zechariah. The prophet described many scenes in which he had taken part in the night of the twenty-fourth νυχθήμερον of the eleventh month; for he had seen and heard and at certain moments himself had asked a word. In the first of these visions there is an incident recorded which may be selected

---

attention is called to. The same period is spoken of, Zech. viii. 9, 10 where, in verse 9, the sense is, "Ye that hear in these days, so many of you as were in the day when the foundation of this house was laid." For the pronoun "Ye" is the antecedent of both the relative clauses that follow in succession—the clause "That hear in these days &c," and the clause, "Which were in the day that the foundation of the house was laid."

[k] Hagg. ii. 10-19.

for our purpose. An angel of Jehovah who talked with the prophet, made intercession and said; "O Jehovah Sabaoth, how long wilt not Thou have mercy on Jerusalem and on the cities of Judah, against which Thou hast had indignation these three-score and ten years?" And Jehovah "answered the angel with good words and comfortable words." So the angel bade Zechariah; "Cry thou, Thus saith Jehovah Sabaoth; I am jealous for Jerusalem and for Zion with a great jealousy; and I am very sore displeased with the heathen that are at ease; for I was but a little displeased, and they helped forward the affliction. Therefore, thus saith Jehovah, I am returned to Jerusalem with mercies: My house shall be built in it, saith Jehovah Sabaoth : and a line shall be stretched forth upon Jerusalem." The angel said moreover to the prophet; "Cry again: Thus saith Jehovah Sabaoth, My cities through prosperity shall yet be spread abroad; and Jehovah shall yet comfort Zion, and shall yet choose Jerusalem."[1]

Thus, more plainly than before, was the epoch announced at Jerusalem of a new era in the divine government. Seventy years of indignation had elapsed: henceforth God will again be gracious to Jerusalem. Nay, He is already returned with mercies to her, and those who were the too eager instruments of His former displeasure, will themselves be punished. But when did those three-score and ten years begin? If we count them backward from the date of the announcement by Zechariah, which is the twenty-fourth day of Shebât in B. C. 519, we arrive at the twenty-fourth day of the same Assyrian and Jewish month in B. C. 589. But what commencement of indignation do we find manifested against Jerusalem then? Why, that last and fatal siege of Jerusalem by Nebukhadrezzar king of Babylon is lately begun. The siege, which at last in the eleventh year of king Zedekiah in B. C. 587 ended in its thirty-first month with the capture of the city, and then was followed in the ensuing month by the burning of the temple and the palaces and by

[1] Zech. i. 7, 12-17.

the demolition of the city walls, had now been going on for the last six weeks, ever since the tenth day of the previous month Tebeth in the ninth year of Zedekiah.[m]

[m] 2 Kings xxv. 1–10, Jerem. xxxix. 1–8; lii. 4–14, Ezek. xxiv. 1–2. Compare Baruch 1. 2. where ἵνα is a mistake of the pretended Baruch for μηνὶ in the date ἐν τῷ ἐνὶ τῷ εἴματτι ἰβδόμῃ or ἐν ἰβδόμῃ) τοῦ μηνός. The threescore and ten years of Zech. i. 12 and vii. 5 are the same as the threescore and ten of 2 Chron. xxxvi. 21. But reference to Jeremiah's prophecies is made in this last passage as in Dan. ix. 2. where the conclusion is made in the first year of Darius the Mede (which year by Chaldæan reckoning began with Markhesvan, by Assyrian probably with Nisan, B. C. 538, but by that of Ptolemy's Canon with the year E. N. 210, that is, on the 5th of January B. C. 538). Seventy years are in fact foretold by Jeremiah xxv. 11, 12. and xxix. 10.

In the latter place seventy years captivity of the Jews at Babylon are clearly spoken of; and the period is the same which Ezra i. 1. alludes to, as terminated in the first year of Cyrus king of Persia (called king of Babylon, Ezra v. 13) that is, in a year which by Chaldæan reckoning would begin with Markhesvan, by Assyrian with Nisan, B. C. 536. But the seventy years of the former prophecy are (in one respect at least) the duration of the supremacy of Babylon B. C. 608–538, which was expired in the first year of Darius the Mede: as Daniel understood by documentary evidence; though he was too sanguine in supposing that the desolations of Jerusalem were to last no longer. But (according to a suggestion by the Rev. Geo. H. Forbes of Burntisland, that three weeks of years are predicted in the 21 days of Dan. x. 13) the prophet was admonished in the 3rd year of Cyrus that the Angel Prince of the kingdom of Persia, by the power given to him of resistance, would delay the fulfilment of Daniel's prayer for the city and the Temple of God, till the end by Chaldæan computation of the 4th year of Darius at Babylon and of the 70th since the end of the year of Nebukhadrezzar in which Jerusalem was destroyed—if we reckon from the beginning of the reign of Darius the Mede in B. C. 538 : or rather (if we reckon from B. C. 536, the first year of Cyrus at Babylon, when the exhortation to the Jews was issued to go up and build the temple at Jerusalem, and when the holy vessels of the former temple were restored to them ; Ezra i. 1–11) till the end of the sixth year of Darius at Babylon in which year the temple was finished at Jerusalem ; Ezra vi. 15–22. On the whole, we observe that the seventy years of Zechariah, recognized also as so many sabbath years of the soil of Judah in 2 Chron. xxxvi. 21 (and there said to have been foretold by the prophet Jeremiah) are a period known to us only from the retrospect in Zechariah, not being found previously announced to the people from God in the recorded words of Jeremiah. However, the theory may be suggested, that the predicted punishment of the king of Babylon when 70 years should be accomplished, was to be more than once fulfilled, not

Thenceforward, the tenth of Tebeth became a yearly fast: and undoubtedly, the anniversary had been a day of mourning at Jerusalem at its late return, although this was since the message through Haggai had been received whereby God promised on the twenty-fourth of Khisleu last past, "From this day will I bless you." It appears, then, that the ninth of Zedekiah is the first of the seventy years that the indignation lasted against Jerusalem and against the other cities of Judah. Now, this year began with Tisri B. C. 590, being the seventeenth year of Nebukhadrezzar's dominion over the kings of Judah, and the fifteenth of his reign at Babylon in succession to Nabopolassar his father. Consequently, the seventy-first year—the year of God's return with mercies, the year of His first promises of blessing by Haggai and Zechariah, began with Tisri B. C. 520.[n]

When those promises, one of which we have cited, were made through Zechariah on the twenty-fourth day of Shebât in the second year of Darius, the work in the house of God had been proceeding anew for five full months,

only in the death of Belshazzar when Babylon was taken by Cyrus, B. C. 538, but in the execution of the first pretender styled Nebukhadrezzar son of Nabunit after Darius's first seizure of Babylon in Anamaka in the first year of his reign, towards the end of December B. C. 521 or early in January B. C. 520; and a third time, in the execution of the second pretender of the same assumed designation at the second capture of Babylon by Darius B. C. 516 in Markazana (June?) of the 6th year of his reign by Assyrian and Jewish calculation, or the 5th by Chaldean registration. Now, the supposed fulfilment in the first year of Darius, marks the last of the seventy years' indignation against Jerusalem which we have cited from Zech. i. 12. The capture of Babylon in B. C. 516 happened in the 71st year after the end of the Jewish civil year (the eleventh of Zedekiah) in which Jerusalem was taken and burnt by Nebukhadrezzar, or in the 71st year of a series which began with the month Tisri in B. C. 587. It is an obvious objection, however, to thus supposing Jerem. xxv. 11, 12 to refer to the disasters which befell Babylon and her king both in B. C. 521-20 and in B. C. 517-16 as well as in B. C. 538, that the supposed dates of fulfilment are not both 70th or both 71st years, but one a 70th and the other a 71st year, from epochs in Jewish history.

[n] For the fast on the tenth of Tebeth commemorating the commencement of Nebukhadrezzar's last siege, see Zech. viii. 19; vii. 1, 5.

since it had been resumed, as we have seen at God's command. So, it was probably soon after, if not before this that the proof to which we have alluded, of zeal and activity in their master's service was exhibited by Darius's governor and other officers west of the Euphrates.

This chief commissioner for the administration of the king's affairs in Syria, probably resided principally (or in ordinary times would have resided principally) at the capital or in its neighbourhood. The distance of Damascus, which there is reason to fix upon as the chief city of Syria under the Persian kings, is not, indeed, great, yet vigilance and activity are indicated by the fact that the governor, named Tatnai,° came to Jerusalem in person, with others in his company by whom his responsibility was shared, and it is probable that the business on which he is recorded to have been engaged during his stay, was that which brought him. The doings of the Jews seem to have been reported with the suggestion, that what they were about was unauthorized; though no great stress could be laid on the fact that the late usurper's government had forbidden them to proceed. Arrived in the province of Judæa, at the place which in their subsequent report to Darius they designated not as a city (in which respect it was not worth speaking of) but as the site of the house of the Great God, the governor and other officials found this house built of ponderous stones, with timber laid in the walls, and the whole work going on fast and prospering. Then, they asked the elders of the people, by whose command they were building that house and rearing those walls (around it). They also took down the names of the men that were the chief among those engaged in the work, to report them with the authority they pleaded for the building. But by God's blessing it happened that Tatnai and his companions were contented to refer the matter to Darius, and did not think proper to stop the work till his decision

---

° The name תתני in Ezra v. 3, 6; vi. 13, which as now pointed is *Tatnai*, is rendered Σισίννης in Esdras ά vi. 3, 7, 27; vii. i. Σισίννης in Josephus Ant. xi. 4 §§ 4-7, xi. 1. § 3. In Esdras β' v. 3, 6, vi 13, the reading of the Vatican MS. in the Roman edition is Θανθαναι, that of the Alex. MS Ταθθαναι.

should arrive. The builders were reported to the king, as representing themselves to be the servants of the God of the heavens and the earth, and their work to be the rebuilding of a house that a great king of Israel had set up in old time, but which was destroyed within the memory of men still alive, by Nebukhadrezzar king of Babylon the Khaldæan, when, their fathers having provoked the God of the heavens unto wrath, He delivered them into the hand of Nebukhadrezzar, and they were carried captive to Babylon. As to the authority by which they were engaged in repairing the destruction Nebukhadrezzar had made, King Cyrus had issued a decree "in the first year of Cyrus king of Babylon," to build this house of God, and the vessels also of gold and silver of the house of God, which Nebukhadrezzar took out of the temple at Jerusalem and brought into the temple at Babylon, Cyrus the king did take out of the temple at Babylon, and they were delivered unto one named Sheshbazzar whom he had made captain or governor, and who was commanded to carry the vessels into the temple at Jerusalem, and to cause the house of God to be rebuilt in its place. By Sheshbazzar, "the prince of Judah" was meant, who (except when he is spoken of in an official manner) is called Zerubbabel.[p]

So much the elders of the people answered Tatnai as to their authority. They added that this Sheshbazzar (whom of course they pointed out among them) had accordingly come from Babylon and laid the foundation of that house of God at Jerusalem; and that from that time to the present the house had been in building, and was not finished. To this deposition of the Jews, Tatnai and those who were in commission with him, subjoined their counsel as to what was to be done. They advised that if it seemed good unto the king, a search should be made in the king's treasure-house there at Babylon, to ascertain whether in fact a decree had been made of Cyrus the king to build this house of God at Jerusalem: and they requested the king to send them his pleasure in the matter.[q]

[p] The Sheshbazzar of Ezra i. 11; v. 14, 16, is called "prince of Judah," Ezra i. 8.   [q] Ezra v. 3–17.

This despatch seems to assume a fact which we have learnt from the Behistun inscription, that the king was not only master of Babylon but resident there at that time. Their advice was complied with, and, search having been made not only at Babylon but also at Agbatana, the decree of Cyrus was discovered at the latter place, and an order most favourable to the Jews was thereupon issued by Darius.[r] But this result may not have taken place till after the overthrow of the king's Median rival, which seems to have happened so late as in October of B. C. 519, in Darius's third regnal year according to the Assyrian and Jewish computation. For it is not certain that, while the power of Frawartish lasted, Darius (even if his people held the palace-fort at Agbatana) was able, without an extraordinary effort, to send thither and make the search which his lieutenant of Syria advised.

V.

FROM Judæa, where the prophets Haggai and Zechariah have now published the termination of the Divine Wrath denounced by Jeremiah and Ezekiel, under which Jerusalem and the other towns of the country had lain in desolation for full seventy years, return we to Armenia where Darius's record of fresh successes indicates that the struggle still subsisted, in which the victories of Dadarshish had been obtained.

We have seen that the king's lieutenants, Vidarna and Dadarshish, had been stationary;—Vidarna, for many months after defeating once the forces of Frawartish in south-western Media, and Dadarshish, after three later conflicts with the enemy in Armenia; both generals waiting, as Darius appears to have directed them, as soon as the enemy was checked, till he himself should be arrived with an overwhelming force in Media, the centre of his competitor's strength. His stay, however, at Baby-

[r] Ezra vi. 1-12.

lon being prolonged, and support meanwhile or a fresh leader being required by his troops in Armenia, a Persian general was despatched, Vaumisa by name, to that province, where he arrived about the beginning of B. C. 519 and fought two battles with the Medes or their allies. His commission (like that of Vidarna and that of Dadarshish) was to exterminate all rebels, but it is not recorded in his case, more than in that of Dadarshish, that he was accompanied by any detachment from the king's army. We may conclude, that any fresh men he may have brought with him, were not Persians or Medes.

As no more mention is made of Dadarshish the Armenian (though we shall hereafter meet with one of this name, a Persian) it may be that he was dead or had been recalled, and that Vaumisa was despatched, not so much in aid, but rather to replace Dadarshish in Armenia. But the enemies of Darius appear to have gained new strength, for Vaumisa had not yet crossed the Armenian frontier when he was assailed by the rebels on the fifteenth day of the month Anâmaka, or in January B. C. 519, in a district belonging to Assyria, another of the provinces that are said to have revolted while the king was at Babylon; and this fact may suggest that the revolt in Assyria had taken place since the last success of Dadarshish, and had created the necessity for the despatch of Vaumisa to support the king's interest in Armenia. However, Vaumisa inflicted a severe repulse upon the rebels. The name of the Assyrian district in which the battle was fought (as we learn from the Kissian text of Darius's great inscription) was Atchidu. On this occasion the Assyrian text again adds a particular not found in the two other versions—the number of the enemy's slain. It was two thousand and twenty-four.

Six weeks after their disaster in Assyria, and six days after the message by Zechariah in Judæa of the return of Jehovah Sabaoth with mercies to Jerusalem, Darius's general having meanwhile followed them across the border into Armenia, the enemy returned to the attack. It was at the close, or, as the Assyrian text has it, on the thirtieth of the month called in Aryan Thuravâhara, the

Assyrian and Jewish Sabatu or Shebat, answering to the first month alike of the spring and of the year according to the Chinese reckoning,* or nearly the Julian February. Again, however, they were defeated, in a district of Armenia called Autiyâra, and with greater slaughter than before; for, as we find it announced to all who understood the Assyrian language, two thousand and forty-four of them were killed in action; and (besides one or two thousands, the notation of which has been obliterated from the rock by time) fifteen hundred and fifty-nine that had been taken alive, were executed afterwards.

This victory having been achieved, no further attacks on the king's forces are recorded to have been made; or rather to have been signally defeated. Vaumisa, thus far successful, having now acquired a secure position in the country, made no further advance but waited, as Dadarshish had already resolved to wait in Armenia, and as Vidarna was still waiting in Kampadéné, till the king should himself arrive in Media to assail the main body of a revolt rooted (as it seems) in the northern and eastern as well as in the central parts of that country, whence, though now checked in the west and south-west, it had extended itself in other directions into the neighbouring provinces.

Before the expiry of the month after Vaumisa's last success, that is, of the mid-spring month called by the Aryans Viyakhana, by the Assyrians Adarru, Darius, as we calculate, had quitted Babylon. But before we accompany him, there is yet a matter to be related which had previously occupied the king, though how long we

* The Chinese subdivide their twelve signs of the Zodiac into two apiece, and the names of these twenty-four subdivisions are applied respectively to the days when the Sun is in the first and the 15th degree of each of the twelve signs. Spring, summer, autumn, winter, have each its six of these sub-signs or fortnightly Zodiacal divisions. The first of these, coinciding with the first day of the sign Tiger (Aquarius) and of the spring quarter, is called *Lih-tchun*, "commencing spring." In 1843 it was the fifth, in 1855 it was the 8th, day of our February; See *Real Life in China* by the Rev. W. G. Milne, pp. 137-140, 142 of the 2nd edit. of Tasset's French Translation, with Introduction and notes by G. Pauthier.

are not able to determine. This was the fresh appearance of a rival in Susiana ᵇ who proclaimed himself king of the country: though apparently with a smaller measure of support than Assina or Atrina, the former adventurer, had found at the outset of his attempt. The new danger is thus briefly recorded by Darius; "There was a man named Martiya son of Chi(n)chikrish, whose place of abode was in Persis at a town named Kuganakâ" (in Aryan, but in Kissian Kukkannakan.) "This man arose in Susiana and said to the people, I am Immannis ᶜ king of Susiana."

Assuming kingship, a man put on the peculiar dress and ornaments of royalty. So, too, it was thought necessary, more or less perhaps for every one, but chiefly of course for a man of the lowest previous station or fame, to abandon his former name, as a petty, vulgar or ill-beseeming garb, and to invest himself with an appellation such as by

ᵇ In *Afardi* (the country of the *Afarti-fa*) according to the Kissian version; in '*Uwaja*, according to the Aryan. The name in the Assyrian text is not as usual expressed by the three characters commonly deciphered *Nu va* (or *ma*) *ki*, whereof the last (being found also after the names Babylon and Asshur) may be set aside as no part but a predicate of the name. The second, too, of the three characters is supposed not absolutely necessary to the expression of the name, which is sometimes represented by the first and third alone. See Journal R. A. S. vol. xiv p. xvi. To the first character, in one of the ancient vocabularies, the meaning or else the phonetic power is assigned of *Elam*. See Journal R. A. S. vol. xv p. 236, note. So much for the usual Assyrian expression of this name. The expression used here, *(Beh. Inscr. Assyrian text*, line 41) consists of three characters deciphered *E lu ti.* But the third character, which is also the predeterminative of a province, has likewise the sound or meaning *mat*. See Sir H. C. Rawlinson's observations, Journal R. A. S. vol. xiv. *Analysis* p. xxiii. also *Memoir* p. 6. We may, therefore, believe that according to the expression of the Assyrian text, Martiya arose in *Elumat;* and we may see in this name the 'Ελυμαΐδα of the Greeks; *e. g.* Strabo xvi. 1 § 17.

ᶜ We select the Kissian spelling as deciphered by Norris, supposing the name to have been indigenous. The Assyrian text of the "Detached Inscriptions," No. 5, has the name written *Yammanesu,* Journal R. A. S. vol. xiv. The true Aryan form is found to be *Imanish.* See Sir H. C. Rawlinson in the "Note" appended to Journal R. A. S. vol. xii, p. xviii, where the statement of vol. x. p. xlvii. (in a note on the Aryan text, col. 2 line 10) is corrected.

its signification, by the memories it suggested, or by its mere difference from the old one, might denote a new and exalted character. We may presume that Immannis (as the Kissian text spells it,) was a name no less fit to win homage in Susiana than Nebukhadrezzar had been lately and was again to be considered in Babylonia. We shall see (and we have noted it already) that as his rival Frawartish took the name Khshathrita among the Medes, so Darius now desired or consented to be called, as Cambyses had been new-named before him, Akhshurush, that is, Khshurush; because apparently that name which had been borne by at least one king of the Median line previously,[d] was suitably put on, when allegiance was claimed by a Persian from the nation of the Medes. But possibly Immannis may be identical with *Umman*, the name of a deity after whom the king of Susa in the time of Sennacherib king of Assyria was addressed as " Eldest son of Umman." This Umman, again, may have been the same with Strabo's "Persic" deity *Omanes*.[e] Immannis, however, may be an Aryan name; for the two last syllables, whether in the Aryan writing of it (lmanish) or in the

---

[d] See Daniel ix. i, and compare Tobit, at the end of the book.

[e] The name *Omanes* is employed by Strabo in the genitive form, 'Ωμανῦ only; Strab. xi. 8 § 4 and xv. 3 § 15, and this genitive may have had for its nominative, 'Ωμανὶς. This deity Sir H. C. Rawlinson (Journal R. A. S. vol. xi p. 96, note) takes to be the same as the *Khomœan Apollo* of Ammianus xxiii. 6, who was worshipped at *Humânia*, the Χοὐμανα of Ptolemy v. 20. Mr H. Fox Talbot tells us (Journal R. A. S. vol. xviii, p. 48) on the authority of an inscription, that some fugitives from Babylon, defeated by Sennacherib or his generals, flying to the court of the king of Susa, address him thus; "Eldest son of Umman! send thine army to help us." Observing that Umman was the great national deity of the Susians, and reminding the learned that among the hieroglyphics of Karnak there is a scene where the ambassadors of an eastern nation asking peace of Pharaoh Ramses, begin their supplication, "Oh Son of Ammon" (and thus employ the title assumed by Alexander the Macedonian) Mr Talbot conjectures the Susian Umman to be identical with the Egyptian Ammon. Both nations were Hamite; Mizraim son of Ham being the father, or the tribe, from whom the Egyptians descended, and Kush son of Ham being the father not only of the Kush or Ethiopians of the Upper Nile but of Nimrod and the Asiatic Ethiopians to whom the Kissians belonged.

Kissian, are also the two last of Hakhâmanish, (in Kissian, Akkamannis) the name of the great progenitor of Cyrus and Darius.

We have seen that Darius declares Martiya to have been originally an inhabitant of Parsa or Fars, that is, Persis. Moreover, in a later passage of his record, a recapitulation of the nine competitors he had overcome, Darius calls this fifth that arose, but fourth that fell before him, a Persian.[f] There seems, however, to be some ground for suspecting him to have not been, what Darius in the inscription upon his own tomb calls himself, " a Persian the son of a Persian, an Aryan of Aryan race."[g] We cannot, indeed, positively affirm that the quality of a Persian used to be bestowed (like the citizenship of Rome) on men having none of the blood of the nation to which the name of Persian properly belonged. Yet, if there was a population in Persis descended from one that occupied the country when the Perso-Aryan immigration happened, this race (which is thought to have been akin to the neighbouring Kissians) may have had more or less of the privileges of Persians conceded to it by that nobler or stronger race, especially since the wars in which the great Cyrus commanded. For to Cyrus, at the outset of the struggle between the Medes and Persians on the one side, and the Assyrian or Chaldæo-Assyrian power seated at Babylon, on the other, Xenophon attributes a measure, for making the auxiliary army from his native Persis more effective, whereby the common people were put upon an equality in arms and military prospects with the nobles, the ὁμότιμοι, and he is represented as admitting zealous auxiliaries of whatever nation, to an equal share with distinguished Persians in the fruits of the ultimate conquest.[h] Or we might suppose Martiya to have been in the case of the children of the Athenian Metiokhus, the

---

[f] Beh. Inscr. *Aryan* col. iv. line 16 ; *Kissian* col. iii. line 52.

[g] See Journal R. A. S. vol. x. p. 292; vol. xv. p. 150. In the Assyrian text the one clause, " A Persian the son of a Persian," is all ; the other clause being omitted. See H. F. Talbot's "Assyrian text of the Naksh-i-Rustam Inscription of Darius ; " Journal R. A. S. vol. xix pp. 261-273.

[h] Xenoph. Cyrop. ii. 1 §§ 9-19; vii. 4 § 28.

eldest son of the great Miltiades. These, being born of a
Persian mother given in marriage to their father by king
Darius when, many years after this time, Metiokhus had
become Darius's prisoner, were accounted Persians.[i] Certainly, we suspect Martiya to have been neither Persian
nor Aryan by unmixed descent, but to have come of the
old Képhénes, as Hellenic legends styled the nation,—a
stock on which the Persian off-shoot of the Aryan race
had become engrafted when in the country of the Képhénes
it probably found wives as well as lands. Now, these
Képhénes appear to have been of Ethiopian race, that
is to say, a branch of the race of Kush son of Ham son of
Noah; and if so, to have been of the same blood with the
Kissians or Kossæans of adjacent Susiana. For Képheus,
from whose daughter according to the legend the Persians
were descended, is himself son of Belus[j] and king of
Ethiopia.[k] That is to say, he and his people were
Kushites of Babylonia. Accordingly, there is a fragment
extant of the first book of his Persian history, in which
Hellanicus asserts that "after the death of Képheus, the
people left Babylon and occupied Khogé, so that the
country (of Babylon) was now no longer called Képhénia
nor the people Képhénes, but the people Khaldæans and
the whole country Khaldaica." Another account represents
Perses the son of Perseus and Andromeda, as expelled
with his Képhénes by the Khaldæans after his grandfather's death, and as establishing himself among the
Artæans or people of Aryan race.[l]

[i] Herod. vi. 41.   [j] Herod. vii. 61, 150; vi. 54.
[k] Apollodorus, Bibliothec. ii. 4 §§ 2, 4. Also Deinias the Argive
and other history-writers of his school, cited by Agatharkhides ap. Phot.
cod. 250. See *Fragm. Historic. Græc.* tom. i. p. 131; tom. iii. p. 25.
[l] See Hellanicus, in *Frag. Hist. Gr.* tom. i. p. 67. Perhaps, it was in
the belief that the Kissians and builders of Susa came from beyond the
Tigris, that Babylon has been called the mother-city (μητρόπολις) of the
Persians. Eustathius in his commentary on Dionysius Periegetes, verse
1005 cites Arrian (probably his *Parthica*, now lost) thus; τοὺς δὲ Πέρσας, ὧν
μητρόπολις ἡ Βαβυλών, Κηφῆνάς ποτε καλεῖσθαί φησιν ὁ Ἀρριανός· See *Fr. Hist. Gr.*
tom. iii. p. 601 and C. Muller's *Geogr. Gr. Minores* tom. ii. p. 390.

514

In regard of Martiya's nationality, the ground of our suspicion is principally the fact, that he, an inhabitant of Persis, thought to make himself king of Susiana. It may be conceived that, being by blood and language connected

But the parenthesis ἐν μητρόπολις ἡ Βαβυλών, perhaps is not Arrian's but expresses a notion derived by Eustathius from later writers whose Persians were those under the Sassanian kings, and who by Babylon the metropolis, meant Seleukeia on the Tigris, which (with the adjoining Ktesiphon) was the capital of the Sassanian as well as of the Arsacian kings. The passage of Hellanicus, above referred to, is preserved by Stephen of Byzantium. In it, for Χογη, Salmasius, it seems (ad Solin. p. 1226B,) proposed to read Χωχη an unwalled town not far from the Tigris and also apparently not far from the capital Seleukeia, the mention of which is cited by Stephen of Byzantium from the tenth book of Arrian's Parthica. This Χωχη is identified with the *Coche* of Ammianus xxiv. 6; see *Frag. Historic. Gr.* tom. iii. p. 588. For Κωχη (a form of the name corresponding exactly with the *Coche* of Ammianus) C. Muller refers us also to Gregorius Nazianz. Or. 2 in Jul. p. 203 ;—and he bids us compare Eutropius 9, 18. We are inclined to think the Khogè of Hellanicus to be the '*Uwaja* (Khoja) of the Aryan text of the Behistun inscription. But in the same first book of his Persian history from which comes the passage of Hellanicus given in the text, another is cited by the same Stephen, in which Hellanicus described 'Αρταίαν the country of the Artæi, as Περσικὴν χώραν ἣν ἐπιόλισι Πιερίδι (perhaps Πίερας) ὁ Πιερίων καὶ 'Ανδρομίδας. It would seem, then, that Hellanicus supposed Khogè, the new settlement of the Képhénes, to be a part of Artæa; which would be sufficiently consistent with the statement of Herodotus vii. 61, that of old the Persians were called by the Greeks Képhénes, but by themselves and their neighbours *Artæi*. There is also this remarkable passage of a scholiast on Dionysius Periegetes, verse 1053, cited by C. Muller in *Frag. Historic. Gr.* tom. iii. p. 365, note, and by him supposed to be taken from Hellanicus:

Πίερη (C. M. reads Πιερίη) ἐξ 'Ανδρομίδας γίνεται υἱὸς, ὃν ὁ πάππος Κηφεὺς παρ' ἑαυτῷ τρέφων Πίερην ὀνόμασι, καὶ τελευτῶν αὐτῷ κατέλιπε τὴν τῶν Κηφήνων ἀρχήν. Χαλδαίοις δὲ ἐπιθέμενος αὐτῷ ἐξήλασεν τῆς χώρας. 'Ο δὲ τῶν Κηφήνων οὐκ ὀλίγους ἐπαγόμενος ἀπήλθεν εἰς τὸ 'Αργεῖον (C. M. reads 'Αρταῖον) ἔθνος, καὶ ἐπανίζεται ἰθαγενὴς προσθέμενος τι θυσίαις κρατεῖ, καὶ Πίερας ἀφ' ἑαυτοῦ ὀνομάζει. Καὶ ἔσχεν υἱὸν 'Αχαιμενίαν ἀφ' οὗ 'Αχαιμενίδαι οἱ Πίεραι ἐκλήθησαν.

There seem to be two elements of the Persian nation acknowledged here; one, Képhénian, the other, Artæan. We have expressed the opinion above p. 13 that the appellation Artæan is nearly equivalent to Aryan; appealing to Dr Donaldson's account of αρτα the initial element of many both Mede and Persian names, that it is the perfect passive participle of the Sanskrit root *Ri*. That Artæi is thus derived and signifies " Men honoured," is agreeable to the statement of Stephen

with the Kushite population of Persis, he had more encouragement to try his luck at the game of aggrandizement amid the Kushites of Susiana, whose position in respect of other inhabitants was probably higher than in Persis,

the Byzantine, that the appellation is connected with the αερα of many Persian names, and that in old time the Persians called men *artæans*, as the Greeks called them *heroes*. Others would refer 'Αςταίων to the native name of the Kissians, *Afarti-fa* (which Mr Norris compares with 'Αμαρδοι) and Mr Norris was inclined to connect the word with a Kissian root, *ir* or *irs*, allied to the Magyar *eros* and the Ostiak *ar*, "great." See Journal R. A. S. vol. xv. p 205, and note on Herod. vii. 61 in G. Rawlinson's Herodotus.

From the Ethiopians of the kingdom of Kepheus, who migrated to Khogé and into the Artæan country or country (afterwards) occupied by an Aryan race—let us pass to the Ethiopians led by Memnon to the relief of Priam after Hector's death. At Delphi in one of the paintings by Herodotus's contemporary Polygnotus, there was a figure, having two special tokens whereby it was understood to represent the hero, called by Pausanias in his account of the picture, "Memnon, a king of the Ethiop race, who came to Ilium from Susa of the Persians and from the river Khoaspes." On his *Khlamys* (rendered *scarf* in Smith's "Dict. of Greek and Roman Antiquities") were birds painted representing those called Memnonides, which (as the Hellespontians said) came on certain days every year to the grave of Memnon, and with their wings wet from the water of the Æsépus, both swept and sprinkled so much of the mound as was bare of trees or herbage. This is one of the marks by which Polygnotus had indicated the person he intended. The other was this. Beside the figure, there was painted an Ethiop boy naked. Thus, the hero was not himself presented as an Ethiop, but the boy who attended him was painted black; see Pausanias x. 31 § 7. As to the quarter from which Memnon's Ethiopian troops were supposed to have been brought, at the time when this painting was executed, Herodotus tells us that the palace at Susa was called the Memnonian palace and Susa itself the Memnonian city or Memnonian Susa; see Herod. v. 53, 54; vii. 151, and compare Strabo xv. 3 § 2. So too Pausanias, iv. 31 § 5, mentions τὰ Μεμνόνια τὰ ἐν Σούσοις τείχη. Two rock-sculptured figures of a conqueror armed with bow and spear and in a dress half-Egyptian half-Ethiopian (one of them on the road between Sardis and Smyrna, the other on the road from Ephesus to Phocæa) were thought by many Greek spectators to represent Memnon, though Herodotus attributed them to Sesostris, ii. 106. A sculpture still extant and supposed to be one of these, is represented in G. Rawlinson's Herodotus. But in later times, when the Ethiopians of Asia were forgotten, the Greeks supposed that Memnon came to Ilium

and their history more illustrious. That Martiya was not of pure Aryan blood, may also perhaps be indicated both by the name of his father and by that of his domicile in Persis. In the Aryan text he is surnamed " Chichikhráish

(originally at least) from the Ethiopia above Egypt, and travelling in Egypt, fancied or were persuaded by their (perhaps Ethiopian) guides, that they had found his statue at Thebes, though the Egyptian inhabitants gave it to a different personage: see Pausanias i. 42 § 3 and compare Diodorus ii. 22 § 4.

Another historian of the age of Polygnotus, namely Hellanicus, described Memnon as a son borne by the goddess *Hemera*, or "Day," to Tithonus a son of Laomedon and brother of Priam; see Schol. Hom. Iliad, iii. 151. But that Memnon figured in the *Persica* of Hellanicus, as he should have done if Hellanicus believed that the hero led his Ethiopians from Susa or elsewhere in the East, we cannot affirm. Indeed, we shall presently notice a reason for supposing that Hellanicus brought Memnon from the south. By Carl Muller, the Scholiast on the above-noted passage of the Iliad is supposed to quote from the *Troica* of Hellanicus. It seems to be the same passage which the Scholiast (without acknowledging his author) has used more fully at Hom. Iliad. xi. 1. where Memnon is also qualified as king of the Ethiopians. So much for the age of Polygnotus, Hellanicus, and Herodotus. But we turn to the older authorities. By Homer in the Odyssey, the hero is briefly alluded to as a son ot Eôs (the goddess Morn) who slew Antilokhus son of Nestor; and again, in a passage where Ulysses in answer to the enquiries of the shade of Achilles, commends Eurypylus, a champion slain by Achilles' son Neoptolemus, as next to Memnon the finest man he had seen,—that is, on the Trojan side, we may suppose; and after the death of Hector; see Hom. Odys. iv. 18. xi. 52. But it is to be remembered that Homer withal makes Eôs rise from the bed of Tithonus to carry light to gods and men; Iliad, xi. 1; and he describes Tithonus as son, and apparently eldest son of Laomedon; Iliad. xx. 237. Memnon, thus sketched by Homer, is in Hesiod's Theogony 984,985, king of the Ethiopians and (along with king Emathion) son of Tithonus by Eôs or the Morn. A like story is briefly repeated by Apollodorus (Bibl. iii. 12 § 4) thus: Tithonus (who stands first, as in Homer's account, on a previous list of the sons of Laomedon son of Ilus) was carried off for love by the Morn into Ethiopia, where she bore him two sons, Emathion and Memnon. Remark we, that Ethiopia, the home of the Morn goddess, 'Ηώς, agrees better with Susiana than with the country above Egypt: and we are thus reminded that Hellanicus may have changed the mother from Morn to Day, in order to accommodate the legend to his belief that Memnon came from the South, the land of Mid-day. Homer seems to own both Ethiopias,

putra," that is, " Son of Chi(n)chikhrish." In the Assyrian, for this addition we have " assa Sinsakhris," " Who (was son) of Sinsakhris." But in the corresponding Kissian surname, "Issanzakris sakri," "son of Issanzakris," the but eastern and western rather than eastern and southern, Od. i. 23–24 quoted above p. 298, note. From Homer and Hesiod let us descend to the Epic-verse maker, Arktinus the Milesian ; who flourished, however, three hundred years before Hellanicus, Polygnotus, and Herodotus; see Clinton, F. H. vol. i pp 152, 155, 355, B. C. 775 and 761. In one of his poems, the *Æthiopis*, which was preserved to the time of Proclus in the Epic Cycle, "probably formed by the Alexandrian critics," the story of Memnon son of ·Ηώς, or "Morn," followed that of Penthesileia, and seems to have formed the main subject of the poem. He is son of Ηώς and slays Antilokhus, as in the Odyssey. That he was represented as the head of Ethiopian forces, we should not know if we had only the argument left by Proclus of the poem : but the title of the work proves the fact, in conjunction with the second book of the *Posthomerica* of Quintus Smyrnæus who is believed to have taken his materials from Arktinus. That Memnon (like Penthesileia) was described by Arktinus to have been killed by Achilles, we know from Proclus, and we might have conjectured from its being so related by Quintus Smyrnæus. But the same is perhaps intimated in the Odyssey xi. 52, where Ulysses gives to the ghost of Achilles some account of events at Ilium that had happened after the hero's death. That Arktinus represented Memnon as a Trojan by his father, may be inferred from Quintus's *Posthomerica* ii. 494, where Memnon is described as son of Tithonus and Eôs ; also from *Posthom.* xiv. 135 where he is termed the son of Tithonus. In *Posthom.* vi. 2 Eôs is described (as by Homer) leaving the bed of Tithonus to discharge her office in the sky. Arktinus, too, it may be presumed, placed the tomb of Memnon by the river Æsepus, and had a tale of the Ethiopians who attended his obsequies being changed into Memnon birds and fighting together till all were killed at his tomb; see the *Posthom.* ii. 587–655. In the generation preceding that of the painter and the two historians whom we began by citing, Pindar (the contemporary of the tragic poet Æschylus) calls Memnon, "the Ethiop son of Eôs," and like Arktinus, numbers him among the slain of Achilles ; Ol. ii. 148, comp. Nem. vi. 84 ; Isthm. v. 51 ; viii. 15. Like Arktinus, too, and like Homer in the Odyssey, he makes Antilokhus to have been slain by Memnon, whom he styles the *stratarch* or commander of the Ethiopians. Perhaps, it is also from Arktinus that Pindar took the circumstance that Antilokhus met his death in the defence of his father Nestor, one of whose chariot-horses had been disabled by an arrow from the bow of Paris ; Pyth. vi. 31. For Quintus Smyrnæus makes Antilokhus draw off Memnon's

word "sakri," signifying "son," may seem discernible also in the name of the father, as forming the latter portion of that name. But, if this really is the case, it indicates that the name of Martiya's father was Kissian.

attack from his father upon himself; Posthom. ii. 243–259. Pindar like Arktinus owns the relationship of Memnon to Priam; for he styles him "cousin of Helenus;" Nem. iii. 111. Pindar's contemporary Æschylus, in some lost drama, appears to have made Memnon's mother a Kissian; see Strabo xv. 3 § 2. This shows that the poet's καλαὸι Κίσσιοι Ἱππεις in the Persæ (cited above p. 19) though mistaken for a different place from Susa, means the τεῖχος Μεμνόνιον at Susa. Thus, Tithonus's bed in the East was considered by Æschylus to be that of an Ethiop or Kush-descended wife. The name Memnon seems to belong to a language which embraced Agamemnon's Achæans no less than Priam's Trojan and Dardan subjects; but his mother may have been of Kushite race as well as the forces which he led from the east. We conclude by giving his story as told by Diodorus ii. 22 out of Ktesias's tales of Assyrian history. "The supremacy (ἡγεμονία) of the Assyrians from the reign of Ninyas son of Semiramis to that of Sardanapallus (when it passed to the Medes) lasted 30 generations and more than 1300 years." But Ktesias gave nothing but the names and lengths of reign of a line of kings till he came to the 20th, Teutamus; pretending (or leaving Diodorus to infer) that there had been no achievements hitherto worthy of remembrance; and that the aid then sent by the Assyrians to the Trojans, under the command of Memnon (the only matter recorded by himself) was also the only event of which the memory had been preserved by an Assyrian inscription. It seems that the legend concerning Perseus and Andromeda was not used by him. But now at last, he has something to tell us, and he tells it thus; "They say that it was in the reign of Teutamus, who was the 20th from Ninyas son of Semiramis, that the Greeks with Agamemnon went upon the war against Troy: at which time the Assyrians had held the supremacy of Asia for more than a thousand years." Such, indeed, may have been the belief at the court of Artaxerxes Mnemon king of Persia, of those with whom Ktesias possibly conversed about the Trojan war. Well; "Priam king of the Troad, finding the war more than he could bear, and being a vassal of the king of Assyria, sent to his lord for succour: whereupon Teutamus despatched 10,000 Ethiopians and as many more Susianians." We stop to remark, that we should like to know whether Susiané, the name of the country which Diodorus always uses (for example in the story of Ninus; Diod. ii. 2 § 3) was found by him in Ktesias's narrative. To proceed: "These forces, besides 200 chariots, were placed under the command of Memnon son of Tithonus. Now, Tithonus was at that time the general in command of Persis; and he

Again, the name of the town in Fars or Persis where Martiya had his abode, is written in the Aryan text, "Kuganakâ," in the Assyrian, "Kugunakka," but in the Kissian, "Kukkannakan." Here it may be imagined,

had more credit with the king than any of the governors that were established over the provinces." Note we, that he who told this, conceived of Persis as of a province which comprehended Susiané or had Susa for its chief city; a state of things resembling the actual condition in the time of Ktesias's master Artaxerxes Mnemon, when (instead of Pasargadæ or even Persepolis) Susa was become the chief residence of the Akhæmenian king. But our author proceeds; "Memnon also was in the prime of age, excellent both for valour and for splendour of spirit; and he had built upon the hill-top (or citadel, ἄκρας) the palace at Susa that subsisted to the time of the supremacy of the Persians, and was called from him Memnoneia." Here, we may be content to ascribe, not to Diodorus but to Ktesias, the past tense of the verb "subsisted," and we may suppose that the palace of Memnon, at the time of Artaxerxes Mnemon, had been replaced by another—perhaps the building (begun at least by Darius son of Hystaspes) where Artaxerxes introduced the idols Mithra and Anakhita, as the inscription found in its ruins by Mr Loftus still informs us. But we are inclined to read ἐπὶ τῆς ἄκρας τῆς ἐν Σούσοις βασιλεία τὰ διαμείναντα κ. τ. λ. i. e. 'upon the citadel or fort-hill in Susa a palace that subsisted &c.' "Memnon had also constructed a high-way, λεωφόρον ὁδὸν, through the country that to this day" (said Ktesias, as we suppose, not Diodorus of his own knowledge) "is named Memnoneion." After noticing the claim made by the Ethiopians "about Egypt," that Memnon was born there, and the ancient palace which they said was still called Memnoneia, our author goes on with his story thus : "Well; Memnon is said to have re-inforced the Trojans with 20,000 foot and 200 chariots, to have exhibited wonderful valour, and destroyed many of the Greeks in his battles, but to have been at last cut to pieces in an ambuscade by the Thessalians. The Ethiopians, however, got possession of his body, and having burnt it, carried back the bones to Tithonus." It is plainly Ktesias not Diodorus who then subjoins; "Some such story as this about Memnon, the Barbarians say is told in the royal records," ἐν ταῖς βασιλικαῖς ἀναγραφαῖς. The doctor's informants, we may dare to say, were ready enough to allege βασιλικὰς διφθέρας (as Ktesias does, Diod. ii. 32) records to which they had no access, or inscriptions on slab and cylinder which (if exposed to public gaze) they yet perhaps could not read or understand. That Memnon brought an Ethiopian force to the defence of Troy, from parts beyond the remotest eastern districts mentioned by Homer in the second book of the Iliad, we are quite ready to believe. That the Kissians were considered Ethiopian by those who thought they had found in their country the

that the absence of the final *n* in the Aryan and Assyrian transcripts, is not necessarily due to elision, which supposes the Kissian to be the proper form of the name, but may be accounted for by supposing the previous vowel to have had a nasal sound inherent in it, according to the Aryan and Assyrian pronunciation, which had to be expressed by a separate letter in Kissian speech. Never-

seat whereto Tithonus had emigrated in the east, seems also manifest: and the judgment may be allowed to have weight. Whether, however, the country from which Memnon led his father's Ethiopians, was really situated on the Khoaspes, may still be regarded as a mere conjecture rather than a matter of authentic record. However, we incline to think that the description of Memnon's forces, cited from Ktesias, which makes them 10,000 Ethiopians *and* 10,000 men of Susiané, is not the trace of a twofold realm of which Teutamus was king, comprehending (say) both Susiané and Babylonia, but rather a story in which the people of Susiané were originally described as Ethiopian, but which was disfigured in the report of it, by persons who considered them of different race—as in later times perhaps they were; so far at least, as the inhabitants of the city and surrounding district of Susa itself were concerned. Let us conclude by owning, that, though at the technical date assigned by Eratosthenes to the taking of Troy, B.C. 1183, the Assyrian arms are thought to have been carried as far westward as Cappadocia, we find no Teutamus king of Asshur at that time when Asshur, the modern Kileh-Shergat on the right bank of the Tigris, 60 miles south of Nineveh, was still the capital; see Rawlinson's Herod. vol. i. pp. 455–460. The name Teutamos would rather remind one of Thothmes, the name of four kings of the 18th Egyptian dynasty, of whom the third about B. C. 1440 extended his conquests to Assyria; Rawl. Herod. vol. ii. pp. 356–360. And his Ethiopians would be from the Nile. We would observe that the Syrians of Cappadocia (perhaps an Assyrian colony; see Scylax § 85) may have been called " White Syrians " by the Greeks (Scymnus of Chios v. 917. Strabo xvi. 1 § 2. xii. 3. §§ 5, 9, 25 citing Meandrius) to distinguish them from others of a swarthier hue. These, an author cited by a Scholiast on Apollon. Rhodius ii. 140, took to be the Syrians in Phœnicé, and Strabo intimates something equivalent. According to Simonides (who was born seven years before Darius son of Hystaspes and 31 years before the poet Æschylus) in an ode entitled Memnon, the hero was buried near Paltus (now Beldeh) on the part of the Syrian coast belonging to the island Arad; Strabo xv. 3 § 2; xvi. 2 § 12. For the dates see Clinton's Fasti Hellenici. We may perhaps infer that the Kissian land when Simonides was in middle age, was not yet supposed by the Greeks to be Memnon's native country.

theless, with or without the final *n*, the latter part of the name seems to mark it as a Kissian compound. For, speaking of the Kush or Kissians who settled in the country called (after its first proprietor) by the Hebrews and Assyrians "Elam," and having asserted that they gave to their capital the vernacular appellation "Shus" (a variety of their patronymic Kush) Sir H. C. Rawlinson adds, that in one of the older inscriptions found in the ruins of Susa, there occurs in almost every line the name "Susinaga." This name he takes for a synonym of the Sushan or Shushan of the Assyrians and Hebrews; and of the Susa, not only used by Greek writers but found in a later inscription, discovered by Colonel Williams in the ruins of the city and thought by Sir H. C. Rawlinson to be of the age of Darius Hystaspes'. son; for in Colonel Williams's inscription the name is stated to be "Shusa."[m]

[m] See Journal R. A. S. vol. xv. p. 239, note; and vol. xiv. *Analysis*, p. xvii, note. The older description of records of Susiana Sir H. C. Rawlinson describes as an extensive collection of legends, on bricks and slabs, belonging to a series of kings who from their language must be judged of Hamite race. Of these inscriptions the character he affirms to be almost the same as the "hieratic Chaldæan" of the early bricks of Lower Babylonia; but the language seems to resemble the Scythic (Kissian) of the Akhæmenian trilingual tablets, rather than the primitive language of Babylonia. See Geo. Rawlinson's Herodotus, vol. i. p. 448. At page 445 Sir Henry had stated that for the most part the inscriptions at Susa belong to the 8th cent. B. C.; the kings named in the legends being (by the mention of them probably in the Assyrian annals, proved to be) contemporary with Sennacherib, Sargon and their immediate predecessors, kings of Assyria. However, in the long inscription of *Sutruk Nakhunta* on the broken obelisk at Susa, he notes what may he thinks be dates; two sets of numbers occurring, which may be read 2455 and 2465, and, if they be numbers of years, indicate an epoch nearly 3200 years B. C. The Cushites, he observes, pp. 448, 449, (if we may judge from the works of which the citadel at Susa is an example, or from the extent of country over which Susian monuments are found) could hardly have been inferior in power or civilization to the Chaldæans who ruled on the Lower Euphrates. Bricks of the Susian type and bearing Scythic (Kissian) legends, have been found amid the ruins of *Rishire*, (near Bushire,) and of *Taurie* (*Siraf* of the Arabs); and in all probability, the line of mounds which may be traced along

But, whether Martiya was or was not, partly at least, of Kissian blood, notwithstanding the regal name which he assumed of Immannis, his enterprise was ill-supported. In consequence as it seems of an advance upon the province made by Darius in person from Babylon, a change took place in the temper of the people of Susiana, which we may ascribe to the encouragement now given to Darius's friends and to the dismay produced among his enemies. In the end, Martiya was seized and slain by those who had owned him their chief.[n]

the whole extent of the eastern shores of the Persian gulf, contains similar relics.

With the names *Shus* and *Avar*, found in Elam or Susiana, Sir H. C. Rawlinson connects the Hyk-sôs invaders of Egypt and their famous city Avaris (on the east of the Bubastite river or Nile-mouth, according to Manetho) Journal R. A. S. vol. xv. p. 239. We would ask, Whether the space of twelve years, during which the kings of Sodom, Gomorrah, and the neighbouring cities served Chedorlaomer king of Elam and the three kings his confederates, together with the 13th year in which they rebelled (Genesis xiv. 3, 4,) may not be the very 13 years of Egypt mentioned by Manetho (in Joseph. *cont. Apion* i. 26) during which Egypt was in subjection to invaders from Palestine, descended from the expelled Hyk-sôs, and called in to their aid by a body of Egyptian lepers and unclean. From Genesis xiv. 4, 5, 9 we might infer that the coalition of four kings was made up of two confederacies, each consisting of a pair of kings; that for the rank of his kingdom Amraphel king of Shinar was the first, but that Chedorlaomer king of Elam was foremost in action. If, however, he is rightly identified with Kudur-Mabuk, a king apparently of Elamite origin and paramount at Babylon (see Geo. Rawlinson's Bampton Lectures pp. 72, 359) we must suppose Amraphel king of Shinaar subordinate to Chedorlaomer. By Aristobulus and Khares, companions of Alexander's, the name Susa was derived from Suson, σύσον, a native word equivalent to the Greek κρίνον, "a lily;" Athenæus xii. p. 113. In his *Chaldæa and Susiana*, Mr Loftus tells us, that during nine months the whole country is burnt up by the sun. At the beginning of January, however, under the heavy rains which fall from December to the end of March (*i. e.* to the beginning of the Aryan *Garmapada*) the young grass is brought forth and increases with a truly tropical rapidity and luxuriance, plentifully interspersed with a sweet and delicate *iris* which has suggested to some that the name of the ancient city Shushan (which also means "a lily") was hence derived.

[n] The brief record of the change of mind in Susiana, its occasion, and the issue of it, appears to be this; "And forasmuch as I was moving (?)

Thus Darius, whether he pursued his march from Babylon or whether for the present he deferred his visit to Susiana, had now the road before him through this province unobstructed, whether towards Media north-

towards Susiana, then the people of Susiana, influenced (? or "frightened?) by me, seized that Martiya who was their chief, and killed him." Of this, the clause which accounts for the change of purpose in Martiya's supporters, is wholly lost in the Assyrian but is perfect in the Kissian, and by aid of the latter can be fully or sufficiently restored in the Aryan. But as yet the meaning of certain words remains doubtful in both texts. The Aryan is, [. . . . ada]kya adam ashaniya aham abiya 'Uwajam. The Kissian is deciphered thus, hiak Hu avasîr Affarti inkanna sennigat. Of this Kissian text, the first word hiak, "and," is a conjunction which has not always its correspondent in the Aryan text; but there is room for one here on the rock tablet, uta. The Aryan word adakya is restored with certainty, because it is elsewhere (viz. in Aryan, col. ii, 24, iii. 81 and 82) the correspondent of the word found here in the Kissian counterpart avasîr; see the Kissian, col. ii. 17; iii. 93. Now, the word avasîr signifies, "when, whereas, forasmuch as, since": see Mr Norris's Glossary; Journal R. A. S. vol. xv. p. 166. The Aryan word ashaniya does not occur in the inscriptions elsewhere. With some hesitation Sir H. C. Rawlinson explains it as a present participle, or rather gerund admitting no inflexion, and derived from the Sanskrit root ash, "to go." The termination aniya for an, he justifies by the examples chartaniya, "joining," which occurs frequently: thastaniya, "stopping," and vataniya; See Journal R. A. S. vol. xi pp. 66, 141, 175. On the Aryan text, then, we take our stand, accepting Mr Norris's explanation of adakya and Sir H. C. Rawlinson's of ashaniya. As to the Kissian, we have only to observe; 1. That while in the Aryan we have 'Uwaja the name of the country, in the clause now cited, and in the next clause, 'Uwajiya the name of the inhabiting people, we have in both the corresponding places of the Kissian, the same word, an appellation deciphered (doubtfully as to the first syllable) Affarti and considered identical with Afarti-fa (Kissian, col. i. 57, 58; iii. 50, 53 and in Detached Inscriptions C and F.) that is, the people of the country called Afardi; this name of the country being written with a letter supposed to be to the other as the cerebral d to t. 2. Of the Aryan phrase, ashaniya aham abiya 'Uwajam, "going was (l) towards Khoja," the counterpart in the Kissian is, Af (?) farti inkanna sennigat, and we might take inkanna for a post-position conveying at least as much as the Aryan preposition abiya, "to, towards," iwi, but more than abiya, if the Kissian word sennigat here, corresponds only with the Aryan aham; as in Kissian col. ii. 48 and col. iii. 35 it corresponds with the mere

ward or towards Persis to the east: and thus, the master whom they seemed to reject, might now (according to an image of the united nations shewn to the prophet Daniel not more than five-and-thirty years before this time) proceed at his choice to seize upon the Aryan Ram by either horn.° For in Persis as well as in Media reigned a revolt, over which, probably from the first, there presided a king of its own, a new pretended Smerdis.

dham of the Aryan, col. ii. 6 and col. iii. 76. Perhaps *inkanna* means "near" or "approaching." 3. The Kissian word, of which the Aryan correspondent is effaced in the clause following the one quoted and expressing the change of the Susian mind, and which is rendered conjecturally "*influenced*" or "*alarmed;*" though he has here read it *fanifa*, may (says Mr Norris) be *tanifa*, as in VI. (the Kissian tomb inscription) 14. There we read in Mr Norris's decipherment, *vasîr tanifa*. And there (if *vasîr* be equivalent to *avasîr*) the meaning may be "*because in awe,*" or "*as in dread (of me).*" Though the words appear to have no exact correspondents in the Aryan or Assyrian, one might suppose from the Assyrian the meaning of them to be "*as they were commanded.*"

° Daniel viii. 3, 4. Can there be any etymological connection between the Latin *aries*, "a ram" and the Sanskrit predicate *Arya*, "honourable"? The ram may have been regarded as the *honourable one* of the flock.

CHAP. IV.

I.

It is distinctly attested by the Behistun inscription, that it was not till *after* [a] the fifth victory of his forces in Armenia, which was Vaumisa's second victory; that is, it was not till after Thuravâhara or February, the first month of the Persian spring, in B. C. 519, that Darius moved from Babylon. The same record attests also, that it was not before the twenty-sixth of Adukanish, that the king defeated his rival Frawartish in Media. But it was before this achievement, as we have shewn (whether very shortly, or by an interval of many months) that an advance of Darius from Babylon caused another antagonist, Martiya, who had arisen later in Susiana, to be destroyed by the very men who had owned him for their king. And, if we have rightly identified Darius with the Akhshurush or Khshurush of the book Esther, he must have resided at Susa in this year B. C. 519 for more than six months after the commencement of his regnal year, that is, after the first day of Nisan or Gar-

[a] See Beh. Inscr. Aryan text, col. 2 line 64 (para. 12); Kissian text, col. 2 line 49; where the relation in time between the preceding and the ensuing achievement is denoted by the word *pasáwa* in the former and *vasní* in the latter, that is, "afterwards."

mapada, the last month of a quarter of the year, which in that latitude, may be wholly regarded as the spring. We, therefore, conclude, that in Viyakhana (which answered to the last month of the Assyrian twelve, Adarru, and which in the Persian twelvemonth stood between Thuraváhara and Garmapada) Darius went from Babylon to Susa; a distance of twenty days' journey; [b] that he spent the first of Nisannu, the Assyrian New year's day (say, the first of April) at that capital; that it was in the seventh Assyrian month, Tasritu, the Jewish Tisri, and after the seventh day of that month, when he left Susa for Media, and lastly, that this month was the Adukanish of the Aryan text of the Behistun inscription, on the twenty-sixth day of which he defeated Frawartish in Media.

With regard to the last of these conclusions, that the Aryan Adukanish corresponded with the Assyrian Tasritu, we rely upon the indication furnished us by the narrative in Esther. For the Behistun inscription enables us only to affirm that Adukanish was the Aryan name for either the third, the fourth, the fifth, the sixth, or the seventh month of the Assyrian and of the Jewish Calendars. And, therefore, but for the evidence of the book Esther that Darius stayed at least 187 days at Susa of the third Assyrian year of his reign, the chances would be four to one against Tasritu being the Assyrian month with which Adukanish corresponded. From the paragraph in the Behistun inscription containing the date, "twenty-sixth of Adukanish," all notice of the king's stay at Susa was excluded by the plan of the inscription, which is a record of battles gained and rivals overthrown. Yet the clauses introducing its subject—the battle in Media upon the twenty-sixth of Adukanish—are so worded as to be compatible with, if they do not obscurely intimate a stay of the king's at some place between Babylon and the spot

[b] Alexander the Great (B. C. 331) did it in 20 days; Arrian Exp. Al. iii. 16 § 6. Antigonus (B. C. 315) marched with a heavy train from Susa to Babylon in 22 days; Diod. xix. 55 § 1, 2.

where ultimately he crossed the Median frontier. His march from Babylon into Media may have been made at twice. He records two moves, successive but disconnected. For the paragraph (which is the one just after the record of Vaumisa's second victory in Armenia) begins thus; "Afterwards I went out from Babylon : I proceeded to Media." [c]

We presume that Darius's stay at Susa was employed in securing his interest in a province which, since his reign began, had already twice attempted to recover its ancient independence, by setting up a king of its own. He was also, probably, in the course of this summer receiving reinforcements from all parts of the empire where he could command or influence. Himself, from wealthy Babylon along with his army, and perhaps a train of Jews (including Mordecai and his household) glad to exchange the Chaldæan capital for the king's protection at Susa,[d] it must be supposed that Darius had brought every supply required for the fitting reception of the expected re-inforcements; for the entertainments with which he proposed to dignify his residence at Susa ; or for the campaign which (when the summer heats were past) he meant to conduct in the country where Frawartish was still called king, beyond the neighbouring mountains. While forces were mustering, councils must have been held continually, not only on the internal administration and civil affairs of Susiana and the other subject provinces, but on the war and on the measures to be

[c] The disjunction is expressed both in the Aryan and in the Kissian; the Assyrian text is here defaced; See Journal R. A. S. vol. x. p. 222; vol. xv. p. 113.

[d] We follow Josephus (Antiq. xi. 6. § 2) so far as to regard Babylon the native place of Mordecai and Esther, though he is contradicted by the book Esther (ii. 5.) in the statement that they were still at Babylon when Esther was taken for the king's Hareem, that is, at latest in the 6th year of his reign. The condition of Babylon at that time and during the previous rule of the second pretender to the name Nebukhadrezzar while the city was being besieged by Darius's forces, shews that Josephus cannot possibly be accurate in this respect. How so, will be seen below.

adopted in respect of provinces where a wavering might be perceptible in allegiance or in hostility on the part of satraps or subjects. Feasts (according to Herodotus) were especially occasions whereon, amid the wine in which they much indulged, the Persians were wont to canvass matters of importance.°

But into these particulars—not being a political history—the book Esther does not enter. So much only is related of what happened at this time, as was needed to explain how Hadassah, that is Esther the Jewess, became Darius's queen, so as in that position to be the means about five years later of saving her nation from destruction. We are told that, "Like the sitting of king Akhshurush on his chair of kingdom, that was at Shushan the palace, in the third year of his reign, he made a feast unto all his lords and his servants, while, before a host of Persis and Media, and the presidents ʄ and lords of the provinces, he

---

°. Herod. i. 133, where commentators cite the similar conduct of the Germans, from Tacitus, Germ. § 22. But Plato (in his "Laws," Book 1. p. 637, E.) is cited by G. Rawlinson as saying, that the practice prevailed among the Thracians, the Scythians, the Celts, the Iberians, and the Carthaginians. The ancestors of Tacitus's Germans (it seems probable) had not yet occupied Germany, or, at least, had not yet driven the Celts across the Rhine, in the days of Plato, B. C. 428–347.

ʄ The *partmim* פַּרְתְּמִים of Esther i. 3, vi. 9, are persons named by a title supposed to be a Persian one, corresponding with the Sanskrit *pratama*, which exists (it is said) in Zend in the form *fratemó* and in Pehlevi as *pardom*. See Lee and Gesenius. This may seem incompatible with the fact, that Daniel (i. 3) designates princes of Judah *partmim*. But this chapter (from the last verse of it) seems to have been written at earliest in the first regnal year of Cyrus at Babylon, the date of the proclamation by which the king summoned the people of Jehovah the God of the heavens, to go up to Jerusalem in Judah and there rebuild the temple which Nebukhadrezzar had destroyed. At that time there had been an Aryan government (that of the Medes) at Babylon for full two years already; so that the word in its peculiar application, might be in use. That these *partmim* were "lords," as we have rendered the term *Sarim* שָׂרִים but of higher rank, appears in part from Est. i. 3, but particularly from the expression of Est. vi. 9, *ish mis-saréi ham-melek hap-partmím*, "a man among the king's lords, the partmim."

displayed the riches of the glory of his kingdom and the honour of the splendour of his majesty for one hundred and eighty days." By this we may understand, that on taking his seat as king at Susa, when he arrived there for the first time, Darius judged it suitable to the occasion, befitting the inauguration of his kingdom, as he had with him a Perso-Median army with many great men both of his court and of the provinces, for part of a display of his wealth and splendour, to provide every day a banquet for all his satraps and military leaders, as well as for those of his court and palace, during the space of six whole months. But he went further: for the book adds that "when those days were expired," and when, we may presume, all his troops were now assembled, "the king made a feast to all the people that were found in Shushan the palace, to both great and small, seven days, in the court of the garden of the king's palace." His Persians and Medes were here; his soldiers of other provinces of his empire; and with them, perhaps, the citizens of Susa, certainly so many as had been levied for the army. The assemblage was marshalled under awnings,⁸ white, green,

We have rendered it "*presidents*," as the English version of Daniel vi. 2, 3, 4, 6, 7 calls the three *sarkin*, סָרְכִין, to whom the Mede Darius's hundred and twenty *satraps* accounted for the king's revenue. From Esther i. 3, where they may seem opposed to the lords of the provinces, one might take them for court lords, dignitaries of the central government. We find from Esth. vi. 10 that Haman the son of Hammedatha the Agagite (after the king had advanced him and set his seat above all the lords that were with him, Esth. iii. 1) was one of the *partmim*, though not of Aryan race nor a Persian by blood. It is, therefore, to be supposed that Mordecai the Jew became one also, when he succeeded to the place of Haman, receiving the king's signet-ring which the king had before entrusted to Haman: see Esth. iii. 10; viii. 2, 15; ix. 4. Perhaps, the seven lords named Esth. i. 14, were of the same class. Compare Ezra vii. 14, 28. Also Cyrus's council of war, Περσέων τοὺς πρώτους, Herod. i. 206.

⁸ Josephus Antiq. xi. 6 § 1 gives this explanation (derived perhaps from the Septuagint paraphrase)

σκήνωμα πηξάμενος ἐκ χρυσίων καὶ ἀργυρίων κιόνων, ὕφη λίνεα καὶ πορφύρεα κατ' αὐτῶν διατείνασιν, ὥστε πολλὰς μυριάδας κατακλίνεσθαι·

With Darius's great entertainment at Susa in B. C. 519, we may

and blue, hung by silver rings on pillars of marble. Thus sheltered from the sun, they were all made to recline, probably in companies and battalions, or in tribes and nations, under their respective leaders, on beds of gold and silver, ranged upon a pavement of red, blue, white, and black marble. The royal wine was supplied in golden

compare another at Persepolis in B. C. 316. Here, Peukestes was the Macedonian Satrap of Persis and we might conclude, of the Uxian territory also, if we did not consider this as more probably an appendage of Susiana, which was claimed as his satrapy by Antigenes, another of those who co-operated at this time against Antigonus with Eumenes. And here Peukestes feasted a confederate army, of which his own was by far the most numerous contingent, after it had under Eumenes foiled Antigonus on the Pasitigris, the western boundary of the Uxian territory. Antigonus had since crossed the mountains into Media, the satrap of which was in his army, and the confederates under Eumenes had reached Persepolis, thence to proceed to the Parætakenian frontier (Diod. xix. 34 ₴ 7. Corn. Nepos, *Eumenes*, cap. 8) to stop the invasion of Antigonus in that quarter ; see Diod. xix. 24 ₴ 4 and compare Arrian Exp. Alex. iii. 19 ₴ 2 ; Curtius v. 35.

A vast number of animals supplied from every part of the province, were sacrificed to the gods and to Alexander and Philip. The altars formed the common centre of four circles in which the army reclined, and ate the flesh of the sacrifices. The inmost circle was distant 202 feet from the altars, having a circumference of two Stades or 1212 feet. It was reserved (where not crossed by roads from the altars to the outer circles) for the beds of the generals, the leaders of the cavalry, and the Persians of greatest distinction. At the distance of another 202 feet, (that is, 404 feet from the altars) a second circle of four stades circumference was filled with leaders of second rank, generals unattached, friends, and the men of the cavalry. The breadth of space between the first and second circles was doubled for the interval between the second circle and the third ; this last being eight stades in circumference and distant 808 feet from the altars. It was occupied by the Macedonian infantry brigade called *Argyraspids* or " Silver-shields ; and by such of the *Hetæri* or " Companions " as had served with Alexander. The outermost circle of all was as near to the third as the second circle was to the first ; the interval being 202 feet. It was ten stades in circumference; distant, therefore, from the altars 1010 feet ; and filled with the mercenaries and allies. The guests thus assembled appear to have been over 40,000 men ; compare Diod. xix. 14 and 28. The beds, κλισιαι, on which they stretched themselves, were of the leafage of trees ; and over thes were awnings (?) αὐλαιαι, and coverlets, τιςιστςώματα, of every sort ; Diod. xix. 22.

vessels,[h] with a liberality befitting the riches of the king. Rules of diet or of drinking, if they existed, as among the castes of India now,—were respected. No one was compelled to drink; the officers of the king's house being directed to comply with the humour of each guest in the matter. With seven eunuchs waiting before him, the king himself, as well as his lords, partook of the feast and surveyed the multitude—his name Darius superseded by one that bespoke him, it would seem, king of the Medes. If this name Akhshurush (or rather Khshurush) signified the same as did what appears the softened form Khurush among the Persians, "*The Sun*," it asserted the majesty of him who bore it; though it was more suited to the mouths of others than to his own.[i] But after all, one

---

[h] Compare the furniture of the Persian tents which fell into the power of the Greeks after the battle at Platæa, B. C. 479 :—

κλίνας ἐπιχρύσους καὶ ἐπαργύρους, κρητῆρας τε χρυσίους καὶ φιάλας τε καὶ ἄλλα ἐκπόματα.

Herod. ix. 30, and again the supper furniture of Mardonius's tent,

κλίνας τε χρυσίας καὶ ἀργυρίας εὖ ἐστρωμένας καὶ τραπέζας τε χρυσίας καὶ ἀργυρίας καὶ παρασκευὴν μεγαλοπρεπέα τοῦ δείπνου

Herod. ix. 82. The Septuagint Esth. i. 7 (as many places in this book) has no pretence to be a translation :—

ποτήρια χρυσᾶ καὶ ἀργυρᾶ καὶ ἀνθράκινον κυλίκιον προκείμενον ἀπὸ ταλάντων τρισμυρίων.

[i] This may help to explain why (if Akhshurush was his regal name) the son of Hystaspes calls himself not Akhshurush but Darius *(Darya-vush)* in all his inscriptions. Perhaps Darius assumed the name Akhshurush before the overthrow of Frawartish, to shew a claim to the throne of the Medes, and may afterwards have neglected it; though the author of the book Esther uses it throughout. We have instances of Chinese emperors, after having received a name of state, speaking of themselves by their petty name; out of humility or the polite affectation of it. 1. Thus an emperor of the third or *Cheoo* dynasty, though in the reign of his son he is called by that son (as he is also called invariably by Chinese commentators) *Kang-Wang*, is found just after his accession, in an address to the great officers and vassals of the empire, calling himself *Chao*, as he had been lately called before his accession by his still living father. See the *Shoo-king* iv. 22 §§ 7, 9; 23 § 4; and 25 § 2. 2. Again, this emperor's grandfather (who completed the downfall of the second, the *Shang* or *Yu* dynasty, and the elevation of the *Cheoo* dynasty) was called *Woo-wang*. He is so called thrice in §§ 1, 12 and 16 by the author of the sixth chapter of the fourth part of the Shoo-king; a chapter which recites an incident of the emperor's last illness, and must be a document or founded on a document written shortly after the emperor's death. But in an address to a great assembly of lords from neighbouring states

may incline to think that of the two names, Darius was the royal and Khshurush the prior private name.[j]

and of officers, civil and military, shortly before the complete overthrow of the last emperor of the Shang dynasty, he calls himself modestly *Fa*. He does the same in a subsequent address to his army. Likewise, at the outset of his expedition, in an address to the Spirits of the mountains and the rivers; See the *Shoo-king,* iv. 1 § 6; 2 § 7; 5 § 2 or, according to an older arrangement of the chapter, 5 § 6. 3. Again, this emperor's famous brother, *Cheoo-kong,* though so called by others, in an instruction to the Son and Heir of Heaven the young emperor his nephew, names himself *Tan;* See the *Shoo-king,* iv. 19 § 18. So, too, during his royal brother's illness in a prayer to the Spirits of the three preceding kings, his fathers, he calls himself *Tan*, though not only the narrator calls him *Cheoo-kong* but afterwards the new king, his nephew, does so too; see iv. 6 §§ 3, 5, 6, 10, &c. and especially 18. In the fourth classic book of Chinese Moral and Political Philosophy, one which bears the name of the sage *Meng-tse,* we often find persons designated by one name but calling themselves by another. At ii. 8 §§ 25, 29 we read of *Hao-seng* whose "little" or "petty" name was *Poo-hai;* also of *Y-ching* whose petty name was *Kwo.* In this last case, the person is afterwards called by the two names together, *Y-ching-Kwo;* according to which precedent, the Artaxerxes of Xenophon's time for instance, would be called Artaxerxes Arsakes; his son Artaxerxes Okhus and his father Darius Okhus. Compare the third Chinese Classic, the book *Lun-Yu* ii, 14 § 14; and the *Meng-tse* ii. 8 § 36 in the *Livres sacrés de l' Orient par G. Pauthier.*

[j] It is a great objection to the explanation attempted in the last note, of Darius's not calling himself Akhshurush in his inscriptions (which fact seems to contradict the theory that Akhshurush or Khshurush was the regal name assumed by the son of Hystaspes) that in inscriptions of Darius's successors it is the regal not the private name which we find employed, where we know both. The last Artaxerxes, whose private name Okhus is usually given him by Greek authors, drops this name in his inscription at Persepolis (Journal R. A. S. vol. x. pp. 341, 342) and calls himself Artakhshatra only. His father, too, Artaxerxes (Mnemon) whose original name was Arsakes, he names Artakhshatra only. His grandfather Darius (Nothus) whose original name like his own was Okhus, he calls by the regal designation only, Daryavush. His great-grandfather Artaxerxes Makrokheir, whose original name (according to Josephus) was Cyrus, he calls only Artakhshatra. The father and grandfather of this last king he calls Khshayârsha (Xerxes) and Daryavush (Darius) respectively. We do not know of any other name which the first of these possessed, and, therefore, he may be omitted: but if the son of Hystaspes had two names, Akhshurush and Darius, the inference from Artaxerxes Okhus's practice in the four other cases is, that Khshurush or Akhshurush was the original and private name

Meanwhile, within the palace also, the ladies of Persia and Media, also probably the wives of men of other countries of low as well as high degree, were feasted by Vashti the queen. She seems to have been that daughter of Gobryas by whom king Darius was already the father of three sons, when he seized the throne: and whom we have attempted to identify with his much-loved queen, called Artystoné by Herodotus. Well; on the seventh and last day of this general entertainment within and without the palace, his heart being merry with wine, the Sun of Persia commanded his seven eunuchs to bring forth before him the queen in the *kitaris* of kingdom,[k] the royal tiara, that he might cause the nations and the lords to behold her beauty; for she was excellent of appearance. Vashti refused to come. The summons probably found her with the crowd of female guests before her. She might have been loth at another time to obey, but while they

while Darius was the regal name; just as in the case of his queen, Esther was the private and Hadassah the regal name. The same nomenclature of himself and of the kings his ancestors, had been employed by Artaxerxes Okhus's father; and the inference is, of course, the same, see Artaxerxes Mnemon's inscription at Susa; Journal R. A. S. vol. xv. pp. 158, 159. It should be noted that descent from the kings of the Medes, and a claim to inherit from them, was asserted at least as obviously by the name Darius as by the name Akhshurush. As to this name אֲחַשְׁוֵרוֹשׁ that we have done well in taking the first *vau* no less than the last for a vowel, is indicated by the omission of both this and the last *vau* in Esther x. 1. where the name is written אֲחַשְׁרֹשׁ. If the ordinary mode of writing the name be taken to explain this form, it gives Akhshorosh or Akhshurush.

[k] The Persian term which we give in the Greek form of it, *kitaris* or *kidaris*, is in Esther i. 11. *kether*. It has been disputed, whether the term was confined to the tiara of the king, or was of a more extensive application. But from this passage with Esth. ii. 17 and vi. 8 we may infer that the latter is the more correct opinion: for in those passages it is uniformly modified by the subjoined term *malkooth*, "of kingdom." Thus *kisseh*, "a seat" (as Haman's, Esth. iii. 1, or Bath-sheba's, 1 Kings ii. 19, or that seat at Jerusalem in Nehemiah's time, which was reserved for the Satrap of the countries west of the Euphrates at any visit of his to Jerusalem, Nehem. iii. 7) requires the subjoining of the same term *malkooth*, which makes it "a seat of kingdom," in order to signify in particular *a throne*, as we in English generally apply that term;—*a royal chair*. Esth. i. 2.

looked on, it was a severer trial to be required to abdicate her dignity, and, confessing her royal state *his* bounty, to cast, as it were, her crown before his footstool, going forth, though as the most precious of his jewels, to swell the magnificence of the king's display. On the other hand, the king, thus slighted in the presence of his assembled people, was inflamed with anger; yet, without the assent of his sages who "knew law and judgment," he would do nothing. At the head of these there appears to have been a council of "discerners of the times," or men trusted as skilful to distinguish the seasonable from the unseasonable, the expedient from the inexpedient,— seven lords of united Persis and Media "who saw the king's face and had the first seats in the kingdom."[1] They even seem to have been present when the cause arose, and nearest to Darius's person. But, whether so or not, to them whose names, according to the Jewish vowel-pointing of the text of the book Esther, were, Carshena,

---

[1] Compare Ezra vii. 14, 28. All the king's great lords (to borrow a term from this last passage) if they had passed through the course of Persian education described by Xenophon and Strabo, were supposed to understand "law and judgment," or "Righteousness," but though all of them casuists, not all would be "knowing of times." As to the council of seven, the language of Josephus (Antiq. xi. 6 § 1) would lead one to think that it still existed in his time under the Parthian kings; for he describes them as

τοὺς ἑπτὰ τῶν Περσῶν οἱ τὴν τῶν νόμων ἐξήγησιν ἔχουσιν παρ' αὐτοῖς·

This, too, reminds us, of the "royal judges" mentioned by Greek writers, Herod. iii. 14, 13 and v. 25, Plutarch Artax. § 29. Of these the highest court, not the sole court, must have been one in attendance upon the king. But as the Satrap's court had its "royal secretary," Herod. iii. 128, so we may suppose it supplied with a "royal judge" or bench of judges. Compare the court convoked by Cyrus "the Younger" for the trial of the traitor Orontes, Xenoph. Anab. i. 6. § 4.

Περσῶν τοὺς ἀρίστους τῶν περὶ αὐτὸν ἑπτὰ·

In addition, the Lacedæmonian general Klearkhus was called in as a σύμβουλος, and, though the last (like Memucan by Darius) was called upon to give his opinion first. Every satrap great or small would need the advice and sanction of men versed in the royal edicts, the laws of the Persians and Medes, no less than the king himself. Perhaps the "Master of the edicts" (rendered in our English Vulgate, "chancellor") whose authority is exhibited in the sub-province Samaria by Ezra iv. 8, 9, 17, 23, was such a judge appointed by the king.

Shethar, Adnatha, Tarshish, Meres, Marsena, Memucan, sitting partly as counsellors, partly as judges, the king put the question, What shall we do unto the queen Vashti, according to law, because she hath not performed the king Akhshurush's commandment by the eunuchs? Then, the last of the seven, Memucan, answered before the king and the lords, to this effect; Queen Vashti's offence is against the master of the house as well as against the king. It affects not the king Akhshurush alone, but also the lords and all the nations that are in all the king's provinces. For the queen's word will go forth through all the wives, to the causing of contempt of their masters[m] in their eyes, when they say, King Akhshurush spake to cause Vashti the queen to come before him, and she came not. Also, this day, the ladies of Persis and Media will say what they heard of the queen's speech, to all the king's lords; and like the abundance of the contempt, will the exasperation be also. If it seem good unto the king, there shall a word of kingdom go forth from before him, and it shall be written in the laws of Persis and Media, and shall not pass away; that Vashti (for queen she shall be called no longer) shall not come before the king Akhshurush, and her royalty the king shall give to her companion that is better than she. And, men shall say, It was heard, was the king's decree, that he shall make, in all his kingdom, great as it is, and all the wives give honour to their masters, great and small!"

The counsel in the eyes of the king and the lords was good; and the king did according to the word of Memucan. He sent letters to all the king's provinces, to province after province, according to its writing, and to people after people, according to its tongue, for every man to be constituted a bearer of lordship in his house and a giver of sentence according to the tongue of his people. The purpose, then, for which the king's letters were sent throughout all the provinces seemed to be, that everywhere every householder should be master of his own house, and that his word there should be law among people of

[m] *baalim*, compare Hosea ii. 16; also *Manu* v. 151, 154.

his own language.ⁿ But this enactment, it would seem, was prefaced by a recital of Queen Vashti's offence and of the punishment which had been awarded her. From other instances we know it was customary, that matters of joy or mourning for the king and his household, should be communicated to all the nations, that all men might take their part and manifest their sympathy.º But on this occasion, it appeared as if the king's action was prompted, not so much by the desire of obtaining the general assent to his decision in the case of Vashti, as by that of promoting the general good; and his charter, besides authority to householders in their families, might seem by analogy to grant the same to lords of nationalities or heads of tribes, in cases where none but men of the same language were concerned. Like many other charters since, this no doubt was very generally but a dead letter from the first. Yet it seemed to affirm a principle which courts of justice might enforce upon appeal—that as the king was an image of God upon the earth, or within his empire, so every man should be in his own household. In the law of some countries the maxim has been asserted, that every man's house is his castle, making him a baron within his own doors; but Darius may seem to have laid it down, that every man's house is his kingdom, and his word there a sentence from which there is no appeal. This we suppose to be quite in accordance with the sentiment of the old laws and customs of other Indo-Germanic nations.ᵖ Indeed, in the primitive state of man-

ⁿ Perhaps this decree of the king's would not have been interpreted as giving Metiokhus son of Miltiades the same power over his Persian wife; Herod. vi. 41.

º When Cyrus lost his wife, Kassandanè, he made great mourning himself and gave notice to all the subjects of his empire to mourn likewise; Herod. ii. 1. On his marriage with Atossa or Hadassah, that is, Esther, our Darius not only made a feast for his lords and his servants, but he made a release to the provinces and gave gifts according to the state of the king; Esth. ii. 18. So Gaumâta the Magian in the character of Smerdis son of Cyrus, taking possession of the throne, sent immediately to every nation a three years' release from military service and tribute; Herod. iii. 67.

ᵖ For the Hindu law regarding females, see particularly *Manu* v. 147–156; In § 152 observe the absolute power of the husband is made to arise from the wife's having been given him by her father.

kind throughout the world, every man's house was his sphere of a theoretically absolute power, like the caves and mountain solitudes of the Cyclop giants, who, according to Homer,[q] had no meetings for counsel or for decisions of law, but every one gave law to his children and his wives.

However, Darius's charter has been pronounced ludicrous to modern ears by the author of the History of the Jews in the Family Library.[r] Of course, his opinion must have been the same of the Hindu legislator's ordinances respecting the fair sex. To us, if there be any feature in the history which might tempt a smile, it is not the matter of the counsel but the art of the counsellor. We admire the courtier-like address and the judicial solemnity of Memucan, in affecting to merge Darius's cause in that of all the husbands and fathers in the empire. Yet the homage thus rendered to public opinion, and to the rule of considering the public interest in every act of the royal will, is not ludicrous; nor yet the counsellor's care for the king's dignity. Perhaps, the writer we refer to, meant simply that the world is now old enough (in Europe at least and in America) to know that law against the will of the ladies is unavailing. For if to modern ears Darius's decree (supposing always that it was unarmed with penal terrors) seems only ludicrous; could those ears in our author's opinion, be required to receive with reverence certain injunctions to the wives of Christendom pronounced by apostles of the King of kings? That in fact, those precepts are little reverenced, we know; but would our author have said that he, too, thought them ludicrous?

As to Darius's law, there are questions of interest to be solved. Was each master of a house left to maintain his right by his own force and discretion, or was he to appeal to such courts of justice as existed in his nation or his neighbourhood? And if he was to appeal to the magistrates, what were the punishments they were empowered to award? Or were these left to the discretion

[q] Hom. Od. ix. 106-115 quoted in part by Strabo xiii. 1 § 25.
[r] vol. 2 p. 18, second edition, London 1830.

of the judge? Or, to the custom of each country? In the case of Vashti, the punishment which Darius's supreme court awarded her on his demand, was not a divorce but degradation. It deprived her of her privilege as a wife, and of her dignity as the queen; but it left her still in her husband's custody, dependant on him alone for the necessaries and comforts of life.

It seems an error to suppose her behaviour to have been a mere compliance with the absolute requirement, according to alleged Oriental notions, of female "modesty." If it had been the king's marriage-feast that was held out of doors, what was now required of Vashti would have been a matter of course.* Besides, the term "modesty" in pleadings of commentators desiring the praise of chapel or drawingroom, is probably used by substitution, for " a sense of female and queenly dignity." Now, this obligation of self-respect is precisely what, according to

* So talk the commentators we have seen, who appear to confound Musulman and Oriental. Josephus, indeed, Antiq. xi. 6 § 1 writes:—

ἡ δὲ, φυλακῇ τῶν παρὰ Πέρσαις νόμων, οἱ τοῖς ἀλλοτρίοις βλέπεσθαι τὰς γυναῖκας ἀπηγορεύκασιν, οὐκ ἐποίησε πρὸς τὸν βασιλέα.

But if such was the law under the Parthians of the time of Josephus, it by no means follows that it was the old law or custom at Pasargadœ in the boyhood of Darius. We have reason to think, that among the primitive Persians, women had as much freedom as with the republican Romans or the Homeric Greeks. As to the compliance required of Vashti, it was (at the utmost) that of the Persian bride at the close of the marriage feast of her new husband and his companions. After the return from India, when Alexander the Great celebrated fourscore marriages at Susa, taking Barsinè daughter of the dethroned and slain Darius for himself, and giving the principal ladies of Persia and Media to the "companions."

οἱ γάμοι ἐποιήθησαν νόμῳ τῷ Περσικῷ. θρόνοι ἐτέθησαν τοῖς νυμφίοις ἐξεξῆς, καὶ μετὰ τὸν πότον ἧκον αἱ γαμούμεναι καὶ παρεκαθίζοντο ἑκάστη τῷ ἑαυτῆς· οἱ δὲ ἰδεξιώσαντό τε αὐτὰς καὶ ἐφίλησαν· πρῶτος δὲ ὁ βασιλεὺς ἦρξεν· ἐν τῷ αὐτῷ γὰρ πάντως ἐγίγνοντο οἱ γάμοι .. Οἱ δὲ παραλαβόντες ἀπῆγον τὴν ἑαυτοῦ ἕκαστος· πρῶικας δὲ ξυμπάσαις ἐπέδωκεν Ἀλέξανδρος.

He also gave gifts on the occasion to as many as 10,000 other Macedonians, who had previously married Asiatic women; Arrian Exp. Alex. vii. 4 §§ 7, 8. Compare the conduct of the Persian envoys in Macedonia in the time of our Darius; Herod. v. 18-20. We may believe that they said truly; "We Persians have a custom when we make a great feast, to bring with us to the board our wives and concubines, and make them sit beside us."

Oriental notions of duty to the husband and the king, Vashti should have esteemed less authoritative and less forcible than Darius's command. In regard of the king's conduct, it may be owned that he was not above his age; if it be fair to put aside the consideration of what his kingly character may have required. It may be admitted that in thus punishing his wife for no adultery, he evinced a hardness of heart to which, even in the Church of God, the Mosaic Law still permitted scope, in the complaints of husbands; though by analogy, it had become evident already, and it was soon to be authoritatively declared by a Prophet,[t] that the God of Israel hated the putting away of wives. But our modern handlers of Scripture histories might as reasonably and usefully exclaim at Darius's revels, as at his legislation in the matter of husbands and wives, fathers and children. His revels, no less than his laws, shew him to have been a true Persian, of the times when the Persians were supreme, and in the countries where their supremacy was exercised far from their native or ancestral land. If he had disregarded Vashti's publicly-exhibited contempt of his command, it would not have been a noble forbearance; it would have been because he was insensible to dishonour; or at least, because he feared dishonour less than he feared his wife. In either case, he would have been contemned by his assembled host. The nations and their lords for such a king would hardly have marched with ardour against the Mede.

However (as Herodotus sometimes subjoins to a disputable opinion) "every reader is at liberty to judge the matter as he will."[u]

[t] Malachi ii. 16.
[u] It would probably require a volume to illustrate the hypothesis that Darius's law which he published on the occasion of Vashti's disobedience, was in accordance with the general notions of right in the Persian empire. An apostle tells us that the husband is the head of the wife; and more with which we are familiar: the Zoroastrian doctors say that the husband is a Mithra or Sun-god to his (more than one) wife: "fœminis salutationem non injungunt Soli, eodem modo quo viri faciunt: sed fœminis præscribunt salutationem, nempe, Ut quotidie euntes ad maritos tam mane quàm tempore precis secundæ," (i. e. at midday) "et muni-

II.

AMONG the governors of provinces who attended the court at Susa in B. C. 519, bringing probably each his re-inforcement to the king's army, Oroites, certainly, did not appear. He was a Persian whom Cyrus, father of the late king Cambyses, had made his lieutenant at Sardis the Lydian capital.* Whether, at the time of this appointment he had or had not been invested with a superiority over all

bus ad latera applicatis, eis dicant, *Quid præcipis? An bene quievisti? Quid cogitas ut nos faciamus? Num quicquid præceperis id facturæ sumus.* Quicquid enim maritus præceperit, id statim præstare debent. Mariti contentationem quærant: et die nocteque sic se gerant. Nam quando maritus contentus est, Dominus etiam contentus erit. Cum fœmina sic fecerit, ea est multo præstantior. Paradisæa et beata erit, quando erga maritum linguâ blandiloquâ fuerit, et ad eum die nocteque judicium suum detulerit. At si marito non obedierit, sed duo crumenæ duo corda fuerint, tum illa vocabitur irreverens, impudens, infernalis, et polluta. Nam marito non contento, quamvis multa merita habuerit, quandonam talia merita ad Animam ejus pertingent? Quandonam à gehennâ liberabitur? Si vero maritus ejus contentus erit, talis fœmina in hoc mundo Paradisæa erit." See the book Sad-der, cap. 65. For the command to men to salute the Sun thrice a day or twice at the least; instead of which the wives are here enjoined to salute their husbands twice; also for the command to salute Fire and the Moon in like manner, see *Sadder* cap. 96: (Hyde, *De relig. vet. Persarum* pp. 487, 509). We have already referred to the Laws concerning females in the Hindu code of Manu. We cite a specimen of them from the " Livres sacrés de l' Orient par G. Pauthier " p. 386; "Quoique la conduite de son epoux soit blamable, bien qu'il se livre à d'autres amours, et soit depourvu de bonnes qualités, une femme vertueuse doit coustamment le révérer comme un dieu." Manu v. 154. But the most ungallant of all, is this; " Une petite fille, une jeune femme, une femme avancée en age, ne doivent jamais rien faire selon leur propre volonté, même dans leur maison." *Manu* v. 147. For some assert that *women like to have their own way*. The incessant obedience " die nocteque " required of the wife by our Zoroastrian author, is recorded by Darius Hystaspes' son, of the provinces of his empire. It is "both by night and by day " in the Aryan, col. 1. line 20; but the corresponding Kissian expression, col. i. line 16 Mr Norris renders " by day and night," though doubtfully; Journal R. A. S. vol xv. pp 97, 98, 174, 198. If he is right, the Magian phrase is *more Kissian than Aryan*.

* Σαρδίων ὑπαρχος, Herod. iii. 120.

governors of provinces lately subject to the Lydian monarchy,[b] we find his authority now extending greatly beyond the border of the dominion of Crœsus, the last of the kings that had reigned at Sardis. Of the twenty satrapies into which, for fiscal purposes at least, Darius's dominions in Asia and Africa were afterwards divided,[c] three—the Phrygian, the Lydian, and the Ionian, including not fewer than eighteen distinct nationalities—were held at this time by Oroites.[d] In the Ionian satrapy, Herodotus

[b] After the establishment of his power at Babylon, the Great Cyrus is represented by Xenophon as having in the first instance, sent Artabatas satrap into Cappadocia, Artakamas into Great Phrygia, Khrysantas into Lydia and Ionia, Adusius into Caria, and finally, Pharnukhus into Phrygia on the Hellespont and Æolis. But of Cilicia, Cyprus and the Paphlagonians he sent not satraps, because they had willingly taken part in the expedition against Babylon, though he appointed them tributes to pay like the others; Cyrop. viii. 6 §§ 7, 8. A similar distribution of the main-land of Asia Minor into seven governments, five under satraps and two under native kings, seems to have existed in Xenophon's own time, and may, indeed, have been the ground, or one of the grounds, on which he relied in his account of the dispositions made by the founder of the Persian empire. For, to Lydia the satrapy of Artimas, Phrygia (the Greater) the satrapy of Artakamas, Lycaonia and Cappadocia that of Mithridates, Bithynia that of Pharnabazus, with Cilicia the province of the native king Syennesis and Paphlagonia that of the native Korylas (which Xenophon enumerates among those the Greek ten-thousand had traversed, Anab. vii. 8 § 25) we may add Caria as the satrapy of Tissaphernes (Hellenic. iii. 2 § 12) and divide the Greek cities on the Ægean and Hellespontian shores between him and Pharnabazus. The native kings, even of the very independent Paphlagonians and Cilicians, may have accounted with neighbouring satraps for their tribute to the king. If so, this may explain the supply of money obtained by young Cyrus from the wife of Syennesis king of Cilicia; Anab. i. 2. § 12.

[c] Herod. iii. 89; Esther x. 1.

[d] Herod. iii. 127 comparing iii. 90. With this power of Oroites, compare that granted to his younger son Cyrus, by Okhus Darius (Nothus). Cyrus was sent down satrap (in chief, at least; see the last note but one) of Lydia, of Great Phrygia, and of Cappadocia; and, withal, appointed commander in-chief of all military forces, the duty of which it was to muster in the plain of the Castolus; that is, apparently, of all the provinces bordering on the Ægean; see Xenophon, Anab. i. 9 § 7 with Hellenic. i 4 § 3 and Anab. i. 1 § 2; i. 2 § 7; and compare the case of Tissaphernes, who after the death of Cyrus, besides his own satrapy and

specifies seven populations, Ionians, Asiatic Magnesians, Æolians, Carians (including Dorian colonies from Greece of which he does not make a separate people as he had considered them before in his list of the nations subject to Crœsus, though his native city Halicarnassus was one of them) also Lycians, Milyans, Pamphylians. In the Lydian satrapy, he enumerates five nations: Mysians, Lydians, Lasonians, Cabalians, and Hygenneans or Hytenneans. In the Phrygian division, six; Hellespontians of the Asiatic shore, Phrygians, the Thracian immigrants called Bithynians, Paphlagonians, Mariandynians, and Cappadocians, called by the Greeks Syrians or White-Syrians.* Of these eighteen names, two at least belong to nations that were not subject to Crœsus; the Syrians of

that of Cyrus, was appointed commander-in-chief, and acts as such when Pharnabazus with his forces is present; Hellenic. iii. 1 § 3 and iii. 2 §§ 13, 18. After Tissaphernes by the king's order had been beheaded, Pharnabazus protested to Agesilaus, that should any other be sent down as general, and he himself be put under that general, he would embrace the alliance of the Lacedæmonians; but if the command should be assigned to himself, he would do his utmost against them; Hellen. iv. 1 § 37; also Vit. Agesil. 3 § 5. Note, that Okhus Darius's letter which his son Cyrus carried to all upon the coast,

κατατίμων Κύρον κάρανον τῶν εἰς Καστωλὸν ἀθροιζομένων.

Xenoph. Hellen. i. 4 § 3; was thus written by the king's scribes; because Xenophon proceeds to explain κάρανον (compare κοίρανος, κέρνος, κάρη, and κάρα) to mean κύριος. The letters in young Cyrus's favour, (like those obtained from Darius Akhshurush son of Hystaspes by Haman and by Mordecai; Esth. iii. 12, viii. 9) being circular, were written in the languages of the several nations that were addressed.

* See Herod. iii. 90. For the non-Hellenic nations of Herodotus's Phrygian (and Hellespontian) satrapy in the army of Xerxes, compare Herod. vii. 72, 73, 75; for those of the Lydian satrapy, Herod. vii. 74, 76, 77; for those of the Ionian satrapy, who all (except the Milyans) served on board the fleet, Herod. vii. 77, 91, 92, 93. On the Cabâlians of Herodotus's Lydian satrapy (Herod. iii. 90) and of the army of Xerxes (Herod. vii. 76, 77) one portion of whom was by descent Mæonian and by proper name Lasonian, while the rest (or Cabâlians proper) seem to have been considered by some as of the same Solymæan origin which Herodotus ascribes to the Milyans; see above pp 113–115, note. For the designation "White-Syrians" applied to the Cappadokians or Syrians of Cappadocia, see Strabo xvi. 1 § 2, xii. 3 § 5 xii. 3 §§ 9, 12, 25; also Marcianus of Herakleia in his Epitome of Menippus's Periplus of the Inner Sea; *Geogr. Græc. Minores*, ed. C. Muller, tom. i. p. 571.

Cappadocia and the Lycians.[f] Besides the followers of the provincial lords whose tenure required them to attend at the vice-regal gate, and besides the king's troops occupying fortresses or charged with the peace of districts—forces which Oroites, without the commission of commander in chief, would be able to influence as governor-general and as their pay-master, though it was the king himself ordinarily who appointed their captains [g]—he had a body-guard of a thousand Persians. Such was his formidable position in Lower Asia at the time of Darius's great muster and splendid entertainments at Susa.

Oroites had lately got rid of two powerful neighbours who (whether they were esteemed in any respect his subordinates or not) had given him offence or umbrage. Once, during the reign of Cambyses, happening to be seated in the assembly of those who did duty by attending at the king's gate, he had been publicly reproached by a Persian named Mitrobates, the satrap resident at Daskyleium on the south side of the Propontis, for suffering

[f] Herod. i. 28, 71-76.
[g] For the independence in regard of the satraps in which it was the rule of the Persian government to maintain τοὺς ἐν ταῖς ἄκραις φρουράρχους and τοὺς χιλιάρχους τῶν κατὰ τὴν χώραν φυλακῶν, see Xenoph. *Cyrop.* viii. 6 §§ 1-9. If Orontes captain of the citadel at Sardis (in Xenoph. Anab. i. 6 § 6) is called by Cyrus son of Darius Nothus, his ὑπήκοος, a subordinate bound to obey him, he may have spoken rather as commander-in-chief on the Western Coast than as Satrap of Lydia. For sometimes one of the satraps (as we have observed in his case and in that of Tissaphernes) was invested with a military command more extensive than the borders of his own province. The case of Dadarshish satrap of Baktria, commissioned to put down the Margian revolt, and of Vibanus satrap of Arakhotia, defending the province against those who were sent by the second pretended Smerdis to invade it, Beh. Inscrip. col. 3 para. 2 and col. 3 paras. 9, 10, 11, are perhaps of two sorts, namely, case of a satrap acting under a special commission and case of one exercising his ordinary powers. It would seem that commanders of the king's troops within a satrap's borders, required his order upon the provincial treasury for their pay; for Xenophon's King Cyrus describes his first intended satraps as men,

οἵτινες ἄρξουσι τῶν ἐνοικούντων, καὶ τὸν δασμὸν λαμβάνοντες, τοῖς τε φρουροῖς δώσουσι μισθὸν, καὶ ἄλλο τελέσουσιν ὅ,τι ἂν δέῃ.

Cyrop. viii. 6 § 3. For the vassals who waited upon the satrap and whose children were trained at his gate, see Cyrop. viii. 6 § 10.

the naval power of the Ionian Polycrates, tyrant of Samos, to grow up and flourish independently, close to the coast of his satrapy. Polycrates (we may be sure) was already odious to the ruler of Sardis; very possibly Mitrobates was so too. In like manner, in a later generation, we find the satrap resident at Daskyleium and ruler of a great part of the Phrygian satrapy of Herodotus, Pharnabazus son of Pharnakes,[h] during a series of years regarded

[h] Pharnabazus son of Pharnakes seems to have enjoyed an hereditary satrapy. With Thucyd. viii. 6 (B. C. 412) where he is himself introduced, compare Thucyd. ii. 67 (B. C. 430) where his father seems to be the person who in the same situation is called Pharnakes son of Pharnabazus, and who afterwards (B. C. 422) gave Atramyttium to the people expelled by the Athenians from Delos; Thuc. v. 1. In a preceding generation (B. C. 478) we have Artabazus son of Pharnakes (for whose former history, see Herod. vii. 66, viii. 126, ix. 41, 66, 89,) sent down to the coast by Xerxes with orders
τήν τε Δασκυλῖτιν σατραπίαν παραλαβεῖν, Μεγαβάτην ἀπαλλάξαντα ὃς πρότερον ἦρχε καὶ περὶ Παυσανίαν κ. τ. λ.
see Thuc. i. 129 with 94, 95, and Herod. v. 32. Compare the treaty of the Lacedæmonians and allies concerning the king's affairs and their's
πρὸς Τισσαφέρνην καὶ Ἱεραμένην καὶ τοὺς Φαρνάκου παῖδας.
Thuc. viii. 58, where, perhaps, we have Tissaphernes as the chief of the satraps of Ionia, Lydia, and Hellespontian Phrygia. And note, that part of the Lacedæmonian force was then to be sent under the command of Klearkhus to Pharnabazus son of Pharnakes on the Hellespont; see cap. 39. Certainly, the beautiful buildings with the choicely wooded parks full of wild animals, at Daskyleium, which Agesilaus's army cut down and burnt, had been left to Pharnabazus by his father; see Xenoph. Hellenic. iv. 1 § 33. In another work, Xenophon describes Pharnabazus as βασιλέως ἄρχων, Anab. vi. 8 § 25; where the Phrygia assigned to another satrap, is clearly Great Phrygia, that country which the army had traversed between Lydia and Lycaonia; that is, from the river Mæander (through Kolossæ, Kelænæ, and other places) to Iconium. For it had already been intimated (Anab. vi, 4. § 24) that the Phrygia adjoining Bithynia was Pharnabazus's, and it is plainly intimated (v. 7 § 24) that Æolis, Troas, and (Hellespontian) Phrygia belonged to Pharnabazus, without constituting the whole of his government. On the Bosporus, Khalkêdôn was his; Xenoph. Hellen. i. 1 § 26; i. 3 §§ 5–13; also Antandrus; ibid.; Kyzicus, too; Hellen. i. 1 § 14. A part only of Æolis (as it seems) belonged to Pharnabazus: and of this a native Dardan had the " satrapy: " Hellen. iii. 1 § 10. " Pharnabazus's Phrygia " was invaded by Agesilaus (Hellen. iii. 4 § 26 and iv. 1 § 1) who wintered at Daskyleium, the place in Phrygia where Pharnabazus had his viceregal residence, with many large villages around, supplying all neces-

with jealousy by Tissaphernes, who (even while Cyrus son of Okhus Darius Nothus ruled at Sardis) was still satrap of all or most part of the above-described Ionian satrapy, and who, before as well as after Cyrus, seems in addition to this territorial dominion to have been invested with the principal military command in all the coast provinces of at least the West of Asia Minor. Moreover, besides the Iono-Carian satrapy, he may seem, before Cyrus's time, to have possessed the satrapy of Lydia also, which we have express authority to say, was held by him afterwards in addition to Ionia and Caria.[1]

saries plentifully:—also chaces of perfect beauty, θῆραι σύγκαλαι, partly uninclosed, partly parked. It was girdled, too, by a river abounding with fish and water-fowl; Hellen. iii. 4 § 13, iv. 1 § 15. Geo. Rawlinson justly contends, that the satrap did not live on the coast; and from Strabo xii. 8 § 10, 11, xiii. 1 § 3 infers, that his mansion was on the river now called *Lufer Su*, where that stream forms a lake called by Strabo Daskylitis, before its junction with the Rhyndakus, which presently after enters the Propontis on its south coast. A site within a bend of the river seems intimated by Xenophon's expression, περιέρχε- δὶ καὶ ποταμός. From Strabo's language it seems clear, that of three lakes in this neighbourhood, the waters of which ran off into the sea by the mouth of the Rhyndakus, the lake Daskylitis was the smallest, also the nearest to the coast. Skylax in his Periplus §§ 94, 95, 96, assigns to Phrygia (besides Æolis and Troas) a coast of its own on the Propontis and Hellespont, enumerates its Greek cities (of which Kyzicus abovementioned is one) and notes the mouth of the river Rhyndakus. For the lake Daskylitis and the river Rhyndakus, see also Plutarch, Lucull. capp. 9, 11. To the same family which we have observed for about 100 years invested with the satrapy of Hellespontian Phrygia, a contemporary of Philip the Macedonian, Artabazus, and his son Pharnabazus a contemporary of Alexander son of Philip, may have belonged. The name Pharnabazus seems made up from those other family names Pharnakes and Artabazus.

[1] In B. C. 412 when, after the destruction of the great Athenian fleet and army in Sicily, Tissaphernes as well as the subjects of Athens invited the Lacedæmonians into Ionia, the former
ἐς βασιλεῖ Δαρείῳ τῷ Ἀρταξέρξου στρατηγὸς ἦν τῶν κάτω·
because
ὑπὸ βασιλέως νεωστὶ ἐτύγχανε πεπραγμένος τοὺς ἐκ τῆς ἑαυτοῦ ἀρχῆς φόρους, οὓς δι' Ἀθηναίους ἀπὸ τῶν Ἑλληνίδων πόλεων οὐ δυνάμενος πράσσεσθαι, ἐπωφείλησεν.
Thuc. viii. 5 :—that is, because he was in arrear in the payment lately required by the king, of tributes from the Greek cities in his government

But, to return ; whether there was, or was not, already
a feud between Oroites and his neighbour-satrap of Daskyleium, which had prevented a co-operation, (perhaps
desired by Mitrobates) against Polycrates, (just as the
selfish jealousy of the faithless Tissaphernes forbad the
concert of measures with Pharnabazus, both in the first
instance when the question was, How best to employ the
Lacedæmonians and their allies against the Athenians;
and again, after Athens was conquered and prince Cyrus
was dead, when the matter now to be considered was,
How best to meet the successive invasions of the king's
country by the Lacedæmonians,) it seems certain that,
after what had been said before the gate of Cambyses,
Oroites resolved, as soon as opportunities offered, to
punish both Mitrobates and Polycrates.¹

which he was unable to levy on account of the Athenians. The tribute
which Tissaphernes could not levy, was not (perhaps) the land-tax of
which we have made mention above p. 174. The military description
of Tissaphernes, though given by mistake (perhaps of Ephorus) to
Pharnabazus, is thus expressed by Diodorus xiii. 36;
ὁ τῶν ἐπὶ θαλάττης τόπων ἔχων τὴν στρατηγίαν.
that his satrapy included both Caria and Ionia, the whole narrative of
the operations in which he assists the Peloponnesian fleet, evinces. In
Xenoph. Hellen. i. 1 § 9 we find him imprisoning Alcibiades at Sardis.
This may denote him satrap also of Lydia ; in which case it will follow
that he lost this satrapy as well as his military appointment, by the
subsequent mission of the king's son Cyrus. But perhaps the fortress
at Sardis was his, because the king's governor was his subordinate not
in his Satrapial but in his military capacity. After the death of Cyrus
in reward for his services he was sent back, Xenophon tells us (Hellen.
iii. 1 § 3)
σατράπης ὢν τι αὐτὸς πρόσθεν ἦρχε καὶ ὧν Κῦρος.
Thus he had probably three-fourths of the territory which Oroites ruled
at last. He was also appointed, subsequently at least, στρατηγὸς τῶν πάντων.
in which capacity when Pharnabazus with forces joined him, he still
commanded in chief ; Hellen. iii. 2 § 13.
¹ For Mitrobates as satrap of Daskyleium, see Herod. iii. 120, 126. In
a former note, we have mentioned Kyzicus as belonging to "Pharnabazus's Phrygia." During the suppression of the revolt of the Asiatic
Greeks in the latter part of our Darius's reign, this city was saved from
the Phœnician fleet by a previous surrender to Oibares son of Megabazus, the lieutenant, ὕπαρχον at Daskyleium, Herod. vi. 33. When, after

Though Polycrates formerly (like other island lords of the Ægæan[k]) had obeyed and even (it was said) had solicited the command of king Cambyses to send a contingent to the naval forces, which were to attack king Amasis by sea while the king of Persia led his army into Egypt by land (a project executed in B. C. 525) the ordinary independence of Polycrates may have been looked upon as treason to the Great King, and insolence to the king's lieutenants, notwithstanding apologies and amends made by him on occasions of special complaint. With a hundred fifty-oared galleys, having a fighting force on board of a thousand Samian bowmen, he had carried on a piratical warfare abroad among the islands and on the Asian coast, reducing not only islands of the Ægæan but even towns on the main-land, to be his dependents; while with a standing force of foreign mercenaries he maintained his authority at home. By these operations (in the course of which he plundered friends and foes without distinction, though he used afterwards to make amends to his friends) he certainly must have incensed the satraps seated at Sardis and Daskyleium whose own interests undoubtedly, as well as the interests of their subject towns, had often suffered. In particular, his war with Miletus (wherein he defeated the Lesbians at sea, when they came with all their forces to the succour of the Ionian city, which Polycrates apparently was blockading) must have involved the interests not only of Oroites but of Mitrobates as well. For (not to speak of a likely community of interests between the Æolians of Lesbos and some of those cities on the continent which with their respective territories made up the district called Æolis proper,) the Æolian towns of Mitrobates's province in the

the death of Mitrobates, Oroites is represented as lord not only of Ionia and Lydia but also of Phrygia, we must understand by Phrygia the satrapy of Mitrobates.

[k] It was a trireme of Mytilénê that carried the summons of Cambyses to Memphis. Mitrobates probably had summoned the Æolian islanders in the name of the king.

35*

old Trojan territory near Mount Ida, were probably still under the supremacy of the Lesbian city Mytilené. Certainly, before the Medes under Cyrus conquered their continental master, the Lydian Crœsus, these towns, having been originally founded by colonies from Lesbos, owned Mitylené for their metropolis.[1]

Herodotus could not tell for certain, whether the Samian malcontents that Polycrates packed aboard of forty ships to join the naval muster of Cambyses, ever reached the king's fleet. By one account, they turned back when they had gone no further than the island Carpathus. Another story was, that they deserted from Egypt. After the subjugation of Lower Egypt, the king of Persia's fleet, or the Greek portion of it, was detained at Memphis till the return of Cambyses from his expedition through Upper Egypt into Ethiopia. Afterwards, the Greeks were suffered to depart; and the Samian squadron may have left with the rest. However, that they returned and with hostile purpose, was well-known. They were able to effect a landing, notwithstanding the resistance which they encountered at sea: and this success is less surprising if their vessels were triremes, as Herodotus terms them, for the fleet with which Polycrates scoured the coasts is said to have consisted of penteconters only. Polycrates, however, holding the fort and city, defied the invaders. They, on the other hand, succeeded in obtaining the aid of the Lacedæmonians and Corinthians, given (it was said) the more readily because in the reigns of the last two Lydian kings at Sardis, on several occasions the friendly intercourse of those Peloponnesian states with Alyattes

---

[1] For the war of Polycrates with those of Miletus and their Lesbian allies, see Herod. iii. 39 : for the Æolian towns of the Troad, Herod. i. 151, v. 94. Herodotus mentions Sigæum and Akhillæum as belonging to the Mytilenians. Strabo says that "Arkhainnax" a Mytilenian, settling at Sigæum, fortified it with stones from the ruins of old Ilium; and that the Lesbians claimed almost the whole of the Troad, nearly all the settlements there being Lesbian plantations; see Strabo, xiii. 1 § 38. The district of Astura and Adramyttium is called Lesbian by Skylax, in his *Periplus* § 98.

and with both Crœsus and his ally Amasis king of Egypt, had been stopped by the audacity of the Samian people. Once, the Samians had enabled 300 Corcyræan boys to escape from those whom Periander lord of Corinth had employed to convey them to Alyattes to be made eunuchs. More recently, at a time when the project had been formed to support the supremacy of the Babylonian empire, when Labynetus or Nabunita was regent, by a coalition against the Medes, in which the infantry of Greece under the leading of the Lacedæmonians was to play a part, the Samians had intercepted one present intended by the Lacedæmonians for Crœsus and another despatched by Amasis for the Lacedæmonians.

So now, the Lacedæmonians and their allies went in great force against Polycrates, but after landing and besieging him for forty days, they relinquished their enterprize and returned to the Peloponnesus, while the squadron manned by the malcontents whom they were to have put into power in the island, went off to seek their fortune as rovers or to find their home upon a foreign shore.[m]

All this was past in B. C. 521, at the commencement of which year Cambyses seems to have been still in Egypt. Polycrates may have represented himself as a sufferer in the cause of the Persians, whose friend he may have appeared in the view of the Lacedæmonians; but his friendship was valued at its proper worth by the Persians themselves. In Egypt at the gate of Cambyses, his acts and his designs would be denounced by Samian exiles. One of these who was at Memphis during the stay of Cambyses, we have named. This was SYLOSON, a younger brother of Polycrates, with whom and another brother, Pantagnotus, on his first success, when he rose against the state with but fifteen men that had spear and shield, Polycrates had shared the island and his authority; though afterwards, he slew Pantagnotus and banished Syloson.

Having been dismissed by Cambyses—whether in

[m] Herod. iii. 39–60.

Egypt, or after his arrival in Syria as the king was on his way back towards the Agbatana of Media which he never reached—Oroites appeared again in his government in the summer of B. C. 521; he took up his residence at the inland city of the Magnesians on the river Mæander, and he proceeded to lure Polycrates within his reach. He sent a confidential person to Samos with this message for Polycrates,—that well knowing the desire of Polycrates, so to increase his naval forces as to be able to make himself master of Ionia and the islands, Oroites now was willing to supply the means, his death being meditated by his master Cambyses. If, then, Polycrates would convey away the imperilled satrap, he should be repaid with such a share of the satrap's treasures as might make him master of all Greece. Meanwhile, if Polycrates would send a trusty servant to view them, Oroites would shew what treasures he had selected to carry off with him.

The message was received with joy. To assure himself, however, of the value of the prize thus offered, Polycrates sent over a citizen of Samos his clerk, γραμματιστὴν, named Maiandrius son of Maiandrius, to see and report upon it. Oroites, apprized of the envoy's approach, had filled eight chests with stones to within a very little of the top, had covered the surface with gold, had corded up the chests, and now kept them ready. Maiandrius came, beheld, and reported what he had seen to his lord. Hereupon, the ever-prosperous Polycrates went over to the continent in person to visit Oroites, taking many of his friends with him, and among them Démokédés, a famous mediciner who had been driven by his father's ill-usage from the Greek city Crotona in Italy and to whom Polycrates gave two talents the year for his services, having out-bidden both the Æginetans and the Athenians with whom Démokédés had served before. Arrived at Magnesia, Polycrates was destroyed (we are told) in a manner unworthy alike of the man and of his aspirations. For, except the tyrants of Syracuse, not one of the usurpers of monarchical power in Greek republics did Herodotus think worthy to be compared with Polycrates. Oroites, then (the historian repeats it) killed his guest in a manner disgraceful to tell, and afterwards impaled the body, ἀνεσταύρωσε, thus fulfilling a dream which his victim's daughter had in vain related to prevent her father's departure. She had seen him in the air bathed by the god of Rain, and after his bath anointed by the Sun. This horrible mode of executing a living man, or exposing the corpse of one already put to death, is exhibited in Assyrian sculptures; a pole, such as a stout young tree stript of its branches might become, had its smaller end thrust with an upward direction into the front of a man's body below the breast bone, then the tree, with the body thus spitted on the intended upper end, was hoisted upright in the air, so that the lower end being pitched firmly in the ground, the man hung stooping over the top, the legs and lower part of the trunk on one side of the wood, the head, chest, and drooping arms on the other. Thus hung Polycrates in the air, bathed when it rained, and when the Sun shone upon him, oiled or anointed with the exuding juices of his own body, which it is likely had been previously mangled with rod or lash and mutilated with the knife. Such was the death, awarded to the vilest Persian malefactors, that ended the fortunate and admired career in life of Polycrates. All foreign Greeks, of whom Démokédés was one, and all slaves that had been of his company, were appropriated by Oroites as his spoil. The Samians of the party he sent home free, bidding them thank him for the death of their tyrant. Thus did he colour his treachery, hoping (it would seem) to gain an influence in Samos.[a]

[a] Of personal provocation to the satrap, given in word or deed by Polycrates, Herodotus denies the existence. Yet some alleged (he says) that when Oroites once sent over a herald with a request to Samos, Polycrates happened to be "in hall," ἐν ἀνδρεῶνι, and Anacreon of Teos with him. He was lying down (perhaps on a divan) with his face to the wall; and when the herald came in and spoke with him, rehearsing the business of Oroites, he neither turned round nor answered;

If Oroites reported his good service, he must have done so, it would seem from Herodotus's account, to the Magian the successor of Cambyses. For even if, when the deed was perpetrated, the king was still living at whose gate Oroites, by the taunts he received and the danger of the royal displeasure which he incurred, was stimulated to the destruction of Polycrates, an announcement that Smerdis son of Cyrus had been acknowledged for their king by the Persians and Medes, and that he was now sitting on his father's throne at Agbatana, circulated everywhere throughout the empire, must have reached Oroites before the news of the death of Cambyses, because Cambyses himself had received it in Syria before he gave himself (accidentally or by purpose) the fatal wound. And if on the first intelligence, Oroites hesitated between the pretended Smerdis and Cambyses, the next news that Cambyses was dead must have decided his profession of allegiance. Eight months later, the Magian was slain and succeeded by Darius. But Darius's pretensions had ever since been disputed, (as we have seen) during the sixteen months or more that had elapsed since the Magian's death, before his appearance in Susa. Therefore, though he had acknowledged Darius as his king, and though at least three revolts from Darius had been successfully quelled, yet as Frawartish was still owned by the Medes and other nations for their king, Oroites continued to keep aloof at his seat of government. Nay, since the death of Polycrates he had taken advantage of the confusion of the empire, to gratify his animosity and increase his power by slaying both Mitrobates and his son Cranaspes, and by seizing on the satrapy of Daskyleium.

Herod. iii. 121. The furniture, κόσμος, of this hall was worth seeing; and was afterwards deposited by Maiandrius in the temple of Héra; Herod. iii. 123. The following is a story ascribed to Diodorus x. frag. 15, but from what author Diodorus took it, does not appear; "Certain Lydians, flying from the power of Oroites the satrap, landed at Samos with much treasure, and became Polycrates's suppliants. At first he received them in an affable manner, but shortly after he slew them all, and became master of the treasure."

Ruler, therefore, now of the Ionian, the Lydian, and the Phrygian or Hellespontian satrapies (constituting, as described by Herodotus, a larger part of Asia Minor than the Lydian monarchy at its best) his demeanour lately had been sullen and disloyal. Besides other outrages of his, an express from the king, ἀγγαρήϊον Δαρείου, whose message being embarrassing was to seem not to have reached him or his answer to it to have miscarried (for, indeed, it summoned him to Darius's gate) he had caused to be way-laid and murdered on his return : taking care that neither the horse nor the body of the rider should prove the violence. If the measures ultimately adopted against Oroites had not yet been thought necessary (as we suppose they had not) when the muster was made and the entertainment was begun at Susa, in the summer of the year B. C. 519, the absence of the satrap then, must have made such measures appear more necessary and pressing. Darius had too much on his hands, to despatch an army against Oroites, even if the nature of his crimes and disaffection had seemed to require that course. However, the king called together Περσέων τοὺς δοκιμωτάτους, as Herodotus tells us, those of the highest distinction or most approved deserts at his court. Perhaps, they were or at least comprehended the *partmim* of the book Esther—or "presidents," as we have rendered the term. He had a service (he told them) which he desired one of them to undertake, and which he wished to be accomplished without force or disturbance, by device and cleverness only: for force, he said, was out of place in a matter of wit. "Which of you," he asked, "will either bring me Oroites alive or else put him to death?" Then, to justify his purpose he detailed the conduct of Oroites. On the one hand, this governor of the country to the west of Armenia had given them no aid in their past difficulties; had made away with two of their body, Mitrobates and his son; and now, when summoned to court, he kills the king's messengers. Immediately, of those who listened to this exposition, thirty persons° offered each to undertake the service

° Was it a *council of thirty* that Darius addressed? Was it a committee of Elders like that (οἱ βουλιώτατι γεραίτεροι) which chose their king's son to

alone. Lots then were cast; the dangerous prize fell to Bagaios son of Artontes; and he proceeded thus. He caused many papers [p] to be written, royal orders on a variety of subjects, and had them stamped with the king's seal. With these despatches (one of which might be imagined to be the decree founded on Queen Vashti's offence, if the mission to Sardis was so late in the year) Darius's envoy set out. When he had reached his destination and had been introduced to the presence of Oroites to transact his business, he began to take the king's letters one by one from their wrappers, and hand them to the king's secretary in the satrap's court, who, according to the duty of his office (first having, we may presume, pronounced them genuine) read them off aloud.[q]

By this method of proceeding, Bagaios intended to try the temper of the guards who surrounded Oroites, and to judge whether they might be induced to desert him for the king. Therefore, when he beheld them doing great worship to the documents themselves and yet greater to what was read out of them, he gives now another letter to the secretary in which it was written, "Persians, king

command the auxiliary army required by the king of the Medes when threatened by the king of Babylon (Neriglissar?); Xenoph. Cyrop. i. 5 § 5. These suffered Cyrus to choose himself 200 of the ὁμότιμοι to accompany him, each of whom was also permitted to select four others of the same class: while to the thousand thus obtained, the council allotted *thirty* common soldiers apiece.

[p] Herodotus's term βιβλία, according to the general practice of the Septuagint elsewhere, should translate the סְפָרִים of Esth. i. 22, iii. 13, viii. 5, 10, ix. 20, 25, 30. Compare βιβλία in 1 Maccab. i. 44. In Plutarch, Lysand. cap. 20 the same document is called successively ἐπιστολὴ, βιβλίον and γράμματα. All these terms are used in the Septuagint Esther.

[q] Herod. iii. 128,

τῶν βιβλίων ἓν ἕκαστον περιαιρεύμενος, ἐδίδου τῷ γραμματιστῇ τῷ βασιληίῳ ἐπιλέγεσθαι. γραμματιστὰς δὲ βασιληίους οἱ πάντες ὕπαρχοι ἔχουσι.

With this testimony compare Ezra iv. 8, 9, 17, 23, where the officer second in rank in the under-government of Samaria appears to have been סָפַר which Aramaic predicate (equivalent to the Hebrew סֹפֵר " a writer " or " accountant," and like the Hebrew word rendered in the Septuagint γραμματεὺς) is akin to the term cited in the last note, and signifying " writs," " books," " letters."

Darius forbids you to be body-guards to Oroites." Hearing this "word of the king" the guards let drop their spears; whereupon, seeing their obedience, Bagaios put into the secretary's hand the last of the sealed writs. It contained these words, "King Darius commands the Persians at Sardis to kill Oroites," which the guards no sooner heard than they obeyed.[r] Drawing their short straight poniard-like swords, which as men of warrior caste they had retained when they relinquished their duty as guards of the body to Oroites, (as the adherents of Martiya had done in Susiana) they slew the man whom they had lately served.[s] Thus, in his death no less than

[r] The "word of the king" being law, whether carried by the mouth of a messenger or written upon paper, seems to have been prefaced by such a formula as in Thucydides the letter of Xerxes to Pausanias begins with,
Ὅδε λέγει βασιλεὺς Ξέρξης Παυσανίᾳ.
Thuc. i. 129; or such as commences the proclamation of Cyrus to the Jews, Ezra i. 2, and rendered in the Septuagint
οὕτως εἶπε Κῦρος βασιλεὺς Περσῶν.
In the letter of Artaxerxes (son of Xerxes) to Ezra, the words, "Thus saith," or, "Thus did say," are omitted; see Ezra vii. 12. But the paragraphs of the Behistun inscription begin each in the Aryan thus, *Thâtiya Dârayavush khshâyathiya*, "Saith Darius (the) king:" or in the Kissian, *Tariyavaus Ko(?)nanri*, "Darius (the) king saith." The Assyrian formula so far as deciphered by Sir H. C. Rawlinson in Journal R. A. S. vol. xiv. *Analysis* pp. iii. iv. has *Dariyavas sarru ... yagabbi* "Darius (the) king ... saith."

Note, that the Greek historians (e. g. Thucydides and Xenophon) use βασιλεὺς without the article as a sort of proper name, to denote the king of Persia. The formula we have been studying, prefixed to a written or oral message, is much older than the Persian kings · see 1 Kings xx. 2; "Thus saith (lit. "said" or "spake") Benhadad." 2 Kings xviii. 19; "Thus saith (spake) the great king, the king of Assyria." Compare 2 Kings ix. 18, 19; 2 Chron. xviii. 26; 2 Kings xviii. 29. The formula resembles that used to commence their messages by the prophets of God.

[s] Herod. iii. 128. The weapon used was the ἀκινάκης. This weapon was the image of the god of war worshipped by the Scythians of Herodotus; see Herod iv. 62. It was carried by the Caspians in the army of Xerxes; Herod. vii. 67. Herodotus explains the term by another, Περσικὸν ξίφος· vii. 54. It is expressly stated to have been straight, by Josephus (Antiq. xx. 7 § 10) and is very frequently represented

in his policy, Oroites resembled Tissaphernes. All the property of which the satrap had possessed himself, whereof his slaves (including Demokedes) were of course a no inconsiderable part, was seized for the king's use, and was carried up, not perhaps to Susa (for this may be a name of the king's residence which Herodotus or his informant merely presumed) but rather to where Darius happened to be at the time. And this may have been Agbatana the capital of Media, where Darius arrived before the end of B. C. 519, if he left Susa and defeated Frawartish in Media during the last month of autumn in that year.

III.

IT was in the month called by the Persians Adukanish and corresponding as we suppose with the Tasritu or Tisri of the Assyrians and Jews; perhaps, as early as the eighth of that month, when Darius (if we have rightly identified him with the Akhshurush of the book Esther) set forth for Media, after the seven days' feast wherewith he regaled his whole army at Susa. To do this, had undoubtedly been his purpose when in the spring he arrived at Susa from Babylon. His first task, therefore, now was to cross the mountainous region to the northward, called by modern Persians Luristan, through which (if ordinary maps are to be trusted) the waters from Media, penetrate by two large rivers to the plains of Khuzistan, where the ruins of Susa are still seen between them in the latitude of their nearest approach to one another.

in ancient sculptures, both in and out of the scabbard. It was worn on the outside of the right thigh; see Geo. Rawlinson's note and woodcuts on Herod. vii. 54. May we compare the weapon of the northern invaders of Thuringia, after which " mutato nomine quæ ad id temporis Turingia, ex longis cultellis sed victoriosis postmodum vocata est non Saxonia sed Anglico elemento Sæxonia ; " see the continuation of Florence of Worcester's Chronicle, vol. 2 p. 101 ed. Thorpe; who tells us the tradition comes from Widukind (ap. Leibnitz, tom. i. p. 73 sq.)

Our description will be rightly understood to exclude the little river which skirts the west side of the mounds, whereon once stood the fortress and palace of Susa. It will be applied to the river Kerkhah (or Kerrah) which crosses the latitude of Susa on the west, and to the river (called by Sir R. K. Porter, Afzal) which having passed by Diz-ful (that is, Diz-bridge) city, crosses the same latitude to the east of Susa, and afterwards (at Bend-i-kir or Benderghil) discharges its waters into the Karûn,* to be by that conveyed to the Persian gulf at a point a little east of the mouth of the Shat-el-Arab—so the Tigris is called after it has received the waters of the Euphrates from the right and those of the above-named Kerkhah from the left. Of these rivers, then, which after their descent into the plain, approach the ruins of Susa so nearly, the course of one or other through Luristan might suggest something like the line (or principal line) of march by which Darius reached Media from Susa. But the upper waters of the Kerkhah (which seems to bé the more considerable river) are derived from streams of the district Kampada or Campadéné, a part of Media already occupied when Darius began his march, by the forces under Hydarnes, which might serve as a vanguard to the king's army as it advanced, and might secure the supply of all that it would require on its arrival in Media. We may, therefore, think that the Kerkhah shews the likelier line of Darius's march. This also seems to be the river which Antigonus regained after Eumenes had defeated his attempt by crossing the line of the Koprates and the Pasitigris (that is the Afzal and the Karun) to advance

* Higher up the Karûn river is Shuster, a capital created for himself by the Sassanian Shapoor, the conqueror of the Roman Valerian. The name (according to Macdonald Kinnier) was given in allusion to that of the ancient capital not fifty miles distant, which is still Shus; for Shus (says he) is a Pehlevi word signifying "pleasant," and Shuster signifies "more pleasant." See Sir R. K. Porter's Travels vol. ii. p. 411. If this word *Shus* be connected with *Khûsh* (which also signifies "pleasant" in modern Persian; see D. Forbes's Hind. Dict. p. 251) it is plain that the city might really have derived its name from Kush son of Ham.

upon Persis from Susa where a part of his troops blockaded the fortress. Finding his condition critical, Antigonus determined to move northward into Media, and to make that province, whose satrap accompanied him, the base of his future operations. His first step was a retrograde march of great hardship to his army, from the west bank of the Koprates to the Eulæus and a town upon it named Badaké, where he recovered his forces from their fatigue by a rest of several days. He then attempted the passage of the mountains. This he effected in nine days, notwithstanding the opposition of the Kossæans, the warlike race by which the hill-region was inhabited.[b]

[b] Diodor. xix. 19. The names of the rivers of Susiana are much confounded by Greek writers. The Eulæus of Diodorus xix. 19, is evidently distinguished not only from the Tigris or Pasitigris of the previous narrative, but also from the Koprates, an affluent of the Pasitigris on the right (that is, Antigonus's) side of that river. It is clearly the westermost of the three rivers, and thus corresponds with the Khoaspes of Strabo in this one passage; Strabo xv. 3 § 6

μετὰ γὰρ τὸν Χοάσπην ὁ Κοπράτας ἐστὶ καὶ ὁ Πασίτιγρις, ὃς ἐκ τῆς Οὐξίας καὶ αὐτὸς ῥεῖ.

Here the words καὶ αὐτὸς refer to the Khoaspes, of which, in § 4 (confounding it with the Pasitigris) he had said, not only that it rises in the Uxian country between Persis and Susiana, but also that it runs into the sea which bounds Susiana on the south. In other authors the name Eulæus is substituted for Pasitigris. For, the Pasitigris river by which Nearkhus and the fleet from the Indus sailed up as far as the σχεδία or raft, across which Alexander was about to lead the army on its way from Persepolis to Susa (see Arrian, Indica cap. 42) is plainly the river (called, however, Eulæus) by which on quitting Susa, having handed over the land-army to the conduct of Hephæstion, Alexander himself sailed down to the sea: thence to proceed to the mouth of the Tigris (the Shat-el-Arab) and to sail up that river as far as Opis. So that not only he passed the spot where a canal from the Eulæus brought into the Shat-el-Arab the greater part of the fleet by an inland navigation, but also the place on the right bank where Hephæstion on his arrival crossed the Tigris to encamp—that is, apparently,

ἐν ταῖς Κάραις καλουμέναις κώμαις.

Diod. xvii. 110 § 3.

τῆς Βαβυλωνίας ἐν ταῖς ὀνομαζομέναις Καρῶν κώμαις.

Diod. xix. 12 § 1; the nearest point of the Tigris to which, appears to have been 300 stades (i. e. the distance of Seleukeia and of the spot at which on his approach from Ekbatana, Alexander was met by the warning Khaldæan deputation) from Babylon, ibid. § 3. (in Diod. xviii. 73 § 3 the names Tigris and Euphrates appear to have been transposed

It may well be doubted, whether Darius's Median rival had ever been in possession of the royal residence, the fortress at Agbatana. His possession seems negatived by the fact preserved to us by Ezra, that Cyrus's edict for

by mistake; comp. Diod. xix. 13). See Arrian, Exp. Alex. vii. 7 §§ 1, 6. Thus, the same river is by Arrian called Pasitigris when (as it seems) he follows Nearkhus, and Eulæus when he follows another writer. From Strabo's citations it is at least clear, that Nearkhus himself called the river Pasitigris. In Diodor. xvii. 67 we have a good account of the rise and course of the (Pasi)tigris, and hence it appears (as it does also from Curtius v. 10 § 1) that the river was reached on the fourth march from Susa towards the frontier of Persis. At this point probably (which should not have been higher than that at which the Karûn receives the Afzal or Diz river) was the Raft of Arrian, *Indica* cap. 42. The ζεῦγμα τοῦ Τίγριδος of Diod. xix. 18 § 4 must have been above the confluence of those rivers; that is, higher up the Pasitigris by however short a distance than the spot by which the Koprates entered it. As to the town of Badakè, whence Antigonus started to cross the country of the Kossæans, (and which, it seems, has been identified by Sir H. C. Rawlinson with *Madakta*, a royal city which, when in the 7th year of his reign Sennacherib king of Assyria invaded Susiana, he boasts to have taken from the Elamite; Journal R. A. S. vol. xix. p. 158) it may not have been exactly on the Kerkhah, though the Kerkhah is meant by the Eulæus on which Diodorus places it. It was, perhaps, on a small affluent which seems to join that river from the right on the south side of the mountains: for the Map of the Turkish Empire published under the superintendence of the Society for the Diffusion of Useful Knowledge (in Stanford's Harrow Atlas) seems to place a town named Patak in that situation.

But to return to the narrative of Diodorus referred to at the commencement of this note; there is a difficulty created by the statement (Diod. xix. 17 § 3) of the distance from Susa of the river (Pasi)tigris, to the further side of which, on Antigonus's approach from the west, Eumenes transported his army after that in conjunction (it is to be supposed) with Antigenes who commanded his "Silver-shields" and had been appointed satrap of Susiana, he had given charge to the keeper of the royal fort and treasure at Susa to listen to no demands of his antagonist. It is stated that, at the point where the river joins (ἴχεται, "holds to" or "takes in hand,") the country of the independent mountaineers called Uxians, the (Pasi)Tigris was a day's journey distant from Susa. This may be true of the river on which Diz-ful now stands, and it may, therefore, be thought that this river (which modern geographers make the tributary of the Karun) was by Diodorus's author considered the main stream. But if, of the rivers which unite

the rebuilding of the temple of Jehovah at Jerusalem, was found among the archives at Agbatana in the palace, in consequence of an order to search for it issued by Darius as early (it would seem) as in the second year of his reign; whereupon a search was made at Babylon, but apparently without success.° The extent of the sway of Frawartish

at Bend-i-kir, he took the westerly stream to be the principal, there seems no room left for that tributary of the Pasitigris on the Susian side, the Koprates; Diod. xix. 18 § 3; unless, indeed, with the violence dealt to the Gordian knot, we suppose the state of the river Kerkhah at that time to have been what according to Mr Loftus it plainly has been once—that where it enters the plain, the Kerkhah (whether naturally or by the labour of men) did then throw off a branch to the south-eastward (described as 900 feet wide and from ten to 20 feet deep) which branch carried a portion of its waters to the Karun, while the remainder of the river pursued its course (as the entire river does now) to the Shat-el Arab; though by a channel (now dry and overgrown with timber) which passes within 600 yards to the west of the mound of Susa. Such a branch from the Kerkhah might be the Koprates, while the river whereon Dizful stands, was considered the principal river of the two which meet at Bend-i-kir. A water communication between the Kerkhah and the Karun might also excuse the above-noted diversity in the application of the name Eulæus by Arrian and by Diodorus. But after all, it is a more probable solution of the difficulty created by the statement in Diod. xix. 17 § 3, that his author (or rather, he in citing that author) mis-stated the distance or applied it to the wrong river.

° See Ezra vi. 1. 2. For "in Agbatana in the palace that (is) in Media the province," our own translation, and for
ἐν ʼΕκβατάνοις τῇ βάρει τῇ ἐν Μηδίᾳ χώρᾳ.
the translation of Esdras α, vi. 23, (followed by Josephus Antiq. xi. 4 § 6 though for the last three words he has ἐν Μηδίᾳ only) we have in the Aramaic original

בְּאַחְמְתָא בְּבִירְתָא דִּי בְּמָדַי מְדִינְתָּא:

Here we might long for authority to read Akhmethan, but the *n* final is subject to elision, as is proved by the instances Susa for Shushan, Rakkan for Ragâ, and Kuganakâ for Kukkannakan. Calmet asserts that the Syriac version here has Ahmathan; compare "Shushan the palace" in Hebrew שׁוּשַׁן הַבִּירָה Esth. i. 2, 5; ii. 3, 5, 8; iii. 15; viii. 14; ix. 6, 11, 12 and Nehem. ii. 1. As Ezra adds the province to Agbatana, so does Daniel to Susa. We have in Dan. viii. 2.

בְּשׁוּשַׁן הַבִּירָה אֲשֶׁר בְּעֵילָם הַמְּדִינָה:

"at Shushan the palace which (is) in Elam the province." We have seen

had certainly been cramped in Media from the first, by the defeat of his forces at Marus or Varus in the beginning of the year B. C. 520; since which Darius's lieutenant Hydarnes seems to have maintained himself in Campadéné. The partisans of the king of the Medes had also been repeatedly worsted in Armenia; and the forces of Darius in that province must have been now in a condition to invade Media from the north-west. But neither from the north-west nor from Campadéné did Darius's lieutenants propose to advance, till their master should arrive in Media; and this he may have now at last accomplished from Susa, with greater ease and in less time than Antigonus did afterwards, if (as is probable) the inhabitants of the mountains were in his interest. He had, perhaps, been ten days in Media, when Frawartish came against him with an army, and a battle was fought at a town named Ku(n)drush of which the situation is as yet unknown to us. It was on the twenty-sixth of Adukanish (say, October) B. C. 519; and a victory was obtained by Darius which Herodotus, not in his history of Darius's reign but writing of Cyrus, has acknowledged.[d]

From the scene of his defeat, Frawartish and some who still remained with him escaped on their horses into the district of Ragâ. For it is as a district and not as a city, that the name of the locality is characterized in the

בְּיָרָה translated βαξις. It is otherwise translated in Diodorus xix. 18 § 1 where we read—

ἥκων εἰς Σοῦσα τὸ βασίλειον·

compare—

προῆγον τῆς Περσίδος εἰς Περσέπολιν τὸ βασίλειον.

Diod. xix. 21 § 2, and—

ἥκων εἰς Περσίπολιν τὸ βασίλειον.

Diod. xix. 22 § 1. Somewhat differently we have

εἰς τὸ βασίλειον ὃ καλεῖται Περσέπολις.

Diod. xix. 46 § 6. These phrases were perhaps borrowed from the historian Hieronymus of Cardia, who served Eumenes, and, after the death of that accomplished soldier, was well treated and employed by Antigonus.

[d] Herod. i. 130. In the history of Darius in the third book, the first pretended Smerdis, the Magian, is supposed to be a Mede (compare i. 101) and the head of a revolt of the Medes, but no battle is related to have been fought in which his supposed partisans were defeated.

Assyrian as well as in the Aryan text of the Behistun inscription; and a division of Media is so named by Diodorus.* Under the Parthian empire, Isidore of Kharax appears to mean the same (or partly the same) district, by the one he calls Rhagiané of Media. This last was traversed by the road from Agbatana to the Caspian Gates for the last 58 skhœnes, that is, the last 145 miles, of the interval. At the city of the same name with the district (the ruins of which, now called Rey, are about four miles distant from the modern Persian capital, Teheran) Alexander arrived on the eleventh day from Agbatana, in pursuit of Darius Codomannus.[f] He killed many horses on the way, left many of his foot soldiers behind; and if Teheran be 198 miles distant from Hamadan, as it is said, he must for those many successive days have made eighteen miles a day.

That Frawartish directed the course of his flight towards the Caspian Gates,[g] and the border of the united

---

* Who tells us (xix. 44 § 4) how Antigonus after his victory (having caused his prisoner Eumenes to die by starvation) distributed his army into winter quarters throughout Media; and especially

εἰς τὴν ἐσχατίαν τὴν προσαγορευομένην 'Ῥάγας.

The Aryan name Ragâ in Beh. insc. col. 3 para. 1, is said to be a feminine singular. If the same word were considered a plural masculine, it would correspond in number with the Greek 'Ῥάγαι and might be supposed to signify properly not the city but the name of a tribe, as Sakâ (Aryan) is in Greek Σάκαι. With Isidore of Kharax the name of the city which was then the greatest in Media is ἡ 'Ῥάγα, a singular feminine; see C. Müller's Geogr. Græc. Minores tom. i. p. 251. In one place, too, the singular 'Ῥάγα is used by Strabo xi. 13 § 6. In Tobit vi. 9 τῆ 'Ῥάγῃ has been put (apparently by a mis-correction) for τῆς 'Ἐκβατάνοις. Elsewhere in that book, we have ἐν 'Ῥάγοις τῆς Μηδίας, Tob. i. 14. iv. 1, 20, v. 5. ix. 2. Also, ἐκ 'Ῥαγῶν, Tob. vi. 12. These oblique cases may be referred to a neuter plural nominative 'Ῥάγα, as we have 'Ἐκβάτανα, Tob. vi. 17. xiv. 12 and ἐν 'Ἐκβατάνοις, Tob. iii. 7; xiv. 15.

[f] Arrian, Exp. Alex. iii. 20 § 2.

[g] Said to be 500 stades from Ragâ city on the one side, and 1260 from Hecatompylos, τὰ τῶν Παρθυαίων βασίλεια on the other; Strabo xi. 9 § 1, and xi. 13 § 6. Eratosthenes is cited as making the distance from the Caspian Gates to Hecatompylos, 1960 stades; Strabo xi. 8 § 9. Apollodorus of Artemita was Strabo's authority for the distance between 'Ῥάγα and the Gates.

provinces of Parthia and Hyrcania, is implied in the statement which we gather from Darius's narrative, that being already in Media, whether west or south of the district Ragâ, he fled into that district. We shall see presently, that the people of those provinces beyond the Gates [h] were in arms for his cause. But, pursued from the field at Kundrush by a detachment of the victors, the king preferred by the Medes was captured and brought before his Persian conqueror; who might be supposed to be now on his way or his return to Agbatana. But in truth, Darius's movements, both before and after the battle, are not recorded, and to assist in divining them, we want a knowledge of the position of Kundrush.

What he did, on beholding his prisoner, Darius tells us thus; "I cropped off his nose, his ears, and his hair; (?) [i]

[h] Isidore's road beyond the Gates passes through Khoaréné and Komiséné before reaching Hyrkania, Astauéné, and Parthyéné. Those two districts, according to Strabo (if we understand him aright) formerly belonged to Media, and if they did so in B. C. 519, lying between the Caspian mountain-pass and other countries favourable to Frawartish, they might furnish him friends on his flight into Parthia. The words of Strabo are these

μέρη δ' ἐστὶ τῆς Παρθυηνῆς ἥ τε Κωμισηνὴ καὶ ἡ Χωρηνή, σχεδὸν δί τε καὶ τὰ μέχρι πυλῶν Κασπίων καὶ Ῥαγῶν καὶ Ταπύρων, ὄντα τῆς Μηδίας πρότερον.

In the previous context our author attests, what is clear from the Behistun inscription and other authorities, that under the Persian, and for long under the Macedonians,

ἡ Παρθυαία συντελεῖ μετὰ τῶν Ὑρκανῶν.

Strabo, xi. 9 § 1. In the *Khrestomathies from Strabo* xi. 35, 37, we find it noted, that the Caspian Gates form the border between Media to the Sunset, Parthia towards the wind Eurus, and Hyrkania towards the wind Kækhias; also, that the Caspian Gates are the boundary of Great Media on the one hand, and of Parthia and Hyrkania on the other: see C. Muller's *Geogr. Græc. Minores tom.* ii. pp 597, 598. The compiler here and elsewhere, seems to have gone upon other authorities besides Strabo. It would appear from Arrian's "Post-Alexandrian History" § 35, (so far as Photius has preserved it in Bibl. cod. 92) that the Caspian Gates divided Python, or Pithon's satrapy of Media, from Philippus's satrapy of Parthia, under the second division of the empire, (the one made by Antipater at Triparadisus in Syria B. C. 321 according to Diodorus xviii. 39).

[i] See the Behistun inscription (Aryan text) col. 2 para. 13 (or lines 71, 78) in Journal R. A. S. vol. x pp. 223–225; and (Kissian text) col. 2

... he was held in chains at my gate, all the host beheld him, and then, at Hagamatana " (or, as the Assyrian, more precise in designating localities, expresses the same, " at the town Hagamatanu ") " I put him on the gibbet ; " (1 impaled him.) Here, if not exhausted by his previous sufferings, the claimant of the rights of the Median blood-

lines 54, 58 in Journal R. A. S. vol. xv p. 113. A portion only of the narrative is preserved in lines 59, 60 of the Assyrian text, in Journal R. A. S. vol. xiv ; nor does this include the mutilations inflicted before crucifixion. Of the term expressing the third subject of mutilation, in the Aryan text, Sir H. C. Rawlinson, who supposed it to signify "lips," on re-examining the rock, recovered the termination, and pronounces it to be of the singular number. He is, therefore, disposed to render it "tongue." The Kissian term (which is *tit*) corresponding with the imperfect Aryan term, Mr Norris compares with the Ostiak word *tut* signifying a "mouth ; " compare Herod. ix. 112. But possibly, *hair* which we have given in our text, will not be repudiated by the reader, merely as a provisional translation : Compare the λώζη, inflicted by Zopyrus on his own person; Herod. iii. 154.

ἀποταμὼν ἑαυτοῦ τὴν ῥῖνα καὶ τὰ ὦτα, καὶ τὴν κόμην κακῶς περικείρας, καὶ μαστιγώσας, ἦλθε παρὰ Δαρεῖον.

The sculptures shew that (no less than the Assyrians) the Persians cultivated long hair ; as did a probably cognate race, the Homeric καρηκομόωντες Ἀχαιοί. In early modern times, the long hair of the Anglo-saxon nobles who followed their conqueror William in his first return to Normandy, attracted the eyes of all ; so tells us Ordericus Vitalis, tom. ii. p. 168. Where we find the shaving of head and face used as a token of grief, we may be sure that the people regarded the loss as an abasement or dishonour. For other indignities were submitted to for the like purpose. A remarkable instance is the exposure of their persons by Egyptian women, in mourning for the dead. It is pourtrayed in some of the plates which accompany Sir J. G. Wilkinson's Manners &c. of Ancient Egypt, and it is alluded to as an exhibition of woe by Hebrew prophets. See Isaiah's prophetic picture of the Daughter of Babylon ; xlvii. 1-3. Of the Moabites, in a time of coming calamity it is foretold ; "On all their heads shall be baldness and every beard shall be cut off ; " Isai. xv. 2. The Assyrians were the oppressors then ; but a like woe to Moab, of which the Khaldæans must have been the instruments, is denounced by Jeremiah, xlviii. 37. On this self-inflicted demonstration of misery, compare Jerem. xli. 5 ; Ezra ix. 3 ; Ezekiel v. 1 : Isai. vii. 20 ; 2 Sam. x. 4. To return to the passage on which this note is written ; after the three clippings, a fourth insult seems recorded ; but both Sir H. C. Rawlinson on the Aryan and Mr E. Norris on the Kissian text, can only conjecture as to the meaning.

royal may yet have lingered. For we read of one who (his sentence being revoked) was taken down from the tree alive. The principal abettors of Frawartish (including, it may be, others than Medes) were also punished within the fortress at the same city;¹ but in what way is a point not yet (it would seem) determined by the translators. It seems probable, that while their chief was exposed in his death, and was made to suffer as much dishonour as he had aspired to of dignity, they (like captives that had been paraded in a Roman triumph as far as the ascent to the Capitol) were slaughtered in prison.

Darius's treatment of his Median rival was, perhaps, little, if at all, less cruel than that which the aspiring Ionian Polycrates had suffered at the hands of the satrap of Sardis. In both cases the would-be lord is punished by his more fortunate rival, as a fugitive slave might have been by his master. Probably, the course pursued was counted both politic and just. The degradation of the conquered was supposed to heighten the superiority of the victor. But, unlike Oroites, king Darius cannot fairly be supposed to have employed any falsehood, even by his people, to entrap his enemy. He did not torture to death and load with ignominy the man whom he had lured into his grasp by cries for help.

The king now remained for a considerable time in Media: his head-quarters (we may suppose) being generally at Agbatana; of which the representative now is found, east of Mount Elwend or Alwand, in a city named Hamadan. From accounts of the old city, relating to times later than those of which we write by rather more than 300 years, it is described by Polybius as the original seat of the

---

¹ The expression in the Aryan text is, Hagamatânaiya atara didâm; "Ecbatanis intra arcem"; col. 2 lines 77, 78; in the Kissian, Akvatana Afvarris-va; col. 2 lines 57, 58. Mr Norris notes, that Afvarris is the correspondent of the Persian *dida*, and he compares the Magyar nouns *var* and *varos*, "fort" and "city." Perhaps, the first syllable *af* is allied to Afs, the Kissian term signifying "a town;" in Persian *vardanam*. In Hebrew and Aramaic, we find Afvarris expressed by בִּירָה See Ezra vi. 2; Esther i. 2, and more above, in a former note.

kingdom of the Medes,[k] and as seeming still by the sumptuousness of its building to have greatly surpassed all the provincial cities of Media; which, since the Macedonian conquest, according to a policy commenced by Alexander the Great himself, had been planted with Greeks. It was situated, Diodorus says, in the plain at the distance of twelve stades from a mountain, twenty-five stades in ascent, named Orontes, from a reservoir beyond the water shed of which an artificial tunnel brought an abundant supply of water to the city.[1] But, to return to our first author; Polybius places Agbatana under the ridge-side of the Orontes; and reports it unwalled;[m] being in this last particular like Susa, like Sardis, like Memphis, and perhaps like Nineveh taken in the widest sense of the name, and like Egyptian Thebes. But as Susa and Sardis had their citadels, and Memphis its " White Fort,"

[k] ἦν δὲ βασίλιιον ἐξ ἀρχῆς Μήδων.
It will be observed, that Polybius (like previous Greek writers) has no notion of any Ekbatana of Media in Atropaténé or elsewhere, besides the town now Hamadan; though 500 years after the accounts followed by Polybius, there was extolled a second Ekbatana in Atropaténé; see above p. 61. As to the fact that Ekbatana is described by Polybius as "adjacent to the parts of Asia about the Mæotis and the Euxine," the description though vague will be found applicable, if we remember that Polybius's Lake Mæotis, which receives the waters of the Tanais (Polyb. x. 48) is most assuredly (as the context shows) the modern Lake Aral which receives the Syr river, the ancient Jaxartes; the equivocal nomenclature being due to the persuasion of the first Macedonian conquerors when they arrived on the south bank of the Jaxartes, that they had reached the Tanais and that the plains beyond the river were those of Europe to the right of the river Don or Tanais. Therefore, in Polyb. x. 27 we must understand by the Mæotis and the Euxine, the Aral and the Caspian sea; though in x. 48 Polybius calls the Caspian by a name which was proper to it, "the Hyrcanian sea."
[1] See Diodorus ii. 13 §§ 6, 7. At xvii. 110 § 7 he writes; "They say its circumference is one of 250 stades."
[m] κεῖται μὲν οὖν ὑπὸ τὴν παρωρείαν τὴν παρὰ τὸν Ὀρόντην, ἀτείχιστος οὖσα.
Perhaps we should have written, Under the side-hills which run along the flank of Mount Orontes; unless τὴν after παρωρείαν be an interpolation; in which case Polybius describes the city as lying alongside of Mount Orontes under the flank of the mountain. See Polyb. Book x (fragments of) chap. 27.

so Agbatana had within it a citadel which was entirely artificial and wonderfully constructed for security.[n] Under the citadel was a palace nearly seven stades (or 1414 yards) in compass, which by the sumptuousness of its particular buildings, shewed the wealth of the original founders: for, though the wood-work was all of cedar and cypress, no part was left naked; but the beams and panels of the ceilings and the pillars in the porticos and peristyles were overlaid with a coating, some of silver some of gold; and the roof-tiles were of silver, all of them. Of these, the greater part was stript off at the invasion of Alexander and the Macedonians, and the remainder under the dominion of Antigonus and Seleucus Nikator.[o] Nevertheless, at the arrival of Antiochus called the Great (who was grandson's grandson to Seleucus) in his war with the second Arsakes, king of Parthia, the sanctuary of the goddess Anahita (which, as at Susa, was a part of the palace) had still the surrounding pillars gilded; a great many tiles of silver had been put together within; there were also some few bricks of gold, and there remained a great many of silver. Out of all these was struck off for the king's use the sum of little less than 4000 talents of coin.

This palace, we may be confident, was the work of times subsequent to those of which we write; though, later in his reign, Darius son of Hystaspes may have

[n] Polybius proceeds

ἄκραν δ' ἐν αὐτῇ χειροποίητον ἔχει, θαυμασίως πρὸς ὀχυρότητα κατεσκευασμένην· ὑπὸ δὲ ταύτην ἐστὶ βασίλεια περὶ ὧν καὶ τὸ λέγειν κατὰ μέρος καὶ τὸ παρασιωπᾶν ἔχει τινὰ ἀπορίαν.

[o] The text of Polybius has Σιλικέου τοῦ Νικάνορος. Seleucus is usually surnamed Nikator. It was by defeating Nikanor, a general left in command by Antigonus in Media and the countries thereabout, that, having already recovered his satrapy of Babylonia since the defeat of Demetrius son of Antigonus by Ptolemy satrap of Egypt, at Gaza (B. C. 312) Seleucus added to it Media and Susiana; Diodor. xix. 92. But this Nikanor is called Nikator in Appian, de Reb. Syr. cap. 55. and Appian says that Seleucus acquired the surname Nικάτωρ for his great success in his wars, rather than because (as it was said) he had killed Antigonus's general, Nikator; ibid. cap. 57. On the other hand, Eusebius p. 184 (quoted by Clinton F. H. vol. 3 Appendix chap. 3 " Kings of Syria ") says " ex câque (victoriâ) dictus est Nikanor."

begun it. At the date of the Macedonian conquest there appears to have been another palace in the neighbourhood of Agbatana, in which Antigonus spent the remainder of the winter after the defeat and death of Eumenes.[p] A palace, in the neighbourhood of Susa rather than within it, may likewise have been the scene of our Darius's late entertainments.

When Polybius tells us, that the citadel was artificial, made by hand of man, he certainly must be understood to say that it was not (like that at Sardis or like the Acropolis at Athens) a hill or rock, the natural advantages of which had been seized upon and improved by art. We might even suspect an intimation that (like the citadel at Susa) it consisted partly of an artificial mound which gave it an elevation above the surrounding city. Accordingly, Herodotus asserts that the fortress at Agbatana, surrounded (as he relates) by seven concentric circles of wall, stood on a mound, κολωνος, which accident assisted to produce the desired effect, that every inner circle in succession should be elevated to the view of the spectator above the circle immediately without it, by the height of the battlements alone. In the inmost circle stood the palace and

---

[p] Diod. xix. 44 § 4.

ἐν τινι κώμῃ ταριχευμασιν, οὐσῃ πλησιον 'Εκβατανων, ἡ ἡ τῆς χώρας ἐκεινης ἐστι τὰ βασιλεια·

Compare Isidore's

'Αδραπαναι τὰ βασιλεια τῶν ἐν Βαταναις.

twelve skhœnes on the great road west from the metropolis; and seven skhœnes east from Κογκοβαρ, now called Kangavár and distant 45 miles from Hamadan; See "Mansiones Parthic." § 6 ed. C. Muller, and Journal R. A. S. vol. xii. p. 100. Ruins of this palace, as Sir H. C. Rawlinson thought, exist "at the delightful village of Artaman near the western foot of the mountain;" Journal R. A. S. vol. x. p. 321. note. Mr Masson tells us (Journal R. A. S vol. xii. p. 123) that south of the modern city Hamadan are conspicuous mounds: the principal of which, known to the inhabitants as the treasury of Darab (Darius), suggests the site of the citadel of Deiokes. We add, that these mounds to the southward indicate a quarter over which the old city extended. So modern Rome has shrunk, as it were, into a corner of the imperial city. The treasury and temple of Anaitis which Isidore mentions at the metropolis, seem to mark respectively the citadel and the palace below it.

the treasure-houses or magazines. Five different colours distinguished the five outer walls in succession, white, black, red, blue, orange; the sixth and the seventh (which was the inmost wall) had their battlements coated respectively with silver and with gold. Within this seven-circled fortress, lived the king; outside were the habitations of the people: whence arises a confirmation of the statement by Polybius, that the city was unwalled.ꝗ When Herodotus tells us that the outer circle of wall about the fortress was about as large as the circle of Athens, we know that Athens proper, or the upper city, is meant; but one is led to suspect, that the historian's informant should rather have compared the fortress at Agbatana (if he did not really compare it) with the Acropolis only of Athens which, indeed, before the reign of Theseus was the "city," πόλις, and which was still called pre-eminently the "City," when the capital had acquired its greatest dimensions.ʳ If, then, compared with this Athenian citadel, that at Agbatana was called artificial, we must suppose that, however the natural shape of the site within might have assisted the work, yet, viewed from without in the faces of its successive terraces, it presented to the eye nothing but the masonry of man from the bottom to the top.

ꝗ See Herod. i. 98, 99. For many subjects of discussion which Herodotus's account has occasioned, see particularly the notes of Geo. Rawlinson and his brother Sir H. C. Rawlinson. It seems obvious (though we do not find it noted) that for οὕτω πάντων τῶν κύκλων, near the end of the chapter, we should read οὕτω τῶν πέντε κύκλων.

ʳ See Thuc. ii. 15.

τὸ δὲ πρὸ τούτου (Θησέως) ἡ ἀκρόπολις, ἡ νῦν οὖσα, πόλις ἦν, καὶ τὸ ὑπ' αὐτὴν πρὸς νότον μάλιστα τετραμμένον.

He ends the chapter thus;

καλεῖται δὲ διὰ τὴν παλαιὰν ταύτῃ κατοίκησιν καὶ ἡ ἀκρόπολις μέχρι τοῦδε ἔτι ὑπ' Ἀθηναίων πόλις.

Liddell and Scott in their Lexicon, add that the rest of the city was called ἄστυ, referring to Aristophanes, Eq. 1093; Lys. 245, and illustrating these by the above-cited Thuc. ii. 15 to which they add ἐν τῇ πόλει, seemingly used for ἐν τῇ ἀκροπόλει (of Athens); Xenoph. Anab. vii. 1 § 27.

IV.

THE next of Darius's successes recorded at Behistun, was the result of his conflict with a nation of warlike herdsmen, the *Asagartiyas* or Sagartians, of whom Herodotus's description, that they were of the same stock with the Persians, perhaps means only that, like both Medes and Persians, they boasted to be of Aryan race. One Chitra(n)takhma proclaimed in the host, or the free muster of his nation; "I am descended from (Kh)uwakhshatara." And here we suppose (as in regard of the similar claim made by Frawartish among the Medes) that the celebrated king of the Medes, the father of Astyages, is meant, whose name (according to Greek and Roman writers) is Kuakhshara or Cyaxares. Having declared his right of blood, the bold speaker added; "I am king in *Asagarta*." So is the country named on the Akhæmenian monuments.[a]

It is, perhaps, a difficult question to answer that arises here, not so much this—When did the Sagartian revolt take place, but rather—When was it that Chitra(n)takhma required of his people an allegiance due to a representative of the Median line of kings. Like the Hyrkanians, who shared the Parthian revolt, as it will be seen hereafter, and like the Margians, who revolted alone, the Sagartians are not separately mentioned in the list of the nations, the inheritance of Cambyses, wrested from Gaumâta the Magian by Darius. But, unlike the Margians and like the Hyrkanians, they are also not enumerated among those who revolted while Darius remained at Babylon after the overthrow of Naditabel. From the former omission we may conclude, of the Sagartians also as of the Hyrkanians and Margians, that they were considered an appendage of some greater nation or country than their

[a] There is the locative case, Asagartaiya (which we have rendered in our text) found in the Aryan copy of the Behistun inscription, col. 2 lines 80, 81; and there is the nominative, Asagarta, in Darius's Persepolitan list of provinces, found in an Aryan inscription only; see Journal R. A. S. vol. x p. 280.

own. Now, if that greater country, unlike to Baktria which remained in obedience when the Margians revolted, but like to Parthia, was one that threw off its allegiance while Darius was at Babylon, the revolt of the Sagartians though happening at the same time, would not be separately mentioned. Therefore, the omission of the name of the Sagartians in the list of the nations that revolted before Darius left Babylon in March B. C. 519 to go by way of Susa into Media, must not be held to prove that they revolted afterwards, in which case Darius in his introduction to the record of his success against them, would have added where he was when their revolt occurred, as he has done in the case of the Babylonians who revolted after he had left their city. The omission of their name in the list of nations that revolted, must be regarded a proof that the Sagartians are included under one of the names enumerated. Next, that the Sagartian country at this time was considered to belong to Media rather than to Persis (as might have been concluded from Herodotus) may fairly be presumed from Darius's counting, as he does, the defeat of its people for a part of what he had achieved in Media.[b] Herodotus himself, by a fact which he attests, seems to warn us not to reckon the Sagartians to Persis; for, whereas the Persians (he informs us) were exempt from tribute,[c] he enumerates the Sagartians as tributary to the king of Persia in the same section of the empire not, indeed, with the Medes but with the Sarangas and others.[d] On the whole, then, we conclude, that the Sagartians, though at a later date allotted to a satrapy on their eastern border, yet when Darius seized the throne,

[b] Beh. Inscr. col. 2 para. 15. On the other hand, see Herod. i. 125, vii. 18.

[c] Herod. iii. 97.

[d] Herod. iii. 93. See above p. 170. The Sarangas are the province called on the monuments, Zaraka in Aryan, Sarranka in Kissian (in the text of Darius's tomb inscription) and Zaranga in Assyrian; the 14th province on the Behistun list given above at pp. 417, 418, and the 8th on the tomb list; Journal R. A. S. vol. x. p. 294; vol. xv. p. 150; vol. xix. p. 262.

were held to belong to Media. That their country was to the east of Media, we infer from the fact, that in the only list where they are named (in consequence of their being for the time regarded as a separate people and province) Darius's list on a slab built into the southern face of the great platform at Persepolis, they stand the first of the file of "eastern provinces" that is, of the countries to the east of Media and Persis. This region seems to be that afterwards called "the desert of Carmania."* That, when Darius made himself king, or (as he says) when Anramazda gave him the kingdom, the Sagartians were more closely connected with the Medes than with the Persians, seems also intimated by the very record that one of their own nation recommended himself as fitter to be their king than Darius (who was of the Persian royal family, descended from Akhæmenes) because he, Chitra(n)takhma, was descended from the great king of the Medes, Khuwakhshatara. By the bye, descent through a female was probably not all that the Sagartian was understood and intended to claim; particularly, if he lied, as Darius asserts; for a descent from the royal line of Media might have been truly asserted not only by Cyrus the Persian and his sons and perhaps (as we have contended) by Darius himself, but, probably, by many a noble family of nations whose kings or rulers formerly were allies of the Mede. Yet, if he and they were equally supposed to derive their royal blood through princesses of the family of Khuwakhshatara, he at least had the advantage in the eyes of his people, of being a Sagartian.

But, however nearly connected with the Medes, and though in their revolt (if it was not a simultaneous one,) they may have followed the example of the Medes, it is

* ἔξημος Καρμανία. Marcian's "Periplus Exteri Maris," in the Geogr. Græc. Minores tom. i. p. 531. Sir H. C. Rawlinson places the permanent seats of the Asagartiyas between Parthia and Media; see his interesting speculations on this branch of the Aryan race, in Journal R. A. S. vol. xi. pp 424, 425. The Carmanian Desert seems to have extended northward from Carmania to Parthia: see Strab. xv. 2 § 14.

contrary to evidence to suppose that the Sagartians did
not accept Chitra(n)takhma for their master till after the
defeat, on the field at Kundrush, of the king to whom the
Medes had given themselves. We have evidence which
shews that, boasting among the high-spirited Sagartians
the like of that descent which Frawartish asserted to the
Medes, Chitra(n)takhma either produced the first open
revolt of his people from Darius or soon became its head.
Indeed, that by his pretension he caused the revolt, is in
one place declared by Darius's record in the very words
used of Frawartish and the other pretenders.ᶠ It is also
attested by the order of figures in Darius's sculpture,
that he declared himself king in his own country before
the new pretender to the name and rights of Smerdis son
of Cyrus appeared in Persis, and, therefore, probably if
not certainly (as will be explained hereafter) before Darius
quitted Babylon in March B. C. 519. But, though from
the beginning of their revolt acknowledged by the Sagartians for their king, he may have acted at the head of his
wild forces as an ally of the Median pretender. Accordingly, we shall meet with a fact that may indicate the
plains of Assyria, one of the provinces that revolted while
Darius yet stayed at Babylon, or even Armenia which
seems to have been invaded on behalf of Frawartish,
rather than his native Sagartian deserts, as a quarter in
which he had been conspicuous before his overthrow.
Our idea of the levies he commanded, must (in some
features at least) be shaped or coloured by Herodotus's
description of the Sagartian contingent in the great army
mustered for his invasion of Europe by Darius's son
Xerxes. In number this consisted of eight thousand
men, in dress half-Persian half-Paktyan, and for arms
carrying only a lasso and a dagger.

It seems to have been after the defeat of Frawartish
that Darius turned his attention to the Sagartian pretender. From his head quarters, apparently in Media, he

---

ᶠ See the recapitulation; Beh. Insc. col. 4 para. 2.

sent against Chitrantakhma a column, the command of which we are surprised to find given to a Mede named Takhmaspâda.[g] But we shall meet with a more remarkable instance of high trust reposed by the conqueror of Frawartish in a Median commander. The king's commission now given to the forces of which Takhmaspâda was made the chief, was like the one we have seen delivered to the column led by the Persian Vidarna or Hydarnes, which marched first from Babylon into Media at the beginning of the year B. C. 520.[h] It was this; "Go ye forth ; Smite ye the insurgent people that do not call themselves mine."

In our poverty of materials, we must not omit this circumstance, that the force commanded by Takhmaspâda, though described as "Persian and Mede" in both the Aryan text and the Kissian, was designated in the corresponding but now unfortunately mutilated passage of the Assyrian, either as "of Media" only, or (if any other name of a province was originally added) as "of Media," with precedence over that other.[i] To act against

[g] Or Khamaspâda, according to the Aryan text. But Mr Norris observes in his Kissian Vocabulary (Journal R. A. S. vol. xv. p. 185.) "it may be suspected that an initial *t* is wanting." In the Assyrian, the name is gone in both places. We have assumed the initial from the Kissian orthography, which (as deciphered by Mr Norris) is Takmasbata.

[h] The commission in these two instances (and also in the case of the army with a Mede for its chief, afterwards sent against Babylon) is given to the chief (in Aryan, mathishta) and the rest collectively, by plural imperatives, Pritâ and Jatâ. A like collective commission on the other side was given after this by the second Pseudo-Smerdis to a lieutenant despatched against Darius's satrap of Arakhotia. But in two instances—in the case of Dadarshish the Armenian and Vaumisa the Persian—we have seen the commission addressed by the singular imperatives, pridiya and jadiya, to the chiefs alone. So it will be in the case of the commission to the satrap of Baktria to put down the rebellion in the Margian country; but in those cases no forces appear to have been furnished by the king himself to the persons charged with his commission. That Vidarna's men were "Persians and Medes" is not expressly stated, but seems implied by the context.

[i] See Journal R. A. S. vol. xiv; "Assyrian text of the Behistun Inscription," line 61.

the Sagartians, the force must have been composed (chiefly at least) of cavalry, and we know that the best horses of the Perso-Median empire were bred in the plains of the Nisæan district in Media: also, that (according to Xenophon) it was not till the time of Cyrus that the Persians obtained horses and learnt to ride.ʲ

The expedition was successful; or, indeed, it would have been unnoticed at Behistun. The success is thus briefly inscribed upon the rock; " When they had received their commission, Takhmaspâda marched with the people. They encountered Chitrantakhma in battle. Auramazda was Darius's helper. By the grace of Auramazda they smote the army of Chitrantakhma. They took Chitrantakhma himself and brought him before Darius." Then, with one omission, the mutilations inflicted on Frawartish are recorded as having been repeated upon the person of the Sagartian pretender. Darius proclaims to his empire and to future generations, "I cut off his nose and his ears." Then he adds a circumstance which (as in the case of Frawartish, where it is also found) our translators have not yet been able to explain; ᵏ and he concludes the account by tell-

---

ʲ Herod. vii. 40; Xenoph. Cyrop. iv. 3.

ᵏ Here, as before in the case of Frawartish, one particular of torture is untranslated. In the Kissian (col. 2 lines 56, 65) as deciphered by Mr Norris, it is expressed by *Redakiduva*, which (he says) is "likely to be a verb of the first person singular;" "something like *I smote* or *I killed:*" see Journal R. A. S. vol. xv. pp. 114 and 205. But in the prefixed grammatical observations, p. 80, he implies that the phrase consists of two words *reda* and *kiduva*, and says of the latter that it is "certainly a first person singular" of the past tense. The Aryan, unfortunately, wants the two first characters of the object of the verb. If these be expressed by *x* and *y*, the whole expression will be *utáshaiya* xy *sh(a)m awajam*, "also his . . . . I smote (or, I took off?) " See Sir H. C. Rawlinson's notes on col. 2 lines 75, 89, after revisiting Behistun. Elsewhere, of the verb *awajam*, Sir H. C. Rawlinson says, " It should be the first person active imperfect of the verb which occurs in the third person middle imperfect in col. 1 line 32." Now, as in col. 3 line 74 we have *awája*, so in col. 1 lines 31, 32 we have twice the verb *awája*, "he (Cambyses) killed" or "took off;" and once, the verb *awajata*, "he (Smerdis) was killed or taken off." That putting and being put to death is directly or indirectly

ing us; "He was held in bonds at my gate: all the people beheld him: then I gibbeted him," (stuck him upon the sharp top of a pole planted upright in the ground) " at the town " (as, with its unvarying precision of expression, the Assyrian text defines the name of the locality) "Arbira." So Persians and Medes pronounced the name; but the Assyrian text gives us the genuine form, Arbil, signifying "city of Bel," the Arbela of the Greeks.[1] The fact that this place is not particularly explained to be a town, and is not referred to its province (as Agbatana also before, was not) in either the Aryan or the Kissian text, may mark the place not only as well known to Aryans and Kissians but as a capital. We may suppose it to have become the seat of provincial government in Assyria, not perhaps

expressed, appears from the Kissian counterpart, and also (it is said) the Assyrian. Of the Aryan *awája* and *awajata*, the respective Kissian correspondents are *afpis* and *afpika*. So, too, the Aryan *awájanam* (col. i. lines 57, 59, 83, col. 2 line 5) is represented by the Kissian *afpiya*, "I killed." And the third person *awájaniyá*, twice (col. i. lines 51, 52) is represented by the Kissian *afpis*, "he killed." But the Kissian *afpiya* and its equivalent *Hu afpi*, represent also the Aryan *ajanam*, col. i. lines 89 and 95, col. 2 line 89, col. 4 line 6-7; while the Kissian *afpis* represents the Aryan *aja* in col. 2 lines 26, 36, 55, 87. col. 3 lines 6, 18, 39, 46, 62, 67. It would appear, then, that the Aryan *ajanam* and *awajanam*; also *aja*, *awája* and *awájaniyá*; are respectively equivalents. See Norris (Journal R. A. S. vol. xv. p. 176) on the verb *afpi*. This verb represents, also, the Aryan imperatives *jadiya* and *jatá*, "smite thou " and "smite ye." Part of the ignominious and cruel usage of offenders by Persian masters, was *scourging*, as we may learn from the description given of the mal-treatment of the mummy of Amasis by Cambyses, and of his own person by Zopyrus. Compare the beating with rods, which preceded the use of the lictor's axe in the case of condemned citizens at Rome, and preceded crucifixion in the case of aliens.

[1] See Journal R. A. S. vol. xi. p. 39 *sub voce*. Rawlinson cites Dion Cassius lxxviii. 1, as affirming Arbela to have been a place of royal sepulture under the Parthian kings; also Curtius v. 1. as testifying that at the time of the Macedonian conquest it contained the royal treasures. If Darius's army stores are not meant, we may suppose the fact reported to be, that the provincial treasury was here. Rawlinson would infer its consequence from Strabo's describing it as *βασιλείαν Ἀξιόλογον*. xvi. 1 § 3.

immediately after the fall of imperial Nineveh in B. C. 608, but at least, since the second calamity which befell that city and the neighbouring Calah (called by Xenophon, Mespila and Larissa) when Cyrus in B. C. 558 at the head of the revolted Medes and of the Persians, having previously made Astyages king of the Medes his prisoner at Agbatana, seems immediately to have invaded this province of the Babylonian empire.^m For Astyages was old,ⁿ and perhaps attached to the state of things in which he had long enjoyed his power; identifying his own interest, as vassal or ally, with that of Babylon. It may be further conjectured that, being thus the first conquest made by the Medes and Persians under the successor of Astyages, the lands of Assyria Proper fell into the hands of Median lords exclusively, the Persians being only auxiliaries and their country distant, while that of the Medes was near. Arbela must have been the chief city of the province in B. C. 331 when the Macedonian Alexander flew thither, a distance of 600 stades, or rather twenty parasangs, from his victory at Gaugamela or Camel's House, a village on the bûmòdus which joined the Lycus or Zab from the right, and when the conqueror by so doing, caused the name of Arbela to be given to the battle. And under Alexander's first successors (coupled with Mesopotamia in a single satrapy) we find a province called after this capital, Arbelitis.^o To this day the name of the city subsists; and

^m See Xenoph. Anab. iii. 4 §§ 7-9; and an article by the present writer; "Ptolemy's Chronology of reigns at Babylon," printed in the Journal R. A. S. vol. xviii.

ⁿ He was the young Persian general's grandfather; and already in B. C. 600, seems to have been the father of Darius the Mede.

^o See Arrian, De successoribus Alexandri (apud Phot. cod. xcii § 35), and Diod. xviii. 39 § 6. By Arbelitis we may understand the province more properly called Adiabéné; to which belonged both Arbela and Gaugamela according to Dio Cassius lviii. 26. For the field of the battle of Arbela, see Arrian Exp. Alex. iii. 8, § 7; 15 §§ 4, 5; and (quoting Aristobulus and Ptolemy) vi. 11 § 5; Strabo xvi. 1 § 3; Plut. Vit. Alex. cap. 31. Itin. Alex. §§ 57, 64. The 600 stades' distance of Gaugamela from Arbela being divisible by 30, the number of stades generally assigned to a parasang, while the shorter distance of 500 stades which

the great mound of Arbil is described as an imposing object of view.

To intimidate the Medo-Assyrian population of the province, which was one that had joined the revolt of the Medes while Darius was at Babylon, must have been the king's intention when he exposed the body of the Sagartian transfixed upon a pole at Arbela, as he had exposed that of the Median pretender at Agbatana. But the suspicion is here suggested, that Chitrantakhma, the pretended descendant from the Mede who shared the conquest of Nineveh with a revolted vassal of Assyria, the Babylonian Nabopolassar, had been well known among the Median lords of the soil in the Assyrian province, though the field of his last struggle with the forces and the fortune of Darius may rather be supposed to have been some obscure spot within his native wildernesses.

As the place is unnamed, so too the date of the defeat and capture of the Sagartian is not given by Darius; though in most cases of success recorded at Behistun, these particulars are added: but having placed the victory upon the list of his achievements, he sums up with the words, "This did I in Media."

Now, in this and in the other like cases, the peculiarity is not to be disregarded. Here, as wherever else it occurs, we believe the omission of the date to be intentional. The date was not inserted, because it would here have been out of its place in the series of dates; though for the record of the matter itself, here was the fittest opportunity, it being desired by the king that the account of the Median war might be presented complete, and that the story of the Parthian war to which he had next to proceed, might neither interrupt that of his achievements in Media nor be itself interrupted by the detail of one of them. Just as we have seen the death of Martiya undated,

---

some laid down, is not so divisible, it seems that the local estimate of the distance was 20 parasangs, which some made 600 stades, others (at 25 stades or three Roman *millia passuum* or 5000 English yards to the parasang) 500 stades.

and just as the story of his unfortunate revolt in Susiana is prefixed to that of the operations against Frawartish in Media and Armenia, while it is plain from the Behistun sculpture that Martiya's enterprise began after that of Frawartish (though the Behistun inscription illustrated by the Book Esther shows that it ended first) even so the case stands here. In like manner as, not to interrupt the tale of the war with Frawartish, that of Martiya's revolt which was the first to end in disaster, is related from beginning to end before the other is begun, so, in order not to interrupt the more important narrative of the successes in Parthia, and at the same time not to disconnect the defeat of the Sagartians from the other successes of Darius's forces in Media, the expedition against Chitrantakhma is put first in the narrative, though in fact it was not terminated till a date later at the least than that of Darius's first victory in Parthia, and perhaps later than the suppression of the revolt in that country towards the end of spring in B. C. 518. But, as in these particular cases he had forsaken the order of time in his narrative, he omits their dates.

If we have now rightly answered, Why the destruction of Martiya in Susiana, and why the defeat, the capture, and the execution of Chitrantakhma, the one catastrophè no less than the other, is undated in the Behistun inscription, we are prepared to meet a doubt that may occur to the reader hereafter, as to the year which certain dated transactions in Arakhotia belong to. But the question, now we hope well answered, if it had suggested itself before might have led us to place the undated termination of the first revolt in Susiana, when Atrina proclaimed himself king of that country, not where it stands in Darius's narrative, that is, before the first of the king's operations against Naditabel the Babylonian, but in the midst of those operations. Atrina's discomfiture is not dated, because it is not told by Darius in the place of its occurrence according to the order of time. And this particular matter is not related in the order of time, because, if it had been so placed among the events of his narrative, it would have interrupted the story of his war with Naditabel.ᵖ

V.

IT was Darius's maxim That force is needless when address will do the business; or that where policy will suffice, it is always to be preferred to violence. Probably, the king had many a success to boast of in these years, which had been gained either by clever conduct of his own or by the dexterous service of his officers. These achievements, however, like the events at Susa in the third year of his reign which the book Esther preserves, it was no part of Darius's design to publish at Behistun. Nevertheless, when they were the acts of the king's servants, they were noted to the credit of the doers in the king's private records; like the information of the plot against his life which (about four years after this) he obtained from Mordecai. Successes of this noiseless description, in which individuals or parties rather than large armed musters succumbed, may be presumed to have been obtained, if not exactly in the revolts which we have chronicled of Susiana, yet in those of provinces, whose desertion of allegiance to Darius while the king was at

---

ᵖ See above pp 475, 476. Atrina and Naditabel arose about the same time and the risings are recorded together, before the relation of the suppression of either. See Behistun inscription (Aryan text) col. i. parn. 16. But if there was a priority, we may assign it to Atrina, because in the sculpture the figure of Atrina stands in front of that of Naditabel. Again, the Susian catastrophe ("Atrina was taken and bound and brought before Darius, who put him to death;" col. i. para. 17) must be placed before the execution of Naditabel by Darius at Babylon (col. 2 para. 1.) And not being dated, we suppose it to have happened after the first dated event of the campaign against Naditabel, that is, later than the 26th of Atriyadiya (December B. C. 521). Indeed, we may conjecture that it was immediately after his victory over the Babylonians at the passage of the Tigris, that Darius sent with such effect to Susiana; col. i. para. 17. It is the slaughter of Gaumâta and his friends rather than the capture of Atrina, that (with the final capture of Babylon) makes up the 19 combats of col. 4 line 5.

Babylon (but nothing more concerning them) is commemorated in the Behistun inscription. And the method which we have seen used for preventing a great revolt in Lower Asia, by suddenly cutting off the perfidious Oroites, may give a good idea of some of these triumphs.

Supposing that Bagaios did not depart on his mission to Sardis before the end of the entertainments at Susa where Oroites should have appeared (that is, not before the date when the king himself, resuming his march from Babylon, proceeded in person against his Median rival) we shall be led to presume that the confiscated effects of Oroites, including the Greek doctor Demokedes and the other proceeds of the satrap's success in luring Polycrates into his power, reached Darius's palace at Susa or Darius himself in Media, at a date not later than that assigned by the king to the next of the achievements recorded at Behistun.

The journey from Sardis to the Kissian capital was reckoned by the Ionian Aristagoras during Darius's reign to be one of three months, and that statement (made in connection with the first recorded project of the descendants of those who fought at Troy, to upset the throne of an Asiatic king of kings) is confirmed by Herodotus; who contributes an account, obtained in his own time, of the stages and distances on the king's road between the two cities; making it (at five parasangs a day) a journey (for an army) of ninety days exactly.[a] The journey from Sardis to the capital of Media would not be longer. As he went down to Sardis, the king's commissioner may fairly be supposed to have travelled with a light train and to have used far greater despatch; so that the news

[a] Herod. v. 50-53; "On our construction," says James Rennell, late Major of Engineers and Surveyor General in Bengal, "there is found an aggregate of about 1120 Geographical miles between Sardis and Susa, take nthrough the points of Issus and Mosul which, divided by 450, the number of parasangas" (Herod. v. 53), "gives 2.489 Geographical miles for each parasanga, or nearly two (geographical) miles and a half;" see "Geography of Herodotus," 2nd ed. vol. i p. 436. Rennell identified the ancient Susa with the modern Sus; pp. 268, 440.

of his success carried by relays of couriers, sometimes riders sometimes runners, might have reached the king in ten or fifteen days ; but the conveying to Darius of the property of Oroites—the gold, the silver, the brass, the garments, the cattle, the slaves [b]—might consume the full three months. For, though Major Rennell observes that the slowest of travellers (namely, those who travel in caravans) far outstrip an army, the 90 days of Herodotus are exclusive of days of rest.

The news, then, of the death of Oroites may have reached Darius before the end of December B. C. 519, and the satrap's spoils may have arrived in the March following—the month in which the king's forces achieved the first defeat of the Parthians and Hyrkanians. Of these, the former only were mentioned in the list of the nations that revolted during Darius's stay of fourteen months at Babylon; but the Hyrkanians (who are not mentioned as a separate people or country in any of the general lists of provinces bequeathed by Darius) were undoubtedly included in the name of the more numerous nation. They stood higher, however, than the Parthians in the esteem of the kings of Persia. Accordingly, they are ranked the fourth in Herodotus's list of the nations that formed the infantry in the famous host of Xerxes, while the Parthians are but the twelfth.[c]

Nevertheless, the same writer attests the geographical connection between the Hyrkanians and the Parthians ; [d] and (unless they are the Parikanians of the tenth on his list of the fiscal divisions of Darius's Asiatic and African dominions) he does not give a separate place to the Hyrkanians in that survey of the Persian empire.[e] Xenophon describes them as a nation of no great number, bordering on, and military vassals of, the Babylonian or New Assyrian empire in the reign of Kuakhshara or Cyaxares son of Astyages king of the Medes, when the war broke out in which Cyrus commanded the Medes and Persians

[b] Herod. v. 49.
[d] Herod. iii. 117.
[c] Herod. vii. 62 : also above pp. 112, 113.
[e] See above p. 170.

against the king of Babylon. " They were then as now," says Xenophon, "esteemed excellent horsemen." When, in the first campaign, the Babylonian army had been obliged to leave an entrenched position to the Medes and Persians, it is told that a thousand Hyrkanian horsemen who formed the rear-guard of the retreating army, transferred themselves with their carts and followers to Cyrus, and at once assisted him to surprize the enemy, on condition that they should be of no less esteem than Medes or Persians. " Accordingly," says our author, " you may see Hyrkanians in trust and in possession of commands, no less than such of the Persians and Medes, as are thought of rank sufficient for the like."[f] The Sakas (in Aryan Saká, in Greek Σακαι) who according to the same writer, subsequently followed the example of their Hyrkanian neighbours in joining the army of Cyrus, seem to be the Parthians; whom Xenophon nowhere mentions under this peculiar name, and who are represented by Trogus Pompeius and others as of Sakan (or, as they term it, Scythian) origin.

But the question, whether the Hyrkanians were not usually reckoned to Parthia, seems authoritatively decided in the affirmative by the language in which (after recording the two victories now gained over the Parthians and Hyrkanians) Darius first expresses the result ; " Then the province became mine," and next sums up the matter ; " This I did in Parthia."[g]

[f] Xenoph. Cyrop. iv. 2 §§ 1, 8.
[g] Beh. Insc. col. 3 para. 2. The Hyrkanians (whose name in Zend, answering to the Persian Gurgan, Sir H. C. Rawlinson interprets "wolves") are referred to the Aryan race ; while the Parthians are considered to have been principally Turanian. See Geo. Rawlinson's Herodotus, vol. i. pp. 649, 650, 674. The Scythians Proper (described by Herodotus as inhabiting what was before the Kimmerian country, a land north of the Euxine sea) appear to have been of Indo-Germanic race ; see G. Rawlinson's Essay on the subject. Ktesias's version of the debt of Cyrus and the Persians to the Hyrkanians, may be seen in the new fragments of Nicolaus Damascenus in the *Fragm. Historic. Græc.* vol. 3. p. 406.

Here are authorities for the Sakan origin of the Parthians : 1. Trogus

The record of his achievements in Parthia had been introduced with this brief explanation; " The Parthians and Hyrkanians revolted from me and called themselves Frawartish's (people)."[b] This happened before Darius left Babylon in the spring of B. C. 519 : because (as has been said) the Parthians are inscribed among the nations who threw off their allegiance during the abode of the king in that capital, which began with the year B. C. 520

Pompeius (in Justin, xli. 1.) "Parthi, penes quos. .. nunc Orientis imperium est, Scytharum exsules fuere. Hoc etiam ipsorum vocabulo manifestatur; nam Scythico sermone, Parthi exsules dicuntur.... Hi domesticis seditionibus Scythiâ pulsi, solitudines inter Hyrkaniam et Dahas et Areos et Sparnos et Margianos furtim occupavere..." (cap. 2) ... "Sermo his inter Scythicum Medicumque medius est; utrinque mixtus."

2. Eustathius (on Dionysius Periegetes, verse 1039) in O. Müller's *Geographi Græci Minores* tom. ii. p 394.

τοὺς δὶ Πάρθους καὶ Παρθυαίους καλοῦσί τινες καὶ φῦλον εἶναί φασι Σκυθικὸν μετοικῆσαι ἐπὶ Μήδους ἐκ φυγῆς· διὸ καὶ οὕτω κληθῆναι· Πάρθους γὰρ Σκύθας τοὺς φυγάδας φασίν.

3. Quintus Curtius (iv. 45 § 11) enumerating the nations of the column that formed the line of Darius Codomannus's left wing at Arbela, has these words, "Parthyæorum (?) deinde gens incolentium terras quas nunc Parthi Scythiâ profecti tenent, claudebant agmen." In vi. 6 § 14 he says, "The Scythians who founded the Parthians" *(Scythæ qui Parthos condidere)* came no doubt from beyond the Tanais : " by which name his Greek author meant the Jaxartes, because Alexander's companions when they reached the left bank of the Jaxartes, and beheld the Sakas beyond, thought they were arrived upon the left bank of the Tanais (now the Don river) which falls into the Mœotis or Sea of Azoff.

[b] In the Aryan text *Parthva* and *Varkâna* (that is, the countries) are said to have revolted : in the Kissian, plural nouns are used (signifying the men of those countries respectively) *Parthuvas-pa* and *Virkaniya-fa*. Of these names of peoples, the derivation of the first is curious ; for it consists of a plural termination subjoined to the name of a country ; *Parthuras* occurring four times in the subsequent context as the correspondent of the Aryan *Parthva*. The plural *Virkaniya-fa* consists perhaps of the Aryan term for a man of Varkâna, with a Kissian plural ending. See Beh. Insc. col. 2 paras. 16, 17, 18. Before (col. 1 para. 6) in the list of provinces to the dominion over which Darius had succeeded, we have *Parthuva-pa*, and in col. 2 para. 2 (the list of the provinces that revolted while Darius was at Babylon) we have *Parthuva-fa*, in the Kissian for the Aryan *Parthva*. In the list in Darius's tomb inscription, the Aryan *Parthva* is in the Kissian text, *Parthuva* not *Parthuras*.

and lasted about fourteen months. Darius's explanatory preface proceeds; " Vishtâspa my father was in Parthia; the people forsook him and revolted." It seems the most obvious sense, here suggested, that Hystaspes was already in Parthia when the revolt took place—the revolt from him being the revolt before-mentioned from the king, and not another. If so, and if at the same time we believe that Darius had left his father in Persis (as Herodotus's story would have it) when he came and slew the Magian on the tenth of Bagayadish (November) B. C. 521, the revolt in Parthia would not appear to have been consummated at any early day of the king's residence at Babylon; time being allowed for the mission of Hystaspes, which must have been designed to secure the eastern provinces from the contagion of the Median revolt. We might suspect, however, that on his son's accession, Hystaspes was endowed with the revenues of the province, as Astyages the Mede (it would seem) had been of Hyrkania after he yielded up the throne.

Having thus introduced his father's campaign against the revolted Parthians and Hyrkanians, the king proceeds to say; "Afterwards, Vishtâspa marched with his people;[1] he fought a battle with the rebels at a town in Parthia

---

[1] In the Kissian text (which alone is perfect here) *Tassunos appo tavini itaka thak*, "people who his with, marched." The third (which is the important word here) is the only doubtful one. Mr Norris remarks; "*Tavi-ni* must be identical with *ni-tavi;* but the transposition is curious." In his glossary he renders *Nitavi*, "his," and refers to seven places of the Behistun inscription; see Journal R. A. S. vol. xv. pp. 116, 196, 182. That Darius should say, "Vishtâspa marched with *his* people," instead of saying, "he marched with *my* people," is consistent with the respect for his father which afterwards makes him say of both the victories, "Vishtâspa smote the rebels," instead of (as is his wont when a lieutenant or deputy is in command) "My people smote them." From the fragments which he recovered on a later visit to the rock, of the paragraph in the Aryan text, Sir H. C. Rawlinson seems to have concluded that the phrase there used signified, " with the people who were under his rule;" see his "Note on the Persian Inscriptions at Behistun," p. v; where the word *anushiyá* recovered in col. 2 line 95, is rendered by him "Sub jugo."

named Vispauzatish; Auramazda was my helper; By the favour of Auramazda, Vishtâspa smote the rebel people mightily. It was on the twenty-second day of the month Viyakhana that thus they fought the battle." We are here surprised to find ourselves brought to so late a date as the twenty-second of Viyakhana (March) B. C. 518, only four days short of five full months since the defeat of Frawartish at Ku(n)drush on the twenty-sixth of Adukanish B. C. 519. During this considerable interval after the overthrow of the man acknowledged for their king by the enemy, Hystaspes, it would appear, was unable till at last to assume the offensive. Before his son's victory in Media, he must have been living still longer in a state of unwilling inactivity within the walls of some strong-hold. The ere-while companion-in-arms of the great Cyrus may have not been more than fifty or fifty-five years old at this time. Indeed, we can hardly suppose him older, having no reason for believing that Darius was not the son of a wife of his youth. Victorious at Vispauzatish, he, however, needed re-inforcement; and Darius sent him immediately a body of Persians from Rhagâ[J] in Media, where Frawartish had been taken after his flight from Ku(n)drush. At Rhagâ Darius had now, perhaps, his head-quarters, during the double war that he was waging both in Parthia and in the Sagartian country. For, if we have reasoned well, Chitra(n)takhma was not taken till after the first victory gained by Hystaspes in Parthia at the earliest. And that the operations were simultaneous, is confirmed by the fact that a force, not of Persians and Medes but of Persians only, is said to have been sent to the aid of Hystaspes; while we have already observed, that the troops despatched under a Median leader against the Sagartian, though called in the Aryan and Kissian an army of "Persis and Media," were in

[J] In the Aryan, *hachá Ragáyá*. This name, Rawlinson tells us, "is the ablative singular of a feminine theme in long *a*." This feminine noun *Ragá* (as we have seen) was before described both in the Aryan and the Assyrian as a district.

fact principally or wholly of the Median portion of the united kingdom; as the language of the Assyrian text of the inscription evinces.

When the Persian force arrived, Hystaspes marched at the head of it; for no more mention is made of the troops he employed before. He fought a battle with the rebels at a town called Patigrabana in Parthia, only nine days after his first fight. The result is related by Darius thus; "Auramazda was my helper. By the favour of Auramazda, Vishtâspa smote the rebel army mightily. It was on the first day of the month Garmapada (April B.C. 518) that thus they fought the battle." Here, being entire, the Assyrian text (as before in the case of three out of the five engagements in Armenia, and after this in the case of the defeat of the Margians) adds the numbers slain of the enemy in the fight and afterwards; "He killed of them 6,560 and executed of the prisoners 4,182."[k]

With this terrible punishment the revolt in Parthia ended; or, as Darius expresses the result, "Then the province became mine." The day of this victory, if the Aryan months corresponded day for day with the Assyrian (as the Behistun inscription supposes) was the first day of Darius's fourth year, according to the Assyrian and the Jewish computation.

VI.

THE death of Oroites was probably known already, and perhaps his spoils were arrived at the residence of the king, when (taking advantage, it would seem, of the change of government at Sardis) SYLOSON appeared, to sue for the political inheritance of his brother Polycrates;

[k] The word of the Assyrian here (and in other like places) used, is deciphered by Sir H. C. Rawlinson *bullu*, and translated conjecturally "hung." The same word is used with respect (as it seems) to followers of Chitra(n)takhma's (not mentioned in the Aryan or Kissian text) who appear to have been punished at the same time when their leader was put upon the tree (or crucified.) Beheading seems the most likely capital punishment to have been inflicted—on large numbers especially; and we have instances of it in the Assyrian sculptures.

and that the hands in which Oroites had allowed it to
remain, should be dispossessed in his favour. The new
comer seated himself in the assembly mustered at the Royal
Gate, and announced himself one of the king's benefactors.
This was duly reported within; and Syloson was admitted
into the king's presence. There, standing in the midst,
on the enquiry of the interpreters Who he was, and By
what act he claimed to be the king's benefactor, he told
the story of the shawl or cloak which he had given when
Cambyses was alive at Memphis. Thereupon, Darius
graciously acknowledged himself under obligation, and
Syloson for his recompense asked neither gold nor silver,
but that the king of kings should recover for him as a
home, and give to him for a possession, the place of his
birth, from which he was still an exile, as when he
encountered Darius in Egypt, and the lordship of which
(since the death of his brother Polycrates) belonged to him,
though it was now held by the servant to whom it had
been left in trust, when Polycrates set out on his fatal
visit to Oroites. "Give me the island called Samos,"
said Syloson, "without killing any of the inhabitants or
carrying them off for slaves." King Darius assented;
and, as Herodotus proceeds to relate, entrusted a force to
Otanes, one of the Six who had helped him to slay
Gaumata the Magian, with the commission to go and
accomplish for Syloson all that he had asked. Otanes,
therefore, (the 'Utana of the Behistun inscription in its
Aryan text) went down to the sea and embarked his
army.*

To grant Syloson's request was to destroy a source of
annoyance on the frontier, to add another, though not in

---

* See Herod. iii. 140, 141. In this Ionic narrative we have στρατιὴν
for the *kâram* of the Aryan and the *tassunos* of the Kissian speech.
Also στρατηγὸν for the Aryan superlative *mathishtam* ("chief," "Most
great") and the Kissian *irsarra*; which last word, used as an adjective,
corresponds also with the Aryan adjective, *wazarka*, in the composition
of the terms expressive of "Great king" and "Great God." For the
Aryan form of the name Otanes, the Kissian substitute is *Yuttana*, the
Assyrian *Huvittan'u*.

appearance an important, state to the Persian empire, and to invest with the government a vassal whose only policy would be to preserve the advantages of his new position by maintaining the obedience of the people in his charge to all the king's demands,—whether fixed duties or extraordinary services. But that Otanes was sent down to the sea merely to accomplish the desire of Syloson, as Herodotus's story would make one believe, cannot be supposed by any critical reader; particularly if acquainted, as we are, with the circumstances in which Darius at this time was placed.

The mission of Otanes was unquestionably the completion of a great political undertaking, the successful commencement of which had been the removal of Oroites; and it may be supposed, that Otanes went either simply to succeed Oroites in the exercise of all the powers which that Satrap had possessed, or (whatever might be the portion of the other's satrapies that he was endowed with) to exercise in chief the military command in those Low Countries over which the authority of Oroites had extended. Syloson's petition, therefore, was put in at a seasonable moment. Oroites (who besides graver matters, had been blamed for not annexing Samos to the province of which he was governor) was now dead, and Otanes was commissioned to make good the omissions of the other as well as to reverse all acts prejudicial to Darius's authority. Firmly to establish this authority, power was to be delegated to able and faithful officers, the king's friends were to be rewarded, and the guilty or worthless were to be displaced and punished. The new Chief was, therefore, charged in particular with the execution of Darius's promise to Syloson.

It is plain, then, that, though Herodotus says only that Otanes having received his commission went down to the sea, he did not mean the sea-board of Phœnicia or Cilicia but that of Ionia; [b] and we need not doubt but that it

[b] When a Persian fleet, bound for the Ægœan, consisted in the main of Phœnicians, Cypriots, Cilicians and Egyptians, the rendezvous in two

was in the ports of the Asiatic coast of the Ægæan that transports were procured for the forces with which Otanes afterwards invaded Samos; also, war-galleys, if there was reason to expect a conflict with any remainder of the fleet maintained by Polycrates, whether at sea in the short passage from the mainland, or off the port or sea-beach of Samos.

When the Persian armament reached the island, none at first made any resistance. Maiandrius, who still held the power his master Polycrates had left in his keeping, professed his readiness to abandon the Samian city and island, if he might do so without hindrance or molestation. The Chief of Darius's forces consented; and a formal treaty to that effect is said to have been concluded, or in fact, perhaps, was begun. On this peaceable appearance of things, in order to complete their remaining business, the Persians of note (probably, the men in authority, of whom in particular Otanes was the Mathishta) had their chairs placed opposite the acropolis or city-fort, and there seated themselves with their attendants around them.[e] Meanwhile, Maiandrius prepared to slip away by himself through a covered passage unknown to his garrison, and leading from the acropolis to the sea-shore. Here he was able to put his valuables on board of a ship. At the same time (perhaps to distract attention from his escape by the confusion that would ensue,) he permitted a mad brother of his who had been till now in custody, to sally

well-known cases of this reign, was in Cilicia. These are (1.) the expedition of Mardonius which failed at the doubling of Mount Athos: and (2) the expedition of Datis and Artaphernes, which carried the army defeated by the Athenians and Platæans at Marathon; see Herod. vi. 43, 95. On the latter occasion, the part of Cilicia is mentioned—the Aleian plain bordered by the sea, between the rivers Sarus *(Syhûn)* and the ancient course of the Pyramus *(Jyhûn);* see Geo. Rawlinson's note on the passage. The fleet of Datis was reinforced to some extent by ships of the lately re-conquered Ionian and Æolian states; but these, probably, did not join the fleet before it reached Samos; (Herod. vi. 95). They seem to have all joined, before Datis left Delos for Eretria; Herod. vi. 98.

[e] Compare Jeremiah xxxix. 3.

out and attack the Persians in front of the fortress, at the head of those mercenaries by whom the authority of Polycrates had always been maintained at home, and who, perhaps, had reason to dread the ill-will of the citizens, should they now be expelled from their stronghold and be disarmed by Syloson and the Persians. For, even if he possessed the means, and might have been permitted to carry off his garrison with him, perhaps these soldiers would have been far from unanimous in the disposition either to accompany their present paymaster in his flight or to let him go off with his wealth alone. Probably, had they accompanied him they would only have embarrassed his plans for the future; and he who had little sympathy for their profession (which it was but by chance that he had been obliged to make use of) foresaw this, and chose to sacrifice them rather than forego his own desire. As to the citizens of Samos, we are informed that certain terms, on which he had offered, when the news of the death of Polycrates arrived, to restore them their freedom, had been scornfully and with threats rejected. And hence we may be sure, that, on the present invasion of their island, it had been plainly aversion for their actual ruler that destroyed the little inclination of the Samians to resist the brother of Polycrates coming to seize the lordship, with the Great King's forces at his back. It is, therefore, credible enough that, as Herodotus relates, Maiandrius wished to do as much mischief as possible to all parties at his departure. So he went now quietly off himself, and sailed for Lacedæmon. On the other hand, the mercenaries with the mad fellow at their head, rushed out upon the unsuspecting Persians and set to work, killing such as were carried in chairs,[d] as the persons it

---

[d] τοὺς διφροφορευμένους. Compare in the Assyrian sculptures, the chairs wherein images of gods are seen carried on men's shoulders. These, with poles lashed to them, and carried along thereby, would bear comparison with the wheel-mounted seats or bodies of chariots, δίφροι, becoming vehicles: like the European sedan-chair. When set down upon the ground, they would again be ἕδραι, chairs.

was most important to be rid of. However, the rest of the Persian troops coming speedily to the rescue, the assailants were presently beaten off and driven back again into their fortress. Then, Otanes thinking that he had been long enough executing his commission in the manner prescribed, "without killing or making slave of a single person," as if he had been absolved from this way of proceeding by the conduct of those who held the acropolis, determined to forget his instructions, and to deal with the Samians in his own way. He ordered a general massacre of all, "whether men or boys, whether in sanctuary or out of sanctuary," to be executed by one division of his forces, while the rest blockaded the acropolis. At last, when (according to our historian) they had as with a net completely dragged the island, the Persians handed it over thus depopulated, but, if not its ordinary buildings, with its temples at least (as we happen to know[e]) not completely gutted, to the little-to-be-envied Syloson. However, afterwards—warned it was said by a Vision, and afflicted by a disease which perhaps was taken for an omen that he should be childless or that his posterity should perish—Otanes did what seems to bespeak him, not only a commander of Persian troops but the person we have supposed, the successor of Oroites in Lower Asia. He assisted Syloson to re-people the city thus bereaved of her children. He may have sent back women and girls, perhaps even men and boys whose value as plunder, rather than pity, may have caused them to be spared by some of his soldiers in the massacre. Other Samians, and volunteers who were not Samians yet like them Ionians, may have been collected in the ports and towns of the main-land; and to the Samian exiles who, in the time of Polycrates were numerous, and many of whom had sought their fortunes beyond the sway of Persian satraps in the West, Syloson may have offered terms such as induced them, the opposite faction being destroyed, to return to their old or their fathers' home.

[e] The furniture of Polycrates's hall remained in Herodotus's time in the temple of Hera, where Maiandrius had dedicated it; Herod. iii. 123.

When Ionia revolted in the latter part of Darius's reign, Samos was able to furnish sixty trireme galleys for the war.ᶠ These, to row and fight them, needed not less than twelve thousand men; of whom the rowers, however, may have been mostly or largely slaves. Nevertheless, we learn that it is not in our own century only, or in new worlds, that cities in some situations grow with great rapidity. Herodotus asserts, that of all the states, Greek or Barbarian, which (in following what seems to have been considered the peculiar vocation of a king or at least of one claiming to be a king of kings) Darius added to the empire left by Cambyses, Samos was his first conquest.ᵍ Thenceforth, Syloson ruled it as a vassal of the king's, and probably in subordination to the king's satrap at Sardis.

ᶠ Herod. vi. 8. This is Geo. Rawlinson's remark.
ᵍ Herod. iii. 139.

CHAPTER V.

I.

HERODOTUS has certainly cramped up into a space much narrower than the real length of time, the events which he relates, belonging to the early years of Darius's reign. When we say this, we exclude (however deserving of the censure) the regnal position certainly given to the king's assessment of tributes to be paid by " the countries which he possessed besides Persis;"* also, the position apparently assigned to the adventures of Demokédés, the Greek physician in Darius's service. We speak only of the events which it falls within our own plan to relate. How it came to pass that the historian omitted some of them and abridged the time occupied by all together, we may learn from the Behistun inscription. From that testimony of Darius himself it appears, that there was a second revolt of Babylon, that it detained part of his forces during a protracted conflict in the land of his ancestors, where he was engaged with a second pretended Smerdis, and that it was not crushed till after that rival and his adherent chiefs had been destroyed. This revolt Herodotus plainly failed to distinguish, in the notices which he had collected, from that former one which the

* See Darius's tomb inscription.

same Behistun inscription has shown us breaking out and speedily extinguished in B. C. 521, immediately after the seven months of the same year during which the first that assumed the character of Smerdis (namely Gaumâta the Magian) was acknowledged king throughout the realm of Cambyses. The two revolts of Babylon in the first few years of Darius's reign were, as Herodotus viewed them, blended into a single object, which he places where the first revolt has its date, investing it with all the interesting circumstances that attended the second revolt. And the intervening struggle of Darius with Frawartish the Mede, extending from Media Proper into Armenia and Assyria on the one hand and into Parthia and Hyrkania on the other—this, together with the rebellions in Susiana, Sagartia, Margiana, Persis and elsewhere, (though he was not altogether unacquainted with them, as disturbances which favoured the insubordination of the satrap whose jurisdiction his own Ionians at that time belonged to) he seems to have considered a commotion not requiring any special attention from him, but the very natural result of the killing of the only pretended Smerdis he knew of, by Darius the son of Hystaspes the Akhæmenian. Believing the tribe Gaumâta sprang from, to be Medes in the same sense as the descendants, among whom they were scattered, of an immigrant Aryan nation he supposed the Magian usurper of the throne of Cambyses to be, in the disguise of the brother of Cambyses, what Frawartish was really and without disguise, the champion of that Median nation which (under the first Frawartish or Phraortes and his successors, Cyaxares, Astyages and Darius the Mede) not only had been independent at home, but had acquired a sovereignty over many neighbouring nations. However, though he used his excellent, perhaps ample but probably fragmentary, information, with little regard to unpicturesque details, which were not invested with interest by a desire on his part to restore them to their proper relative positions, Herodotus has (accidentally as it were) preserved one particular, important to us as a note of time, since it no longer misleads us as to the date of the death of Oroites and that of the expedition through which Syloson was put in possession of Samos. We perceive it now to be the connection in time between the conquest of that island by the forces of Darius and a revolt of Babylon considerably later than the one with which our historian confounded it. He tells us; [b] "While the armament was gone to Samos, the Babylonians revolted," and (as when they revolted before, at the beginning of Darius's reign) again gave their allegiance (we may add) to a pretended son of the Labynetus or Nabonedus of the Greeks, called by the great name of Nebukhadrezzar.

Now, if the subsequent siege of Babylon, which we shall have to recite from Herodotus, lasted so long as he proceeds to relate, that is, one year and eight months; and if the month, called by the Aryans Markazana, in which Darius tells us the capture of the city happened, was the eighth month (as Herodotus's narrative seems to indicate) of the Babylonian, that is, the Khaldæan regnal year, (which we have found him referring to before, and which for its first month seems to have begun with the Assyrian "eighth month," named in the Calendar of the Jews Markhesvan, the Aryan Bâgayâdish) then, the first month of the siege will be that same first month of the Khaldæan regnal year, coinciding nearly with November in the year B. C.

---

[b] Herod. iii. 150. The Greek is,

ἐπὶ δὲ Σάμον (not Σάμου) στρατεύματος ταυτικοῦ οἰχομένου.

Compare ἐν τῇ παροιχομένῃ νυκτί, "last night;" Herod. i. 209; also μετὰ Σόλωνα οἰχόμενον, "after Solon was gone;" Herod. i. 34. That οἴχεσθαι signifies not "to be going" but "to be gone," is everywhere evident. It appears in the saying of Xenophon's Gadatas to Cyrus after a narrow escape,

Νῦν τὸ μὲν ἐπ' ἐμοὶ οἴχομαι, τὸ δ' ἐπὶ σοὶ σέσωσμαι.

Cyropæd. v. 4 § 11. But the fact has not been always recognized. In the present passage of Herodotus οἰχομένου is translated by Cary, "While it was on its way." Such a date for the Babylonian revolt would have been wonderfully precise. The truth is implied in Geo. Rawlinson's paraphrase; "After the armament of Otanes had sailed for Samos." But Herodotus says, "During the absence of the armament." At this time, perhaps, the news arrived at Sardis and in Ionia.

518. Thus, the siege will have begun fully seven months after the final victory gained in Parthia by Darius's father Hystaspes, on the first of Garmapada, that is, on the Aryan correspondent of the Assyrian New-year's Day, the first day of Darius's fourth regnal year by Assyrian and Jewish computation. Equally long, or still longer, must the siege have begun after Otanes received his commission respecting not only the countries of which Sardis might still be counted the capital, but the island called Samos also.

However, we are inclined to think that Herodotus's twenty months (beginning where we infer that they began) were the measure (derived from the Khaldæan annals) of the reign of the second pretended Nebukhadrezzar son of Nabunita; rather than the measure of the length of the siege which Babylon sustained in his reign;—however speedily the beleaguerment may have begun after the adventurer had made himself master of that city. We may be certain that the length of this third Nebukhadrezzar's reign was a matter of authentic record at Babylon ; but, whether authentic information as to the beginning of the siege which ended in his ruin was also accessible, we may doubt; as well as the likelihood of its having begun (of all the days in the year) on the first of Markhesvan, the Khaldæan New-year's day.

Now, according to this view of ours, the pretender probably proclaimed himself before Markhesvan in B. C. 518; because (as we have shewn in a former chapter[c]) the first year of a king of Babylon by the Khaldæan annals was not reckoned to begin till the New-year's day after his accession to the throne. But, though we suppose this

[c] See above pp 439 and following. According to this rule, the reign of the first pretender to the name of Nebukhadrezzar son of Nabunita, though he was recognized by all, would not be found in the annals; because no New-Year's day arrived after his accession to the throne. It was after Gaumata's death on the 10th of Bagayádish (the correspondent of the Khaldæan first month of the regnal year) when he was proclaimed king; and he was put to death in Anamaka, which corresponds with the third month of that Khaldæan year.

second revolt of Babylon to have begun before "eighth month" of the Assyrian (that is, before Markhesvan of the Jewish) year in B. C. 518, we do not suppose it to have broken out till after the harvest had been secured in April and May of that year, and we should hardly date the sailing of Otanes with Syloson for Samos, later than in August.

But before and (as we shall endeavour to shew) much before these contemporary events, the second revolt of Babylon and the conquest of Samos by Darius's lieutenant, it appears that the throne of Cyrus and Cambyses, (which, since the death of the first who personated the lawful heir, Darius had occupied) was again claimed by an adventurer who put himself forth as Smerdis son of Cyrus, Smerdis brother of Cambyses, Smerdis the sole representative not only of Akhæmenes in Persis but of Cyrus and Cambyses in United Persis and Media and in every part of that empire which Cyrus had conquered—which Cambyses had inherited and enlarged.

Darius introduces the record of his subsequent successes against this pretender by telling us; "There was a man named Vahyazdâta dwelling in Pârsa" (that is, Fars or Persis) "at a town named Târvâ," but which the Kissians called Tarrahuva, "in a district named Yutiyà," or (according to the Kissian text) "Ihutiyas." When we notice these differing Aryan and Kissian names of town or district in Persis, where the Persians (properly so called) were an immigrant people, it occurs as likely, that the Kissian orthography exhibits the more genuine name;[d]

[d] On the other hand, we prefer the Aryan form of the pretender's name, in which *ahya* is represented by the single vowel *i* in the Kissian substitute, *Vistadta*. See Behistun Inscription ; Aryan text, col. 3 lines 22 and 23; Kissian text, col. 3 lines 1 and 2. The Assyrian form deciphered *Huvisdata*, is related to the Kissian form, as the Assyrian *Huvidarna* is to *Vidarna*, the Aryan and Kissian correspondent. The Kissian *Ihutiyas* for *Yatiyá*, with other Kissian proper names, may suggest that what Herodotus says of Persian names, is more applicable to their Kissian than to their Aryan forms—that they end in the letter which the Ionians call *sigma* and the Dorians *san*.

nay, that the original population were akin to the Kissians as we have already on other grounds contended. But Darius proceeds to say; "This man a second time arose in Persis, and said among the people, I am Bardiya son of Kurush. Then the Persian people, that were with their families, remote from communication,* revolted from me. They went over to that Vahyazdàta. He became king in Persis." But though owned in Persis only, it is certain that he claimed—indeed, he was in consistency obliged to claim—all that Cyrus, all that Cambyses had possessed elsewhere.⨍

We have now to enquire as to the epoch at which this revolt of the Persians took place in favour of Vahyazdâta. The order of the figures of Darius's rivals in the Behistun rock-sculpture proves, we say, two points as to this revolt. The first is, that it was one of older date than the second

* The words, "remote from communication" (not added in the case of the Medes, col. 2 para. 5 and which seem to be an excuse for the Persians) are a doubtful interpretation we have been led to by Sir H. C. Rawlinson's remarks; Journal R. A. S. vol. x. p. 232. The Kissian counterpart seems as yet to yield no help; unless in ground for doubt; ibid. vol. xv p. 119. The Assyrian is here effaced.

⨍ This appears from the legend of his figure in the sculpture, where his claim is expressed to have been—not, "I am king of Persis" (as, according to their legends, the others claimed to be kings of Susiana, or Babylon, or Media, or Sagartia, or Margiana) but—the same that (according to his legend) had been the claim of the first false Smerdis, the Magian Gaumâta,—"I am king," that is, "I am the king;" see the legends in the Aryan and Kissian. In the Assyrian, Gaumâta and Vahyazdûta (the two who claimed to be Smerdis) Naditabel and Arakha (the two who claimed to be Nebukhadrezzar son of Nabunita) and the Mede Frawartish, claim no kingdom, but only each of them to be a differently named person of a certain regal stock; while Chitrantakhma the Sagartian claims to be of such a stock, without pretending to any other name than his own. The three others all claim to be kings in their several provinces (two successively in Susiana, and one among the Margians). Martiya alone, the author of the second revolt in Susiana, takes also a new name *Yammanesu* as well as the title of king in Susiana. None of the three claim a royal descent; not even Martiya, in assuming a new name, appears thereby to pretend to be some one having a title which he did not possess himself.

revolt of Babylon; the date of which we have concluded to be about August in B. C. 518. The other point proved by the sculpture is, that Vahyazdâta presented himself to the Persians after the date of the like conduct of Chitrantakhma among the Sagartians.

Now, we have supposed, of Chitrantakhma's rebellion, that (though he did not present himself to the Sagartians till after Frawartish had been owned for their king by the Medes) Darius's inscription includes it in that of the Medes; and, therefore, that it happened before Darius quitted Babylon in March B. C. 519: because, though the Sagartians are not separately named among the provinces that rebelled while the king was still at that capital, they are also not said to have revolted while he was in Susiana, between March and October of the same year, nor yet (as it is specified of the Babylonians on the mention of their second revolt) after the king arrived "in Persis and Media;" while there is evidence to persuade us that they were a people appended at that time to the nation of the Medes.

Both Chitrantakhma's reign among the Sagartians and the reign of Vahyazdâta which afterwards began in Persis (the latter no less than the former) may have begun while Darius was yet in Babylon; though (as the order of the figures in the king's sculpture mutely intimates) at points in that period successively subsequent to the appearance not only of Frawartish as king of the Medes but also of Martiya, the second pretender to the Susian throne. But that this was really so, we have evidence in the case of the Persian reign which may terminate doubts as to the Sagartian reign also. In the inscription added to Darius's sculpture at Behistun, the Persians are found in a list of the nations that revolted before he quitted Babylon.[s] Again, where it introduces the person of Vahyazdâta (in order to recount to us the battles Darius's forces defeated him in, and the capital punishment inflicted upon him at last) the inscription (as we have seen) declares that,

[s] See Behistun Inscription, col. 2 para. 2, cited above p 480.

Vahyazdâta having pretended to be the younger son of Cyrus and brother of Cambyses, the people of Persis revolted from Darius and went over to Vahyazdâta. This revolt, therefore, being made not from Frawartish the Mede or any other rival, but from Darius himself, cannot be distinguished from the revolt of the Persians which happened before Darius left Babylon, without the violent supposition (equivalent to the interpolation of a sentence in the inscription) that when Vahyazdâta offered himself, they were returned, (perhaps since the defeat of the Mede at Kundrush,) from the revolt they had been guilty of while Darius was at Babylon. We, therefore, feel obliged to conclude, that before March in B. C. 519 when Darius advanced from Babylon to Susa, (and when it might have been a matter of doubt whether it was Media or Persis that he meditated to invade) the people in Persis had preferred to him, though he was descended from the founder of their royal family, not a Mede of the family of the famous king of the Medes, Khuwakhshatara, but a Persian,[h] pretending to be the long-missing and now only-surviving son of their beloved "Cyrus, the king, the descended from Akhæmenes." A former re-appearance among them (as it was supposed to be) of Smerdis son of Cyrus, had caused them to set an example of revolt from the mis-government of Cambyses, which was followed by the Medes and by the other nations, in B. C. 521: for it was in Persis that Gaumâta first showed himself and was first owned as Smerdis and as the king.[i] And now, a second time, upon Vahyazdâta's counterfeiting the same

[h] Vahyazdâta is expressly called a Persian; Behistun Inscription, col. 4 line 26 of the Aryan, col. 3 line 57 of the Kissian.
[i] Behistun Inscription; col. i. para. 11, cited above p 328. In Darius's recapitulation (Behistun Inscription, col. 4 para. 2) we read. "One (of the nine kings) named Gaumâta was a liar: he said thus, I am Bardiya son of Kurush. He made Pârsa (Persis) to revolt." The same acts in the same words are ascribed to Vahyazdâta. The town and district of Persis Vahyazdâta belonged to, are named, Behistun Inscription, col. 3 para. 5. The place where Gaumâta arose is named, col. i. para. 11, and evidently attested to belong to Persis, in col. 3 para. 7.

character, they did likewise. There was no intermediate revolt of the Persians, either from Gaumâta or from Darius. The second rising of a pretended Smerdis produced (not a third but) the second rebellion of the inhabitants in Persis who, having revolted before from Cambyses, now revolted from Darius; just as afterwards, the second appearance of a pretended Nebukhadrezzar son of Nabunita, produced a second revolt of the Babylonians.ʲ Accordingly, in a third passage of Darius's inscription, where he summarily recapitulates the previous story of the defeat of nine rival kings in nineteen fights,ᵏ two—and only two—revolts are recorded of Persis; the one caused by Gaumâta's lie, the other by that of Vahyazdâta; just as two, and only two, Babylonian revolts are there recorded; the one, kindled by Naditabel's lie, the other (as we shall presently see) by the similar lie of a new adventurer.

On the whole, we conclude that the new pretended son of Cyrus cannot have appeared in Persis later, though he may have appeared there earlier by months, than February B. C. 519: and if so, it follows that a hostile government subsisted in that province, all the while that Darius stayed at Susa and all the while that the operations

ʲ The addition, "For a second time" (in Aryan *duvitiyam*) which is made to qualify the appearance of Vahyazdâta in Persis (Behistun Inscription, col. 3 para 5) is attached to the act of the Babylonians, in accepting for their king the second that called himself Nebukhadrezzar son of Nabunita, in col. 3 para. 13. Only in this last passage it is with a preposition, *patiya duvitiyam*.

ᵏ Behistun Inscription, col. 4 lines 5 and 7 of the Aryan; col. 3 lines 48 and 49 of the Kissian text. The corresponding part of the Assyrian contains the nine kings, but the mention of the nineteen engagements is obliterated. The nineteen actions seem exclusive of the slaughter (by Darius and the Six) of the first enumerated of the nine kings, Gaumâta; also, of the slaughter of Martiya, the second pretender in Susiana, who was destroyed by his own people. But if so, the number nineteen must include the capture of Babylon by Vindafrâ or Vintaparna the Mede. That this should be counted, is probable, even because it is the only recorded success of the second struggle with the Babylonians. But the record seems to be an argument for believing that (as Herodotus expressly relates) the city was taken by assault.

already noticed were being carried on, in Media by Darius in person, in Parthia by his father Hystaspes, and among the Sagartians by his lieutenant Takhmaspâda the Mede. If a combined resistance to Darius had been otherwise practicable, one obstacle is apparent. The pretensions of a king who called himself son of the Persian Cyrus and brother of the Persian Cambyses, were hardly to be reconciled with those of a descendant from Cyaxares the Mede. The Medes, indeed, on Gaumâta's proclaiming himself Smerdis, had followed the Persians in owning him king in place of Cambyses: but the claim of Frawartish, as descended from the great Cyaxares, which seems to have extended to the whole dominion ultimately obtained by the Medes and Persians, was not recognized in Persis; the inhabitants of which did not revolt from Darius till Vahyazdàta presented himself in the character of Smerdis.

II.

AFTER that Media, Parthia, and the Sagartian country were subdued, Darius's attention must have been directed almost exclusively to Persis, and the pretended son of Cyrus who, for more than a year, as we may safely say, had there been acknowledged king. The last victory in Parthia had been obtained on the first of Garmapada, the Assyrian Nisannu, when (by Assyrian and Jewish computation) Darius's fourth regnal year began, about April in B. C. 518. After the ensuing hot weather, during which season he may naturally have determined to rest his forces, to add to their numbers, and to renovate their organization and equipment, Darius probably had planned to invade Persis, an operation which would seem to be of easier execution from Media than from the side of Susa where the preceding season of heat had been spent. But, during the repose of his troops and while his thoughts were busy with his proposed undertaking, news came that the Babylonians had again revolted and that a new

"Nebukhadrezzar son of Nabunita" was owned their king. Darius's account of this matter is given, merely to introduce and explain the last great success of his five years' struggle to win and keep that inheritance of Cambyses, the whole or some one or other member of which (formerly an independent kingdom) was claimed by (all together) nine rival pretenders. He says; "While I was in Persis and Media,[a] the Babylonians for the second time became revolters from me. A man arose in Babylon, named Arakha, an Armenian, son of Handita.[b] From the district" (or as the king says in the Kissian text, "from the town") "Dubâna he arose: He lied thus, I am Nebukhadrezzar son of Nabunita. Then, the Babylonian people revolted from me. To that Arakha it went. He seized Babylon. He became king in Babylon."

The intercourse between Armenia and Babylon was constant: for the great Khaldæan capital was supplied by water-carriage from the hill-country of Armenia whence the Tigris and Euphrates take their rise, with commodities which no doubt had formerly found their mart at Nineveh and the sister cities on the Upper Tigris. Herodotus mentions in particular, wine; meaning that of the grape; which may have come from nearer places on the way.[c]

[a] Beh. Insc. col. 3 para. 13. As to the expression, "While I was in Persis and Media," observe, that it states the king's whereabout in a general way. The king says, "While I was in the United Kingdom," instead of saying more particularly, "While I was in Media." So above (col. 2 para. 14) the "army of Persis and Media" sent under Takhmaspâda the Mede against the Sagartians, seems from the imperfect Assyrian text to have consisted of soldiers from Media only.

[b] *Handita* for *Nandita* is a correction made by Sir H. C. Rawlinson on revisiting Behistun. But the value of the Aryan letter represented by *n* in the names *Handita* and *Dubuna* is considered doubtful. Arakha, the proper name of the son of Handita, occurs also in the topographical nomenclature of Babylon, attached apparently to a ditch or canal : see the India House Inscription ; Rawlinson's Herod. vol. 2 p. 585.

[c] Herod. i. 194. For the vines of Albania on the left of the Kυρος, now Kûr, river, which falls into the Caspian from the west, see Strabo xi. 4 § 3. Sir H. C. Rawlinson tells us, that grape wine is now brought to Baghdad from *Kirkûk*, but that the vine does not grow in Armenia.

Possibly, Arakha was a Khaldæan of Armenia and, therefore, better qualified by his mother tongue to win the confidence of those who spoke the Akhad language—if it was still spoken by any—in Babylonia. But the extant inscriptions of his pretended father Nabunita are in Assyrian; a language with which a native of Armenia might also easily be familiar. Long before the revolt, according to Herodotus—perhaps, ever since Darius left the place, in March B. C. 519; since which date two harvests had been gathered in;—stores of victual had been quietly accumulated, not perhaps in the capital alone, but at points in the country connected with Babylon by river or canal, so that at the outbreak the city was immediately provided with subsistence for a siege.[d] But although it is unnoticed (not only as we might have expected in Darius's rehearsal of his victories at Behistun, but also by Herodotus) there was a Persian governor with his garrison, in possession of palace, armoury, and strong-hold, who had to be overpowered or surprized, before Arakha could call himself master of Babylon and believe himself able to hold it against Darius. So, when in Photius's abstract of Ktesias's Persian history we study the only story of a Babylonian revolt, and find it stated that the Babylonians revolted, killing Zopyrus their general in the absence of king Xerxes son of Darius at Agbatana, we are led to think, that a mistake of the father for the son has been made, with respect both to the king and to his lieutenant; so that, as in the case of the king, the name of Xerxes is substituted for that of Darius, so in the case of the governor, Zopyrus the son is put in place of Megabyzus the father, one of the Six whose name (according to the

---

For vines in Assyria, Mr Layard (in "Nineveh and its Remains" vol. 2 p. 425) cites 2 Kings xviii. 32. May not Armenian boats have brought wine from intermediate points on the rivers; *e. g.* from Khalybonitis in Syria; compare Strabo xv. 3 § 22.

[d] Herod. iii. 150.

Βαβυλώνιοι ἀπίστησαν κάρτα εὖ παρεσκευασμένοι· ἐν ὅσῳ γὰρ ὅ τε Μάγος ἦρχε καὶ οἱ ἑπτὰ ἐπανέστησαν ἐν τούτῳ παντὶ τῷ χρόνῳ καὶ τῇ ταραχῇ ἐς τὴν πολιορκίην παρεσκευάδατο, καὶ κως ταῦτα ποιεῦντες ἐλάνθανον.

Aryan orthography) is Bâgabukhsha.* In this correction of Ktesias's story, we are confirmed by finding as we

* Photii Cod. lxxii. § 20,

ὁ δὲ Ξέρξης στρατεύει ἐπὶ τοὺς Ἕλληνας ... Πρότερον δὲ εἰς Βαβυλῶνα ἀφίκετο, καὶ ἰδεῖν ἐπεθύμησε τὸν Βελιτανᾶ τάφον, καὶ εἶδε διὰ Μαρδονίου, καὶ τὴν πύελον ἐλαίου οὐκ ἴσχυσεν ὥσπερ καὶ ἐγέγραπτο πληρῶσαι. Ἐξελαύνει Ξέρξης εἰς Ἐκβάτανα, καὶ ἀγγέλλεται αὐτῷ ἀπόστασις Βαβυλωνίων καὶ Ζωπύρου τοῦ στρατηγοῦ αὐτῶν ὑπὸ σφῶν ἀναίρεσις. Οὕτω καὶ περὶ τούτων φησὶ Κτησίας καὶ οὐχ ὡς Ἡρόδοτος. Ἃ δὲ περὶ Ζωπύρου ἐκεῖνος λέγει (πλὴν ὅτι ἡμίονος αὐτῷ ἔτεκεν) ἐπεὶ τά γε ἄλλα, Μεγάβυζον οὗτος λέγει δια–ράξασθαι, ὃς ἦν γαμβρὸς ἐπὶ τῇ θυγατρὶ Ἀμύτι τοῦ Ξέρξου. Οὕτω μὲν ἧλω διὰ τοῦ Μεγαβύζου Βαβυλών. Δίδωσι δὲ αὐτῷ Ξέρξης ἄλλα τε πολλὰ καὶ μύλην χρυσῆν, ἐξ ἕλκουσαν τάλαντα· ὃ τιμιώτατον τῶν βασιλικῶν δώρων παρὰ Πέρσαις ἐστί. Ξέρξης δὲ ... ἤλαυνεν ἐπὶ τὴν Ἑλλάδα.

It was really a revolt of Egypt, that Xerxes found upon his accession and suppressed before he went against Greece. But in the latter expedition, Megabyzus son of Zopyrus is named the sixth and last of the generals in chief; Herod. vii. 82. The part of the story of which the title is,

Ξέρξης ὁ Δαρείου παῖς τοῦ Βήλου τοῦ ἀρχαίου διασκάψας τὸ μνῆμα.

is cited by Carl Müller from Ælian *Var. Hist.* xiv. 3 where it is told more at length. This "Bel of old time," whose tomb was said to be at Babylon, will be the same Belus who was said to have built the original wall of the city, whom also Nebukhadrezzar in the *Indica* of Megasthenes speaks of, when he is made to say that his ancestor Belus and queen Beltis were powerless to persuade the Fates to turn away the calamity of Babylon which ·he foretold; see Abydenus in Euseb. Pr. Ev. tom. ii. p. 440 ed. Gaisford. Abydenus seems to identify the Belus who walled Babylon, with the Belus to whom the Babylonians ascribed the new creation at the time when all was water on the face of the earth. It is clear that the "Belus the Old" of Ælian is the Belitanâ of Photius's epitome of Ktesias. The latter (in G. Rawlinson's Herod. vol. i. p 628, note,) Sir H. C. Rawlinson observes, is the Βιλιθὰν of the Phœnicians: and he cites Damascius ap. Photium, p. 343. He also supposes בל אית to signify Βῆλος ὁ ἀρχαῖος. Now, Gesenius makes *perennitas* the primary, and *firmitas* the mere secondary meaning of אֵיתָן or אִיתָן But "to be from of old" is not the same as "to have been of old;" and even if both the senses may be given to ὁ ἀρχαῖος, neither of them is equivalent to *perennitas* or "everlastingness." Moreover, the Anglican version of the Hebrew holy writings seems to recognize Gesenius's secondary for the principal sense: as does Professor Lee in his Hebrew Lexicon. With Perizonius, therefore, (as cited by C. Müller) we may render τὸν Βελιτανᾶ τάφον, "the tomb of Bel the Strong." But this Bel, being also termed Βῆλος ὁ ἀρχαῖος, "the Bel of old time," may be properly

proceed, that to a son of this Zopyrus (one named, like his grandfather, Megabyzus, and who by his wife Amytis was son to Xerxes and brother to Artaxerxes the Long-armed) Ktesias assigns the feat whereby Babylon was said to have been regained; although the same Megabyzus's contemporary, Herodotus, ascribes it not to him but to his father Zopyrus. For, if here the truth be certainly on the side of the son's contemporary (when he relates that the stratagem of the father, that is, of Zopyrus, recovered Babylon for Darius) and not on the side of Ktesias, who with his informants lived three generations later (when he represents the son, Megabyzus, as having recovered the same city by the same stratagem for Xerxes) it follows that the preceding portion of Ktesias's account requires a corresponding rectification; and we conclude, That it was not Zopyrus in the service of Xerxes (as stated by Ktesias) but it was Zopyrus's father, the Megabyzus Darius had been served by against the Magian, who was στρατηγὸς (as Ktesias terms him) that is, Mathishta, as the Persians said, or Chief of the forces—

identified by Sir H. C. Rawlinson (citing Chwolson vol. 2 p. 39) with the Bel called by the Sabæans of Harran, " the grave old man." In the Khaldæan worship there is found a Bel at a city the site of which is now named *Niffer*, by corruption of the old Semitic name *Nipur* and identified by the tract Yoma in the Talmud (where it is called Nopher) with the Calneh of Genesis x. 10 but of which Sir H. C. Rawlinson thinks the old (Ilamite) name was the same as that of its god, and that it is perhaps the Βίλβη of Ptolemy; G. Rawlinson's Herod. vol. i. pp. 437, 596. This Bel—who stood third of the thirteen or second of the twelve chief gods,—was often identified or confounded with the Bel of Babylon, namely Merodakh, who was but the 10th of the 13 or 9th of the 12 gods. See Sir H. C. Rawlinson's Essay, " On the Religion of the Babylonians and Assyrians," in the first volume of his brother's Herodotus. The Bel to whom Berosus ascribed the creation of the present order of things upon the earth, with that of the animated races that now inhabit the earth, does not seem to have been distinguished by him, any more than by Abydenus, from the Bel of Babylon; and this Bel (Merodakh) seems to have been the Bel, who was said to have first surrounded the city with a wall and whose tomb Xerxes was said to have broken open. For the same great building is called the temple of Bel (Merodakh) at Babylon and the tomb of Bel.

not of Xerxes but, of Darius the father of Xerxes, in Babylon while the king was absent, "at Agbatana," as Ktesias related, or, as Darius's inscription has it more indefinitely, "in (the united kingdom of) Persis and Media." Having shewn himself worthy of high trust and ample recompense, the father of Zopyrus (Bàgabukhsha son of Dâduhya, as the Behistun Inscription calls him) had been left in charge of Babylon, when Darius departed thence for Susa and Media, in the spring of the year B. C. 519; and he was now slain there in the summer of B. C. 518, when the inhabitants revolted from his master, and gave their allegiance to the Armenian Arakha.[f]

[f] Behistun inscription, col. 4 line 85. The whole passage of the Aryan text in which Darius enumerates those who aided him against the Magian, as copied from the rock on Sir H. C. Rawlinson's after visit to Behistun, is given in his Supplementary Note, pp. xi. xii.

It may be suspected that *Dâduhya* was an Aryan name, of which *Zopyrus* was a Greek substitute, current at Athens after the date at which Zopyrus, son of the second Megabyzus, took refuge there: See Herod. iii. 160, Ktesias ap. Photium cod. lxxii § 43. As to *Dâduhya*, we find in Hindustani (derived from the Sanskrit) the nouns *dáh* and *dahan*, "burning," and the verbs *dahna* and *dáhna*, "to burn" in the neuter sense and "to burn" transitively; see Forbes's Hind. Dict. pp. 255, 275. We may add the Greek noun feminine (in the acc. singular) δαΐδα or δᾶδα with the cognate Latin correspondent (in the nominative) *táeda*, "a torch, piece of light-wood;" also the Greek verbs δαίω and δαίεθαι (which last has the perfect δέδηε) "to kindle," and "to burn" or "blaze." As to the name Ζώπυρος, the Greek substitute (as we suppose) for Dâduhya, and compounded of words conveying the ideas of our words "live" and "fire;" the neuter ζώπυρον is explained, "a spark, bit of burning coal, match to light a fire with;" and the verb ζωπυρῶ is "to kindle, set a-blaze;" see Liddell and Scott's Greek and English Dictionary. If our conjecture should be verified, it would follow that the custom common among the Greeks, of giving to the (eldest?) son the name of his grandfather (a custom long followed formerly in the family of the writer of this, at Kettleby in Lincolnshire, and doubtless in other English families elsewhere) was observed in this Perso-Aryan family, at least three times in five generations. We shall have 1. Dâduhya (Zopyrus) the father of Bâgabukhsha (Megabyzus) in the Behistun inscription; 2. Bâgabukhsha in the inscription, or Megabyzus in Herodotus, the comrade of Darius; 3. Zopyrus son of Megabyzus, who recovered Babylon and then was made Darius's governor there, according to Herodotus; owned also as governor of Babylon by Ktesias; 4. Mega-

The plan of the Babylonians was not this time to risk battles, but to rely on their walls. With these, completing the design of his father Nabopolassar,[g] the Great Nebukhadrezzar, and subsequently Belshazzar's guardian Nabunita or Labynetus, the husband of Queen Nitokris, had surrounded the city, on the outside and along both banks of the Euphrates within, where the river divided the city into two.[h] For of three circuits of wall which (ac-

byzus son of Zopyrus, who recovered Egypt for Darius's grandson, mentioned by Herodotus, Thucydides, and Ktesias ; 5. Zopyrus son of the last Megabyzus by Amytis the daughter of Xerxes, his wife, who fled to Athens, according to Herodotus and Ktesias; the person (as we suppose) who gave currency to the Greek name Zopyrus as a substitute for the Aryan Dâdubya. A brother of his, named Artyphius, is mentioned by Ktesias. If Darius's comrade Megabyzus was killed (as we infer) at Babylon in B. C. 518, this fact would be a complete proof that the Megabazus who conquered the maritime parts of Thrace (Herod. iv. and v.) was not the same person, as some have thought.

[g] For Nabopolassar's share, see his son's "Standard," or "India House Inscription ; " Rawlinson's Herod. vol. ii. p. 585.

[h] See Berosus, as cited by Josephus *cont. Apion.* i. 19, 20, and *Antiq. Jud.* x. 11. § 1 comparing Herod. i. 178—181, 186; also iii. 159. Perhaps Herodotus's δύο φέρεα τῆς πόλεως,—portions of the city eastward and westward, divided by the river,—were the inner, ἡ ἔνδον, and the outer city, ἡ ἔξω πόλις, of Berosus; these designations having respect to the Euphrates and signifying, ἡ ἐντὸς τοῦ Εὐφράτου πόλις καὶ ἡ ἐκτὸς τοῦ Εὐφράτου respectively. Then would arise the question, Whether the inner and original Babylon was the eastern or the western φέρος, but this seems to be decided by the actual position on the east bank, of the ruin of the palace of Nabopolassar the father of Nebukhadrezzar; for such the mound of Amrûm proves to be; see Rawlinson's Herod. vol. ii. pp. 577, 578. The phraseology "Within and without the Euphrates," is employed (apparently after Eratosthenes) by Strabo ii. 1. § 31, where the Euphrates is considered as the western side of the third geographical σφραγίς or oblong parallelogram in Eratosthenes's division of the continent from east to west: these first three divisions being in succession, the Indian, the Aryan, and the Assyrian. To some, Berosus's language perhaps might convey the idea, not that after having added, but, that by adding an outer Babylon to the original city, Nebukhadrezzar sought to hinder its besiegers from having it any longer in their power to turn back the river in order to build siege-works, or to make of the river itself an engine against the city. But his real meaning seems to be, That having added a new city

cording to Berosus) it possessed when it was captured for Darius the Mede by Cyrus, only one (according to Herodotus's description of the defences) had been de-

to the old one, the king was not content any longer with water defences which (by turning off the river) might be made dry ditches. The news of his father Nabopolassar's death having brought him back from the conquest of Syria to take possession of the government at Babylon, and the captives of his war who afterwards arrived, having been distributed by his direction into proper settlements throughout the country

αὐτὸς δὲ ἀπὸ τῶν ἐκ τοῦ πολέμου λαφύρων τό τι τοῦ Βήλου ἱερὸν καὶ τὰ λοιπὰ κοσμήσας φιλοτίμως, τήν τι ὑπάρχουσαν ἐξ ἀρχῆς πόλιν ἀνακαινίσας, καὶ ἑτέραν (ἔξωθεν cont. *Apion* and so Syncellus,) κατασκευασάμενος, (Sync. has προσκατασκευασάμενος, Josephus himself cont. *Apion*. προσχαρισάμενος)

πρὸς τὸ μηκέτι δύνασθαι τοὺς πολιορκοῦντας τὸν ποταμὸν ἀναστρέφοντας ἐπὶ τὴν πόλιν κατασκευάζειν, ὑπεριβάλετο τρεῖς μὲν τῆς ἔνδον πόλιως περιβόλους, τρεῖς δὲ τῆς ἔξω· τούτων δὲ (so I read for want of better, instead of the variants τοῦτο δὲ in Joseph. *Antiq.* and τούτων in Joseph. cont. *Apion*. respectively;—and so I find does Georgius Syncellus, citing the same passage of Berosus, p. 417 ed. Dindorf)

τοὺς μὲν ἐξ ὀπτῆς πλίνθου καὶ ἀσφάλτου, τοὺς δὲ ἐξ αὐτῆς τῆς πλίνθου.

Here it might be understood that, of the two triple lines of fortification the one which surrounded the old city was built of kiln-burnt bricks laid in bitumen, while the triple line defending the new city was composed of terraces of sun-dried brick, but we prefer supposing Berosus's meaning to be, that each city's outermost περίβολος, or girdle of defence, was of sun-dried brick only. Afterwards, in his notice of Nabunita's reign (calling him Nabonnedus, as Herodotus names him Labynetus) he adds

ἐπὶ τούτου τὰ περὶ τὸν ποταμὸν τείχη τῆς Βαβυλωνίων πόλιως ἐξ ὀπτῆς πλίνθου καὶ ἀσφάλτου κατασκευμήθη. These walls on the river side of each division of the city are described by Herodotus i. 180 ; also, the brick edging and lining of the river channel's sides, Herod. i. 186. By the bye, be it observed as to the last mentioned king and as to the walls of Babylon, that Abydenus in his work upon the Assyrians (himself rather than Megasthenes, the fourth book of whose *Indica* he had just cited) asserted expressly what could not be more than probably inferred, if we had only the Jewish historian's citations of Berosus's account to go upon; that Nabonnêdus, whom Abydenus calls Nabannidokhus or Namannêdokhus, was in no way related to the preceding king of Babylon : see Euseb. *Præp. Evang.* tom. ii. p. 442 ed. Gaisford. where Eusebius also cites a statement of Abydenus's, that "the city of Babylon was first walled by Belus: " as to which, compare Curtius v. 4, and note that, perhaps it is not Nebukhadrezzar's palace but the one represented by the mound of Amrâm, which we have called Nabopolassar's, that Curtius means

molished in that historian's time. The outermost circumvallation had been destroyed (as Berosus related) by the

> by his "still standing palace of Belus." Abydenus goes on to say;
> "But this fortification having disappeared in process of time, again
> Nebukhadrezzar built the one which subsisted until the reign of the
> Macedonians, having gates of brass." These were the walls of which
> Kleitarkhus and others, the companions of Alexander, gave the
> measurements cited by Diodorus; and of which, Curtius (probably
> citing Kleitarkhus) says, that they were covered with spectators at the
> entry of Alexander into Babylon, Curt. v. 3, while Nearkhus related,
> that as Alexander arrived at them he saw a number of crows fighting
> and beating one another, and some of them fell beside him: Plut. *vit.
> Alex.* cap. 73. These, too, were the walls, of which, we are told, Alexander caused ten stades' length to be pulled down to furnish burnt
> bricks, and (as it seems) after the ground had been levelled, room for
> the funeral pile of his beloved friend Hephæstion, a square structure,
> the sides of which at the base were each a stade in length and the
> height of the whole more than 130 cubits; Diodor. xvii. 115. Nebukhadnezzar's walls, according to the same Abydenus, constituted a triple
> line of defence;
>   Βαβυλῶνα ἐτείχισε τρισλῷ περιβόλῳ.
> But Berosus, writing in early Macedonian times, after having described Nebukhadrezzar's walls as τρεῖς περιβόλους, "three circumvallations,"
> relates that Cyrus who had previously (he says) issued forth from Persis
> with a numerous army and subdued the rest of Asia, after having
> invaded Babylonia, defeated Nabonnedus and taken Babylon, gave orders
>   τὰ ἔξω τῆς πόλεως τείχη κατασκάψαι,
> "to demolish the outer walls of the city." Therefore the walls at the
> time of the Macedonian conquest and as they existed in Berosus's time,
> were at the utmost a double line only. As to the demolition attested
> by Berosus, it is to be observed that Herodotus, writing less than a
> century after the capture of the city by Cyrus, in the time of the king
> the grandson of Darius Hystaspes' son, makes the double assertion that
> Cyrus did not, but that Darius did, order it. He says of Darius
>   τὸ τεῖχος περιεῖλε καὶ τὰς πύλας πάσας ἀπέσπασε· τὸ γὰρ πρότερον, ἑλὼν Κῦρος τὴν
>   Βαβυλῶνα ἐποίησε τούτων οὐδέτερον.
> Herod. iii. 159. But here it seems strange at first sight that the
> demolition of the surrounding wall having been mentioned, the writer
> should add, that all the gates were torn away, as if this particular was
> not included in the demolition of the wall. The difficulty, however, is
> removed by Berosus's account, which enables us to perceive that, after
> the wall was taken away according to the order of Darius, there still
> remained interior defences; indeed, a double line of them, as is evinced
> by Herodotus's own account of the city, as it existed in his time; an

command of Cyrus, after he had made himself master of

account which, though placed in his first book, appears to have been written (like another passage in that book relating to the history of Darius) after the third book of his history had been finished. It was, therefore, of these interior walls described by Herodotus, Ktesias, and Kleitarkhus, that Darius caused the gates to be taken away, in addition to the demolition of the outer wall. We have already cited the passage in which Berosus describes the three circuits of wall constituting the defences of the city as originally completed : we now cite from Herodotus's account of the defences, where the present tense is used throughout, the words which attest but two remaining circumvallations :—

τάφρος μὲν πρῶτά μιν . . περιθεῖν μετὰ δὲ τεῖχος.
(Herod. i. 178.)

τοῦτο μὲν δὴ τὸ τεῖχος θώρηξ ἐστί· ἕτερον δὲ ἔσωθεν τεῖχος [περιθεῖ] οὐ πολλῷ τέῳ ἀσθενέστερον τοῦ ἑτέρου τείχεος, στεινότερον δέ.

Herod. i. 181. When this description, then, was first given, that is (as, after having doubted, we are now sufficiently assured) when Artaxerxes the Long-armed resided in Babylon and Herodotus visited the city, the outermost of the three circumvallations attested by Berosus had been demolished. This work, ascribed to Cyrus by Berosus and to Darius by Herodotus, was all the easier if, as we have interpreted Berosus's description already, the outer περίβολος, or girdle of defence, was composed entirely of " mere brick," that is, sun-dried brick, cemented with mud. Such an embankment might be overturned into the trench or other excavations outside, from which it had been raised, and the surface afterwards be levelled for suburban buildings, fields, and gardens so as (after the lapse of some generations at least) to exhibit no very evident or continuous traces of the rampart which had been thrown down. Even the outer wall described by Herodotus must have been merely cased with burnt brick. While by degrees this choice building material in the lapse of generations was stripped off for various employment, far and near; and perhaps most of all, for the walling by Seleucus Nikator, of the place on the Tigris which (whatever was its former name) he called Seleukeia and made the capital (see Strabo xvi. 1 § 5) there probably went on a simultaneous process of levelling the interior mass of mere earth and filling up ditches and other excavations out of it, in order to turn the ground to profit by cultivation. In Strabo's time the city was for the most part deserted ; so that what a line of comedy said punningly of the Arcadian Megalopolis, was tragically true of Babylon ;

ἐρημία μεγάλη 'στὶν ἡ μεγάλη πόλις.

the mighty city was become a mighty desolation.

The works Berosus attributed to the reign of Nabonnedus, certainly included the wall of burnt brick described by Herodotus, i. 180, as running along the brink of the river on both sides within the city and

the city; but Herodotus, writing at least 150 years before

as having narrow gates affording communication between the river and the streets which ran thitherward. They include also some of the works attributed by Herodotus to Queen Nitokris,—the bridge, the stairs, descending to the water from each gate in the river-side walls, and the facing of brickwork with which she protected the sides of the bed of the river; Herod. i. 186; for she was the wife of the historian's τύραννος. Labynetus, the Nabonnedus of Berosus; see Herod. i. 77, 188. Indeed, an existing relic of these works is an embankment now washed into by the Euphrates, the bricks of which are stamped with the name and titles of Nabunita: see G. Rawlinson's Herod. vol. ii. p. 579. These works of Queen Nitokris and her consort (to whom we also confidently attribute the outermost of the three lines of fortification described by Berosus, though he gives all to Nebukhadrezzar;) and with them all the works of Nebukhadrezzar and his predecessors, except the Hanging Gardens, are assigned to the Assyrian queen Semiramis in the account of Babylon derived by Diodorus principally perhaps from Ktesias; though in this particular Curtius's usual authority, sometimes cited by Diodorus also, Kleitarkhus, seems to have agreed with or rather perhaps echoed his predecessor: see Curtius v. 4. Diodor. ii. 7-10. This idea which Berosus complained of as a Greek blunder, does not appear to have been entertained by Herodotus; for while he attributes many particular works to Nitokris (whom he judges of the two, the queen of the greater intelligence) he allows Semiramis only a share in the others; except certain prodigious embankments in the plain which he attributes to this queen entirely. He says, "There came to be kings many others, of whom I will make mention in my Assyrian accounts, and who went on in the ordering" (or "who added to the order and array" οἱ ἐπεκόσμησαν) "of both the walls and the temples, but among them it seems two women also. She that reigned before, whose name was Semiramis, and who came into being five generations before her that reigned afterwards," perhaps B. C. 538+17 regnal years of Nabonnedus+130 years of five generations, or about B. C. 700 at the utmost, "exhibited for her part throughout the plain, embankments worth beholding; for previously the river had used to shew like a sea over all the plain:" Herod. i. 184. Some works, we have seen, that really belonged to Nitokris and her consort, were attributed by the school of Ktesias to Semiramis. Now, this fact may add strength to the reason which the defensive character of the work suggests for ascribing to Nabonnedus and Nitokris the Wall of Media mentioned by Xenophon (Anab. i. 7 § 15) and described by him (Anab. ii. 4 § 12) as built of kiln-burnt bricks, and 20 feet thick, 100 feet high, and (it was said) 20 parasangs long; the same wall which Strabo citing Eratosthenes calls "the Cross-wall (διατείχισμα) of Semiramis," extending apparently from the right bank of the river Tigris

Berosus,[1] while he affirms expressly that Cyrus did nothing of the sort, ascribes the demolition (as we shall see) to our Darius, after the capture of the city by his lieutenant Vindafrà the Mede. We know not what account (if any) Berosus gave of the siege under Darius, but, if the Khaldæan writer and his more famous Ionian predecessor be granted us as generally trust-worthy authorities, we may use Herodotus to justify Berosus and Berosus to reconcile Herodotus's description of Babylon in his first book with the (probably previously written) account in his third book of the measures adopted against the city, after its capture in the reign of Darius. We, therefore, conclude that Babylon was substantially as well fortified, when it revolted from Darius the Persian the son of Hystaspes, and prepared for a second siege, as when it was assailed by the Medes and Persians under Cyrus at the close of the regency of Nabunita and the reign of the last native sovereign, Belshazzar. On both occasions, it would appear to have possessed a triple circumvallation;[2] of which the exterior line seems to have been added the last, and to have been finished at least after the death of the great Nebukhadrezzar.

In order that their provisions might serve the longer, Herodotus reports, That having reserved, each man of

opposite the City Opis, across the mid-river region to the Euphrates, Strabo ii. 1 § 26; xi. 14 § 8. And we may suppose it built when Astyages having been overthrown at Agbatana, Assyria Proper having been conquered by the Medes, and the coalition against the rising power having terminated in the overthrow of Crœsus, the Babylonians began to dread invasion, and to employ the skill, the labour, and the wealth they had at their command in the construction of defences.

[1] Berosus in his youth was a contemporary of Alexander, but his Chaldæan history was brought out in the reign of Antiokhus Soter who succeeded to the throne of his father Seleucus, Nikator, B. C. 280. For this is cited Tatian Or. advers. Gr. § 58.

[2] Nebukhadrezzar in the Standard Inscription, G. Rawlinson's Herod. vol. 2 pp. 585, 587, seems to own only that double circumvallation which Herodotus describes. We conclude that the outer line was added or at least completed by Nabunita.

them his mother and one other woman of his household [k] to make his bread, the Babylonians mustered together the rest of the female population and strangled them all on the spot.

But Babylon in the hands of a new pretended Nebukhadrezzar son of Nabunita, was not all that distracted Darius in the midst of his purpose to crush the pretended son of Cyrus, now reigning in Pârsa-land. To the north of a territory then called Hariva, watered by the Arius or Hari river, and now belonging to Herat, is another country, watered by the Margos of Greek writers, and bounded on the south by the mountains whence that river descends, while its north side is skirted by a desert, into the bosom of whose sands the river discharges its waters at last. This region lay between the satrapy of the united Parthians and Hyrkanians on the west, and that of Baktria on the east; being the Margianè of the Greeks. By Darius it is called Margush in Aryan: by the modern Persians it is known as Merv and its river as the Murgh-âb or Murgh Water. It is not set down as a separate province by Darius, at Behistun, at Persepolis, or at his tomb, in his lists of the countries that called him master. Nor does Herodotus mention this people separately, either in the host of Xerxes or among Darius's tributaries. But before the point in his narrative at which we are now arrived, Darius had already named them among those that threw off their allegiance to him, during his stay at Babylon in the first and second of his regnal years. Perhaps, like their western neighbours, the Parthians and Hyrkanians, they had at first called themselves the liege men of Frawartish the Mede. But certain it is, that after the death of Frawartish and when the Parthians and Hyrkanians were subdued, having (for the time at least of the hot weather) been left to themselves, and probably

---

[k] ἐκ τοῦ ἑωυτοῦ οἰκίου, "out of his own house" seems to be the reading of most MSS, Herod. iii. 150. There seems, however, to be some authority for οἰκηΐων, "persons of the family." Compare ὑπὸ τῶν ἑωυτοῦ οἰκηϊοτάτων, "by his own brother;" Herod iii. 65.

encouraged by the revolt of Babylon, they put a leader of their own at their head, who then called himself king in Margiana. We date his appearance, by the order wherein Darius's rivals are presented to view in the Behistun sculpture; for there, the Margian stands last of the Nine, behind the second so-called Nebukhadrezzar son of Nabunita. Nevertheless (as the catalogue of Darius's victories informs us) the Margian was overthrown, not only before that pretender but before the Persian who repeated the imposture of Gaumâta the Magian and who stands seventh in the file; that is to say, next in front of the second Nebukhadrezzar.

The account in the Behistun Inscription is this: " Saith Darius the king, A province named Margush became my enemy. A certain man named Frâda a Mârgava " (or, as we should say, " a Margian ") " him they made Mathishta. Afterwards, I sent to a Persian, a servant of mine, the satrap in Baktria, named Dâdarshish. Thus I said to him : Go thou, smite thou that people which is not called mine. Afterwards, Dâdarshish went with a people. He made battle with the Margavas. Auramazdâ brought me help. By the will of Auramazdâ my people smote that rebel people mightily. On the twenty-third day of the month Atriyâdiya, then it was that the battle was made them thus. Saith Darius the king ; Afterwards the province became mine. This is what was done by me in Baktria."[1]

---

[1] See Behistun inscription, Aryan text, col. 3. para. 3. For Margava signifying a man of Margush, one should have expected Mârguviya, after the analogy of Bâbiruviya in col. i. lines 77, 79. Perhaps this and Margayaibish (the dative or ablative plural) col. 3 line 16 are contracted forms. As to the Margian territory, Strabo, ii. 1 § 14, extols the climate and fertility of Hyrkania, Aria, Margiané and Baktriané. Of Margiané in particular he reports it to have been said, that the vine stock is often found so large as to require two men to clip it with their extended arms. This he repeats xi. 10 § 2 with the addition that the clusters would be often of two cubits (length ?). In the previous section, xi. 10 § 1, he had introduced Aria and Margiané together as a single division of his

Here we perceive the reason, why this province does not appear under its own name in the lists of the countries subject; having before, in xi. 8 § 1, more expressly made them one by calling them

τὸ τῶν Μαργιανῶν καὶ τῶν 'Αρίων ἔθνος.

This unity may have been administrative and peculiar to the times of the geographer's authors. In some passages, even under the single name Aria, he may seem to comprize both countries, their mountains of which he speaks, and their plains watered respectively by the rivers Arius (now Hari) and Margos (now Murgh). It is incidentally remarked, after Aristobulus, by Strabo xi. 12 § 5 (as by Arrian Exp. Alex. iv. 6 § 6, where also, on the same Aristobulus's authority no doubt, Arrian asserts that the river gives its name to the people or country) that the Arius is ultimately swallowed up in the sand of the desert. The corrupt passage which follows the mention of both rivers in Strab. xi. 10 § 1 may seem to be one in which either Aria comprehends Margiané or else Margiané is comprehended in Baktria. It is this,

'Ομορεῖ δὲ ἡ 'Αρία τῇ Βακτριανῇ καὶ τῆν ὑποττάσει ὁρη τῷ ἔχοντι τὴν Βακτριανήν.

Here the editor of Didot's Strabo, Carl Muller, dispels the chief obscurity, by a felicitous conjecture. For ὑποττάσει ὁρη he reads ὑπὸ Στασάνορι· observing that, according to Diodorus xviii. 39 § 6; xix. 48 § 1 and Arrian de Success. Alex. § 36 (p. 245 of Didot's Arrian) Antipater in B. C. 321 and Antigonus in B. C. 316 had entrusted Stasanor with Baktrianê and Sogdianê. To correct the previous part of the passage, C. Muller offers us the choice of three less happy conjectures. 1. He proposes τῇ Μαργιανῇ τῇ instead of τῇ Βακτριανῇ καὶ τὴν; 2. Or καὶ [τῇ Μαργιανῇ] τῇ instead of καὶ τὴν. Or lastly καὶ [τῇ Λοιπῇ] τῇ instead of the same καὶ τὴν. We would amend the words preceding the restored ὑπὸ Στασάνορι by merely substituting καὶ γ' ἦν for καὶ τὴν. So that altogether the passage in English will be; "Aria borders upon Baktrianê, and indeed it was under Stasanor who had (the satrapy of) Baktrianô." This would intimate Strabo's belief that Aria had at one time formed part of Stasanor's Baktrian satrapy; and we own that we do not find evidence of that fact. But we find that Stasanor had been made by Alexander the Great his satrap, first of Aria, then of the Zarangæ or Drangæ also ; see Arrian Exp. Alex. iii. 29 § 5; iv. 18 §§ 1, 3; vi. 27 § 3; and we find that on the death of Alexander he was confirmed in the government of these two nations by the guardian of the empire, Perdiccas, in B. C. 323 ; Diod. xviii. 3 § 3; compare Arrian de Succ. Alex. § 8. While Stasanor was thus satrap of Aria and Drangæ, the satrap of Baktrianê and Sogdianê was Philip, and the satrap of Parthia and Hyrkania was Phrataphernes; but when Antipater, succeeding to Perdiccas, assigned the satrapies in B. C. 321, Philip was transferred to the satrapy of Phrataphernes, Stasanor to that of Philip, and Stasandrus (like Stasanor a native of Cyprus) was put into Stasanor's place as satrap of

subject to Darius. The Margian rebels quelled by the satrap of Baktria, are held by the king to belong to

Aria and Drangéné; Diod. xviii. 39 § 6; Arrian, de Succ. Alex. § 36. This Stasandrus, having joined the confederacy under Eumenes against Antigonus (see Diod. xix. 14 § 7) was succeeded in his satrapy (on Antigonus's victory) by Euitus, who, dying shortly after, was succeeded by Euagoras (Diod. xix. 48 § 2) Stasanor remaining still satrap of Baktriané and Sogdiané.

As to our remark that in the amended passage Strabo xi. 10 § 1, it may seem either that the term Aria comprehends Margiané or that Margiané is included under Baktriané, observe that Aria is made to have a part of Baktria adjoining it to the north, though that country in general is said to lie to the east of Aria; Strab. xi. 11 § 1. In Strab. xi. 8 § 1 Baktriané follows Aria in the progress eastward from the Caspian or Hyrkanian sea. In Strabo ii. 1 § 14 Margiané follows Aria, but is coupled with Baktriané instead of being coupled with Aria.

If to the emendations embraced above, of Strabo xi. 10 § 1, it be proposed for the sake of greater historical accuracy, to add the substitution of Drangiané or Zarangiané for Baktriané, we object that in the context following, Strabo adds what would then be tautological;

συντελής δ' ἦν αὐτῇ (i. e. τῇ 'Αρίᾳ) καὶ ἡ Δραγγιανὴ μέχρι Καρμανίας.

C. Muller's first and second proposed emendations of the former part of the passage, which introduce Margiané into the text, either by substitution for the former Baktriané or in addition to it, seem likewise excluded for the similar reason that the words which presently follow (xi. 10. § 2) παραπλησία δ' ἐστὶ καὶ ἡ Μαργιανή would then be a tautology.

Strabo gives to Aria three cities; Artakaena, the original capital (for Arrian writes Ἀρτακάανα πόλιν ἵνα τὸ βασίλειον ἦν τῶν Ἀρείων, Exp. Alex. iii. 25 § 5) with Alexandreia and Akhaia, cities named after their founders. These seem to be the Kharacene Isidore's three cities in Aria (Stathmi Parthici § 15) named Kandak, Artakauan and Alexandreia ἡ Ἀρείοις. the last of which is taken for Herat. From Antiokheia ἡ Ἰνδέρς in Margiané northward (Stathm. Parthic. § 14) a place identified with the *Merv al rud*, that is, "Merv on the River," of our maps—Isidore travels to Kandak in Aria southward, while Strabo in his enumeration proceeds from Akaia in Aria southward to Isidore's single Margian city Antiokeia northward; and this seems to confirm the inference that arises from the comparison of names in the two lists, that Strabo's city Akaia is Isidore's city Kandak. Strabo tells us that Antiokhus Soter (B. C. 280–261) admiring the excellent nature of the Margian plain, surrounded it with a wall of 1500 stades (either $\frac{1500}{30}$=50, or $\frac{1500}{25}$=60 parasangs) in extent; and built a city Antiokeia. This city according to Pliny N. H. vi. 18 had been previously built by Alexander the Great. Pliny's words are quoted by Isidore's editor C. Muller thus; "Sequitur

Baktria: though it seems that the Satrap did not march against them without an express order from his master.ᵐ

regio Margiane apricitatis inclutæ, sola (?) in eo tractu vitifera, undique inclusa montibus amœnis, ambitu stadiorum MD, difficilis aditu propter harenosas solitudines per CXX m. p." (i. e. 40 parasangs at 3 *millia passuum* or 25 stades to the parasang) "et ipsa contra Parthiæ tractum sita; in quâ Alexander Alexandriam condiderat. Quâ dirutâ à barbaris, Antiochus Seleuci filius eodem loco restituit Syriam; nam interfluente Margo, qui conrivatur in Zothale, is maluerat illam Antiochiam appellari. Urbis amplitudo circumitur stadiis LXX." This last sum, not being a multiple either of 30 or 25, seems not to represent a Persian measurement. Of another Margian city, Merv Shah Jehan in N. Lat. 37 deg. 26 min. on the same Murgh water but more than a hundred miles lower down, we are not able to produce any notice from Greek authors.

ᵐ For *satrap* the Aryan word both here col. 3 line 14 and at col. 3 line 55, is *Khshatrapává*, and this written after the Kissian pronunciation is *Saksabavana*; see the Kissian text col. 2 line 80, and col. 3 line 22; though how far in the latter passage the word is Mr Norris's restoration we do not know. *Khshadrapan*, the singular form indicated by the plural אֲחַשְׁדַּרְפְּנִים found in Esther, and the Aramaic correspondent in Daniel, seems the contraction of *Khshatrapávan*, a form indicated by the above-cited Kissian pronunciation. In the Sanskrit legends on the coins of no less than 13 rulers of Surâshtra (an Indian kingdom " of which the peninsula of Guzerat may be taken as the metropolitan province") the word *Kshatrapasa* is a genitive form equivalent to the Greek σατράπου. These rulers were of the Sâh dynasty, placed in the two centuries next before the Christian era, and may have been (originally at least) vassals of the Græco-Baktrian kingdom. See Strabo xi. 11 § 1 and Journal R. A. S. vol. xii. pp 1–72. The Perso-Aryan word represented by the Greek nom. sing. σατράπης, Sir H. C. Rawlinson takes to have been *Khshatrapá*, and the last syllable he identifies with the Sanskrit verb-root *pá*, interpreting it " preserving " or " who preserves; " Journal R. A. S. vol. xi. p. 117. For some Sanskrit verbal nouns having this termination with the same meaning, see Wilson's Sanskrit Grammar p. 32. Thus the whole word signifies " Preserver of the kingdom : " for that *Khshatra* signifies "crown," "sceptre," or "kingdom," is abundantly clear from the cuneiform inscriptions. To this etymology Xenophon's Cyrus the Elder may seem to bear witness, *Cyrop.* viii. 6 § 11, when he promises that the satrap who in proportion to his power shall shew most chariots, with most and ablest horsemen, he will honour ὡς ἀγαθὸν σύμμαχον καὶ ὡς ἀγαθὸν συμφύλακα Πέρσαις τε καὶ ἐμοὶ τῆς ἀρχῆς. Compare his συμφύλακις τῆς βασιλείας. ibid. 7 § 14. We would ask the Sanskrit scholar if, in the form of the title Satrap which the Kissian text of the Behistun inscription attests, the termination *pávan* (from which we

Of Frâda in the Kissian text (where his name is deciphered Farrata) it is said, that he was made by the Margians their king: not their Irsarra, which term is elsewhere always the correspondent of the Aryan Mathishta. Accordingly, in Darius's recapitulation of the Nine Kings and their several pretensions, we read (in the Aryan no less than in the Kissian text) as follows; " One named Frâda, he lied: He said thus, I am king in Margush." And then it is added of him, as well as of the others, that he was author of the revolt he headed. That Frâda lied, calling himself king in Margiana, is also asserted by the legend belonging to his figure in the sculpture, in all three texts, in the Aryan and Assyrian no less than in the Kissian. But by his position in the file, and also by the language of Darius in the narrative where he is first introduced, language importing previous hostility to Darius on the part of the Margians and that it was of their own movement this people made Frâda their chief, we are warned not to take the words of the recapitulating paragraph so strictly in this as in the other cases; but to be content to understand, That the revolt of which Frâda had now been made the leader, could not have gone on without him, being a revival of a previous state of hostility,[n] during which also he may have been the

suppose *pan*, the termination of the Hebrew form to be a contraction) may not be an active present participle of *pá*: see Wilson's Sanskrit Grammar p. 171. Professor Dowson reads *Chhatrapa*, *Chhatrapasi*, and *Chhatrapasisa*, in a Baktrian Pali inscription from the Punjâb. Of the three he takes the last for a genitive and the second for a mere variant of the first; Journal R. A. S. vol. xx pp. 222-225, 228. See other instances in this language, pp 245, 249, 250.

[n] See Behistun inscription, Aryan text, col. 4 lines 23-26. The Kissian word *Irsarra* in Behistun inscription, Kissian text col. 2 lines 8, 14, 17, 61; col. 3 lines 7, 21, 30, 33, 40, represents the *Mathishta* of the Aryan text col. 2 lines 13, 20, 24, 83: col. 3 lines 30, 32, 56, 69, 70, 84. But concerning the Margian leader, the Aryan phrase col. 3 line 12 *awam mathishtam akunavatá*, " Him chief they made," is in the Kissian, col. 2 lines 79, 80, *yufri Ko appini ir yuttás*, " He king of them they made him." Now the monosyllabic character which Mr Norris temporarily expresses by *Ko*, is everywhere the expression of the

principal Margian supporter of Darius's Median rival Frawartish.

Of his fate there is no mention made, as of that of Darius's other rivals in the record of their defeat. He must have saved himself from capture and a felon's death, either by being slain in the battle or by a flight which carried him beyond the border of the Persian empire: and for this perhaps, the Khorazmian desert to the northward afforded facility. According to what seems to have been the custom of the Assyrian copy of the Behistun inscription, in the case of victories obtained by lieutenants of the king's, the loss sustained by the Margians in their defeat is given; and we learn that the slain in fight were 4203; besides some tens, of which the notation on the rock has perished. Of the prisoners (as the statement was translated in 1851) the prodigious multitude, 6562 was butchered. Possibly it may turn out when the language of the record is more perfectly understood, that both here and on former occasions, the numbers given of captives did not suffer death but were treated as spoil, being sold or distributed for slaves.

III.

THE slaughter of the revolted Margians was achieved on the twenty-third of Atriyâdiya (the month called Kisilivu or Khisleu by the Assyrians and Jews) in the year B. C. 518.

Nearly three weeks before, on the fourth day of this month, which was the ninth of Darius's fourth regnal year by the Jewish calculation, an enquiry had been made at Jerusalem by the Church, and a Divine answer had been returned, which must not be left unmentioned, because

---

Kissian correspondent to the Aryan term *Khshâyathiya*, in modern Persian *Shah*, " a king." As an adjective, *Irsarra* corresponds with the Aryan *wazarka*, " great ; " see Behistun inscription (both texts) col. 1. line 1 ; The tomb inscription (both texts) line 1, &c.

they refer not to the past merely, nor to the Jews alone, but to the fresh contrast now presented to view between the fortune of Babylon and that of Jerusalem. The former prosperity and adversity had changed sides, and below we shall have to mark some great epochs in the progress of woe at Babylon and blessing at Jerusalem.

Certain deputies had been appointed by the people,[a] to go unto the House of God to entreat the Face of Jehovah. They were to propound a question to the priests in the House of Jehovah Sabaoth, and to the prophets; of whom the chief at least were Haggai and Zechariah. Of themselves God had declared in old time; "Israel is My Son, even My First-born;"[b] and now their spokesmen were to ask as from one man; "Should I weep in the fifth month, separating myself (for that purpose) as I have done these so many years."

The mourning thus put forward, was in memory of the day, whether the seventh or the tenth of the fifth month when Nebukhadrezzar king of Babylon's "captain of the guard," according to the sentence pronounced by his master, entered Jerusalem and there set fire to the House of Jehovah, to the king's house, and to all the great houses, after which with his forces he broke down the wall round about the city.[c] In the prosperity which had lately returned according to previous notifications from God, and especially when they beheld the new House of Jehovah

---

[a] By *they* in Zech. vii. 2 (as by *them* in Zech. i. 3, and perhaps by the second *they* in Zech. i. 6 remarked on in a former note) we understand the people of Israelites, the returned captivity.

[b] Exod. iv. 22, 23.

[c] 2 Kings xxv. 8, 10; Jeremiah lii. 12. The 10th day of the 5th month, four full years before the event, is the date of the last of the prophecies against Judah and Jerusalem delivered by Ezekiel in the land of the Khaldæans, in the 5th, 6th, and 7th years of Jeconiah's captivity and Zedekiah's reign; see Ezek. xx. 1 with i. 1–3. These prophecies having been delivered in former years, the day of the commencement of the siege, when it arrived, was announced by him in the distant Khaldæan land; being the 10th of the tenth month of the 9th regnal year of Zedekiah. See Ezek. xxiv. 1–2.

far advanced towards its completion, many of the people began to think the yearly mourning for the destruction of the former temple no longer suitable, while others probably maintained the sanctity and the continual obligation of the ordinance. Perhaps the debate at this time was occasioned or revived, by the approach of a similar observance in the tenth month, ordained it is likely along with the other, and in which they commemorated with fasting and wailing the tenth day of the month Tebeth in the ninth year of King Zedekiah, when the king of Babylon came with all his army and began the siege of Jerusalem.[d] For, if it was no longer proper to mourn, because they were now so comforted that it would be ungrateful to grieve even for the great calamity of all, the destruction of God's holy habitation in the fifth month; certainly neither the commencement of the siege in the tenth month of the ninth year, nor the capture of the city on the ninth day of the fourth month in the eleventh year of Zedekiah,[e] ought any longer to be a matter of national mourning. For the reason of these observances was the same in one and all.

The question, therefore, having been put, as in the presence of God, the Word of Jehovah Sabaoth came to Zechariah, one of the prophets then present, commanding him to repeat the answer of God to all the people of the land, and above all to the priests, who had the chief share in ordaining and conducting ritual observances. The prophet did this by portions as the answer came to him, and as he conceived it further and further from God.

First, by this answer, God seems to have repudiated the fasts, upon which He had been consulted, as neither instituted by His command, nor observed on His account. "When ye fasted" said He, "and mourned in the fifth and seventh month, even these seventy years,[f] did ye fast

---

[d] 2 Kings xxv. 1; Jerem. lii. 4; Ezek. xxiv. 1–2.
[e] 2 Kings xxv. 4; Jerem. lii. 6; xxxix. 2.
[f] Not *those &c.* as printed in the English Bible. Literally, *This seventy year*. The same phrase Zech. i. 12, is rendered in the Septuagint τοῦτο

at all unto Me ?" It seems intimated, that their object was not to glorify God for His righteous judgments by humbling themselves before Him, but to indulge a complaining spirit; just as they ate and drank, not for holy joy and thankfulness to God, but, like the lower animals to gladden themselves without Him. By their mourning, they had rather accused God than condemned themselves; had evinced perhaps a rebellious rather than a contrite and submissive disposition.

It should be observed, that the fast in the seventh month coupled by the answer of God with the fast specified in the enquiry of the people, (perhaps merely because it was the one that had then been observed the last) was kept in remembrance of the massacre of Gedaliah and other Jews whom the conquerors had left in charge of a few country-folk, that were to have occupied the land of Judah and to have preserved it from utter desolation, while the other survivors of the destruction of Jerusalem were carried off to Babylon.[g] This last event in the process of destruction and desolation marked the commencement of what by the Jewish civil calendar and in the annals of Judah, should have been the twelfth regnal year of Zedekiah at Jerusalem; but we would rather lay stress upon the fact, that it also closed the nineteenth year of Nebukhadrezzar, according to the Hebrews, which was his seventeenth regnal year, according to the Khaldæans; if we were right when we concluded in a former chapter, that the Khaldæan regnal year began with the eighth month of the Assyrian and Jewish year; the month called Markhesvan by the Jews.

The words of the answer also suggest an enquiry as to the seventy years' commemoration which it mentions of

---

ἐβδομηκοστὸν ἔτος. compare τῶν τρίτων. Numb. xxiv. 10. In their rendering here (Zech. vii. 5) ἰδοὺ ἐβδομήκοντα ἔτη, for ἰδοὺ perhaps we should read ἤδη as before in ver. 3 ἤδη ἱκανὰ ἔτη. Compare Genesis xxvii. 36 where for ָ הֲכִי διότιμος τῶν of the Roman Ed. the Alex. MS. gives ἤδη δ. τ. But perhaps ἰδοὺ, ἤδη and ἤδη τῶν are alike genuine Septuagint renderings of הֲכִי.

[g] Jerem. xl and xli; 2 Kings xxv. 22-26.

the events lamented in the fifth and seventh month, if not in the tenth and fourth month also. It has been shewn that in the annals of Babylon, the first Nebukhadrezzar's reign was computed from the New-year's day next after his father's death; that is, from the first of Markhesvan B. C. 604; whereas in Judah his reign was computed to begin two years earlier, along with the fourth year of Jehoiakim king of Judah, on the first of Tisri B. C. 606. Therefore, the year in which Jerusalem was taken, the temple burnt, and Gedaliah slain, being the nineteenth year of his reign at Jerusalem, was the seventeenth year at Babylon, and ended there with Tisri B. C. 587. If so, the first year of sad commemoration began there the next day; that is, on the first of Markhesvan B. C. 587. And the seventieth year had begun with the month last past at the date where we are now, in Khisleu of the fourth year of Darius the Persian, B. C. (587-69=) 518. So that the seventieth year of commemoration (a period to be distinguished from that of God's indignation spoken of in Zechariah's hearing in the second year of Darius) was now in its second month, as was Darius's fourth year also, by the Khaldæan account.

The answer of God added, that because the people would not listen to the former prophets, when Jerusalem was inhabited and in prosperity, with her cities round about her, when men inhabited the South and the Plain; because they then disregarded ordinances respecting weightier matters than fasts or feasts, saying; "Judge ye judgement of Truth; and shew ye mercy and compassion, every one to his brother, and oppress ye not the widow, nor the fatherless, the stranger, nor the poor; and let none of you imagine evil against his brother in your heart," therefore came the great wrath from Jehovah Sabaoth, certain memorable epochs of which they lamented in their fasts. As Jehovah cried and they would not hear, so they cried and Jehovah would not hear; but scattered them with a whirlwind among all the nations whom they knew not. Thus, the land was desolate after them, so that no man passed through nor returned; for they laid the Pleasant Land desolate. All that had befallen both them and their land, was of their own doing.

Thus did God's answer to the people refer to the past and to the causes of all their calamities. But the Word came yet again saying; "Thus saith Jehovah, I am returned unto Zion, and I will dwell in the midst of Jerusalem, and Jerusalem shall be called The city of the Truth; and the mountain of Jehovah Sabaoth, the Holy mountain." "There shall yet old men and old women dwell in the streets of Jerusalem, and every man with his staff in his hand for multitude of days; and the streets of the city shall be full of boys and girls, playing in the streets thereof. I will save My people from the east country and from the country of the going down of the sun, and I will bring them, and they shall dwell in the midst of Jerusalem, and they shall be My people, and I will be their God in Truth and Righteousness. I will not be unto the residue of this people as in the former days; for the seed shall be prosperous; the vine shall give her fruit; and the ground shall give her increase; and the heavens shall give their dew; and I will cause the remnant of this people to possess all these things. And it shall come to pass, that as ye were a curse among the nations, O house of Judah and house of Israel, so will I save you and ye shall be a blessing. Fear ye not, let your hands be strong. For as I thought to punish you, when your fathers provoked Me to wrath, and I repented not; so again have I thought in these days to do well unto Jerusalem; Fear ye not."

Lastly, the Word said to Zechariah; "Thus saith Jehovah Sabaoth, The fast of the fourth month, and the fast of the fifth, and the fast of the seventh, and the fast of the tenth, shall be to the house of Judah joy and gladness and cheerful feasts; therefore, love ye the truth and peace. Thus saith Jehovah, There shall come great tribes and strong nations to seek Jehovah Sabaoth in

Jerusalem and to entreat the face of Jehovah. Thus saith Jehovah Sabaoth, In those days it shall come to pass that ten men shall " (humbly and reverently) " take hold out of all languages of the nations, even shall take hold of the skirt of him that is a Jew, saying; We will go with you; for we have heard that God is with you." [h]

So much for the enquiry proposed and the answer returned at Jerusalem on the fourth of Khisleu B. C. 518, in the fourth year of Darius's reign. It must be supposed that at least by this time (more than a year since the defeat of Darius's Median rival) the capital city of the Medes had yielded to the conqueror's searchers the record of the decree whereby Cyrus had commanded the rebuilding of the House of God at Jerusalem. For such a decree there was:—besides Cyrus's letter, proclamation, or injunction, to the people of God; and, as we have already related,[i] at Agbatana in the Fort, the only regal residence then existing there, the record was found; if not while Frawartish was still called king, and still possessed an army in Media, yet at least after his defeat. It seems to have been a memorial of the decree, rather than a copy of it, that was found. The contents were recited by Darius in a letter which he caused to be written in his name to his lieutenant, and others in Syria who had advised the search, and had petitioned for a notification of the king's pleasure as to the work whereon the people returned from Babylon were engaged at Jerusalem. Subjoined to the recital, as his decision thereon, the king sent this order to his officers, " Be ye far from them. Let the work of this House of God alone. Let the governour of the Jews and the elders of the Jews build this House of God in its place."

Thus had the builders at Jerusalem been released from all fear of molestation on the part of the civil power, and the faith in God's promises by His prophets which before sustained them had been fully justified. But the king's letter had done more than forbid the offering of any

---

[h] See Zech. vii. and viii.   [i] pp. 243, 244, 507.

obstruction to the fulfilment of Cyrus's command, or any molestation of those whom Cyrus had charged with the matter. It concluded with a further order of Darius's own; "Moreover, by me is made a decree, what ye shall do to the elders of the Jews for the building of this House of God: That of the king's goods, of the tribute beyond the river (Euphrates), forthwith expenses be given unto these men, that they be not hindered: and that which they have need of—both young bullocks and rams and lambs, for the burnt-offerings of the God of the Heavens wheat, salt, wine, and oil, according to the appointment of the priests that are at Jerusalem—let it be given them, day by day, without fail:[j] that they may offer sacrifices of sweet savour unto the God of the Heavens, and pray for the life of the king and of his sons. Also, I have decreed that, whoever shall alter this word, let timber be pulled down from his house, and being set up, let him be clapped upon it:" (that is, impaled thereon) "and let his house be made a dunghill for this. And the God That hath caused His Name to dwell there, throw down every king and people that shall put-to their hand to alter and to destroy this House of God which is in Jerusalem. I Darius have made a decree. Let it be done with speed."[k]

Such was the king's despatch which Tatnai, and the inferior officers who were of the commission with him, had received. They had acted upon it immediately, and the elders of the Jews had gone on building and prospering.

It is plain from this account, that king Darius (whether after or before the making of the reference to him concerning the building at Jerusalem) had obtained minute

[j] There appear to have been stores at Jerusalem of the king's share of the produce of the soil of the country, and perhaps there were in the pastures herds and flocks belonging to the king as his share of the animal increase; the tribute, except poll-tax, being apparently paid in the natural products of the country. Subsidies of money are erroneously asserted to have been made by the king towards the building of the holy house and the maintenance of the daily sacrifices, in the compilation called Esdras [e], or 1 Esdras, iv. 51, 52.

[k] Ezra vi. 1-12.

information concerning the Jewish worship; even if the language of his decree be not thought to express the counsel of some trusted Jewish servant.¹ It may be presumed, that during the two years next before the dates at which we are now arrived; namely, That of the reply to the enquiry at Jerusalem concerning the fasts, (the fourth of Khisleu) and That of the destruction of the Margian rebels, (the 23rd of the same month) there had been a continual influx of Jews into Jerusalem, especially from Babylonia,ᵐ where also their residence, since the commencement of the late revolt, must have now become full of danger, while yet perhaps it could not be so easily enforced, if they wished to abandon it.

¹ One like Zerubbabel or rather Joakhim son of Zerubbabel in the apocryphal story found in Esdras *. See that book in the Anglican version of the Apocrypha; 1 Esdras iv. 13, 43–46; v. 5.

ᵐ See Zech. vi. 10. We even think it not altogether devoid of probability that, as stated 1 Esdras v. 2, a large body of Jews may have emigrated from Babylon to Jerusalem under an escort granted them by Darius of a thousand horsemen. For this is not a circumstance (like the subsequent enumeration in 1 Esdras v. 1 &c.) which belongs properly to the emigration under Zerubbabel and which the compiler has borrowed from the genuine book of Ezra.

IV.

WHEN the Margians were crushed, in Khisleu, or December, the ninth month of the Assyrians and Jews, in the year B. C. 518, the people of Babylon, (having been thrown into revolt by Arakha before Frâda became the Margian Chief) were probably already beset, more or less closely, in their vast walled capital. Indeed, according to Herodotus (if we have rightly interpreted his story of the length of their siege) they had been environed by Darius's forces from the very beginning of the regnal year now current according to their own Khaldæan reckoning; that is to say, since the first day of the eighth month, called Markhesvan by the Jews, the Bagâyâdish of the Persians and Medes. For Darius's fourth regnal year, which was now in its ninth month as reckoned by the Jews, was but in its second according to the Khaldæan method.

The army threatening Babylon had for its Mathishta or Chief a Mede, called in the Aryan text of the Behistun inscription Vidafrâ, a name, however, which we will henceforth write Vindafrâ.[a] But the force despatched

---

[a] See Behistun inscription, Aryan text, col. 3 line 83. The Kissian record col. 3 lines 42, 43, calls him *Vintaparna*, the name it also gives, col. 3 lines 89, 90, to the *Intaphernes* of Herodotus, (the first of Darius's Persian Six) who in the Aryan text col. 4 line 83, is named *Vidafrand*. Perhaps Vidafrâ and Vidafranâ are correspondents in different Aryan dialects, as Median and Persian. In the Assyrian text the name is lost.

by Darius and confided to Vindafrâ is not stated to have been one of "Persians and Medes." Therefore, in this absence of a description elsewhere given in like cases, it may be presumed to have been a soldiery drawn from nations ranked as subject to the two-horned Aryan Ram; though the leader may have been attended by a body of his Median countrymen. To this column, on its arrival from Darius's head-quarters in Media, reinforcements flowed in, we may presume, from the satraps whose provinces bordered on Babylonia. Such to the north-west and west were Syria and Arabia, and such a one to the east was Susiana. The army received the usual charge from their king, " Go, smite that people at Babylon that is not called by my name."

By the story which Herodotus had obtained for his hearers, the Babylonians cared little for the number or the valour of their besiegers. They mounted their walls,[b]

[b] ἀναβαίνοντες ἐπὶ τοὺς προμαχιῶνας τοῦ τείχεος.
Herod. iii. 151. Liddell and Scott explain the word προμαχιῶνις by the Latin term *propugnacula*. For examples of this term, the Latin Lexicon of Andrews cites from an account of the preparations for the defence of Placentia for Othó against Vitellius's lieutenant Cæcina (Tacit. Hist. ii. 19) " Solidati muri, propugnacula addita, auctæ turres; " also, ibid. iii. 84, of the Vitellian soldiery besieged in the Prætorian camp at Rome; " Multi semianimes super turres et propugnacula mœnium exspiravere." One might imagine projecting platforms, moveable or immoveable, and with or without a shield before them (such as " bartizans " are described to have been) rather than a simple parapet or breast-work shielding those by whom a wall was manned. Other instances of the word προμαχιὼν, are found Herod. i. 98, 164. In the former we have rendered it " battlement," p. 568. At top of the outer of the two walls described by Herodotus (that is, seemingly, the outer of the two walls attested by Nebukhadrezzar's "Standard Inscription," but the middle one of the three lines of fortification that, according to Berosus, the city possessed before it was taken by Cyrus) there were along the edges, two rows of chambers or single-roomed houses, οἰκήματα μονόχωλα, facing each other and leaving a space between, broad enough for the passage of a car drawn by four horses all abreast; Herod. i. 179. From the flat roof of the outer row the duty of the defence would be carried on; and within both rows of rooms, the troops not on duty would be lodged, arms and victual would be stored.

they danced and mocked at Darius and his army: one voice was heard to sing out, "Why sit ye here? Begone! Mules must have foals, before ye can take this city!" Here it would seem was an allusion to that better than Vindafrâ the Mede, who had commanded for a better, as the besieged esteemed him, than Darius the Persian, namely Cyrus. For in the days of Herodotus it was said that Cyrus had been designated in prophecy "a Persian mule," his mother having been of a better sort a Mede, and his father a Persian; and it was Cyrus who, at the head of the army of the son of Akhshurush Darius the Mede, his uncle, had taken Babylon twenty years ago.[c] But Cyrus was dead; and it would be long before another would arise like him. If the son of Hystaspes, too, as we suspect, might have been no less properly nick-named "a Persian mule," at least his lieutenant Vindafrâ the Mede was not one. The prophecy, therefore, against Babylon, the citizens thought, had been fulfilled in that fortunate commander, who, taking advantage of their fathers' want of vigilance, had won the city before. There was now little cause for fear. They should not neglect the defence! Such was the state of things for many months at Babylon.

Meanwhile, Darius was carrying on a dangerous struggle

[c] See the oracle said to have been given to the envoys of Crœsus at Delphi; Herod. i. 55, 91; also, the prophecy put into the mouth of the great Nebukhadrezzar by Abydenus, alleging Khaldæan authority; (Euseb. *Pr. Evang.* ix. 41 tom. ii. p. 441 of Gaisford's ed) Abydenus wrote,

Λίγεται γὰρ Χαλδαίων ὡς ἀναβὰς ἐπὶ τὰ βασιλήϊα κατασχεθείη τῳ ὅτεῳ δὴ, φθεγξάμενος δὲ εἴπει, Οὗτος ἐγὼ Ναβουκοδρόσορος, ὦ Βαβυλώνιοι, τὴν μέλλουσαν ὑμῖν προαγγέλλω συμφορὴν, τὴν ὅ τε Βῆλος, ἐμὸς προγόνος, ἥ τε βασίλεια Βῆλτις ἀποτρέψαι Μοίρας τίσαι ἀσθενοῦσιν. Ἥξει Πέρσης ἡμίονος, τοῖσιν ὑμετέροισι δαίμοσι χρεώμενος συμμάχοισιν, ἐπάξει δὲ δουλοσύνην. Οὗ δὴ συναίτιος ἔσται Μήδης, τὸ Ἀσσύριον αὔχημα. . . Ὁ μὲν θεσπίσας παραχρῆμα ἠφάνιστο.

It has been thought, (but erroneously according to Clinton, upon more mature reflexion) that in this story as well as in what precedes it, Abydenus quoted Megasthenes, the contemporary of Seleucus Nikator, the companion of the first Macedonian satrap of Arakhosia and Gedrosia, Sibyrtius, and the envoy to the great king of the Hindus, Sandracottus or Chandragupta; see Clinton F. H. vol. 3, Appendix chap. 12, "Greek authors;" No. 12 "Megasthenes."

with the impostor owned in Persis as Smerdis son of Cyrus and rightful heir to Cambyses. Darius's headquarters seem to have been still in Media; although an expression of his has been thought to indicate a temporary absence from the province and a subsequent return to it with fresh Persian forces.[d] We have remarked already,

---

[d] The Assyrian preposition *itti* answering to אֵת in Hebrew (one of the three forms in which the prepositive particle את is found connected with the pronouns) translates the prepositions *pasā* and *hadā* of the Aryan, with their respective Kissian correspondents, *kik* and *itaka*; compare Behistun Inscription, Assyrian text, line 73 with the Aryan text col. 3 lines 32, 33 and the Kissian text col. 3, lines 7 and 8. That *hadā* Aryan, and *itaka* Kissian, mean "with," may be granted. But may not *ittiya*, the preposition combined with a pronoun, of the Assyrian line 73, be equivalent to the French "chez moi? Compare אֵת Genes. xxx. 29 which Gesenius renders "apud me" *i. e.* "me pastore." The question is, How to render the Aryan phrase (Behistun Inscription col. 3, line 32) *hya aniya kāra Pārsa pasā manā ashiyava Mādam*, or the Kissian words corresponding to the four last of that phrase, *ir-porik Mata-pa-ikki Hu-kik;* which in the Assyrian again are, *ittiya itriku'a Mādai*. Mr Norris renders the Kissian *kik* according to Sir H. C. Rawlinson's rendering of the Aryan *pasā*, "after." But query, if *kik* (which seems to occur but this once and is written with the same two characters which in the reverse order form frequently a postposition read *ikki*) have not the same meaning as *ikki*, "to"? Again, if in Aryan *pasā* be to *pasāwa* (which last occurs in almost every paragraph of the Behistun Inscription) as in Latin *post* to *postea;* and also, if the words *pasā manā* be rightly constructed together as signifying "after me;" still, the meaning of this need not be "at my heels." Perhaps the phrase intimates, that what other Persian troops Darius had, besides those with him which he intended to despatch with Artavardiya against Vahyazdāta, all came to Media to join him, to place themselves under his command, or, simply, to be with him. Compare such instances as these in Greek of the construction of μετὰ with an accusative (a preposition which with the genitive signifies "along with") ἰέναι μετὰ Νέστορα Hom Il. x. 73; "to go after Nestor," *i. e.* to go to fetch him : βῆναι μετά τινα, Hom. Il. v. 152; "to go after a person," *i. e.* in order to slay him: πλεῖν μετὰ χαλκὸν Hom. Od. i. 184; "to sail after brass," *i. e.* in order to get some : βῆναι μετὰ πατρὸς ἀκουήν, Hom. Od. ii. 308; "to go after hearsay of (thy) father," *i. e.* in order to get and bring back news of him. The Assyrian phrase above cited, *ittiya itriku'a Mādai* was rendered by Rawlinson in 1851, " cum me rediëre (ad) Mediam." But *itriku'a* elsewhere answers (as it does here) to the Aryan *ashiyava*, "went."

that the army investing Babylon under Vindafrâ the Mede appears to have been mustered from the subjects of the Perso-Median nation in the conquered provinces. Against the Aryan population which supported the rival king in Pârsa-land, Darius used forces of higher repute; such as had not only the remembrance of late successes to encourage them, but had never suffered defeat from the enemy they were now to face. The deluded Persian population was to be encountered by an army entirely of their own race and partly of their own country. The "Persians and Medes" who had conquered, in Media and in Parthia, all that called Frawartish their king, and who still attended upon Darius after the despatch of his other forces under Vindafrâ against Babylon, had been reserved for this service. They were reinforced out of a people commemorated by Darius's trilingual record in its Kissian text alone. The additional clause, now mutilated or as yet at least but incompletely copied, describes them as having "remained faithful" to Darius. This characteristic, though their name is missing, joined to the fact that the clause which concerns them never had its correspondent in the Aryan text, nor perhaps in the Assyrian either, seems to indicate inhabitants of the country now in revolt, but men of a stock which spoke the Kissian language, being not of Aryan race but descended from the older population whose land the immigrant or invading Aryans had called Persian after the name of their own tribe.

Of the whole column the command was given to a Persian named Artavardiya: but the usual commission to destroy all who owned any other than Darius for their king, is not in this case recorded. Perhaps it was respect for the feelings of Persian hearers rather than a special forbearance which he had practised in the case of his revolted countrymen, that caused the omission. Before

For instance, compare line 16 of the Assyrian (where Rawlinson renders *itriku'a*, "transibant") with col. i. line 41, where he renders *ashiyava* also "transibat."

the army departed, whatever Persian soldiery the king had at his command elsewhere, detachments or what not, he appears to have summoned into Media, to remain with him, (perhaps at Agbatana) forming the nucleus of a reserve with which he surrounded his person and of which he kept the command in his own hands. When this relief arrived, Artavardiya set forth for Persis with the force of which he had been made the chief. Having entered that country, he was encountered at a town named Rakhâ (in the Kissian, Rakkan) by Darius's rival, the pretended Smerdis, Vahyazdâta. A battle ensued, wherein Darius's army obtained a complete victory, on the twelfth day of the month Thuravâhara, that is Sabatu or Sebat, the eleventh month of the Assyrians and Jews, coinciding nearly with the February of B. C. 517. The so-called Smerdis, with a cavalry of trusty adherents, effected a retreat to Pishiyâ'uwâdâ or Pishiyakhòdâ, the district where, in Mount Arakadrish, the former pretended Smerdis, Gaumâta the Magian, first shewed himself.[e] Thence, with strength recruited, he came again, and at a mountain (or town, as the Kissian version calls the place) named Parga,[f] fifty-four days after the first fight, he again assailed the advancing army of Darius. It was the sixth of Garmapada, the Assyrian and Jewish Nisannu or Nisan, answering nearly to our April; and the day was a fatal one for him. He was again totally defeated, nor was he able as before to escape : he was taken alive. And now we leave it to Darius himself to tell the rest of the story. " Afterwards, I impaled that Vahyazdâta and his principal adherents at a town of Pàrsa-land named 'Uwâdaidaya, or Khodaidaya."[g] To this, in the Kissian and Assyrian

[e] See p. 328; where, however, the mention of a town is unauthorized, and the 14th of Viyakhana (the Assyrian Adarru or Jewish Adar) is interpreted according to a scheme which, on Mr Norris's communication of the discovery of the Assyrian month names, we were obliged to surrender; see pp. 425, 437, 446.
[f] Geo. Rawlinson would identify this place with the modern *Fahraj* situated between *Shiraz* and *Kermàn*.
[g] See Behistun Inscription, Aryan text, col. 3. para. 8.

versions, we find added (what may have been but accidentally omitted in the text intended for Aryan ears) "This I did in Pârsa-land."

However, just as, after Darius's successful operations against Frawartish in Media, the flame propagated to Parthia remained to be quenched by Vishtaspa the king's father; so now, after Vahyazdâta's defeat in Persis, the partisans of that pretended Smerdis had still to be conquered in Arakhotia. It appears that Vahyazdâta was not followed by all the forces of his kingdom when he resisted the invasion conducted by Artavardiya. From that total are to be deducted such as may have been employed in guarding the western frontier, towards Susiana; or in maintaining the pretender's authority in disaffected or lawless parts of the interior. We have also to take account of the difficulty there must have been found, to muster, at a distance from the men's homes, and still more to keep for many weeks together, as an army, any very large moiety of a population which though warlike and hardy, depended (it is probable) for the most part, even when gathered together in arms, every man on the stores supplied from his own field or pastures. But further, it appears that, either in anticipation of an invasion from that quarter, or probably invited by the state of the province, the pretended Smerdis (how long, we know not, before he was himself invaded from Media) had detached a force against Hara'uwatish or Arakhotia, where a servant of Darius's was satrap, called Vivâna, or as the name has been latinized Vibanus : and he had given it in kingly style, the commission to go and smite Vivâna with all others in that country who owned Darius for their lord. Probably at this time, not being yet separated from Pârsa-land (among the tribes of which Herodotus names the Germanians, not wandering herdsmen but settled tillers of the soil[h]) the cultivated part of Carmania

---

[h] Herodotus, i. 125, enumerates ten Persian tribes, which he distinguishes as ruling and dependent tribes, and again as cultivators, ἀροτῆρες and pasturers, νομάδες. The three ruling tribes and three others includ-

belonged to the area where Vahyazdâta's pretensions were admitted; while on the other hand, the government of Vivâna (like that of Sibyrtius, the Macedonian, left satrap of Arakhotia at the death of Alexander the Great,) may have extended over Gedrosia.[1] Thus Vivâna would have been the neighbour whom the ruler of Pârsa-land had to trespass upon or to resist on his eastern frontier: and the pretended Smerdis seems to have resolved upon making himself master of Vivâna's province, desiring to push the authority of a son and heir of Cyrus; just as it appears to have been with the view of extending the dominion of Frawartish king of the Medes to the boundary of that of the great Cyaxares, from whom he claimed to descend, that the attempt was made, in the first two years of Darius's reign, to wrest Armenia from the lieutenants of Darius.

Against the invaders of Arakhotia Darius had no victory of his satrap's to boast of, till no less than eleven months had elapsed since the first defeat, and nine months since the final overthrow, of Vahyazdáta in Pârsa-land, that is, Fars or Persis. This fact may be regarded as a sign that Arakhotia had been invaded by Darius's enemies under favourable circumstances, and with a considerable measure of success.

But on the thirteenth day of the Anâmaka that followed

ing as the last of them, the Γυμάνιοι, were cultivators. The remaining four tribes of which the Σαγάρτιοι is the one last mentioned, were pasturing tribes. We have had occasion to express the opinion that the Sagartii, with their horses, herds, and flocks, lived in a region to the northward, sometimes called the Carmanian Desert. Stephen of Byzantium citing the above passage of Herodotus, for Γυμάνιοι writes Καρμάνιοι. For an instance of variation from γα to κι see the next note.

[1] When Alexander on his return from India, arrived ἰς τῶς Γαδρωσίων τὰ βασίλεια (named by Arrian, Exp. Alex. vi. 24 § 1, Πούρα) he deposed the satrap Apollophanes and appointed Thoas in his place; but Thoas dying, he transferred Sibyrtius from the satrapy of Carmania to that of the Arakhoti and Gadrosii; Arrian, Exp. Alex. vi. 27 § 1. After Alexander's death, Perdiccas Σιβυρτίῳ μὲν ἰδωκεν 'Αραχωσίαν καὶ Κιδρωσίαν, in this and other cases confirming Alexander's former appointments; Diod. xviii. 3 § 3. Strabo and others write Γαδρωσίαν.

next after the date of Vahyazdâta's ruin; that is to say, on the thirteenth day of a month corresponding with the Assyrian and Jewish Thabitu or Tebeth, and coinciding most closely with the January of the Julian year B. C. 516, Vivâna being attacked at a fort in Arakhotia named Kapishkanish, inflicted a severe blow upon the invaders of his province. They rallied, however, and fifty-four days afterwards, on the seventh of the month Viyakhana (the Assyrian and Jewish Adarru or Adar, agreeing most nearly with the Julian March) they again attacked the Satrap in a district called Gadutava or Kanduvata.ʲ They were completely defeated. Their leader along with his mounted associates, keeping together in their flight, took refuge in a certain fort named Arshâda which in the Kissian version is further described as Vivâna's Irvael, that is (as Mr Norris concludes, not without support from Ugrian analogies) a possession and dwelling-place of the satrap's. It seems clear, that at least since their first defeat, the invaders had been losing ground which before they had held in the country; that the district where they suffered their final defeat, had been occupied by them; and that Vivâna's fort, the present refuge of their leader and his companions, was likewise an acquisition they had made in a former flow of success. It did not shelter them long. They were followed up by the victorious satrap and his people, taken, and put to death. "Then," says Darius, "the province became mine. This I did in Arakhotia."ᵏ

The very considerable interval of time which we find between even the latest date that can be assigned to Vahyazdâta's despatch of the army which invaded Arakhotia, and the date of its first defeat by the satrap of the

---

ʲ See Behistun Inscription col. 3, line 28 of the Kissian text with Norris's observations; and col. 3, line 65, of the Aryan. This district, Sir H. C. Rawlinson thought, may be marked by the modern *Kaddah* on the *Khash-rúd* conterminous with *Seistan*: Journal R. A. S. vol. xi p. 128.

ᵏ Behistun Inscription col. 3 para. 12.

province, has led us to suppose that the enterprise was at first successful. That it ended, however, in the destruction of those by whom it had been conducted, does not surprise us: because we know that the ruler of their native land, whose commission they bore, had since been overthrown, and the land conquered; so that while the victorious general Artavardiya was probably able to send succours to Vivâna, their antagonist, no like support could any longer come to them from that quarter. But their success at first must be ascribed to causes quite unknown to us. It is conceivable, however, that the satrap of Arakhotia was in some degree distracted in his measures, or obliged to confine himself to defensive operations, by the late or still subsisting revolt from Darius, of another neighbouring province. For such was THATAGUSH, the country of Herodotus's Sattagydas; if this, as we conclude, was the western division of a region that stretched away from the border of Hariva, eastward to the Indus, lying between Baktria on the north side and Arakhotia on the south. This tract of country, which Herodotus appears to designate the Paktyan land, Strabo's authority Eratosthenes certainly called the Paropamisadan province, though the Assyrian text of the Behistun inscription limits this appellation to its eastern division, that is, to the part of it called Gadâra or Kantâra (according as the name was engraved for Perso-Median or for Kissian reading) and which was occupied by the Gandaræ of Hecatæus, the Gandarii of Herodotus.[1] The part we speak of—the country

[1] The most warlike of the Hindus, those that went after the gold (of which the diggers and owners were "ants;" and out of which the Hindus paid 360 talents a-year, tribute to Darius; Herod. iii. 94, 95, 98) lived furthest toward the north and resembled the Baktrians in their manner of life. These according to Herodotus, iii. 102, Κασπατύρω τι πόλι καὶ τῇ Πακτυϊκῇ χόρῃ ιἰσὶ πρόσουροι. The expedition accompanied by Skylax of Caryanda (in Caria) which Darius despatched to sail down the Indus and from the mouth of that river, crossing the Erythræan sea and circumnavigating the Arabian peninsula, to reach Egypt by the Arabian gulf (our Red Sea) started ἰκ Κασπατύρου (or according to the Sancroft MS Κασπατύρου) τι πόλιος καὶ τῆς Πακτυϊκῆς γῆς. Herod. iv. 44. The name of this city upon the Indus seems more correctly written in the San-

of the Sattagydas—is enumerated by Darius among the provinces that revolted from him while he was at Babylon, in the first two years of his reign : but, being entirely uninformed by what means and when it was reduced to obedience, we can only suppose the success to have been attained without any of those violent collisions of the mustered forces of both sides, which, when they ended in the defeat of the enemy, it was Darius's plan to commemorate by his Behistun inscription. Moreover, it is probable that the submission of the Sattagydas, if not yielded immediately after the destruction of the Margian rebels by Dâdarshish the satrap of Baktria, was, at the utmost, not protracted long after the recovery of Arakhotia by the satrap Vivâna.[m]

croft MS *Kastapura*; but the true name perhaps is *Kaspapura*; which may be made up out of both readings; commencing with Κασπα according to all the MSS of Herod. iii. 102 as well as most MSS Herod. iv. 44; and ending with πυρος, as in the Sancroft MS Herod. iv. 44. For, from the *Periegesis of Asia* by Hecatæus the Milesian, a writer with whom our Halicarnassian was familiar and who was a contemporary of Darius, Herod. v. 125, this fragment has been preserved by Stephen of Byzantium, Κασπάπυρος πόλις Γανδαρική Σκυθῶν ἀκτή. See Hecatæus's Fragments, No. 179, in the *Fragmenta Scriptorum Græcorum* edited for Didot by Carl and Theodore Muller, tom. i. p. 12. By comparing the two writers we may learn, that a part at least, of the Paktyan land lying upon the (right hand bank of the upper) Indus, was occupied by the nation termed Γανδάριοι by Herodotus iii. 91, vii. 66, and Γανδαραι as well as Γανδάριοι by Hecatæus, who withal made them 'Ινδῶν ἔθνος, "a Hindu people," though by Herodotus as well as by Darius's Inscriptions they are distinguished from the Hindus of Darius's dominion (who were those conquered by Darius himself: Herod. iv. 44: whereas the Gandarian nation was inherited from Cambyses, as the Behistun list evinces) see Hecatæus, frag. 178. Here, then, is a confirmation of our opinion of Herodotus's confusion of the 7th and 13th satrapies, in Herod. iii. 91, 93; see above pp 169, 170. It may also be suspected on a comparison of Herodotus and Hecatæus, that the Paktyans were in some sense " Scythians," for while Kaspapura is placed in the Paktyan land by Herodotus, this city of an Indian and, therefore, Aryan, race is referred by Hecatæus to the Scythian region.

[m] Besides the list of provinces that revolted from Darius about B. C. 520, all Darius's three general lists of subject provinces contain Thatagush. In two, namely at Behistun and at Persepolis, the name pre-

The two battles, gained by Vivâna on the thirteenth of Anâmaka and the seventh of Viyakhana, we have assigned to the year B. C. 516 ; concluding that the order of time cedes, in one (the tomb-inscription) it follows, Hara'uwatish or Arakhotia. At Persepolis it stands between 'Uwarazmiya, or Khorasmia, and Arakhotia ; but we attach little importance here to the juxtaposition with Khorasmia ; because after Khorasmia the enumerator seems to have been obliged to return, having reached the extremity of the empire in this direction. Perhaps a like remark is appropriate in the case of the Behistun list, where Thatagush follows Saka.

But in the tomb list, after Zaraka and Hara'uwatish (that is, the Zarangas or Drangas and Arakhoti, which formed a line from west to east towards India, Strabo. xv. 2 § 8) we have Thatagush, Gadâra Hi(n)dush. Here it seems strongly indicated, that these last three also follow in a line from west to east ; that is to say, from the eastern border of Hariva, or Herat, which had been before enumerated, to within the western frontier of the Panjâb, the country where lived the Hindus conquered by Darius, near the Gandarian city Kaspapura but on the left bank of the Indus. If so, Thatagush was a country east of Hariva, within the limits given (from Eratosthenes) by Strabo xv. 2 § 9 to the Paropamisadas, the people inhabiting between the river Indus on the east and Aria or country of the Arii (Hariva) on the west, also between Bactriané on the north (in which direction the ridge of Paropamisus was their strong border) and Arakhotia on the south.

We will here remark on a passage of the preceding section (where Strabo describes the direct road to India after arriving from the Caspian Gates through Parthia at Alexandreia ἡ 'Αρίοις) that for Βακτριανῆς we ought to read 'Αρίανῆς. The passage we would thus correct is this :—

ἀλλ' ἡ μὲν ἐπ' εὐθείας διὰ τῆς Βακτριανῆς καὶ τῆς ὑπερβάσεως τοῦ ὄρους εἰς 'Ορτόσπανα ἐπὶ τὴν ἐκ Βακτρων τρίοδον, ἥ τις ἐστὶν ἐν τοῖς Παροπαμισάδαις.

We are inclined to suppose that the Sattagydas (Thatagush) and the Aparytas who in Herod. iii. 91. are linked, the one to the other, by the Gandarians and the Dadikas (of whom the former are the Gandaræ of Hecatæus, the Kantara of Darius's tomb-inscription in the Kissian version, and the Gadâra of the Aryan inscriptions) are included in the general ethnic name of Paktyes in Herod. vii. 67. For in Herod. vii. 66, the Gandarians and Dadikas form a separate command together ; while the Sattagydas and Aparytas are not mentioned at all by their proper names in the host of Xerxes. And according to our correction (referred to in the last note) of the statement made by Herodotus iii. 91, 93 concerning the 7th and 13th satrapies, the four nations that are linked together, as we have said, in Herod. iii. 91—the Sattagydas, the Gandarii, the Dadikas, and the Aparytas, belong to the Paktyan satrapy which is to be separated entirely from Armenia.

in which they happened was the same as the order of place which they hold in the Behistun narrative; that is, that they happened both of them after the overthrow of

It would appear, then, that the Paropamisadas of Eratosthenes are broken into two nations in the lists of Darius, the Thatagush and another, which in the Kissian and Assyrian versions of the Behistun list was termed Parrupamisanna but in the Aryan text Gadâra. Also it would appear that, though distinct for military employment in the time of Xerxes, yet for payment of tribute and for their civil government the two formed but one satrapy, before the end of our Darius's reign no less than at the date of the death of Alexander the Great. This satrapy formed what Herodotus calls the Paktyan land, if our correction be admitted of what we call the historian's mistake, Herod. iii. 91, 93. Thus, the Paropamisadan satrapy of Alexander's historians and of the geographer Eratosthenes, is identified with the Paktyan country of Herodotus, and with a satrapy which Darius son of Hystaspes formed out of four nations, the Sattagydas, the Gandarii, the Dadikas, and the Aparytas. We are, therefore, well prepared to subscribe to a theory which has been proposed—That the name Paktyan is connected etymologically with a title the Affghans give themselves, Pushtun or Puhtan : (see Malte-Brun, *Annales nouvelles des Voyages* tom. ii. pp. 344 etc. cited by G. Rawlinson, Herod. vol. iv. p. 215) confirmed as the notion is, by this judgment of Viscount Strangford's in an article on the Pushtu, or language of the Affghans; Journal R. A. S. vol. xx p. 60. "There is no reason for doubting that the forms Πάκτυες and Πακτυϊκὴ χώρα, met with in Herodotus, express the modern national name of Pushtu in the pronunciation of the eastern Affghans, with whose geographical position they completely coincide." It seems, moreover, plain that the Gandarii and Dadikas, though they lived in Paktyan land, were not Paktyans as the Sattagydas were. They formed a separate command in the army of Xerxes, and (like the Parthians, the Khorasmians and the Sogdians) they were armed and attired in the Baktrian fashion, whereas the Paktyans proper, armed with their country bows and with daggers, were also σισυρηφόροι, " wearers of sheepskin or goatskin cloaks." But two other commands are expressly said to have been attired in the Paktyan fashion ; that of the Οὔτιοι and Μύκοι and that of the Παρικάνιοι. These three nations are the 20th, 21st and 22nd of p. 113. The skin-cloak, σίσυρα, was also worn by the Caspians, the 17th nation of p. 113. Several questions arise here.

1. Were the people called by Herodotus Paktyans (part of whose country had been occupied by the Gandarians from India) themselves of Aryan race ?

2. Should we add to the Sattagydas and Aparytas, as also Paktyan, a people placed by Alexander's historians on the border of the Gedrosians

the second pretended Smerdis in Pârsa-land. For if not, they must have been fought, either both of them before the victories gained for Darius by Artavardiya, or partly between the Zarangæ and the Arakhoti, that had received from Cyrus the title of " Benefactors" but were otherwise called Arimaspi?

3. But from their name Arimaspi according to Diod. xvii. 81 may we not suspect these "Benefactors" of Cyrus's to have been of Mongolian race; and their language to have been akin to the Kissian? For the last syllable of this name may easily have been the Kissian plural termination *pa*, altered according to the analogy of Greek; and there was a remote nation of Arimaspi whose name was fancifully interpreted to mean " One-eyed," placed by Herodotus beyond the Issedones; see Herod. iv. 13 and iii. 116; compare Diod. ii. 43 § 5. We have elsewhere suggested, that Πάκτυες represents the vernacular equivalent of the title " Benefactors;" since *pikti* in the Kissian phrase *Auramasta pikti Hu-tas* answering to the Aryan *Auramazdāmiya upastām abara*, if it does not mean "*help*" like *upastām*, must mean "helper." The Arimaspi, if of Mongolian race, might come under the general Persian appellation *Saka* (which the Greeks interpreted " Scythian ") and they may have been the people of the Kharacene Isidorus's Sakastanê lying on the road between Zarangianê and Arakhosia; see the Stathmi Parthici § 18. But as to the argument founded on the proper name of Cyrus's Benefactors, it will of course be replied that Arrian, who places this people on the river Etymander, Exp. Alex. iv. 6 § 6 makes their name to have been Ariaspas 'Αριάσπαι, Exp. Alex. iii. 27 §§ 4, 5 which is no other in the singular than 'Αριάσπης, the name of a Mede, one of the companions of Cyrus in Xenoph. Cyrop. v. 1 § 2 &c. or Ariaspes father of Atossa, in Hellanicus frag. 163; and, like that, is in both its parts of Aryan derivation, being equivalent to the Greek proper name Kalippus. However, *Arimaspos* rather than *Ariaspas* seems to have been the reading of Curtius vii. 11 where all Zumpt's eleven Florence and Berne MSS have the corrupt *armatos*, though a Leyden MS which Zumpt notes as *Voss*. 2. is said to have *Armaspos*. In the *Itinerarium Alexandri* discovered among the Ambrosian MSS by Cardinal Mai, and printed with the Pseudo-Callisthenes at the end of the Arrian published by Didot, immediately after an incidental mention in cap. 87 of the Etymander river running through the country of the *Evergetæ* or Benefactors, (parallel with that of Arrian *Exp. Alex.* iv. 6 § 6) we read at the beginning of cap. 88, " Hieme igitur apud Arimaspos declinatâ," where the blunder Arimaspos for *Zariaspa*, the capital of Baktria (Arrian, *Exp. Alex.* iv. 1 § 5 Strabo xi. 11 § 2) seems to indicate the name which the mention of the Evergetæ had suggested to the compiler's mind or the name which his author had given to the Evergetæ. We will only add a conjecture as to Sakastanê, that its other

before and partly after those successes in Persis. Now, if the victories in Arakhotia, of Anâmaka and Viyakhana, had happened both of them before the earliest victory in Persis, they would also have been related first. Indeed, they would have belonged to a previous year; for Viyakhana, the date of the latest of the supposed preceding victories (a month answering to our March) if it belonged to the same year, would be later than Thuravâhara, (that is, February) when the first victory was gained in Persis. Again, if the successes in Arakhotia had been obtained partly before and partly after those in Persis; that is, if the victory in Arakhotia of Anâmaka had happened before the victory in Persis of Thuravâhara, but the victory in Arakhotia, of Viyakhana, after it (though withal before the victory in Persis of Garmapada in the same year B.C. 517) in that case (as we conclude from Darius's former practice in relating the suppression of the two revolts in Susiana and the campaign of his lieutenant Takhmaspâda the Mede against the Sagartians) they would have been left undated on the monument." We are, therefore, satisfied that we have done well in identifying the Anâmaka and Viyakhana marked by Vivâna's victories, with the January and March of our year B. C. 516. In other words, we fully believe that these successes in Arakhotia belong to the year after the one in which two great blows in Persis destroyed the kingly power of the pretended Smerdis, Vahyazdâta.

name Παςαιτακηνή given it by Isidore, if it cannot by a more correct orthography be connected with the (Paktyan?) 'Αταςίται of Herod. iii. 91, may be supposed to be derived from a colony of Παςαιτάκαι from Baktria (comp. Arrian, *Exp. Al.* iv. capp. 21 and 22) rather than from Media.

ᵈ See above p. 579.

V.

AFTER the recovery of Arakhotia, completed in March of the year B. C. 516, except in beleaguered Babylon, no resistance to Darius was anywhere prolonged, whether in behalf of a rival claiming to be the nearer heir of Cyrus and Cambyses, or in the hope of separating a nation from the dominion of the Persian, and re-establishing it in possession of a king of its own with prospect of possible aggrandizement in time to come. Many nations had drunk of the cup of chastisement; and now "the king of Sheshak," Nebukhadrezzar son of Nabunita, as the Armenian adventurer had fatally styled himself, was to drink after them; one that, more like the inmate of a prison, than the head of a powerful nation, inhabited the palace and sat on the throne of the victorious Nebukhadrezzar.[a]

The regnal year of the Khaldæans actually current, was the second of this phantom Nebukhadrezzar, and the fifth of Darius, as rival kings of Babylon. The lapse of it had reached the fifth month; for its first had been in the order of the Assyrian and Jewish twelve, the eighth month called by the Jews Markhesvan and answering nearly to the November of the year B. C. 517. The year before this—that is, the new Nebukhadrezzar's first—had been the last of a term of seventy years that began with the eighteenth year of the son of Nabopolassar and ended with the fourth year of the son of Hystaspes, according to the Khaldæan registers;[b] and while all these seventy

[a] See Jerem. xxv. 26. The Sheshak of this text seems explained by Jerem. li. 41, "How is Sheshak taken! and how is the praise of the whole earth surprised! How is Babylon become an astonishment among the nations!"

[b] Darius's first regnal year, by the Assyrian and Jewish reckoning, began, (as has often been intimated) with the first month of the Assyrian and Judæo-Assyrian Calendar; being the first month (say, April in B. C. 521) of the reign of the Magian who assumed the character of Smerdis son of Cyrus This is the reckoning of the books, Haggai,

years lasted, the Jews had continually commemorated the anniversaries of four signal epochs in those disastrous years which closed the reign of their last native king Zedekiah. But we have seen that, when the seventieth year was not two months old, when of the four mournings the last they had kept was the one which for the sixty-ninth time had recalled to their minds the murder of

Zechariah, and Esther. But, according to the Khaldæan account which we detected in the report of Herodotus, and which seems to be followed in the case of Artaxerxes the Long-armed in the book of Nehemiah, Darius's first year began with the Magian's eighth month in B. C. 521; that being the month which the regnal year of the Khaldæan registers began with. As to the regnal years of the son of Nabopolassar, it is well known that, by Khaldæan account, he was not king in the 4th year of Jehoiakim king of Judah (which the Hebrews considered his first) because during the whole of this year his father was yet alive. Nor did the Khaldæan annalists write him king in the fifth year of Jehoiakim king of Judah, though Nabopolassar's death probably took place before the close of that Jewish civil year or at least before the end of the first month of the following civil year, the 6th of Jehoiakim; because the Khaldæan method was the reverse of that of Ptolemy's canon. The canon reckons the whole of the (Egyptian) year in which a king began to reign at Babylon, to the new king as his first; whereas the Khaldæans reckoned the whole of the (Khaldæan) year in which such king began to reign at Babylon to the predecessor. Thus, the 70 years' grief for the temple were the (43—17=the) 26 last years of the Great Nebukhadrezzar + the two years of his son Evil-Merodakh + the four years of the usurper Neriglissar + the 17 years given to Nabonedus, + the (2 of Darius the Mede + 7 of Cyrus=) 9 years ascribed to Cyrus + the 8 years including the first seven months of the Magian's reign but ascribed entirely to Cambyses + the first 4 years of Darius. For these items, see Berosus's Fragments, Ptolemy's Canon, and, for the last of them, Zech. vii. 5, where (as mentioned in a former note) the words translated "those seventy years," should rather be rendered "this seventy years," that is, "this now (in Khisleu) seventieth year." The after years, therefore, during which the Babylonians might triumph for their victory, while the men of Judah might sorrow and cry to the God of Israel for the punishment of their oppressors, began with Markhesvan B. C. 587 and ended with Tisri, the Assyrian Tasritu, B. C. 517. For the year of the capture of Jerusalem (which began with Markhesvan B. C. 588 and was the 19th of Nebukhadrezzar's reign according to the Hebrews, or his 17th according to the Khaldæan date of his accession to the throne) see 2 Kings xxv. 1–4, 8; Jerem. lii. 4–6, 12.

Gedaliah in their seventh month, the twelfth of the Khaldæan year, and when the first mourning of the seventieth year by the Khaldæan reckoning was now approaching, namely the fast for the commencement of the siege of Jerusalem by Nebukhadrezzar's army in the tenth month of their own Mosaic and of the Assyrian twelve—just then, in reply to a consultation regarding them, the Word of God by the prophet Zechariah had given a promise that these four seasons of mourning should be to the House of Judah joy and gladness and cheerful feasts. However, during the seventieth year, the first counted by his adherents to the new Nebukhadrezzar at Babylon, the four fasts had been held (we suppose) as usual at Jerusalem, and it had not yet seemed clear (while in Persis and Arakhotia, as well as at Babylon, the pretensions of Darius were disputed by armed opponents) that the promise was fulfilled. In the present year, too, the seventy-first, which was now five months old, the anniversary of the tenth of Tebeth when the Babylonians began the siege of Jerusalem, had probably been remembered there by the appointed fast, though in Arakhotia on the thirteenth Darius's enemy sustained his first defeat. But in March B. C. 516 that enemy vanished; and before the next fast of the year arrived, there occurred an event which made it impossible for the Jews to keep in the manner prescribed either this which commemorated the entry of the Khaldæans into Jerusalem in the fourth Mosaic month, or the great fast of all in the month following which reminded them of the execution of Nebukhadrezzar's sentence upon the city in the burning of the temple and great houses, and in the demolition of the walls. The event which was thus to make all mourning cease, was a great retaliation upon their conquerors, the capture of Babylon by the forces of the king under favour of whom they had for some time been prospering in the re-building of the temple as well as in their private affairs ; and whose stores now supplied the daily service of that altar of burnt-offering which stood before the door of the unfinished House ; having been put up before the building was commenced,

and when the people first returned from Babylon under
Zerubbabel the Prince of Judah and Jeshua the High Priest
of the sons of Aaron.

During a year and five months, that is, for the time
already elapsed at the point of the history where we now
find ourselves, and for two months yet to come, according
to Herodotus the city was blockaded in vain; although
all possible plans and devices had been employed to take
it.[c] We are assured that among these attempts the
stratagem had not been forgotten by which Cyrus had
suddenly succeeded, having made his preparations without
being discovered and having selected for the execution
the time of a festival within the city at which (as Xenophon adds to Herodotus's account and to that of Daniel)
" the people of Babylon were in the habit of drinking and
revelling all night long." But during this long second
siege the Babylonians were vigilant; all above forty years
of age remembering well how they had been taken before;
the interior walls along the river sides were never deserted;
their posterns affording communication between the city
and the river, were never left open or unguarded. Therefore, at the season when the Euphrates is lowest, which
Darius's army had spent before Babylon twice in the
winters of his fourth and fifth regnal years, if the water
of the river was ever turned off from its natural course
to run upon the country westward through the outlets and
into the prodigious reservoirs which former kings had
excavated for the irrigation of that region and perhaps
also in part for its defence against Arab depredators as
well as to facilitate building at the bottom and sides of
the river and its canals within the walls of Babylon, however shallow the stream may have been rendered that
still followed the bed of the river, the city it traversed
was nevertheless in no danger of being taken by assault
from the river; [d] and it was still abundantly supplied with

[c] Herod. iii. 152.
[d] For the method of the capture by Cyrus, see Herod. i. 191. For
Xenophon's similar account, and for his testimony (confirming Daniel

drinking water not only from wells but from vast tanks within the walls.*

v. 30, 31) that among those slain in the capture was the king of Babylon (the son according to Herod. i. 188 of Labynetus's wife Nitokris) named, not as Herodotus asserts, "Labynetus like his father," but really Belshazzar, as we learn from Daniel, or *Bel-shar-uzzur* according to the inscription on his father (that is, we think, his step-father's) cylinders found by Mr J. E. Taylor at *Muqcyer* or Mugheir, and of which Mr H. F. Talbot has given a decipherment and translation in Journal R. A. S. vol. xix p. 194) see Xenoph. Cyrop. vii. 5 §§ 7–31. Of one sentence in the chapter referred to of Herodotus, we would offer a correction. It is this

εἰ μέν νυν προετύθοντο οἱ Βαβυλώνιοι, ἢ ἔμαθον, τὰ ἐκ τοῦ Κύρου ποιεύμενα οὐδ᾽ ἂν περιιδόντες τοὺς Πέρσας ἐσελθεῖν ἐς τὴν πόλιν διέφθειραν κάκιστα.

To make sense of this, it might seem necessary to read διεφθάρησαν, for διέφθειραν, translating, *If the Babylonians had received previous information, or had comprehended what was doing by Cyrus, they would not have perished miserably, even if they had permitted the Persians to enter the city,* or rather, the channel of the Euphrates between the two divisions of the city. But we would not correct the text thus. We would merely substitute οἱ δ᾽ ἂν, for οὐδ᾽ ἂν, that is, read an iota for a upsilon; whereby we obtain a text which may be translated thus; "If the Babylonians had been informed beforehand or had comprehended what was being done of Cyrus, why then, after having suffered the Persians to enter into the city, they would have destroyed them miserably." How so, the next sentence explains. We do not see what is gained by Schweighæuser's correction οἱ· for οὐδ· (nor yet by substituting οἱ μὲν, the variant of some MSS, for οὐδ᾽ ἂν) if we do not at the same time change διέφθειραν into διεφθάρησαν. In what we have proposed as the genuine text, it may be remarked that (although not essential to the construction) the words οἱ δὲ make the connection pointed and the sense therefore clearer. We find a similar sentence to the one which we have restored, in Schweighæuser's Lexicon Herodotæum, cited from Herod. vi. 30, εἰ μέν νυν, ὡς ἐξηγρέθη, ἀνάχθη ἀγόμενος πρὸς βασιλέα Δαρεῖον, ὁ δ᾽ οὔτ᾽ ἂν ἔπαθε κακὸν οὐδὲν, κ. τ. λ.

On this Schweighæuser observes that both the *δ* and the *ἂν* might have been left out. In the passage of Herod i. 191 that we are considering, it may be thought that the infinitive ἐσελθεῖν was preferred to the participle ἐσελθόντας, as more euphonious after the preceding word περιιδόντες. However, we believe that when περιιδεῖν signifies "to permit willingly," it may be followed by an infinitive though the participle is used when it is preceded by that verb in the sense of "suffering through negligence." There are two cases of the use of the infinitive, in Herod. i. 24 and Herod. iv. 11, where, as here, consent is obviously implied in the preceding verb.

* The following description in Curtius v. 4 was probably taken from

The extent and the height of these external defences have been exaggerated. Greek visitors, if they were not purposely deceived by those who shewed them the wonders of the place, were certainly very ready to mis-apprehend and mis-report what they were told of the sights which amazed them. But some advance perhaps may be made towards a more correct conception of these great works, by confronting our informants, one with another, and by marking for especial investigation the points on which they are not agreed. The date of each testimony is also to be observed; although those whom we cite, Herodotus, Ktesias, and Kleitarkhus, all describe the city as they found it at successive and nearly equal intervals of time after the period we are engaged upon. Herodotus professes to tell what the city was when he visited it in the reign of our Darius's grandson, the first Artaxerxes of the Greeks. The account of Ktesias belongs to the reign of the second Artaxerxes, the grandson of the first. That of Kleitarkhus may be considered contemporary with the overthrow of the last Akhæmenian king of kings, the third Darius, the great-nephew of Ktesias's master; though

---

Kleitarkhus; "Euphrates interfluit magnæque molis crepidinibus coercetur. Sed omnium operum magnitudinem circumveniunt cavernæ ingentes, in altitudinem pressæ, ad accipiendum impetum fluminis, quod ubi appositæ crepidinis fastigium excessit, urbis tecta corriperet nisi essent specus lacusque qui exciperent. Coctili laterculo structi sunt: totum opus bitumine adstringitur." This passage helps us to discern an event that must have led to the disappearance of smaller buildings in the desolation of Babylon; to wit, the choking up of these great receptacles of the river's overflow. But, till they were utterly neglected, these reservoirs replenished at the season of high water (in summer) as the tanks of India are in the season of rain, preserved a store of water for the rest of the year. In Nebukhadrezzar's India-House inscription, of which an account is given with a partial translation in Geo. Rawlinson's Herodotus, vol. ii. pp 585-587, we find repeated mention of the Yapur Shapu, the great reservoir of Babylon, and how the inundation of the gates of the great wall of Babylon, and of the palace called Taprati-nisi; also how the damage to the foundation of that palace, by the overflow of its waters in the flood-season, had been counteracted by Nebukhadrezzar.

the work of Kleitarkhus on the conquest of Asia, seems to have been produced under Ptolemy son of Lagus who was at first Satrap and ultimately king of Egypt after the death of Alexander the Great.

As to the height of the walls that girdled the great city Herodotus and Ktesias seem to have agreed; the former reporting it 200 royal cubits, the latter (if we may trust Diodorus's quotation) 50 fathoms: [f] for four cubits, or lengths of a man's arm from elbow to tip of middle finger, were counted by the Greeks to a fathom, that is, to a man's reach with his two extended arms. But that walls so high, encompassing an extensive city, should have been erected by mere men for defence in a great plain against creatures like themselves, is utterly incredible. However witnesses belonging to the Macedonian period (Kleitarkhus in particular, who is named by Diodorus and silently followed by Strabo and Curtius[g]) are said to have estimated the height at fifty cubits or one-fourth part only of the former computation. But even this is too much; and (according to a suggestion made by Sir H. C. Rawlinson) we suspect the native account, which our three Greek reports were founded on, to have been merely this; That the height of the wall was two hundred hand-breadths, making fifty feet.[h] And this estimate may sometimes have been expressed in bricks, or layers of brick; just as, in the description Herodotus gives of the method of the building, we are told that at intervals of 30 layers of brick a bed of reed-matting was introduced into the wall.

[f] See Herod. i. 178, Diodorus ii. 7 § 4.
[g] See Diodorus as before, Strabo xvi. 1 § 5, Curtius v. 4. The number 365 stades circuit is reasonably restored to Curtius by Zumpt. Strabo's 385 seems an error of the copy he used.
[h] This Herodotus turned into 200 cubits height and 50 cubits thickness, supposing (as it would appear) that two dimensions were spoken of, when height only was really referred to; also, that instead of palms and feet respectively, the two sums had a common unit of measure, the royal cubit. That Herodotus's eye was not practised to judge correctly of height, appears from his obelisks in Egypt 100 cubits high. None now existing reach 100 feet; see Sir J. G. Wilkinson on Herod. ii. 111.

Herodotus may have been told that the wall was two hundred bricks high, and at the same time it may have been intimated that thirty rows of brick made five cubits height, or six bricks a single royal cubit. That some explanation was offered on this occasion of the Babylonian measures of length, there is an indication in the fact that with his report of the height of the walls he connects the statement, That the length of the royal cubit exceeded that of the middle sized one by three finger-breadths. Certainly Ktesias (the author chiefly followed, as it would appear, in Diodorus's description of Babylon) estimates the thickness of walls in that city by bricks; and of the kiln-burnt bricks, belonging to the age of Babylonian supremacy, those which have been thoroughly burnt may be described as measuring one hand-breadth in thickness and four hand-breadths both in length and breadth: for they are mostly square though sometimes they are found shorter in one horizontal direction than in the other.[1] We may

[1] See especially in Journal R. A. S. vol. xvi p. 261 Mr J. E. Taylor's account of the inscribed kiln-burnt bricks which in the Ziggurrat of the temple at Mugheir, form the casing of the second stage, story, or πύργος as Herodotus calls the corresponding portion of the ziggurrat or tower in the temple at Babylon. The bricks which case the second stage (16 feet 8 inches high) have Nabunita's stamp upon them. They are described as 13 inches square, 3 inches thick, and the stamp upon them 8 inches by 4. The bricks which form the coating of the first story, belong to a primitive Khaldæan king. They are described as $11\frac{1}{4}$ inches square, $2\frac{1}{4}$ inches thick, with a stamp upon them $3\frac{1}{4}$ inches square. For Ktesias's measurements by bricks, see Diod. ii. 8 § 5; where, of "Semiramis's" two palaces on opposite sides of the Euphrates, is described the larger and more magnificent, the one on the "west" (query, *east*) bank, having alongside of it (as he tells us afterwards; Diod. ii. 10, § 1) the famous Hanging Garden, and composed of an acropolis with a first, a second, and a third rampart round it, 20, 40, and 60 stades long respectively. Diodorus writes of the middle wall.

οὗτος ὁ περίβολος ἦν τὸ μὲν μῆκος σταδίων τετταράκοντα, τὸ δὲ πλάτος ἐπὶ τριακοσίας (query τριάκοντα) πλίνθους, τὸ δὲ ὕψος, ὥς Κτησίας φησίν, ἐργυιῶν ἑκατόν, τῶν δὲ πύργων ὑπῆρχε τὸ ὕψος ὀργυιῶν ὀγδοήκοντα.

The palace on the opposite side of the river (which, according to him, must have been the east side, but seems to have been really the west bank) was but 30 stades in circumference. This seems to be the palace of Neriglissar, and to have adjoined the παράδεισος to which Alexander

remark, however, that the wattled reeds spread out and stamped upon the top of every thirtieth layer of the brick, if they extended to the outside of the wall, seem to betoken not only that the interior of the great wall was as usual built only of large sun-dried bricks but that the casing also, even the outermost, was not of thoroughburnt bricks; nor the cement above the ditch, either bitumen or the fine mortar of lime found in the ruins of the buildings most carefully executed by Nebukhadrezzar.[J]

We have thus come to two hundred bricks, or handbreadths, as the estimate of the height of the wall of Babylon which the natives gave to Herodotus in the reign of our Darius's grandson. But this height, perhaps, was calculated not from the level of the plain in which the city was built, but from the bottom of the broad moat which had supplied the material for the wall and surrounded it on the outside; for we learn from Herodotus that this moat was lined with burnt brick; and, therefore, the two hundred bricks, each three inches or three and a half inches thick, may have been the whole number when

---

crossed the river in the early part of his fever and whence he was brought back to the palace before his death; see Arrian Exp. Alex. vii. 25 §§ 3, 6. That there was a house or palace on the same side with "the paradise on the other side of the river" would appear from the narratives both of Arrian and of Plutarch, but it is especially intimated in the term applied in Plutarch to the palace he was brought back to; τὰ πέραν βασίλεια, Plut. vit. Alex. cap. 76. Again, in ii. 9 § 2 is described a cutting walled and arched with burnt brick and bitumen, shut up at each end with gates of brass and carried under the river from one palace to the other; to make which "Semiramis" turned off the river for seven days into a receiver 300 stades square and 35 feet deep in the lowest part of the Babylonian soil : and Diodorus says—
τῆς δὲ διώρυχος ὅσηχον οἱ μὲν τοίχοι τὸ πλάτος ἐπὶ πλίνθους εἴκοσι, τὸ δὲ ὕψος χωρὶς τῆς καμαρώσεως ψαλίδος πόδας δώδεκα, τὸ δὲ πλάτος ποδῶν δεκαπέντε.

[J] Mr J. E. Taylor in Journal R. A. S. vol. xv p. 265 writes of the temple rebuilt by Nabunita at the place now called Mugheir; "The whole building is built of sun-dried bricks in the centre, with a thick coating of massive partially-burnt bricks of a light red colour with layers of reeds between them; the whole being cased by a wall of kiln-burnt bricks." Evidence of the use of such layers of reeds in genuine Babylonian remains has been supposed to be wanting.

counted one above another from the bottom of the moat to the top of the wall.

The towers upon the wall, 250 only in number by the later accounts, (because the city being to a great extent surrounded with marsh, towers had been deemed unnecessary in the parts of the wall so protected), are described by Curtius who, without doubt, as usual follows Kleitarkhus, to have been ten feet higher than the intervening wall the thickness of which (as we judge from the consenting reports of Curtius and Strabo) he stated at 32 feet; room enough, it is added, for two cars each having four horses abreast, to pass one another at top with ease. It would seem that, since the time to which Herodotus's description related, the two rows of cells or chambers had been removed which then extended along the top of the wall, one on each side, and (having perhaps loop-holes outward) were entered, it is said, from a road between them, broad enough for a car to pass drawn by four horses abreast. This provision for the permanent occupying of the ramparts by the troops required for their defence, with another particular which Herodotus subjoins, still more needful to make the ramparts of use, That there stood in the wall an hundred gates all made of brass; and their jambs and lintels likewise; seems to indicate that the historian describes the great wall not exactly as it was when he visited Babylon but rather as it had been before Darius dismantled it. For that the brazen gates were taken away by Darius he elsewhere expressly testifies.[k]

But, returning to Kleitarkhus, we would observe, That the fact of his stating the thickness of the wall and also the height of the towers above it, not in cubits but in feet, suggests the question, whether the height of the great wall itself as originally reported by him may not have been fifty feet instead of fifty cubits, and whether the term

---

[k] Herod. i. 179; iii. 159. To the latter particular of his description (the brasen gates of the wall) as no longer existing, he may alone allude when he subjoins to the term Διὸς Βήλου ἱρὸν the words which we would place between commas, χαλκέπυλον καὶ ἐς ἐμὲ τοῦτο ἔτι ἐὸν· Herod. i. 181.

cubits found in Diodorus, Strabo and Curtius, may not be due to early transcribers of Kleitarkhus.[1] In like manner we may hope, that even Ktesias's exaggeration of the same height, was not in the original manuscript fifty fathoms, as cited by Diodorus, but fifty cubits only. For Diodorus had already repeated Ktesias's assertion, That no one since Ninus had ever built so great a city as Nineveh (which the Medes demolished when they broke up the Assyrian kingdom) not only for the bigness of its compass, which was 480 stades (the area inclosed being 150 stades in length and 90 stades in breadth) but moreover for the grandeur of the wall, which was 100 feet high, was broad enough for three chariots to pass abreast, and had 1500 towers in it, each 200 feet high.[m] But if by Ktesias's estimate the wall of Babylon had been fifty fathoms high, he must have believed it to be three times as high as the wall of Nineveh, which yet he said had never been equalled. For 50 fathoms is 300 feet. We

---

[1] It is further to be observed that Strabo, xvi. 1 § 5, though plainly following Curtius's author, instead of representing the towers as rising ten feet higher than the intervals of wall, makes them 60 cubits high; that is, 10 cubits more than 50 cubits high. His words are

ὕψος δὲ τῶν μὲν μεσοπυργίων πήχεις πεντήκοντα, τῶν δὲ πύργων ἑξήκοντα. For the πήχεις of the copy used by Strabo, we suppose the original MS of Kleitarkhus's work had πόδες. Again, Curtius's author (we may be allowed to say) puts not cubits but feet only for Ktesias's fathoms, in the height of the citadel towers. Ktesias asserted (in Diod. ii. 8 § 6) that the citadel, 20 stades in circumference, exceeded (in the height and thickness of its walls) the nearer one of two outer walls which successively surrounded it; and this nearer or middle wall, he had described as 40 stades long, 300 bricks thick, fifty fathoms high, and its towers 70 fathoms high. Now Curtius (following, as we suppose, Kleitarkhus) writes thus; "Arcem quoque ambitu XX stadia complexam habent. XXX pedes in terram turrium fundamenta demissa sunt; ad LXXX summum munimenti fastigium pervenit." For this last number of feet, LXXX, we should read LXX, and so make the sole difference between Ktesias and Kleitarkhus to lie in the unit of length. With this correction, the height of the towers (including 30 foot foundations) will have been represented by Kleitarkhus as 100 feet.

[m] For Ktesias's wall of Nineveh 100 feet high; see Diodor. ii. 3. For his wall of Babylon 50 fathoms high; see Diodor. ii. 7.

are inclined to think that Ktesias made the walls of
Babylon fifty cubits high; and, therefore, less lofty than
the pretended walls of Nineveh. Then, perhaps, the
transcribers of Kleitarkhus substituted cubits for feet on
the authority of older and uncorrupted copies which they
possessed of Ktesias; whereas transcribers or persons
superintending the transcription of the work of Ktesias
substituted fathoms for cubits, not to fall short of Herodotus. And now to confirm the conjecture that Herodotus's 200 cubits height is the misreport of 200 hand-
breadths in a native account (equal to 50 feet) we will only
say that in the Annals of Sennacherib king of Assyria,
speaking of a great mound which he raised at Nineveh
in order to build thereon a palace more suitable to the
majesty of a king of Assyria than that which had hitherto
been used, the king says " Two hundred tibki " (that is, as
the Hebrew term almost identical with the Assyrian is
cited to explain, 200 hand-breadths) " in height I raised
its wall." [a]

[a] See the Taylor Cylinder Inscription, being Annals of Sennacherib
during his first eight years of reign, transliterated into Roman character
and rendered in English by Mr H. Fox Talbot in Journal R. A. S. vol.
xix p. 167. The Hebrew noun which explains the Assyrian term is
variously pointed טפח and טפח the first of which in 1 Kings vii. 20 is
rendered παλαιστή in the Alex. MS of the Septuagint; also in 2 Chron.
iv. 5; also in Psalm xxxix. 6. The latter form is rendered παλαιστής and
παλαιστή by the Septuagint in Exod. xxv. 25; Ezek. xl. 5, 43 and xliii.
13. The 200 *tibki* of the Taylor Cylinder Inscription, Mr H. Fox
Talbot informs us, are expressed in the parallel passage of a duplicate,
which he calls the Constantinople Inscription, " three *vas* and twenty
tibki." Whence it appears, that the Assyrians had a measure called
the *vas*, equal to 60 hand-breadths or to ten cubits. From the Michaux
Inscription (Journal R. A. S. vol. xviii p. 55) we obtain a measure called
susi in the plural, that is, "Sixties," the σωσσι of Berosus, or in the
singular *sus*; three of which appear to have been double the length of
one *sus* and 50 *gar*. If the *sus* be sixty cubits (or six *vas*) the *gar* will
be three-fifths of a cubit; that is (if of a royal cubit of twenty and a half
inches) twelve and three-tenths English inches; and, therefore, may be
regarded as the Babylonian foot. In Sennacherib's Bellino Inscription,
lines 54, 55 (Journal R. A. S. vol. xviii. p. 81) we have 20 *tibki* + 160
tibki = 180 *tibki* lengths of inscriptions. In the same Cylinder, containing annals of the first two years of Sennacherib's reign, we have the

Thus as to the height of the great wall of Babylon, described by Herodotus, Ktesias, and Kleitarkhus, we conclude, that it was more probably fifty feet than fifty fathoms or even fifty cubits; though the royal cubit of Babylon, if it exceeded the Greek cubit by three finger-breadths or one eighth of such a cubit,° being about

sides of the old palace pulled down by Sennacherib, measuring 360, 80, 134 and 95 "half-*hus*" respectively; a measure which seems opposed to the "big *hu*" or *hu-reblu* of the Michaux Inscription, line 1. Of Sennacherib's New palace, the four sides, according to the Bellino Cylinder lines 51, 52, measured *Shukli rebti* 1700, 162, 217 and 386. These "big *shukli*" seem opposed to the "half *hu*" and to be identical with the *hu-rebti*. *Shukli*, rendered "measures" by Mr H. F. Talbot, he takes for the plural of an Assyrian correspondent to the Hebrew שֶׁקֶל *shekel*, but a length not a weight. The *hu* (thought to be an old Hamite term) is proved to be synonymous with the *amma* (in the plural, *ammat*) of Nebukhadrezzar's inscriptions, by a comparison, first made by Dr Hincks of two passages in the India House Inscription, viz. vi. 25 and viii. 45; see Journal R. A. S. vol. xviii. p. 45. The *amma* is explained by the Hebrew and Aramaic אַמָּה. Of itinerary measures we have the half-*kasbu* or "small *kasbu*" in the Bellino Cylinder, line 61, and Taylor Cylinder in Journal R. A. S. vol. xix, p. 165. Mr H. F. Talbot says in Journal R. A. S. vol. xviii p. 102, that the *kasbu* of time was two hours. If this be correct, the half *kasbu* of distance will be equivalent to a *parasang*.

° Herodotus says; "The royal cubit (of Babylon) is longer by three fingers than the moderate, average, or middle-sized cubit, τοῦ μετρίου πήχεος· l. 178; and he tells of a woman whose height was three fingers short of four cubits; l. 60. Elsewhere he tells us; "A hundred fathoms, ὀργυιαὶ fair, are a stade of six plethrums, πλέθρου ἑξαπλέθρου, if the fathom measure six feet and four cubits, and if the feet are of four handbreadths each and the cubit of six hand-breadths; Herod. ii. 149. The hand-breadth, παλαιστή or παλαιστή here named, is the Septuagint rendering (as has been said) of the טֶפַח which was divided into four אֶצְבָּעוֹת (in the Septuagint δακτύλοι) "finger-breadths;" compare Jerem. lii. 21 with 1 Kings vii. 26 and 2 Chron. iv. 5. Herodotus (we have seen) speaks of feet of four hand-breadths and cubits of six hand-breadths; as if he knew of feet and cubits measuring otherwise. We are told that "from a tolerably extensive field of enquiry M. Oppert (in the *Athenæum Français*, 1854, p. 370) has valued the length of the Babylonian foot at 315 millimètres, which is as nearly as possible twelve and two-fifths English inches; also, that the Babylonian cubit was to this foot, not as 3 to 2, the proportion of the Greek cubit to the Greek foot, but as 5 to 3; being twenty English inches and a half, the Babylonian foot or brick-length (if two-thirds of this length) would exceed

in fact a cubit of 5 hand-breadths each of 5 fingers, while the foot was divided into three such hand-breadths; " see Rawlinson's Herodotus, vol. 1 p. 315 notes. The foot spoken of by M. Oppert seems to be the *gar* cited above from the Michaux inscription. Sir H. C. Rawlinson was led by his researches to believe the ordinary Babylonian foot less than the Greek foot and less even than the English: and, so, to compare it rather with the Roman foot of 11.6496 English inches. Perhaps, in the long period of Khaldæan and Assyrian history, the foot measure at Babylon varied in its length. The bricks of two sizes in the ruin at Muqeyer or Mugheir, of the temple of the Moon, those of the founder (who was the earliest or one of the earliest known Chaldæan kings) eleven and a quarter inches square and the fifth of this or two and a quarter thick, and those of Nabunita (who in B. C. 555–538 rebuilt the temple) 13 inches square and 3 inches thick, might suggest that the ancient foot fell short of the English foot; though the foot of latter times exceeded the same in length; see Mr J. E. Taylor's account; Journal R. A. S. vol. xv p. 261. The notion that Herodotus's μέτριος πῆχυς was the cubit of one and a half Greek feet, and that the royal cubit of Babylon was three fingers, or one-eighth of a Greek cubit, longer than such a cubit, seems confirmed when we find the length of the royal cubit of Babylon, thus obtained, to be almost exactly that of the Egyptian cubit. In the Nile island, Elephantinê, on one of the walls of a stair that leads down to the river, is a succession of graduated scales, each containing one or two cubits, with inscriptions recording the rise of the water at various dates during the rule of the Cæsars. Every cubit is divided into fourteen parts, each of two digits (finger-breadths) giving 28 digits to the cubit. The length of the cubits here, according to Sir J. G. Wilkinson who carefully measured them all, and was guided by the general length as well as by the average of the whole, is 20.625 inches. This gives 0.736 decimal of an inch to each of the 28 digits. Again, there are wooden cubits from Egypt, divided and subdivided into palms (7) double digits (14) and digits (28) besides other parts. One found at Memphis, is stated by M. Jomard (in his *Etalon Métrique* and *Lettre à M. Abel Remusat sur une nouvelle mesure de coudée*) to be 520 millimetres or (if, according to the Table in Dr Lardner's Arithmetic, one Millimètre is .03937 decimal of an inch) 20.4724 English inches. One in the Museum at Turin he states to be 522.7 millimètres or 20.57869 English inches. Others are particularized, which, on account of some seeming error in the typography, we do not report from Sir J. G. Wilkinson. But the average of wooden cubits M. Jomard is said to state at 523.506 millimetres, that is, 20.610195 English inches. A measure discovered at Karnak and proved by the position in which it

the English foot by about one inch and two-thirds, so that the height of fifty feet would be all but fifty-seven English feet. But the Michaux Inscription seems to make the Babylonian foot three-fifths only of the cubit, so that, if the cubit was twenty inches and a half long, fifty Babylonian feet would exceed fifty English feet, by fifteen inches only.

But we have also to consider the reported circumference of this rampart; and here, too, we have a diversity of statement to begin with. Herodotus tells us that the city was four-cornered, and that each face or front measured 120 stades, so that the stades of its whole compass were in all 480. The later accounts of Ktesias and Kleitarkhus seem to be connected both of them with a story, told perhaps not by Ktesias but by Kleitarkhus and the Macedonians only, that the whole rampart had been completed in one year; the number of stades in the length of the whole being equal to the number of days in a year, and one stade's length having been built every day. Others more plausibly told the story thus; Semiramis distributed the 360 or 365 stades of wall to as many of her courtiers, who, being provided with work-people and materials, carried on the building in every lot simultaneously, so as to finish it in a year; every one superintending the building of his own share. The wall may in fact have been placed (in Magian times at least) under the tutelage of the 360 or 365 guardians of the circle of the year. But (in connection, as we have said, with this story) Ktèsias

---

was found to belong to the 18th Egyptian dynasty, is a double cubit divided into 14 parts, each the double of the 14th part of the cubits above-mentioned. It is 41.3 English inches long; so that the half or single cubit is 20.65. This double cubit has its first 14th part halved and its second quartered; the halves being the 14th parts of the single cubit, and the quarters the 28th parts or digits; See Sir J. G. Wilkinson's *Manners and Customs of the Ancient Egyptians*, second series, vol. 1 pp 29–33. These double and single Egyptian cubits correspond at least, if their lengths were not also respectively the same, with " big *hu* " and half-*hu* of the last note.

42*

related that the wall measured 360 stades ; Kleitarkhus made the length 365 stades.

To reconcile this testimony with that of Herodotus, as to the length of a wall with which Babylon was still encompassed after the demolition of an outer bulwark by Darius son of Hystaspes, we do not suppose that Herodotus has transmitted to us by mistake the measurement of the wall which had disappeared so long before his visit, and that Ktesias has given the measurement of that remaining outer line of wall which both he and Herodotus beheld. This, however, seems to be the ground on which it has been supposed that Babylon was once girt by a quadrangular rampart, each of the four sides of which was 120 stades long, but that in the days of Ktesias there remained only the wall of an interior city, the four sides of which were each ninety stades in length. We ascribe to Herodotus a different error; considering the outer and inner Babylon of Berosus to have been separated by the Euphrates. We believe Herodotus erred in supposing that the breadth of the quadrilateral figure, presented to him by the city, was equal to the length ; that he mistook a rectangular parallelogram (which we often improperly call a square) for the perfect square, which is such a parallelogram having also equal sides. Mistaking an oblong figure for a square, and having heard its length proclaimed to be 120 stades, he inferred that the wall which surrounded it was four times as long. Ktesias's account, that the whole circuit of wall was 360 stades, seems to rest upon the same estimate of the length from end to end of the inclosure. He seems to have regarded the area of the city as a parallelogram of 120 stades by 60, that is, just half the square of Herodotus. The error which we impute to Herodotus in respect of the figure formed by the rampart of Babylon, is the more probable, inasmuch as he appears to have committed it again in the same description of Babylon. Of the temple of Zeus Belus, that is, the sacred precinct of Bel Merodakh, he describes both the inclosure and the tower within to be square; saying that the inclosure measured two stades each way, and the tower, one; whereas the analogy of other temples (as that of Nebo at Borsippa and that of Sin, or the Moon, at the place now called Muqeyer or Mugheir) leads us to expect that both tower and inclosure were oblong; while in fact the great mound at Babylon called by the Arabs of the present day Babel, and which seems now to be unanimously considered the wreck of the tower, is oblong. Again, we are justified in supposing that 120 stades was the length not of the shorter but of the two greater sides of the area of Babylon, because in the case of the temple of Belus our historian seems to have given, as the length common to all the four sides, what was in fact only the length of the two greater sides. As we have already stated, he says that the temple was four-angled and measured two stades every way, while a solid eight-storied tower built in the midst measured at bottom one stade both in length and in breadth. Now, Mr Rich gives 200 yards (that is, one stade) length as the measure of one of the two greater sides of the existing mound.[p]

That Babylon was indeed surrounded by a quadrilateral rampart, as Herodotus intimates, of which the total length according to Ktesias was 360 stades, and nevertheless that the four sides were not considered by Ktesias equal, that is, each of them ninety stades lóng, but that in his view of the matter, the inclosure was twice as long one way as it was the other, or 120 stades long and 60 stades broad, is, moreover, a conclusion that one should be led to by Ktesias's purely imaginary account of the

[p] Herod. i. 181. The dimensions of the mound as given by Mr Rich are: The northern side, 200 yards in length; south side, 219 yards; east side, 182 yards; west side, 136 yards; see Layard's Nineveh and Babylon p. 502, note, also Geo. Rawlinson, Herodotus vol. 2 p. 575 citing Rich's First Memoir, p. 28. Sir R. K. Porter, ii. p. 340, makes the north face 551 feet; the south 552 feet long; and gives the length of 230 feet to each of the other sides; ibid. The stade, Herodotus's estimate of the length of each side of the many-storied tower, was of course 600 Greek feet, or 606 English feet, equal to 202 yards.

former and (as he boasted) the far larger Assyrian capital, Ninus, which the Medes had demolished two centuries before his time. By that account, already cited, Nineveh was quadrangular but longer one way than by the other; being 150 stades in length and 90 in breadth; so that all four sides put together, measured 480 stades.[q] Not only, then, must we believe the supposed parallelogram to have been greater than the Babylon with which Ktesias must have had a better personal acquaintance than Herodotus could have acquired by his visit; but we may perceive the fact, that if Babylon could have been set down in the middle of it, its shape being similar to that of Babylon, its boundaries would have stretched beyond Babylon in every direction, so as to leave an interval of fifteen stades between each of its sides and the adjacent parallel wall of Babylon. In short, the description of Ktesias's Nineveh seems to have been based on the shape and dimensions of the existing Assyrian capital; for such was Babylon in the estimation of Herodotus, Xenophon, and the Greeks in general.

[q] This is exactly the circumference attributed by Herodotus to what Ktesias represented as the smaller city of the two; being the quadruple of 120 stades, which Herodotus made to be the length of every side of that great quadrangle Babylon. But if the imaginary Nineveh of Ktesias measured 150 stades in length by 90 in breadth, it contained but 13,500 square stades; while Babylon, the smaller city of Ktesias, contained 14,400 square stades according to the dimensions given to it by Herodotus. If it should be suggested that this larger area of Babylon was not the area actually walled in the time of Herodotus, but the area reported to have been bounded by that outer wall which the evidence of Berosus and Herodotus put together makes us suppose to have been destroyed by Darius; and that the report of this previous larger area was transformed into a description of the former Assyrian capital Nineveh; the observation is still just,—That Ktesias's plan of the larger city intimates the Babylon which he beheld, which Herodotus had seen before him and which the companions of Alexander occupied after him, to have been not a square but an oblong parallelogram. It is to be noted that 480 stades' circumference, at the rate established by Herodotus and Xenophon of 30 to the parasang, gives three (army) marches, each one-third of a parasang longer than usual; and we behold an exceeding great city of three days' journey in circuit; see Jonah iii. 3.

. According, then, to the best Greek testimony, the area of Babylon, measuring 120 stades in length and sixty stades in breadth, appears to have been a parallelogram containing 7,200 square stades. Now, if we take the side of the square stade to have been the true Greek stade 202 yards long, Babylon will be supposed to have measured 24,240 yards, or more than thirteen miles, six furlongs, in length; and 12,120 yards, or more than six miles, seven furlongs, in breadth; and, therefore, to have contained a surface of nearly ninety-five square miles. Now, after deducting the space taken up by the moat, the ramparts, and a roadway two plethrums or one-third of a stade in breadth, behind the rampart; also, the ground covered by the walls that ran along both banks of the river and by the Euphrates itself; also, the area occupied by the palaces, the temple of Bel Merodakh, the great reservoir, the canals; nay, after allowing for a great extent of ground kept under cultivation within the city, the size of the area remaining may still seem incredible.[r] We may be driven

[r] For the open space, ὅσος διάλειμμα, left between the houses of the city and the wall, throughout the whole circumference, see Diodorus ii. 7 § 5; and compare Curtius v. 4; "Ædificia non sunt admota muris sed ferè spatium jugeri unius absunt." The Roman jugerum, considered as a measure of length, was the side of two square actus or "droves" that is (120 × 2=) 240 Roman feet. As to the proportion of the area occupied by houses and employed for the purposes of cultivation, Curtius proceeds, "Ac ne totam quidem urbem tectis occupaverunt: per LXXX stadia" (so Zumpt after seven MSS, instead of the commonly printed "XC stadia") "habitatur: nec omnia continua sunt: credo quia tutiùs visum est pluribus locis spargi. Cœtera serunt coluntque ut si externa vis ingruat, obsessis alimenta ex ipsius urbis solo subministrentur." It may be questioned, however, whether these grounds under cultivation when Kleitarkhus wrote or when the Macedonians became masters of Babylon, were so extensive in the days of Cyrus and Darius son of Hystaspes. For the deduction from the inhabited surface to be made on account of the river, see Diod. ii. 8 § 3, where he tells of Semiramis.

ἐξ ἑκατέρου δὲ μέρους τοῦ ποταμοῦ κρηπῖδα πολυτελῆ κατεσκεύασε παραπλησίαν κατὰ τὸ πλάτος τοῖς τείχεσιν ἐπὶ σταδίους ἑκατὸν ἑξήκοντα·

Here we have two river-side walls, each ten yards thick (for Kleitarkhus stated the equal thickness of the ramparts at 32 feet or room for eight horses abreast, at 4 feet (the width of the Roman actus or "drove") to a

to suppose, that besides the exaggeration which made the breadth of the quadrilateral city equal to its length, there horse. The two walls, then, taken together, may be put at one-tenth of a stade in thickness, which multiplied by the length of 160 stades, gives 16 square stades covered by these walls. Again, the breadth of the river stated by Xenophon, Cyrop. vii. 5 § 8 to be more than two stades in the part that traversed Babylon, if multiplied by 160 stades' length of the intramural river, gives 320 square stades covered by the river. Strabo, however, says that the river flows through the city σταδίαίος τό πλάτος, xvi. 1 § 5; while Diodorus ii. 8 § 2 represents the bridge, built in the narrowest part of the river, by Semiramis (or rather, according to Herodotus, by Nitokris) as five stades long. Mr Layard in *Nineveh and Babylon* p. 489 (with a reference to Col. Chesney's *Expedition for the Survey of the Euphrates and Tigris* vol. 1 p. 57) describes the Euphrates flowing through Hillah, a modern town, occupying probably the site of an extramural settlement on the south side of the old city, as a noble stream with a gentle current, about 200 yards wide and 15 feet deep. This account confirms that of Strabo; and from this we cannot suppose more than 160 square stades to have been covered by the river within the circuit of the walls. We have seen Curtius's account of the extent of land devoted to cultivation within the walls, at the time of the Macedonian conquest, and with this state of things the fact is consistent, that B. C. 312, 311 in the struggle of Seleucus with the generals of Antigonus to recover and preserve the satrapy of Babylonia, we read of no attempt on either side to defend the city. Seleucus stormed the citadel in which his children and friends had been placed in custody by Antigonus; and where the partisans of Antigonus had taken refuge. And afterwards, when Seleucus's general Patrokles was invaded by Demetrius son of Antigonus, though his master had the good-will of the people, he was obliged to order the evacuation of the city by its inhabitants, and he only placed garrisons in two citadels (perhaps the palaces on opposite sides of the river described by Diodorus ii. 8). Of these, one was captured and given up to pillage by Demetrius; the siege of the other he left to be finished by a subordinate when he himself was obliged to leave for the Mediterranean coast with the greater part of his forces; see Diodor. xix. 91, 100. This was before the foundation of Seleukeia on the Tigris. Writing as of his own time, Diodorus tells us ii. 9 § 9.

καὶ γὰρ αὐτῆς τῆς Βαβυλῶνος τὸ βραχύ τι μέρος οἰκεῖται, τὸ δὲ πλεῖστον ἐντὸς τείχους γεωργεῖται.

And Strabo, remarking on the result of the transfer of the remaining dignity of Babylon to Seleukeia, says, xvi. 1 § 5—

καὶ δὴ καὶ νῦν ἡ μὲν γέγονε Βαβυλῶνος μείζων· ἡ δ' ἐρήμως ἡ πολλή.

Such was the state of Babylon about the time of the first Roman emperor, and when our Lord appeared. The Babylon of the New Testament is a city standing in the same relation to Jerusalem as had

was another source of error in a substitution by the Greek reporters of their own stade for a much smaller Babylonian unit of length.

Observing that Nebukhadrezzar, in the India House Tablet, gives the measure of his lengths of wall in hundreds of "ammas," that is, as the same term in Hebrew signifies, "cubits;" and remarking that the hundred cubits has the same relation to the palm or hand-breadth which the stade has to the foot, being six hundred palms, one might suspect that in the Greek reports the term stade was substituted for a Babylonian term signifying the measure of a hundred ammas, each about twenty English inches and a half long,* and that the walled parallelogram been occupied of old by the city on the Euphrates. This is incontestible as to the Babylon of the Apocalypse; and as to 1 S. Pet. v. 13,

ἀσπάζεται ὑμᾶς ἡ ἐν Βαβυλῶνι συνεκλεκτή.

observe, that as ἡ συνεκλεκτή is not to be taken literally, as some commentators have done very laughably; but, "she who is your fellow-elect" signifies mystically, the Church in the place from which S. Peter wrote (as Churches are signified by the Elect Lady and her Elect sister, in 2 S. John 1, 13) so the city wherein this mystical person lived, is spoken of not by its proper but by its mystical name. Trajan visited Babylon in A. D. 116.

κατά τι τὴν φήμην (ἧς οὐδὲν ἄξιον ἰδεῖν ὅτι μὴ χώματα καὶ λίθους καὶ ἐρείπια) καὶ διὰ τὸν 'Αλέξανδρον, ᾧ καὶ ἐνήγισεν ἐν τῷ οἰκήματι ἐν ᾧ ἐτετελευτήκει.

So Dion Cassius (according to the abridgement of Xiphilinus) lxxxviii 30. Trajan may have found the palace still habitable where Alexander died.

* The Babel-Assyrian inscription on the Michaux stone is strangely connected by an inscription in the British Museum, with the reign of Marduk-haddon, or Marduk-adan-akhi king of Babylon; who, again, by the Inscription of Bavian is proved to have been a contemporary of the first known Tiglath-Pilezer king of Assyria, at about B. C. 1120. This very ancient inscription was long ago brought to Paris by the traveller Michaux from a palace on the banks of the Tigris, one day's journey below Baghdad, not far from the site of the ancient Ktesiphon. It is given in Roman characters and accompanied with an English translation by Mr H. F. Talbot in the Journal R. A. S. vol. xviii. pp 52–76. Here we have a field measuring 3 susi in length and apparently half that, or 1 sus and 50 gar, in breadth. Of this sus or "Sixty" (applied to length of space, as Berosus applies the σάρος, νῆρος, and σῶσος, to length of time viz. 60 and 60 × 10 and 60 × 10 × 6 years) the unit is supposed to be the hu mentioned in the first line of the same inscription and proved by Dr Hincks to be identical with the amma or "cubit" of

described by Ktesias was but 12,000 ammas long and 6,000 broad, or 3 miles, 1553 yards long and one mile, 1656 yards broad. But this figure, in circuit eleven miles 1140 yards and containing a little more than seven square miles and a half, seems too small, or at least not to have sufficient length, when applied to the existing field of heaps traversed and briefly described by Mr Layard;*

Nebukhadrezzar's inscriptions. The whole *Sus* is equal to 100 *gar* if (as it is argued) the breadth was half the length of the field, and if so, one *gar* (equal to three-fifths of a *hu, amma* or "cubit") must have been the Babylonian measure answering to the Greek and Roman foot, and the Sixty of cubits or the Hundred of Babylonian feet must have been the correspondent of the Greek *plethrum* ; and six such Babylonian *plethra*, would correspond with the Greek stade or measure of six Greek *plethra*. Perhaps, such a *Sus* or Babylonian *plethrum* is meant when Strabo (xvi. 1 § 5) reports the length of each side of the Hanging Garden at Babylon to have been four *plethra*, and when Diodorus (repeating here, it would seem, Curtius's authority, Kleitarkhus) reports the space left vacant between the houses and the city wall at Babylon to have been two *plethra* wide; Diod. ii. 7 § 5. Such a *Sus* or Babylonian plethrum seems to have been converted by Diodorus's authority (probably Ktesias) into a stade, where he reports the bridge over the Euphrates at Babylon five stades long ; Diod. ii. 8 § 2. Berosus, too, on one occasion seems to have mis-translated such a *Sus* or plethrum into a stade. For, whereas in Genesis vi. 15 the length of Noah's ark is 300 *ammahs*, that is cubits, the ark of Khshisuthrus is five stades long ; Berosus, quoted by Geo. Syncellus ; ed. Dindorf. p. 54, and in the Armenian Eusebius p. 14, ed. Mai. It is true, that the breadths are not in like proportion, 50 cubits and two stades.

* From Amran, the last and most southerly of the great mounds, to Hillah is about an hour's ride; Layard *Nineveh and Babylon* p. 484. From a line of earth-works on the south bank of a wide and deep canal, crossed near the village Mohawill on the road to Hillah from Baghdad, the distance to the most northerly of the great mounds, the one now called by the Arabs Babel, is about four miles, a tract of low mounds and canal banks. Between this and the southern extremity of the Amran mound, or for a distance of nearly three miles southward from the Babel mound, there is almost an uninterrupted line of mounds, the ruins of vast edifices, within a triangular space that has the Euphrates for its base, and for its sides two earthen ramparts whereof the one to the north leaves the foot of Babel and makes the apex of the enclosure by joining the south rampart about two and a half miles east-ward of the river. From the most southerly point of

though the walls of Rome commenced by Aurelian in A. D. 271, including those of the Trastevere and the Vatican, are but from twelve to thirteen miles in circuit.ᵘ

But again, it may be thought that the 120 stades length of one longer side of the area of Babylon, and 360 stades, the length of all four sides of that oblong rectangle, as we have learnt to regard the place, may have been parasangs in the original information, and that these (according to the custom of Herodotus and Xenophon) may have been reckoned equal each to 30 stades; though for our own part (as for instance, on the road from Seleukeia on the Tigris to Agbatana) we have hitherto had reason to regard the parasang as equal to no more than two and a half English miles or 4,400 yards. This suspicion that parasangs in the original information, or similar Babylonian measures, were converted into stades in the Greek reports, at the rate of thirty stades to one parasang, is strengthened when we observe that the rectangle imagined (or credulously accepted) by Ktesias for the area of the vanished and, therefore, more prodigious Nineveh, may, no less than that of Babylon, be measured exactly by parasangs of thirty stades a-piece, and that thus measured, it becomes exactly one parasang, both in length and breadth, bigger than Babylon. If, then, we reduce to parasangs the numbers of stades given in the Greek measurement of Babylon which we have accepted as the most authentic, we find the outer line of the defences, as it remained after the execution of the orders issued by Darius in B. C. 516, to be four parasangs or ten English miles long, and two parasangs or five miles broad: and thus we make it appear that the circumference of the city was thirty English miles, and its surface fifty square miles,

---

this tract of great mounds to the town Hillah, as between the Mohawill village and the Babel mound, can only be traced low heaps and embankments scattered irregularly over the plain: ibid. pp. 491, 492. The longer side of a parallelogram of 12,000 *ammas* by 6000, might extend from a little north of Babel to a little south of Amran.

ᵘ See Murray's Hand-book of Rome and its Environs, ed. 1862, p. 5.

according to Ktesias, and apparently according to a standard reckoning of which Kleitarkhus's is but an attempted emendation.

But it is further to be observed, that in such an original description of the circuit of Babylon (with which we may compare that of Nineveh in the Prophet Jonah, " a very great city of three days' journey ") the parasang may have been a measure of time in travelling, an hour, and may have represented (by the custom of the country, or owing to various obstructions to progress in the neighbourhood of Babylon) a distance as much inferior to two and a half miles as is the length of the Indian coss, which is hardly two miles;[v] so that the city might be not more than eight miles long and four miles broad, with a circumference about the double of that of Rome, and a surface of thirty-two square miles. Of what we have termed the most authentic dimensions reported by Greeks, it is perhaps the breadth, or its proportion to the length, which is the most doubtful.

We will now leave the enquiry; with a misgiving that recent surveys and investigations on the spot, may have rendered it superfluous, by supplying a surer basis of calculation than the testimonies of ancient Greek writers. In the matter of numbers, our readers may be of opinion that a method of dealing with those testimonies, better than our calculations, is suggested by the example of Strabo and of Mr Layard in the case of Xenophon's estimate of the breadth of the Euphrates at Babylon. Xenophon states it at two stades or about 400 yards; whereas according to Strabo (probably following Kleitarkhus) and according to Mr Layard, appealing to Colonel Chesney, it is but one stade or 200 yards.

[v] In Messrs Allen's Map of India, 1844, also in Messrs Walker's Map of India in Elphinstone's Hist. of India, ed. 1857, the degree of 60 geographical or 69.12 British miles is divided into 42 cosses of Hindustan. Four of these by two form a parallelogram of six and a-quarter by three and an-eighth English miles.

VI.

AFTER a year and seven months had elapsed, Herodotus tells us, " Darius was troubled and all his army with him; not having it in their power to take the Babylonians." But in the twentieth month (whether of the siege, as Herodotus says, or of the new Nebukhadrezzar's reign, as reckoned by the Khaldæans, or, both of the siege and of the space in some Tables of years assigned to the new reign) there befell a change. To shew what this was, let us first repeat the story told by Herodotus, then, make certain observations which it suggests, and lastly, offer a correction which seems necessary to restore it to its original shape. " In the twentieth month," says Herodotus,[a] (that is, as his previous context intimates, in the eighth month of the second Khaldæan year) "a marvellous thing happened to Zopyrus, a son of one of the Seven that the Magian was pulled down by, namely Megabyzus. It was this; one of the pack-animals used by Zopyrus to bring victual to the siege—a she-mule—dropped a foal. Having convinced himself of the fact, and remembering what had been shouted from the rampart, that mules must have foals before the city could be taken, he commanded his servants to keep the matter secret, believing that the impossible condition having by divine power been brought to pass, the city might now be taken, and that he himself was specially invited to be the great Benefactor by whom the service to the king should be achieved. However, he could not devise any plan likely to succeed, except this; to desert to the besieged, win their confidence, and then betray them into Darius's hands. But how should he make them trust him? Why, he cut off his own nose and ears, he clipped off the hair round about his head in rascal fashion; he laid stripes upon his back, and in this mangled condition, the high-caste Persian came before his king. At sight of him, Darius started up from

[a] Herod. iii. 152-158.

his throne with a loud exclamation, and asked, Who had treated him so vilely? and What had he done? Zopyrus said he had resolved that the Persians should no longer be laughed at by a set of Assyrians; and that he had executed what was necessary for his part, before communicating with the king, who would have refused his consent to a scheme that was to cost his servant so dear; but now, Darius had nothing to do but to perform his own part, and they would take Babylon. He would desert to the city, tell the besieged that Darius had treated him thus, and get a command. Then, on the tenth day after the one on which he should have entered the city, the king should post a thousand men over against the gate of Semiramis; and again, on the seventh day after the tenth, a couple of thousands over against the Gate of the Ninians; then, let twenty days go by, and bring four thousand men and set them down over against the gate of the Khaldæans. On none of these days were the troops so posted to be of a choice description or well provided for resistance. They might have their side-arms, that is daggers or short swords, but no other weapons; and so, the Babylonians sallying out upon them, headed by Zopyrus, were to be able to destroy them. Then, after the twentieth day, straightway Darius was to command an assault of all his forces upon every side of the city; posting the Persians over against two gates, the Belidan and the Kissian. Upon that, Zopyrus who would now be trusted with the keys, promised to let them in, and with those good troops to finish the business. These measures having been concerted, Zopyrus left the king and went off towards the gate of the city, turning from time to time to look behind him, as a real deserter might have done in fear of pursuit. Then, the watchmen posted on the (gate) towers, seeing him approach, ran down, and pushing one of the leaves of the gate a little aside, asked him, Who he was, and What he wanted. His answer preserved him from hurt and gained him admittance; he was led before the authorities, was believed, and obtained a command of troops. Then, on the tenth day, according to the plan concerted with Darius, he led out his Babylonians, made a circuit to the rear [b] of the thousand men that Darius had posted first, and cut them all to pieces. The citizens were delighted, and became more ready to second him than before. Again, after the days agreed upon had elapsed, he led out a picked body of men and cut to pieces Darius's two thousand; thereby gaining extraordinary applause in the city. Again he let the days agreed upon go by, then led forth to the point that had been named, and taking them in the rear cut to pieces the four thousand. This achievement raised the credit of Zopyrus among the Babylonians to the highest pitch; so that they made him commander of the forces and keeper of the walls. Then Darius, as it had been agreed, ordered a general assault upon the wall, attacking the place on every side, and Zopyrus shewed what sort of game he had been playing. For, while the Babylonians mounted the walls and were engaged in repelling the assaults, Zopyrus threw open the leaves both of the Belidan and of the Kissian Gate; and let in the Persians within the rampart. Then the Babylonians, as many as had seen the deed, fled to the sacred precinct of Zeus Belus; while those who had not, remained every man at his post, till they, too, found that they were betrayed."

Such is the tale of Herodotus, abridged in merely decorative particulars. We must remark upon it in the first place, that king Darius was not with his army when Babylon fell into his power. This is plain from his own account of the event, engraved on the rock at Behistun. Next, we would observe that the foaling of a she mule in Zopyrus's quarter is clearly an embellishment of the story of the capture, added on repetition by one who bore in mind how it had been jeeringly said that mules must produce their like before the city could be taken; but, not understanding the reference to Cyrus, took this for a

[b] The expressions of Herod. iii. 157 which we have ventured to interpret, not "surrounding" but "getting round" the enemy, are συκλωσάμενος τοὺς χιλίους, and again, συκλωσάμενοι κατιφόνευσι τοὺς τετρακισχιλίους.

prophecy, the fulfilment of which in the condition as well as in the consequence, was necessary to complete the story.

The prodigy, then, which Zopyrus was related to have witnessed, with the effect which it is said to have produced upon his determination, must be discarded by us, as in fact it was omitted in Ktesias's account of this matter.[e] Yet we are not the less able to assign a special motive for Zopyrus's acceptance of any hazard or loss involved in an attempt to recover Babylon. Besides the desire (shared we doubt not by a multitude of bold spirits) to achieve the honour and rewards prepared for the servant who should be named a special benefactor of his lord the king, Zopyrus had perhaps to retrieve a neglect of duty or a supineness of his father's, which might have been Darius's ruin though it was over-ruled to the woe of Babylon. Certainly, he had his father's death to revenge; for we have found that, when the Babylonians revolted, Darius's military governor who was slain, was Zopyrus's father.

Again, as to the tale told by Herodotus; its ascribing the recovery of the great city in such a degree to the device and self-devotion of Zopyrus seems incompatible—not, indeed, with Darius's silence as to the man and his exploit in the Behistun Inscription, but—with the extraordinary compliment there paid to his general Vindafrâ the Mede. Commonly, when Darius commemorates on that monument a victory granted him by the will of Auramazdâ at a time and place where he was not present in person, he makes no special mention of the Chief, but says, "My people defeated the enemy." But the capture of Babylon he ascribes to Vindafrâ alone; just as he had, the victories in Parthia to his father Hystaspes. We, therefore, cannot but believe that the services in the siege of Babylon rendered him from first to last by Vindafrâ were far more important than those of any other person whatever. So great, indeed, that reading Hero-

[e] See Ktesias ap. Photium, cod. 72 § 22.

dotus's story of the fate of Intaphernes, that is, Vidafranâ (a name which, like what seems to be its abbreviation Vidafrâ,[d] is in Kissian Vintaparna) one might even be led to doubt whether it was the first of the Persian Six, or this Mede of like or the same name, who, presuming upon his past services, was guilty of such arrogant and violent acts as to forfeit his own life and (like Haman) the lives of his sons and all his kinsmen also.

Notwithstanding, when we consider that Zopyrus was the father of that Megabyzus who (while he recovered Egypt for his wife's brother, our Darius's grandson) seems to have laid the Athenians and other Greeks their allies under a great obligation by his conduct to more than 6000 prisoners;[e] when we consider, too, that a son of this Megabyzus, named like his grandfather Zopyrus, so relied upon the credit of his family at Athens as to fly thither from the king;[f] and, indeed, that he lost his life in attempting to put the Athenians and their allies in possession of Kaunus; we see a connection involving more than ordinary means of information, and we suppose that a story about one who was father of Megabyzus and grandfather of the man that took shelter at Athens; a story current among that refugee and his father's Greek contemporaries; countenanced, too, in some degree by the fact, that after the recovery of Babylon the former Zopyrus had become its governor, must have stood upon a foundation of truth. At the same time we admit, that the actual service rendered to King Darius may have been greatly exaggerated; nay, altogether mis-represented; and we grant that a prominence in the story of Babylon was

[d] We think Vidafrâ may be an abbreviation of Vidafranâ, as *Khshatrapává* (Beh. Insc. Aryan text col. 3 line 14) seems to be an abbreviation of Khshatrapávaná, a form indicated by the Kissian *Saksabavana*, col. 2 line 80.

[e] Ktesias ap. Phot. cod. 72, §§ 33–37. Thucyd. i. 110.

[f] εἰς Ἀθήνας ἀφίκετο κατὰ τὴν τῆς μητρὸς (Amytis wife of Megabyzus) εἰς αὐτοὺς εὐεργεσίαν,
says Ktesias ap. Phot. § 43.
εἰς Ἀθήνας αὐτομόλησεν ἐκ Περσῶν.
Herod. iii. 160.

given to Zopyrus—more unjust even than that which
(perhaps while he was Darius's lieutenant at Sardis) Otanes
obtained among the Greeks; when he was extolled as the
one of the Six, the Persians were most indebted to for the
overthrow of that pretended Smerdis, the Magian Gaumâta; and also as one who had counselled the adoption
by the Persians of a democratic form of government for
the future.

Nor do we venture altogether to discredit the fact, that
Zopyrus, whom Darius made governor of Babylon, was a
man who had lost his nose and ears. This has been
represented a misfortune quite incompatible with the
authority of a commander among Asiatic troops. The
objection would tell most strongly against Megabyzus, the
substitute for Zopyrus in Ktesias's account of the recovery
of Babylon; for this Megabyzus (as we have said) was the
commander who re-conquered Egypt; he had previously
been one of the six generals-in-chief of the great army
Xerxes invaded Europe with; and subsequently, when
governor of Syria, he was able to carry on a war against
Artaxerxes, with so much credit and success as at last to
obtain a reconciliation with the king. But the substitution of Megabyzus for his father in the story of Babylon,
we have shewn to be an error; and, therefore, another
objection is of no moment which applies to Megabyzus
alone, that king Xerxes would not have given his
daughter to a man whose ears and nose had been cut
off. But after the reduction of Babylon, it is not related
that Zopyrus led armies or conducted campaigns, for
Darius. We are merely told, that he had Babylon
given him, to hold as his estate rent-free as long as he
lived.⁵ If so, in that vanquished city his mutilated face
would make him more terrible to the natives; while,
with the large Persian force that henceforth formed rather
an army of occupation than a garrison, it would serve for
a perpetual memorial both of the service he had rendered

---

⁵ τὴν Βαβυλῶνά οἱ Δαρεῖς ἀτελία νέμεσθαι, μέχρι τῆς ἐκείνου ζόης.
Herod. iii. 160.

to the king and of the guilt of those whom they were themselves employed to coerce. Therefore, though Darius was not present when Babylon was taken; though no she-mule foaled in any camp of the besiegers; though the chief merit of their success belonged not to Zopyrus but to their commander, the Mede Vindafrà; yet will we continue to suppose on the authority of Herodotus, that before the city was taken, some feigned attacks having been repulsed with much appearance of advantage on the part of the besieged, their confidence either in themselves or in certain false friends became a means whereby Darius's forces afterwards got possession of a couple of gates, and so entered the city. We will suppose, that Vindafrà had found the means to correspond with friends within the walls, one of whom was Zopyrus, whether he sustained the character of a deserter or was a prisoner. If a prisoner, it is possible that he had been in the hands of the new Nebukhadrezzar, ever since the Babylonians had been excited to revolt and had slain their governor, the father of Zopyrus; and though the captive's life was spared, his person may then have been subjected to a treatment not only ignominious but cruel, the traces of which were ineffaceable.

But as to the time employed in those four successive attacks upon the city, which, after being thrice triumphantly defeated, ended in the sudden capture of the besieged population, Herodotus or a previous narrator appears to have misunderstood the story he had undertaken to repeat, and consequently to have made in this part of it a representation inconsistent with the evident purpose of what he had already rehearsed. This earlier part of the story had first recounted, How for one year and seven months the city had defied all the efforts of its assailants. Next, had come the words, "Then in the twentieth month." And hereupon had followed the narrative we have given, which extends from the mule's foaling to the capture of Babylon. But no later month than the twentieth is mentioned, and it seems plain that, according to the view of the original recorder or expounder of the matter, it

was in the twentieth month (the month which is said to
have arrived after one year and seven months had been
wearily spent by the besiegers in unavailing efforts) that
the city fell into their hands at last. But, as the tale is
repeated by Herodotus, though for dates we have this
twentieth month given us, together with three, if not
four, days of a certain series, described by their number,
yet we have not one occurrence really dated, unless it be
the prodigy which did not happen at all. The only
purpose the mention of the twentieth month appears to
serve, is to let us know when the mule foaled. The first
three attacks upon the city (if not the fourth also) are
epochs, indeed, that seem fixed to their proper days; but
those days, being counted from the desertion of Zopyrus
which is itself undated, lose the character of dates: they
might be supposed to belong to a twenty-first and twenty-
second month of siege, though no such months are spoken
of. This mis-apprehension was probably occasioned by
the fact, that the connection, originally apparent, between
the twentieth month previously, and the tenth day subsequently, noted, had been destroyed, or made obscure, to
the romance-loving and unarithmetical hearer, through the
foisting of the she-mule and her foal into the chronicle.
However, this interpolation being banished, the original
connection is easily guessed. Accordingly, the correction
we propose of Herodotus's account is, that the first two
days of attack, described as the tenth and seventeenth
of a certain series, be regarded as the tenth and seventeenth of the before-mentioned twentieth month :—further,
that after the repulse of their second menace of attack,
it be supposed, not that the besiegers let twenty days
pass by idly, and then feigned a third attempt, but
that they waited till the twentieth day of the month.
Then, the day whereon the city was taken is not indeed
numbered, and yet the attack being described as made
" straightway after the twentieth "[h] may be considered
to be placed on the twenty-first of the same month ; and

[h] μετὰ τὴν εἰκοστὴν ἡμέρην ἰθέως.
Herod. iii. 155.

this date of the capture agrees surprisingly with the statement of the Behistun Inscription so far as it survives "Auramazdâ was my helper," says the king. "By the will of Auramazdâ Vindafrâ took Babylon. He made the people my prisoners. On the twenty-second day of the month Markazana, then it was that Arakha, who said I am Nebukhadrezzar, was thus seized." [1]

On these two nearly coinciding dates, the 21st of the month, discernible (in spite of the mis-telling of his story by Herodotus) as the date, according to that story, of the successful assault, and the 22d, given by Darius as the date of the seizure of Arakha, it is hardly necessary to observe, that (though the gates and ramparts of Babylon may have been occupied and the city itself may have been penetrated on the 21st) we ought not to be surprized if Darius's rival did not fall into Vindafrâ's hands till the morrow; whether he was seized in the principal palace (where Belshazzar had been feasting and was slain, when Cyrus took the city) or in any other stronghold or lurking place in the wide extent of Babylon. So, in Xenophon's account of the capture by Cyrus we are told, that—the city having been surprized, the palace entered, and the king slain in a certain night—after it was day, the forts or citadels within the city surrendered. However, we must not omit the remark, that if, as we have often assumed it, the first month of the Khaldæan twelve has been really discovered in " Eighth-month " or Markhesvan of the Assyrians and Jews, and if we have rightly concluded that Herodotus's twenty months of Babylonian siege begin with Markhesvan in the year B. C. 518, it follows that this period expired with Sivannu or Sivan, the third month of the Assyrians and Jews, corresponding nearly with June of B. C. 516. If, then, Babylon was really taken in this twentieth month of siege or eighth of a second Khaldæan year of its new king's reign, it will be seen

[1] See col. 3 lines 42–44 of the Kissian text (which is the most complete of the three) Journal R. A. S. vol. xv. p. 124. also, line 87 of the Assyrian text, in vol. xiv ; and col. 3, lines 86–88 of the Aryan, in vol. x p. 239.

that this is the month that the Aryans called Markazana or Margazana. For, as we have seen, according to Darius, the new Nebukhadrezzar fell into the hands of Vindafrâ on the 22d of Markazana.

It was on these conclusions, that an observation formerly made was founded, that before the second of the four yearly fasts of the Jews arrived in Darius's fifth, and his rival the upstart Nebukhadrezzar's second, Khaldæan year; or (in other words) before the seventy-first anniversary arrived of the capture of Jerusalem by the forces of the first Nebukhadrezzar, in the eleventh year of Zedekiah king of Judah, the news of the fall of Babylon and the capture of its third Nebukhadrezzar, must have reached Jerusalem and there filled the children of the captivity with exultation and thankfulness. For Jerusalem had been taken on the ninth day of the Jewish and Assyrian fourth month, Thammuz, corresponding with the ninth month of the Khaldean twelve; so that the sad anniversary in B. C. 516 did not arrive till nearly three weeks after the calamity of Babylon and the reply therein given by the God of Israel to the lamentations wherewith, since Jerusalem had been taken and burnt, His people had yearly solicited Him.

On the great success achieved by the lieutenant of Darius, we may adopt a remark of Herodotus, that this is the second capture of Babylon which happened within the limits of our history; the first having been accomplished by Cyrus. The statement is not incorrect, though Herodotus was not himself aware of the fact that the city had once before rebelled against Darius, and that, on the defeat of its army by the king himself, it had been entered and long occupied by the conqueror. For the gates on that occasion appear to have been opened by the inhabitants, not forced by Darius. Indeed, though upon the occasion, we called Darius's taking possession a "capture," we offered a reason for believing that no considerable resistance had been made to the king's entering.[j] On the present occasion, the besiegers made

[j] p. 478.

themselves masters of the city in spite of every effort of those who had taken shelter within its walls.

As, after it had been a first time besieged and taken by the Khaldæans, Jerusalem revolted once, and surrendered; but again revolting, was, after a long siege, taken by them a second time;[k] so it had happened to the Khaldæan capital itself in relation with the Medes and Persians. As with Poland in our days, it was their own rebellion or patriotism that drew down the full measure of calamity upon both the cities; though Jerusalem at least had been fore-warned of the consequences. By rejecting the counsel of God, they made their rebellion against the king of Babylon a rebellion against their God.

In order to complete the present section we have more to subjoin. From the king's own record at Behistun, we learn that after Vindafrâ had won Babylon and all that it contained for him, Darius caused Arakha, who called himself Nebukhadrezzar, to be there put to death along with all his principal adherents. It seems to have been also recorded, that they were impaled.[l] It is certain that Herodotus tells us, the king impaled at Babylon those who were about the principal men of the city, to the number of three thousand.[m] Here, possibly, we have

[k] See Daniel i. 1; 2 Kings xxiv. 10–17; xxv. 1–7.

[l] That Darius put them to death at Babylon, is evident from the Kissian, col. 3 lines 45, 46, in Journal R. A. S. vol. xv p. 124. That they were impaled seems intimated by the word deciphered *altakan* in line 88 of the Assyrian text, in Journal R. A. S. vol. xiv; comparing therewith *as sakip altakan* of line 60, rendered " *ad crucem affixi.*" Thus ἀψῶσαι indicates crucifixion; S. John iii. 14, viii. 28, xii. 32, 34.

[m] τῶν ἀνδρῶν τοὺς κορυφαίους μάλιστα, εἰς τρισχιλίους ἀνεσκολόπισε.
Herod. iii. 159. To shew that ἀνασκολοπίσαι is equivalent to ἀνασταυρῶσαι Schweighæuser cites Herod. ix. 78, where, the charge having been made against Xerxes and Mardonius,

Αἰωνίδεω ἀποθανόντος ἀποταμόντος τὴν κεφαλὴν ἀνεσταύρωσαν.

Pausanias is recommended to retaliate on the dead body of Mardonius, Μαρδόνιον ἀνασκολοπίσαι. In the case referred to of Leonidas, it had been related, Herod. vii. 238,

ἐκέλευσε ἀποταμόντας τὴν κεφαλὴν ἀνασταυρῶσαι.

It seems to have been the *head* of Leonidas that was to have been stuck upon a pole, while Pausanias is invited to impale the entire body of Mardonius. When Saul king of Israel was slain in battle on Mount

the retribution rendered by the Babylonians for having slaughtered Megabyzus their governor and other Persians and Medes with him at the time of their revolt. This, at the rate of ten for one (which after the taking of Memphis by Cambyses, the king's judges sentenced the Egyptians to pay for the Mytilenian crew they had massacred [n]) would make those who perished with Megabyzus, three hundred. If in this part of it, the Assyrian version of the Behistun Inscription had been less defaced, we should probably have been furnished with details beyond those recorded in the least mutilated, the Kissian

---

Gilboa, his head and his armour, having been carried about in the land of the Philistines, the armour was deposited in a temple of Ashtaroth and his head pitched in the temple of Dagon; while his body was set up as a trophy upon the wall of Bethshan, near which city the battle had been fought; see 1 Sam. xxxi. 8–10; 1 Chron. x. 8–10. In the first passage, the expression in the Septuagint is τὸ σῶμα αὐτοῦ κατέπηξαν ἐν τῷ τείχει Βηθσάν, or, in the Vat. ed. Βαιθσάμ.   Josephus, Antiq. vi. 14 § 8 (writing of Saul's three sons as well as of Saul himself) expresses the same particular thus;

τὰ δὲ σώματα ἀνεσταύρωσαν πρὸς τὰ τείχη τῆς Βηθσὰν πόλεως, ἣ νῦν Σκυθόπολις καλεῖται.

For κατέπηξαν or ἀνεσταύρωσαν, we have יִתְקְעוּ in both the Scripture texts above referred to.

Of such trophies in rude times, or among rude nations, we will add some other instances. Regarding the body of Patroklus, Iris brings word of Hector to Achilles; Iliad. xviii. 176, 177.

κεφαλὴν δέ ἑ θυμὸς ἀνώγει
πῆξαι ἀνὰ σκολόπεσσι ταμόνθ' ἁπαλῆς ἀπὸ δειρῆς.

So, Thoas king of the Tauri (in the Kimmerian country) calling his people to the pursuit of Orestes, is made to say, σκολοψι πέξωμεν δέμας, Eurip. Iph. in Taur. ed. Matth. v. 395. Orestes, again, having bid Electra give the body of Ægisthus to wild beasts if she liked, proposes an alternative.

ἢ σκῦλον οἰωνοῖσιν, αἰθέρος τέκνοις,
πῆξας' ἔρεισον σκόλοπι.

Eurip. Elect. ed. Matth. lines 901, 902.

The σκόλοψ, like the Roman *vallus*, was a palisade used in fortification; see Hom. Il. viii. 343; Od. vii. 45; Herod. ix. 97. In Xenophon Anab. v. 2 the same stockade is called σκόλοπες, "pales" § 5, and σταυρώματα, §§ 15, 19, 27; also apparently χαράκωμα, "a paling" § 26; Further, to make their way through this, we read, τοὺς σταυροὺς ἐξαιροῦντες, τοὺς καθ' αὑτοὺς, διέκοπτον. § 21.   A comparison of the Greek and Roman χάρακες or *valli* is found in Polyb. xviii. 1. and Livy xxxiii. 5.

[n] Herod. iii. 14.

text. In particular, we should have had, as in the accounts of other victories in the Assyrian text, the number of those that were executed; a record for which ample space appears to remain in the obliterated portion of the lines, as well as for the matters related in the Kissian text. Whether, indeed, Darius commemorated also that demolition of fortifications which, as Herodotus informs us, he proceeded to, is beyond conjecture. Whether recorded at Behistun or not, the act was his, not that of Cyrus, to whom Berosus erroneously ascribed it. The elder historian briefly states; " He stripped them of their wall and tore off all their gates, for the former time when Cyrus took Babylon he did neither the one of these things nor the other."º The truth, indeed, of this would seem to be incompatible with the account of the walls in his first book, which our travelled historian gives us as one who had surveyed them himself. But (as we have observed before) Berosus reconciles the inconsistency. For, having asserted in his account of the great Nebukhadrezzar's reign, that the city was fortified with three circuits of wall, he relates afterwards that Cyrus the Persian, as soon as he had got Babylon into his hands, gave orders to demolish the outer walls of the city.ᵖ Here, when we have substituted Darius for Cyrus, we are taught to restrict to the outermost rampart that phrase of Herodotus's which credits Darius with "stripping Babylon of its wall;" though the historian, under the reign of Darius's grandson, describes the city as possessing still two circuits of wall. And, while we thus interpret our author's " wall of Babylon " that the city was stript of, to mean the outermost of three circuits of wall that it possessed at the commencement of the siege, we are justified by his adding of himself, that Darius moreover tore away all the gates. For the mention of this particular supposes walls which survived the afore-

---

º Herod. iii. 159. His words (which we have translated, " He stript them of their wall ") are,
 σφέων τὸ τεῖχος περιεῖλε.
ᵖ τὰ ἔξω τῆς πόλεως τείχη.
Berosus, ap. Joseph. *cont. Apion.* 1. 20.

mentioned demolition of fortifications, but which were to be made unserviceable. The purpose we have reason to believe, was effected, not only by the taking away of the gates, but also, by the pulling down of the housing provided for men, military stores, and victual, in the rows of chambers which, like two huge parapets, ran at top along the edges of the outermost at least of the two remaining circumvallations.ᑫ The entire demolition of the outermost of the three ramparts was an easier work, by reason of the nature of its materials. For, while both the walls which survived seem to have been at least cased thickly with burnt-brick, well cemented, we learn from Berosus (when his expression is restricted to the utmost) that *one* rampart was made of " mere brick without bitumen," or (we may venture to add) any other cement except mud ; for by this "mere brick" we understand sun-dried brick.ʳ If the outermost of all the ramparts at Babylon was composed entirely of this material, obtained from a trench dug on the outside of it, the labour would be comparatively little to throw it down again into its ditch ; and there would be this advantage immediately accruing, that the area of both ditch and wall might at once be devoted to cultivation. This wall may have had no gates of its own, but may have been bent inward in a series of curves ; its moat joining that of the second wall on each side of every gate of the city.

Five gates of Babylon are named in Herodotus's story

ᑫ Herod. i. 179. The space left at top of the wall between the two rows of building, the historian calls, τιθρίππῳ περίλασιν. The demolition of the upper-works is implied by the statement (of Kleitarkhus) in Curtius and Strabo, that the wall was 32 feet broad ; wide enough for *two* chariots to pass, having each four horses harnessed abreast. Thus, each horse is allowed four feet of road, the width of the Roman actus or " drove " (left for man or animal to pass, between every two lots of land 120 feet square ; the pair or yoke of which was called *jugus* or *jugerum* and each one *actus quadratus ;* see Smith's Dictionary of Greek and Roman Antiquities). To overturn the πρμαχιῶνας, seems to have been a dismantling of a place commonly resorted to by the captors ; see Herod. i. 164.

ʳ See Berosus ap. Joseph. *Antiq.* x. 11. and *cont. Apion.* i. 19.

of the capture; the gate of Semiramis, the gate of the Ninians, that is apparently Ninevites, the gate of the Khaldæans, the Belidan gate, and the Kissian gate.[s] Of these, the second, the third, and the fifth seem obviously named after the people to which the quarter they opened from was appropriated;[t] and it may be observed in passing, that on the fall of Nineveh in B. C. 608, a large number of the inhabitants may have been transplanted to Babylon. The gate of Semiramis, we may be induced to identify with the one where, (as Herodotus says in his first book) the body of Nitokris was entombed over-head, and which was disused in consequence; people generally shrinking from a passage that led underneath a dead body.[u] For, as in later Greek accounts of Babylon we find

[s] See Zopyrus's explanation of his plan; Herod. iii. 155. The last two gates, the Kissian and the Belid or Belidan, are again named in the account of the execution of the plan; chap. 118.

[t] Compare S. John, Revel. xxi. 12, 13; Ezek. xliii. 30–34; Numb. ii. 1–30.

[u] Herod. i. 187. As to the gates, perhaps that of Semiramis and that of the Ninians may be identified with the gate of Mula and the gate of Nin, in Nebukhadrezzar's India House Inscription (G. Rawlinson's Herodotus vol. ii. p. 585). Here, Mula and Nin appear to be deities presiding over their respective gates. Is Mula the deity called in the Akkad language Mulita and in Assyrian Bilta, the Μυλιττα and Βηλτις of the Greeks, who was regarded as the wife both of Bel-Nimrud and of Nin his son? See Sir H. C. Rawlinson's Essay on the Religion of the Babylonians &c. in G. Rawlinson's Herodotus vol. i. pp. 595, 603, 604, 625. The Belidan gate, in Nebukhadrezzar's wall of Babylon, Sir H. C. Rawlinson supposes to have been so named because the road through it went forth to a city the ruins of which are called Niffer, a corruption of the name in Semitic cuneiform, which was *Nipur;* the Nopher of the tract Yoma in the Talmud, which that tract identifies with Calneh, one of Nimrod's capitals. The original Hamite cuneiform name of this city was identical with that of the god it was dedicated to, as yet unknown, the 2d of the twelve gods and also of the first triad of the twelve, who is called for convenience Bel-Nimrud. The city is mentioned by this name in the titles of the Khaldæan king, Ismi-dagon, whose accession is approximately fixed at B. C. 1861; see Sir H. C. Rawlinson's Essay on the Early History of Babylonia, in G. Rawlinson's Herodotus vol. i p. 437, note; also his Essay on the Religion of the Babylonians and Assyrians p. 596. But, even if we suppose the corners of the (oblong)

Semiramis taking the place of Nitokris, so here Nitokris may have been put into that of Semiramis. It is difficult to imagine that such a tomb should have been assigned to a queen who survived the death of the native king her son and the surrender of the regent her husband when Babylon was taken from its former kings by Cyrus. The Belidan and the Kissian gates must have been situated both of them at no great distance from the temple of Merodakh (or as Herodotus and other Greeks call him, Zeus Belus) whereof the mound now named Babel by the Arabs is supposed to be the ruin; because we are told that such of the Babylonians as saw Darius's troops gain possession of the two gates fled to this temple. For they must have been near the gates to have seen what happened there; while yet the temple they fled to, must have been the nearest place that, by its sanctity rather than strength and stores, seemed capable of protecting them. Our conclusion, as to the situation of the gates, is not a little confirmed by the name of one of them, the Belidan, which seems to show that the god was its special guardian; though, on this occasion, traitor or impotent; and that the quarter whence it afforded issue, was the one in which the god's temple stood, if it was not also inhabited by a tribe of Khaldæans considered as his children and after him called Belidan. Of the two gates, one might suppose

quadrilateral rampart of Babylon, to have pointed as did probably the corners of the temple of Zeus Belus, N. S. E. and W. (in which case the side nearest the temple, supposing the temple to be represented by the present Babel mound, would run from N. to E.) the situation of Niffer seems too far south of the latitude of Babylon east-ward to allow of the direct road thither from Babylon to have issued from a gate which Herodotus's narrative places near the Belus temple, that is, the Babel mound. The Belus or Bel of Babylon (who is the Merodakh of the great Nebukhadrezzar's Inscriptions) seems to have been sometimes identified in those inscriptions with the Bel of Nipur; though properly he was a distinct deity, the ninth of the twelve gods; see the above-cited Essay, p. 598, note. As to the Kissian gate, it may be thought to help the proof that this opened the way to the Kissian country, that Nineveh, too, had its *Nuva* (that is, Kissian or Elamite country) gate; See Sennacherib's Inscription on the Taylor cylinder, translated by Mr. H. Fox Talbot; Journal R. A. S. vol. xix p. 169.

the Kissian, to have been in the outer, and the Belidan in the inner of the two walls, which survived in Herodotus's times; though our author in this part of his work (not distinguishing more than one circuit of wall in the defences of Babylon) supposes them to have been threatened and seized by two distinct bodies of Persians furnished by Vindafrâ's army. On which, by the bye, it may be appropriate to remark that these "Persians" would probably have been called "Persians and Medes" if Darius had told the story. But Darius does not acknowledge any Persian and Median division in the army; and hence perhaps, his special mention of Vindafrâ.

At the time of the city's capture, Merodakh's precinct we may suppose, in the midst of which rose, tower above tower, the high place of the sanctuary of the god, had been crowded with fugitives. Afterwards (whether it had been able to protect them or not) it was allowed we know to retain its brazen or copper plated gates.[v] Indeed, the reason of this is obvious. They were necessary for the security of the treasures which it was still permitted to possess. For, though we may be sure that its hoards were largely confiscated by Darius, the idol, sitting beside a table, which Herodotus saw in a shrine at the bottom of the tower, with the altar before the door of that lower or (as we may term it) downstairs sanctuary of Bel (for so using a title for his name, the people called the god) though idol, chair, table, altar, were all of gold, must have been at that time in existence and left in the temple by Darius for the worship of the people. Indeed, Sir H. C. Rawlinson considers the idol described by Herodotus to be certainly the same as the great idol of Merodakh in the temple of Babylon, so curious an account of which has been left (he says) by Nebukhadrezzar. It had been made of silver by an earlier king; but it was overlaid with plates of gold by Nebukhadrezzar.[w] The like

[v] Herod. i. 181.
[w] Sir H. C. Rawlinson cites the India House Inscription col. 3. lines 1 to 7; see his Essay on the Religion of the Babylonians and Assyrians in G. Rawlinson's Herodotus vol. i p. 629, note. Sir H. C. Rawlinson

indulgence must have been extended by the Persian conqueror to the golden table set beside a bed of large dimensions in the sacred chamber at the top of the seventh stage of the tower. There was also in the court below, when Vindafrâ took Babylon, an image of a man,[z] made of gold, twelve cubits high, and solid; of which it was afterwards related in particular, that Darius was much disposed to carry it off, though he refrained. It was no longer standing in the precinct at the time of Herodotus's visit, having been taken away by Xerxes; who also slew

says "in the temple of Bit Saggat," understanding by the Bit Saggat or Beth Saggath the great temple of Babylon; and he concludes that it was the great idol in this temple that had the special name of Bel. On col. 1 line 5 of the Birs Nimrud Inscription Mr H. Fox Talbot remarks; "At first I supposed that Beth Shagathu was an individual temple so named at Babylon, and that Beth Zida was another; but I have since found that in almost every great city there were buildings so named; and, therefore, I now think that it has the general meaning of "Temple" or "Place of worship." It is derived, I believe, from *Shagad*, "to worship, fall down in adoration before an image &c." Heb. סגד (Gesen. p. 763) from whence, as Gesenius well observes, is derived the Arabic *shejed*, "to adore" and *mesjid*, "a house of prayer," which latter word [signifying a Mahommedan place of worship in Hindustani, see Forbes Hind. Dict. p. 494] has become in English "a mosque." I find (continues Mr H. F. Talbot) that Mr Cureton in his Syriac Gospels p. xlvii. says that *Bith Shagadtha* means "a house of worship," and *mashgad*, "worship." And Castelli's *Lex. Syr.* p. 578, has *Shagad*, "adoravit;" see Journal R. A. S. vol. xviii pp. 36, 44. In lines 15 and 16 of the same column, the particular temple at Babylon is called in Mr H. F. Talbot's decipherment, *beth shagathu beth rab shamie u irtsit, subat bel ...... ilu Marduk;* which he renders, "the house of worship (in Babylon), the palace of heaven and earth, the dwelling of Merodakh king of the race of the gods." Perhaps, the tower particularly specified in line 23, represented the heavens or stages of heaven; and the court around it, the earth. Note, that this temple of Bel or Merodakh was pre-eminently τὸ ἐν Βαβυλῶνι ἱερὸν, as Herodotus calls it, i. 183, or "the temple of Babylon," as it is twice called by the elders of the Jews in Ezra v. 14, in opposition to "the temple in Jerusalem." The word הֵיכַל which forms part of both terms (in its emphatic or definite form הֵיכְלָא) is equivalent to *beth-rab*, in the above cited designation of the temple of Bel, that is, "a palace, great house."

[z] ἀνδριὰς, Herod. i. 183, to be distinguished from ἄγαλμα in chapters 183 and 181.

the Priest as he was in the act of prohibiting the removal. This image probably represented some famous personage of the prosperous days of Babylon; perhaps Nebukhadrezzar; and was judged legitimate plunder; the property, not of the god but of the Aryan conqueror. The Khaldæans asserted, in Herodotus's time, that the Bel which he saw with its chair, table, and the step or stand, (βάθρον i. e. βάσις), whereon the sitting figure, (if not the entire group) was elevated, were made out of eight hundred talents of gold.ʸ They should have known, if they did not take into

ʸ See Herod. i. 181–183. According to Herodotus, the "Babylonian talent" in which the silver tributes were paid to Darius, weighed one-sixth more than "the Euboic" in which the gold was paid; its sixty *minas* being of equal weight with seventy Euboic *minas*; see Herod. iii. 89. But a more exact account is supposed to be found in the ancient writer followed by Ælian *Var. Hist.* i. 22 who made the Babylonian talent equal to 72 Attic minas; meaning thereby, *old* Attic, the same as Euboic and still used in commerce after the legislation of Solon had introduced at Athens the smaller talent and mina, afterwards distinguished as Attic. This Babylonian talent, weighing one-fifth more than the Euboic, is shewn to have been identical with the Æginetan talent, from Pollux ix. 76, 86; each containing 10,000 of Solon's drachmas. The oriental origin of the Euboic as well as of the Æginetan weights is acknowledged; see the article on the word *Pondera* by Philip Smith in Dr William Smith's "Dictionary of Greek and Roman Antiquities." Two Hebrew talents, standing to one another as sixty shekels to fifty (the proportion of the Babylonian to the Euboic talent) are inferred from Exodus xxxviii. 24 &c. Ezek. xlv. 12 and a comparison of three manahs in 1 Kings x. 17 with 300 bekahs or half shekels, 2 Chron. ix. 16. Mr E. Norris argues for two Hebrew talents, that of the Sanctuary and that of the King; the first the double of the latter; and he cites the testimony of the Rabbins in the Aruch; "The legal shekel is equal to four *dinarin* and the *dinar* is the *zuz* (or drachma). The shekel of our Rabbins is but one-half and contains two dinars." He also cites the testimony of the Targum on Samuel, which translates "the fourth part of a shekel," 1 Sam. ix. 8 by זיו אחדא "one drachma," illustrating the fact that though the *shekel* (that is, two bekahs) was equal to an ordinary στατηρ or *tetradrachma*, that is, a four-drachma piece or two didrachmas (S. Matt. xvii. 27) the Septuagint sometimes translates it, didrachma, meaning the two-drachma piece of Alexandria which numismatists inform us was equal to the Attic four-drachma piece. Mr Norris has passed to this question from the main subject of an article on Assyrian and Babylonian Weights, in Journal

account, the fact above cited, that, under the exterior of gold, the idol was of silver.

Herodotus's account of this temple, contemporary with the reign of the son of Xerxes, shows how entirely false was the story, told to the companions of Alexander in B. C. 331-323, that the ruin in which it then lay was the work of the celebrated invader of their country, Xerxes.* After the battle of Arbela in B. C. 331, Alexander, on his arrival at Babylon, ordered the fallen tower to be put up again; but between this visit and his return in B. C. 324,

R. A. S. vol. xvi, in which from ancient weights found at Nineveh it is shewn conclusively, that the Assyrian Fifteen, Five, Three, Two and One manah weights, also Quarter manahs and Fifths of a manah, weighed twice as much as weights of the same denomination among the Babylonians ; the fifteen-manah Assyrian (or thirty-manah Babylonian) weight being something more than forty-one pounds English and (at sixty manahs to the talent) intimating the existence of an Assyrian talent of 164 pounds weight and a Babylonian of eighty-two pounds.

The Babylonian talent, which the Greeks called Æginetan, was understood by Josephus (*Antiq.* iii. 6 § 7) to be intended by the *kikkar* of Exod. xxv. 39, which the Septuagint render τάλαντον. The original form of this Hebrew word, according to Gesenius, was *kirkar;* but Josephus writes it in Greek κιγχάς. On the weight of the golden candlestick, recorded in that passage of Moses, Josephus has the words,

λυχνία .. σταθμὸν ἔχουσα μνᾶς ἑκατὸν ἃς 'Εβραῖοι μὲν καλοῦσι κίγχαρις

(read κιγχάς, striking off the last syllable which seems to have grown out of a reduplication of the preposition which follows)

εἰς δὶ τὴν 'Ελληνικὴν μεταβαλλόμενον γλῶσσαν, σημαίνει τάλαντον.

These hundred minas, making one Æginetan or Babylonian talent, are *Attic minas of Solon;* whereof three-fifths, that is sixty, weighed a little Attic or Solonian talent, and five-sixths, that is eighty-three and a-third, a big Attic or Euboic talent, while each one of them was the weight of 100 Attic drachmas. Accordingly, we learn from Pollux, ix. 76, 86 that the Æginetan talent contained 10,000 Attic drachmas while the Attic talent contained but 6000. That is, the Æginetan talent contained 100 (new) Attic minas, and the (new) Attic talent, sixty. Thus, the New Attic or Solonian talent was to the Æginetan or Babylonian, as three to five, while the old Attic or Euboic was to the same as five to six.

* See Strabo xvi. 1 § 5 ; Arrian, Exp. Alex. iii. 16 § 3, vii. 17 §§ 2-4. The ruined state of the temple of Belus in the days of Kleitarkhus must be the cause of the entire omission of this great wonder of the place in Curtius's description of Babylon.

the preliminary business of clearing the spot had been feebly prosecuted, and the king thought to set about it with his whole army. Merely to remove the fallen mass of earth and rubbish, we are told, was " two months' work for ten thousand men," and after Alexander's death in B. C. 323, nobody troubled himself further with the enterprize. Indeed, it would seem, the Khaldæan priests themselves were by no means eager for the restoration; or desirous (as perhaps we might express it) that the " tomb of Bel " should become once more the " temple of Bel." Arrian relates, that when, early in the year before that of his death, Alexander approached Babylon from Agbatana, as soon as he had crossed to the right bank of the Tigris (at a point distant, as we learn from Diodorus, 300 stades from Babylon; perhaps the place subsequently made the capital and called after his own name by Seleucus) he was warned from Bel by a deputation of learned Khaldæans, not at that time to enter the city, or at any rate not with his face toward the sun-down or leading his army in that direction; but when he came, to approach the city with his face towards the sun-rise. But Alexander suspected (not without appearance of reason, we may be sure) that it was on their own account they wished to keep him away.*

<hr>

* Though Alexander thus suspected the oracle, yet his companion Aristobulus (as cited by Arrian) tells us, he resolved to obey its admonition in respect of the direction of his course when he should enter the city. Accordingly, he encamped the first day beside the Euphrates; (that is, having heard the message of the god, he crossed from the right bank of the Tigris to the left bank of the Euphrates and there encamped for the first night, after a march of 200 stades as it would seem from Diodorus xvii. 112 § 4). Then, on the morrow, he kept the river on his right hand and took his way along-side of it (that is, down the stream on the left bank). It is said, that he did thus,
ἐθέλοντα ἐπιβάλλειν τῆς πόλεως τὸ μέρος τὸ ἐς δυσμὰς τετραμμένον ὡς ταύτῃ ἐπιστρέψαντα πρὸς ἕω ἄγειν. 'Αλλ' οὐ γὰρ δυνηθῆναι ὑπὸ δυσχωρίας οὕτως ἐλάσαι σὺν τῇ στρατιᾷ
" desiring to get beyond the part of the city that faced the west, and then to wheel about and lead his army towards the east; but the difficulty of the ground made it impossible to proceed with the army thus "—And why?
ὅτι τὰ ἀπὸ δυσμῶν τῆς πόλεως εἰσιόντι, εἰ ταύτῃ πρὸς ἕω ἐπιστρέψει, ἰλύδη τε καὶ τεναγώδη ἦν. Καὶ οὕτω καὶ ἴσχετα κα ἄκοντα ἐπιθέσεαι τῷ Θεῷ.
Arrian, Exp. Alex. vii. 17. From this account the inference seems to

For he was full of his purpose to restore the temple of
Bel; while the god had much land that he had been
endowed with of the Assyrian kings; also, much gold; and
out of this (ἀπὸ τοῦ; query ἀπὸ τούτου) of old the temple used
to be repaired and the sacrifices offered to the god; but at
that time the produce of the god's property went to the
Khaldæans; there being nothing to spend it upon.[b] To
restore the temple and to renew the services of it, might
therefore increase the labour and diminish the revenue of
the priesthood.

The fall of the upper stages of the tower in the temple
of Bel, with the sacred chamber of the god that had been
at top of all, is exemplified and one (probably the chief)
cause of it is mentioned, in the description given by the
king who repaired the structure last, of the state in which
he found the similar but smaller temple-tower at Borsippa;
the famous pyramidal wreck of which in our days is called
by the Arabs Birs Nimrûd. "From the lapse of time,"
says the great Nebukhadrezzar's inscription (which is
repeated on two cylinders obtained from the wreck of the
King's restorations by Sir H. C. Rawlinson) the head of it
having meanwhile been left unfinished, "the building had
become ruined. They had not taken care of the exits of
the waters. So the rain and wet had penetrated into the
brick-work. The casing of burnt brick had burst open;
and the crude brick of the bulk of it was poured out in
heaps."[c] The condition of the tower of the temple of Bel

---

arise, that the angles of the Babylon city-wall pointed due North, South
East, and West; and that Alexander wished to reach the North-west
face. Diodorus xvii. 112 (the place referred to in the text) evidently
following Nearkhus, represents the Khaldæans as saying the king
might escape the danger by stopping his intended march and *passing
the city*, ἐὰν παρέλθῃ τὴν πόλιν. Here, too, may be meant not getting beyond
a north-west angle but rather passing an angle of the city-wall which
pointed to the North but was east of the Euphrates.

[b] This statement would imply that the sacrifices and burning of incense
spoken of by Herodotus as performed at two altars in the court at foot
of the tower and in front of what we may call the earthly sanctuary,
were no longer celebrated in B. C. 324.

[c] See Sir H. C. Rawlinson's translation (sent from Baghdad Nov. 1854

may have been worse than this when Alexander first arrived at Babylon; and it is to Alexander's labour, preliminary to rebuilding,—it is to the clearing away of the crude brick, turned to earth, and of the rubbish of the harder materials of the fallen mass, that we may attribute the fact, reported of the mound Babel, that the shape is not conical but flat-topped: shewing no traces of former upper stages.[d] In spite of this appearance, therefore, we may still give credit to Herodotus's description of the pile which Babel is believed to represent; at least so far as the attestation goes, that it consisted of seven solid quadrangular towers ($\pi\acute{\nu}\rho\gamma o\iota$, or masses of

but not printed by the R. A. S. till 1859) at p. 51 of an article intended for the first of vol. xviii. of the Journal but stitched up with Part 2 of vol. xvii. We have substituted "burst open" for "bulged out;" the Assyrian word *uptaddiru* being (as Mr H. F. Talbot in 1860 informs us) the T conjugation of the verb פטר "to split," Gesen. p. 818. For "the terraces of crude brick," we have substituted "the crude brick of the bulk of it;" the Assyrian word *kum* in the term *libitti-kummi-sha* meaning, according to Mr H. F. Talbot, "mound" or "mass" and being related to the Hebrew and Aramaic קום "surgere," whence the Heb. קוֹמָה "height" Also, for "lay scattered" we have substituted "was poured out;" being taught by Mr Talbot that *ishapik* (in the Senkereh Inscription, 15, *ishapku*) is the passive of שָׁפַךְ "effundere," Gesen. p. 1032. Compare *ishshafek* 3 pers. masc. sing, of the present tense Niphal in Genesis ix. 6 of which the plural would be *ishshafku*. The whole passage in Mr Talbot's independent translation (presented to the R. A. S. May 1861, without any such alterations as Sir H. C. Rawlinson's then recently published translation might have suggested) is this; "Ob dies antiquos in ruinâ ceciderat; non curati fuerant canales aquarum ejus; propriâ ruinâ ceciderant lateres ejus; lateres pulchri vestientes eam disrupti erant; lateres formantes molem ejus effusi erant cum ruinâ;" see Journal R. A. S. vol. xviii p. 38 comparing notes, p. 47. As to the clause "propria ruinâ ceciderant lateres ejus," in his Additional Notes pp. 362, 363, Mr Talbot gives some forcible reasons that had induced him to abandon it in favour of Sir H. C. Rawlinson's translation. Further, we think that the term *agurri*, rendered by Mr Talbot, "lateres pulchri," is well proved by Sir H. C. Rawlinson in Journal R. A. S. vol. xviii p. 9) to mean "lateres coctiles," and that he also teaches us well to regard the opposed term *libitti (i.e. libinti)* as signifying bricks in the raw state, "crudi laterculi," sun-dried bricks, such as Berosus seems to mean by his "mere brick."
[d] See G. Rawlinson's Herodotus vol. ii. p. 576.

earth and brick work) raised one on the top of another; the smaller upon the larger; and on the summit of the whole, an eighth story, not solid but having within it a sanctuary, shrine or holy lodging, νηός, wherein was a table of gold, beside a large bed; but no image of the god; who, indeed, in this lofty habitation was said to pass the night in his proper person with the one of all the women of Babylon whom he had chosen according to the priests to share his bed. From this account, and from our historian's silence as to its existence, one should infer that the sanctuary contained no coffin or trough-like receptacle, πύελος, such as appears in Ktesias's story of the sacrilegious visit of King Xerxes to the "Tomb of Bel."* Perhaps, the sepulchral chamber was believed to be situate in some other part of the building; but the pile seen by Herodotus may have been already a ruin in the time of Ktesias. By this author's story Xerxes is made to have entered the tomb (whether through roof or wall) διασκάψας, "by a breach." It is certain that the gigantic pile described by Herodotus, is by Greek writers sometimes termed the " tomb of Belus."† As to the

---

* Ktesias ap. Ælian. Var. Hist. xiv. 3 and ap. Photium, Biblioth. cod. 72 § 21. In such a πύελος was deposited the body of Cyrus, in his tomb at Pasargadæ; see Aristobulus in Arrian Exp. Alex. vi. 29 and Strabo xv. 3 § 7. In the romance of the Life of Alexander by a Pseudo Callisthenes, the King when he was at Persepolis, is said to have seen among others the tomb of Cyrus;

ἦν δὲ πύργος αἰθριος δωδεκάστεγος, ἐν δὲ τῇ ἄνω στέγῃ ἔκειτο αὐτὸς ἐν χρυσῇ πυέλῃ, (read πυέλῳ) καὶ ἄλλαι σεμιαίχυντο αὐτῷ, ὥστε τὸ τείχωμα αὐτοῦ φαίνεσθαι, καὶ αὐτὸν δὲ ὅλον, διὰ τοῦ ὅλου.

Ps. Call. ii. 18. This romance is printed for the first time along with the Arrian edited for M. Didot by C. Müller. One might fancy our extract an improvement upon the story of Onesicritus, of whom Strabo writes, xv. 3 § 7;

τὸν πύργον διακάστεγον ἔφησε καὶ ἐν μὲν τῇ ἀνωτάτω στέγῃ κεῖσθαι τὸν Κῦρον.

† The author followed by Diodorus xvii. 112 § 3 spoke of Alexander's raising up again the *tomb* of Belus which the Persians had pulled down; whereas in Diodorus ii. 9 § 4 the building is called a *temple*;

ἱερὸν Διὸς ὃν καλοῦσιν οἱ Βαβυλώνιοι Βῆλον.

Strabo, too, speaking of Babylon, xvi. 1 § 5 says, "The tomb of Belus is there; now indeed demolished (and Xerxes, they say, pulled it down); but it was a four-cornered pyramid of burnt brick, itself a stade

means of access to the sanctuary on the summit, Herodotus says; " There is an ascent formed to the towers on the outside, going in a circle round them all." From this one should suppose, that stairs led to the bottom of each higher tower in succession, not as at Borsippa on the same side, the north-eastern, but on every side in its turn; so that the top of the seventh tower (that is to say, the terrace supporting the eighth tower) would be reached from the side, or quarter of the horizon, opposite to that at which the ascent began. For example, if the ascent began, as at Borsippa, on the North-east (not as in the Mugheir and Abu-Shahreyn temples of southern Babylonia on the South-east) it would reach the top of the seventh tower on the South-west side ; supposing the four corners of the structure to be right opposite to the cardinal points of the horizon.* By this interpretation of Herodotus we

high and each of its sides a stade long; the which Alexander wished to put together again (*ἀνασκεύασαι*.)" Herodotus must certainly have blundered when he made the lowest story of this pyramid a stade high.
* The notices we have seen, extracted from Rich and Porter, of the Babel mound, intimate that its two longer sides face the North and South, and its two shorter sides East and West. But we venture to presume the same inaccuracy here as that remarked by Sir H. C. Rawlinson in the case of the Borsippa mound, the Birs-Nimrûd of the Arabs. He tells us, that Rich and Porter have both described the sides of the Birs as facing the four cardinal points; whereas in reality, it is the four corners which (with a slight error) face those points; and the titles of of Ker Porter's plates (vol ii. plates 67 and 70) must be thus altered throughout the series ; his western face being south-western ; southern face, south-eastern ; eastern face, north-eastern ; and northern face, north-western. The North-east face is the front of the temple ; the South-west, the back ; and the other two are the sides. So Sir H. C. Rawlinson in the article on the Birs Nimrûd ; Journal R. A. S. vol. xviii p. 5, note. It is very plain that a similar inaccuracy (natural, perhaps, in the case of an *oblong* rectangle, having its corners opposite to the cardinal points of the horizon) has been made by Mr J. E. Taylor in his account of "the big two-storied ruin " at Muqeyer or Mugheir, being the Temple of the Moon-god, Sin, repaired by Nabunita (B. C. 555–538). He speaks throughout his article (Journal R A. S. vol. xv pp. 260-265) as if the sides of that parallelogram faced the cardinal points and the angles the intermediate points of the horizon. Thus he says (p. 261) that the longest sides are to the east and west ; adding presently, that the northern face of the first story has four buttresses

are led to conceive, that each tower in the course of the ascent bore the one above it on its centre ; and that each besides two corner ones ; and the western side, seven besides the corner ones ; and on the eastern side a stair-case three yards broad with sidewalls a yard broad, leading up to the basement of the second story ; besides the after-mentioned ascent to the top of the second story which was the basement of a chamber but lately destroyed. Again (p. 262) he writes ; A curious feature in the building is the position of the second story, which is close upon the northern end of the first story: the southern side being an inclined plane from the base of the first to the summit of the second story. Accordingly, in pp. 263, 264 he speaks of a South-west corner, a North-west corner, and a South-east corner. But his "Plan of Muqeyer Ruins" shews that the angles of the two-storied ruin are opposite to the cardinal points and the sides to the intermediate arcs of the horizon ; so that the longer sides face the North-east and South-west : the shorter sides, the North-west and South-east ; and the inclined plane by which the sanctuary at top was reached, ascends on the South-east side from the base of the first to the summit of the second story. This difference between the verbal description and the plan is (generally) avoided in the same explorer's Notes on the ruins of Abu Shahreyn, in the Journal R. A. S. vol. xv p. 405. Of the four-sided pyramidal building at the "north" (north-west) end of a walled platform, the site of an ancient town, the angles point North, South, East, and West respectively, while the parallel sides face the sky-lines connecting those points. Like the principal ascent of the two-storied ruin at Muqeyer, so here, the only ascent from the platform at bottom is on the South-east side ; which with the opposite North-west side (as at Muqeyer) is shorter than the North-east and South-west sides. For its first flight from the platform, this single ascent is a stair-case, fifteen feet broad and seventy feet in sloping height ; the steps of which were formed originally of marble slabs.

We will close this note with some of the dimensions of the ruined Muqeyer temple, which had till lately (as we have said) a chamber at top of all, forming a third story. The second story, according to Mr Taylor, is sixteen feet eight inches high : the length of the entire building is 198 feet, the breadth 133 feet, according to Mr Loftus's *Chaldæa and Susiana*, as cited in Rawlinson's Herodotus vol. 2 p. 576. Of these measurements, it is observable that the first may be reduced to the exact product of fifty times a unit of four inches' length, say fifty palms or hand-breadths equal to ten cubits of twenty inches each. The second measurement is equal to 600 such palms all but six ; the third to 400 such all but one. Perhaps, it may yet be found that the breadth more exactly measured, is 133 feet 4 inches, that is 400 palms of four inches or eighty cubits of twenty inches. It is, however, hardly to be supposed that in the length so great an error of measurement has been made as one of two feet.

terrace, or the top of each of the first seven towers, was scaled by a straight stair in the middle of one of its four sides. But it would also accord with the language of Herodotus, to suppose the direction of the stair-case diagonal from bottom to top of each tower, as the ascent was pursued circuitously, along the successive faces of masonry. The existing examples of this style of temple-tower would lead us to expect, that in the great temple at Babylon likewise, the stair-cases to all the stages approached from the same quarter, and that the upper stories of the pile receded from the centre of the lowest as the ascent advanced. Moreover, the reported oblong figure of the ground-plan of the existing mound inclines (though it does not, perhaps, compel) us to the same conclusion.

The account Diodorus has reported of the three golden idols at the top of the tower-stairs of the temple of Belus, representing Zeus, Hera, and Rhea respectively, must be rejected in the first place, for the extravagance of the size and weight of these images, their table, and their furniture; secondly, for the inconsistency of this description with that of Herodotus; thirdly, on account of Diodorus's previous statement that it was not possible to tell the truth about this temple inasmuch as the pile by reason of its age had fallen down, and the accounts of historians were discordant; though all agreed that it was extraordinarily lofty, and that there the Khaldæan astrologers used to make their observations; the risings and settings of the stars being beheld with accuracy on account of the height of the building.[h]

[h] See Diodorus ii. 9. One would be glad to know whether the complaint of discordance in the accounts of authors is Diodorus's own; and whether his detailed account of the idols, their table, and its costly plate, is borrowed from Ktesias. Kleitarkhus and the Macedonian conquerors were without doubt unable to give any account of the pyramidal pile: but is there any evidence that the fall of the upper stages had taken place in the time of Ktesias; that is (let us say) before the accession of Arsakes Artaxerxes Mnemon? We suspect that such was the fact, and that the story of the triad of idols at top, is earlier than Macedonian times, having been borrowed by Diodorus from Ktesias.

When Darius had exacted from the people of Babylon the full measure of retribution due in blood, he restored the city to the remnant to dwell in; having probably (as, in the days of Xenophon, Cyrus was said to have done) distributed among his friends, houses of private persons and residences of hereditary or temporary rulers, giving them lordship and authority over the body of the people. Zopyrus was made governor. That is, the mutilated Persian having helped to repair the loss which had befallen his master when Megabyzus his father was governor, was consoled and rewarded by being put in his father's place. A large body of Persian soldiers was established as a permanent garrison in Babylon. These were maintained at the expense of the population whose submission they enforced. The practice subsisted still in the reign of Arsakes Artaxerxes Mnemon, and that it was then of long standing, we learn from the good authority of Xenophon. But when the same writer ascribes the measure to Cyrus, his report is of little weight. Like the demolition of the outer line of fortification which, though ascribed by Berosus to Cyrus, we have learnt from earlier testimony to attribute to Darius, we suppose the policy of the Persian government, in respect of its military occupation of Babylon, to have been first adopted by Darius.[1] The two revolts of the city in the first four years of his reign may be accepted as proof sufficient of the fact.

[1] We apply to Darius son of Hystaspes what Xenophon (in Cyrop. vii 5 §§ 69, 70) has told of Cyrus.

νομίσας δὲ καὶ Βαβυλῶνος ὕλης φύλακας δεῖν εἶναι ἱκανοὺς, εἶτ᾽ ἐπιδημῶν αὐτὸς τύγχανοι

when he had his own body-guard just before mentioned, of 10,000 Persians.

ἔτι καὶ ἀποδημῶν, κατέστησε καὶ ἐν Βαβυλῶνι φρουροὺς ἱκανοὺς· μισθὸν δὲ καὶ τούτοις (as well as to his body guards)

Βαβυλωνίους ἔταξε παρέχειν· βουλόμενος αὐτοὺς ὡς ἀμηχανωτάτους εἶναι ὅπως ὅτι ταπεινότατοί καὶ εὐκαθεκτότατοι ὦσιν.

Xenophon adds, what we accept without modification.

αὕτη μὲν δὴ .. ἡ ἐν Βαβυλῶνι (φυλακὴ) τότε κατεστάθισα καὶ νῦν ἔτι οὕτως ἔχουσα διαμένει.

VII.

THE capture of Babylon was the prosperous termination of those manifold dangers with which Darius had been hitherto engrossed. His rivals now were everywhere overthrown. None of his nation could now gainsay the assertion, that Auramazda had given him the kingdom which the family he belonged to, the Akhæmenians, had been dispossessed of when Persis and Media and the other provinces revolted from Cambyses and owned Gaumáta the Magian for their king. The date of his last achievement—the 22d of the Persian Markazana, the Sivannu or Sivan of the Assyrians and Jews, in the year B. C. 516—is, therefore, the commencement of a season of calm and comparative inactivity which may fairly be regarded as that in which, as the Hebrew book Esther relates, the King Akhshurush (being probably again at Susa) remembered Vashti, her offence, and his own irrevocable decree. His sentence had been, that she should never more come into his presence and that her queenly rank should be given to another and a better than herself. Rich as he was with the pillage of Babylon, and perhaps full of the impression produced by its works of the sculptor's and the founder's art, he might now cause (as at some date or other he seems in fact to have commanded) her image in gold, to preserve and honour her memory; but, breathless, speechless, cold, that could not supply the loss of her living self.[a] Therefore (as the final clause of the decree which banished Vashti warranted them) those who waited on him in the interior of the palace suggested, that he should appoint officers in all the provinces of his kingdom to send up the fairest young maidens that might

---

[a] See Esther ii. 1, and compare Herodotus vii. 69 where it is related that Artystoné ("daughter of Cyrus," as queen, though daughter of Gobryas by birth, and identical with Vashti, according to our finding) was the best-beloved of Darius's wives, and that it was she whose image Darius caused to be wrought in gold; compare the expecting widower Admetus's promise to Alcestis; Euripid. Alcest. vv. 360–366.

be found, to the royal residence at Susa, the king's partiality for which seems to have been already declared. There, in the House of Women, in the custody of Hegai, the eunuch, they might abide; and when they had passed through the prescribed term of purification, the king might admit them to his presence and select one of them to be queen instead of Vashti. Darius acquiesced.

In Susa itself, there lived a Jew called Mordecai, a name akin to that by which the Babylonians distinguished the planet next to Saturn the remotest visible to the unaided human eye. In Roman mythology this planet was connected with the god Jupiter, whose name it still bears with us. At Babylon it was associated with the god to whom the citizens rendered their highest worship, Marduk or Merodakh. This was their Bel, who, though he occupied at first an inferior place among the Twelve gods, seems, as the greatness of Babylon grew, to have supplanted the Bel of the first triad; as Zeus among the Greeks usurped the throne of Kronos.

Mordecai was son of Jair son of Shimei son of Kish a Benjamite. This Kish from his name, from that of his son, and from his tribe, may be supposed to have belonged to the house of Mephibosheth son of Jonathan son of Saul king of Israel; and, indeed, that he was of the family of Saul is asserted by Josephus. He was one of the captives that, along with Jeconiah son of Jehoiakim king of Judah, the great Nebukhadrezzar had brought to Babylon in the eighth year, both of his sway as the king of Judah's lord and of that first captivity of Jews at Babylon which included Daniel and his companions. Thus, the great grandfather of Mordecai had shared in that second deportation of men of Judah to Babylon, which took place when Jerusalem, having revolted from her lord paramount under Jehoiakim, surrendered under his son; and the king of Babylon left her, as his under-king, Mattaniah brother of Jehoiakim, having changed his name to Zedekiah.[b]

[b] 2 Kings xxiv. 10–16. The descent of Mordecai from Kish the captive, is stated in Esth. ii. 5, 6. The clause "who had been carried away . . ." or a "Benjamite who had been carried away . . ." has been referred by

In the house of Mordecai, bred up as his own child, was his cousin Hadassah, that is Esther, the orphan daughter of his uncle Abihail.[c] Her original name by which she was known among her own people seems to have been Esther; and this appellation we would refer to the Assyrian ISHTAR, signifying "goddess" in general and the one represented by the planet Venus in particular, as on the authority of Assyrian inscriptions Sir H. C. Rawlinson undertakes to affirm. The name Hadassah or Atossa, one might suppose to have been already celebrated among the Persians, if we gave heed to fragments of Hellanicus and to a pedigree of Kappadocian kings preserved by Diodorus out of the histories of the successors of Alexander the Great. In ordinary use, perhaps, it was either Assyrian or Aramaic. In the cognate Hebrew of the children of Israel it signified "a branch of myrtle." The name may have been bestowed upon Esther when she was received by Hegai into the House of maidens, or on her introduction to the king, or, perhaps, on the promotion she attained to afterwards.

But at the time of which we now speak (after the subjugation of Babylon in the month Sivan, or about June, of the year B. C. 516) the King's decree ordering the fairest maidens in every quarter to be sent to Susa, was issued; and after a while, many such having accordingly been gathered together there in the royal mansion under keeping of Hegai, Esther also was taken from her home in the adjoining city and placed in the same eunuch's hands.[d] Josephus relates, that Babylon was the place

some commentators not to "Kish a Benjamite" or to "Kish" (in the respective cases) the person last before mentioned, but to Mordecai, the person from whom the ascent to Kish begins. By this method, which has been urged not merely as possible but as the only one admissible, we might make strange nonsense of the fifteenth verse; "Now when the turn of Esther the daughter of Abihail the uncle of Mordecai who had taken her for his own daughter, was come . . ." We might insist that the clause, "Who had taken her for his own daughter" related not to the antecedent Mordecai but to the first name of the string, "Esther."

[c] Esth. ii. 7–15. [d] Esth. ii. 8.

where the beautiful maiden was found,* and that her uncle (as he miscalls her cousin Mordecai) removed from Babylon to Susa for love of her. This tradition we may so far regard, as to believe, that Mordecai and Esther were both natives of the Khaldæan capital, whither their ancestor Kish had been transplanted from Jerusalem in B. C. 598; but that before the second revolt of the city in B. C. 518, (perhaps as shortly before as when Darius left Babylon in March B. C. 519 to proceed first to Susa and thence into Media) they had transferred their residence to Susa.

The keeper of the women was greatly pleased with Esther. Not knowing her people or her kindred, (for these particulars were naturally of little interest to him, and Mordecai, who seems to have generally kept them back in his own case, had instructed her not to divulge them⸠) the eunuch may have referred her to that part of the Babylonian population whereof she spoke the language, probably the Aramaic. He supplied her speedily with all she needed in order without delay to enter upon her twelve months of purification, or rather, perhaps, her twelve monthly purifications. Not till this term of preparation was past, could she be presented to the king.

A measure for another purpose, but of a character very similar to this of the levy of maidens for the king's house, is assigned by Herodotus to this time. In fact, one of these measures may have been subservient to the other; and both may have been carried out by the same machinery if they were not even both decreed by a single edict, combining a matter in which the king alone was concerned with one urgently required by the condition of one of the principal kingdoms of the empire. And this may have been the case, although of the two measures (or perhaps, parts of the same royal order) one was disregarded as not to his purpose by the writer of Esther, while the other, if known to Herodotus's informants, was a matter either considered not worth telling or which they gladly left in oblivion.

* Joseph. Antiq. xi. 6 § 2.   f Esth. ii. 10; iii. 4.

Dreadful sufferings had been endured by the people of Babylon, the consequence of their revolt, of their long resistance, and of their forcible capture. The desolation denounced by prophecy as finally to befall, and which, accordingly, has now long since befallen, the great city, may have seemed already imminent. In particular (as we have seen) the female population, except a generally unprolific remnant, consisting of every man's mother and a handmaid to grind his grain and make his bread, had been strangled by the revolters themselves at the beginning of the siege. Therefore, to replace these wives and daughters, Darius imposed on the surrounding nations a levy of 50,000 women; each nation having also to deliver at Babylon the portion at which it was rated. The edict was heard and obeyed; and from the supply of women thus poured into the place, were descended the Babylonians of Herodotus's time; which was that of Darius's grandson, Artaxerxes son of Xerxes.

How the imported women were assigned to their husbands our historian does not inform us. According to the usage before prevalent and which our Greek traveller thought (or perhaps affected to think) so clever, no father could dispose of his own daughter. The law took this matter out of his hands. In every ward of the city and every village of the country, the maidens of marriageable age were assembled yearly, and hurdled up together, while the men stood round them, outside the pen. Then, a crier began to put up the handsome girls, one by one, to be sold for wives to the highest bidders. When all had been disposed of, for whose charms any money could be obtained, the presiding officer next put up the ill-favoured girls, beginning with the ugliest, to be given successively each of them in marriage to the man who offered to take her for the smallest marriage portion or gratuity; all such dowries being paid out of the fund which had accrued from the sale or disposal in marriage of the good-looking damsels.

Such, by Herodotus's account, was the rule according to which till Babylon was impoverished by its revolt in

B. C. 518 and its capture in B. C. 516, the maidens, handsome or not, who had reached maturity, were married off on a particular day of every year; rich men buying the beauties, and poor husbands being purchased for the illfavoured girls.[g] To the discontinuance of the wholesome custom thus established, Herodotus attributes the prostitution which in his day was the usual manner of life, and means of subsistence, followed by the young women of Babylon.[h] It seems probable, however, that the former yearly auctions for the settlement of new-grown maidens in marriage had originated among, if they were not also always confined to, the Hamite population of the country.

VIII.

WHILE Esther at Susa was in the course of what we might figuratively term her sanctification for the presence of earth's King of kings, the House of the God of the Heavens was at last completed at Jerusalem. We have the date of this event in the book of Ezra, that illustrious man of God, who states what was the descent from Aaron

[g] See Herod. i. 196 and iii. 159.
[h] The disregard at Babylon for the chastity of wives, daughters, sisters, except as a marketable commodity, is not surprising among a people who made it a matter of religious obligation that every female among them should wait in the holy precinct of a goddess till she was able for once at least to offer to the temple treasury the price of her own whoredom; see Herod. i. 199. This estimate of female purity at Babylon is attested on the occasion of Alexander's arrival in B. C. 331 after the battle of Arbela. It is, probably, after Kleitarkhus, that Curtius tells us, v. 5; "Nihil urbis ejus corruptius moribus; nihil ad irritandas illiciendasque immodicas cupiditates instructius. Liberos conjugesque cum hospitibus stupro coire, modo pretium flagitii detur, parentes maritique patiuntur. Convivales ludi totâ Perside regibus purpuratisque cordi sunt. Babylonii maximè in vinum et quæ ebrietatem sequuntur effusi sunt. Fœminarum convivia ineuntium in principio modestus est habitus; dein summa quæque amicula exuunt, paulatimque pudorem profanant; ad ultimum (honos auribus habitus sit) ima corporum velamenta projiciunt. Nec meretricum hoc dedecus est, sed matronarum virginumque; apud quas comitas habetur vulgati corporis vilitas."

which made him a priest in Israel and describes himself, by the business of his life, as " a scribe of the words of the commandments of Jehovah, and of His statutes to Israel ; " while we find him, accordingly, styled in the commission he received from our Darius's grandson, " a scribe of the God of the Heavens."[a]

Ezra records it, that the " House was finished on the third day of the month Adar which was in the sixth year of the reign of Darius the King.[b] We cannot tell whether

---

[a] Ezra vii. 11-12.

[b] Ezra vi. 15. In the Esdras α of the Septuagint, the materials of which come chiefly from canonical books of Hebrew Scripture, at vii. 5 the date is in the same month Adar of Darius's sixth regnal year, but the day of the month is the twenty-third instead of the third. Josephus, *Antiq.* xi. 4 § 7 makes the twenty-third of Adar to be the day of the year, but he substitutes the ninth for the sixth year of Darius. In this departure from Esdras α, a book which we have found to be his authority elsewhere, Josephus seems to exhibit an element of the popular but (almost of course) erroneous calculation made by the Jews of Herodian times and alleged by them to our Lord (S. John iii. 20) that it had taken forty six years to rebuild the temple in the days of Zerubbabel and Jeshua. For nine years (assigned by Josephus as the age of Darius's reign when the temple was completed at Jerusalem) added to eight years assigned to the previous reign of Cambyses by Herodotus (who divides the months of the Magian usurper's reign between the last year of Cambyses and the first year of Darius) ; and added to twenty-nine years assigned by Herodotus to the reign of Cyrus (on the supposition that it commenced immediately after the overthrow of Astyages) amount to forty-six years. Other chronologers contrived to make up the fabulous forty-six years without corrupting Ezra's date for the completion of the temple. We find them lengthening Cyrus's supposed reign as Astyages's successor (that is, lengthening the interval between Astyages and Cambyses) from twenty-nine to thirty-one years ; and they interpolate a year for the reign of the Magian, though in fact he had no such year assigned him in Tables of Reigns ; his eight months being (as we have said) the end of the eighth of Cambyses and the beginning of the first year of Darius. But this manipulation $31+8+1+6$ gives forty-six years. The great exaggeration of the length of time that the rebuilding of the temple lasted, was due to the ignoring of a Median reign which intervened between those of Astyages and Cyrus and was described by Xenophon as the reign of Cyaxares son of Astyages, by Daniel as that of Darius the Mede the son of Akhshurush. The next step was to identify the first year of Astyages's successor with the first

it was Ezra's practice to count the regnal years of the Persian kings, like the author of the book Esther and like the prophets Haggai and Zechariah, by the Assyrian and Jewish calendar, or whether like Nehemiah, his younger contemporary, he used the method of Babylon and counted as regnal years a parcel of the years of Khaldæan tables beginning with the New-year's day next after the king's accession. However, there is no doubt arising hence as to the number of the year before the commencement of our era in which the House at Jerusalem was finished. For it is the same month Adar, whether the sixth year of Darius began with the Khaldæans on the first day of Markhesvan B. C. 516 or with the Assyrians and Jews on the first of Nisan in the same year. Only this Adar or Adarru would be the fifth month of the Khaldæan regnal year, and the twelfth month of the Assyrian. It, therefore, coincides nearly with March B. C. 515.

The House of the God of Israel being now finished, the Priests, the other Levites, and the rest of the Children of the Captivity, kept the Dedication of it with joy. In front, on the altar of burnt-offering they offered 100 bullocks, 200 rams, 400 lambs ; and also, for a sin-offering in behalf of all Israel wherever scattered, twelve he-goats, according to the number of the tribes sprung respectively from the sons of that Jacob unto whom the word of Jehovah came, saying, Israel shall be thy name.

In the following month, the first of the Assyrian calendar year as it was also of the Mosaic, the children of the captivity kept the passover on the fourteenth day of the month, according to the Law of Moses. The males of the house of Aaron, the heirs of their ancestor's priesthood, with those of the other families of the tribe of Levi, who inherited the subordinate functions of the holy ministry—not such only as belonged to the particular divisions whose turn it happened to be to serve them before God, but all who were of lawful age—purified

year of Cyrus, spoken of in Ezra i. 1 ; that is, a year which began (according to Herodotus) November B. C. 558, with a year commencing November B. C. 536 by Khaldæan registration.

themselves for duty, and killed the passover-lambs for
the general multitude, as well as for their brethren of
the sacerdotal tribe and for themselves. So, all of Israel
that were returned to their own land, whether out of the
Babylonian or perchance some of them out of the Assyrian
captivity, and together with them all such persons as,
having separated themselves by circumcision of their
males from the filthiness of the heathen of the land, had
joined themselves to the children of Israel to seek Jehovah
the God of Israel, did eat the passover. Also, they kept
the feast of Unleavened Bread with joy on the seven days
following; because Jehovah had made them joyful. For
it was by Him, their God and our's, the Only God, that
the heart of " the king of Assyria " (so they called
the present possessor, though a Persian, of all the
dominions of their old Assyrian masters) had been inclined
to favour them, and to strengthen their hands in the
work of the House which God had condescended to accept
at Jerusalem.º

They had possessed an altar of burnt-offering; the
daily sacrifices had been renewed and carried on there
continually, ever since the beginning of Tisri (as, after
the corresponding Assyrian seventh, that seventh of the
Mosaic months was called) the first month of their old
civil calendar in the year B. C. 536. This we say,
supposing the first of Cyrus recorded by Ezra to have
begun with the Nisan of that year. Otherwise, if the
regnal year be meant beginning with the first of

º See Ezra vi. 16-22. The appellation " King of Babylon " is given by
Nehemiah, xiii. 6, to our Darius's grandson, the king under whom he
as well as Ezra served the people of God. There is some evidence to
justify the view taken by Herodotus, by Xenophon in his Cyropædia,
and by others (among whom we single out Ptolemy in his Canon of
Reigns Assyrian and Mede at Babylon) that after the fall of Nineveh
and before the capture of Babylon by Cyrus, the Kings of Babylon not
only possessed Assyria and were *in fact* kings of Assyria, but sometimes
or in some parts of their empire styled themselves " kings of Assyria "
although the contemporary Hebrew writers designate them " Kings of
Babylon " or " Kings of the Khaldæans ; " see Mr Norris's article on
Assyrian and Babylonian Weights, in Journal R. A. S. vol. xvi p. 218.

Markhesvan in B. C. 536, the erection of the altar at Jerusalem by Zerubbabel and Jeshua must be referred to the first of Tisri B. C. 535. But, whether it was in B. C. 535 or B. C. 536, ever since that event they would have been justified if, for the fast in the month Tisri whereby they deplored the calamity sustained by the nation many years before in the death of Gedaliah, they had substituted a feast of joy and thankfulness on account of the returning mercy of God and the mitigation of His chastisements. Yet, till now in B. C. 515, during seven years of Cyrus, eight of Cambyses and six of Darius, for want of a Dwelling-place of God's to look to and pass into from the altar, the Mosaic services for one-and-twenty years since the termination of the seventy years' captivity at Babylon, had been very imperfectly performed at Jerusalem.[d]

[d] We remind the reader that we have noticed four distinct periods, having alike a duration of seventy years:—1. The seventy years' supremacy of Babylon, which lasted from the overthrow of Nineveh in B C. 608 till its own capture by the Medes and Persians under Cyrus in B. C. 538. 2. The seventy years' Captivity of Judah at Babylon, from the beginning of the fourth of Jehoiakim to the end of the last year assigned in the Khaldæan annals to Darius the Mede; B. C. 606–536. (These periods are both foretold by the Prophet Jeremiah.) 3. The seventy years of indignation against Jerusalem and the cities of Judah, spoken of as already past in Zechariah i. 12; the same which we suppose to have begun with the ninth year of Zedekiah king of Judah (or rather the year of Nebukhadrezzar therewith corresponding) and to have ended with the first year of Darius son of Hystaspes as reckoned at Babylon; B. C. 590–520. 4. The seventy years mentioned Zech. vii. 5 during which the fasts of the fifth and of the seventh months had been first commemorated in Israel; commencing, we suppose, with what would have been the twelfth year of Zedekiah (or rather a month later, with the year of Nebukhadrezzar at Babylon therewith corresponding) on the first of Markhesvan B. C. 587; and ending with the month Tisri B. C. 517, the end of the fourth year of Darius as reckoned at Babylon.

In a manner somewhat similar, there seem to be two periods of twenty-one years, in which the mercy of God to Judah is obstructed. These seem to be supplementary respectively to the two spaces of seventy years foretold by Jeremiah:—the first beginning (and, therefore, ending) two years before the second. These seem typified by twenty-three out of the twenty-four days of Nisan in the third year of Cyrus (Nisan B. C. 534) mentioned Dan. x. 1–4, 13. During three full

IX.

It has been related, that when many maidens had been gathered together at Shushan the palace, to the custody of Hegai, Esther was brought also unto the king's house. It is likewise to be remembered, that the maiden pleased the keeper of the women ; so that he speedily gave her every thing needed for purification, with her allowances and her appointed suite of seven maids out of the king's

weeks or twenty-one days of this time, Daniel fasted and prayed ; and on the twenty-fourth and last day he received a reply mentioning a resistance which it had encountered for one and twenty days. The years corresponding with the whole twenty-four days, seem to be two of Darius the Mede + 7 of Cyrus + 8 of Cambyses, + 7 of Darius the Persian, beginning by the Assyrian calculation with Nisan, or by the Babylonian with Markhesvan of B. C. 538. Now, in the last year of the series, the seventh of Darius son of Hystaspes, if it be reckoned to begin with Nisan B. C. 515, we have an evident declaration that obstruction is at an end, in the recommencement at Jerusalem of the services of the newly-completed Sanctuary. In the tenth month of the same Assyrian and Mosaic year, we have the marriage of Esther to the great king; and this sign may still be cited, if the twenty-fourth year of the series, the seventh regnal year of the son of Hystaspes, be reckoned (as at Babylon) from Markhesvan B. C. 515. But, as to the question, which are the two distinguishable periods of twenty-one years in this space of twenty-four years, we may say :—1. The first period of twenty-one years, beginning with the first regnal year of Darius the Mede at Babylon, ended with the fourth of Darius the Persian by Babylonian registration. It completed seventy years after and exclusive of the year by Babylonian registers in which the army of Nebukhadrezzar destroyed Jerusalem ; for at the first of Markhesvan B. C. 538, the beginning of the first year assigned to Darius the Mede, forty-nine years only had elapsed since the expiration of the one in which Jerusalem perished. And thus, it also completed a period of ninety-one years or thirteen weeks of years since Babylon began to sit as a queen, in B. C. 608. 2. The second space of twenty-one years is the one we have mentioned in the text. It was that in which the men of Judah, being returned from their captivity of seventy years at Babylon, struggled to restore the Temple of God, from Tisri B. C. 536, when the altar was rebuilt on the first of the month till the eve of that day in B. C. 515, the end of the civil year in which the Sanctuary had been finished and its services recommenced. It was a space the extremities of which were the first regnal year of Cyrus and the sixth of Darius son of Hystaspes at

45*

house. He also changed her and her maids to the best place or quarter of the House of Women. Under these circumstances we may be certain, that no time was lost before her " twelve months began according to the manner of women; " wherein, besides other things for the purifying of women, oil of myrrh was used for six months and sweet odours for six months.

" Now when every maid's turn was come to go in to King Akhshurush " after she had passed her twelve months' preparation, " then came she to the king in this manner. Whatsoever she desired was given her to go with her out of the House of Women into the King's

Babylon, and it completed a period of ninety-one years or thirteen weeks of years since the expiration of the third year of Jehoiakim king of Judah in which Jerusalem first yielded to a Babylonian conqueror.

And here, to us it seems worth remarking further, that between the close of this period and the commencement (as we calculate it) of Daniel's seventy weeks of years (that is, the first of Tisri B. C. 459) is an interval which may be measured by weeks of years no less than by years; being fifty-six years or eight weeks of years, in duration, and comprizing the last thirty years of our Darius, the twenty-one of Xerxes, and the first five of Artaxerxes Makrokheir. Moreover, the Jewish civil years from and after the one which expired with Elul in A. D. 32 (the close, by our calculation, of Daniel's seventy weeks) to the end of Elul in the present autumn of A. D. 1866, fill up 262 weeks of years exactly; whereof eighty-two extend to the end of Elul in A. D. 606. From that time or about the commencement of an apostacy in the mystical Babylon, shortly before denounced as such by Gregory the Great when it threatened to appear elsewhere, exactly 180 weeks of years have since elapsed. The 1260 years which go to these 180 weeks of years have seemed to many commentators to be the forty-two mystic months or 1260 mystic days of prophecy; and to be the whole reign of the popish apostacy at Rome, set up by Phocas the Greek emperor in A. D. 606 and about to be abandoned, as it would seem, by the Frank emperor, Napoleon in A. D. 1866. Thus, from B. C. 606 to A. D. 1866, we remark, in the history of Israel ancient and modern a series of periods consisting of weeks of years; Israel's captivity at Babylon, seventy years; struggle for the rebuilding of the Temple at Jerusalem, twenty-one years; interval before the rebuilding of the walls in the sixth year of Artaxerxes Makrokheir fifty-six years; the Seventy Week period, 490 years; the growth of the Church from the call of the Gentiles till the Roman apostacy, 574 years; Usurpation of Supremacy by the Bishops of Rome, 1260 years.

house. In the evening she went thither, and on the morrow she returned into the second House of Women; to the custody of Shaashgaz, the king's eunuch which kept the concubines. She came in unto the king no more, except the king delighted in her, and that she were called by name."

So, when it came to be Esther's turn to go in unto the king, she would not exercise her privilege of choosing whatever she desired to carry with her; " she required nothing but what Hegai the king's eunuch, the keeper of the women, appointed." Thus did she shew herself docile, unexacting, and self-controuled, on an occasion for self-indulgence which might never again be offered her, and at a moment when a desire to please the king's eunuch for the sake of future advantage could not have been a motive; inasmuch as she was not to return any more to his custody. She was ever, we may believe, no less winning by her behaviour than by the beauty which had caused her to be selected for the king at first. It is said, "Esther obtained favour in the sight of all them that looked upon her."

. Thus was Esther taken unto king Akhshurush, into his House Royal, in the tenth month, called by the Jews Tebeth, as by the Assyrians Thabitu, in the seventh year of his reign. It was the tenth month of his seventh year, according to the Jewish and (we make no doubt) the Assyrian reckoning; but it was the third month of his seventh year, by the Khaldæan account so often explained. As Tebeth is one of the five months, from Markhesvan to Adar, counted to regnal years of the same number whether Jewish or Khaldæan, no doubt as to the year before our era in which Esther was brought to the king could arise from a question whether the regnal years of the book Esther are calendar years of the Assyrians and Jews or calendar years of Babylon. This Tebeth of Khshurush Darius's seventh regnal year answered nearly to January of the year B. C. 514.*

* If we follow the indications given by Josephus and Philo, we shall place Tebeth as the month next after midwinter in the Jewish twelve-

"Then the king loved Esther above all the women; and she obtained grace and favour before him, more than all the virgins." His choice was fixed. None that had been already introduced could compare with her and after her he had no desire or curiosity to see any one who had not yet been presented. So he set the crown royal upon her head, and made her queen instead of Vashti.

We have seen all reality of mourning destroyed at Jerusalem, both at the fast of the fourth month, Thammuz, and at the fast in the fifth month, Ab, in the year B. C. 516, by the news of Darius's having taken Babylon on the twenty-first or twenty-second of the month before Thammuz. This change to joy fulfilled (as we have observed) a promise of God's, made in Khisleu B. C. 518, that their fasts, commemorating national calamities for the seventieth time in the year then recently begun, should be turned to feasts and rejoicings. Long before (as we have lately noted) even at their first return from Babylon, the month Tisri had furnished an occasion for yearly thankfulness, to balance the death of Gedaliah for which the fast in that month had been ordained. And now, the mournful memory of the month Tebeth and the fast for the commencement of the fatal siege of Jerusalem, might justly give place to joyful recollections in the years

month. According to the adaptation of the Jewish months to the Julian year preserved by Geo. Syncellus and referred to above, p. 107 note, the tenth of Tebeth was the first of January. Instead of the month Tebeth, the book Esther in the Septuagint (followed by Josephus) substitutes, "the twelfth month Adar." For the text of the Septuagint Esther, we appeal to the Roman Edition, to the Alex. MS, and to Tischendorf's MS Frid-August. The text of this last MS (a portion, it is said, of the now famous *Codex Sinaiticus*) differs as left by the first scribe, in this only, that it reads 'Αδὼς for 'Αδὰς. The correction of the text by a later but ancient hand from Origen's Hexapla, has been already cited above p. 106 note; see Tischendorf's Septuagint, ed. 1856 *in loco* and Prolegom. § 31. In the note on p. 106 there is expressed an inclination to the belief, that "the Persians began their year at the same season with the Jewish Church." We have since learnt that the Mosaic year began at the same season of the year as the Assyrian; and in latter times derived its month-names from those of the Assyrian months.

at least that followed this. That in the month Tebeth Esther became the Great King's crowned wife, was enough to make it no more a month of mourning but of gladness.

On the occasion itself, "the king made a great feast, to all his princes and his servants, even Esther's feast; and he made a release to the provinces and gave gifts according to the state of the king." Thus, not only a sense of their duty as subjects, to sympathize with the joy of the king, but the royal bounty on this occasion, when announced to the provinces, must have spread festivity throughout the empire.[b]

It seems to have been at this time and for the purpose of this feast, as well as perhaps for the preliminary ceremony of a public selection by the king of the one among so many on whom he intended to bestow the queenly crown, that (as we read) "the virgins were gathered together the second time." The record may be taken to express, that whether they had passed in their turn to the house of concubines or whether they remained still in the first house where the maidens were kept, all who had been gathered to the royal fortress at Susa from their several homes, in distant or in neighbouring provinces, were now re-assembled. If the purpose was, as we have conceived it, honour to Esther, bounty to her late

[b] Josephus follows some other authority than that of the Septuagint, when he makes the virgins 400. He is certainly incorrect in reporting the term of their purification to have been six months. He also writes of the king,

διαπέμψας τοὺς ἀγγάρους λεγομένους εἰς πᾶν ἔθνος ἱεράζειν αὐτοῖς τοὺς γάμους παραγγίλλων· αὐτὸς δὲ Πέρσας καὶ τοὺς Μήδους καὶ τοὺς πρώτους τῶν ἰθνῶν ἰστία ἐπὶ μῆνα ὅλον ὑπὲρ τῶν γάμων αὐτοῦ.

Antiq. xi. 6 § 2. Here the authority followed was acquainted with the constitution and customs of the monarchy under the Akhœmenian dynasty. It is supposable, that the feast ordained by the king was held at Jerusalem in Adar: and that hence originated the error common to Josephus and the Septuagint, of placing Esther's marriage in Adar instead of Tebeth, the twelfth instead of the tenth month of the king's seventh regnal year, as reckoned in the book Esther. The command to the provinces to make merry, is probable; Herodotus relates, that on the death of Kassandané, his consort, Cyrus made a great mourning for her, and commanded all the subjects of his empire to do the like; Herod. ii. 1.

companions, and a pompous display before the assembled people, it may further be supposed that during the days of the marriage-feast (still keeping to herself the knowledge of her nation and parentage, in obedience to Mordecai's injunction) Esther presided among those beautiful daughters of many nations from among whom the king had selected herself. For so, we remember, had Vashti formerly feasted the ladies of Persis and Media within the palace, while out of doors the throng of men, both high and low, was entertained by the king. As for Mordecai, who before the introduction of Esther to the king used to walk daily in front of the court of the House of Women for tidings of his cousin, he now took up his seat as one ready for the king's service, among those who were obliged and those who made it their duty, to wait upon the king at his gate.° According to the Septuagint

---

° After being installed in the palace at Babylon, the Cyrus of Xenophon's historical " consciousness " assembles,

τοὺς τε ὁμοτίμους (of the Persians) καὶ (of all the nations) πάντας ὅσοις ἐπίσει ἐπικαίριοι ὅσαι καὶ ἀξιχρεώτατοι αὐτῷ ἰδόκουν κοινωνοὶ εἶναι καὶ τίνων καὶ ἀγαθῶν.

Addressing them respectively as friends and allies, he says,

"Ὅτστε ἡ Πέρσαις ἐπὶ τοῖς ἀρχαίοις οἱ ὁμότιμοι διάγουσι, οὕτω καὶ ἡμᾶς φημὶ χρῆναι ἐνθάδε ὄντας τοὺς ἐντίμους πάντας ἄπερ καὶ Ἰαῦ ἐπιτηδεύειν.

Accordingly, it was resolved,

τοὺς ἐντίμους ἀεὶ ταςείναι ἐπὶ θύρας καὶ παρέχειν αὐτοὺς χρῆσθαι, ὅ,τι ἂν βούληται ἕως ἂν ἀφίῃ Κῦρος.

Then, the author, offering himself now as a witness to a contemporary matter of fact, subjoins,

'Ὃς δὲ τότε ἔδοξεν, οὕτω καὶ νῦν ἔτι ποιοῦσιν οἱ κατὰ τὴν 'Ασίαν ὑπὸ Βασιλεῖ ὄντες. Θεραπεύουσι τὰς τῶν ἀρχόντων θύρας.

Cyropæd. vii. 5 §§ 71, 85; viii 1 § 6. Xenophon further relates by what penalties Cyrus enforced this "waiting upon the Gate," as attendance there is called. Absentees were enquired for;

'Ὁπόσοι ὄντες ἱκανοὶ ἄλλων ἐργαζομένων τρέφεσθαι, μὴ παρεῖεν ἐπὶ τὰς θύρας, τούτους ἐπιζήτει ...

And here again as a witness to existing matters of fact, Xenophon adds,

ἐπιζητεῖ δὲ καὶ ὁ νῦν βασιλεὺς ἤν τις ἀπῇ οἷς τάξωσιν καθήκει.

Ibid. viii. 1 §§ 16, 20. Great decorum was enforced at the gate: ibid. §§ 33, 40–42; and, perhaps, it was only zeal for the king's service which excused the upbraiding of Oroites there in insulting terms, on account of Polycrates. Like military service, attendance at door of king or satrap was a vassal's duty. For, after that Xenophon's Pheraulas had proposed to endow his Sakan guest with all the wealth that had been bestowed upon himself by Cyrus, on condition that the Saka

version (which seems to exhibit some Targum or Paraphrase of Esther rather than the original Hebrew text of the book) the king's feast to his great men and his should maintain him at table as a guest (though in fact this was but to make the Saka his steward) he is represented as promising to get the Saka exempted both from door service and from service in war; without loss of any of the profits of service. Pheraulas tells his friend;

καὶ ἄλλα γί σοι, ὦ Σάκα, τχιοδιαστράξομαι παρὰ Κύρου, μήτε θύρας τὰς Κύρου θεραπεύειν μήτε στρατεύεσθαι. 'Αλλὰ σὺ μὲν (says he) πλουτῶν οἴκοι μένε· ἐγὼ δὲ ταῦτα ποιήσω καὶ ὑπὲρ σοῦ καὶ ὑπὲρ ἐμοῦ· καὶ ἐάν τι ἀγαθὸν προσλαμβάνω διὰ τὴν Κύρου θεραπείαν, ἦ καὶ ἀπὸ στρατείας τινὸς, εἴσω πρές σε, ἵνα ἔτι πλείονων ἄρχης μόνος, ἔφη, ἐμὲ ἀπόλυσον ταύτης τῆς ἐπιμελίας·

Ibid. viii. 3 § 47. Part of the duty of every satrap was;

ἐπίσοι ἂν γῆν καὶ ἀρχὴν λάβωσιν, ἀναγκάζειν τούτους ἐπὶ θύρας ἰέναι καὶ εὐφρεσύνης ἐπιμελουμένους ταρίχειν ἑαυτοὺς τῇ σατραπῶν χρῆσθαι ἦ τι δήπταν.

Ibid. viii. 6 § 10; also § 14. Those who owed attendance at the King's or satrap's gate, owed also military service if required of them. Indeed, it was that they might be ready to execute the king's behests, whether by head or hand, at home or abroad, that they were required to be ever in attendance.

We will conclude with some observations on the attendance at the king's gate mentioned in the book Esther, as illustrated by the language of the version or paraphrase of that book in the Septuagint. To the term of the Anglican version "*the king's gate*," answers in the Greek the term αὐλή, that is *Court*, or *Court yard;* the outer court being meant; see Esth. ii. 19, iii. 2, 3; iv. 2 *(bis)*; v. 9, 13; vi. 10, 12. But the same Greek term corresponds with the term *court* of the Anglican Version in Esther vi. 4, 5; where the outer court is meant. In Esth. iv. 11. the English phrase "*into the inner court*" answers to this in the Septuagint εἰς τὴν αὐλὴν τὴν ἐσωτέραν. But it is not surprizing that in Esth. vi. 4 for the English expression "into the outward court" we have simply ἐν τῇ αὐλῇ in the Greek. In one passage the Septuagint version is obliged to distinguish between the *Gate* and the (outer) *Court* of the king. In Esth. iv. 2 we read,

ἦλθεν ἕως τῆς πύλης (but αὐλῆς in the Alex. MS.) τοῦ βασιλέως καὶ ἔστη· οὐ γὰρ ἦν αὐτῷ ἐξὸν εἰσελθεῖν εἰς τὴν αὐλὴν σάκκον ἔχοντι καὶ σποδόν.

(as the cup-bearer Nehemiah was in danger of offending king Artaxerxes by appearing before him with a sad countenance). It is to be noted that men came to the king's gate to ask redress; Cyrop. viii 1 §§ 17, 18; or requital, as Syloson did; for here, justice was administered; Cyrop. viii. 8 § 13. According to the belief of the Greek translator (whether his work represents the Hebrew book or an Aramaic Targum of it) those who, in his phrase, ἐθεράπευον ἐν τῇ αὐλῇ, or (as Xenophon expresses it) ἐθεράπευον τὰς θύρας τοῦ βασιλέως, sat *within* the gate of the outer court of the palace at Susa. This view seems confirmed by the language of the original in Esth. iv. 2. In front of that outer court gate was a πλατεῖα, "a broad street," or a *piazza* in the proper sense of the term,

servants on this occasion, as when Vashti formerly presided among the Aryan ladies, lasted seven days. During these days, apparently, it was, that two of the eunuchs who had the office of King's Gatekeeper, conceived offence and plotted to kill their master. The Hellenist paraphrase makes envy of Mordecai's promotion the cause. But this must be a mere fancy of the later Jews, not a tradition delivered them from their fathers, the contemporaries of the events. For if the ill-will of the gate keepers had been provoked by Mordecai's presence (a piece of homage perhaps on his part rather than in any degree a sign of the king's favour to him) Mordecai should have been the aim of their revenge, not the king. However, owing to his place at the gate, Mordecai was fortunate enough, being also plainly a man of great sagacity and penetration, to discover the conspiracy. Josephus pretends that it was through a brother Jew, the servant of one of the eunuchs, that he was made acquainted with the secret. However, through Esther he communicated it to the king; who, after an enquiry by which the guilt of the two eunuchs was established, caused them to be impaled. The whole transaction was written in the book of the chronicles before the king.[d]

that is, what we call a "square." Perhaps "the court of the House of the Women" opened into the outer court of the King's House; as may Queen Esther's house or apartments, though opening also into the Garden of the palace. Into the inner court of the king's house no man might enter without a special summons, on pain of being instantly put to death, if the king did not hold out the golden sceptre for him to touch; see Esth. iv. 11; v. 1, 2; viii. 4.

[d] See Esth. ii. 23. In Esther vi. 1 (where is mentioned the reading of this record to the king during a sleepless night) the Version or Paraphrase in the Septuagint, calls it γράμματα μνημόσυνα τῶν ἡμερῶν, or λόγων τῶν ἡμερῶν, as the text is said to be corrected by a later hand in the Frid.-Aug. MS from Origen's Hexapla. Here in Esth. ii. 23, the good service of Mordecai is said to have been deposited for a memorial ἐν τῇ βασιλικῇ βιβλιοθήκῃ. By his own account Ktesias, while in the service of Arsakes Artaxerxes Mnemon, derived the history which he published after his return to Greece,

ἐκ τῶν βασιλικῶν διφθερῶν ἐν αἷς οἱ Πέρσαι τὰς παλαιὰς πράξεις κατὰ τινα νόμον εἶχον συντεταγμένας.

see Diodor. ii. 32. If he really got anything from this authentic

There, for several years, it lay unnoticed, till (on the occasion of a terrible jeopardy which threatened the whole scattered people of Israel far and near in every province of the empire) it spoke to the king and along with Esther's intercession against their enemies, it operated to a preservation which is still commemorated yearly by the Jews in their present wider dispersion upon the earth But the story of Haman son of Hammedatha the Agagite belongs to the 12th year of Darius's reign, which, according to the Assyrian calculation followed in the book Esther, began with Nisan of the year B. C. 510, whereas it is with the festival on account of Esther's marriage in the beginning of the year B. C. 514, that our undertaking is accomplished; a contribution towards the connection of ancient Israelite with ancient Gentile history.

The period is brief that we have studied; yet the result is important; if (as we think) it has been our happy lot—though in an inferior department of labour—to find the true position in history of one of the Sacred Records, and thereby (as it happens) to vindicate it alike from that absolute denial of its historical character which some critics have pronounced, and from the perhaps more insulting treatment which others have thought necessary, when (in order only to misapply it) they have perverted or ignored its testimony in the chief particulars. It is now found consistent in all respects with the rest of the extant history of the reign it refers to, without having suffered violence in its statements as to either time, place,

---

source, we may be sure that it related to times then recent; and probably, was obtained at second-hand, as from some eunuch's report of what he professed to have heard recited by the king's reader or *munshi*, διδάσκαλος. For instead of ἐπὶ τῷ διακόνῳ αὐτοῦ, "he commanded his waiting-man" in Esth. vi. 1, the Alex. and Frid. Aug. MSS have ἐπὶ τῷ διδασκάλῳ αὐτοῦ. With the Greek word διφθέρα, *a skin*, Sir William Ouseley connects *defter*, which in modern Persian means "a register." *Travels*, vol. 2, p. 353 note.

character, or incident. Viewed, too, as following the fall of Babylon and the restoration of the House of God at Jerusalem, the Marriage of Esther may by some students of Revelation be suspected to possess a typical and prophetic as well as an historical value; so that while it belongs to the past, it may at the same time darkly exhibit a phase in the future condition of the Church of God.

APPENDIX.

I.

Notes on the Comparative Table of Descents.

WE promised this article of our Appendix, in a note at the foot of page 91, opposite to which page, the Table is placed. The reader who hardly otherwise than by skips may have attended us thus far, will permit us to be more brief than we had proposed to be.

A.

However, on the Descent of the kings of Egypt of Manetho's 26th Dynasty, exhibited in the first column of our Table from Nekho the First to that Psammenitus son of Amasis who was conquered by Cambyses the Persian, the reader cannot be satisfied without some justification of so obscure a portion of history.

The authorities which have furnished the means for compiling this genealogy are, 1. *Herodotus* from ii. 152 to iii. 15. 2. *Manetho* (or *Manethoth* the Egyptian) as represented by the two chronologers, Africanus and Eusebius, whose statements are preserved by Georgius the Syncellus. (We have used Dindorf's edition published at Bonn in 1829). 3. *Egyptian monuments*, whose evidence we owe principally to Sir J. G. Wilkinson in the Notes and Appendix furnished to the Euterpè in Rawlinson's Herodotus. 4. *The Annals of Assurbanipal* son of Esarhaddon king of Assyria, as reported by Sir H. C. Rawlinson, 14 Aug. 1860 to the Athenæum. 5. *Diodorus* also has been used; and 6, a *List of the kings of Egypt*, 86 in number, from Mestraim or Menes to Amôsis (Amasis) and the conquest of Egypt by Cambyses in the fifth year of his reign, given from time to time in sixteen sets, by the Syncellus (vol. 1 pp. 170-397). But only in the case of one out of six kings of the 26th dynasty have we found this table correct in the number of regnal years. Diodorus (to whom we owe an important confirmation of the date of the conquest of Egypt by Cambyses) gives the lengths of the reigns of Amasis and Apries only; and gives them wrong.

The eight years' reign of the first Nekhao or Nekho we obtain from Manetho through both Africanus and Eusebius. See Geo. Syncellus, vol. 1 pp. 141, 143. And the same number is given him in the List of 86 kings; Syncell. vol. 1 p. 396.

The 54 years' reign of Psammitikhus, Psammetikus, or Psametik, we obtain from Herodotus ii. 157; from Africanus's not Eusebius's Manetho; and from Wilkinson's assertion, that one of the Apis stelæ (whose depository was discovered by M. Mariette) records this king's 54th year; see Sir J. G. Wilkinson's note on Herod. ii. 157 and his Appendix, chap. 8 § 33, vol. 2 p. 381 of Rawlinson's Herodotus.

The 16 years of Nekho the Second we obtain from Herod. ii. 159 and from monumental evidence. The six years, instead of sixteen, assigned by Manetho (according to both Africanus and Eusebius) look like a transcriber's error, omitting the *iota*. The monumental evidence is in particular that of an Apis stela, which (according to Wilkinson in Rawlinson's Herod. vol. 2 p. 385) states that an Apis born in the 16th year of Nekho, was consecrated at Memphis at the end of the first year of Psametik (the Second, called by Herodotus, Psammis) and died in the 12th year of Apries, aged almost 18 years. Another stela of Psametik a priest, in the Egyptian Museum at Florence (numbered 2551 in Migliarini's Guide to that Museum) also negatives six years and confirms 16 as the length of Nekho the Second's reign. But we will cite it under the reign of Apries.

The six years of Psammis or Psametik the Second (called Psammuthis, by Manetho and in the List of 86 Egyptian kings) are assigned him on the authority of Herod. ii. 161 and of Africanus' not Eusebius's Manetho and are fully confirmed by the Apis stela already mentioned; which records a bull born in the 16th year of Nekho and dying, when nearly 18 years old, in the 12th year of Apries.

The 18 years of Apries or Hophra, the Vaphris of Manetho, these (followed, perhaps, by a 19th year which by right was his too, but in which he was defeated by Amasis and lived a prisoner in his own house at Sais; Herod. ii. 169; and which, after he had been put to death, was counted the first regnal year of Amasis) are assigned in our table to Apries on existing monumental evidence; namely, that of the stela at Florence named above under Nekho, and that of a Leyden monument. Beginning with the Florence monumental inscription, it will be necessary to furnish the reader, with the varying accounts that have fallen into our way, as well as with our criticism and determination thereon. According to Wilkinson in Rawlinson's Herodotus vol. 2 p. 381, it "reckons only 71 years 4 months and 8 days from (a certain point in) the 35th year of Amasis (back) to (a certain point in) the 3d of Neco." Now from this account it becomes probable (but only probable) that Apries reigned 18 years. For the difference between the 16 years, we know that Nekho reigned in all, and the more than two years of his reign that had elapsed at the beginning of the period of 71 years and more, the term of a certain life, is 13 years and more. If now, to this difference, forming the earliest section of the life, we add the 6 years already proved to have constituted the reign of Nekho's successor, Psammis or Psametik the 2d, in Egyptian Tables of years; and also add the 34 years and more which the life lasted after the reign of Amasis was counted to have begun, we get 53 years and more. And this deducted from the whole life of 71 years and more, leaves for the part of the life given by Egyptian Tables to the reign of Apries, probably 18 years; because certainly the length assigned to a reign in Tables of years distributed into reigns, was never either a fraction of a year or a term compounded of a year or years and some excess, the fraction of another year.

A minuter account of this monument (given at p. 21 of Migliarini's Guide to the Egyptian Museum at Florence, published in 1859) is this: "2551. Stèle en grès. Adoration, accompli par mari et femme avec un enfant, à Osiris, dans son naos, à Thoth et autres dieux (perdus par la fracture de la pierre). L' inscription qui suit porte des dates chronologiques précieuses; et grace aux recherches des savants, elles nous ont fourni des éclaircissements, très utiles pour l' histoire ancienne, touchant l' epoque. L' année 3me, le 1er du mois *Epep* sous le regne de Nechao [ii] (609 ans avant notre ère) est enregistrée la naissance du prêtre Psammétik. Après on trouve fixée la durée de sa vie, 71 ans 4 mois et 6 jours; étant mort l' année 35me le 6 du mois de *Paini*, sous le regne d' Amasis . . ." Now the month *Epep* was the 11th and the month *Paoni* the 10th of the year, according to the Egyptian Calendar given by Wilkinson in chap. 1 of his Appendix to the Euterpē, vol. 2 p. 283 of Rawlinson's Herodotus. See also above, our list of Egyptian months in *Table A*, which fronts p. 431 of this volume. Now, according to these particulars the reign of Apries would seem to have had 17 years and about 5 months allotted to it. But this reign, as well as every other in the Egyptian registers of years, was expressed by a single number of years, not by the compound of years and parts of a year. The account, then, of the stela at Florence in Migliarini's Guide must be inaccurate.

Accordingly, we have found a different account in a learned edition of Manetho's Remains, occupying pages 511–616 of the *Fragmenta Historic. Græcorum* edited by Carl Muller for the Paris Publisher A. F. Didot. At p. 594 we read as follows; "Scilicet stelâ funebri (v. Rosselini, tom. ii. p. 150; Bœckh. p. 345; Bunsen, iii. p. 143) Florentinâ Psammetichus quidam natus esse dicitur Nechoi anno tertio, *Paoni (i. e.* mensis decimi) die primo; vixisse 71 annos 4 menses 6 dies; mortuus esse Aahmi regis anno trigesimo quinto, ac quidem anni hujus mense (secundo) *Paopi* ejusque die secundo." We have here the measure of the whole life, confirming Migliarini's report and less by two days than Wilkinson's account. But we have for the birth-day, the first of *Paoni* (the 10th month) instead of Migliarini's first of *Epep* (the 11th month) and for the death-day, we have the 2d of *Paopi* (the 2d month) instead of Migliarini's 6th of *Paini* (the tenth month). And the results will now be quite satisfactory.

Therefore, according to Carl Muller's account of the inscription on this stela, the part of the deceased's life spent under Nekho, including his birth-day, was 13 years 3 months and another small fraction of the 3d year, the 5 days supplementary at the end of the birth-year. The years following under Psammis or Psametik the 2d, were 6, as we have proved already; and the latter part of his life, after Apries was replaced by Amasis, was 34 years 1 month and 1 day, exclusive of the day of death. Hence it appears, that the number of years assigned to the reign of Apries in the Tables used by the authors of the inscription, after the death of the person it records, was 18. For this is the exact difference between the sum of the parts of the lifetime assigned to the reigns of Nekho, Psammis, and Amasis (that is, 53 years 4 months 6 days) and the measure of the whole life, that is 71 years 4 months and 6 days.

From this proof supplied by the Florentine stela, we pass to the other furnished by a Leyden inscription, the account of which we owe to the same commentary by Carl Muller on Manetho's 26th Dynasty, which supplied us with the best report of the inscription at Florence. Our commentator writes thus *(Fragm. Hist. Græc.* vol. 2 p. 594 col. 2) " Porro in duabus stelis Leidensibus inscripta hæc sunt. Psammetichus, Ochubeni filius, vixit 65 annos 10 menses 2 dies. Natus est die primo Epiphi mensis (undecimi) anno primo regis Nechai. Mortuus est die vigesimo octavo Pharmuthi mensis (secundi) anno vigesimo septimo (sc. regis Amasis)" But here for *secundi* we must read *octavi;* for Pharmuthi was the 8th month; see Wilkinson in Rawlinson's Herodotus vol. 2 p. 282. It is an error of the press; for the author in the argument he founds upon the statement we have cited, treats the month of death as the eighth month of the 27th regnal year of Amasis. Let us now see what was the length of the reign of Apries according to this Leyden stela. Dying the 28th day of the 8th month of the 27th year of Amasis, the person commemorated had lived under Amasis 26 years 7 months and 27 days, exclusive of the death day. Born the first day of the 11th month of the first year of Nekho (that is, born 10 months after the beginning of the 16 regnal years of Nekho) he had lived under Nekho the last 15 years of that king and the last 2 months and 5 days (supplementary) of the first year of Nekho. Of the intervening reigns, those of Psammis and Apries, that of Psammis it has been already shewn numbered 6 years. Therefore, the Tables used by the author of the inscription, assigned to Apries a reign of 18 years. For, the sum of the days spent by the deceased in regnal years of Nekho, Psammis, and Amasis, being 47 years 10 months 2 days, if deducted from the whole lifetime (65 years 10 months 2 days) leaves exactly 18 years. It is certain, then, that the Tables of years used in the reign of Amasis (or at least in the latter part of his reign) assigned 18 years only to Apries.

But according to Africanus's report, oftener faithful than that of Eusebius, Manetho gave to Apries a reign of 19 years; while not only Eusebius, but Herodotus at ii. 161 assigns him 25 years. Now when we consider Manetho's description as reported by both Africanus and Eusebius, of the king placed by them in the 26th dynasty between the second Nekho and Apries, that is, Ψάμμουθις ἕτερος, "another Psammuthis," while the former king to whom allusion at first would seem to be made in this description of the second Psametik of the monuments, had been called by both reproducers of Manetho (according to Georgius Syncellus) not Psammuthis but Psammetikhus, we are inclined to conjecture the original statement of Manetho to have been one that recognized the third Psametik of the monuments, saying, "After Nekho (or, as Africanus and Eusebius report the name, Nekhao) the 2d, Psammuthis reigned for six years, then Apries for 19 years, and *another Psammuthis for 6 years*, altogether 25 years." Thus, while we suppose (as we intimated at first) that Manetho's 19th year of Apries represents the year in which Apries was defeated and captured by Amasis and was permitted for a while to survive a prisoner in his own house at Sais, we take the next six years, making up the 25 ascribed to him by Herodotus and Eusebius, to be the reign of the third Psametik at Thebes; who by his wife *Neith-akri (i. e.* Nitokris) as Sir J. G. Wilkinson informs us on the authority of monuments still existing at Thebes (see Rawlinson's Herodotus vol. 2 p. 387) was son of Psametik the 2d and was brother of Apries, while (by a daughter of his) he was father of Amasis. The relationship of this Psametik the 3d to Apries, calls to mind that of Neriglissar to Evil Merodakh at Babylon; while his relationship to Amasis recalls to mind that of the Mede Cyaxares the 2d (Darius the Mede) to Cyrus the Persian. And, as in Ptolemy's Canon we find the two years of Darius the Mede counted to his successor Cyrus, so we suppose the years of Psametik the 3d along with the nineteenth year of Apries to have been counted (after his death) as the earlier ones of the 44 of Amasis. If Amasis reigned alone for the last 37 years only of the 44 years ascribed to his reign, the first year of his sole reign will be that which in Ptolemy's Canon is the last of Nebukhadrezzar king of Babylon, whose vassal we may suppose Apries to have been at the time of his dethronement, considering the prophecy of Nebukhadrezzar's conquest of Egypt delivered on the first of Nisan B. C. 571 (Ezek. xxix. 17–19). For the last year given to Nebukhadrezzar in the Canon is the Egyptian year E. N. 186; and this, as it may be learnt from the sequel of this discourse, was the 8th from the beginning or the 37th from the end of the 44 years of Amasis.

These 44 years are assigned in our Table to Amasis (or Amôsis) on the authority of Herodotus iii. 10 and of Africanus' not Eusebius's Manetho. And the same is confirmed by monumental evidences; for (according to Sir J. G. Wilkinson) the 44th year of Aahmes or Ames (that is, Amôsis) is a date in inscriptions that still exist; see his note on Herod. iii. 10.

Six months are assigned in our Table to Psammenitus, on the authority of Herod. iii. 14 and of Africanus's Manetho. He is left out of Manetho's 26th dynasty by Eusebius; nor have any monuments been found bearing his name; into the composition of which (according to Wilkinson) *Neith* enters, the name of the goddess of his royal city, Sais, in whose temple-court was buried both Amasis (who, Wilkinson says, had the title *Neith-se* or " Son of Neith ") and also his predecessors of the 26th dynasty; see Wilkinson on Herod. iii. 10. Africanus's Manetho according to the MSS of the Syncellus, calls him, Ψαμμιχεϱίτης, *Psammekherites*, and it might be dreamt that this name contains in it that of the sixth Egyptian month, Mekhir, the Μιχιϱ and Μιχιιϱ of MSS of the Syncellus's work (vol. 1 p. 13) the month (as we calculate) in which Psammenitus was captured by Cambyses.

For, as to the six months that Psammenitus or Psammekberites reigned, they were undoubtedly the first six months of the Calendar Egyptian year in which Amasis died and he himself succeeded to the throne; for (after the method pursued in Ptolemy's Canon) that Calendar year was counted his first regnal year. It was the year in which Cambyses had thought to find Amasis still on the throne; but, when he led his invading army into Egypt, he found Amasis dead; he defeated Psammenitus the son and successor of Amasis in a great battle; and after a siege, he took both Memphis the capital city of Lower Egypt and the person of king Psammenitus; no doubt before *high Nile*. Now, according to Manetho (as represented by Eusebius at least), it was in the 5th year of Cambyses that the Persian conquered Egypt. Moreover, Manetho's evidence as reported by Africanus seems to be in reality the same in this point as that of Eusebius. For the ἔτει of Africanus in Dindorf's Syncellus (ed. 1829) vol. 1 p. 141 line 17 seem to be a misprint for ἔτει i the reading of Eusebius. Goar's Latin version has "quinto anno," and we are not warned by a note that the reading of Goar's Greek text was ἔτει i but that one or both of the Paris MSS (used for the emendation of the text by Dindorf) give ἔτει i. Moreover, that ἔτει i was the reading of the old text, appears from its being found in Routh's Africanus; see Routh *Reliq. Sacræ*, vol. 2 p. 147 ed. 1814. This also is the reading at p. 596 vol. 2 of the edition of Manetho's remains in the *Fragmenta Hist. Græcorum*. The same fifth year of Cambyses, occurring as the date of the conquest of Egypt by the Persians in Geo. Syncell. vol. 1 p. 397, seems taken from a document already noticed (exhibiting a list of 86 kings of Egypt from Mencs to Cambyses) his 16th and last extract from which, the Syncellus had just given. According to Ptolemy's Canon, the fifth year of Cambyses was the year E. N. 223, the first month of which, Thoth, began at midnight with the 2d day of January in the year B. C. 525, and its sixth month, Mekhir, ended (6 × 30═) 180 days afterwards; on the 30th of June. We suppose, then, that Memphis was taken and king Psammenitus became the Persian's bondsman, in June B. C. 525, and that is before the annual Nile-flood. As all the previous Egyptian dates exhibited in our Table depend upon this, we will add that Eusebius elsewhere (quoted by Clinton) not only assumes Cambyses to have made himself master of Egypt in his fifth regnal year, but withal places the event in the 3d year of the 63d period of four full years which began with the Olympic games; his expression being; " *Ol.* 63. 3, Cambyses obtinuit Ægyptum anno quinto regni sui." Now, this Olympic year began with the moon of which the full was the first after midsummer-day B. C. (776–62½ × 4, or 250 years═) 526; for, in the first year of every four, the games were celebrated during the five days next after the 10th of this moon, (see Bœckh on Pindar's scholiast, Olymp. iii. 35. referred to in the article *Olympia* from the pen of the editor of Dr. Smith's " Dictionary of Greek and Roman Antiquities," 2d Edit.) and we may venture, perhaps, to ascribe this time of the games as the third *five-day week* of the particular moon. Well, the Olympic year specified by Eusebius. which began thus about Midsummer B. C. 526, ended likewise about Midsummer B. C. 525; and it is the latter half of it which coincides nearly with the first half of the year E. N. 223, the fifth regnal year of Cambyses according to Ptolemy's Canon. To Diodorus also (i. 68) we are referred by Clinton for a corroboration of Eusebius. Diodorus says, that Amasis died what time Cambyses king of the Persians made his expedition against Egypt, in the 3rd year of the 63d Olympiad, the festival at which Parmenides of Camarina won the foot-race. It may be remarked, that the position in the Egyptian annals of this great epoch, the Persian conquest, was easy for the Greeks to obtain out of Egyptian Tables of years and reigns, and had in fact become well known to the Greeks of Alexandria in the time of the Ptolemæan dynasty. Accordingly, Diodorus gives it in a place where he does not appear to have been obliged in any degree by his subject to hazard an assertion for which he had not very good authority. Of his tenth book, which contained the history of Cambyses and where the date of his conquest of Egypt might justly be called for, fragments only remain, whereof one or two only concern Cambyses.

For the nature of the succession in the 26th dynasty, between the first Nekho and Apries, that it is a descent from father to son; also, for the fact, that Psammenitus was son of Amasis, we are indebted to Herodotus. The connection between Amasis and the preceding king Apries, by a wife of Amasis who was daughter of that Psametik the 3d who reigned at Thebes and whose wife Neith-akri was sister to Apries, is given us by Sir J. G. Wilkinson on monumental evidence, in Rawlinson's Herodotus vol. 2 p. 387.

If, then, as we have concluded, the reign of Psammenitus was counted to begin with the first day of the 223d revolution of a circle of 365 days from mid-day the 26th of February B. C. 747; that is, if it began at midnight with the 2d of January B. C. 525; then, the reign of Amasis was computed to have begun with the first day of Thoth E. N. (223—44==) 179 or at midnight with the 13th of January B. C. (525+44==) 569; the reign of Apries, with the first day of Thoth E. N. (179—18==) 161; or mid-day 17th January B. C. (569+18==) 587; the reign of Psametik the 2d, with 1st of Thoth E. N. (161—6==) 155 or at midnight with the 19th of January B. C. (587+6==) 593; the reign of Nekho the 2d, with the first of Thoth E. N. (155—16==) 139 or at midnight with the 23d January B. C. (593+16==) 609; the reign of Psametik 1st, with the first day of Thoth E. N. (139—54==) 85 or mid-day 5th Feb. B. C. (609+54==) 663; and lastly, the reign of Nekho the First or his sub-kingship in a district of Lower Egypt, with the 1st of Thoth E. N. (85—8==) 77; or mid-day 7th Feb. B. C. (663+8==) 671.

Thus, have we shewn the evidence on which the dates in the Egyptian column of our "Comparative Table" have been given. It will be observed, however, that the last date now mentioned, or the earliest in the Table, the commencement of the reign of Nekho 1st, stands on evidence inferior to that by which all the subsequent dates are established.

This father of Psametik the 1st, in the 21st year of the reign of his son, the year E. N. 105, beginning 31 Jan. B. C. 643, was not counted by that son's subjects the priests at Memphis to have been the predecessor of his son upon the throne. For (according to Sir J. G. Wilkinson in Rawlinson's Herod. vol. 2 p. 380) an Apis stela testifies, that a sacred bull born in the 26th year of Tehrak, died in the 21st year of Psametik aged 21 years; the reign of Tehrak having continued only ten months and four days after the birth of this Apis. If, then, at the time in Psametik's reign when the bull died, Tehrak was held to have been the last preceding king, it is clear the eight years assigned by Manetho to Psametik's father Nekho, also the six years ascribed to Nekho's predecessor, Nekhepsô, and the seven years of Nekhepsô's predecessor, Stephinates, the first Saite of the 26th dynasty, were regnal years of Egypt in which Tarkus or Tarakus, the last of the three Ethiopians who fill Manetho's 25th dynasty, was the real king of Egypt in the estimation of the highest Egyptian authorities of the year B. C. 643. The 26 years, ascribed to *Tehrak* by the Apis stela and placed immediately before the reign of Psametik, began, therefore, with the first day of Thoth E. N. (85—26==) 59, or at midnight with the 12th of February B. C. (663+26==) 689; about ten years after the encounter within the Syrian border between the forces of Tirhaqah king of Kush (that is, Ethiopia) and those of the Assyrian Sennacherib

(2 Kings xix. 9 ; Isai. xxxvii. 9) at which time the second Shebek (called by Manetho, Sebikhôs son of Sabakôn) must have been the Ethiopian on the throne of Egypt.

It would appear from the annals of Assurbanipal king of Assyria, who (if his father Esarhaddon be intended by the Assaradinus king of Babylon in Ptolemy's Canon) came to the throne B. N. 81, or in B. C. 667, that his father Esarhaddon had over-run Egypt, had driven out the unnamed Ethiopian master of the country, and had established rulers in the various Nomes or districts of both Upper and Lower Egypt, who were called kings and depended immediately upon the king of Assyria. These nomarkhs or district-kings, however, were afterwards put down by the Ethiopian king *Tarku*; to punish whom, Assurbanipal at the very beginning of his reign led his forces against Egypt. He found Tarku in Memphis, and drove him to Thebes, called by him *Ni'a* or *No* as in Scripture. He re-established the petty kings in the several sections of the land, twenty in all; the first of whom is no other than Psametik's father, "Niku king of Mimpi and Tsai:" while the last is "Mantimi-ankhé king of Ni'a," or No. He then withdrew from the country, having regulated the tributes that were to be paid him by the kings. But these afterwards rose against the garrisons that the king of Assyria had left in Memphis and Thebes. Tarku re-entered Egypt from Ethiopia. Both Niku and another nomarkh of Lower Egypt, Pakruru ruler of Pi-sebet, (that is, Pi-beseth or Bubastis) are mentioned in the struggle that followed, in which the Assyrian leaders are said to have suppressed the insurrection. Sir H. C. Rawlinson (from whose account in the Athenæum of Assurbanipal's annals these particulars have been taken) remarks, that the 20 provincial kings represent the Dodecarchy of Herodotus, and we find Sir J. G. Wilkinson previously regarding the same Dodecarchy or Twelve-king administration (of Lower Egypt) as a government subordinate to the king of Ethiopia. Both are probably right: though the mode of administration is only noticed by Herodotus as existing after the departure of the Ethiopian at the end of fifty years; a sum equivalent, as it happens, to the total of the 26 years given by the Apis stela to the last Ethiopian Tehrak and the 24 years divided equally by Eusebius's Manetho between the two Sabakos. Rawlinson understands Assurbanipal to say, that Niku had a share in the revolt of the states of Egypt from the Assyrian, but Herodotus, ii. 152, relates that he was put to death by Sabakôs the Ethiopian king, and that thereupon, his son Psametik fled into Syria, that is, beyond the border of Egypt and within the Assyrian empire. It is true, that though there were three Ethiopian kings, Herodotus has but one name for them all, Sabakôs, who both conquered Egypt at first, and at last after a reign of 50 years voluntarily retired from the country. If Niku was slain by the Ethiopian king, he was certainly slain not by Sabakôs, either the father or the son, but by the Tarkus of Manetho, the Tarku of the

Assyrian annals, the Tehrak of Egyptian monuments. The execution of Niku and flight of his son into Syria, shew clearly enough both how the governor of Memphis and Sais was looked upon by Tehrak, and that the Ethiopian at last recovered Egypt from the Assyrians. The return of Niku's son into Egypt, there to become one of the Twelve kings by whom Lower Egypt at least was jointly governed, is dated by Herodotus on the retirement, induced by a dream, of the Ethiopian who had put his father to death ; and he was brought back by those of the Saite nome ; Herod. ii. 152, 151. When he was again obliged to take shelter in the marshlands of the Delta, suspected by his eleven colleagues of aspiring to be sole ruler of the country, it may be hard to say, whether his treason was to the eleven, as Herodotus thought, or to a distant suzerain, either Ethiopian, or, as we should say, Assyrian. The monuments attest that (at a later time of his life, perhaps) he had for wife a daughter of an Ethiopian king called Pionkhe, and of Queen Araunatis who ruled at Napata, the chief Ethiopian city of the time, under "the sacred mountain," now called Gebel Berkal ; see Sir J. G. W. in Rawlinson's Herodotus vol. 2 p. 381. This fact may be taken for proof sufficient, that, ultimately at least, he was acknowledged by the Ethiopian to be his brother the king of Egypt. Also, the fact owned during his own reign, that Tehrak (the Ethiopian) was his immediate predecessor, seems to urge the conclusion that, after Tehrak's death or resignation of the government, Psametik having (either then or previously) aspired to become king instead of nomarkh, and having had to fly to the marshlands in consequence, ultimately compassed his desire ; and that afterwards, his regnal years were counted (whatever the interval may have been before he really became king) as if they had followed those of Tehrak without dispute or interruption.

The story told by Herodotus, that this king captured Azotus (Ashdod) a great city of (Philistine) Syria, after a siege of nine and twenty years (Herod. ii. 157) looks like the distortion of a much more credible fact that, having been at war with the Assyrians by whom the Philistine country was occupied, from the beginning of his reign, at last in his 29th year he made himself master of Azotus. The 29th of Psametik would seem from our Table to be the last but one of the reign of Phraortes the first king of the Medes, who became a formidable neighbour to Assyria; though he miscarried at last: Herod. i. 102. It was some six or seven years at the least after this supposed date of the capture of Azotus, when the Scythians (Herod. i. 105) by whose aid the Assyrians had lately vanquished Cyaxares son of Phraortes king of the Medes, and seem to have recovered for a while their dominion in Asia, marching against Egypt, were met by Psametik within the border of Syria, and were induced by gifts and fair speeches to retire. Yet the temple which they pillaged on their way as they went off by Askalon, being nearer to Egypt than Ashdod, may have been situate within the range of Psametik's acquisitions in Syria; though the Assyrians might seem to have been still in possession of Gaza (Kadytis) the southernmost of the Philistine cities, if we believed, as Herodotus tells us, that it was taken by Psametik's son, Nekho, in consequence of a victory which he gained over the Syrians in Magdolus. But, as Herodotus has probably substituted a defeat of the Syrians at Migdol or Magdolus on the confines of Egypt for the defeat of Josiah king of Judah "at Megiddo; " " in the valley of Megiddo," that is (apparently) in the valley of the river Kishon, two or three marches from the northernmost Philistine city, so he seems to have substituted Kadytis (that is, Gaza) for Karkemish on the Euphrates, Nekho's object, which the king after his victory probably obtained, or Jerusalem which certainly fell into his power ; see Herod. ii. 159 ; 2 Kings xxiii. 29-35, 2 Chron. xxxv. 20-24. xxxvi. 3, 4. For Migdol or Magdolus, see Exod. xiv. 2, Jerem. xlvi. 14 (or in the Septuagint xxvi. 14) Ezek. xxix. 10, and xxx. 6 as translated in the Septuagint. For Megiddo, see "Lands of the Bible" vol. 2 p. 86 where the author Dr Wilson remarks, that the Waters of Megiddo in Judg. v. 19 probably mean the Kishon, now called *Makatt'a*. Nekho certainly advanced after his victory as far as Riblah in the land of Hamath ; 2 Kings xxiii. 33. Herodotus (or rather his informants) whom we suppose mistaken in the geography of Nekho's wars, certainly erred in dating them later in his reign than his digging of the canal from the Nile to the Red Sea; for it will be seen from our Table that his first expedition to Karkemish was in the very first year of his reign B. C. 609 and his second (when his enemy was no longer the Assyrian but the Chaldæan inheritor of the power of fallen Nineveh, and when he suffered a great defeat) was in B. C. 605, the fifth of his reign ; see Jerem. xlvi. 2. It may be a trivial observation suggested by the Table, that Astyages king of the Medes and Nekho's son Psametik the 2d, began to reign in the same year; but it is not such to remark that Psametik the 2d, was succeeded by Apries, that is, by Pharaoh-hophra, in the very year when Jerusalem was at last taken and destroyed by Nebukhadrezzar ; because it suggests that the sudden retreat of the Egyptian army and the resumption of the siege of Jerusalem by the Chaldæans, who had abandoned it on the approach of the Egyptians, may have been connected with the death of the Egyptian king ; see Jeremiah xxxvii. 5-15 ; xxxiv. 21, 22. We will say no more of the reign of Apries than this ; That his sea-fight with "the Tyrian," and his expedition against Sidon, if accurately ascribed to him by Herodotus ii. 161 must have happened during the reign of Eithobal king of Tyre, when Nebukhadrezzar besieged Tyre for 13 years according to the Phœnician annals of Philostratus cited by Josephus, *cont. Apion.* i. 21 and *Antiq.* x. 11. For, after Tyre (the old Tyre on the mainland) was taken by Nebukhadrezzar, Apries was invaded about B. C. 571 ; see Ezek. xxix. 17-20, Jerem. xliv. 30, xliii. 10, xlvi, 13, 26. And in B. C. 569 it appears from the Table, he was a prisoner in the hands of Amasis: while, divided apparently for a time between Amasis and Psametik the 3d, the latter reigning in Upper Egypt and Amasis in the Lower, the whole country came into a state of vassalage to Babylon.

On the remaining personages of this column, mention will be made in the second article of this Appendix, "On the position in Persian History of the 28th, 29th, and 30th, Egyptian dynasties."

B.

As to the succeeding columns of our Table, the reader is given to understand, by a note added to the Table itself, that Ptolemy's Canon of Reigns is the authority for all the dates in the Column of *Kings of Babylon;* for the dates of the reigns of Cyrus the 3d and Cambyses the 3d, in the Column of *Median Kings;* and for the dates in the column of *Persian Kings,* attached all of them to reigns following that of Cambyses the 3d, and like his, like his father's, and like those of the kings in the second column, reigns at Babylon belonging to Ptolemy's List. An inaccuracy in this statement shall be noticed in the next section to this. (Section C.)

The relationships or consanguinities exhibited in our column of (Native) kings of Babylon, are warranted for the first four kings by the Khaldæan historian Berosus, as cited by Josephus *Antiq.* xi. 11 and *cont. Apion.* i. 19, 20. In the same passages, Berosus confirms the Canon of Ptolemy as to the length of each of these reigns and also of that of Nabonnedus (the Nabunita or Nabunahita of the monuments) who in the Canon is named Nabonadius. These five numerical particulars are found in the second column of Ptolemy's Canon, the column of Years of the Reigns; where also each of them stands, on the same line from left to right with the king it belongs to in Ptolemy's first column; the column of Kings. The Canon will be exhibited below in Article iii. of this Appendix.

That Nebukhadrezzar was son of Nabopolassar, is also established by existing monumental evidence. Nebukhadrezzar king of Babylon calls himself eldest son of Nabopolassar king of Babylon, on a Cylinder now in the British Museum, which was found by Mr W. K. Loftus at Senkereh, in the ruin of the Temple of the Sun, and a copy of which in the Roman character with an English translation and notes is given by Mr H. Fox Talbot in the R. A. S.'s Journal vol. xix. pp. 187–192. Also, Nebukhadrezzar makes a similar assertion on the Birs Nimrud Cylinders, obtained by Sir H. C. Rawlinson, and given in Roman character with English translation and notes by Mr H. F. Talbot in the Journal R. A. S. vol. xviii. pp. 35–52.

That Evil-Merodakh (mentioned 2 Kings xxv. 27 and Jerem. lii. 31) was a son, and that Belshazzar (whose reign is recorded by Daniel) was a son's son, of Nebukhadrezzar, is intimated by Jeremiah, at xxvii. 7, where it is related how having ordered the prophet to preface his words with a parable in dumb-shew, making bonds and yokes, putting them on his neck; and then taking them off and sending them to the king of Edom, the king of Moab, the king of Ammon, the king of Tyre, and the king of Zidon, by the hand of messengers that had come from those kings to Zedekiah (Nebukhadrezzar's vassal, who had rebelled or was purposing rebellion at Jerusalem) God dictated a message to be added from Himself, the God of Israel, Who had made the earth with the man and the beast that are upon it, and had given it to whomsoever it seemed meet to Him, that He now had given all these countries into the hand of Nebukhadrezzar king of Babylon His servant, and that all nations thereof were to serve Nebukhadrezzar and his son and his son's son until the very end of his land should come.

This evidence, however, would not be sufficient alone to establish the relationship of either Evil-Merodakh or Belshazzar to Nebukhadrezzar. But in the case of Evil-Merodakh, we have the positive testimony of Berosus, already referred to, that he was the son as well as the successor of Nebukhadrezzar. And Berosus in this and his other statements of relationship, is confirmed as we shall see by Abydenus.

But that Belshazzar is referred to in the term, "son's son" of the passage above cited from Jeremiah, might be disputed with the greater force, because (in a passage already referred to) Berosus records that Evil-Merodakh's sister's husband Neriglissar murdered Evil-Merodakh, succeeded him on the throne, reigned (as Ptolemy's Canon likewise testifies) four years, and left the throne to his son Laborosoarkhod; who in fact (till on whatever occasion he was beaten to death by the courtiers) occupied it for nine months, though no year was assigned him in Tables of Years and Reigns at Babylon. For Laborosoarkhod may be presumed to have been son of Neriglissar by his wife, the sister of Evil-Merodakh, in which case the boy would be by his mother, grandson of Nebukhadrezzar; and might, perhaps, even be not incorrectly called his son's son; Neriglissar his father, being perhaps considered to have been made by his marriage a son of Nebukhadrezzar. (Note, that Neriglissar was, perhaps, the son of a person who had filled Nebukhadrezzar's place for seven years during Nebukhadrezzar's abasement to the mental condition of a brute animal; for, in inscriptions of his he calls himself son of *Bil-zikkar-iskun king of Babylon*; see G. Rawlinson's Herodotus vol. 1 p. 518).

On what authority, then, have we in our Comparative Table of Descents exhibited Belshazzar as son of a son of Nebukhadrezzar's, probably Evil-Merodakh, by a queen Nitokris, afterwards wife of Nabonnedus or Nabanita?

It is well known, that before certain late discoveries of monumental evidence, the statement joined in by Berosus and by Ptolemy's Canon on the one hand and the Book of the Prophet Daniel on the other, seemed to offer us irreconcilable facts. The former evidence omitted all mention of Belshazzar and stated that, on the murder of Laborosoarkhod, the conspirators met and invested a certain Babylonian named Nabonnedus, one of their number, with the royal authority, and that he exercised it till, in the 17th year of his reign, Cyrus the Persian invaded the country; whereupon Nabonnedus, having been defeated in battle, took refuge in Borsippa and on the capture of Babylon by Cyrus, surrendered himself with his stronghold to the conqueror, by whom he was well treated and sent away to spend the rest of his days in Karmania. On the other hand, according to Daniel (chap. v) Belshazzar was the king of Babylon when what Jeremiah calls "the very end of Nebukhadrezzar's land " arrived, and the kingdom was given into the hands of the Medes and Persians. We are told that he was giving a great feast when the sentence of God was declared; that he was slain the same night; and that Darius the Mede took the kingdom. That the place of the feast and of Belshazzar's death was Babylon, appears, perhaps from all the circumstances, but certainly from this; that among the vessels of gold upon the banquet table, were those that Nebukhadrezzar had brought out of the temple of the God of Israel at Jerusalem and had deposited in the temple (of Bel) at Babylon; Compare Daniel v. 2 with Ezra i. 7; v. 14; vi. 5. Therefore, since not only the names are different but the fortunes also of Nabonnedus and Belshazzar, (the latter slain in the capture of Babylon, the other surviving that event,) we cannot, without violence to the evidence, identify Belshazzar with Nabonnedus; though Josephus did so of old, and Prideaux has done the same in modern times; see Joseph. *Antiq.* x. 12, and Prideaux's, " Connection of the history of the Old and New Testament," vol. 1 p. 158 ed. 1820. Moreover, the special particular in which Daniel's Belshazzar differs from the Nabonnedus of Berosus, is attested by Xenophon *Cyrop.* vii. 5 §§ 28–30 where he describes minutely how the king of Babylon was slain in that night of banqueting within, when Cyrus at the head of the Medes and Persians surprized the city and won it from the confederates.

Nevertheless, it was impossible with due regard for the testimony of the witnesses concerning the end of Belshazzar's reign and the end of that of Nabonnedus, to separate the time of the one reign from the time of the other; the first and third years of which appear as dates of visions of Daniel (in Dan. vii. 1 and Dan. viii. 1). This, however, has been attempted; e. g. in the document (a corrupted edition of Ptolemy's Canon) preserved by Geo. Syncellus under the name of the Ecclesiastical Canon, where Belshazzar is identified with Neriglissar, while Nabonnedus, Astyages, Darius son of Ahasuerus and Artaxerxes are made to be one and the same person ; see Geo. Syncell. ed. Dindorf. vol. 1 p. 393. But the two kings manifestly jostled one another in the same period at Babylon.

To wait for fresh evidence before deciding on the reconciliation of Daniel's narrative with that of Berosus and others, was all that remained for fair and prudent men to do. Nevertheless, to deal with the difficulty, as with the Gordian Knot, by refusing credence to one or other of the seemingly opposite accounts, was a more congenial course to many. Besides, such hasty decision would have been accounted bigotry in those only who being persuaded of the Hebrew prophet's credibility, might be so rash as to reject the Khaldæan evidence. For to have discarded Daniel's story as unworthy of attention, being only that of one of the Church's prophets, might be regarded in a certain boastful school which enjoys great credit in the literary world, as a laudable freedom from prejudice or a piece of Philosophic Liberality. But after all, what would have happened? Stores are accumulated of disinterred relics of Assyria and Babylon. Among these are numerous records of Nabonnedus's reign, which, for a while, indeed, might delight us by their confirmation of the premises at least of our rationalistic argument, "There was a Nabonnedus; therefore, there never was a Belshazzar." But by and bye, to our confusion out come four cylinders from their several holes within the solid brickwork of the four corners of an old Khaldæan ruin at the place now called Muqeyer or Mugheir. The prisons which had preserved them so long, were broken open, and they were brought forth in triumph to be placed in the British Museum by Mr J. E. Taylor; and the reader may find the single inscription repeated for safety's sake on all the cylinders, still more likely to survive the vicissitudes of time, as long as men shall live upon the earth, by its transliteration into the Roman character, and its appearing with an English Version and Notes (the work of Mr H. Fox Talbot) in the R. A. S.'s Journal vol. xix. pp. 193–198, (to say nothing of the copies in paper and print of the cuneiform text itself, which we believe the authorities of the British Museum have issued to the world). For the discovery of the cylinders by Mr. Taylor, see the R. A. S.'s Journal vol. xv. pp. 263, 264. Inscribed upon them are words of Nabunita, Nabo-Nid, or Nabunahid; the Nabonnedus, Labynetus, or Nabonadius of Berosus, Herodotus, and Ptolemy's Canon. He commemorates in the first of two columns of inscription, his rebuilding of the structure in which the cylinders were deposited; a temple-tower dedicated to the Moon-god and reared at first in the earliest period of the Khaldæan monarchy. The second and last column is a prayer to the god whose name was *San* or *Sin*: (compare Sir H. C. Rawlinson's account of this god in his brother's Herodotus, vol. 1 pp. 614–618). After other petitions come the following, according to Mr Talbot's translation; "And as for me, Nabo-Nid king of Babylon; preserve thou me in the pure faith of thy great divinity: Give me abundance of length of days, even to overflowing! And to *Bel-sar-ussur*, my eldest son, my rising hope, fix firmly in his heart the awe of thy great divinity!"

Belshazzar, then, was the eldest son of Nabonnedus, or at least was so entitled. But it seems to be an honour not commonly given to a son, to be introduced by name into such a prayer, as the king's partner in the benefits for which the god that has been propitiated is solicited.

Having, then, adduced an unexceptionable contemporary testimony that there was a Belshazzar as related by Daniel, no less than a Nabonnedus as attested by Berosus and others, who lived at one and the same time in the kingdom of Babylon, we would now proceed to infer, as it has been generally inferred by others from the narrative of Daniel (in Dan. v. 2, 11, 13, 18, 22) that Belshazzar may safely be regarded as a son or grandson of the great Nebukhadrezzar. We do not here adduce as a proof of the same, either Jerem. xxvii. 7 already quoted, or 2 Chron. xxxvi. 20 (perhaps written by Ezra) where it is said that what the sword had left when Jerusalem was taken and destroyed, Nebukhadrezzar carried away to Babylon where they were servants to him and his sons till the reign of the kingdom of Persia. Confining ourselves here to the passage indicated of the book of Daniel, we find Nebukhadrezzar repeatedly called Belshazzar's father, alike by the writer of the narrative and by personages he introduces; and we find Belshazzar once called son of Nebukhadrezzar. The narrator calls Nebukhadrezzar Belshazzar's father, in beginning the story; and of the personages concerned in the action of it, we have first the queen entering the banquet-house where Belshazzar with his wives and concubines had been feasting and drinking wine before a thousand of his lords, but where all were now in terror and confusion because there had appeared fingers of a man's hand, and they had written words over against the candlestick on the plaister of the wall, such as the wise men of Babylon, having been called in immediately, had been unable to read and interpret. She quiets the king's fears, and counsels him to call in one Daniel, who, for the spirit of divine wisdom that was in him, "King Nebukhadrezzar thy father" (said she to Belshazzar) "made master of the magicians, astrologers, Khaldæans, and soothsayers," naming him Belteshazzar. Next, we read how Daniel was brought in before the king, "and the king spake and said unto Daniel; Art thou that Daniel of the children of the captivity of Judah, whom the king my father brought out of Jewry?" And presently after, he reiterates to Daniel a promise which he had already made in vain to the wise men of Babylon; "Now, if thou canst read the writing and make known to me the interpretation thereof, thou shalt be clothed with scarlet and a chain of gold about thy neck, and thou shalt be the third ruler in the kingdom." Apparently, there was already in the kingdom a second ruler. Thus the Queen calls Nebukhadrezzar the king's father; the king himself calls Nebukhadrezzar his father; and now in his replies we shall see that Daniel does no less.

He declines the gifts, he promises to read the writing to the king and to make known to him the interpretation. He goes on to say; "O thou king, the most high God gave Nebukhadrezzar thy father a kingdom and majesty and glory and honour." He describes the greatness of Nebukhadrezzar's majesty and power. He adds; "But when his heart was lifted up and his mind hardened to deal proudly, he was made to come down from his kingly throne and they took his glory from him; and he was driven from the sons of men, and his heart was made like the beasts, and his dwelling was with the wild asses; and they fed him with grass like oxen, and his body was wet with the dew of heaven, till he knew that the Most High God ruled in the kingdom of men and that He appointeth over it whomsoever He will. And thou, his son, O Belshazzar, hast not humbled thine heart, though thou knewest all this..." We have cited enough.

Now, if Belshazzar, whom Nabonnedus calls his son, was Nebukhadrezzar's grandson, it was not through Nabonnedus. For we are expressly told by Abydenus, in his work upon the Assyrians, quoted by Eusebius *Præp. Evang.* ix. 41 that they appointed to be king *Nabannidokhus* (so he calls Nabonnedus, for he is not merely repeating Berosus) although this Nabannidokhus was in no way related to his predecessor, that is, Neriglissar's son Laborosoarkhod: and that, when Cyrus took Babylon, he bestowed upon Nabannidokhus the government of Karmania. In thus describing Nabonnedus as unconnected with the royal family, Abydenus does but express plainly what Berosus (as already cited) certainly intimates. The same is confirmed by cuneiform inscriptions in which Nabonnedus appears as himself a king but not as the son of a king of Babylon; only of one in high office. See G. Rawlinson's *Herodotus* vol. 1 p. 520 note.

But was Belshazzar *through his mother* Nebukhadrezzar's son or son's son? It seems to be his mother who presents herself to us in the shape of that Queen recorded by Daniel, who enters the banqueting-house, amid the general alarm, and advises king Belshazzar to call in a man to solve the mystery, who had been promoted above all the wise men of Babylon by the king's father because "the spirit of the Holy Gods was in him." She who thus tells Belshazzar what Nebukhadrezzar his father had done, is distinguished broadly from the king's wives and concubines who had been sharers in his feast; see Dan. v. 3, 23. She is greater than a wife; she is older and wiser than a wife of Belshazzar; she is the Queen. She cannot, then, be any other than Belshazzar's mother; the Queen Daniel shews us, is the Queen-mother.

Was Belshazzar's mother, then, a daughter of Nebukhadrezzar, married to Nabonnedus? Married to Nabonnedus she may have been, but she can hardly have been Nebukhadrezzar's daughter, or surely Berosus and Abydenus would have mentioned this connection in the case of Nabonnedus as they had in the case of Neriglissar. For Berosus's very particular account of this, and all the relationships in our 2d column, for which we have cited him, is sufficiently confirmed by Abydenus, in the passage of Eusebius lately referred to. Abydenus describes Neriglissar as the *ανδρωσις*, or "connexion by marriage," of Evil-Merodakh; whereas he immediately describes Nabonnedus as not in any way connected with Laborosoarkhod, *τροσήκοντά οἱ οὐδέν*. He cannot have known him to be Laborosoarkhod's uncle by marriage, his mother's sister's husband.

But we know who Belshazzar's mother was. She was Herodotus's Queen Nitokris, to whom he assigns works attributed by the Khaldæan historian to Nabonnedus, and bricks of which still bear Nabonnedus's name. For Herodotus i. 188, tells us, that it was against *this queen's son* that Cyrus waged the war in which he took Babylon. Moreover, Herodotus calls Labynetus (that is, Nabonnedus) *the father* of this same king, the son of Nitokris; thus confirming the cylinder above-cited of Nabonnedus, and explaining the fact that Berosus ascribes to Nabonnedus the very works which he for his part had ascribed to Nitokris. It is, indeed, by no means surprizing that Berosus should ascribe them to the husband; but the degree of surprize that may be felt at their being attributed by Herodotus to the wife, will presently be removed when we find, that there was a respect in which Nitokris commanded a higher degree of honour and regard from the Babylonians than could her husband Labynetus.

Yet this Nitokris, Belshazzar's mother (we have already given reason for believing) was not a daughter of Nebukhadrezzar's; and, therefore it was not on account of her birth that she stood higher than her husband in the estimate of the people. And now, we confirm this negative conclusion by observing, that she is proved by her name to have been an Egyptian princess by birth. Herodotus himself remarks (ii. 100) that the name of a female sovereign once read to him by the priests in Egypt out of a catalogue of their kings, was the same as that of the Babylonian queen Nitokris. This Egyptian queen was placed by Manetho (according to Africanus and Eusebius) in his 6th Dynasty and described by him as a spirited and beautiful woman, the builder of the third Pyramid. Africanus makes her the sixth and last sovereign that ruled at Memphis of this dynasty; see Geo. Syncellus ed. Dindorf. vol. i. pp. 108, 109. She is also found as the 22d on a list of 38 "kings of them of Thebes" which bit by bit, as he proceeds, the Syncellus transcribes for us out of Apollodorus [ἡ] χρονικὴ, this last having borrowed it from Eratosthenes, who said he got his knowledge from Egyptian records through the temple scribes or professors of hieratic writing, ἱερογραμματεῖς, at Diospolis (Thebes) and translated it by the king's command out of Egyptian into Greek. See Geo. Syncell. vol. 1 p. 195 and pp. 171 and 279. In this document, the name Nitokris is stated to signify 'Αθηνᾶ Νικηφόρος. Lastly, the same early female sovereign is attested by the Turin Papyrus where she is named *Neitakri*. See in G. Rawlinson's Herodotus, Sir J. G. Wilkinson's note on Herod. ii. 100, where he exhibits her two hieroglyphic name-shields, adding; "There was another Nitokris of the 26th dynasty, written *Neitakri* with the usual name of the goddess Neith " (as an element in it) .... "The name is perfectly Egyptian .." The Nitôkris of Manetho's sixth dynasty is related by Herodotus to have been placed upon the throne of a brother that his subjects had put to death. By Eratosthenes she is described as ruling "instead of her husband." According to

Egyptian law, the same person might be both her brother and her husband. He had reigned but one year, according both to Manetho and Eratosthenes, who, however, call him by different names. Manetho calls him Menthesûphis and makes him to have been the 2d of that name in the same dynasty. The description of his wife or sister Nitokris seems to indicate some admixture at least of foreign blood. She was ξανθή τὴν χροιάν, and may have been born of a fair complexioned mother: comp. Genes. xii. 10–20. This description of her complexion, added to the feat of having built the third pyramid, is suggested to have occasioned the confusion with a certain Rhodopis, celebrated as a courtezan in Egypt in the time of Amasis; see Herod. ii. 134, 135 and notes of Sir J. G. Wilkinson. According to Wilkinson, there are monuments which shew this dynasty of Memphite kings (Manetho's sixth Egyptian dynasty) to have been contemporary with another, Manetho's 11th, which was ruling in the Thebaid; as well as with Manetho's 7th, 8th, 9th, and 10th dynasties, which were ruling in other parts of Egypt. Further, the predecessor of Nitokris's late husband or brother, is stated in a papyrus (according to Brugsch) to have been censured by one of those kings of the Thebaid for favouring the Shepherd invaders, (perhaps, we should rather say, immigrants and intruders). See Wilkinson in G. Rawlinson's Herodotus vol. 2 pp. 347, 348.

Nitokris, then, the wife of the ruler of Babylon, Nabonnedus or Labynetus, and the mother of Bel-sar-ussur or Belshazzar, is proved by her name to have been of Egyptian parentage. How, then, can Belshazzar be son or son's son to Nebukhadrezzar, as we should conclude from Daniel and Jeremiah, if neither his father nor his mother belonged to Nebukhadrezzar's family? The only answer appears to be this. He must have been either the son of Nabonnedus by a former wife, a daughter of Nebukhadrezzar's, or the son of a former husband of Nitôkris—whether a son of Nebukhadrezzar's or Nebukhadrezzar himself. But that Nabonnedus before his marriage with Nitokris had received in marriage any daughter of Nebukhadrezzar's, is a supposition contradicted (as we have seen already) by the conduct of Berosus and Abydenus, who, while they lay stress on the fact that Neriglissar, Evil-Merodakh's successor, had married a daughter of Nebukhadrezzar's, say immediately with equal emphasis, that Nabonnedus was unconnected with his predecessor Nebukhadrezzar's grandson, Laborosoarkhod. It remains, then, that Nitokris was the widow either of Nebukhadrezzar or of a son of Nebukhadrezzar's, and that by that former marriage she was already the mother of Belshazzar at the time when she became the wife of Nabonnedus or Labynetus. As to her parentage, we cannot help suspecting strongly, not merely that she was of the Egyptian royal family (which will probably be conceded) but further, (what we find also Sir J. G. Wilkinson apparently inclined to believe) that she was the daughter of Apries, said to have been sent to his Asiatic suzerain by Amasis; see Herod. iii. 1-3. This daughter of Apries was, it is true, according to the story, called Nitêtis. On the other hand, the name Nitôkris, or rather *Neith-akri*, is found in the family of Apries: it had belonged to a sister of his, the wife of that third Psametik, who during the earlier years of the reign of Amasis appears to have been Nebukhadrezzar's deputy-king in Upper Egypt; see Wilkinson in G. Rawlinson's Herodotus, vol. 2 p. 387. In both the names—Nitetis no less than Nitokris—the name of the great goddess of Sais, the patroness of the 26th dynasty, is the principal element; and the two are at least not more dissimilar than are (for instance) the appellations given by Herodotus and Manetho to the father of Apries, from that which the monuments give him. Nitetis is as near to Nitokris as either Psammis or Psammûthis to Psametik.

Nebukhadrezzar, who invaded Apries and pillaged Egypt not earlier than 1 Nisan B. C. 571, may have carried off Nitokris among his trophies, or she may have been sent to him afterwards, when Apries had been superseded by Amasis in the Lower country and by Psametik the 3d in Upper Egypt, in B. C. 569. She may have been given by the conqueror to his son Evil-Merodakh as the daughter of Alyattes king of Lydia was required by Cyaxares king of the Medes for his son Astyages, or as a daughter of Cyaxares was asked by Nabopolassar, the last king of Nineveh's deputy on the throne of Babylon, for his son Nebukhadrezzar. Belshazzar's birth can hardly be placed before B. C. 568, or after the last year of Evil-Merodakh B. C. 560. After the death of Evil-Merodakh and the succession of the murderer, his sister's husband, to the throne, the widow of Evil-Merodakh may have been glad to embrace the protection to herself and child which a marriage with one of the powerful nobility of Babylon might afford. And when, a few years afterwards, the nobles, and her new husband Nabonnedus among them, put Neriglissar's son and successor out of the way of her son Belshazzar's recovery of his father's throne, the selection of Nabonnedus, as the person by whom the royal authority was to be administered immediately, may have been due in part at least to his marriage with Nitokris. As mother of Nebukhadrezzar's heir, during the childhood at least of her son, Nitokris, especially if a woman of much natural capacity, would be very generally regarded (at least in the capital) as her husband Nabonnedus's superior, a new Semiramis. His true position seems to result from a comparison of his inscriptions where he styles himself king of Babylon, with the narrative already cited from the book of Daniel where the place of second ruler in the kingdom is indicated as existing and filled by some one who could not be removed. We suppose, then, that Nabonnedus was but second king; yet that, supported by his consort, he was in possession of almost all the regal power outside of Babylon, while Nitokris swayed her son within the capital.

We hope, we have now shewn cause for entirely dissenting from an opinion thus expressed in Rawlinson's Herodotus vol. 1 p. 520 note; "The theories which regard Nitokris as the wife of Evil Merodach (Wesseling *ad Herod.* i. 185) or of Nebukhadnezzar (Heeren, *As. Nat.* vol. ii. p. 179, Eng. Trans; Niebuhr, *Lectures on Anc. Hist.* vol. i. p. 37; Clinton, F. H. vol. i. p. 279 note) are devoid of any sure foundation." Good grounds, it is hoped, have been shewn to exist for the belief, that the famous consort of Labynetus or Nabonnedus, was Belshazzar's mother by a former husband; and that this husband, if not (which is possible) Nebukhadrezzar himself, must have been a son of his, most probably Evil-Merodakh.

We have cited Herodotus to prove the fact, that Nitokris was the mother of that ruler of the Assyrian (*i. e.* Chaldæo-Assyrian) empire who was attacked in Babylon by Cyrus; and to prove also the fact, that she was wife of Nabonnedus or Labynetus. It would not be quite fair to leave unnoticed some other propositions, either intimated or expressly asserted by Herodotus, in respect of Nitokris, her husband, and her son.

1. The historian evinces pretty plainly his belief that Nitokris was a widowed mother when the works he attributes to her were being constructed at Babylon. Now, she was, indeed, all the while the widow of Belshazzar's father but not (as our historian naturally concluded) of Labynetus.

2. Again, Herodotus i. 188 affirms that the son of Nitokris was named Labynetus like his father. This is only his own inference, (but an erroneous one) from two facts, which we believe as well as he did, first, That Belshazzar's father was then dead; and, second, that there was one in power named Labynetus when Cyrus attacked Babylon. The Labynetus, however, then in power was neither the son of Nitokris nor his natural father, but his step-father, the second husband of Nitokris.

3. But this second husband of Nitokris is rightly recognized by Herodotus i. 77 as alive and in power at Babylon at an earlier date, when the Lydian Crœsus and his capital were taken by Cyrus. In the story of Crœsus he had told us that when, after the indecisive battle with Cyrus, fought beyond the river Halys, the Lydian king returned to Sardis, intending after the approaching winter was past, to renew his invasion with a larger army, he despatched heralds not only to the Lacedæmonians but to the Egyptians, with whose "king" Amasis he had sworn a league before he entered into alliance with the Lacedæmonians, and also to the Babylonians whose "tyrant" was Labynetus; the heralds were charged to warn these confederates to be at Sardis in the fifth month from that time. But as soon as this was done and his army, so far as it consisted of troops hired from abroad, was dismissed, Cyrus appeared at the head of his army; the Lydians mustered but were defeated, and Sardis was taken after the siege of a fortnight. Now, Herodotus relates that this, according to the Delphian answer to the complaint of Crœsus, happened three years after the predestined time

on account of the presents sent by Crœsus to Delphi when he first consulted the oracle ; see Herod. i. 91 : he also (as we understand his narrative) places the year of the capture of Sardis two years more, that is (3+2=) five years in all, after the reign began of the monarch substituted for Astyages on the throne of the Medes ; see Herod. i. 45. Now, the 29 years' interval reckoned by Herodotus, i. 214, between the reigns of Astyages and Cambyses son of Cyrus, will begin (according to Ptolemy's Canon) with the year E. N. (219—29=)190 or about 10 Jan. B. C. 558. The year also in which Crœsus sent to Delphi, being the third of the reign after that of Astyages (compare the above-cited Herod. i. 45, and 91) will be E. N. 192, beginning 8 Jan. B. C. 556. And this conclusion is sufficiently confirmed by the authority of the Parian Marble, which placed Crœsus's mission to Delphi in the archonship at Athens of Euthydemus, 292 years before the archonship at Athens of Diognetus which began Midsummer B. C. 264, that is, in a year beginning Midsummer B. C. 556 as does the first year of the 56th Olympiad ; see the Parian Marble in the *Fragmenta Historic. Græcorum* tom. 1. p. 549. Lastly, the year in which Sardis was taken (or fifth year of Astyages's successor and third year from the mission of Crœsus) will be E. N. 194 B. C. 554 and the 3d year of the 56th Olympiad just before winter. Now, at this time (according to Ptolemy's Canon) Nabonadius or Nabonedus was already king of Babylon, the first of his 17 years being identified with E. N. 193, commencing 8 January B. C. 555. We remark in conclusion, that no more opposition is intended by Herodotus betwixt king and tyrant in the case of Amasis and Labynetus (Herod. i. 77) than in that of Astyages and Cyaxares, Herod. i. 72.

4. The last passage we have to notice of Herodotus, touching this subject of Nitokris, Labynetus, and the son of Nitokris, is Herod. i. 75 ; where, telling how the Cilician and the Babylonian acted as arbitrators between Cyaxares the Mede and Alyattes the Lydian, after their battle had been stopped by an eclipse of the sun, he names the Babylonian, Labynetus. This is clearly a mistake. The king of Babylon at that time was Nebukhadrezzar son of Nabopolassar. For, according to Herodotus himself (Herod. i. 107, 130) Cyaxares's reign of 40 years extended to B. C. (558+35=)593 or E. N. (190—35=) 155, the first year of his son and successor Astyages, and the 12th year of Nebukhadrezzar's 43 years' reign as Nabopolassar's successor. We have contended in the R. A. S.'s Journal vol. xviii. on " Ptolemy's Chronology of Babylonian reigns," that the eclipse was the one in the forenoon of 18 May B. C. 603, being the 6th year after the fall of Nineveh in B. C. 608 and the 28th year of the absence of the Scythians on service in Asia, which was 22 years under the Assyrians and 6 years under the Lydians ; borrowing the number 6 from Herod. i. 74 ; the number 28 from Herod. i. 106 and iv. 1 ; and the number 22 from Herod. i. 130 where to make up 150, the years to be added to 128 are 22. But

the fact attested by Herodotus, that Cyaxares was king of the Medes when the eclipse happened, proves that the eclipse of May B. C. 585 was not the one (as some have contended) which led to the arbitration of the kings of Cilicia and Babylon between the contending kings of the Lydians and of the Medes.

Since the identification of Belshazzar given in this section was written, we have found Mr Talbot, in his notes on the last sentence of the inscription on the four cylinders extracted from the four corners of the second story of the temple tower at Mugheir, referring to "the great inscription of Nabonidus col. 2. line 27, where the king prays the gods to bless his son," (Belshazzar). Perhaps this "great inscription" is the one on "the fragments of the barrel cylinder" found by Mr Taylor while excavating a mass of fallen rubbish at top of the first story of the same temple-tower; see Journal R. A. S. vol. xv. pp. 202, 203.

C.

A NOTE added to the comparative Table itself, and cited at the beginning of the Section preceding this, (sect. B.) gives the reader to understand that, not only the regnal years of Cambyses the 3d, in the column of Median kings, and those of his successors, in the column of Persian kings, but the regnal years of his father, the Great Cyrus, are taken from the Canon of Ptolemy. But this is not exact. The truth is, that the interval of nine years between those assigned in the Canon to Nabonadius and those assigned to Cambyses (the third of the name in our Table) is given there entirely to the Great Cyrus, as the same space of nine years was also given him by Berosus; see a fragment of the account derived from Berosus by Alexander Polyhistor, preserved in the Armenian Eusebius, ed. Mai, and thence transferred to the *Fragmenta Histor. Græc.* t. ii. pp. 504, 505 where we read; "Regnavit autem Babylone Cyrus annis novem, donec in planitie Daharum alio prælio conserto periit. Tunc imperium tenuit Cambyses annis octo. Deinde Darius annis sex et triginta. Deinde Xerxes cæterique Persarum reges." Whereas, we have divided those nine years, assigning the first two of them to a Mede by whom Cyrus was preceded, whose name is omitted in the Canon and by Berosus but who is called in our Table Cyaxares the 2d. To Cyrus we have given the seven remaining years only; and for that allotment, we plead not only the arithmetical argument derived from the fact, that seventy years preceded the reign of Cyrus, of which 45 belong to Nebukhadrezzar, 2 to Evil Merodakh, 4 to Neriglissar, and 17 to Nabonnedus, but we refer the reader to the authority of Xenophon *Cyrop.* xviii. 7 § 1 a passage which we have commented on, above pp. 252–254. But we do not find like authority for the space we have given to Cyrus's predecessor, called by Xenophon, "Cyaxares son of Astyages," by Josephus, *Antiq.* x. 11 § 4, "Darius son of Astyages," and in the book of Daniel, "Darius son of Akhshurush of the seed of the Medes." We must have been trusting to memory and speaking without book, when formerly we named Josephus as a witness to the two years during which this king was master of the kingdom of Babylon.

The reader will also observe in regard to our Comparative Table, that the 29 years' interval between Astyages and Cambyses son of Cyrus, described by Herodotus i. 214 as the reign of Cyrus, is by us divided between Darius or Cyaxares son of Astyages, and his nephew who succeeded him, Cyrus. That he preceded Cyrus on the Median throne, we are convinced by the books of Daniel and Ezra (the passage of the latter book to which we refer, Ezra vi. 2-3, has been commented on, above p. 244) also by the Cyropædia of Xenophon and by Josephus. When he succeeded his father in B. C. 558, the seat of his kingdom was of course Agbatana: and, even after the capture of Babylon by the Medes and Persians, when he succeeded to the throne of Supreme King, for the short time that he survived, he may have continued, during the greater part of the year at least, to reside at the Median capital. Indeed, it is in Media that Josephus places Daniel's presidency and the lions' den; *Antiq.* x. 11 §§ 4-7; and he proceeds to ascribe to Daniel a certain beautiful building at Agbatana of wonderful construction, looking still as fresh as ever, where they buried the Median, Persian, and Parthian kings down to his days; the person in charge of it being a Jewish Priest. He calls it βᾶριν, saying ᾠκοδόμησεν ἐν 'Εκβατάνοις τοῖς Μηδικοῖς βᾶριν and θάπτουσι δ' ἐν τῇ βάρει. One cannot think that the royal fortress built by Deiokes (see above pp. 568, 569) could in Josephus's time either be fresh-looking or be ascribed to Daniel. This seems intended in 1 Esdras vi. 23 and Joseph. *Antiq.* xi. 4 § 6, where we read οἰκίθη ἐν 'Εκβατάνοις τῇ βάρει τῇ ἐν Μηδίᾳ χώρᾳ. Nor can Daniel's βᾶρις be the palace afterwards built under the fort: see above p. 567. One might rather liken it to a burial-tower of the Parsis (Zoroastrians) of India. In reference to the continued residence of the Mede at Agbatana, it may be observed that this is Xenophon's representation also.

For the lengths of the preceding Median reigns, we follow Herodotus. As to Astyages and his 35 years, see Herod. i. 107-130. As to Cyaxares the first, and his 40 years, "including those of the Scythian dominion," σὺν ταῖσι Σκύθαι ἦξαν, Herod. i. 103-105; also 73, 74; As to Phraortes and his 22 years, Herod. i. 102; as to Deiokes and his 53 years, Herod. i. 90-102. For the whole 128 years during which the Medes bore rule, πάρεξ ἢ ὅσον οἱ Σκύθαι ἦρχον, i. e. " *exclusively* of the Scythian rule" of 22 years, see Herod. i. 130.

The first year of Cambyses being adjusted in Ptolemy's Canon to the year E. N. 219 beginning 2 January B. C. 529, the year of Egyptian registers in which Cyrus died and he succeeded, the first years of the several preceding kings will be found according to the same rule, by the adding to the year B. C. 529, and the subtracting from the year E. N. 219, of the intermediate regnal years.

These same reigns, however, when adjusted to Khaldœan Tables of Years, would appear to begin about ten months later. For from Herodotus iii. 66, 67, 68 and from the Behistun Inscription (as interpreted in matter of month-dates by the lately discovered Assyrian Calendar containing the Assyrian as well as the old Khaldœan monthnames) we have learnt that the 8 years ascribed to Cambyses, by Berosus in a passage lately quoted and by Ptolemy in the Canon, concluded with a space of seven months during which the Magian was king, and the last of which was the month called Tasritu or Tisri by the Assyrians and Jews, say, October B. C. 521. Consequently, by this reckoning, the first year of Cambyses began with the first of Markhesvan (say, 1 Nov.) B. C. 529. Whereas (as we have seen by Ptolemy's Canon) the eight years of Cambyses were the years E. N. 219-226, beginning the first of the Egyptian month Thoth, or 2 January B. C. 529 and ending with the last of the five supplementary days, the 31st of December B. C. 522. Therefore, the reigns preceding that of Cambyses must also, by the Khaldœan reckoning, have commenced with the Markhesvan next after the commencement of the Egyptian year of Nabonassar to which the first year of each reign would have to be adjusted on the rule of Ptolemy's Canon. For instance, the reign of Deiokes will begin with the first day of the Assyrian Markhesvan instead of the first day of the Egyptian Thoth, (that is, with about the first of the Roman November instead of the 10th of the Roman February) B. C. 708 or E. N. 40; see above pp. 433-435, 427, and Table B. which fronts p. 431.

As to Darius the Mede the son of Akhshurush, exhibited to us by Daniel as the predecessor of Cyrus, and who stands in our Table as he is named by Xenophon, Cyaxares son of Astyages; we have observed that Josephus (who remarks, by the way, that the Greeks gave him another name) calls him Darius son of Astyages. This identification of Astyages with the Akhshurush of Dan. ix. 1, is countenanced by the last verse of the Book Tobit, where it is said of Tobit's son Tobias, that " before he died, he heard of the destruction of Nineveh, which was taken captive by Nabukhodonosor and Asuerus (or Ahasuerus) and he rejoiced over Nineveh before he died." For, though the confederate vassals who overthrew Nineveh in B. C. 609 were Nabopolassar king of Babylon and Cyaxares (first of the name) king of Media, yet, as in B. C. 606 we find it expressly stated by Berosus that Nabukhodonosor (or Nebukhadrezzar) commanded his father Nabopolassar's army that crossed the Euphrates and invaded Syria and Phœnicia, we may readily believe that he had also commanded his father's forces before in the attack upon Nineveh. And if Nabopolassar was represented there by his son, we may readily believe that Cyaxares also kept himself in reserve, giving the command of the Medes that took the field, to his son Astyages. If so, it is Astyages that in the book Tobit (written it appears originally in Chaldee, for Jerome's Latin version was made from a (modern)

Chaldee, that is, an Aramaic copy) the Hellenist translator calls 'Ασουηρος or 'Ασουηρος, the name which in Hellenist versions of Daniel and Ezra represents the one which the Hebrews wrote אֲחַשְׁוֵרוֹשׁ and in Esth. x. 1 אֲחַשְׁוֵרֹשׁ that is, Akhshurush, and which the Aryans of Media pronounced as we suppose, *Khshurush*.

According to our Table, a sister of Astyages named *Amyité* was wife of Nebukhadrezzar. We obtain this form of the name ('Αμυίτη) from Geo. Syncellus, p. 210 B, (ed. Dindorf. vol. 1 p. 396) who had before him the Greek text of Eusebius's Chronicon i. 4, 9 with the citations there made from Alexander Polyhistor and from Abydenus; while we have only the same in S. Jerome's Latin version and in an Armenian version published at Milan in Latin by Mai and Zohrab, and in both Armenian and Latin by Aucher at Venice. In the Armenian, the name of the Median daughter-in-law of Nabopolassar, the wife of Nebukhadrezzar, is *Amuhia* not (as we might have expected) *Amuhida*. But that the Syncellus has given us a pretty correct form used by the Polyhistor and Abydenus, may be believed from its near resemblance to *Amytis*,"Αμυτις, the name of Cyrus's Median wife, and also of that daughter of Xerxes who was wedded to Megabyzus the second; see Ktesias *ap. Photium*, Cod. lxxii. §§ 2, 3, 5, 10, 11, 20, 22, 28, 30, 40, 41, 42, 43.

The "satrap of Media," as he is called, who gave his daughter to be the wife of Nebukhadrezzar, is called Astyages (by the Syncellus, or *Asduhages* in Mai's version of the Armenian Eusebius) from Alexander Polyhistor and Abydenus. But, according to the history and also the chronology of Herodotus as well as the fact that the son of Astyages, Darius the Mede, was 62 years old in B. C. 538, seventy years after the fall of Nineveh, and, therefore, was not born till eight years after the marriage of Nebukhadrezzar, prove that the Astyages of Abydenus and the Polyhistor is a misnomer for Cyaxares.

The Syncellus in the passage above indicated, though he names Alexander Polyhistor only, must have also had in view the passage quoted by Eusebius from Abydenus; because he relates not only that Nabopolassar sent to the satrap of Media and obtained a daughter of his as a wife for his son Nebukhadrezzar, but also the result of this proceeding; how, though bearing the commission of Sarakus's general, he marched against Sarakus king of the Chaldæans (or rather, Assyrians, as Abydenus expresses it) to Nineveh, where Sarakus set fire to his own palace and perished in the flames. For this result of the contract between the Babylonian and the Mede, is not contained in Eusebius's citation from the Polyhistor, as represented in the Armenian version; which says only, " Is ad Asdahagem qui erat Mediæ gentis præses et satrapa, copias auxiliares misit; videlicet ut filio suo Nabucodroasoro desponderet Amuhiam è filiabus Asdahagis unam. Deinde Nabucodrossorus dominatus est tribus annis supra quadraginta." The more valuable account given by Abydenus, of the decline and fall of Nineveh is this; " Ægyptum prœterea partesque inferiores Syriæ acquirebat Axerdis" (Esarhaddon). "Hinc Sardanapallus" (Asshurbanipal) "exortus est. Post quem Saracus" (Assbur-irik-kin, Sir H. C. Rawlinson in Athenæum Aug. 22, 1863) "imperitabat Assyriis; qui quidem, certior factus turmarum vulgi collectitiarum quæ a mari adversûs se adventarent, continuo [Na]busalussorum militiæ ducem Babylonem mittebat. Sed enim hic capto rebellandi concilio Amubiam Asdahagis Medorum principis filiam nato suo Nabucodrossoro despondebat; moxque raptim contra Ninum, seu Nineven, urbem impetum faciebat. Re omni cognitâ rex Saracus regiam, Evoritam, inflammabat. Tum verô Nabucodrossorus, summâ rerum potitus firmis mœnibus Babylonem cingebat." Eusebius adds; "Iis narratis reliqua etiam Nabucodrossori gesta ita persequitur Abydenus ut à libris Hebræorum prorsus non abhorreat." These extracts from Mai's edition of the Armenian Eusebius, pp. 19-25, are given along with the passage from the Syncellus, by Clinton, F. H. vol. 1 pp. 270, 271 and by G. Rawlinson, Herod. vol. 1 p. 487 note. The passage of Syncellus and Eusebius's extracts from the Polyhistor (whose authority certainly was Berosus) are to be found among the fragments of Berosus in the *Frag. Hist. Græcorum* tom. ii. Eusebius's extract from Abydenus is to be found among the fragments of that writer, tom. iv. p. 482. Berosus also related that it was for the sake of his Median consort that Nebukhadrezzar erected the famous Garden in the Air, or Suspended Garden, at Babylon; see Josephus *Antiq.* x. 11; *Cont. Apion.* i. 19; *Fragm. Hist. Græc.* tom. ii. p. 507. She is miscalled a Persian (probably after Ktesias) by Diodorus, ii. 10; compare Curtius v. 5.

D.

IN the column of Persian Kings, the genealogy from Akhemenes to Xerxes is taken from Herodotus vii. 11. It seems to be confirmed by the statement in the Behistun Inscription, that eight of the Akhæmenian family had reigned before Darius son of Hystaspes; though the same inscription places Darius in only the fifth degree of sonship from Akhæmenes, omitting the first Teispes, the first Cambyses, and the first Cyrus, the son, the grandson, and the great-grandson of Akhæmenes in the Herodotean pedigree. We suppose that at the time of the engraving of the inscription, the Teispes father of Ariaramnes was (by no very strange error) confounded with another Teispes, his great-grandfather, and an immediate son of Akhæmenes; see above pp. 231, 232.

Cyrus father of Cambyses and grandfather of the Great Cyrus, occurs Herod. i. 111. For Cambyses the father of Cyrus, the legend on a brick found at Senkereh in Lower Chaldæa is cited by Sir H. C. Rawlinson in which Cyrus calls himself "son of Cambyses the powerful king." For the same Cambyses, the grandfather of the well-known Cambyses the conqueror of Egypt, (also, for Mandane, daughter of Astyages, his wife), see Herod. i. 107-9 and Xenophon e. g. *Cyrop.* i. 2 § 1 where the *Perseidæ* (as the family Cambyses belonged to, is named) are the Akhæmenidæ (for whom, see Herod. i. 123. iii. 65) regarded as sprung from the Greek hero Perseus; for so by Greek genealogists Akhæmenes was reckoned. Among the Aryans, he was regarded merely as a descendant from Parsa, but by the Greeks as the immediate offspring of Perses who was son of their own Perseus by Andromeda the daughter of Kepheus. For Perses son of Perseus, see Herod. vii. 61, 150. For Akhæmenes son of Perses, see Nicolaus of Damascus (as cited in the Etymologicum Magnum) and the Scholiast (who seems to be quoting Hellanicus) on Dionysius Periegetes line 1053. In this last passage the double assertion is made (apparently by a contemporary of Herodotus) that Perses son of Perseus had a son named Akhæmenes and that he gave name to the united nation of Artæans (So C. Müller corrects Argeians) and Kephenians; see the *Fragm. Hist. Græc.* tom. iii. p. 365, also *Geogr. Græc. Minores* tom. 2 p. 456 and compare what we have said already, p. 514 note.

The line of descent from the second Teispes down to Okhus Artaxerxes or Artaxerxes the 3d, gathered from Greek writers, is fully established by the cuneiform inscriptions of Darius son of Hystaspes, of Xerxes, of Artaxerxes Mnemon or Artaxerxes the 2d, and of Okhus Artaxerxes; see Journal R. A. S. vol. x pp. 196, 320, 323, 324, 327, 334, 337: vol. xv p. 159; vol. x pp. 341-2. The inscription here last referred to, has the line from Arsames to Artaxerxes the 3d: the one next before it, the line from Hystaspes to the second Artaxerxes: the first of all, the line from the second Teispes to Hystaspes.

That Arses was the son of the third Artaxerxes, also our statement of the descent of the Darius Codomannus from Darius Okhus commonly called Nothus or the Bastard, both appear from Diodorus xvii 5 §§ 3, 5.

As to the dates of the eight reigns, they are given (as it has been said) on the authority of Ptolemy's Table of Reigns at Babylon; where the 190 years from E. N. 227 to E. N. 416, are assigned to them respectively, in the eight portions following, 36, 21, 41, 19, 46, 21, 2, 4, from the 1st of January B. C. 521 to the 13th of November B. C. 332. These same eight reigns in the Khaldæan Tables, probably extended from the 1st of Markhesvan B. C. 521 to the last day of Tisri B. C. 331; see our argument as to the previous reigns, grounded on the case of the last Cambyses, in the Section C. page 741. In Assyrian and Jewish Tables of Reigns, we may conclude from the books of Haggai, Zechariah, and Esther, that these same eight reigns, following that of Cambyses, extended from 1 Nisan B. C. 521 to 1 Nisan B. C. 331.

Before we pass from this Column of Persian Kings to the next, we will give place here to some notes as to Hystaspes the father and Artaxerxes the grandson of our Darius Khshurush. The grandson according to Josephus, *Antiq.* xi 6 § 1, was Kurush (which he writes in Greek fashion, Κῦρος, the name transcribed by the Latins, *Cyrus*) though the Greeks (adds our Jewish historian) call him Artaxerxes. Perhaps (as we have already observed above p. 2 note) this assertion was not made on authority but was an inference from the book Esther, the story of which Josephus places in the reign of Artaxerxes. Such an inference would imply a belief in Josephus that Κῦρος was the same as *Khshurush* and that *Khshurush* was the name written in the Hebrew books אֲחַשְׁוֵרוֹשׁ. But it would also imply that Josephus's pronunciation of the Hebrew word was not the one indicated by the present pointing. We ourselves suppose *Kurush* to be the Persian and *Khshurush* the Median form of the same name; according to which conclusion it will have been Darius's private name in the form celebrated among the Medes, and his grandson's in the since more celebrated Persian form. The epithet given to the grandson μακρόχειρ, "long-arm," "long-armed," in Latin "Longimanus" may have indicated in its original Persian form, no personal peculiarity but only an attribute of every Persian monarch, his reach of power. This attribute is urged upon the Athenians by the Macedonian of the day when Mardonius offered them to be the king's allies, δύναμις οὐκ ἀνθρώπου ἢ βασιλέος ἐστὶ καὶ χεὶρ ὑπερμήκης. Herod. viii. 140.

As to the father and mother of Darius, according to Ktesias their death was strangely connected with the tomb of Darius, which has now been recognized, and has had three of its inscriptions copied, at *Nakhsh-i-Rustam*. In Photius's epitome, Ktesias's story is this; "Darius commands a tomb to be constructed for himself in the Double Mountain; and it is constructed. But having conceived a strong desire to see it, he is restrained by both the Khaldæans and his parents. But his parents having determined to go up, fell and died; because the priests that drew them up saw [serpents] and were terrified and in their terror let go the ropes. And Darius was grieved exceedingly: and the heads were cut off of them that drew them up, being forty men." This incident stands in Photius (Cod. lxxii. § 15) before Darius's expedition against the Scythians, the nation that then possessed what was once the country of the Cimmerians, north of the Danube and of the Euxine sea. The word *serpents* is bracketed because ὄφις, which it expresses has been inserted in the Greek text on but slender authority. The *Double Mountain*, τὸ δισσὸν ὄρος of Ktesias, where Darius's tomb was made, has been shewn by Von Hammer to be a different one from the βασιλικὸν ὄρος, or "Royal Mountain" of Diodorus xvii. 71, four *plethra* distant from the citadel at Persepolis, towards the east, and having rock-tombs to which the bodies of the kings had been hauled up for burial by engines. The double mountain of Ktesias is one to the north of Persepolis, that has been called by Persian geographers *Duta*, an equivalent of Ktesias's δισσὸν, the monuments and tombs of which, travellers call *Naksh-i-Rustam*. The mountain spoken of by Diodorus is the one called by the Persians *Naghant* or *Rahmet* or *Rakhmed*, rising behind the ruins of Persepolis towards the east, and having two large royal sepulchres; see the note of Didot's editor of Ktesias, C. Müller, pp. 64, 65.

E.

As to the Column of Benjamite Captives, there is little to observe. The genealogy is derived entirely from Esth. ii. 5, 6, 7, and 15. The first ancestor of Mordecai and Esther, is named and described as "Kish a Benjamite, who had been carried away from Jerusalem with the captivity, which was carried away with Jeconiah king of Judah, whom Nebukhadrezzar the king of Babylon had carried away." This description and explanation, though possibly not written the whole of it at one time, is thoroughly authoritative. Now, the first year of the captivity of Kish or Jeconiah is the first year of the reign of Zedekiah king of Judah: compare Ezek. xxiv. 1-2 (as explained by Ezek. i. 2, viii. 1, xx. 1, and xl. 1) with 2 Kings xxv. 1, Jerem. xxxix. 1. And this, according to our Column of Kings of Judah, to be treated of lower down in this section, was with the Jews their civil year, beginning with the first of Tisri B. C. 598; but with the Khaldæans, perhaps it was a year of theirs that began a month later, with the first of Markhesvan.

Therefore, since his captivity was counted to have commenced with the Tisri or the Markhesvan (say, the October or November) of the year B. C. 598, Kish is rightly placed in the Comparative Table as of the same generation with Jeconiah in the Column of Kings of Judah, who was 18 years old when he began his 3 months' reign in B. C. 598 (see 2 Kings xxiv. 8) and 55 years old at the accession of Evil Merodakh son of Nebukhadrezzar, (for $18+37=55$; see 2 Kings xxv. 27). And if Kish was of Jeconiah's generation, he was also of Seraiah's, in the column of High Priests; he was of Nebukhadrezzar's, in the Column of Kings of Babylon; he was of Psammis's, in the Column of Kings of Egypt; he belonged to the generation of the Great Cyrus's Median and Persian grandfathers, the former of whom was by marriage Nebukhadrezzar's brother; and lastly, in the Column of Persian kings, the ancestors and descendants of our Darius, he belonged to the generation of Hystaspes's grandfather.

But some have understood the passage referred to of Esther, to signify that Mordecai the descendant (not Kish the ancestor) was carried captive by Nebukhadrezzar from Jerusalem, along with Jeconiah. But this conclusion is quite inadmissible, unless we are prepared to believe that the Khshurush of the book Esther is Nebukhadrezzar; which would be absurd, and not worth the trouble of refuting; though we have already shewn that he cannot be Nebukhadrezzar's brother by marriage, Astyages, a supposition scarcely less preposterous; see above p. 29. It may further be observed, that there is no other purpose imaginable for which the genealogy was given in the book Esther, than that of connecting Mordecai and Esther with the land of Israel, or with Jerusalem the common capital of Judah and Benjamin, by the description subjoined to the name of Kish the last person in the line of ascent. If this description is applied to the first person in the ascending chain, Mordecai the son of Jair, the son of Shimei, the son of Kish, it must be owned that the names which follow, referring to persons otherwise unknown are quite useless. But, any such objection as this notwithstanding, it has been contended that the description, "A Benjamite who had been carried away from Jerusalem &c." which follows the chain of persons, must according to the inflexible usage of correct diction, be applied to the first and not to the last person of that chain. To disprove this assertion it is sufficient to cite an instance in which the first person and the last of an ascending lineage being known to us, it is found that a description at the end of the chain is applicable to the person last mentioned but not at all to the one with whom the chain begins. Now, such an instance occurs in Ezra vii. 1–5; where we have this genealogy given; "Ezra the son of Seraiah the son of Azariah the son of Hilkiah the son of Shallum the son of Zadok the son of Ahitub the son of Amariah the son of Azariah the son of Meraioth the son of Zerahiah the son of Uzzi the son of Bukki the son of Abishua the son of Phinehas the son of Eleazar the son of Aaron *the chief priest.*" Now here the description appended to the latter end of the chain of names, "the chief (or head) priest" (Heb. *hak-kohen ha-rosh*)—applied also to Seraiah in 2 Kings xxv. 18 and to Azariah in 2 Chron. xxxi. 10,—is very suitable to Aaron; for at the institution of the Levitical priesthood, after having been anointed, along with his four sons, Aaron certainly was chief of the actual priesthood as well as ancestor of the priests of all future times of the Mosaic polity. But to Ezra, the first person in the chain, the description is not applicable. He is described as "the Scribe-priest" (Heb. *hak-kohen has-sopher*) Ezra vii. 11; and in his days the son and grandson of Joshua the son of Jehozadak were successively head priests at Jerusalem; see the Column of Priests of Judah. But even when this chain connects but two persons, the description appended may apply to the latter, as in this, "Jonathan the son of Shimeah the brother of David." 2 Sam. xxi. 21.

2. We come now to the Column of Kings of Judah, lately appealed to, when we borrowed the date 1 Tisri B. C. 598 for the commencement of the captivity of Mordecai's ancestor Kish.

For the genealogy of this Column from Uzziah to Jeconiah son of Jehoiakim whose captivity was shared by Kish (also by the prophet Ezekiel then 25 years old; see Ezek. i. 2, xl. 1) the reader is referred to the holy books of the Hebrews, the 2d of Kings from the 15th chapter forward, and the 2d of Chronicles from the 26th chapter forward. Of the three successive descendants of Jeconiah, the last, Joiakim son of Zerubbabel, is placed within brackets to distinguish him as *apocryphal*, because we have no other authority for him than 1 Esdras v. 5, 6. But Zerubbabel and his father Shealtiel are abundantly attested in the books of Haggai, Zechariah, and Ezra. Besides, for them as well as for the chain of descent from Zerubbabel to Joseph the husband of the Blessed Mary (who, while a betrothed wife but still a maiden, by the power of the Holy Spirit of God conceived and bore a son, the Lord Jesus Christ) we are able to appeal to the genealogy preserved by S. Matthew, where, as in the Hellenist compilation Esdras α (or 1 Esdras) and in the Septuagint versions of Ezra, Haggai, Zechariah, and Chronicles; also in Josephus, *Antiq.* xi. 3 § 10, they are called Salathiel and Zorobabel.

For the fact, that Shealtiel or Salathiel was son of Jeconiah, Coniah, or Jehoiakin, we refer the reader, first to the above mentioned genealogy in S. Matthew's Gospel; S. Matt. i. 12; and to illustrate that testimony we would adduce the prophecy, delivered in the reign of his father, concerning Jeconiah's seed that should be cast out, and none of whom should prosper, sitting on the throne of David and ruling any more in Judah; Jerem. xxii. 24, 30. But that Shealtiel or Salathiel was son of Jeconiah, is a fact attested also in 1 Chron. iii. 17. Here we have a genealogy of many descendants from Jeconiah, seeming to reach as low as the last generation that was subject to the Persian empire. The record, therefore, in its present form, is of no earlier date than that of the descendants of Jeshua son of Jehozadak, the Priest, in Nehem. xii. 10, 11. Mistakes there certainly are in it. Thus, in verse 15, Shallum is described as a "fourth" son of Josiah, distinct from "the first-born Johanan," *i. e.* Jehoahaz, "the second Jehoiakim," and "the third Zedekiah." Whereas from Jerem. xxii. 11 compared with 2 Kings xxiii. 30, it is plain that Shallum was another, perhaps a previous, name of Jehoahaz son of Josiah. We pass over the substitution of Johanan for Joahaz, or Jehoahaz, as due perhaps to error of transcription only; but we observe it as another inaccuracy, that Jehoahaz is described as Josiah's first-born. He was, indeed, older than Zedekiah, being the elder of two sons that Josiah had by Hamutal the daughter of Jeremiah of Libnah, the younger of whom was Mattaniah whose name king Nebukhadrezzar changed to Zedekiah on making him king; see 2 Kings xxiii. 31, xxiv. 17, 18. But Jehoahaz was younger than his half-brother Jehoiakim son of Josiah by Zebudah the daughter of Pedaiah of Rumah; see 2 Kings xxiii. 31, 36.

For the lengths of the several reigns from Uzziah's to that of Zedekiah, we refer to the authorities already cited for the lineage of Jeconiah son of Jehoiakim.

But we have now to justify the position assigned by our Table in the time before Christ, to these same lengths of reign, both severally considered, and in their total of $(52+16+16+29+55+2+31+11+11=)$ 223 years. We have also to justify ourselves for taking these years to begin and end at the same points in the circle of the seasons, in a uniform manner; to be, in fact, a series of civil calendar years of

Judah, beginning with the first of Tisri B. C. 810 and ending with the eve of the first of Tisri, that is, with the last *νυχθήμερον* or last four and twenty hours of dark and light, belonging to the month Elul, B. C. 587.

First, then, let us shew good reason for believing the regnal years of these kings of Judah to be years of the civil calendar of Judah.

To do this, we begin by observing that the three months' reign of Shallum, otherwise Jehoahaz, son of Josiah (2 Kings xxiii. 31; 2 Chron. xxxvi. 2) which intervened between the reigns of Josiah and Jehoiakim, was included in that 31st and last regnal year of Josiah which began, we say, 1 Tisri B. C. 610, and ended with Elul B. C. 609. For Josiah was slain at Megiddo as he attempted to stop the march of Nekho king of Egypt against Karkhemish on the Euphrates, a dependency of Assyria ; and Jehoahaz was arrested by Nekho on his return and carried with him into Egypt. Now, summer is the usual season of military operations, and Nekho in particular (it may be supposed) would choose to be absent from his own country during the Nile-flood. We say, then, that Josiah was slain and Jehoahaz succeeded him in the summer (perhaps, *early* in the summer) of the year B. C. 609, the first summer of Nekho's reign ; see 2 Kings xxiii. 29–34, and 2 Chron. from xxxv. 20 to xxxvi. 4. As to the chronology of Nekho's reign, see above section A. For Jehoiakim's regnal year began so late in the round of seasons as to be but recently begun on the arrival of the ninth month (Khisleu), say December ; compare Jerem. xxxvi. 1–9. Therefore, the three months of Jehoahaz in the year B. C. 609 cannot have been included in the first regnal year of Jehoiakim. And yet, the years of Josiah and Jehoiakim formed an uninterrupted series. For in the fourth year of Jehoiakim, we find the prophet Jeremiah affirming, "from the 13th year of Josiah the son of Amon king of Judah even unto this day; that is, the three and twentieth year, the word of the Lord hath come unto me and I have spoken unto you . . . but ye have not hearkened ; " see Jerem. xxv. 1-3. Now, since Josiah reigned 31 years, the twenty-three years of the prophet beginning with Josiah's 13th and ending with Jehoiakim's 4th, being 19+4, shew no interval between the end of the last year of Josiah and the beginning of the first of Jehoiakim. Therefore, the three months' reign of Jehoahaz, which intervened in fact and which were certainly not counted to Jehoiakim his successor, were reckoned in the annals as part of the last regnal year of Josiah.

Next we observe, that the three months, or (as the reign is also computed) the three months and ten days, of Jeconiah son of Jehoiakim (2 Kings xxiv. 8; 2 Chron. xxxvi. 9) which intervened between the reigns of Jehoiakim and Zedekiah, were included in the 11th and last year of the preceding reign, which ended with Elul B. C. 598 ; according to the same rule (as it would seem) which had caused the months of Jehoahaz to be reckoned not to the following but to the preceding regnal year. For, as we have lately had occasion to shew, and as we shewed above p. 442 note, the first eleven years of the captivity which followed the brief reign of Jeconiah, being of course exclusive of his reign, were con-numerary with the eleven regnal years of the king who succeeded him, his uncle Zedekiah. Moreover, the carrying away of Jeconiah from Jerusalem, the end of his reign, is assigned to the eighth year of Nebukhadrezzar (2 Kings xxiv. 12) that is, to the 11th and last of Jehoiakim his father. For Jehoiakim's fourth was the first year assigned by the annalists of Judah to their king's new lord paramount, whom they saw only in the face of Nebukhadrezzar (see Jerem. xxv. 1 comparing therewith Dan. i. 1) and Jehoiakim was reckoned to have reigned 11 years in all. Thus, Jeconiah's reign, the fraction of a year, was included in the last year of Jehoiakim, which ended (as we have seen) not very long before Khisleu, or, say, December, in the round of seasons. With this conclusion coincides the expression, that "at the return of the year Nebukhadrezzar sent and fetched Jeconiah to Babylon;" 2 Chron. xxxvi. 10. Thus, Jeconiah's reign ends with the 11th regnal year of Jehoiakim his father, and his captivity is registered as commencing with the reign of his successor Zedekiah. Accordingly, the years of Jehoiakim and Zedekiah (like those of Josiah and Jehoiakim, already remarked upon) succeed one another without any odd time, or fraction of a year, intervening. Jehoiakim's reign has 11 years counted to it (2 Kings xxiii. 36; 2 Chron. xxvi. 5) whereof the last eight are the first eight years of Nebukhadrezzar, because the fourth of them, as we have seen (Jerem. xxv. 1) was counted the first of Nebukhadrezzar. Moreover, the 10th and 11th regnal years of Jehoiakim's successor Zedekiah are counted the 18th and 19th regnal years of Nebukhadrezzar (Jerem. xxxii. 1; lii. 12; 2 Kings xxv. 8). Therefore, these ordinals denote the last years of the two totals, 8 years and 10 and 8 years and 11, without acknowledging any intervening space for Jeconiah.

But we have seen that Jeconiah was carried into captivity at the return of the year; and that his successor Zedekiah's first regnal year (which finished not long after the 5th Mosaic month; comp. Jerem. i. 3) had not been long current when the 9th Mosaic month arrived. The year, then, *that returned* was (apparently enough) the new civil year, commencing with the 7th Mosaic month; and the reigns, not only of Zedekiah but also of his predecessors Jehoiakim and Josiah, also the subsequent years of the captivity of Jeconiah whereof we know (37—11=) twenty-six con-numerary with the years that were counted by Ezekiel after the destruction of Jerusalem (comp. Ezek. xl. 1)—which years, formed an uninterrupted series of $31+11+11+26=79$ years—were years of the civil calendar of Judah. Can we hesitate to conclude further, that the lengths of reign assigned to previous kings were also certain numbers of civil calendar years? The accounts we have of Hezekiah's first year which shew him to have been already king when the first Mosaic month (the month of the Passover) afterwards called

Nisan—arrived, prove that his years were not years of the Mosaic calendar (see 2 Chron. xxix. 3, 17 &c). The same conclusion arises from the record of Josiah's 18th year; see 2 Chron. from xxxiv. 8 to xxxv. 19, and 2 Kings from xxii. 3 to xxiii. 23. But we have already concluded of Josiah's years, that they were of the same type as those of Jehoiakim—calendar years beginning shortly before the 9th month (see Jerem. xxxvi. 1-9) that is, years of the civil calendar beginning with the 7th Mosaic month.

When the regnal years of a line of kings were years of the calendar of the state, the question speedily arose, how to assign the year which a demise of the crown divided between two kings. We have seen by the cases of Jehoahaz and Jeconiah, that the rule of the annalists of Judah was, to count that year altogether to the former possessor of the crown; while we observe the contrary practice followed by the Egyptians in Ptolemy's "Table of Reigns at Babylon;" where a calendar year of Egypt broken by a transfer of the crown, is counted entire to the successor as the first of his regnal years. But the rule of the annalists of the house of David was the same as that of the contemporary Assyrians; as is shewn by the cuneiform annals of Sennacherib inscribed on the Taylor Cylinder; see above p. 442. And that the rule continued to be observed at Babylon when the supremacy which had passed thither from Nineveh was now in the hands of the Persians and Medes, is evinced by Herodotus's account which we have often dwelt upon, of the composition of the last of those eight years which this historian as well as Berosus assigned to Cambyses; see above pp. 432—435.

It was, therefore, in exact accordance with the method followed at Babylon no less than with their own, that chroniclers of Judah counted Nebukhadrezzar's first regnal year as lord paramount of Judah, to begin not at that point in the third year of Jehoiakim at which he had taken Jerusalem and its king, but at the beginning of the fourth year of Jehoiakim who was permitted to remain in the under-kingship; see Dan. i. 1, Jerem. xxv. 1. This new phase of Jehoiakim's reign, in which he was no longer Nekho's vassal, but Nebukhadrezzar's, was dated, not from the actual commencement, but, from the next ensuing New-year's day. Both this method of post-dating a new reign, and that of ante-dating it which we find in Ptolemy's Canon, saved the difficulty of constructing Tables (less useful for chronological computations in general) wherein fractions of years—even such as might not be smaller than months—should be assigned to their proper kings.

The rule observed in Assyria, in Babylonia, and in Judah, seems to be in vigour now among the Chinese; whose manners, laws, and customs, in part at least, date from times as old as those of the earliest Khaldæans and Assyrians. The proof we offer, though it betrays the slenderness of our information, if sufficient, as we think it, for the demonstration in hand, may be acceptable in the absence of a better.

We have noted from newspapers two letters from China, one, a letter from Pekin, dated the 5th of February 1862 and addressed to the Journal called the Overland Friend of China; the other, a letter from Shanghai, dated the 30th of January 1862 and published in the Telegraph newspaper. The writer of the former letter says; "... The new year has opened under the style of *First year of his majesty Tungche*...." The writer of the other, speaking of the night preceding the 30th of January, the day his letter is dated, calls it *New year's Eve*. We conclude, then, that the first year of the Emperor Tung-che is counted to have begun with the Calendar year of China, on the 30th of January A. D. 1862; although in fact, his accession to his father's throne had taken place, as previous advices had informed us, about four months before.

Having now shewn our grounds for believing the regnal years of every king of Judah to have been so many years of the civil calendar of the country, the first of which commenced with the Tisri next after the king's accession to the throne, we proceed to justify the positions in time before Christ, to which we have adjusted the nine reigns contained in our column of kings of Judah; so that the whole number of years in all of them $(52+16+16+29+55+2+31+11+11=)223$, begins with the 1st of Tisri B. C. 810 and ends with the last day of Elul B. C. 587. On the correctness of the position assigned to the last of these reigns (the 11 years of Zedekiah, which are the first eleven of Jeconiah's captivity) depends that of every previous reign. For to this reign of Zedekiah (the first eleven years of captivity for the prophet Ezekiel and for Mordecai's ancestor Kish as well as for Jeconiah) the reigns of Zedekiah's predecessors have been prefixed, each in the order of its precedence, and each covering its recorded number of calendar years. Therefore, if we can justify the position before Christ in which we have placed Zedekiah's reign, the correctness is also established of the position of each previous reign; and withal we demonstrate the correctness of the date for the commencement of Kish's captivity, for which we lately referred to the column now under our consideration.

But, in truth, if we can ascertain the position in time before Christ, of any one of our nine reigns of kings of Judah, or even the position of any one of the 223 calendar years of Judah contained in the whole of those reigns, the position of every other reign or regnal year will then appear with equal certainty, by setting it off at its proper distance, in years before or after, from the first ascertained position. The annals of Rome and the Olympic annals of Greece afford us here no help; for no event of our nine reigns in Judah is dated in those annals. But Ptolemy's Canon, not as garbled in the astronomical and ecclesiastical canons of Georg. Syncellus but as preserved by Theon, a document in which the years of successive reigns and interregnums at Babylon are adjusted to a series of Egyptian years, supplies sufficient assistance. We seem here to recognize at once several epochs of Jewish history, mentioned either during our nine reigns or in notices chronologically connected therewith of the succeeding line from Jeconiah to Zerubbabel.

We remark one year to which the first of Nebukhadrezzar has been adjusted, another and another made in like manner the first of Evil Merodakh, and the first of Cyrus respectively. Looking closer, we find the date of the capture of Babylon by the Medes and Persians under Cyrus which (according to Jewish prophecy) happened seventy years after the capture of Nineveh by the Khaldæans and Medes. Moreover, cuneiform discovery enables us, by the aid of the annals of Sargon king of Assyria, to see in Ptolemy's Canon the date of the capture of Samaria by the Assyrians in the reign of Hezekiah king of Judah.

But on examination we find difficulties arise. The first of Nebukhadrezzar by the Canon follows the last regnal year of Nabopolassar at Babylon; but the year called Nebukhadrezzar's first by his Jewish contemporaries, preceded the death of Nabopolassar; as is evident by a comparison of Berosus's account of the war of Nebukhadrezzar in Syria as commander of his father's forces, with the account in the book of Daniel (i. 1) of the subjugation of Judah in the 3rd year of Jehoiakim, and that in Jerem. xlvi. 2–12 of the defeat of Nekho king of Egypt at Karkhemish on the Euphrates in the 4th year of Jehoiakim and in the fifth, as it would seem, of the occupation of Karkhemish by the Egyptians. For the prophet makes the 4th year of Jehoiakim when Nekho (having come up, as it seems, with all his forces to relieve Karkhemish) was thus defeated, to be the first year of Nebukhadrezzar; see Jerem. xxv. 1. Again, the first of Evil Merodakh, by the Canon as well as by Berosus, is in the 44th year counting from the first of Nebukhadrezzar; whereas, according to the Hebrew writers, it was in not less than the $(8+37=)$ 45th year but, as we contend, in the $(8+37+1=)$ 46th year; see above p. 441. This discrepancy, however, is very useful towards ascertaining the length of the interval between the two commencements of Nebukhadrezzar's reign just observed. Again, the first regnal year of Cyrus in the Canon, follows immediately after the last year of Nabonadius or Nabonnedus, in which (as we learn from Berosus) Cyrus took Babylon. But, according to Daniel, on the capture of Babylon Darius the Mede—then 62 years of age—took the kingdom; so that what the Canon calls the first of Cyrus was more properly the first of Darius the Mede who was afterwards succeeded on the throne by Cyrus, as it also appears from Daniel. Again, however, we have here a discrepancy which aids to explain how it is, that, whereas the Hebrew writers place seventy years captivity of men of Judah at Babylon before the first of Cyrus, and after the earliest capture of Jerusalem by Nebukhadrezzar which was in the 3d year of Jehoiakim king of Judah, the reigns at Babylon of Nebukhadrezzar, Evil Merodakh, Neriglissar, and Nabonnedus amount only to $(43+2+4+17=)66$ years. We perceive that these 66 years end earlier (as we have already had an intimation that they began later) than the 70 years spoken of by the

Hebrews. But the last year of the reign of Nabonadius may be fairly taken for the last of the predicted 70 years of Babylonian reign over the nations, so that the fall of Nineveh is thus dated in the last year but four of the reign at Babylon of Nabopolassar. From this it will follow, that the seventy years of Jewish captivity at Babylon lasted just so long after the capture of Babylon by the Medes and Persians as it began after the capture of Nineveh by the Khaldæans and Medes; or (which is the same thing) that Darius the Mede reigned as long after Nabonnedus and Belshazzar as the fourth year of Jehoiakim king of Judah followed after the commencement of the reign of Babylon in succession to Nineveh. But it seems from the account of Cyrus's reign at the close of Xenophon's Cyropædia, that Cyrus reigned only seven of the nine years between the last of Nabonnedus and the first of Cambyses. Therefore, Darius the Mede reigned two years after Nabonnedus and before Cyrus; and if so, the fourth of Jehoiakim (the first of the 70 years of captivity) began when two years had intervened since the year in which Nineveh was taken; and if so, Nabopolassar, who (as we have found reason to conclude already) reigned four years between the year of the fall of Nineveh and the 43 years ascribed to Nebukhadrezzar's reign by Berosus and the Canon of Ptolemy, was still counted king at Babylon during the 4th and 5th years of Jehoiakim, *i. e.* during the first two years of the captivity of Judah at Babylon and the reign ascribed to Nebukhadrezzar by the prophets and chroniclers of Judah.

If the years thus obtained, the first of Cyrus, as successor to Darius the Mede, the fourth year of Jehoiakim, and the year of the fall of Nineveh, be adjusted to the series of years in Ptolemy's Canon on the principle of the Canon, the capture of Nineveh will stand in the year of Nabonassar 139, beginning January 22 B. C. 609; the fourth year of Jehoiakim will be the year E. N. 142, beginning 21 Jan. B. C. 606; and the first year of Cyrus, according to the Hebrews will be the year E. N. 212, beginning 5th January B. C. 536. But when the commencements of these years are brought down from the first of the Egyptian Thoth to the first of the ensuing Tisri for Jewish dates, and of the ensuing Markhesvan for Khaldæan, the year in which Nineveh was taken, the last year but four of Nabopolassar, will end with Tisri B. C. 608: the first year of Babylonian supremacy will begin on the 1st of Markhesvan the same year B. C. 608; the fourth year of Jehoiakim and first year of the captivity of Judah will commence on the 1st of Tisri B. C. 606; and the first year of Cyrus, as successor to Darius the Mede, will commence, according to the Khaldæans, 1 Markhesvan B. C. 536, though by Jewish reckoning the 70 years captivity had expired with Elul B. C. 536 and the first year of Cyrus would be reckoned to begin on the first of Tisri.

On such conclusions as these, the positions before Christ are calculated in the column of our Table that we are now considering. We have said that if the position of any one of the regnal years in that column be rightly calculated, the correctness of the dates for the rest will follow. If so, the 4th year of Jehoiakim king of Judah being now (by help of Ptolemy's Canon) fixed as having commenced on the first of Tisri B. C. 606, the same aid may be said to have established every other date. For instance, the captivity of Jeconiah and Kish, which began with the first year of Zedekiah, eight full years later has its commencement on the first day of Tisri B. C. 598. Again, the destruction of Jerusalem effected by Nebukhadrezzar's orders in the 11th year of Zedekiah in the 5th Mosaic month (or in the last month but one before the end of the 11th year of Zedekiah) will stand in the month Ab B. C. 587.

The above justification of the regnal dates in our column of Kings of Judah, rests upon our conclusion that the calendar year of Judah which formed the 4th regnal year of Jehoiakim, commencing with the month Tisri (or the corresponding Khaldæan year which began, a month later, with Markhesvan) being the first regnal year of Nebukhadrezzar by the reckoning in Judah, began about the first of October (in the one case) or about the first of November (in the other case) of our year B. C. 606; that is, two years and one month in the one case or two years exactly in the other, before the year of Babylon indicated by the (Egyptian) year of Nabonassar, 144, with which the first regnal year of Nebukhadrezzar is made to correspond in Ptolemy's Canon. Now, this conclusion we think no less worthy of confidence than any chronological conclusion to which the Canon of Ptolemy properly handled may lead. Nor do we think it can be distrusted by any, but those who refuse to believe that the promises of God by the prophet Jeremiah were verified in fact; that the Babylonian supremacy should last 70 years, and that the forced residence of Judah in Babylon should also last 70 years; see Jerem. xxv. 11-14 for the former promise; and the letter of Jeremiah to them of the captivity at Babylon, Jerem. xxix. 10, for the latter promise; remarking withal that the 70 years of desolation at Jerusalem discerned in the former passage by Daniel, Dan. ix. 2, were not fulfilled till 18 full years had elapsed after the supremacy of Babylon ended; Zech. i. 12; also that a 70 years commemoration of the destruction of Jerusalem and of the remnant left in Judah under Gedaliah, did not end till 21 full years had elapsed after the last of the years of Babylonian supremacy; see Zech. vii. 5.

But we will prove to these sceptics, without any presumed verification of divine promise—attested only by the holy prophets of ancient Israel—that the fourth regnal year of Jehoiakim did really precede the year of Judah most nearly corresponding with the one that at Babylon was counted to Nebukhadrezzar as his first, by two years; or that it preceded that Babylonian year itself by two years and one month.

According to the annals of Judah (2 Kings xviii. 10,) Samaria the capital of the ten tribes of Israel that had revolted from Judah was captured by the Assyrians, and its inhabitants carried into captivity, in the 6th year of Hezekiah king of Judah. Now, according to the same annals (2 Kings xviii. 2; xxi. 1, 19; xxii. 1; also 2 Chron. xxix. 1; xxxiii. 1, 21; xxxiv. 1) the sixth regnal year of Hezekiah was the (24th+55th+2nd+31st+3rd=the) 115th year of Judah before that first day of Tisri wherewith the 4th year of Jehoiakim began. But, according to the annals of the first and 12th years of Sargon king of Assyria (referred to in G. Rawlinson's Herodotus vol. 1 p. 472) Samaria was taken and carried captive by the Assyrians in the first year of the reign of Merodakh Baladan king of Babylon, who reigned 12 years; that is, in the first year of the only king of Babylon that reigned 12 years according to Ptolemy's Canon, namely Mardokempadus. Now, the first year of Babylon assigned to Mardokempadus (as we learn from the column of years of reigns and interreigns in Ptolemy's Canon) was the (12th+5th+2nd+3rd+6th+1st+4th+8th+13th+20th+22nd+21st= the) 117th year before the first day of Markhesvan, or New-year's day of the first Calendar year of Babylon that Berosus and the authorities Ptolemy used in constructing his Canon, assigned to Nebukhadrezzar as his first regnal year at Babylon. That is to say, Nebukhadrezzar's reign was counted at Babylon to begin two years and one month later than it was counted to begin at Jerusalem. Or—as by aid of the column of (Egyptian) years of Nabonassar with which these Babylonian years are made to correspond in Ptolemy's Canon we are enabled to say—it appears that the year, counted at Babylon for Nebukhadrezzar's first, began with Markhesvan E. N. 144 (B. C. 604); whereas the year, counted in Judah for Nebukhadrezzar's first, began with Tisri E. N. 142 (B. C. 606). Now, this is what we proved before by aid of the prophecies of Jeremiah, but what (for the sake of the sceptics who would not accept of a conclusion founded on the presumed fulfilment of prophecies or promises of the Holy Scriptures) we undertook to prove without such aid.

We have been addressing ourselves in imagination to a sort of men that is ever ready to welcome a pretence of cavil at Holy Scripture. Therefore, now, before we subjoin a justification (as against Clinton) of our dates for certain previous epochs, we will notice in the history of Hezekiah king of Judah (in order to remove it) an apparent contradiction in respect of a very important date, between the authorities Hebrew and Babylonian which we have just been using with so much pleasure each of them to corroborate the other.

We had occasion to remark, that the city Samaria was taken and its people carried into captivity, in the sixth year of Hezekiah king of Judah and in the first year of Merodakh Baladan, or Mardokempadus, king of Babylon. It was also explained, that the sixth year of Hezekiah began with the month Tisri in B. C. 721, and the first year of Merodakh Baladan a month later, on the first day of Markhesvan; although in Ptolemy's Canon of Reigns at Babylon it is made to correspond with the Egyptian year of Nabonassar 27; which year began on the 19th of the previous February. Since, therefore, the first year of Merodakh Baladan began a month later than Hezekiah's sixth; his twelfth and last (when he was expelled by Sargon) corresponded with Hezekiah's 17th, beginning one month later with the first of the Markhesvan of B. C. 710; while Hezekiah's sickness and miraculous recovery in the (29—15=)the 14th year of his reign, after which he received the congratulations of Merodakh Baladan (2 Kings xx. 1, 6, 12), happened in the 9th year of that king of Babylon. Now, the year of Senacherib's invasion of Judah (which his inscription on the Taylor Cylinder makes to be his third regnal year; see Journal R. A. S. vol. xix. pp. 143–9) was evidently the 27th year of Hezekiah or the 13th that followed after the 9th of Mardokempadus and 14th of Hezekiah. For, not only have we the annals of Sargon king of Assyria for 15 years in the interval, after the first five years of Hezekiah and before the reign of Sennacherib, but Sennacherib's third regnal year coincided (as we will shew presently) with the third and last year of Belibus at Babylon, before whose rule there had been an interregnum of two years, and before that a five years' reign of Arkianus; and before that a three years' remainder of Merodakh Baladan's reign, since the year in which Hezekiah was sick and Merodakh Baladan sent to congratulate him on his recovery. Therefore, Sennacherib, who invaded Judah in the third year of his reign, invaded it also in the (14+13=) 27th of Hezekiah's reign. But, according to Scripture, 2 Kings xviii. 13, it was in the 14th year of king Hezekiah that Sennacherib king of Assyria came up against all the fenced cities of Judah and took them. How shall we reconcile this with the Babylonian annals, just cited, which make the invasion to have happened in the 27th year of Hezekiah?

Before answering this, we give the promised proof that the three years of Belibus at Babylon beginning with Markhesvan B. C. 702, are the first three regnal years of Sennacherib. According to Sennacherib's inscription on the Bellino cylinder, line 14, (see Journal R. A. S. vol. xviii. pp. 84, 78, 90) in " the beginning " of Sennacherib's reign, before the new year came which he counts for his first regnal year, (*i. e.* in the remainder of the year marked by the demise of the crown to him, which year was counted, according to custom, entirely to his predecessor) he made Belib king in the Leshan and Akkad provinces, of which it is plain from Sennacherib's account of his 6th and 8th years on the Taylor Cylinder, that Babylon was the capital, and that they were termed the provinces of Belus; see Journal R. A. S. vol. xix. pp. 155, 160. Belib's regnal years, therefore, began (according to the rule of Sennacherib's regnal years) with the next new-year's day of Babylon, which may also have been the regnal new-year's day at that time, of the Assyrian annals. But, after the campaign in Phœnicia, Philistia, and Judah, in Sennacherib's third regnal year, having in his fourth year conducted an expedition against the same enemy (Merodakh Baladan king of Karduniash, the erewhile king of Babylon) whose restored influence over the princes of Babylon in Leshan and Akkad he had defeated in " the beginning " of his reign, and having now expelled him from his present and perhaps more proper dominion of Beth Yakina, Sennacherib placed on Merodakh Baladan's throne *Asshur-nadan-mu* (seemingly the Apronadius of Ptolemy's Canon) and bestowed upon him the whole land of Leshan and Akkad; see Journal R. A. S. vol. xix. p. 151. Apparently, Belibus had ceased to reign in fact, before Sennacherib began this second expedition against Merodakh Baladan king of Beth Yakina and Karduniash. It seems clear, that the fourth year of Sennacherib is the first year of Apronadius, the successor of Belibus at Babylon; and, accordingly, that the previous three years of Belibus are the first three regnal years of Sennacherib.

Having now brought forward the opposed statements of Hebrew Scripture and of Assyrian and Babylonian annals—that Sennacherib's campaign in Hezekiah's kingdom happened in the 14th year of Hezekiah, and that it happened in a year equivalent to the 27th of Hezekiah— we proceed to reconcile them; for we believe them both.

We suppose (as we urged some years ago in Journal R. A. S. vol. xviii. p. 108) that in their registers of the yearly doings of the king, the chroniclers of Judah (or some of them at least) counted two reigns of Hezekiah, the first of which terminated and the second began at the time of that figure of a death and resurrection, when (having been bidden by God in a grievous sickness to set his house in order, for that he should die; and having nevertheless at his sore entreaty been promised that he should rise from his bed on the third day and go up into the house of the Lord on Mount Moriah and continue to live and reign for fifteen more years) not only was the promise fulfilled to him eventually, (the fulfilment beginning on the third day, as it had been appointed), but it was made credible to him on the instant, by a sign from God. He had asked for a sign that God would do as He had said, and the prophet Isaiah bade him choose whether the shadow on a sundial which he could see from his bed, should go forward ten steps or go ten steps back. Then Hezekiah, thinking the latter the greater sign, asked for that; and Isaiah cried unto Jehovah, and He brought the shadow ten steps backward, by which it had gone down in the dial of Ahaz; see 2 Kings xx. 1-11; Isai. xxxviii. 1-22.

Now, there may have been annals of King Hezekiah's reign which had then reached their 14th year and which were carried on during the remainder of Hezekiah's life, without any deviation from ordinary practice, but in some annals of the reign, we suppose, that a new series of years was begun, and the years of this new series, the years of the new reign may have been counted not from the expiration of the year current when Hezekiah rose to a new life and reign, that is to say, not with the next ensuing Tisri but from the day of the king's figurative resurrection; and thus the 14th year of the new reign during its earlier months, might coincide with the latter part of the 27th year according to the ordinary registration, which 27th year closed with Elul B. C. 699. For example, if we should suppose the three days in which Hezekiah may be regarded as having died and risen again, to have been the same days of the year in which our Lord, the Great Antitype, in A. D. 29 died and rose again, that is, the 14th, 15th, and 16th of the month Nisan, in the middle of the 14th civil year of Judah assigned in the annals to Hezekiah's reign ; in this case, the sickness and recovery would have happened in the Nisan of B. C. 712 ; and the 14th of a series of 15 fresh years commencing on the 16th of that Nisan, would have begun on the 16th of Nisan B. C. 699 in the middle not only of the 27th civil year of Hezekiah, but also of the 3rd year of Bolib and (apparently) of Sennacherib also, by the annals of Babylon ; so that, if Sennacherib reached the land of Israel in his progress between that day and the last of the ensuing month Elul, the invasion would certainly have taken place not only at the date intended by the document on which the compilers of Hezekiah's history relied, but also at the date which the annals of Assyria and Babylon attested.

But we have yet to justify the years of accession which we have assigned in our Table to Uzziah, Jotham, and Ahaz; that is, the years B. C. 810, 758 and 742. It is contended by Clinton in the chapter of "Scripture Chronology" in the Appendix of the first volume of his *Fasti Hellenici*, that of the reigns in Judah contained in our Comparative Table, those of Jotham and Ahaz consisted not—each of 16 years complete, or (as we have concluded) of 16 civil years of Judah, but—each of 16 years current ; and in calculating the total duration of the kingdom of Judah, he counts the reigns of Jotham and Ahaz at 15 years apiece. Consequently, his dates for the accession of Uzziah, Jotham, and Ahaz, are lower than our's, being B. C. 808, 756, and 741 respectively. We propose, then, here to vindicate our dates ; and to shew, that there is no sufficient reason for believing that the years assigned by the records of Judah to reigns of kings of the same country (for we speak not of the kings of Israel) were not uniformly spaces of time measured by entire years ; being sometimes, as in these cases of Jotham and Ahaz, numbers only of years current.

Clinton's proof that the 16th year of Jotham was not a completed year, is drawn from what we read of the years of Pekah king of Israel : and his like assertion in regard of the 16th year of Ahaz, he defends by what we find written of the years of Hoshea king of Israel.

(*a.*) He argues that Jotham's last year was incomplete, because the first of his 16 regnal years is said to have begun in the 2d year of Pekah (2 Kings xv. 32, 33) while it is said that the first year of his successor Ahaz began in the 17th year of Pekah : (2 Kings xvi. 1). Our answer is two-fold. First, we say, it may be true that Jotham's 16th calendar year of reign was not complete when, on the demise of his crown to Ahaz, the exercise of the regal functions by Ahaz began. Nevertheless, the first year of Ahaz in the annals—the first that had not been already assigned to a predecessor and was now, in consequence of his late accession, assigned to him—would not begin till the next ensuing first of Tisri, if the practice of the registrars in Judah was the same with that of the registrars under the contemporary kings of Assyria, as it is clearly exemplified in the formerly-cited annals of Sennacherib. The similar practice of the kings of Judah, we have inferred from the fact that those fractions of a year, the reigns of Jehoahaz and Jeconiah, or so much at least of each of the said fractions as fell within the calendar year that was current at the preceding demise of the crown, was evidently counted by the annalists of Judah to the last regnal year of the predecessor of each. It is supposable, then, that the day of Jotham's accession and also the next ensuing new-year's day, the first of Tisri, happened both of them in the 2nd year of Pekah : and that the last of the 16 calendar years of Jotham, counted from that first of Tisri in the 2nd year of Pekah, was completed with Elul in the 18th year of Pekah, though the crown had passed to Ahaz by the death of his father in the 17th year of Pekah, and this event alone has been recorded.

But our answer was to be twofold. We will, therefore, add in the second place, that, though in 2 Kings xi. 32, 33, Jotham is stated to have begun his reign in the 2nd year of Pekah, yet previously, in verses 27 and 30, it is said, that Pekah having come to the throne in the 52nd and last year of Uzziah or Azariah, Jotham's father, and having reigned 20 years, was slain and succeeded on the throne by the slayer,—not in the 19th as we might have expected, but—in the 20th year of Jotham, that is, in the (20—16$=$) 4th year of Ahaz, since Jotham had reigned but 16 years when Ahaz succeeded him on the throne of Judah. We infer from this, that the first of Jotham's 16 years began but a brief fraction of a year later than Pekah's accession, and that Pekah's 2nd year was counted from the new-year's day next after his accession—whether the new-year's day of Judah, when Jotham's first regnal year began though he had been king in fact before that day, or the new-year's day of Israel, which (for a reason given p. 434) we suspect arrived a month later than the new-year's day of Judah, being the first of Markhesvan. If so, sixteen calendar years of Jotham's might be complete, and the first of Ahaz might begin, within the 17th year current of Pekah. And thus it appears, that the texts concerning Pekah's reign on which Clinton relies to shew that Jotham did not reign 16 whole years, admit of a construction with which our supposition is quite compatible, that his 16 years were complete.

(b.) Again, Clinton argues that the last of the 16 years ascribed to Ahaz was not a complete year, because Hoshea king of Israel is said (in 2 Kings xvii. 1) to have begun to reign nine years in Samaria in the 12th year of Ahaz king of Judah while Hezekiah's 4th year in which the three years' siege of Samaria commenced and Hezekiah's 6th year in which the siege ended in capture and captivity, are said to be respectively the 7th and 9th years of Hoshea (in 2 Kings xviii. 9, 10 ;

with which compare also 2 Kings xvii. 5, 6 and Jos. *Antiq.* ix. 14 § 1.) He reconciles these statements by the supposition above mentioned, against which we contend, and explains that Hoshea began to reign in Samaria before the close of the 12th year of Ahaz at Jerusalem, and entered upon his 4th year before the close of the 15th year of Ahaz; further, that the 4th year of Hoshea comprehended so much of the 16th year of Ahaz as had elapsed at the accession of Hezekiah and that it was still current after the first year of Hezekiah had begun, so that, as the history attests, his 7th year was still current when the 4th year of Hezekiah began, and his 9th year likewise when the 6th year of Hezekiah had begun.

This argument, we think, may be completely neutralized. First, we observe, that the account of Hoshea's reign in 2 Kings comes evidently from more than one source, and consists of information unskilfully combined by the compiler. Clinton's supposition, that the 16th year of Ahaz was but part of a year, appears (as we have seen) to reconcile the statement as to the first year of Hoshea with the statement as to Hoshea's 7th and 9th years, but it does not notice what is also stated concerning the 3rd year of Hoshea (in 2 Kings xviii. 1,) that in this year Hezekiah king of Judah began to reign. This statement, indeed, as to the first year of Hezekiah, may seem reconcilable with the one made afterwards concerning the 4th and 6th years of Hezekiah. It might be supposed, that, though the demise of the throne of Judah from Ahaz to Hezekiah took place in the 3rd year of Hoshea, yet that the next new-year's day, when the first year of Hezekiah began according to the custom of the annals, did not arrive till after the 4th year of Hoshea had commenced. But this explanation contradicts Clinton's conclusion, that the 4th year of Hoshea began before the close of the 15th of Ahaz, and comprehended so much of the 16th of Ahaz as had not elapsed when Hezekiah came to the throne, as well as the beginning of the first year of Hezekiah. Therefore, Clinton's fundamental supposition that Ahaz reigned but a bit of a year more than 15 years, does not commend itself to our acceptance as reconciling all that has been cited from 2 Kings xvii. and xviii. concerning the coincidence of of the 1st, 3rd, 7th, and 9th years of Hoshea with the 12th of Ahaz and the 1st, 4th, and 6th years of Hezekiah.

Moreover, Clinton's hypothesis, though it enables him to count nine years only for Hoshea from the 12th of Ahaz to the capture of Samaria by the Assyrians, is liable to an objection which attaches, of course, primarily to the statement in 2 Kings xvii. 6, and xviii. 10 that the king of Assyria took Samaria in the ninth year of Hoshea. It appears from 2 Kings xvii. 3–5 that after Hoshea had begun to reign, in the 12th year of Ahaz king of Judah (but how long after it, is not recorded) Shalmanezer king of Assyria came up against him and made him his servant. As such, Hoshea gave him presents for some years; but in the end, the king of Assyria found conspiracy in Hoshea; who had sent messengers to So king of Egypt (in Heb. סוֹא in the Septuagint Σηγὼρ Vat. Ed.; but Σωὰ Alex. M.S. and Joseph. *Ant.* ix. 14 § 1:) and had brought no present (*i. e.* apparently, had come before his lord with excuses but without tribute) to the king of Assyria, such as he had brought year by year before; therefore, the king of Assyria shut him up and bound him in prison, and came up throughout all the land, and went up to Samaria, and besieged it three years. Hoshea, therefore, had ceased to reign before the siege began; he had changed his throne in Samaria for a prison within the dominions of the king of Assyria, and he was no more king of Samaria in the sixth than in any subsequent year of Hezekiah's reign at Jerusalem. It may be said, indeed, that the third and last year of the siege sustained by the citizens of Samaria after they had lost their king, is called the ninth year of Hoshea because it would have been his ninth year had he been present in Samaria. But we say, that this is a miscalculation; and, in addition to what we have objected against the supposition which enables Clinton to count that year as Hoshea's ninth, we say on the contrary, that the fourth year of Hezekiah, in which the siege of Samaria was undertaken by the Assyrians, is the real ninth year from the 12th of Ahaz; counting the two extremes and reckoning the 16th year of Ahaz as a complete year. And thus we reconcile the assertion made in 2 Kings xvii. 1, that Hoshea began a reign of nine years over Israel, in the 12th year of Ahaz, with the fact recorded afterwards in the 4th verse, that the king of Assyria threw Hoshea into prison before he besieged Samaria, that is (we conclude) in the fourth year of Hezekiah. As to the statements, which we venture to call entirely erroneous, that the 3d, 7th, and 9th years of Hoshea were the 1st, 4th, and 6th of Hezekiah, we may have something to offer presently.

It is now proper to remind the reader, that we have an entirely different view given us of the reign of Hoshea in 2 Kings xv. 27–30 where we read that Hoshea conspired against Pekah, and slew him, and reigned in his stead in the 20th year of Jotham son of Uzziah; that is, in the 4th year of Ahaz, which was the 20th year from Jotham's first, and would have been Jotham's 20th regnal year if he had not died in the 16th year. By this account, Hoshea is made the ruler in Samaria between the death of Pekah and that 12th year of Ahaz which is made the first of a nine years' reign of his in 2 Kings xvii. 1. And it is remarkable, that this former period also is one of nine years duration, if (as in the other case, and as perhaps we should *in all the reigns of kings of Israel*) we count the two extremes, that is, the 4th and 12th years of Ahaz. In the early part of the latter period, Hoshea was independent; for it was not till Shalmanezer had come against him, that he became Shalmanezer's servant. In the former period, he may have been a mere governor for Pekah's conqueror, Tiglath Pilezer; as Gedaliah was at a later date, in Judah for Nebukhadrezzar king of Babylon, after the destruction of Jerusalem and the deportation of the greater part of the people that survived. But the relations of Pekah at the end of his reign and of Hoshea who succeeded him, with the great king, the king of Assyria, we leave to the learned in Assyrian records.

The whole space from the death of Pekah to the capture of Samaria, is a span of nineteen years, if we count the two extremes, the 4th of Ahaz and the 6th of Hezekiah, reckoning Ahaz's reign at 16 years complete. The years called—as we have thought erroneously—the 3rd, 7th and 9th years of Hoshea, in 2 Kings xviii. 1, 9, 10 and xvii. 6, are the 13th, 17th and 19th of this period; and, perhaps, the ordinal numbers denoting them have been injudiciously altered from these numbers. We will only add, that the first year of Nabonassar (which commences with the Egyptian year at 25½ Feb. B. C. 747 by Ptolemy's canon) seems to have begun with Markhesvan (say, 1 Nov.) of that year by the Babylonian Tables of regnal years; a month later than the 12th of Jotham; and that the campaign of Tiglath Pilezer against Rezin king of Damascus and Pekah king of Samaria, was probably in the 8th year of Nabonassar as counted at Babylon, and in the 3rd of Ahaz; which last year (as our Table shews) extended from Tisri B. C. 740 to Elul B. C. 739, extremes included.

The reader, however, is referred to Sir H. C. Rawlinson's important article (in the Athenæum of 18 May 1867), "*The Assyrian Canon verified by the Record of a Solar Eclipse, B. C. 763*, in the 18th year before the accession of Tiglath Pilezer II." In an abstract of Assyrian dates here given, the overthrow of Rezin and a record of Tiglath Pilezer's having taken tribute from Ahaz, are referred to a two-year's presence of the Assyrians at Damascus, assigned to B. C. 733–32. From the verification of the Canon in question by the eclipse, which certainly occurred in the June of the 18th year before Tiglath Pilezer's first, Sir Henry concludes, that *the numbers in the Hebrew text of the Bible will have to be altered so as to curtail the interval between Hezekiah and Ahab by about* 40 *years*. In his Abstract of Dates, he places the war of the king of Assyria with Hazael king of Aram, and the Assyrians' taking of tribute from Jehu king of Israel, at B. C. 841; whereas by the Hebrew account, Jehu began a reign of 28 years in the year of Ahaziah son of Jehoram son of Jehoshaphat king of Judah; that is, in B. C. 810+29 +40+6+1=886. There may still be a question for the competent, whether an omission of about 40 names may not have occurred in compiling the list of Eponym archons in the existing Assyrian Canon *above the year of the Eclipse*. It will be seen presently, that the testimony of the Hebrew books betrays no inconsistency; so that, if 40 years are to be deducted from the Annals, the same number must likewise be taken from a certain 390 years in Ezekiel; whether, having thus been deducted, they are to be added or not to the other sum of 40 years in the context.

(*c.*) Of the kings of Judah, the predecessors of the first set down in our Comparative Table, Clinton strives to reduce the measure of the united reigns of Jehoshaphat and his son Jehoram from (25+8⸺) 33 years complete, to 31 years complete. Without entering into his argument, we will only call attention to the unsoundness of the grounds on which he founded the necessity for reducing the total number of years assigned by Hebrew history to the kings of Judah. From the first of Rehoboam to the last year of Zedekiah, the total number, as recorded, is $17+3+41+25+8+1+6+40+29+52+16+16+29+55+2+31+11+11=393$ years. This sum Clinton increases by the addition of two quarters of a year, the reigns of Jehoahaz son of Josiah and of Jeconiah son of Jehoiakim, which we have shewn to be fractions respectively of the last calendar year assigned in the annals to Josiah and of the last calendar year assigned there to Jehoiakim. Now, there is a passage of the prophet Ezekiel (Ezek. iv. 1-8) where the years of the iniquity of the house of Israel and of the house of Judah, 390 and 40, are said to have been laid on the prophet to be borne by him (as God had borne them) while he watched, in mimic siege, before a tile whereon the city Jerusalem had been pourtrayed, lying 390 days on his left side for the one, and forty days on his right side for the other. The years thus represented, were years previous to the siege, (that is, to the ninth year of Zedekiah, when the siege began) not, as Clinton has regarded them, years accomplished in that eleventh and last of Zedekiah when the siege terminated in the capture and destruction of Jerusalem. Accordingly, when we have deducted the years of the siege (the last three regnal years of Zedekiah) the particulars derived from the history make up exactly the 390 years spoken of to Ezekiel; for $393-3=390$ years of iniquity from the first of Rehoboam to the 8th of Zedekiah. We have already had occasion to shew, in commenting on Zech. i. 12, that the seventy years of indignation against Jerusalem (the result of the iniquity of Jerusalem) began with that ninth year of Zedekiah in which the Chaldæan besiegers first sat down before Jerusalem. The 40 years of iniquity, signified and commemorated by the prophet's lying 40 days on his right side, seem to be the years of the reign of Solomon, the first of the kings, the sons of David; see 1 Kings xi. 42 and 2 Chron. ix. 30. The three periods put together, $40+390+70$, make up exactly 500 years from the first year of Solomon to the first of Darius son of Hystaspes. But in the important passage of Ezekiel, the terms Israel and Judah would seem more appropriate, if interchanged; for Solomon during his 40 years was king of all Israel, whereas his successors from Rehoboam to Zedekiah, were kings of Judah; that is, Judah and Benjamin only.

We have now, we hope, sufficiently justified *not only* our dates for the three accessions in our column of kings of Judah which Clinton has dated differently. More than this, we have shewn reason for believing all his preceding dates of accession of kings of Judah, with the other dates dependent on these, to be fixed too low. Thus we make the first year of Rehoboam to commence with the month Tisri B. C.

(590+390==) 980 instead of 976, and the first year of Solomon with Tisri B. C. (980+·40==)1020 instead of 1016.

F.

The column of High priests, the last of our Table, must now be justified by our authorities. The first four High priests, from Hilkiah to Jehozadak, are the last four of the line of 22 that begins with Eleazar son of Aaron in 1 Chron. vi. 4-14; where (as in Joseph. *Antiq.* xx. 10) we are told that when the Lord carried away Judah and Jerusalem by the hand of Nebukhadnezzar, Jehozadak son of Seraiah went among them. Seraiah is mentioned in 2 Kings xxv. 18-21, where (after the capture, pillage, and destruction of Jerusalem in B. C. 587) we read that the king of Babylon's captain of the guard took Seraiah the chief priest and Zephaniah the second priest, with many others of highest place in the nation, and brought them to Riblah in the land of Hamath, where the king of Babylon smote them and slew them. For Seraiah and Jehozadak his son, see also Joseph. *Antiq.* x. 9 § 5. In § 6, Josephus adds a list of the high priests from Zadok, who was the first that officiated in Solomon's temple, to Jehozadak, who went into captivity. He says, that they all succeeded, sons to fathers, in the office, and makes Seraiah succeed Hilkiah; thus omitting Azariah, though (according to 1 Chronicles) son of Hilkiah and father of Seraiah. Josephus's list is in other respects still more at variance with the one in 1 Chronicles. But the Hilkiah of both lists may be recognized in Hilkiah the High Priest of that 18th year of king Josiah which began with the month Tisri in the year B. C. 623; see 2 Kings xxii. 4, 8, 10, 12, 14; xxiii. 4, 24; 2 Chron. xxxiv. 9, 14-16, 20-22.

For the line of six from Jeshua to Jaddua, we send the reader to Nehemiah xii. 10-12, 22-23, 26. As to individuals; for Jeshua who returned from Babylon in company with Zerubbabel in the first year of Cyrus, we refer to the books of Haggai and Zechariah (especially Zech. iii. 1-10 and vi. 11-13); to Ezra iii. 2, 9; iv. 3; v. 2. Josephus also following these authorities makes him the contemporary of Darius son of Hystaspes; *Antiq.* xi. 3 § 10. It is to be remembered, that the first year of Cyrus at Babylon, beginning with Markhesvan B. C. 536 according to the contemporary Khaldæan annalists, and with the previous month Tisri according to the practice followed by the old annals of Judah, began probably by the Perso-Median reckoning with the Assyrian Nisannu or Jewish Nisan, the Perso-Median Garmapada.

For Joiakim son of Jeshua, we say in particular, that Josephus places his priesthood in the time of Xerxes; *Antiq.* xi. 5 § 1. There is no other Joiakim than this, who can be meant by the high priest of the same name in that hopelessly unhistorical book Judith (iv. 6, 8, 14, xv. 8) and accordingly, in that book the narrator supposes the Jews to be but recently returned from their captivity; see Jud. iv. 3.

He was succeeded after his death, by his son Eliashib; *Ant.* xi. 5 § 5. We find Eliashib acting as high priest for twelve years and more of the time that Nehemiah was governor at Jerusalem; that is, from 445 to 434 B. C., the 20th to the 32d year (and later still) in the reign of Artaxerxes son of Xerxes; see Nehem. iii, 1; xiii. 4–7.

His death and the succession of his son Joiada, is noted by Josephus, *Ant.* xi. 7 § 1. Now, this Joiada is mentioned, and (apparently) as then high priest, during the second residence of Nehemiah at Jerusalem; Nehem. xiii. 5—7: 28.

Another son of Eliashib named Johanan, occurs Ezra x. 6; Joseph. *Ant.* xi. 5 § 4; but he is not in the line of descent we write of, if, as we take it, the Johanan son of Eliashib in Nehem. xii. 23 be the Johanan of the previous context, a grandson of Eliashib's; whose succession to the priesthood at the death of his father Joiada is attested by Joseph. *Ant.* xi 7 § 1. This Johanan (so called, Nehem. xii. 22, 23; but called Jonathan Neh. xii. 11) was high priest (according to Josephus) in the reign of an Artaxerxes (other than the Artaxerxes son of Xerxes, of his previous chapter) mentioned by him but a few lines before. For he tells us, that Johanan had a brother named Jeshua, a friend of Bagôses, " who was captain for the other Artaxerxes." He certainly means the second of the Akhæmenian kings that reigned under that name, him the Greeks called Mnemon, the grandson of the first. For we cannot join with Prideaux (*Connexion &c.* vol. 2 p. 71) in rejecting Isaac Vossius's emendation (justified it is said by the old Latin version of Rufinus) which substitutes ἄλλου for λαοῦ in Josephus's term descriptive of Bagôses, ὁ στρατηγὸς τοῦ λαοῦ 'Αρταξέρξου, which to us seems manifestly corrupt. With the phraseology as amended, compare a well-known designation, ὁ ἄλλη Μαρίᾳ, S. Mat. xxviii. 1. By this emendation, another Persian king is introduced into the history; and the broad gap in Josephus's enumeration of the regal contemporaries of his high priests, is diminished. Moreover, Artaxerxes the grandson is exactly the king we look for as the contemporary of the high priest, the grandson of Eliashib.

For seven years under the captaincy of Bagôses, the Jews were obliged to pay 50 drachmas a day for each lamb, before they were permitted to offer the daily morning and evening sacrifices. In the reign of Darius son of Hystaspes a very different state of things had been decreed. The king had ordered his officers, that whatever the elders of the Jews needed—both young bullocks and rams and lambs for the burnt-offerings of the God of the Heavens, wheat, salt, wine, and oil—should be given them day by day without fail, according to the appointment of the priests at Jerusalem, that they might offer sacrifices of sweet savours unto the God of the heavens, and pray for the life of the king and of his sons. (Ezra vi. 9–10.) Darius's grandson Artaxerxes, when he sent Ezra to Jerusalem, had certified all the treasurers beyond the river, that touching any of the priests and Levites, singers, porters, Nethinim or ministers of the House of the God of the Heavens at Jerusalem, it should not be lawful to impose toll, tribute, or custom, upon them (Ezra vii. 24). When Josephus states the fine which the commander of the king's troops exacted for every lamb in the time of the second Artaxerxes, the grandson of the first, at 50 drachmas, he probably means the well-known Attic drachmas of Solon; five of which were worth but three Æginetan drachmas, so that 10,000 of them, were required to make up a single Æginetan, that is Babylonian, talent; see his mention of the *kinkhar* or talent weighing 100 *minæ* (that is, the 60 *minæ* of which weighed as much as 100 common *minæ*) Joseph. *Ant.* iii. 6 § 7. The story is, that Bagôses had promised Jeshua to procure for him the high priesthood, which his brother was then invested with. Jeshua on this, presumed to dispute with Johanan "in the sanctuary," ἐν τῷ ναῷ, (not ἐν τῷ ἱερῷ) perhaps obstructing him in his duty or assuming it to himself. Johanan was so exasperated by the provocation (whatever it was) as to give his brother a blow, of which he died on the spot. Hearing of what had happened, Bagôses came up, and with great wrath began saying to the Jews; " What, have ye dared to commit a murder in your sanctuary?" Then, as he was about to enter, when the Jews attempted to stop him, as one " unclean," (for he was neither priest nor Israelite) he exclaimed, " Am not I cleaner than he who slew a man in the sanctuary?" and so went in, followed of course by his armed attendants. This defilement of the temple by the Persians, as Josephus terms the act of Bagôses, seems to have been regarded by the Jews in general a greater calamity and more memorable profanation than the crime which had occasioned it. Nor does Josephus express a different opinion. But he records the indignant sayings of the Gentile Officer; he remarks how dreadful it was that Johanan, while acting as priest, should have committed such an impiety on a brother; he adds it as an aggravation, that no so savage and impious a deed had ever happened among either Greeks or Barbarians; and he concludes, that the pollution of the sanctuary by the Persians and the slavery of the people, that is, (as we may understand him) their being obliged for seven years to submit to the daily exaction of amercements before they could offer the morning and evening sacrifices, were a judgment of God's upon them for the crime that had been committed. Similar conclusions, no doubt, he would have readily suggested, from the various profanations at the hands of Greeks and Romans, which the same temple from time to time sustained; till at last in his own days, its sacrifices and other services were violently abolished in the destruction of the edifice and of the city. And, if the murder of Jeshua (according to the Jewish historian) provoked God to defile His temple by the Persians, the same Josephus ought to have seen the cause of the final calamity of his nation in the death of a greater Jeshua than the brother of Johanan.

Lastly, Josephus confirms our Table, by telling us that, on the death of Johanan, his son Jaddua succeeded to the high priest's office; *Ant.* xi. 7 § 2. For the interesting account of Alexander's visit to Jerusalem, his behaviour to the high priest Jaddua, and the encouragement he received out of the book of Daniel, after his capture of Tyre and Gaza, see Jos. *Ant.* xi. 8 §§ 4, 5.

We are now brought to Josephus's story of Jaddua's brother Manasseh, who was expelled from the privileges and duty of a priest because he had married Nikaso daughter of Sanaballetes, a Khuthæan by race, who had been sent satrap to Samaria "by Darius the last King," ὑπὸ Δαρείου τοῦ τελευταίου βασιλίως, or, "by Darius the last of the name," if, (as we suspect), the word βασιλίως be an interpolation. A notion seems to us implied in the phraseology of Josephus, that Sanaballetes had been sent from the old seat of the Khuthæans to Samaria, when he was entrusted with the government of the colony that, since the days of Esarhaddon king of Assyria (not Shalmanezer, as Josephus supposes, *Ant.* xi. 14 §§ 1–3), had occupied the country of Ephraim. Till that colony was sent from Babylon, Khuthah, and other parts, by Esarhaddon, or till the occurrence of events determining that measure; though the capital Samaria had been taken and no fewer than 27,000 families had been carried away into Assyria in the first year of the reign of Esarhaddon's grandfather Sargon, the land had continued for nearly six and forty years (65—6 years of Hezekiah and 13 of Ahaz; compare Isai. vii. 8) to belong to a remnant of its former inhabitants. Ephraim had not yet been *broken so as to be no more a people;* and, accordingly, their ruler, Menahem, was one of a crowd who came with gifts and homage to Sennacherib; when, after th conquest of Phœnicia in the 3rd year of his reign, he was preparing to enter the Philistine country and Hezekiah's kingdom of Judah: see the Taylor-Cylinder Inscription translated by Mr H. F. Talbot; Journal R. A. S. vol. xix. p. 144.

Josephus supposed Khuthah to be in Persis, meaning, probably, Susiana, but he plainly could not tell where it was; and we may presume he had no notion of its identity with Tiggaba or Digba, although that (it is said) is now fully established by the monuments. Sir H. C. Rawlinson places this city not far from Babylon to the north-east, in a situation marked by ruins now called *Ibrahim;* see Rawlinson's Herodotus; vol. 1 p. 313, 632, vol. 2 p. 587. The name written כּוּתָה and כּוּת in 2 Kings xvii. 24, 30 is transcribed Χουθὰ and Χοὺθ in the Septuagint.

According to Josephus, our sole authority, the son-in-law of Sanaballetes was the brother of Jaddua. He refused to be re-invested with his priestly office at the price of a divorce from his wife; preferring to depend upon his father-in-law's exertions on his behalf. Many others of his nation "both priests and Israelites," who for marrying foreign women (and perhaps other transgressions of the law) had been excommunicated at home, joined Manasseh in Samaria. Sanaballetes gave them lands; and promised to obtain authority from Darius to build them a temple of which Manasseh should be high priest, on a hill overhanging Shechem, named Gerizim. About this time, Alexander son of Philip, having succeeded to the Macedonian throne, invaded the empire of Darius and began a series of conquests, by defeating the king of Persia's satraps at the passage of the river Granicus. Darius mustered a great army, crossed the Euphrates, passed through the defiles of Mount Taurus into Cilicia, to stop the invader's progress. But he was defeated in a great battle at Issus, and was obliged to fly for his life. Sanaballetes had hoped when Darius returned victorious, to obtain from him the permission to build the desired temple on Mount Gerizim. But when Darius fled, and when Alexander entered Syria, took Damascus, and having received possession of Sidon, began the siege of Tyre, Sanaballetes immediately came to his camp with 8,000 men, offering his services and surrendering his districts. He was well received, and obtained from Alexander the license he had looked for at the hands of Darius. Accordingly, the temple was built immediately, that thenceforth all Jews in Samaria and their proselytes might worship there; Manasseh entered on the priesthood, and Sanaballetes who was old, died before the nine months were over, seven of which Alexander employed at Tyre and two at Gaza; Joseph. *Ant.* xi. 7 § 2; 8 § 4.

If we believe this very circumstantial account, Sanaballetes the Khuthæan satrap of Samaria, who died (it says) in the fourth regnal year of the third and last Darius king of Persia, cannot be that Sanballat (in the Septuagint, Sanaballat) the Horonite, who was already governor of Samaria in the 20th year of the reign of Artaxerxes son of Xerxes; that is, in (4+2+21+46+19+22===) the 114th preceding year by Ptolemy's Canon. In other words, the father-in-law of Jaddua's brother cannot be the contemporary of Jaddua's great-grandfather, Eliashib.

But if there were *two* Sanballats, how is it that Josephus knows but of one? To this it is hardly a sufficient reply, that though he gives us an account of Nehemiah's services, Josephus does not appear to have had before him the book of Nehemiah, in which Nehemiah's contemporary Sanballat, the Horonite, is so frequently mentioned. But we believe that, whether from no fault of his own or from neglect, Josephus did not use Nehemiah's record. Not only do we find him in his narrative, going beyond Nehemiah's record, but he contradicts Nehemiah. First, he mentions one Adæus the governor west of the Euphrates, to whom the King's letter in Nehemiah's favour was addressed: *Antiq.* xi. 5 §§ 6, 7; whereas Nehemiah tells us, the king granted him letters to the governors of the different districts, but does not give their names. He attests only a letter to Asaph keeper of the king's forest, to enable him to obtain the timber required for his various buildings. Again, identifying with Xerxes that Artaxerxes who sent Ezra and Nehemiah (as they themselves testify) to Jerusalem, Josephus tells us that Nehemiah arrived there in the 25th year of Xerxes, that he was for two years and four months engaged in rebuilding the walls, and that, in the ninth month of the 28th year of Xerxes, he finished the work; §§ 7, 8. In one at least of our author's three figures, as we read them, some corruption has crept in. To make them consistent, either one might read *the 5th month of the 26th year* for the date of Nehemiah's arrival, or one might substitute *three years and nine months* for the time of building. Also, it is to be noticed, that the authority followed by Josephus can hardly have placed the missions of Ezra and Nehemiah in the reign of Xerxes. It bungled its narrative if it did, for Xerxes (according to Ptolemy's Canon) reigned but 21 years in all. Nehemiah tells us a very different story (Neh. vi. 15) namely, that the wall was finished on the 25th day of Elul, in a space of 52 days, following (as the previous narrative shews) immediately after Nehemiah's arrival at Jerusalem, in the 20th year of Artaxerxes; see Nehem. vi. 15; comparing therewith ii. 1, 11. The author followed by Josephus may have thought 52 days too short a time, as probably it was, for repairing that destruction of the wall of Jerusalem which the Babylonians had accomplished in the year B. C. 587. But Nehemiah's work was to repair a later and less thorough dismantlement, which (apparently, in the course of the war waged by Megabyzus satrap of Syria against the king) had been sustained by a new wall rebuilt, as we have elsewhere inferred, under an order of the present king's, which he issued at about the same date as he did his commission to Ezra.

The conclusion, that Josephus made no use of Nehemiah's own account of his administration, may serve to justify him—not for having omitted a former Sanballat, but rather—for having misplaced the personage in the reign of the last Darius, and in the high priesthood of Jaddus. Prideaux long ago pointed out the gross improbability of the story Josephus has handed to us—that the temple on Mount Gerizim was built by Alexander's permission while that enemy of Darius was engaged in the successive sieges of Tyre and Gaza; see the *Connexion &c.* vol. 2 pp. 67, 69. Alexander's share in the providing of a temple in Samaria for Sanballat's son-in-law the priest Manasseh, looks like a late Samaritan invention.

On the whole, we conclude to follow Prideaux's judgment, that it is one and the same Sanballat governor of Samaria, who figures in the narratives of Nehemiah and Josephus; and we are therefore obliged to believe further, that Sanballat's son-in-law Manasseh was not the brother of Jaddus. We accept the view taken by Prideaux, who sees Manasseh in that un-named son of Joiada son of Eliashib the high priest, who was driven from him by Nehemiah governor of Judah, for having made himself son-in-law of Sanballat the Horonite; Nehem. xiii. 28. By the bye, if Horonite mean a man of Horonaim in Moab, there must be a reference to Sanballat as well as to Tobiah in the citation of the Law of Moses concerning the Ammonite and the Moabite, that is made in Nehem. xiii. 1. Thus, the building of the temple on Mount Gerizim must be placed, we think—not as by Josephus in the time of the third and last of the Akhæmenian kings who reigned by the name of Darius, but—in the time of the second that assumed that regal name, the bastard son and successor of the king who sent Ezra and Nehemiah to Jerusalem. Also, the first high priest of that temple, Manasseh, being not brother of Jaddua but son of Joiada, must have been a brother of the Johanan and Jeshua, whose dispute about the high priesthood in the Holy Place when the second Darius's son, the second Artaxerxes, was king and Bagôses was captain of the Persian garrison at Jerusalem, has been already related.

Prideaux contends, that the expulsion of Manasseh by Nehemiah from Jerusalem, was the final act of the first seven year-weeks of those seventy spoken of to Daniel, which, (by our calculation,) ended with the month Elul A. D. 32. Now, according to the same calculation, the first seven weeks of years ended with Elul B. C. 410 about three months before the end of the year of Nabonassar 338, which in Ptolemy's Canon is given to Darius Nothus as his 14th regnal year. That Manasseh's expulsion coincided with this epoch, Prideaux would shew to be probable, by observing (vol. 2 p. 217 note) that, according to the numbers of years assigned to the high-priests in the *Chronicon Alexandrinum* of Scaliger (or *Chronicon Paschale*, as the enlarged edition of Du Cange is entitled) the first year of Joiada's priesthood is brought down to the 11th regnal year assigned in Ptolemy's Canon to Darius Nothus.

This statement may be explained by adding, that the years of priesthood at Jerusalem after the return from Babylon, are dated in this Chronicle *from the complete restoration of the temple in the reign of Darius son of Hystaspes* and *from the 8th year of Darius son of Hystaspes*, (we pass over the mistaken identification of this year with the 2nd of the 63rd Olympiad); see *Chron. Paschale*, ed. Paris, A. D. 1668, pp. 188, 189. Both here, and repeated at pp. 207, 208, we have a list of 21 priests and their respective years of successive priesthood, amounting to 483 years; termed also 69 weeks of years, and extending to the end of the priesthood of Alexander Jannæus. Among these, be it noted that to the 18th in succession are given (perhaps, by misprint) in the first copy, 18 years' priesthood; for which we should read 8 years with the second copy of the list, p. 208; as the stated total of 483 years requires. The priests and priesthoods we are concerned with here, (the first six) are

Jesus son of Josedek 32 years;
Joakim son of Jesus 30;
Eliasib son of Joiakim 40;
Jodae son of Eliasib 36;
Jannæus son of Jodae 32;

And Jaddus son of Jannæus *in whose time Alexander built Alexandria and came to Jerusalem and worshipped*, 20.

The following 15 priests of whom Alexander Jannæus is the last (it may, by the bye, be briefly noticed) exercised their office, 21+15+14+ 32+26+22+24+16+7+33+17+8+27+1+30 years. These 293 years of the last 15 priests, added to the 190 years of the first six, make up the aforesaid total stated in the Chronicle, 483 years or 69 weeks of years. It appears, then, that since by Ptolemy's Canon, Darius son of Hystaspes reigned 36 years; his son Xerxes 21 years, and Artaxerxes son of Xerxes 41 years; and since the temple, according to Ezra, was finished in Adar of the sixth year of Darius; the 103rd year of subsequent priesthood, being the first year of Jodae or Joiada son of Eliashib, ended with the 11th régnal year of Darius Nothus, reckoned according to the Assyrio-Judæan registers, that is, ended with the month Adarru or Adar B. C. 412; while the first seven weeks of years since Tisri B. C. 459, ended with the sixth month of the 4th year of Joiada's priesthood; the civil year following (or the first year of the second seven weeks) being, apparently, the first Jubilee year of the Prophetic Seventy weeks, as the civil year, beginning with (or marked by) the call of the Gentiles in the person of the centurion Cornelius, and following the 70th week, was a tenth year of Jubilee. But we know not if there be evidence of the original authenticity of the list of high priests, beginning with Jeshua son of Jozadak and preserved in the Chronicon Paschale; nor though that authenticity be owned probable, do we know how far the several priesthoods may have been stretched or curtailed in duration by the arbitrary handling of early Christian criticism. Nor can we say, whether it was on good authority, or merely for the sake of a theory concerning the Prophetic Seventy Weeks, that the 32 years' priesthood of Jeshua were made to begin after the completion of the House of God, in the reign of Darius son of Hystaspes, when on the 10th of Tisri B. C. 515 after 72 years' interruption, the highest function of the priesthood (that on the day of Atonement) could perhaps first be discharged. We observe, that the total of years given to the first six priests, namely, those from Jeshua to Jaddun, is the exact total of years assigned in Ptolemy's Canon to the Reigns of Persian kings from Darius son of Hystaspes to Codomannus Darius son of Arsames. So that Jeshua's priesthood being supposed to begin later than the reign of the son of Hystaspes, that of Jaddun is necessarily extended almost to the end of the reign of the last Darius's successor, Alexander the Macedonian. Georgius Syncellus, too, gives the names of the priests and the years of their office after the return from Babylon, beginning with Jeshua. But the position he assigns to the first priesthood, and consequently to those that came after, differs from that given in the Paschal Chronicle. He makes Jeshua's priesthood extend from the first year of Cyrus to the 20th of Darius son of Hystaspes; an interval which he computes at 60 years, *i. e.* of Cyrus, 31, Cambyses, 8, the Magian, 1, and Darius's first 20. Then, he gives to Joiakim 36 years; to Eliashib 34; to Joiada 36; to Johanan 32; and to Jaddua 20; pp. 240, 248, 255; or in Dindorf's ed. pp. 456, 457, 473, 484. Though the 70 years' total of the first two of these five priesthoods is differently apportioned to Joiakim and Eliashib than in the Paschal Chronicle, the other priesthoods, and the total of the five are the same. But this total 158 years is at least misplaced; since it wants twelve years to fill the interval between, and exclusive of, the 20th of Darius son of Hystaspes, and even the first regnal year at Babylon of the last Darius's successor, Alexander the Great. For that interval by Ptolemy's Canon (Theon's copy) is $16 + 21 + 41 + 19 + 46 + 21 + 2 + 4$, or in all 170 years; though it is true that the Syncellus (after the example of that impudent manipulation of Ptolemy's Canon which he calls " the Ecclesiastical Canon"), having first added 22 years to the previous space (called the reign of Cyrus) between the reigns of Nabonnedus and Cambyses, contracts in turn the 170 years of which we now speak to 153 years. See Geo. Syncellus, ed. Dindorf, pp. 442–487, and for "the Ecclesiastical Canon," pp. 393, 394.

About two centuries after Alexander's conquest, the Samaritan sanctuary on Mount Gerizim (which, to escape the persecution endured by the Jews under Antiokhus Epiphanes, had been declared, by a very "broad" and comprehensive "liberality," a temple of *the Hellenian Zeus*) was laid waste by John (or Johanan) surnamed Hyrcanus, of the Asmonean family, the Jewish high priest and prince, the 19th from Jeshua son of Jehozadak. See Joseph. *Antiq.* xiii. 9, § 1, and Geo. Syncell. p. 289, or ed. Dind. p. 548. That which is now pointed out as the site, is described as in shape a *trapezium* or four-sided figure, of which at least one pair of opposite sides are not parallel; also, as measuring about 14 yards by 16; being cut on the bare and level rock. See Dr. Wilson's "Lands of the Bible," vol. ii. pp. 69, 70. The present priestly family among the Samaritans in Shechem (Nablous, *i.e.* Neapolis), at the foot of Mount Gerizim, is said to be of the tribe of Levi, and the rest of the community claims descent from the tribes of Ephraim and Manasseh, sons of Joseph; vol. ii. p. 63. This appears also from the language of their written documents; see the two Marriage Contracts in the same volume, pp. 689–697.

APPENDIX NO. II.

On the position in Persian History of Manetho's 28th, 29th, and 30th Egyptian Dynasties.—See p. 94, note (a).

A

PROFESSING to report from the Egyptian historian Manetho, the chronologers Africanus and Eusebius, as reported themselves by

Georgius Syncellus (see Goar's Paris ed. pp. 76, 77, as marked in
the margin of the Bonn edition of Dindorf which we use), both place
the whole of Darius Nothus's nineteen years' reign *before* the eight
or nine reigns of native Egyptians which fill up the 28th, 29th, and
30th dynasties. The same epoch, of the recovery of independence in
Egypt, is indicated in a document of which the Syncellus has given
us an abstract, and which he describes as an *Old Egyptian Chronicle;*
though probably it is more recent than Manetho's work. For (after
having stated that the 27th dynasty consisted of five Persians, who
reigned for the space of 124 years in Egypt,—and after an omission
of the 28th dynasty, by the *least* defective of the two Paris MSS. of
our Syncellus's work) that abstract of the Old Chronicle proceeds (in
Geo. Syncellus, ed. Paris, p. 52) to enumerate, as the 29th, a *Tanite*
dynasty that reigned 39 years, and then it concludes with a 30th
dynasty, of a single *Tanite,* who reigned 18 years. Now the several
periods, occupied by these dynasties, and by those which preceded
them, not only are numbered successively (as the reader may gather
from what has been said), but are summed up at last as separate
parts of 3 myriad 6 thousand 5 hundred and 25 years, or 25 times
1461 years,—a period called by Egyptians and Greeks the *Restoration of the Zodiac.* Therefore the 27th dynasty in the Old Chronicle
preceded the 28th, 29th, and 30th entirely; and its 124 years' reign
of five Persians must be taken to denote the same period as the $124\frac{1}{3}$
years of Africanus's 27th dynasty, and as the $120\frac{1}{3}$ years of Eusebius's
27th dynasty, because the number of the dynasty is the same in all,
and the number of years reigned, nearly the same.

This identity is not affected by the fact that by the Old Chronicle
the kings of this dynasty are *five* in number, while according to
Africanus and Eusebius they are *eight.* For the five are found in
Ptolemy's Babylonian Canon also, where they form a series under the
following names: *Cambyses, Darius I., Xerxes, Artaxerxes I.,* and
Darius II.,—reigning $8 + 36 + 21 + 41 + 19 = 125$ years. And the
eight consist of these same five with three other kings (purposely
excluded from the Canon); namely, *Artabanus,* put in after Xerxes;
and *a second Xerxes,* with *a Sogdianus* after him, put in between
Artaxerxes and Darius II. These are the three which make up
Africanus's eight kings. The eight reigns of Eusebius are made up
by the insertion of a Magian reign after Cambyses, instead of an
Artabanus after Xerxes: otherwise they are the same as Africanus's
eight.

As to the duration of the dynasty, Eusebius is nearer the truth than
Africanus and the Old Chronicle. It was four years less than the 125
years at Babylon given to the five kings by Ptolemy's Canon. For
the Egyptians reckoned the fifth year of Cambyses at Babylon, his
first in Egypt; so that while their year of Nabonassar 219 was his
first at Babylon, his first in Egypt was their year of Nabonassar 223.

(The difference between the Egyptian and the Khaldæan years of Nabonassar will be explained in the article next to this.) In the last article we showed the agreement of Africanus and Eusebius in reporting Manetho to have made Cambyses begin his reign over Egypt in the fifth year of his reign over the Persians. Now, as a year in the Annals of Egypt (which Manetho certainly meant by the fifth of Cambyses), the 223d of Nabonassar began with the 2d day of January B.C. 525. This testimony of Manetho is confirmed by Diodorus. For (in i. 68, § 6) he places Cambyses' conquest of Egypt in the third year of the 63d Olympiad, *i.e.* between the midsummers of B.C. 526 and 525. The conquest became an accomplished fact, it would seem, in June B.C. 525; but according to the Egyptian rule, the first year of Cambyses in Egypt *ended with the civil year current at his accession to the kingly power.*

The number, therefore, of Egyptian years attributed in the Annals to the Persian dynasty, from the 223d of Nabonassar, the first of Cambyses in Egypt, to the 243d of Nabonassar, the last year of Darius Nothus's reign there, by Ptolemy's Canon, is 121 years, as we have said. And the time actually reigned is the same. For, not only does Cambyses appear to have completed the conquest of Egypt (as we have elsewhere concluded from Herodotus) in the sixth or seventh month, that is June or July, of B.C. 525, but, according to Diodorus, the last king of the dynasty died shortly before midsummer B.C. 404, or towards the end of the fourth year of the 93d Olympiad. See Diodor. xiii. 8 (comparing 68, 76, 80, 104); also Herod. iii. 14. So that, as it has been observed, Eusebius calculated the length of the reign in Egypt of the 27th dynasty more accurately than Africanus and the compiler of the Old Chronicle.

More than enough has now been said on the identity of the Old Chronicle's 27th dynasty with that of Manetho as reported by Africanus and Eusebius; but a fact is incidentally conspicuous, of some importance to an estimate of the age and authority of the Old Chronicle,—that,· while it agrees with Ptolemy's Babylonian Canon as to the number of kings in the 27th dynasty, it also seems to repeat the error of Africanus's Manetho (or Africanus himself) as to the duration of the dynasty in Egypt.

As to the main question, the position in Persian history of the 28th, 29th, and 30th Egyptian dynasties, we now have adduced Manetho's testimony, as represented by Africanus and Eusebius, and also that of the Old Chronicle,—to the effect, that the Egyptians recovered their independence, and that a native dynasty occupied the throne, after Darius Nothus's reign; that is, not earlier than the Egyptian year of Nabonassar 344, which year began with the 2d of December B.C. 405, and was marked, as it proceeded, by the death of the Persian monarch.

Against this date for the accession of the 28th dynasty, or this assignment of the year in which the revolt from the Persians began, it may be alleged that our Syncellus (Paris ed. p. 256) prefaces his own table of the 28th, 29th, and 30th dynasties thus: *Egypt revolted from the Persians in the second year of Nothus Darius.* Also previously (Paris ed. p. 255), on the same Persian king, he had noted, *In this king's reign, that was surnamed Darius Nothus, the misfortune of the Athenians befell in Sicily, and Egypt revolted from the Persians.* Further, he makes the first year of Darius Nothus to be the World-year 5091, and that of the first independent native king in Egypt to be the World-year 5092. Of the meaning of his testimony, therefore, there is no doubt.

We know not what author our Syncellus followed here; but to us it seems scarcely credible that Egypt should have revolted, even a short time only before Athens surrendered to the Peloponnesians, and Darius Nothus died—events nearly simultaneous in B.C. 404; and that there should have been produced no such effect upon the war, in which the Athenians had been engaged, as either Thucydides, Xenophon, or an author repeated by Diodorus would have been obliged to record,—no stipulation with the Lacedæmonians, on Darius's part, about Egypt,—no subsidy from Egypt received by the Athenians,—while, after the loss of their fleet and army in Sicily, they still struggled to preserve their supremacy over the islands and coasts of the Ægæan Sea. Some such succour might have been lent them as we find the Lacedæmonians obtaining afterwards, when their relation with Artaxerxes Mnemon was what had subsisted between the Athenians and Darius Nothus, at the end of his reign. According to Justin vi. 2, when Artaxerxes' satrap Pharnabazus threatened the Lacedæmonians with a naval war, to be conducted by Conon the Athenian, they received from *Hercynio king of Egypt* 100 trireme galleys and 600,000 bushels of corn. It is immaterial here to ask whether Hercynio (who is not mentioned in the list of kings, and who must have been the contemporary of the first king of the 29th dynasty Nepherites) is properly described. It may be concluded, however, from Diod. xiv. 79, that any business of his was but that of a subordinate in the matter.

Again, in the notices we have given, of our Syncellus's own, respecting a revolt of Egypt from the Persians which was consummated by the accession of the 28th dynasty, there is a perceptible discrepancy. From our second citation of those notices it would seem to follow that the revolt was subsequent to the calamity of the Athenians in Sicily; whereas the notice before cited dates it in the second year of Darius Nothus's reign, that is, in the year of Nabonassar 326, and (according to the Egyptian use of the era of Nabonassar) in the year of Egypt that began the 7th of December B.C. 423,—ten years before the catastrophe in Sicily.

On the whole we conclude that the evidence of Manetho and the

Old Chronicle is of much greater weight than this of the Syncellus, as to the commencement of independence in Egypt under the 28th dynasty: and our own suspicion is that the Syncellus's author really stated the revolt of Egypt to have begun *in the second year of Darius Nothus's son and successor Artaxerxes Mnemon*, otherwise Artaxerxes II. We suppose, then, that the revolt of Egypt from the Persians broke out shortly after the death of Darius Nothus; and that in the Annals of the country the year of Nothus's death—being the 344th of the Egyptian era of Nabonassar, whose first of Thoth was the 2d of December B.C. 405—was made the first year, not of Artaxerxes Mnemon (Nothus's eldest son and successor at Babylon), but of Amyrtæus the Saite, the sole king of the 28th dynasty.

It somewhat countenances this conclusion, that the earliest notices we know of in Persian history respecting the loss of Egypt, are during the expedition of Darius Nothus's younger son Cyrus to dethrone Artaxerxes Mnemon in B.C. 401. After Cyrus was slain in battle at Cunaxa,—when, returning unconquered, the Greek division of Cyrus's army had reached the southern, or left, bank of the (greater) Zab river in Assyria, their camp having been daily furnished with a bazaar for the purchase of necessaries, and their march directed and accompanied, according to terms agreed upon between themselves and the king, by forces under command of the satrap Tissaphernes, who was likewise returning to the coast,—the relation between the two camps had become feverishly mistrustful; and we find Klearkhus, the principal leader of the Greeks, seeking an interview with Tissaphernes, where, to remove misunderstandings, and mitigate ill-will, he confessed the advantages derived from the treaty by his countrymen, and on the other hand pointed out the great profit that might be made out of it by the king. He specified several employments that might be made of the army he commanded in the then present condition of the empire. Of these, one was to *chastise the Egyptians:* see Xenoph. *Anab.* ii. 5, § 15. The same suggestion would seem to have been thrown out before by others, when first, after the battle (in which the Greeks overthrew all they met, but Cyrus was slain), the king Artaxerxes sent to parley with these remaining antagonists: *Anab.* ii. 1, § 14. Hence we are led to suspect that, occurring, as we have shown reason to suppose it did, immediately after his father's death and his brother's accession to the throne, the revolt of Egypt and the prolonged impunity of the revolt, had much assisted in determining the attempt of Cyrus.

B

But how long the native government lasted in Egypt, which sprang up out of the revolt, or in what year of Okhus Artaxerxes' reign the country was reannexed to the Persian empire, it is not easy to decide;

for the evidence, whether as to the duration of the independence, or as to the year in which it terminated, is contradictory.

From Diodorus xvi. 40-51 (comparing for the Olympic year, chapp. 30, 52, 53) it would appear that it was in the winter of the arkhonship of Apollodorus at Athens, the third year of the 107th Olympiad, when the conquest of Egypt was completed by Okhus. That is to say, the last native king, Nectanebôs (or second Nectanebus), left Memphis to the forces of Okhus, and fled into Ethiopia, in the 10th year of Okhus's Persian reign according to Ptolemy's Canon, the year of Nabonassar 399, which, as a year of Egyptian chronology, began with the 19th of November B.C. 350.

Diodorus relates, under the year of Thettalus—the archon by whom Apollodorus was immediately preceded—that Okhus had been roused by the recent further revolt of Phœnicé to make a fresh effort for the recovery of Egypt, in which he proposed to conduct his army in person. He made great levies at Babylon of horsemen, foot-soldiers, arms, victual; while his satraps of Cilicia and Syria were striving to maintain his interests in Phœnicé. On the other hand, Tennes, king of the foremost and wealthiest city at the time in the country, namely, Sidon, had obtained from Nectanebôs king of Egypt a reinforcement of 4000 hired Greeks, commanded by Mentor of Rhodes; and with his Phœnician and other levies aided by these, he defeated the satraps and expelled them from the Phœnician soil. Moreover, imitating what had happened upon the mainland, the nine commonwealths of Cyprus with common consent revolted from the Persians, arming each of them its king with the full powers required for conduct of war. On this Okhus sent a letter to Idrieus lord of Caria, commanding him straightway to gather land and sea forces and to make war upon Cyprus.

Idrieus quickly obeyed, sending 40 galleys and 8000 hired land troops against Salamis, the principal of the island cities. The command was given to Phocion of Athens and Evagoras, who claimed the kingship of Salamis, lately held by Nikokles, son of the famous Evagoras, and now by another member of the family, Pnytagoras. Thus did Okhus provide against the revolt in Cyprus. He sent also to the principal cities of Greece, asking soldiers for the invasion of Egypt; and he himself set forth with all his forces from Babylon. He crossed Syria, arrived in Phœnicé, and encamped not far from Sidon. And now the cause of the revolt was betrayed by its leader, Tennes king of Sidon, who made use of Mentor and the Greek mercenaries in carrying out his new design. Okhus thus obtained possession of a city that was every way prepared to make a formidable resistance by land and sea. The Persian had previously put to death 600 of the principal citizens, 100 of whom had been put into his hands by the treachery of their king; and the rest had thereupon issued forth in procession from the city to ask terms of surrender, displaying all the ensigns proper to suppliants. But the Persian knew how he might obtain possession of the city without their surrender. He approached it, accompanied by Tennes, and was admitted by Mentor. Then the Sidonians, seeing their city surrounded by hostile myriads, and the walls betrayed, shut themselves up, with their wives, their children, and their slaves, and set their houses on fire. Forty thousand bodies are said to have been devoured by the flames, and the city became a heap of ashes. Okhus, who in Mentor and the Greeks had found better auxiliaries for the recovery of Egypt, put Tennes to death; while, terrified by what had happened at Sidon, the other Phœnician cities submitted at once. The ashes of Sidon were a mine of wealth, which the Persian sold for a great sum. These events, according to Diodorus xvi. 42-45, happened in the archonship of Thettalus, or earlier part of the summer B.C. 350.

Apollodorus had succeeded Thettalus at Athens as archon, and the third year of the 107th Olympiad was begun, when, from Thebes and Argos in Greece, and from the Greek towns of Okhus's own dominions, arrived in Phœnicé bands of soldiers, amounting in all to 10,000 men, ready to accompany the king against Egypt. Athens and Sparta, while refusing men, had professed the desire to remain at peace with the king. See Diod. xvi. 46, comparing for the Olympic year, capp. 37, 40. In Cyprus, too, the forces levied by Idrieus, and led against Salamis by Phocion and Evagoras, having made a vast booty, so many volunteers flowed in from Syria and Cilicia to obtain the like, that the numbers originally despatched were doubled; the kings of the island lost courage; and the cities submitted to the Persians, all but Salamis, where Pnytagoras still defied his besiegers, till in the end the complaint made against him by Evagoras having been met by a counter charge against Evagoras himself, Okhus permitted Pnytagoras, on his submission, to retain his office at Salamis; while Evagoras was similarly provided for on the continent.

Okhus therefore proceeded against Egypt, but not, it is to be supposed (whether in the year B.C. 350, as Diodorus relates, or in any subsequent year), before the annual Nile-flood had subsided. Diodorus (xvi. 40) reckons the armaments of the king, with which he originally undertook the war against Phœnicé and Egypt, at the strength of 300 trireme war-galleys with 500 store-ships by sea, and 30 myriads of footmen with 3 myriads of horsemen by land. The magnitude of the sea force would be less surprising if we might understand it to have been assembled after Phœnicé and Cyprus were reduced. On the other hand, for the defence of Egypt, Nectanebôs is said to have had at his disposal 20,000 hired Greeks, as many Libyans, and 60,000 Egyptians of the fighting caste, besides a prodigious number of river-boats fitted for warfare on the inner waters; also every other needful kind of war material. All manner of devices for the defence of the mouths and the eastern bank of the river had been long adopted: the

king's own indiscretion, it is said, was the cause of his ruin. His self-confidence he thought just, when he remembered, says Diodorus, xvi. 48, § 1, his having before defeated the Persians in the previous invasion. For (proceeds our author) he had then possessed generals of distinction, excellent both for valour and for ready strategic wit— namely, Diophantus of Athens, and Lamius of Sparta; and it was by means of them that he succeeded in all things. But on this occasion he trusted to his own sufficiency, and admitted nobody to a share in the command.

The reader will ask, *What* previous invasion of Egypt by the Persians is here spoken of? Diodorus has mentioned none, repelled by Nectanebôs himself, though he has described the failure of a great expedition of the Persians, commanded by Pharnabazus and Iphicrates, in the reign of *Nectanebis* (or the first Nectanebus), who reigned the last but one before the king now spoken of. See Diod. xv. 41, and compare 29.

Our historian, it is true, had related that Takhôs king of Egypt,— being in Syria on an expedition against King Artaxerxes Mnemon, in which his Greek land troops were commanded by Agesilaus king of Sparta, and his fleet by Khabrias the Athenian,—found himself obliged, by the intrigues of his brother, whom he had left regent in Egypt, and that brother's son, Nectanebôs, who had the command of the Egyptian division of his army in Syria, to save himself by a flight across the Arabian desert (to Babylon) and the presence of the Great King. Whereupon he had been pardoned and sent back with a Persian army against his nephew Nectanebôs, who had usurped his throne. See Diod. xv. 92, § 5. Now this invasion, if it was ever carried out, might be placed as late as in B.C. 358, after Nectanebôs, by Agesilaus's aid, had vanquished his Mendesian competitor, and after the departure and death of the Spartan king; for which events see Plutarch, *Vit. Agesilai*, capp. 38-40. For the story has been grossly perverted by Diodorus into a war in which Takhôs, assisted by Agesilaus, vanquished Nectanebôs. From Isocrates, *Orat. ad Philipp.* (to be discussed by ourselves below), Mr. Mitford (chap. 45, sect. 2; or vol. vii. p. 359 of his *History of Greece*) concludes that an expedition against Egypt, under Okhus, was connected with the preparations in the Phœnician harbours which frightened the Athenians into peace with Rhodes, Côs, Chios, and Byzantium, in the archonship of Elpines, B.C. 356-5. See Diodor. xvi. 22. But we defer this question for the present, and we return to Diodorus's story of the arkhonship of Apollodorus, B.C. 350-349.

When Okhus reached Egypt, Nectanebôs (if we rightly understand Diodorus's description) had distributed, as garrisons, among the border towns and other posts selected as points of defence, one-half of his Libyan and Egyptian forces and three-fourths of his Greeks. Pelusium, standing on the easternmost mouth of the Nile at a little distance from the sea, being the first point of attack, had a garrison of no less than 5000 Greeks. Behind these forts on the frontier, King Nectanebôs, with the remainder of his forces forming a moveable force about his person, was employed in watching the passes by which the enemy might attempt to penetrate into the country. On the other hand, having pushed his Greeks close up to the walls of Pelusium, while with the bulk of his army he encamped 40 stades off, and after a first indecisive conflict, Okhus formed three columns of attack, headed each by a brigade of Greeks. One of them, having attached to it the Boeotians under Lacrates of Thebes, was devoted to the siege of Pelusium; a second, with the Argives attached under Nicostratus, was provided with 80 trireme galleys. This column was led by Egyptian pilots along a devious channel (from the sea) to a retired spot, where a landing was effected and a camp entrenched within the enemy's outer line of defences. The intruders indeed were quickly attacked by not less than 7000 mercenaries from the nearest post, commanded by a Greek named Cleinias of Côs; but they completely defeated these, killing their commander and more than 5000 men. Terrified at the news, Nectanebôs believed that the rest of the Persian forces would also casily cross the river. By this remainder we are perhaps to understand the third Persian column, which, as soon as it is spoken of, we find near Bubastus, called by Herodotus Bubastis, on the east side of the Delta, about half way between the base and the apex. Nectanebôs supposed that the enemy's united forces would then march upon Memphis; and he decided that what now above all things demanded his care, was the security of that capital. He therefore returned thither with his army and made preparations to support a siege. This conduct ruined him. As soon as his Greek garrison at Pelusium, who were vigorously defending that important place, heard that they had lost his support, they began to provide for their own safety, by capitulating with their countryman Lacrates, who commanded the assailants. They agreed to give up the place on condition that they should be conveyed, unharmed, to Greece with whatever they might bring with them. Such were the successes of the second and first of the Persian columns, headed respectively by the Argives under Nicostratus, and the Boeotians under Lacrates. The third column, commanded by the eunuch Bagôas, and accompanied by Mentor and the Greeks that had given up Sidon, having arrived near Bubastus (when, or how, we are not told; but perhaps only since the fall of Pelusium, at which Bagôas is spoken of as present; and, if so, in part at least by way of the river), obtained possession of that important place and many other towns in quick succession. For Mentor spread the story among the soldiers, that the Great King's purpose was to treat all with kindness that should surrender of their own accord, whereas those that were taken by force would suffer the fate of the Sidonians. At the same time the guards at the gates received the order to offer no hindrance to any person quitting the camp. Finding this liberty, the Egyptians that had been captured (in the advance of the force to Bubastus) took advantage of it, to make their escape; and Mentor's story was speedily propagated everywhere. Jealousy was created in the garrisons between Greeks and natives; those of each nation fearing that the others would offer to surrender first. Bubastus was given up, and the other cities in succession. Therefore, at Memphis, Nectanebôs hearing of these disasters, thought no longer of defence, but collecting his treasures, fled southward into Ethiopia. Thus Okhus Artaxerxes became master of Egypt in the year of the country whose first of Thoth was the 19th of November B.C. 350, being the 10th of the 21 years (from E.N. 390 to E.N. 410, according to the Egyptians) which are assigned to his reign in Ptolemy's Canon. He dismantled important places; he gathered a quantity of silver and gold by plundering temples; from the ancient temples he also carried off *tablets*—ἀναγραφάς (which afterwards Bagôas restored to the priests for large ransoms); he dismissed his Greek troops with ample rewards to their several homes; and, having established Pherendates satrap of Egypt, he returned with great glory and wealth of spoils to Babylon. So Diodorus tells the conquest of Egypt, xvi. 46–51; and passing in the next chapter to the arkhonship of Callimakhus—the fourth year of the 107th Olympiad—the first matter he relates in that space between the midsummers of 349 and 348 B.C. is the high advancement with which Mentor was honoured by Okhus, in consideration of the services he had rendered in the war with the Egyptians. See Diodor. xvi. 52, 53.

Thus, if it be granted to us, for the reasons we have offered, that Egypt revolted on the death of Darius Nothus, it appears that, according to Diodorus, the independence of the country lasted from that time, or from the beginning of the year of Nabonassar 344, to the beginning of the year of Nab. 399; that is, from 6 P.M. 1st Nov. B.C. 405 to 19th Nov. B.C. 350, exactly 55 years of the Egyptian annals. And this is the very sum of regnal years that we obtain from Georgius the Syncellus's own table of the 28th, 29th, and 30th Egyptian dynasties,—a table which perhaps he derived from the same source as his list of 86 Egyptian kings that reigned before Cambyses. This table is found at pp. 256, 257 of the Paris edition of his Chronography; but the reader is to observe that MS. A, followed by Goar in that edition, omits the reign of the second Nectanebus, and that this reign is supplied by Dindorf in the Bonn edition from MS. B; where, however, this third and last reign of the 30th dynasty is placed *before*, instead of *after*, the reign of Teôs, though Teôs (that is Takhôs) is still *numbered* correctly as the second of the three Sebennyte kings.

The eight kings and reigns of the three dynasties are given thus: I. One Saite, Amyrtæus, 6 years, from World-year 5092. II. Four Mendesians, namely, Nepherites, Akhôris, Psammúthis, and a second

Nepherites; 6, 13, and 2 years; also ⅓d of a year: four periods beginning with the World-years 5098, 5104, 5117, and 5119 respectively. III. Three Sebennytes, namely, Nectanebes, Nectanebus (or, as we may call them, the first and second Nectanebus), and Teôs,—8, 18, and 2 years respectively, beginning with the World-years 5120 (so *Codex B*), 5128, and 5146. Thus the *last* year of the 30th dynasty is made to be the World-year 5147, and the 56th year of independence. But here we have, in excess of the particulars furnished, an error of one year (perhaps intentionally made) on the ground of the four months' reign of the second Nepherites. The four months are counted by our Syncellus, or a predecessor, as a separate year: whereas they should be included either all in the first year of the following reign, or partly in this and partly in the last year of the preceding reign.

Thus our Syncellus's own table, of the reigns of the independent Egyptian kings of the 28th, 29th, and 30th dynasties, confirms Diodorus's date of the conquest of Egypt by Artaxerxes Okhus in the 10th year of his reign, by assigning to those dynasties a total duration of 55 years. This measurement, however, seems to be important only *so far as it indicates that the compiler had found occasion to cut off eight years from Africanus's account of Manetho's 30th Egyptian dynasty*. In respect of the two previous dynasties, this table may be said to agree with both Africanus's version of Manetho's account and that of Eusebius. In regal names and in number of kings it agrees with Africanus. In the number of regnal years assigned to the 29th dynasty it agrees with Eusebius, who adds a fifth reign of one year to the account of Africanus. But as to the 30th dynasty, of which the regnal years according to Eusebius are 10 + 2 + 8, the Syncellus's table, as we have intimated, seems to exhibit Africanus's account, 18 + 2 + 18, shortened arbitrarily by the deduction of 10 years from the first reign. That it is an *arbitrary* shortening of Africanus's account, is proved by this,—that if Egypt was reconquered in the 10th year of Okhus (as the Syncellus's table of the independent kings of Egypt confirms Diodorus in attesting), then it is certain the second Nectanebus did not reign the 18 years assigned to him, not only by Africanus, but by what we may call the amended account of our Syncellus. According to Diodorus xv. 92, comparing 78 and 82, the last native king Nectanebôs dispossessed his uncle Takhôs (the Teôs of Manetho) in the arkhonship of Molôn, the third year of the 104th Olympiad (which began after midsummer B.C. 362),—only 12 years before his own expulsion from Egypt by Okhus, according to the date of this expulsion which we have seen assigned by Diodorus. Again, if the year of Egypt beginning in the third year of the 104th Olympiad,—that is, if the year of Nabonassar (according to the use of Egypt) 387, being the 44th of Artaxerxes Mnemon at Babylon, and of the revolt in Egypt, which began with the 22d of November B.C. 362,—was the first year of Nectanebôs, and if the kings of the Saite and Mendesian houses had ruled the revolt during its first (6 + 21 =) 27 years, as our Syncellus and Eusebius say, instead of the 6 + 20 = 26 years of Africanus, then what follows? Why this, that between the end of the last Mendesian reign and the beginning of the last Sebennyte reign there remain but 16 years to be divided between the first two Sebennyte kings, namely, *Nectanebes* (by Diodorus called Nectanebis) and *Teôs* (by Diodorus, Plutarch, and others called Takhôs); whereas these two kings reigned according to Eusebius 10 + 2 years, according to Africanus 18 + 2 years, and according to our Syncellus 8 + 2 years. Thus do we show, that even if the total of the years assigned by our Syncellus to the 30th dynasty in Egypt be taken to be nearer the truth than either Eusebius's total or that of Africanus, still the items—the particular numbers of years assigned to the several reigns—are not more trustworthy than those of Africanus; which, indeed, appear to be borrowed by our Syncellus, or his author, with one arbitrary alteration.

C

THE account above cited of the 28th and 29th dynasties, in which our Syncellus may be said to agree with Africanus and Eusebius, is sufficiently conformable to the notices in Diodorus's history of native Egyptian kings,—the contemporaries of Artaxerxes Mnemon and the predecessors of Takhôs or Teôs. These notices refer to three Egyptian kings,—the first two Mendesians of the 29th dynasty, Nepherites and Akhôris, and the first Sebennyte of the 30th dynasty, Nectanebis. By Diodorus these three are called Nephereus, Akoris, and Nectanebis.

Of the first, Diodorus relates, xiv. 79, that, in prosecution of the war with Artaxerxes Mnemon,—during the time in which Agesilaus, having been sent to Asia, landed at Ephesus; there increased the army that he brought; marched over the Caystrian plain, ravaging the country as far as Kumé; thence returned to Ephesus, the most part of the summer having been spent in enriching his army, and the town-mob that attended it, with the spoils of (Hellespontian) Phrygia and the parts adjacent,—the Lacedæmonians meanwhile sent to make alliance with *Nephereus king of Egypt*. Instead of men, the Egyptian gave them 50 myriads of corn and *fittings*, σκευήν, for 100 trireme galleys. The Lacedæmonians had at that time a fleet of 120 such war-galleys stationed at Rhodes, and confronting one of 40 triremes in the Great King's service stationed at Kaunus in Caria, and commanded by Conôn the Athenian. They crossed to the mainland, and set about the siege of Kaunus; but the arrival of numerous land forces obliging them to desist, they returned to Rhodes. Afterwards Conôn, with a fleet now augmented to the double of its former number of vessels, sailed in his turn to *Kherronesus*,—apparently a promontory of the mainland, otherwise called Kynosêma, opposite to the city Rhodes.

The citizens, among whom the party opposed to Laconian rule had obtained the ascendancy, or at least a favourable opportunity, shut out the Lacedæmonians and admitted Conôn. Next, those who had been employed to bring the corn from Egypt, not knowing that the Lacedæmonian fleet had been obliged to seek a station elsewhere, arrived off Rhodes, and were carried into port, furnishing victual for the city, and for the fleet commanded by Conôn. See Diodorus (who probably follows Theopompus), xiv. 79. These events are dated (chap. 54) in the arkhonship of Phormion, the year of the 96th Olympic festival; that is, between the midsummers of 396 and 395 B.C. ; a year coinciding most nearly with the 10th of native rule in Egypt according to the annals of that country,—if (as we have concluded) the year of Egypt in which Darius Nothus died and Artaxerxes Mnemon succeeded, the 344th of Nabonassar by Egyptian reckoning, was the year of the first revolt. Now,—as the date of a royal act on the part of Nephereus king of Egypt,—the 10th year of the revolt is consistent with Manetho's account of the times of the first Nepherites (as reported by Africanus, Eusebius, and the above-quoted table of reigns, given by our Syncellus without the name of his authority), that he came to the throne in the seventh year of the independence, and reigned eight years.

The next of the independent kings of Egypt noticed by Diodorus is this king's successor, whom, in the tables reported as Manetho's from Africanus and Eusebius, and in his own table, our Syncellus calls Akhôris, Ἀχωρις. Photius gives the name Akôris, Ἀκωρις, in speaking of Theopompus's account of him in the 16th book of the *Philippica*. See Photius, *Biblioth.* cod. 176, p. 20, cited in C. Muller's *Fragmenta Historic. Græcorum*. Diodorus mentions this king in connection with the expedition which Artaxerxes Mnemon sent against the revolted Evagoras king of Cyprus, in the arkhonship of Mystikhides, the third year of the 98th Olympiad. Diod. xv. 2, 8, 14. This year, bounded by the midsummers of the years 386 and 385 B.C., coincides, for the most part of it, with the year of Nabonassar (according to the Egyptians) 363 ; and this is the 20th year of the independence of Egypt, if we begin to count with the first year assigned to Darius Nothus's successor in Ptolemy's Babylonian Canon,—namely, the year of Nabonassar 344. Now the 20th year of independence falls within the period assigned from Manetho to Akhôris's reign,— the 13th and 12 following years of independence. Diodorus tells us that, besides other succours,—particularly money from Hecatomnus, prince of Caria, who had commanded at sea in a former expedition against him,—Evagoras (who was at first king of Salamis only, but had now extended his authority over the other states of Cyprus, and had even made himself master of Tyre and some other places in Phœnicé) had made alliance with Akoris, Ἀκορις, king of Egypt, an enemy of the Persians, and had received a considerable force from him, as well as soldiers not a few from the king of the Arabs. Also, after the fleet and army of Artaxerxes were arrived in Cyprus, during the contest, Evagoras is said to have received from Akoris corn, money, and other necessaries,—particularly a reinforcement of 50 triremes, which raised Evagoras's fleet to the number of 200 galleys. Again, when Evagoras had been defeated in a great sea-fight, and was blockaded in Salamis, we find him leaving his son Pnytagoras in command of the place, running out of port himself with ten galleys by night, arriving in Egypt and urging Akoris to exert himself in the war with all his might. Then, in the arkhonship of Dexitheus,—that is, after midsummer B.C. 385,—he is said to have returned to Cyprus with aid in treasure, but less than he had hoped for from Akoris. In the end, abandoned by his allies, he began to treat for peace. The negotiation afforded an opportunity for preferring a charge of treason against Tiribazus, the Persian admiral, which, being seized by his colleague Orontes, caused him to be displaced. At last, Evagoras obtained peace from Orontes, now chief commander of the Persian forces; but he was reduced to the rank of king of Salamis, subject to a certain yearly tribute, besides obedience to orders from the Great King. Before this termination, while the war was protracted, the importance to Egypt of Evagoras's ill-success seems to have been diminished for a time by one consequence of Tiribazus's disgrace;—that Glôs, the working admiral of the Persian fleet, to whom was due the naval victory in B.C. 385,—fearing, it is said, to be involved in the danger of Tiribazus, whose daughter had been given him to wife,—quitted the service of Artaxerxes (enabling Evagoras, it is probable, to make a longer and more equal fight), and entered into a compact of his own with the king of Egypt on the one hand, and on the other with the Lacedæmonians, who were meditating a fresh Persian war, and the cultivation of whose good-will was one of the charges against Tiribazus. But, before he could redeem his promises, Glôs was assassinated in the second year of the 99th Olympiad, B.C. 383-2. It would be no improbable suspicion that should attribute his death to an agent, voluntary or commissioned, of the Great King's, or of one of his lieutenants. See Diodor. xv. 18, 14, 15; and for the former detail, xv. 2-4, 8, 9.

So far Diodorus's notices of Akoris are consistent in date, as we have explained already, with the length of his reign and its position in the period of Egyptian independence, attested by Manetho. And the reader will observe that our argument is quite unaffected by a mistake, of which the contemporary statements of Isocrates have been used by Clinton and others to convict Diodorus, in supposing that the events of the two years of the arkhons Mystikhides and Dexitheus, which began after midsummer B.C. 386, were the closing events of a ten years' war between Evagoras and the generals of Artaxerxes Mnemon, —a war which was certainly not concluded in the arkhonship of Demophilus, the sixth arkhon of the series beginning with Mystikhides.

See the *Panegyricus* of Isocrates, §§ 35, 39, quoted in Clinton's Tables F. H., B.C. 380. That the war lasted 10 years is confessed by Diodorus, xv. 9, and asserted by Isocrates in his *Evagoras*, §§ 23, 24. But we hesitate to place, as Clinton does, the termination of the war in B.C. 376; for in the *Panegyricus* (of which Clinton shows the date to be B.C. 380) we understand Isocrates to call the year then current the sixth year, not from the beginning of the war, but from the defeat at sea, just before mentioned, which Evagoras sustained in the arkhonship of Mystikhides. According to Isocrates, *Evag.* §§ 23, 24 (quoted by Clinton, F. H., vol. ii. Appendix, chap. 12, on the Cyprian War), the peace left Evagoras master of all he possessed when the war began. Yet *that* all, it is at the same time intimated, was only Salamis. If so, it was not the ten years' war, but a former one which began either with the aggressions of Evagoras on the other Cypriot kings, or, at least, with the campaign on their behalf conducted by Autophradates, satrap of Lydia, general, and Hecatomnôs, prince of Caria, admiral, under the Great King's commission. This campaign is connected in Diodorus's narrative with events of the arkhonship of Nicoteles, B.C. 391-390. See Diod. xiv. 98, and Theopompus, ap. Photium, cited in the *Fragm. Historic. Græc.* vol. i. p. 295. The ten years' war was begun under Tiribazus; and more will be said of it below. But here, our concern is merely this, the date of the events with which Akoris is connected by Diodorus, whether correctly or inaccurately. However, we may observe that Diodorus's detail, as to Tiribazus, Glôs, and Orontes, in the ten years' war, cannot be thoroughly trusted. Tiribazus's disgrace may have followed and not preceded the defection of Glôs, who perhaps is the same Glôs of whom we read in Xenophon's *Anabasis*. We add that Evagoras (together with his son Puytagoras) was assassinated by the eunuch Thrasydœus, and succeeded as king of Salamis by his son Nikokles, in the year of the arkhon Socratides, the third year of the 101st Olympiad, B.C. 374–373. See Diod. xv. 47, § 8; correcting and supplementing his account (as before) from that of Theopompus ap. Photium, already referred to, and from Isocrates's piece entitled *Nikokles*.

Diodorus mentions Akoris, not only, as we have seen, at a date consistent with Manetho's statement of the lengths of the several reigns in the 28th and 29th Egyptian dynasties (that is to say, under the arkhons Mystikhides and Dexitheus, in years 3 and 4 of the 98th Olympiad, years divided by the midsummer of the year B.C. 385), but later under Kallias, the fourth arkhon of the 100th Olympiad, who took office at midsummer B.C. 377 : see Diod. xv. 29, comparing, for the date, 23, 24, 25, and 28. This year coincides most nearly with the Egyptian year of Nabonassar 372, the 29th of Egyptian independence. But the 29th year was already the second, if not the third, year of the Sebennyte independent dynasty, or 29th dynasty of the entire series, if we give credit to Manetho's totals of years reigned by the Saite and

Mendesian, or 28th and 29th dynasties. As reported in the Syncellus's list and by Eusebius, these two dynasties reigned 6 + 21 years; according to Africanus's Manetho, 6 + 20 years. Thus at Diodorus's later dater in B.C. 377-6 it was no longer Akoris, the second Mendesian, that was king of Egypt according to Manetho, but the first Sebennyte, the king who in Africanus and, Eusebius's reports of Manetho (cited by Georgius Syncellus, Paris ed. pp. 76, 77), no less than in the Syncellus's own list, is called *Nectanebês*, but by Theopompus, ap. Photium, and in Diod. xv. 42, *Nectanebis*, and by ourselves at times *Nectanebus the First*.

Diodorus's story in B.C. 377-6 is this: While the Great King's general Pharnabazus was busy preparing an invasion of Egypt, the king of that revolted province (whom he speaks of by name but once, and then calls *Akoris*) was assembling, by dint of liberal pay and promises, a very considerable force of soldiers hired from abroad, the command of which was accepted by the Athenian Khabrias. On this, Pharnabazus complained to the Athenian commonwealth; warning the citizens that, by this act, Khabrias was alienating from them the good-will of the Great King. The republic immediately ordered its citizen home; but, it would appear (though this is no part of Diodorus's narrative), immediately bestowed upon him an important command in its own service: for we find that he gained them the victory in a great and decisive sea-fight at Naxos, on the 17th of Boedromion, the third month of the following arkhon Kharisander, that is, about September B.C. 376. (See F. H., vol. ii. *Tables;* where Clinton adduces contemporary evidence to prove Diodorus inaccurate in placing Khabrias's victory in the previous arkhonship.) The Athenians not only recalled Khabrias from Egypt, but further gratified Pharnabazus by sending him Iphicrates to occupy in the invading army a post like that relinquished by Khabrias in the defence of Egypt. But we repeat it, Pharnabazus's remonstrance with the Athenians was made in the arkhonship of Callias, the fourth year of the 100th Olympiad.

If then, for the regnal years of the independent Saite and Mendesian, or 28th and 29th dynasties, Manetho's numbers be admitted, it follows that on this second occasion (in xv. 29) Diodorus is incorrect in still naming the king of Egypt Akoris; and that the king at this time was really that same *Nectanebis* whom the historian mentions three years afterwards in the third arkhonship of the 101st Olympiad, the year of the assassination of Evagoras. See Diod. xv. 41, 42. Moreover, from Photius's epitomè of the 12th book of the *Philippica* of Theopompus, we may infer that the inaccuracy was not his author's but Diodorus's own. Photius writes thus: *The 12th book has in it about Akôris king of the Egyptians* . . . ; *and in what way they* (the Lacedæmonians) *made the peace under Antalkidas; and how Tiribazus warred; and how he took counsel against Evagoras; and how Evagoras joined with Orontes in accusing him to the king; and how, Nectanebis having succeeded to the kingship of Egypt, Evagoras sent ambassadors to the Lacedæmonians; and in what way his war in Cyprus was ended for him.* See *Fragm. Historic. Græc.* vol. i. p. 295. Theopompus therefore placed the accession of Nectane*bis* before the end of Evagoras's ten years' war, and represented this event as one that induced an effort on the part of Evagoras to form a new combination against the enemy. Now, according to Manetho, the year in which Nectane*bes* came to the throne was, at latest, the $(6 + 21 + 1 =)$ 28th, or at earliest, the $(6 + 20 + 1 =)$ 27th year of the independence. That is, it was at latest the year of Nabonassar 371, according to the Egyptians, which year began with the 26th day of November B.C. 378; or at earliest it was the year of Nabonassar 370, which began at 25¼ days of November B.C. 379.

This seems to confirm the general correctness of Clinton's conclusion (derived from Isocrates *in Evag.* § 23, and *Panegyric.* § 39), that Diodorus mistook the active operations of the first two years of the ten that the war lasted, begun by Tiribazus, for the final operations of the war. But the ten years need not be made to have commenced with the first of the two arkhons mentioned by Diodorus, namely Mystikhides, at midsummer B.C. 386; and then, continuing under the arkhons Dexitheus, Diotrephes, Panostratus, Evander, Demophilus, Pytheas, Nikôn, Nausistratus, to have concluded with Callias, who went out of office at midsummer B.C. 376, and was arkhon, according to Diodorus, when Pharnabazus, making preparations for the invasion of Egypt, complained at Athens that Khabrias had taken service under the king of Egypt. The expedition against Egypt (whether the preparations began thus simultaneously with the restoration of peace in Cyprus or shortly afterwards) was, we doubt not, facilitated by the peace. But the peace appears to have begun, and the ten years' war sustained by Evagoras to have ended, a year earlier. The ten years seem to have been reckoned by Theopompus to begin with the predecessor of Mystikhides, *the arkhon Theodotus*, under whom (as it is testified by Aristides, tom. ii. p. 286, and by Callisthenes, *ap. Diod.* xv. 117, quoted by Clinton)—and also in the earlier part of his year, or about autumn B.C. 387 (as Clinton further shows)—the general peace of Antalkidas was concluded, and Cyprus was left to be dealt with by Artaxerxes at his pleasure. If then the ten years' war in Cyprus begun by Tiribazus was counted to have commenced with the arkhon under whom the peace of Antalkidas was consented to in Greece, it must have been reckoned to end with Nausistratus, the predecessor of Callias, at midsummer B.C. 377. Then followed the negotiation in the year of Callias between Pharnabazus and the Athenians touching Khabrias's having accepted a command under the king of Egypt.

We have now seen that though Diodorus names this king Akoris, not only does Manetho make the person on the throne to be *Nectanebes*, the first of the three Sebennytes that compose the 30th dynasty, but

Theopompus does the same; telling us that *Nectanebis* succceded to the kingship in Egypt before the peace (in the year of the arkhon Callias at the latest, or rather in the year of Callias's predecessor Nausistratus, or Nausinikus), which ended Evagoras's ten years' war in Cyprus. For,—whether the peace was made in the year of Callias, which ended at midsummer 376, or, as Theopompus appears to have related (counting from the arkhon year in which the peace of Antalkidas was concluded), in the year of Nausinikus, which ended at midsummer B.C. 377,—if Akoris's reign was no more, and that of Nectanebis was begun, before the peace, then it was Nectanebis, not Akoris, who was threatened by Pharnabazus in the year of Callias.

Thus, if Diodorus does not, in this instance, confirm the chronology of Manetho, it is through his calling the king of Egypt in the year of Callias by a wrong name, and not for any fault of Manetho's. For Theopompus confirms Manetho; giving us to conclude that not Akoris, as Diodorus says, but Nectanebes, as Manetho has it, was the name of the king of Egypt whom Khabrias was engaged to, between the midsummers of the years 377 and 376 B.C., in a year (the fourth year of the 100th Olympiad) corresponding for the most part of it with the 30th Egyptian year of independence.

The chronology of Manetho has now been shown to be consistent with that of Diodorus in respect of the Mendesian kings, Nepheritcs the First and Akhôris; also to agree with that of Theopompus in the case of the first of the Sebennyte kings, Nectanebes. But as to this last king, who, for the similarity, if not identity, of his name with that of the Sebennyte conquered by Artaxerxes Okhus, may be called Nectanebus the First, we have also a testimony of Diodorus's, placing him at a date that agrees with the chronology of Manetho. Pharnabazus's preparations to invade Egypt, begun in the year before midsummer B.C. 376, were complete in the year in which Evagoras's assassination is placed, that of Socratides, the third arkhon of the 101st Olympiad, who came into office at midsummer B.C. 374. In xv. 41–43, Diodorus relates how the land forces, numbering 20 myriads, Barbarians, and 20 thousands, Greeks, were united on the coast at Aké (now *Akka* or *Acre*) with a war-fleet of 300 triremes and 200 thirty-oared galleys, besides a multitude of store-ships. From this point the expedition set forth by land and by sea together at the beginning of summer; Pharnabazus being the commander-in-chief, and Iphicrates of Athens the leader of the Greek troops. If the season was the beginning of summer, then, as the year of the invasion, by Greek computation, begins after midsummer B.C. 374, we must date the setting forth from Akka about the beginning of May B.C. 373; that is to say, the summer of the 32d year of the revolt and the 375th of Nabonassar, according to the Egyptians,—a year whose first of Thoth had been the 25th of the preceding November. When the naval forces and land army of the Persians reached Egypt, they found every preparation for defence complete. King Nectanebis had been well informed respecting the great armament mustered to invade him; but the natural strength of the country, and the difficulty of approaching it, encouraged him by every possible means to add to those advantages.

All entrances, by land and by sea, the invaders found admirably fenced. At every mouth of the Nile a town or fort with lofty towers had been built on each side of the stream where it entered the sea; a bridge of wood united the places, and commanded the navigation. But the Pelusiac mouth, being the nearest to the Syrian frontier, and the most likely to be assailed by an enemy from that quarter desiring to force a passage into the country, was the channel where the principal defences were constructed. These were manned in large numbers. Every approach on the land side was flooded; while the creeks, most favourable for the entrance of vessels from the sea, were barred by obstructions of earth and mason-work. The result equalled all that had been hoped. The Pelusiac branch of the Nile defying them, the invaders proposed to make a descent upon the coast at the Mendesian mouth of the river, the squadron entrusted with the operation keeping out of sight of the land during its passage. A landing was effected; the Egyptians, after a severe fight, were driven within their walls, and these again were taken and destroyed. Iphicrates advised to sail up the river immediately and seize Memphis, which he learnt from the prisoners was destitute of troops: but Pharnabazus rejected the project as too dangerous; nor would he and his generals permit Iphicrates to execute it alone, which he offered to do with such Greek mercenaries as were on the spot. His boldness inspired them with jealousy and alarm. Pharnabazus decided to wait till the whole force should be conveyed to the point of which they were in possession. The Egyptians thus gained time to despatch a force to occupy Memphis, and with all their disposable men to hem in the invaders, and to harass them with incessant attacks, which, aided by the difficult nature of the country, did great damage to the Persians. This warfare continued till the Etesian Winds having set in, the rise of the Nile, and the inundations in every quarter, made the country continually stronger for defence. Under these circumstances the Persian generals resolved to abandon the enterprise, and to return to the Syrian coast; whence Iphicrates, remembering the arrest and punishment of Conôn, managed to escape in a vessel by night, and so reached Athens in safety. For the yearly Etesian Winds in the height of summer, Clinton, B.C. 341, cites Ulpian, pp. 35, 41, ed. Par., and *Vit. Pythag. ap. Photium*, cod. 249, p. 1321. For the fate of Conôn, comp. Xenoph. *Hell.* iv. 8, §§ 12–16; Diodor. xiv. 85; Corn. Nep. *Vit. Con.* cap. 5; Isocrat. *Panegyric.* § 41.

D

THE above extracts from Diodorus and Theopompus, it is hoped, have sufficiently confirmed the chronological accounts of the 28th and 29th Egyptian dynasties, derived from Manetho by Africanus, Eusebius, and the author, whoever he was, from whom Georgius Syncellus copied his own list of the kings of those dynasties.

It may therefore here be proper to justify our Comparative Table of Descents (facing p. 91), in the column of *Egyptian Kings*,—where we distinguish Amyrtæus the Saite, who forms alone Manetho's 28th dynasty and reigns six years, as a different person from Amyrtæus, called by Thucydides the "king in the Marshes," who joined the son of Psametikhus, Inarôs the Libyan, in his revolt from the Persians in the reign of the first Artaxerxes. We consider the six years' reign of Amyrtæus the Saite, attested by Manetho, to be the first six years of the reign of Artaxerxes the Second called Mnêmôn; or, which is the same thing, the first six years of that revolt from the Persians, and that establishment of self-government in Egypt, which took place (as the testimony of Manetho, confirmed by the silence of the historians of the previous Peloponnesian war, has led us to conclude) on the death of Darius Nothus in the year B.C. 404.

We had at one time fancied, as others have fancied, that Manetho's 28th dynasty (instead of following the 27th, or Persian, dynasty,— whereof Cambyses was the first king and Darius Nothus the last) was really contemporary with the fourth Persian of the 27th, Artaxerxes Makrokheir, the son of Xerxes. We had identified its position with the period of the war maintained by Inarôs and his Greek allies against the Persians, which after six years (as Thucydides testifies, i. 110) ended disastrously. But besides the improbability, whatever that may be, of Manetho's having committed such an error, it is not till after Inarôs's captivity in B.C. 455 that Amyrtæus, his confederate, is spoken of as "king in the Marshes," maintaining himself through the peculiar character of the district and the martial habits of its inhabitants. He is mentioned last in B.C. 449, during an invasion of Cyprus by the Athenians and their allies under Cimôn, when, being sent to by Amyrtæus, they detached sixty triremes to Egypt, and with 140 remaining besieged Kitium; but, Cimôn dying and a famine following, were compelled to abandon that operation, and, after defeating the Phœnicians and Cilicians on the same day by land and sea on the other side of Salamis, to return home, and the ships from Egypt with them. See Thucyd. i. 112. Here, it is true, we have Amyrtæus alive and holding out against the Persians at the end of another six years, after Inarôs had fallen into the hands of Megabyzus the Persian general. But if these years were intended, in the six given by Manetho to the 28th dynasty, why were not the six of Inarôs prefixed? Or if Manetho's Amyrtæus be the confederate of Inarôs, why does not his son who succeeded him appear in the 28th dynasty? For, as Herodotus assures us, iii. 15, the Persian government permitted Pausiris son of Amyrtæus to succeed to his father's government in Egypt, as it permitted Thannyras son of Inarôs to succeed to his father's Libyan principality.

The identity of the six years, given by Manetho to his Amyrtæus the Saite of the 28th dynasty, with the six years of the revolt of Inarôs, under the reign of Artaxerxes Makrokheir in the 27th dynasty, is regarded with favour by Professor Geo. Rawlinson, in his Note on Herod. iii. 15; and he maintains it as not unlikely, that the summary of Manetho's work used by Eusebius (he does not mention a like summary used by Africanus) misrepresented Manetho here, as it did in other places according to Bunsen (and he cites Bunsen's *Egypt*, vol. i. p. 86, Eng. Trans.), making dynasties seem to be consecutive, which Manetho knew and confessed to be contemporary. A similar opinion (as we learn from Clinton, who rejects it) was expressed by Larcher, and before him by Wesseling, in commenting on the same text of Herodotus; also by Dodwell, in *Annal. Thucyd.* p. 99.

For ourselves, we not only abandon this supposition, but we reject (as does Professor Rawlinson) one retained by Clinton and Sir J. G. Wilkinson, that Manetho's Amyrtæus, being the same person as the Amyrtæus of Herodotus and Thucydides, began his six years' reign in B.C. 414-413, forty years after the defeat and capture of Inarôs. This date, the 11th year of the reign of Darius Nothus, is the one assigned by Eusebius, in *his own* chronology, for the commencement of independent government in Egypt, under the 28th, 29th, and 30th dynasties. As quoted by Clinton (*F. H.* vol. ii. Appendix, chap. 18, "Kings of Persia"), Eusebius's words, in the Latin Version, are these: *Olymp.* 91, 3. *Ægyptus à Persis recessit; et rursum Ægyptiorum renascitur dynastia 28a; et regnavit Amyrtæus annis sex.* We object, first, that Amyrtæus, when he was succeeded in his Egyptian district by his son Pausiris—no less than Inarôs when he was succeeded in his Libyan government by his son Thannyras, as recorded by Herodotus—must be supposed to have been completely removed from the scene of his resistance to the Persians, whether by death or by captivity, long before the 11th year of Darius Nothus. Secondly, we refer to the reasons we have given for believing that the independence of Egypt did not begin till after the death of Darius Nothus in the summer of the year B.C. 404; that is, not till five-and-forty years after the last mention of the confederate of Inarôs in Greek history, and more than fifty years after Inarôs fell into the hands of the Persians.

Amyrtæus the contemporary of the first Artaxerxes may have belonged to the Saite family which reigned in Egypt before the conquest by Cambyses, and formed the 26th dynasty. The relationship will seem probable if we consider that tradition of Asiatic empire which Herodotus calls a Persian principle; and in compliance wherewith the Great King invested Pausiris with the deputy-kingship which his father had misused. Again, Manetho's Amyrtæus the Saite, the contemporary of Artaxerxes Mnemon, may have been a son of Pausiris. This, we now learn from C. Müller (on Manetho's 28th dynasty), is the opinion of Boeckh.

But the dates of Diodorus and Theopompus lately cited—by attesting the general accuracy of the chronology of the 28th and 29th dynasties exhibited by those summaries of Manetho's work, to which alone Africanus and Eusebius are supposed to have had access—destroy the hypothesis, lately cited, that the 28th dynasty did not really follow the 27th, but was in fact contemporary with the Artaxerxes of the 27th dynasty. They destroy also the Eusebian opinion, followed by Clinton, that the accession of the 28th dynasty happened in the third year of the 91st Olympiad, the year after midsummer B.C. 414, coinciding for the most part with the 11th year of Darius Nothus, or 335th of Nabonassar by the Egyptian reckoning; which year began with the 5th of December B.C. 414. Diodorus and Theopompus prove the Amyrtæus of Manetho to be rightly placed as king of Egypt during those six years of the annals of the country that followed the last of Darius Nothus's reign, or followed the year of Nabonassar 343 according to the Egyptians. From the evidence of Diodorus and Theopompus we have produced points of time at which were reigning kings called Nephereus, Akoris, and Nectanebis (the latter being a different person from Nectanebôs, and indeed preceding him by the interval of one reign at least, that of Takhôs). These epochs, as we have shown, fall within the positions assigned by Manetho to the reigns of the manifestly identical kings, Nepherites the First, Akhôris, and Nectanebes. But they only fall into these positions on the supposition that the 28th, 29th, and 30th dynasties followed—where Manetho or his summarizers, as reported by Africanus and Eusebius, have actually placed them—in succession after Darius Nothus, the last of the Persian kings of the 27th dynasty. If Manetho's chronology be thus confirmed in respect of the three kings named, it is also confirmed for the previous reign of Amyrtæus. The account of the reigns of the 29th dynasty receives no confirmation, in the case of the first Nepherites, from the date at which Nephereus is mentioned by Diodorus as the ally of the Lacedæmonians, if we reject the account of the 28th dynasty. And we do reject that account if we suppose the 28th dynasty to have been contemporaneous, either with a part of the reign of Artaxerxes the First, or a part of the reign of Darius the Second. If Nepherites, the earliest king of the 29th dynasty, reigned, as Manetho says, six years, but, instead of following next but one (Amyrtæus) after Darius Nothus, as Manetho places him, be supposed to have followed Darius Nothus immediately, then Nepherites must also be supposed to have been for the last three years succeeded by another, between the midsummers of 396 and 395 B.C., or in the year of Nabonassar 353 according to the Egyptians. That is to say,

Akhôris, not Nephcrites, will have been king already, at the time when the Lacedæmonians, being at war with Artaxerxes Mnemon, and having sent Agesilaus to invade the satraps Tissaphernes and Pharnabazus by land, are related to have procured corn and other necessaries for their fleet from Nephereus king of Egypt. But if Diodorus's mention of Nephereus king of Egypt in B.C. 396-395 be admitted as evidence confirmatory of Manetho's chronology of the 28th and 29th dynasties (according to which Nepherites the First reigned during the seventh and five following years of the revolt, or from 453 to 458 E.N.), then Manetho is withal supposed to have correctly interposed the six years of Amyrtæus the Saite, the only king of the 28th dynasty, between Darius Nothus and Nepherites the First.

E

ENOUGH has been said to justify the assertion that Egypt was not lost to the Persian Empire during the reign of Darius Nothus. It has become sufficiently apparent that the years of independence under the 28th, 29th, and 30th dynasties were counted from that of the death of Nothus and accession of his eldest son Arsakes, who took the name of Artaxerxes and is entitled Mnêmôn. Proceeding too from this date, the times allotted by Manetho to the several reigns of the Saite or 28th and the Mendesian or 29th dynasty, are at least sufficiently accurate in their measurement to coincide with the notices of some of the kings in Greek history. The names of all the kings, as given in Georgius Syncellus's list, have been recited; and they are the same that Africanus is reported to have given from Manetho. Eusebius adds to the Mendesian dynasty a fifth king, *Múthis*, who reigned one year, making the reign of the dynasty 21 years and four months, instead of 20 years and four months, which is the measurement of Africanus. The Syncellus also gives the same space to the 29th dynasty as Eusebius, by allotting to the third king, *Psammúthis*, two years instead of the one he reigned according to Africanus and Eusebius. See Syncell., Paris ed., pp. 76, 77, and pp. 256, 257.

But, as to the date which the reign of the Sebennyte or 30th dynasty extended to, the decision is more difficult. We have already recited Diodorus's account of an expedition conducted by Okhus Artaxerxes, the son and successor of Arsakes Artaxerxes Mnêmôn, during the years of the arkhons at Athens Thettalus and Apollodorus, the point of separation between which is the midsummer of B.C. 350; how under Thettalus he reduced Phœnicé, and, under Apollodorus, Egypt. We have shown that the *curtailment* in the Syncellus's list of the years assigned by Africanus to the three kings of the 30th dynasty conforms exactly to Diodorus's chronology. And here we may add another confirmation of this chronology, or conformity with it, as the case may be decided. It is found in an ancient calculation ascribed by Geo. Syncellus to Manetho, but, as C. Müller thinks (*Frag. Hist. Græc.* tom. ii. p. 537), a *Pseudo-Manetho, known to the Syncellus through Panodôrus*, rather than the Manetho of Africanus and Eusebius. See Geo. Syncell., Paris ed., pp. 52, 53. This Manetho of Panodôrus, if we may so term him, made the last year of the 30th Egyptian dynasty to be about the 15th year before the reign (the Syncellus's expression is κοσμοκρατορία) of Alexander the Macedonian. Now the first year of Alexander, as *king of Macedonia*, being the year of the arkhon Pythodemus (see Arrian, *Exp. Alex.* i. 1), the first of the 111th Olympiad (see Diodor. xv. 91), is the 15th from and *with* that of the arkhon Apollodorus, which was the third year of the 107th Olympiad, and the year in which, according to Diodorus, Okhus by right of conquest began to reign in Egypt. For the 13 intervening arkhons, see Dionysius of Halicarnassus, *de Dinarcho*, § 9, and Diodor. xv. 52, 53, 56, 59, 66, 69, 70, 72, 74, 77, 82, 84, 89. Of the whole 15 years, the first 12 are the remainder of 21 years given to Okhus in Ptolemy's Canon; two are years of his son Arses, according to the same; and one is the first year at Babylon of Darius the Third; and in Macedonia, of Alexander son of Philip. For the two came to their several thrones about the same time. See Diodor. xvii. 6, § 5; also Ptolemy's Canon, which divides 12 years between Darius and Alexander on the throne of Babylon; while Aristobulus tells us, in Arrian, *E. A.* xii. 28, § 1, that, besides the year in which he died, counted by the Canon, in the Egyptian use of it, to Aridæus, his successor, Alexander reigned 12 years; whence it follows that Darius's four years were the first four of Alexander's reign.

It may truly be objected to this argument, that our Syncellus understands the 15 years to extend from the World-year 5147 (which is his last year of the 30th dynasty in Egypt) to the World-year 5162, which is his seventh year of Alexander in Macedonia and first upon the Babylonian throne.

But, according to his own figures (taken, however, it would seem, from the author whom we have called Panodôrus's Manetho), if 3555 years, beginning with the World-year 1586, constitute the duration of the 30 dynasties, they ended with the World-year 5140; and a clear interval of 15 years is found between them and the year of the World 5156, which our Syncellus makes Alexander's first year on the Macedonian throne. See Georg. Syncell., Paris ed., pp. 52, 257, 260, 261.

Still, when all is said, we are unable to accept Diodorus's date for the conquest of Egypt by Okhus Artaxerxes. The evidence of a contemporary exulting, in an address to Philip king of Macedonia four years later, that Okhus's efforts had been ineffectual, is irresistible. It is clear that if an attempt upon Egypt was made in the arkhonship of Apollodorus, B.C. 350-49, it was unsuccessful. For how can we suppose, with Mr. Mitford, that, if the Persian had then recovered Egypt, Isocrates could have thought it proper to pass over the recent success, and insist upon a previous failure, when the business in hand was to show that the state of the Persian empire invited attack? "Who," says he, "that has heard the situation of the country will not be stimulated to wage war with the present king? Egypt indeed had revolted in the time of his father, but then they used to be afraid lest some time or other the king should make an expedition against them in person, and overcome both the difficulties which the country presents to an invader, on account of the river, and all their preparation besides. But now this king has freed them from that fear. For, after having mustered the largest army he possibly could, and marched against them, he came back from thence not only worsted, but covered with ridicule, and having showed himself unfit either to be king or to command an army. Again, Cyprus, and Phœnicé, and Cilicia, and those parts, whence they used to supply themselves with naval forces, in his father's time, when Clearkhus commanded the Greeks in the expedition of Cyrus, belonged to the king; but now they are partly revolted, and partly are involved in war and calamities so great that none of those nations can be serviceable to him; but they will be in a disposition very convenient for *thee*, if thou shouldst wish to war upon him." So writes Isocrates, in the address *To Philip*, § 42. See Dobson's *Oratores Attici*, vol. iii. p. 278. For the date of the address, one indication follows immediately after the extract we have given. It is what Isocrates says of the doubtful relations that existed between Idrieus and the Persian government; in particular, of the hostilities that had taken place between them, though they were not now at war. For we learn from Diodorus that Idrieus was just come to the lordship of Caria (which, in the arkhonship of Lykiscus, the year of the 109th Olympic festival, beginning at midsummer B.C. 344, he had held for seven years), when, in the arkhonship of Thettalus, as we have seen, he received and obeyed an order to attack the revolted island of Cyprus. Diod. xvi. 40, 42, 45, 69. It would seem that his conduct under this commission had not given satisfaction. He may have pursued his own ends, betrayed the king's interests, maintained a correspondence with the enemy. But Clinton, from §§ 8, 21, 31, shows that Isocrates published his *Address to Philip* before the conclusion of the Phocian war, which was in the arkhonship of Arkhias, and some time after the 19th of Elaphébolion, in the previous arkhonship of Themistocles, when peace was made with Philip by the Athenians. The date, therefore, is *early in the summer* of B.C. 346.

It is clear, then (to say nothing of the state of Phœnicé, Cyprus, and Cilicia), that at this date Egypt was still unsubdued, and that the expedition against the country, if there was one, in the year of Apollodorus, had failed. That, indeed, may have been the occasion, alluded to by Diodorus himself, when the success of Nectanebôs was due to his having confided the entire direction of his defence to two able Greek leaders, Diophantus of Athens, and Lamius of Sparta.

Perhaps, also, it was in his first attempt, through want of acquaintance with the locality, that Okhus, after reaching the Serbonid Lake, is said to have lost a part of his army in the passage of the Barathra —an adjoining tract of swamp and quicksand, reckoned by Diodorus among the natural barriers of Egypt, and which may have been fed from the Pelusiac channel, then a chief outlet of the water of the Nile. See Diod. xvi. 40; comparing the description in i. 30, which he himself sends us back to, of the Serbonid Lake, and the *miry plains* of the adjoining desert, *called Barathra:* πεδία τελματώδη, τὰ προσαγορευόμενα Βάραθρα. The existence of an olden communication between the Pelusiac branch of the Nile and the Serbonid Lake has been already suggested above, p. 290, note.

But if Diodorus's date for Okhus's recovery of Egypt, the year of Apollodôrus, be rejected; and if, moreover, the achievement was unaccomplished when King Philip was addressed by Isocrates, towards the close of the arkhonship of Themistocles, which was the fourth from that of Apollodorus,—that is to say, if, far from being conquered in the year which ended at midsummer B.C. 349, Egypt still laughed at Okhus a little before midsummer B.C. 346,—can any later date be proposed, on authority, for the success which he ultimately obtained?

Both Africanus and Eusebius (as copied by Geo. Syncellus, pp. 77, 78, ed. Paris) concur in a statement for which they seem to cite the Third Part (τόμος) of Manetho's Egyptian History. They say that the 31st dynasty of kings in Egypt (consisting of Okhus, Arses, and the Darius who was pulled down by Alexander the Macedonian) began to reign over Egypt in the 20th year of Okhus's Persian reign. But though they alike profess to cite Manetho, they differ in the numbers they assign, of regnal years in Egypt, to Okhus, Arses, and Darius; also in the total number of years that intervened between Okhus's recovery of Egypt and the end of the last Darius's reign; Africanus's figures being $2 + 3 + 4 = 9$ years, and Eusebius's $6 + 4 + 6 = 16$ years.

It is the difference as to the length of Okhus's reign in Egypt that here concerns us chiefly. Both say that, according to Manetho, Okhus became king of Egypt in the 20th year of his Persian reign; but Africanus makes this 20th year the second, while Eusebius makes it the sixth, before the beginning of the reign of his son Arses. Thus Africanus, with Ptolemy's Canon, which also gives 46 years to the second Artaxerxes, the father of Okhus, reckons Okhus to have reigned 21 years in all, while Eusebius extends his reign to 25 years. But it seems to be, as to when Artaxerxes Mnemon was succeeded by Okhus, not as to when Okhus was succeeded by Arses, that they differed. Eusebius seems to have given to Okhus the last four years of Artaxerxes Mnemon, somewhat like Diodorus, according to whom Artaxerxes Mnemon reigned 43 years only (Diod. xiii. 108, xv. 93), and Okhus 23 years (Diod. xv. 93).

If, then, the difference as to the length of the reign of Okhus between

Africanus and Eusebius be a difference as to the date of his accession, the 20th year of his reign has a different meaning as used by the one from that applied to it by the other.

According to Africanus, the 20th year of Okhus, like his 20th by Ptolemy's Canon, is his last year but one. It may therefore seem probable that the year of Egypt intended by Africanus is the year of Nabonassar (according to the Egyptians) 409 ; for that is the 20th year of Okhus according to Ptolemy's Canon. And the year of Nabonassar 409 began 408 Julian years, all but $\frac{408}{4}$ or 102 days, after midday 26th Feb. B.C. 747, or began at mid-day the 16th of November B.C. 340.

Thus the high authority of Manetho, *according to Africanus*, would place the flight of Nectanebos and the accession of Okhus to the throne of Egypt in the year of Egypt which began at mid-day 16th Nov. B.C. 340, in the fifth month or thereabout of the arkhonship of Theophrastus, the year of the 110th Olympic festival.

But this date no less than that of Diodorus is disproved by the language of a contemporary. It is shown to be *too late* by a letter of Philip king of Macedonia to the people of Athens, replied to in a speech of Demosthenes to that people; both the letter and the speech belonging to the arkhonship of Theophrastus, and immediately preceding the war which Philip was understood to threaten, and which the Athenians were moved by Demosthenes to declare. For this date see the authorities in Clinton, *F. H.* vol. ii. Tables B. C. 340, 339, especially the citation from the 6th book of the *Atthis* of Philokhorus, in Dionys. Halic. *ad Ammæum* in Sylburg's edition, vol. ii. p. 123. In the 3d section of the epistle Philip says, " Ye have arrived, *ἀφῖχθε*, at such a degree of recklessness and ill-will that ye have even sent (*ἀπεστάλκατε*) ambassadors to the Persian, to persuade him to make war upon me,—a thing that one might be particularly surprised at ; for before his taking of Egypt and Phœnicé, ye passed a vote, if he should attempt any change in the state of things, *ἄν ἐκεῖνος τι νεωτερίζῃ*, in like manner to summon me and all the other Greeks against him ; but now ye have such a superabundance of hatred to me as to discuss with him the subject of an offensive alliance." See G. S. Dobson's *Oratores Attici*, vol. v. pp. 257, 258.

Thus Africanus's date, the 20th year of Okhus, if it means the year of Nabonassar 409, is below the true date at which Okhus recovered Egypt. But it may justly be contended that the 20th year of Okhus according to Africanus is the 19th year of Okhus according to Ptolemy's Canon, that is, the year of Nabonassar 408 according to the Egyptians, —a year which not began but *ended* at the point in the arkhonship of Theophrastus above mentioned, mid-day November the 16th B.C. 340, beginning 6 hours P.M. 16th November B.C. 341, in the arkhonship of Nicomakhus.

We say that Africanus may justly be thought to have meant this year 408 of Nabonassar by the 20th of Okhus, because this 20th is by him computed to be the 65th year of independence in Egypt, and the ninth before the beginning of the year which in Theon's copies of Ptolemy's Canon is the first of Alexander on the throne of Darius, when the Macedonian occupied Egypt, and marching thence into Assyria, defeated Darius in the province of Arbela. For the 65th year of the revolt of Egypt is the 65th after the end of Darius Nothus's reign by Egyptian registration, that is, the year of Nabonassar $343 + 65 = 408$. And again, the ninth year before the beginning of the year counted to Alexander as his first on the throne of Egypt and of Asia, in Theon's or the unadulterated copies of Ptolemy's Canon, is the year of Nabonassar $417 - 9 = 408$.

It must be here interposed by way of explanation, first, that when we say Africanus computed the 20th regnal year of Okhus to be the ninth before the beginning of Alexander's first on the throne of Asia according to the true Canon of Ptolemy, we give the result of his numerals. He distributes the interval, being the reign in Egypt of the 31st dynasty, thus: to Okhus 2 years, to Arses 3 years, to Darius 4 years; giving the same number to Darius as the Canon does, but one year more to Arses than does the Canon. Secondly, when we say that by Africanus's computation the 20th year of Okhus was the 65th of the Egyptian revolt, we express the result of his numerical statements. He distributes the interval of independence in Egypt, between the end of Darius Nothus's reign and the beginning of the 20th year of Okhus, thus: to Amyrtæus of Sais, and in him the entire 28th dynasty, 6 years; to the 29th dynasty of four Mendesians, Nepherites, Akhôris, Psammúthis, and Nepherites, 6 years, 13 years, 1 year, and 4 months respectively; to the 30th, a Sebennyte dynasty of three kings, Nectanebes, Teôs, and Nectanebus, 18 years, 2 years, and 18 years respectively. See G. Syncell. pp. 76, 77, Paris ed. Now if we consider the four months of the second Nepherites (as we must by the Egyptian rule of registration) to have been either entirely comprehended in the year registered the first of his successor, or to have formed partly the beginning of the year registered as his successor's first and partly the end of his predecessor's last, the other particulars of number given by Africanus as from Manetho amount to 64 years. Therefore the 20th of Okhus in Persia (which was his first in Egypt, because in it, by expelling Nectanebus, he terminated the independence of Egypt and made himself the king of the country) was according to Africanus the 65th of the revolt, though by Ptolemy's Canon the 20th of Okhus was the 66th of the revolt.

This explanation having been made, let us take in hand again the year of Nabonassar 408, commencing in the year of the arkhon Nicomakhus at 15¾ November B.C. 341, and search whether—if Africanus rightly identified it with Manetho's (?) 20th year of Okhus—it is admissible as the date of the recovery of Egypt by Okhus.

In other words, can Egypt perhaps have been recovered when Philip wrote to the people of Athens, so recently as during the winter of the arkhon immediately preceding the one under whom the letter was written, or since November B.C. 341? For we may presume that the season selected for the invasion, especially since the failure of Pharnabazus and Iphicrates, began after the end of the annual Nile-flood. We contend that Egypt was conquered before the year of Nabonassar according to the Egyptians 408, and before the arkhonship of Nicomakhus, which began midsummer B.C. 341. It was at the beginning of this arkhonship that Demosthenes's fourth Philippic was pronounced; in which (sec. 9) he urged particularly and at length the despatch of that embassy to the Great King of which Philip complained a year or more afterwards, when probably the satraps of the Asiatic side had already, by their master Okhus's orders, thrown into Perinthus, which Philip was besieging, a force of mercenaries, under a captain named Apollodorus, that finally saved the place. See Dobson's *Oratores Attici*, vol. v. pp. 235, 236. For proof that the fourth Philippic was spoken in the arkhonship of Nicomakhus, that is after midsummer B.C. 341, see Dionysius Halic. *ad Ammæum*, p. 738, quoted by Clinton, who shows that the state of things under which it was spoken was not altered since the date of the third Philippic, delivered before midsummer B.C. 341, in the arkhonship of Sosigenes. For this date, too, see Dionys. Halic. *ad Ammæum, ibid.* In the third Philippic, too, § 15, *Oratores Attici*, vol. v. p. 223, he had briefly but emphatically named the Great King as one to whom an embassy should be sent, in their quest of succour in men and money against Philip. In the previous harangue on the Khersonesus, under the arkhón Sosigenes, § 18, he had spoken of embassies to every quarter without name of place or person. See Dobson's *Oratores Attici*, vol. v. p. 200.

It appears, then, that before the year of Nabonassar 408, which began 15¾ November B.C. 341, and which Africanus's figures would make the 20th of Okhus, and therefore the year of the recovery of Egypt, the Athenians had been urged to send the embassy which Philip afterwards complained of their having sent. We argue, therefore, that Egypt had been recovered before the Athenians, on the advice of Demosthenes, in the arkhonship of Nicomakhus, sent the embassy; for Philip's complaint in the following arkhonship of Theophrastus is: "Before the Persian recovered Egypt and Phœnicé, ye decreed to call in me and all the Greeks against him, if he attempted to effect a change; but now (*i.e.* since his conquest of Egypt and Phœnicé) your hatred is so great of me that ye treat with him about the offensive alliance (which ye are making)." This seems to intimate not only that Egypt was recovered when the satraps interfered to save Perinthus, but also when the Athenians acted on the advice of the fourth Philippic, not long after midsummer B.C. 341; that is, before 15¾ November B.C. 341, when the 408th year of Nabonassar began, the claims of which to be the date of the conquest we are now considering. It is to be observed, that in advising application against Philip to the Great King, Demosthenes says nothing about Egypt and Phœnicé. Now, if Okhus had been still foiled in his attempts against those provinces, one might have expected some reason why it was not useless for the Athenians to send ambassadors to him; whereas if, as we believe, he had already succeeded, it was prudent in the orator not to dwell upon a known fact, the fear of which had once induced the Athenians to contemplate a general confederacy against the Persian.

But we also remark, that the year 408 of Nabonassar has no claim to be regarded as the date of the recovery of Egypt, except the mere mistake of Africanus in supposing this to be the position of the 20th year of Okhus, in respect to the death of Darius Nothus on the one hand, and the battle of Arbela on the other. It was by omitting a year (which Eusebius's Manetho and the Syncellus's author restored to the 29th dynasty) that Africanus counted only 64 years between the last year of Darius Nothus and the 20th year of Okhus Artaxerxes; and it was by giving an additional year to Arses, to remedy the former mistake, that he counted nine years of Persian rule in Egypt, beginning with the supposed year of the conquest, the 20th of Okhus, and ending with the fourth year of Darius, which Ptolemy's Canon also made to be the last of Darius's reign. If Africanus thought himself justified, in giving three years to the reign of Arses by such authority as Diodorus's, who (in xvii. 5) relates that Arses was slain by Bagôas in the *third* year of his reign, the answer to him is, that by the Egyptian method of Ptolemy in the Canon of Reigns this third year is the same which is counted as the first of Darius Codomannus's four.

The year, then, being too low of the arkhon Nicomakhus (like that of the arkhon Theophrastus), according to the testimony of Philip and Demosthenes, while not only Diodorus's year of the arkhon Apollodorus, but even the date of Isocrates's Address to Philip after the conclusion of a peace between him and the Athenians, the close of the arkhonship of Themistocles, is too high a date for the conquest of Egypt, we are left to seek the year and the season of Okhus's victory in the interval between Themistocles and Nicomakhus, that is, between the midsummer of B.C. 346 and the midsummer of B.C. 341.

There is considerable authority, to terminate doubt, in favour of the arkhonship of Arkhias, which immediately followed that of Themistocles, when Isocrates finished his address to Philip. The Manetho of Eusebius, while making the 20th year of Okhus in his Persian kingdom the year of his accession to the double crown of Egypt, places this 20th year as the $(6+4+6=)$ 16th before the death of Darius Codomannus, or rather before the beginning of the arkhonship of Aristophon, in whose first month Darius was slain, and whose year was the first of the first Calippic Period, beginning at midsummer B.C. 330. For this, according to some chronologers, was the first year of the *kingdom of the Greeks*; and therefore not only in the *Ecclesiastical Canon*, but in the *Astronomical Canon*, preserved for us by Georgius Syncellus, Darius has six regnal years, and the first of Alexander is deferred from the year of the battle of Arbela, where it stands in the authentic Canon of Ptolemy, to the Egyptian year of Nabonassar 419, which began with the 14th of November B.C. 330. See Georg. Syncellus, ed. Paris, pp. 207, 208, 209.

Thus the Eusebian Manetho places Okhus's 20th year of rule among the Persians, his first regnal year in the Egyptian Annals, as the 16th year of Egypt before the midnight between the 13th and 14th days of November B.C. 330, the point at which the year 419 of Nabonassar began. That is, he made the year of the conquest of Egypt by Okhus to be the (419 − 16 =) 403d of Nabonassar, beginning with the 18th November B.C. 346. For it is to be remembered that (like the Ecclesiastical Canon in this particular) he gives four years instead of two to Arses. He also gives 25 years instead of 21 to Okhus at Babylon, because apparently (in this, too, like the Ecclesiastical Canon) he had given but 40 years instead of 46 to Artaxerxes Mnemon. For 40 + 25 + 4 is a sum equal to that of the numbers in both Ptolemy's and the Syncellus's Astronomical Canon, 46 + 21 + 2.

But why should we attach importance to this date, of the Eusebian Manetho, for the conquest of Egypt,—the year which began with the 18th of November B.C. 346? Because we arrive at this date by another path of reasoning. The perfidy of Mentor, by which he gained possession of the person of *Hermeias*, tyrant of Atarneus, and thereby recovered for Okhus all the towns and fortresses held by Hermeias, was, according to Diodorus, the first act of Mentor's administration on the western coast after the conquest of Egypt. Diodorus dates it also in the year of Callimakhus, who came into office at midsummer B.C. 349, being the successor of the arkhon Apollodorus, under whom the conquest of Egypt is placed by the same historian. See Diod. xvi. 52. Against this date we object, not only that Egypt has been shown, from the language used by Isocrates about midsummer B.C. 346, to have been, not even then, subdued,—and therefore that the year after the subjugation could not begin at midsummer B.C. 349,— but we say this: Hermeias certainly did not fall into Mentor's hands before the arkhonship of Eubulus, who succeeded Arkhias at the midsummer of B.C. 345. And therefore, if the year of Mentor's treachery to Hermeias was the year after the conquest of Egypt, this last event must be placed in the arkhonship of Arkhias, the year which began at midsummer of B.C. 346. Now this agrees with our conclusion, as to the date of the conquest, derived from the Eusebian Manetho; for that date was the 403d year of Nabonassar, a year of Egypt beginning at a season most suitable for an invasion of Egypt, namely, with the 18th of November B.C. 346.

That Hermeias was not captured by Mentor before the arkhonship of Eubulus appears thus. Plato died in the year of the 108th Olympic festival, in the arkhonship of Theophilus, according to Apollodorus the chronologer; *ap. Laertium*, v. 9. Athenæus adds (at v. p. 217) that Theophilus was the successor of Callimakhus; that is the arkhon under whom Diodorus misplaces the calamity of Hermeias. Moreover, Hermippus, *ap. Laertium*, iii. 2, placed Plato's death in the same Olympic year. Well: on the death of Plato in the arkhonship of Theophilus, he was succeeded in his school by Speusippus, and *Aristotle went away to Hermeias, tyrant of Atarneus, with whom he passed a space of three years*, and then in the arkhonship of Eubulus parted (ἐχωρίσθη) to Mytiléné. So says Dionysius of Halicarnassus, *ad Ammæum*, p. 728; and so a greater authority, Apollodorus the chronologer, cited by *Laertius*, v. 9. Now Eubulus was the fourth arkhon, counting from and including Theophilus. Accordingly he was also the fourth arkhon of the 108th Olympiad; and came into office, as we have said, at midsummer B.C. 345. Just so Laertius says, v. 9, that Aristotle came to Mytiléné in the arkhonship of Eubulus, in the fourth year of the 108th Olympiad. For these citations, mostly verified by ourselves, see Clinton's Tables. It was probably at the news of his patron's seizure that Aristotle quitted the Asiatic shore for Mytiléné; and this indeed Strabo intimates, xiii.' 1, § 57, by his expression, "*the philosophers escaped*." But he may possibly have quitted before. In any case Hermeias's arrest cannot be placed earlier than in this year; and if, as Diodorus asserts, it was Mentor's first achievement in the year after Okhus's reduction of Egypt, it may, we think, be concluded with great probability that the conquest happened in the winter of B.C. 346-345, in Arkhias's arkhonship, or, as the Eusebian Manetho first led us to suppose, in the Egyptian year of Nabonassar 403.

Very early in the arkhonship of Arkhias, the termination of the Phocian war by King Philip set free a large number of mercenaries that had served both the Phocians and the Thebans. The moment, therefore, would seem to have been favourable for Okhus to increase his force of Greeks for the invasion of Egypt. The first event of Philip's interference in the Phocian war, after his arrival in Locris, was that Phalœkus, the leader of the mercenaries or free companions in the Phocian service, finding Philip too strong for him, began to treat, obtained leave to quit the country, and retired with 8000 comrades into the Peloponnesus. See Diodorus xvi. 50.

It is but a superfluous remark, that in the arkhonship of Arkhias Philip's son Alexander was in his 11th year; though a ridiculous legend related that Nectanebus flying from Egypt, on the occasion which we have dated in that year, came in the disguise of a wizard to Macedonia; where, deceiving Philip's consort Olympias by magic and personating the god Ammon, he became the father of the future founder of Alexandria.

805

APPENDIX NO. III.

On Ptolemy's Canon of Reigns, ending with Alexander's at Babylon, and his Canon of subsequent Reigns at Alexandria: with a notice of the Seleucidan Era.

A

IN a foot-note on page 102 we promised to adduce in this place, *Cases proving the custom of Ptolemy's Canon*, as to the assignment of the year of Nabonassar in which one Babylonian reign ended and another began. But what we have here and elsewhere termed the custom *of the Canon* is in reality the custom of Hellenized Egyptians, or learned Greeks of Egypt, in their use of the numbers, preserved by Babylonian monuments, and perhaps tabulated in a Babylonian canon. For the very same numbers, interpreted according to the Khaldæan use, produce different dates of years before Christ. Whether the Canon ended with the reign of the last Darius, with that of the Macedonian conqueror, or with those of the nominal kings, his brother and son, who succeeded him in partnership, and while they lived had the first Ptolemy for their satrap in Egypt, it is certain, that, at a later date, this Babylonian series of regnal periods was prefixed by chronologers to a series of subsequent Greek reigns (or reigns at first Greek, afterwards Roman) in Egypt. It is also certain that the custom of Egyptian annalists had governed the latter list throughout. The year in which a king had yielded up his throne had always been counted his successor's first, not his own last year; or, to take the converse, however late in the year a demise of the crown might have happened, the twelvemonth in which a king came into the possession of his throne had ever been assigned altogether to him, and not at all to his predecessor. This being the case of the latter list of kings, when the Babylonian line came to be prefixed, the same was perhaps believed and certainly was taken to have been the rule of registration in it. The regnal years at Babylon were treated as so many previous Egyptian years. The Babylonian series was prefixed to the series of Egyptian regnal years, as if the end of the last year of the Khaldæan Register, instead of being overlapped by the beginning of the first year registered in Egypt, had immediately preceded it. Accordingly, the first year of Nabonassar, when the two series of reigns were united in a single canon, became the year of Egypt in the course of which Nabonassar acquired the kingdom at Babylon, or, more correctly, had been first registered king in the Khaldæan Annals. For we have learnt (pp. 438-446) that the Khaldæan adjustment of reigns at Babylon was governed by a rule that differed from the Egyptian. The Khaldæans assigned to each king, as the first of his reign, the

57

calendar year that followed next after the one wherein he became possessed of the kingdom in fact; the compensation being, that they gave him, for his last year of reign, the calendar year in which, early or late, he gave up the kingdom. But it will be observed that the gap between the two commencements of a reign, according to the Egyptian and according to the Khaldæan account, diminishes as we go back towards the first year of Nabonassar; or, to express the same otherwise, augments as years advance from that epoch. This augmentation as we go on, or diminution as we go back, is due to the difference between the Egyptian year and the Khaldæan. For although the years of reign at Babylon were treated in Egypt, by chronologers of the Ptolemæan or Augustan periods, as years of Egypt, that is, years of 365 days apiece,—not fixed by periodical intercalation of days, but *vague*, receding continually in relation to the corresponding tropical year,—nevertheless they were really (as registered by the Khaldæans) *tropical*, or at least lunar years kept *in a fixed relation to the tropical* by intercalation of lunations. Moreover, it has appeared (p. 434) that the regnal year at Babylon began with a month corresponding to the Markhesvan or second Tisri of the Syrians and Jews. Thus the first year of Nabonassar, according to Babylonian records, was a year that began with the Markhesvan next after his accession to the throne at Babylon. Hence, in proportion as the chain of Babylonian reigns lengthens, and the Egyptian first day of Thoth recedes in the tropical year, the interval grows between the Egyptian and the Khaldæan New-years' days. So that, whereas between the Khaldæan and the Egyptian commencements of the reign of Nabonassar the interval had been about eight months, the interval between the same two commencements of Alexander the Great's reign became the space of nearly that whole Egyptian year in the course of which Alexandria was founded and King Darius was overthrown in the province of Arbela.

What has been said will be illustrated by the following *Table of Reigns at Babylon; covering the period from the New-year's day of the first regnal year of Nabonassar to, and inclusive of, the New-year's day of the first of Seleucus Nicator.* The reader withal is here put in possession of the particulars contained in the astronomer Ptolemy's oft-quoted *Canon of Reigns, Assyrian and Mede, at Babylon.* For these, and these only, are exhibited in the first three columns of our Table, in their first 31 particulars. They are all the names and numbers, except such as follow the reign of Alexander the Great, in those columns; and they are taken from the edition of Ptolemy's Canon for which Henry Dodwell collated fresh MS. authorities with the previous edition of Petavius. See H. Dodwell's *Dissertationes Cyprianicæ*, folio edition, p. 24. To this more authentic exhibition of Ptolemy's Canon (supposed to come from that astronomer's commentator Theon) we have added some varieties in the writing of names preserved by Georgius Syncellus in his Astronomical and Ecclesiastical Canons:—

1. Kings and Inter-reigns.	2. Years of each King and Inter-reign.	3. Totals of the Years of Nabonassar at the end of each Reign and Inter-reign.	4. Time elapsed at the Commencement of each Reign and Inter-reign by the Egyptian Method.	5. Commencements of each Reign and Inter-reign by the Khaldæan Method.
NABONASSAR, . .	14	14	25½ Feb. B.C. 747	1st of Markhesvan (say Nov.) B.C. 747
Nadius (or Nabius),	2	16	22¾ Feb. ... 733	 733
Khinzirus and Porus, ...	5	21	21½ Feb. ... 731	 731
Júgæus (or Ilúlæus),	5	26	20¼ Feb. ... 726	 726
Mardokempadus, .	12	38	19 Feb. ... 721	 721
Arkianus, . . .	5	43	16 Feb. ... 709	 709
First Inter-reign,	2	45	14¾ Feb. ... 704	 704
Belibus, ...	3	48	14¼ Feb. ... 702	 702
Apranadius (or Aparanadisus), .	6	54	13½ Feb. ... 699	 699
Rigébelus (or Erigebalus), . .	1	55	12 Feb. ... 693	 693
Mesessimordakus,	4	59	11¾ Feb. ... 692	 692
Second Inter-reign, . . .	8	67	10¾ Feb. ... 688	 688
Assarad (or Isar-ind)inus, . . .	13	80	8¾ Feb. ... 680	 680
Saosdukhinus, . .	20	100	5½ Feb. ... 667	 667
Khyniladanus, . .	22	122	0½ Feb. ... 647	 647
Nabopolassarus, .	21	143	26 Jan. ... 625	 625
Nabokolassarus, .	43	186	20¾ Jan. ... 604	 604
Iloarúdamus, . .	2	188	10 Jan. ... 561	 561
Nirikassolassarus, .	4	192	9½ Jan. ... 559	 559
Nabonadius, . .	17	209	8½ Jan. ... 555	 555
Kyrus (Cyrus), .	9	218	4½ Jan. ... 538	 538
Kambyses, . . .	8	226	2 Jan. ... 529	 529
Darius I., . . .	36	262	31 Dec. ... 522	 521
Xerxes, ...	21	283	22 Dec. ... 486	 485
Artaxerxes I., . .	41	324	16¾ Dec. ... 465	 464
Darius II., . . .	19	343	6½ Dec. ... 424	 423
Artaxerxes II., .	46	389	1¾ Dec. ... 405	 404
Okhus, ...	21	410	20¼ Nov. ... 359	 358
Arses, ...	2	412	15 Nov. ... 338	 337
Darius III., . . .	4	416	14½ Nov. ... 336	 335
Alexander the Macedonian, . .	8	424	13½ Nov. ... 332	 331
Aridæus Philip with Alexander, and afterwards the latter alone,	12	436	11½ Nov. ... 324	 323
SELEUCUS, . . .	...	...	8½ Nov. ... 312	1st Markhesvan B.C. 311

The reader is to understand that in the column of Commencements according to the Khaldæan method, the fifth and last of the Table, each reign or interregnal period begins not after but *with* the first day of Markhesvan. But, in the column of Commencements according to the Egyptian method, each date signifies the point of time *immediately after which* the reign or interregnum noted on the same line in the first column began. Thus, 1. The date *December the 31st B.C.* 522 signifies that the reign of Darius son of Hystaspes was considered to begin τοῦ μεσονυκτίου, *at midnight,* immediately *after* the completion of the Roman and our 31st civil day of December B.C. 522; that is, exactly along with the Julian year B.C. 521. 2. So, too, by the date of the commencement of Xerxes' reign, 22d Dec. B.C. 486, it is to be understood, that, according to Egyptian registration, the reign of that monarch began at midnight with the Roman 23d of December B.C. 486. 3. In like manner, Nabonassar's reign, as fixed by the Egyptians, is to be understood as having begun *immediately after* 25½ (days of) February, or τῆς μεσημβρινῆς, *at mid-day,* immediately after 12 hours of the Roman and our 26th of February B.C. 747. 4. The reign of Naboko(d)lassarus, *i.e.* Nebukhadrezzar or Nebukhadnezzar, began by the Egyptian registration immediately *after* the lapse of 20¾ days in January; that is, ἑσπέρας, *at eventide,* or six hours after noon of the 21st of January B.C. 604. And 5. The reign of Cyrus (or, more properly, of his uncle Darius the Mede) began immediately after the expiration of 4¼ days of January, that is, πρωίας, *in the morning,* or at six hours before noon of the 5th of January B.C. 538.

As to the names Mardokempadus and Nabokolassarus in the first column, the Merodakh Baladan and Nebukhadrezzar of the Bible, we were much disposed to write them *Mardokempa(l)dus* and *Naboko(d)-lassarus*,—thereby suggesting, either that, possibly, the combinations ΛΔ and ΔΛ in the first Greek copy of the Canon, having been mistaken for ΔΔ and ΛΛ respectively, may have been thought sufficiently transcribed by a single Δ and a single Λ; or, more probably, that, when the sounds represented in Greek by those two letters came together, the one preceding was apt to be elided in pronunciation, and thence in writing also.

In respect of the name *Arôgus,* applied to the successor of Okhus, that is, of Artaxerxes the Third in our editions of Theon's copy of the Canon, we have substituted *Arses,* after the Syncellus's Ecclesiastical copy, which, confirmed as it is by Diodorus, has authority in a question about the reading of a name, however depraved in its numbers by a rash and ignorant criticism. We suppose the word ʼΑρώγου in existing MSS. and Edd. of Theon's copy to be a mistranscription of ʽΆρσου ʽΏχου, and that this should be interpreted (*The reign*) *of Arses* (*son*) *of Okhus;* although the Ecclesiastical copy has ʽΆρσου ἀδελφοῦ ʽΏχου, and is followed by the Syncellus, who in his own Table of Persian

Kings has Ἄρσης· Ὤχου ἀδελφός, ed. Dind. p. 487. The Syncellus's Astronomical copy, by a faulty transposition of letters, has Σάρου for Ἄρσου, and the Alexandrian Chronicle, ap. Scalig. Euseb. pp. 245-251, quoted by Clinton, gives Ἀρσίοχος for Ἄρσης.

B

CONCERNING the kings preceding Cyrus in Ptolemy's Canon, some historical notes may be desirable, as an introduction to whatever more may come to light, or may be already known to students of cuneiform writings, though not to general readers. But as to the five kings that stand immediately above Cyrus in the first column of our Table, we would merely refer to Article I. Section B. of this Appendix. As to the names themselves, various Greek forms of them are found elsewhere. Those of Berosus, as quoted by Josephus, may be seen in *Joseph. cont. Apion.* i. 19, 20. Other forms used by Josephus, where he does not appear to be following Berosus, may be seen in *Antiq.* x. 11, § 2. The orthography employed by Alexander Polyhistor, so far as it may be believed to survive, may be found in the Armenian version of Eusebius's *Chronicon*, ed. Mai, as cited in C. Müller's *Fragm. Hist. Græc.* tom. 2, p. 505, No. 12. And how Abydenus wrote the names may in like degree appear from the same, tom. 4, pp. 282-284. These various Greek forms may be useful to decipherers and interpreters of Cuneiform Inscriptions, in which at least four out of the five names have been found in the Babylonian form; for we are told that the interpretation of proper names is one of the most difficult branches of the study; and that, being but rarely expressed phonetically, phonetical equivalents of the wholes or of parts are required. We are not aware that the name of the third king Evil-merodakh has yet been found in any Babylonian inscription; but its Hebrew orthography, as well as two Hebrew forms of the name of Evil-merodakh's father, is preserved in the Bible. For another Greek form of it besides those already referred to, the reader may go to the Ecclesiastical Canon of Syncellus, p. 393, ed. Dind., and to the Syncellus's own list of Khaldæan kings, p. 422. The form of his father's name ordinarily used by Greek ecclesiastical writers is the one given in the Septuagint.

But this second and most celebrated name of the five, together with the fifth name, which is Herodotus's Labynetus, is also found phonetically written in Perso-Aryan and in Kissian cuneiform in the great trilingual inscription at Behistun.

1. Of earlier kings than the five who stand immediately before Cyrus in Ptolemy's Canon we will now say something. We begin with the two immediate predecessors of Nabopolassar, and of these first with SAOSDUKHINUS. A barrel cylinder, writes Sir H. C. Rawlinson (*Athenæum*, 22d Aug. 1863), has been found at Babylon which commemorates the installation of *Saul-mugina* (the reading says he is

not quite certain) on the throne of Babylon by his elder brother Asshur-bani-pal king of Assyria, immediately after the death of his father Esarhaddon. The identity, adds Sir H., of Säul-mugina and the *Saosdukhinus* of Ptolemy's Canon ought to have been recognised long ago, since there is a passage in my published Inscriptions, Plate 8, No. ii. line 11, which commemorates the appointment by Asshur-banipal of his younger brother Säul-mugina to the sovereignty of *Karaduniyas* or Babylon. The *Sammughes* of Polyhistor, continues Sir H., is of course the same king. Of the Polyhistor in this matter we know only through Eusebius, already referred to, and by Clinton recited at length *F. H.*, vol. i. pp. 270, 271. The passage in question is this: " Sub Ezechia Senecherimus regnavit, uti Polyhistor innuit, annis octodecim : post quem ejusdem filius annis octo : tum annis viginti et uno Sammughes : itemque frater hujus viginti et uno : deinde Nabupalassarus annis viginti : denique Nabucodrossorus tribas annis supra quadraginta : ita ut a Senecherimo ad Nabucodrossorum octoginta et octo anni excurrunt." (For 18 + 8 + 21 + 21 + 20 = 88.)

2. On this we must observe that, Sammughes being now identified with *Säul-mugina*, that is, Saosdukhinus, king of Babylon, younger brother of Asshur-bani-pal king of Assyria, the as yet unnamed *brother* by whom Sammughes is said to have been succeeded should be KHYNILADANUS, who, as we have seen, according to Ptolemy's Canon, reigned the space of 22 years between the 20 years of Saosdukhinus and the 21 years of Nabopolassar.

Further on, Eusebius returns to Polyhistor, and, after other particulars, reports him thus: " Jam post Sammughem imperavit Chaldæis Sardanapallus viginti annis et uno." Thus the successor of Sammughes (or Saosdukhinus) in the kingdom of the Khaldæans at Babylon is at length named *Sardanapallus*. But this is a misnomer ; for he was really named Khyniladanus. The blunder apparently is this: the brother of Sammughes who succeeded him at Babylon is called by the name of the elder brother, who placed both him and Sammughes upon the inferior throne, being himself the lord paramount, the king of Assyria. Another blunder follows with which we have nothing to do here,—the ascribing of the part in the overthrow of Nineveh played by Nabopolassar to the successor of Saosdukhinus. This omission of Nabopolassar is due perhaps rather to the negligence of Eusebius than to that of Polyhistor. The true account of Sardanapallus has been preserved to us from Abydenus in Eusebius, *Chron.* p. 24, cited in C. Müller's *Fragm. Hist. Græc.* tom. 4, p. 282, No. 7. Abydenus represents Sardanapallus not as the successor of Sammughes (Saosdukhinus) and the predecessor of Nabopolassar at Babylon, but as the successor of Esarhaddon and predecessor of Sarakus at Nineveh. Following Abydenus, then, *we must identify Sardanapallus with Asshurbani-pal* son of Esarhaddon ; and *Sarakus*, who perished when Nineveh was taken by the Babylonians and Medes, with the successor of

Asshur-bani-pal, the last king whose name appears on the Assyrian monuments. This name in full, Sir H. C. R. tells us (*Athenæum*, Aug. 22, 1863), was apparently *Asshur-irik-ili-kin*, but was contracted to *Asshur-irik-kin*, or *Asshur-irik-ili*. We seem to have the elements of Saraks or Sarakus in the last, and perhaps accented, syllables of the first two elements of the monumental name. Of the last three kings of Nineveh, Abydenus's account, cited by Eusebius, ends thus: ".... Ægyptum præterea partesque inferiores Syriæ acquirebat Axerdis (Esarhaddon). Hinc Sardanapallus exortus est. Post quem Saracus imperitabat Assyriis: qui quidem, certior factus turmarum vulgi collectitiarum, quæ à mari adversus se adventarent, [Na]Busalussorum militiæ ducem Babylonem mittebat. Sedenim hic capto rebellandi consilio, Amuhiam, Asdahagis Medorum principis filiam, nato suo Nabucodrossoro despondebat; moxque raptim contra Ninum, seu Ninivem, urbem impetum faciebat. Re omni cognitâ rex Saracus regiam (Evoritam) inflammabat." Thus the identification of Saosdukhinus with the Säul-mugina of the inscriptions and the Sammughes of Alexander Polyhistor leads to that of Khyniladanus at Babylon, and to that of the Sardanapallus of Alexander Polyhistor and Abydenus at Nineveh.

3. The predecessor of Saosdukhinus at Babylon called ASSARADINUS is satisfactorily identified with the king of Assyria, Esarhaddon (2 Kings xix. 37, Isa. xxxvii. 38, and Ezra iv. 2), who is clearly proved to have reigned in person at Babylon. See Rawlinson's Herodotus, vol. i. p. 482, comparing 2 Chron. xxiii. 11. Thus Esarhaddon and two of his younger sons in succession were the three kings next before Nabopolassar at Babylon.

4 and 5. Next we go back to a point 22 years before the beginning of Assaradinus, and where the 3 + 6 years begin of BELIBUS and APARANADIUS. These have been found to be kings of Babylon appointed successively by the Great King, the king of Assyria, Sennacherib. The former was put upon the throne in B.C. 702, during the interval between the accession and the first New-year's day of the reign of Sennacherib, whether this was the first day of Nisannu or the first day of Markhesvan. Sennacherib made Belibus king after having defeated the forces and pillaged the palace in Babylon of one whom Sargon, the father of Sennacherib, seven years before had expelled from the throne of Babylon—*Marduk-bal-adana king of Karduniash*, the Merodakh Baladan of the Bible,—who, now defeated by Sennacherib, fled within (?) the rivers Agammi and Apparati. Mr. H. Fox Talbot tells us that Dr. Hincks was the first who recognised the Belibus of the Canon in the name of the person on this occasion recorded to have been appointed by Sennacherib king "of Leshan and Akkad" in line 14 of the Bellino Cylinder. The name is written *Beleb* in Mr. Talbot's decipherment, *Journal R. A. S.* vol. xviii. p. 86, and *Bel-ipni* by Sir H. C. Rawlinson in the *Athenæum*, Aug. 22, 1863.

The three years' reign of Belibus, attested by the Canon, is confirmed by Polyhistor, who gives him the honour claimed by Sennacherib of having defeated Merodakh Baladan. According to Mai and Zohrab's translation of the Armenian Eusebius, Polyhistor wrote: "Postquam regno defunctus est *Senecheribi frater* et post Hagisæ in Babylonios dominationem (qui quidem non expleto trigesimo die à Marudacho Baldane interemptus est) Marudachus ipse Baldanes tyrannidem invasit, mensibus sex; donec eum sustulit vir quidam nomine *Elibus*; qui et in regnum successit. Hoc postremo tertium jam annum regnante Senecheribus rex Assyriorum copias adversus Babylonios contrahebat, prælioque cum iis conserto superior evadebat; captumque *Elibum* cum familiaribus ejus in Assyriam transferri jubebat. Is (Senecheribus) igitur Babyloniorum potitus filium suum *Asordanem* eis regem imponebat; ipse autem in Assyriam reditum maturabat." See *Fragm. Hist. Græc.* tom. 2, p. 504.

It would be easy to identify the son of Senacherib, here mentioned as the king by whom Elibus was superseded at Babylon, with the successor given to Belibus in Ptolemy's Canon, if Asordanes, the name of the son of Senacherib, could be identified with Apranadius or Aparanadisus, the name of the king who in Ptolemy's Canon occupies the throne at Babylon for six years in succession to Belibus. It has been suggested that Apranadius may be a corruption of Assaranadius—a very violent remedy. See Rawlinson's Herodotus, vol. i. p. 478, note. Polyhistor's account of Senacherib's substituting his son Asordanes for Elibus on the throne of Babylon is confirmed by a cylinder of the reign of Senacherib. The Bellino cylinder indeed, above quoted, does not reach down to the commencement of the reign of Belibus's successor; for it contains the wars of but two years after the first New-year's day of Senacherib's reign. But the Taylor cylinder records the wars of Senacherib's first eight regnal years, and this is the cylinder we here speak of. In it, as well as in Bellino's cylinder, is recorded the defeat of Merodakh Baladan king of Karduniash between the accession of Senacherib to the throne and the first New-year's day of his reign; but no notice is given, as in the former cylinder, of the appointment of Belibus as Senacherib's viceroy at Babylon. But in the fourth year of Senacherib—that is, the year after the campaign in Judæa—and after the third year counted to Belibus at Babylon, we have an expedition against Beth-Yakina, beyond the rivers Agammi and Apparati, mentioned in the Bellino cylinder. Merodakh Baladan is driven out of the country, and Senacherib places upon that king's throne his own eldest son *Asshur-nadan-mu*, and, what may imply the displacement of Belibus, to whom the country had before been given according to the Bellino cylinder, he bestows upon him "the whole of the land of Lesban and Akkadi." Two years afterwards, that is, in the sixth year of Senacherib, the refugees of Beth-Yakina established over sea (beyond the broad river) in the territory of Susiana having been followed up, their towns having been destroyed, and they themselves, with their gods, and the Susians who had entertained them, having been carried off to Assyria, the position of Asshur-nadan-mu in Beth-Yakina must have been made more secure. At the same time, his authority must have been restored in Leshan and Akkadi; for during the return of the expedition, it is related that a great battle having been fought with *Susubi* prince of Babylon, whom his soldiers had restored to the sovereignty of Leshan and Akkadi, "the provinces of Bil-lu" (an unusual orthography of the name Belus), Susubi's army was destroyed, and he himself was taken alive, loaded with chains, and carried to Assyria. This Susubi had been described as dwelling within (apparently on the Babylonian side of) the river Agammi (a canal, perhaps, from the Euphrates to the Tigris), and as having been defeated in battle when he encountered Senacherib's army on its way to Beth-Yakina, in the fourth year of Senacherib's reign. The river Agammi must have separated the provinces of Belus, Leshan and Akkadi, from Beth-Yakina; and the kingdom of Karduniash must have comprehended the countries on both sides of the river. Two years later, in the eighth year of Senacherib, we find that, Susubi having escaped from Assyria, the princes of Babylon resolved upon war, placed him on the throne, and invested him with royal power over the lands of Leshan and Akkadi. Then, with treasure out of the temples, he hired the Susians to come to his aid. The Susian forces occupied Akkadi, advanced to Babylon, which thus seems to have been situate in Leshan west of Akkadi, concluded a treaty with Susubi, and fought a great battle with the army of Senacherib, in which, however, they were defeated. See *Journal R. A. S.* vol. xix. pp. 149-165.

In this contemporary narrative Asshur-nadan-mu seems clearly to be the same as the Polyhistor's Asordanes son of Sennacherib. But his viceregal residence seems to have been not at Babylon, but at the more distant Beth-Yakina, the former seat of the power of Merodakh Baladan. This leads us to the conjecture, that though Leshan and Akkadi were appended to Beth-Yakina when Sennacherib placed his son here upon the throne, they may have still had an under-king of their own whose name may have been Apranadius.

We have now said all we can on BELIBUS and APRANADIUS, who ruled in Babylon during the first nine years of Sennacherib: but we shall shortly have occasion to return to the passage above adduced from the Polyhistor, on account of the events there said to have preceded the reign of Elibus or Belibus, who was possibly Susubi.

6. We now go back from the reign of Belibus to that of the king called in the Canon MARDOKEMPADUS. This king, who reigned 12 years in Babylon according to the Canon, from the 27th to the 38th of Nabonassar, that is, by the Khaldæan account, from the beginning of Markhesvan B.C. 721 to the end of Tisri B.C. 709, is the Merodakh Baladan mentioned in the annals of Hezekiah king of Judah, in those

of the kings of Assyria Sargon and (as we have lately seen in part) Sennacherib, and also in the fragments remaining of the Polyhistor's narrative. We have elsewhere shown that the sixth year of Hezekiah king of Judah, in which Samaria was taken by the Assyrians, began with Tisri B.C. 721. Now Sargon, or Sargina, king of Assyria, relates that he took Samaria in his first year of reign, and carried into captivity 27,200 persons; also, that in his own 12th year he drove Merodakh Baladan out of Babylon after he had reigned there 12 years. See Rawlinson's Herodotus, vol. i. p. 472. The inscription relating to Samaria is published in Botta's Inscriptions, Plate 70. See the *Athenæum*, Aug. 22, 1863, where Sir H. C. R. offers reasons which may have weight to induce a belief that further draughts were made upon the Israelitish population to be transplanted into Assyria after the one here recorded; though they seem by no means a proof, or even an indication, that the city Samaria was again besieged and captured by the Assyrians in the 13th or a later year of Sargon. The embassy of Merodakh Baladan king of Babylon to Hezekiah, recorded in 2 Kings xx. 12-15 and Isa. xxxix., happened in the 14th year of Hezekiah, or shortly after; for it was occasioned by the news that Hezekiah had been sick and was recovered; the sickness certainly having been in the 14th year of Hezekiah, though not in *the same* 14th year (as we have explained elsewhere) in which Sennacherib invaded him; 2 Kings xviii. 13; Isa. xxxvi. 1,—for Hezekiah after his recovery (which was a miracle and the figure of a resurrection from the dead) had a new reign given him of 15 years, and reigned, it is stated, 29 years in all: see 2 Kings xviii. 2 and 2 Chron. xxix. 1. Thus it was evidently in about the *ninth* year of Merodakh Baladan's reign at Babylon that he sent his letters and present to Hezekiah, or in about the twelvemonth beginning with Markhesvan B.C. 713, and in about the fourth year before his expulsion from Babylon by the arms of the king of Assyria. Of his brief success in an attempt made about seven years afterwards to repossess himself of that city and its dependencies, the Polyhistor's testimony to which fact has been already cited, we shall shortly have occasion to speak. At present, having pointed out the evident identity of the Mardokempadus who reigned at Babylon 12 years according to the Canon, from the 1st of Markhesvan B.C. 721, with the Merodakh Baladan who reigned there during the first 12 years of Sargon king of Assyria, we proceed to his successor on the throne of Babylon.

7. This was ARKIANUS. If this personage be indeed the successor of Merodakh Baladan, as we have just shown, the five years allotted him in Ptolemy's Canon are the years of Sargon extending from the 13th to the 17th according to Assyrian numeration. He was perhaps not merely Sargon's viceroy appointed in the room of Merodakh Baladan, but Sargina or Sargon himself, as first suggested (says Sir H. C. R. in the *Athenæum*, 22d Aug. 1863) by Dr. Hincks. The fifth

and last year of Arkianus at Babylon, ending according to the Khaldæan registration of years with Tisri B.C. 704, and corresponding, as we have intimated, with the 17th year of Sargon, was the last year of Sargon. For, according to an *Assyrian Canon* of yearly officers (like the eponym arkhons of Athens, as observed by Dr. Hincks),—where the names denoting years are assigned in parcels by dividing lines to successive kings,—we are assured by Sir H. C. R. that Sargon reigned 17 years: see the *Athenæum* as before.

The next two years, called *a period without a king*, at Babylon, in Ptolemy's Canon of Babylonian Reigns, and, by Sir H. C. R.'s report, assigned in the Canon of Assyrian Arkhonships to Sennacherib, making his years of reign to be 24 in all, were really a period no less anarchical in Assyria than at Babylon. They certainly preceded the first year counted as Sennacherib's in both the Bellino and the Taylor cylinders, for they are attested by the Babylonian Canon to have preceded the viceroyalty of Belibus, whose first year is shown by the Bellino cylinder to correspond with the first regnal year of Sennacherib. The arkhons whose names form the dates of the Bellino and Taylor cylinders are reported by Sir H. C. R. to be respectively the 4th and the 15th of the 24 arkhons assigned in his *Assyrian Canon* to the reign of Sennacherib. Therefore they held office in the 2d and 13th years of Sennacherib's reign, as that reign is made to have commenced in those cylinders. The two years of interregnum marked in the Babylonian Canon plainly indicate an interval between Sargon and his son Sennacherib, during which the succession to the throne was disputed. It would appear from Polyhistor's account (preserved by Eusebius, and cited above under BELIBUS), that Sennacherib in B.C. 702 succeeded a brother of his upon the throne of Sargon, and that before the viceroyalty of Belibus there had been a ruler at Babylon, named Hagisa, who, whether under an Assyrian commission or self-constituted, had not reigned a month, or, as the Polyhistor said, had not completed his 30th day, when he was slain, and his placed usurped by *Marudachus Baldanes*; who, in his turn, when he had reigned six months, was overthrown by one named Elibus,—the Belibus of Ptolemy's Babylonian Canon. How it came to pass that Merodakh Baladan gave place to Belibus, or at least Sennacherib's account of the matter, we have learnt from the king's cylinders; one of which has also informed us of Merodakh Baladan's further disasters in the land of Beth-Yakina in the fourth year of Sennacherib's reign, or about 15 years after the embassy from Babylon to Hezekiah king of Judah.

C

WITH reference to our Table of Regnal and Interregnal periods at Babylon, from the beginning of Nabonassar's reign to the beginning of that of Selcucus, let us remind the reader of what has been said already, that a document which it contains, the Babylonian Canon (called Ptolemy's, as the lately discovered Assyrian Canon might be called Rawlinson's), ends with the reign of Alexander the Great. So much premised, we observe that Georgius Syncellus distinguishes this piece from another (which he calls the Ecclesiastical Canon) by the titles of the Mathematical, the Astronomical, and, once, the Khaldæan Canon. But even this his Astronomical Canon is marred by uncritical adjustments to Holy Scripture. Wherefore we have followed the more authentic copy, presumed to have been transmitted with less of alteration from the time of Theon, as we find it in Dodwell's Appendix to his *Dissertationes Cyprianicæ*. As to the original document, our Syncellus supposes it older than Claudius Ptolemy; for he justifies its authority in his own time with Greek as well as Khaldæan men of science, by alleging the use of it made by Ptolemy ἐν τῇ μεγάλῃ συντάξει τῇ τῆς ἀστρονομίας, or, as he afterwards expresses himself, ἐν τῇ μεγάλῃ συντάξει τοῦ μεγάλου Πτολεμαίου, not in the Systematic Treatise on Starry Influences, but in the greater one on Astronomy, the title whereof, in its superlative form, enters into the name of the work given by the Arabic translators, *Al-magest*. But though thus used in the great work of Ptolemy (and to verify the assertion, the reader may employ these references given by Dodwell: iv. cap. 6, v. 14, iii. p. 79, iv. p. 102, iv. p. 103; Gr. ed. v. p. 125), this *Khaldæan Canon of Reigns* seems not to be reckoned by the Syncellus a part (or at least an essential part) of the work he calls the πρόχειροι κανόνες, *Manual Tables*, of Ptolemy, and the πρόχειροι τῆς ἀστρονομίας κανόνες, *Manual Tables of Astronomy*. Not only from the Syncellus's language, but from that of the fragment of a commentary (addressed by Theon to his son Epiphanius, and described as a second and more popular commentary) εἰς τοὺς προχείρους κανόνας, on the *Manual Tables* (for which fragment see Dodwell's aforesaid Appendix), it would seem that the civil time-table, used for the astronomical purposes of that work, was, substantially at least, Dodwell's *later* Table, or series of tables, of Reigns. This series of reigns—first Greek, afterwards Roman—begins with the reign next after that of Alexander, the Founder (as the conqueror of Asia was called at his own Alexandria); that is to say, it begins with Philip Aridæus, whose lieutenant, at his accession to the kingship, the first of the Ptolemies was made in Egypt. The principal part of the Manual Tables of Astronomy the Syncellus seems to describe as an astronomical table of 1476 Egyptian years, beginning with the first of Philip; and the Syncellus's language receives light from the fragment of Theon. Accordingly, we are led to conceive that this cycle of 1476 Egyptian or 1475 solar years was divided into a series of 59 lesser periods of 25 solar years apiece; each solar year being computed to be, *not*, as that of Alexandria was, $\frac{1488}{1480}$ths of an Egyptian year, according to the old calculation adopted by Calippus in the time of Alexander the Great, and by Sosigenes in the time of

Julius Cæsar, but $1\frac{1}{4}\frac{7}{7}\frac{5}{5}$ths of the same; that is, 365 days, 5 hours, 56 minutes, 20 seconds, and $\frac{2}{3}\frac{3}{8}$ths of a second: while Hipparkhus's calculation, as reported by Ptolemy, was 365 days, 5 hours, 55 minutes, 12 seconds. See Clinton's *F. H.* vol. ii. Appendix, chap. 19. It was in order to find in this cycle of 1476 years of Philip the dates corresponding with epochs of the Alexandrian eras of Diocletian or of Augustus, that the Canon of Reigns subsequent to that of Alexander the Great (*the Egyptian Canon,* or Canon of the *Egyptian era*, as we may especially term it) was added to the Manual. The years of Alexandria were fixed, and differed from those of Egypt, which were vague, or receding years, by the intercalation of a sixth epagomené, or day supplementary, at the end of every four years or 1460 days; and the method of reducing any date in the series of these years to a date in the cycle of 1476 Egyptian years is explained by Theon. He takes as an example the 77th year of Diocletian, the 22d day of Thoth, the 11th hour of daylight; and he finds the corresponding point of time in the cycle of 1476 years thus: To begin, he turns to the *Canon of Reigns subsequent to Alexander's*, or reigns of the era of Philip Aridæus, and out of the third column, or column of totals, he obtains the number of years from the commencement of the reign of Philip to that of the reign of Diocletian, which is 607. To this he adds the *number of years* in the date given for reduction; that is, 77 years of Diocletian (current). Next, to determine the position of the total, which is 684 years in the Canon (of astronomical positions) for a cycle of 1476 years, he carries the same εἰς τὸ τῶν εἰκοσιπενταετηρίδων πρῶτον σελίδιον, *to the column of twenty-fives of years, which is the first in the lesser Canon thereof.* (For the Greek phrase, understanding its meaning, from what had been said some time previously, to be this, εἰς τὸ τῶν εἰκοσιπενταετηρίδων κανόνιον κατὰ τὸ πρῶτον σελίδιον, we were inclined to propose εἰς τὸ τῶν εἰκοσιπενταετηρίδων, πρῶτον ὄν, σελίδιον. But as the same expression has occurred before, following in the same context the more explicit phraseology, we may rather decide that τῶν εἰκοσιπενταετηρίδων is here the abbreviation of τοῦ τῶν εἰκοσιπενταετηρίδων κανόνιου.) Here Theon finds the number *next less than* 684 *years*. This (consisting of Egyptian years current in so many twenty-fives of solar years) is 676; corresponding with 27 complete twenty-fives of solar years. Therefore 676 is said to be *the first* of the five required κεφάλαια or *heads* of the given date, as contained in the Astronomical Table; that is, the head of εἰκοσιπενταετηρίδες, or 25 *year periods:* while the eight years' remaining surplus (for 684 - 676 = 8), being a fraction of the current 28th period of 25 years, are taken for the ἁπλᾶ ἔτη, single years, the second of the five heads or particulars required in the Canon (of astronomical positions) for 1476 Egyptian years. Now here, when this section was written, we suspected that Theon's figures had been altered, and that they should have been 607 + 77 current = 684th year current; and 684 years current − (27 × 25 =) 675 whole years = 9th year current. But we have since found that Theon reports the canon of planetary positions for the cycle of 1476 years aright. See below, Section E.

Thus, of the five heads or particulars of date in the cycle of 1476 years, two are now obtained, the number of 25 year periods elapsed, which is 27 ; and the number of the year in the current period of 25 years, which number is *eight*.

Next he proceeds to the finding of the other three particulars, the month, the day, and the hour; and he takes from the Canon of Reigns, subsequent to Alexander's, the number of years from the beginning of Augustus to that of Diocletian, 313. This is his first step. The second step in the operation is thus previously explained : The years of Augustus of the Alexandrian register, being fixed in relation to the circle of the seasons by an intercalation like the Julian, formed a series which, having in any commencement of a year coincided with a year of the register of Egyptian years, could not so coincide again till after 1460 Alexandrian years of Augustus, reckoned at 365¼ days apiece, or after 1461 Egyptian years, each consisting of 365 days. But such a coincidence in commencement did take place five years after the beginning of the reign of Augustus; or, as he had said before, in the fifth year of Augustus's reign. The two expressions are this, γενησθαι (read γεγενῆσθαι) μετὰ ἑ ἔτη τῆς ἀρχῆς τοῦ (read τῆς) Αὐγούστου βασιλείας, and this, τῷ πέμπτῳ ἔτει Αὐγούστου βασιλείας. Therefore the step now taken is this : From the before-mentioned 313 Egyptian years he deducts five years, and the remainder 308 he adds to the given 77 of Diocletian. Of the total 313 − 5 + 77 (why not 313 − 4 + 76 ?), that is, in either case 385, he takes the fourth part, that is, 96 and a fraction. Without the fraction, this is the number of the days intercalated at Alexandria since ἡ εἰρημένη διὰ ᾳυξ' ἐτῶν ἀποκατάστασις—*the aforesaid restored coincidence of the Egyptian with the Egypto-Julian year, or solar year of Alexandria* (where it was computed that 1460 solar years are equal to 1461 Egyptian years, each of 365 days). If so, the computation of Egyptian time since the coincidence had again got 96 days ahead of the Alexandrian at the given point of Alexandrian time in the 77th year of Diocletian. These, therefore, must be added either to the number of the month-day of the Alexandrian date in question, if the Greek hour of that day be after noon, or to the next less previous number, if the hour be noon or before noon. In this case the day-hour is the 11th from sunrise of the 22d day of the Alexandrian September, or Alexandrian Thoth, which (except as we shall see in the first year of a τετραετηρις, or four-year period) began with the Roman 29th of August. Therefore the days to which the addition is to be made are 22, the hour being the 11th from sunrise, or the 5th after noon. The total 96 + 22 current, that is, 118 days current, are days of the already found Egyptian year from the beginning of Thoth ; and reach to the 28th day current, that is, to five hours after mid-day and the completion of the 27th day of the fourth Egyptian month, Khoiak by name; 30 days being allowed for each month.

Thus does our instructor obtain from the given date the last three of the five particulars, called by him κεφαλαια, of the cycle date required, namely, the month, the day, and the hour: the other two, the 25 year period, and the year, he had obtained before, as we have seen. Altogether, he seems to arrive at the following date in the cycle of 1476 (Egyptian) years of Philip: the fifth hour of the 28th day of the fourth month of the eighth year after that with which the 25 year period ended for the 27th time; that is, 7 years, 3 months, 27 days, and 5 hours after the lapse of the said 27th period of five-and-twenty years out of the 1476 years' cycle. Now this ought to be an hour of a day of a month of the $607 + 77$ or 684th year of the era which commenced at mid-day 12th Nov. B.C. 324. But if so, ought not Theon to have made his year of the 1476 years' cycle the ninth rather than the eighth of the 28th period of five-and-twenty years? We thought so when the above was written. But we have since found, that the eighth year of the 28th time 25 years, according to the Table in Theon's hands of planetary positions for the hours, days, months, and years of the cycle of 1476 years, was actually the $1 + 25 \times 27 + 8 = 684$th year of the cycle. See below, Section E.

Thus have we essayed to show how the Syncellus's meaning, in what he reports of Ptolemy's Manual Tables, is elucidated by Theon in the fragment printed by Dodwell. We now transcribe the Syncellus's text; suggesting, as we go on, the emendations it seems to require. Τὰς μέντοι ἀπὸ τῆς τελευτῆς Ἀλεξάνδρου ψηφοφορίας τῶν ἀστέρων ὁ αὐτὸς Φιλόσοφος ἐν προχείροις κανόσιν, ἀνος' ἐτῶν περιόδων (perhaps a misprint of Dindorf's edition, for which Goar's Latin would teach us to read περιόδῳ) ἤτοι ἀποκαταστάσει Αἰγυπτιακοῦ ἑνὸς ἔτους (read Αἰγυπτιακοῦ ἐνιαυτοῦ) ἐξέθετο. See Geo. Syncell. ed. Paris, p. 207, A. In juxtaposition with this passage from the chronography of Georgius Syncellus we will exhibit another, with our emendations of it, from the already cited fragment of Theon's popular commentary on the same Manual Tables. First, a brief preface ends with this statement of the *purpose* of the commentary: πρὸς τὸ καταδηλοτέραν αὐτοῖς τὴν ἔκθεσιν τῶν κανονίων τῆς διδασκαλίας καταφαίνεσθαι. Then Theon proceeds: Ἐπεὶ οὖν τὴν (1) τῶν προκειμένων προχείρων κανόνων, περιέχουσαν τὰς κινήσεις τῶν ἀστέρων, ἀπὸ χρόνου τινὸς ἐχρῆν προυφιστάναι, καὶ τοῦ κατ' αὐτὸν (2) τόπου τῶν ἀστέρων (ἐπεὶ καὶ κινήσεώς ἐστιν ἀρχὴ τόπος καὶ χρόνος) πεποίηται αὕτη (3) ἀπὸ τοῦ πρώτου ἔτους Φιλίππου τοῦ μετ' Ἀλέξανδρον τὸν κτίστην κατ' Αἰγυπτίους, καθ' οὓς ἐνιαύσιος χρόνος ἡμερῶν τυγχάνει τξέ μόνον, Θὼθ νουμηνίᾳ (4), τῆς μεσημβρίας. ὅπως ἐστὶ πληρωθείσης ἕκτης ὥρας καὶ ἀρχομένης ἑβδόμης, ὡς πρὸς τὴν ἡμετέραν κατ' Αἴγυπτον Ἀλεξάνδρειαν· διὰ τὸ καὶ παρὰ τὰς χώρας γίνεσθαι κατ' ἄλλον καὶ ἄλλον χρόνον. We have here made three or four corrections: (1) inserting τὴν before τῶν προκειμένων προχείρων κανόνων, and understanding from the preceding context ἔκθεσιν τῆς διδασκαλίας. Dodwell proposes to insert ἀρχήν (we should have preferred περίοδον) between κανόνων and περιέχουσαν. (2) For αὐτήν we have substituted αὐτόν, as referring to χρόνου in the previous context. (3) We have put αὕτη, "*this (beginning)*," for ταύτην. Sense would also have been made by reading τοῦτο, "*this (thing)*," for ταύτην. (4) Dodwell's text has νεομηνία, or the nominative for the dative: perhaps a mere misprint.

The text of Georgius Syncellus, thus illustrated by Theon, is also to be compared with other statements of his own. One at p. 204, C, ed. Paris, runs thus, according to Dindorf: ἀπὸ τῆς ἀρχῆς οὖν τούτου (of Aridæus Philip) οἱ χρόνοι τῶν προχείρων κανόνων κατὰ Πτολεμαῖον ληφθέντες [καὶ τὰ] κατὰ ἀποκατάστασιν Αἰγυπτιακοῦ ἔτους ψηφίζονται, —where the words we have bracketed seem to be a misreading, which the next word corrects, and ought to have superseded. Another passage is at p. 52, A, B. Our author has been speaking of an old chronicle of Egyptian dynasties, thirty in number, and that lasted altogether 36,525 years; that is, τὴν παρ' Αἰγυπτίοις καὶ Ἕλλησιν ἀποκατάστασιν τοῦ ζωδιακοῦ μυθολογουμένην divided into 25 spaces of 1461 years, or 25 computed ἀποκαταστάσεις Αἰγυπτιακοῦ ἐνιαυτοῦ. Hence he traces next the fact, Πτολεμαῖον τὸν Κλαύδιον τοὺς προχείρους κανόνας τῆς ἀστρονομίας διὰ κέ ἐτηρίδων ψηφίζεσθαι θεσπίσαι,—adding (after some words which look like an interpolation), εἰ καὶ διὰ φυοσ' ἐτῶν τὸ κανόνιον τῶν κέ ἐτηρίδων ἐξέθετο διὰ τὸ μὴ ἀπαρτίζειν τὸν αὐξα ἀριθμὸν εἰς κέ ἀλλὰ λείπεσθαι ιδ'. τὴν μέντοι μονάδα περίττην ἔθετο, κ.τ.λ. On the ἀποκατάστασις οὐρανοῦ or κοσμική in 36,525 years, or 25 times the period of 1461 years, see also Syncell. p. 35, D.

From what the Syncellus proceeds to say, p. 207, in the passage which lent us our first quotation, it seems clear that in the copies used in his time of Ptolemy's *Manual Tables of Astronomy* (or Handy Tables for Calculations of the Stars), the Table of Regnal Years, from the end of Alexander's and beginning of Philip's reign, was divided at two points, and these the same that we find in Dodwell's edition of the Tables of Reigns subsequent to Alexander's. Thus there was produced a first section of the series ending with the reign of the last of the Lagidæ at Alexandria, Cleopatra; a second section, beginning with Augustus and ending with Diocletian's predecessor Carus; and a third section or table, beginning with Diocletian and carried down to the Syncellus's time of writing.

The reason of this division is easily assigned. Counting from and including the first of Augustus as Cleopatra's successor, the years of Philip that followed, though Egyptian years, like all that preceded them of the same series, corresponded with the Egypto-Julian years of a new era at Alexandria, the Augustan era. Therefore, to facilitate comparison and the reduction of dates of the one era to dates according to the other, this portion of the years of Philip was placed in a separate table. In like manner, when again the Augustan era gave way at Alexandria to the new era of Diocletian (the years of which were still Egypto-Julian like those of the Augustan era), to exhibit the correspondence between the years of this second series at Alexandria on the one hand, and on the other hand the Egyptian years of the era of Philip, these (beginning with the year of Egypt reckoned as the first of Diocletian) were placed in a separate Table of Reigns. This last table (in order to the longer employment of Ptolemy's astronomical table of 1476 Egyptian years, beginning with the first of Philip) had necessarily been continued, since it was used by Theon on the 25th of November A.D. 364, in the first year of Valentinian, for the dating of an observation made by him at Alexandria in the 81st year of Diocletian, which was the 1112th of Nabonassar, or (1112 − 424 =) the 688th of Philip. For in the years of Nabonassar we find Theon, like Ptolemy in the Magna Syntaxis or Almagest, distinguishing but two parts—one a series of 424 years, from the beginning of Nabonassar to the end of Alexander; the other a remainder of 688 years, from the beginning of Philip Aridæus to the day of the observation. See Theon, ad Ptolem. M. S. pp. 227, 284, 283, cited by Clinton. But the table of reigns beginning with Philip Aridæus reached, of course, only to his own time, when Ptolemy published his *Manual Canons*; and (if the astronomer survived, as Suidas affirms) the whole reign of Antoninus Pius (it is remarked by Clinton) may have been added by him to those already entered in the Canon, and here he may have left it to be from time to time continued by his successors.

Ptolemy dates an observation, which he made at Alexandria, of the vernal equinox, on the 7th of Pakhon (the ninth Egyptian month). He calls the year the 463d from the expiry of Alexander, that is, of the reign rather than the life of Alexander; for he follows the Egyptian reckoning of reigns, according to which the life extended beyond the reign; whereas by the practice of Khaldæan records the reign extended beyond the life. Ptolemy had observed the preceding autumnal equinox at the same place; and he dates it on the 9th of Athyr (the third Egyptian month), *in the third year of Antoninus* (Pius), that is, says he, the 463d year from the expiry (τελευτή) of Alexander. See Ptolem. M. S. iii. 2, p. 62, cited by Clinton in the F. R. under years of Christ 139, 140. After $424 + 462 = 886$ *completed* years of Nabonassar, the next year began $\frac{885}{4}$ ths of a day, or $221\frac{1}{4}$ days, earlier than $25\frac{1}{4}$ Feb. A.D. 140, when 886 Julian years would have expired from the commencement of the era, $25\frac{1}{4}$ Feb. B.C. 747. Accordingly, the 887th year of Nabonassar, or 463d year of Philip, was the year of Egypt which began at midnight between the 19th and 20th of July A.D. 139. Of the year here beginning the 9th of Athyr, being the $30 \times 2 + 9 = 69$th day of the year, was consequently the 26th of

September A.D. 139 : also the 7th of Pakhon, being the 30 × 8 + 7 = 247th day of the year, was the 22d of March in the bissextile A.D. 140.

When Ptolemy made these observations of the equinox in autumn A.D. 139 and spring A.D. 140, his Canon of Reigns subsequent to Alexander's ended with that of Adrian. It is by this Canon that he dates observations of his own; and those made by his predecessors, as Timokharis, Aristarkhus, Hipparkhus, dated at various points in the series of Calippic periods, containing 76 years apiece, he reduces to their positions in the era of Nabonassar or era of Philip. See Ptolem. *M. S.* vii. 3, p. 169; iii. 2, p. 63, p. 62, p. 60; v. pp. 111-113; cited by Clinton.

And here, by the way, the observation may be permitted, that from Ptolemy's statements it is demonstrated (by Clinton, *F. H.* vol. ii., Appendix, chap. *On the Attic Months*) that the first year of the first Calippic six-and-seventy years (being the eighth year of the sixth Metonic 19 year period) was the Attic year of the arkhon Aristophon, which was the third year of the 112th Olympiad, beginning at the new moon nearest midsummer 330. It is said to have been in Hecatombæon, the first Attic month of this Greek year, that Darius Codomannus was murdered: see Arrian, *Exp. Alex.* iii. 22. Accordingly, Alexander's reign at Babylon, by the account of Georgius Syncellus's copy of the Khaldæan, or, as he generally calls it, the Astronomical Canon, began with the year of Nabonassar 419, and the 12 years of Nabonassar occupied by the united reigns of Darius and the Macedonian conqueror are divided in equal shares between the two. But (as the fact is exemplified above in our Table of Babylonian Reigns) this 419th year may be considered in two ways, either as an Egyptian or as a Khaldæan year. If regarded as the 419th year of an *Egyptian* series, beginning with the one in the course of which the Khaldæan year began that was assigned at Babylon to Nabonassar as his first, it began 418 times 365 days later than 25½ Feb. B.C. 747, that is, it began with the 15th of October B.C. 330. But if the 419th year of Nabonassar be taken (as at Babylon no doubt it was taken) for the 419th of a series that began with the Khaldæan New-year's day next after Nabonassar's accession to the throne of king, it began *later* than the 1st of Markhesvan (or Dius, as the Macedonians called the month) in B.C. 747 by 418 completed years of a computation in which the months were lunar, but periods of years by intercalation of months were made equal to solar periods of the same number of years. That is, the 419th year of Nabonassar considered as a year of Babylon began with the 1st day of Markhesvan B.C. 747 − 418 = 329. It is therefore the 419th year of Nabonassar by *Egyptian* calculation (not the Khaldæan year of that number) that must be compared with the first year of the first Calippic period of the Greeks, if the two years, commencing but four months apart, be taken to mark the same political epoch. Such an epoch there certainly was; and the Syncellus's copy of the Khaldæan Canon indicates it, when it makes the 419th year of Nabonassar the first of Alexander on the Perso-Median throne. For this same year was Alexander's *seventh* regnal year as king of the Macedonians; and our Syncellus tells us, p. 261, A, ed. Paris, " *They count the kingdom of the Greeks from the seventh year of Alexander;*" adding, "*From the seventh year of Alexander to the 22d*," and last, "*of Kleopatra*," extremes included, "*are 300 years*." This calculation is correct, and may be regarded confidently as made by Greeks of Alexandria. But the Syncellus's subjoined assertions, that Alexandria was built the same year, that the Samaritans were punished the same year on Alexander's return from Egypt, and that the battle of Arbela was fought the same year, are not true. These events mark the year of Nabonassar by Egyptian computation 417; which began at noon the 14th of November B.C. 332, and was the fifth year of Alexander as king of the Macedonians. The cause of the confusion is, that here begins the Persian reign of Alexander, and therewith "the kingdom of the Greeks," according to the Egyptian computation of the years of Nabonassar, and according to the division of the reigns of Darius and Alexander given in the copy of the Khaldæan Canon which Theon appears to have transmitted, and we have embodied above in our Table of Reigns at Babylon from the first year of Nabonassar to the accession of Seleucus. On the 419th year of Nabonassar we shall discourse again below.

It would seem, then, that the Canon of Reigns subsequent to Alexander's, which Ptolemy had appended to his Table of Astronomical Occurrences for 1476 Egyptian years, having been continued after Ptolemy's death to the time of Theon, had ever afterwards been brought down (as we may learn from our Syncellus's account of it) to each calculator's own time, for the sake of the astronomical table with the use of which it was connected. That the same practice of continuation was followed after the Syncellus's time, the copy in Dodwell's Appendix might be quoted to prove.

D

LET us now turn to the *Year of Adam*, current at the Syncellus's time of writing, whereto the Canon of Reigns is attested by him to have been carried down. It is not the year of Adam 6352 (as given in Goar's Greek text and Latin version of our author's work), but by Dindorf's report, 6302, according to MS. B, the best extant. To find the year of our era is a matter of some difficulty.

In the previous context, p. 207, A, as afterwards, p. 261, C, 327, A, and perhaps elsewhere, the year of Adam 5170 is made to be confessedly the first of the era of Philip; and therefore the point at which the Syncellus's Chronology of Man's History coincides with the commencement of Ptolemy's Manual Tables of Astronomy, and the Table of Reigns subsequent to Alexander's thereto appended. Now, if the chronology of regnal periods in these tables began with the Syncellus's year of Man 5170, and was continued to the Syncellus's year of Man 6302, it follows that the year of Philip, current at the end, was the 1133d year. If, then, according to the table we have given above, the first year of Philip began at mid-day the 12th of November B.C. 324, the 1133d year should begin at mid-day the 2d of February A.D. 809. For the 1132 years *completed*, if they were not Egyptian but Julian years, would reach from mid-day 12th November B.C. 324 to mid-day 12th November A.D. 809. But during those Julian years the Egyptian New-year's day had fallen back $\frac{1132}{4}$ths of a day, or 283 whole days behind, or above, or earlier than the point it stood at, in the Julian circle of 365¼ days, at first. So that the 1133d year of Philip began in A.D. 809, earlier by 283 days than 11½ November; that is, it began 1½ February A.D. 809.

But to our thus reckoning the Syncellus's 6302d year of Man to be nearly the year of our Lord (beginning 25th March) 809, it may be objected, that our author counts 5500 years of man completed before the year of our Lord's nativity (see p. 316, B, *et passim*); and if so, the year of Man in which he wrote, 6302, was the year we call 802 of our Lord,—only beginning, as all the Syncellus's years of the world do, with the 25th of March instead of the 1st day of January. See his p. 1, A.

And in support of this contrary conclusion, that the year of our Syncellus's writing began with the 25th of March A.D. 802 (that is, seven years earlier than the point of commencement which our first conclusion implies), it might be contended further that the era of Philip is made by our author to begin seven years above the true epoch; because if 5169 years of the World (being the number, according to our author, that was completed before the year in which the era of Philip began) be deducted from the 5500 years completed, as he says, before the one in which the nativity of Christ happened, we find an interval of 331 years, so that the era of Philip is made to begin in a year of the same number before our author's era of the Nativity as that before our vulgar era in which began with Alexander the kingdom of the Greeks, according to the Khaldæan computation of the 417th year of Nabonassar. For this 417th year of Nabonassar is the first regnal year of Alexander at Babylon by Ptolemy's Khaldæan Canon, according to what we call Theon's reading of that document. See our Table of Reigns, above, p. 807.

But it seems highly probable, if not hardly to be denied, that the year in which the Syncellus wrote, and which he counted as the 6302d year of Adam, was actually the 1133d of Philip, according to the copy of Ptolemy's Manual Canons then in his hands; and we cannot fairly imagine an interpolation of seven years in that copy's Table of Reigns subsequent to Alexander's. Therefore we argue that it is not the first year of Philip that our Syncellus has put too high, or too far back, in the *Years of the World;* but it is the year of our Lord's nativity which he has put seven years lower in the era of Philip than the year already too low but commonly accepted and used for the date. If, according to the dogma of previous ecclesiastical authorities, he supposed the first year of Philip to be the year of Man or the World 5170, he should have placed the Nativity, as Panodôrus did, in the year of the World 5493. He has no reason, therefore, to complain of the Egyptian monk as he does thus, p. 313, A, ed. Paris: ὁ Πανόδωρος, συμφωνῆσαι σπουδάζων τοῖς ἔξω σοφοῖς περὶ τὴν σφαιρικὴν κίνησιν, ἔτεσιν ζ' διήμαρτε τοῦ ͵εφ' ἔτους, ͵ευ7γ' ἀντὶ ͵ε,φ' στοιχειώσας, καίπερ ἐν ἄλλοις εὐδοκιμήσας παρὰ πολλούς. The same charge of having fallen seven years short of the 5500 years, said to have elapsed at the Incarnation, and of having consequently made the year of the Crucifixion to be the year of the World 5525, had been preferred against Panodôrus at nearly the beginning of our Syncellus's work. See p. 35, C, Paris ed. But it is brought forward with more detail below, pp. 326, 327, ed. Paris; and we will cite the passage, chiefly for the sake of correcting it, and especially of bracketing for that purpose parts that seem to be marginal scribblings which a transcriber thought it his business to introduce into his author's text: Πανόδωρος δέ τις τῶν κατ' Αἴγυπτον, [εἷς μοναχὸς] ἱστορικὸς οὐκ ἄπειρος χρονικῆς ἀκριβείας, ἐν τοῖς χρόνοις ἀκμάσας Ἀρκαδίου βασιλέως (to whose reign Dodwell's Canon of Reigns assigns the 13 Egyptian years from 715 to 727 of Philip, and for whose actual reign the reader may go to Clinton, *F. R.*, A.D. 395–408) καὶ Θεοφίλου Ἀλεξανδρείας ἀρχιεπισκόπου, ἀλήθειαν ἀσπασάμενος ἐν πολλοῖς ζ' διήμαρτεν ἔτεσιν ἐλθὼν εἰς τὴν σωτήριαν σάρκωσιν, τῷ ͵ευ7γ' ἔτει ταύτην συλλογισάμενος. Ἡ δὲ αἰτία τοῦ σφάλματος αὐτοῦ γίγονεν οὕτως. Ἐπὶ γὰρ (read Ἐπεὶ γὰρ) τὸ πρῶτον ἔτος Φιλίππου τοῦ Ἀριδαίου, τοῦ μετὰ Ἀλέξανδρον τὸν Μακεδόνα βασιλεύσαντος Μακεδόνων ά, καθ' ὃ ἔτος καὶ ὁ Κλαύδιος Πτολεμαῖος τὴν τῶν προχείρων κανόνων ψηφηφορίαν ἐπήξατο, [Ἀρχὴν (read ἀρχὴ, or perhaps ἀρχῇ) Αἰγυπτιακοῦ καὶ Ἑλληνικοῦ ἔτους κατὰ τὴν πρώτην τοῦ Θωθ μηνός, παρ' Αἰγυπτίοις λεγομένου, κθ τοῦ Αὐγούστου μηνός] οὖσαν ἀποκαταστατικὴν, ὁμόχρονον ὁμολογουμένως ἐστὶ τῷ ͵ερό ἔτει τοῦ κοσμου, ἀπὸ δὲ τοῦ αὐτοῦ πρώτου ἔτους Φιλίππου μέχρι τῆς καθαιρέσεως Κλεοπάτρας, ἔτη κατὰ (insert τοὺς) ἀστρονομικοὺς κανόνας ἐπισυνάγεται ογδ', [ἀπὸ τοῦ αὐτοῦ ͵ερό κοσμικοῦ ἔτους] ἔτη γίνονται (5169 + 294 =) ͵ευξγ' ἀπὸ Ἀδὰμ ἕως καθαιρέσεως Κλεοπάτρας, κατὰ τοῦτο (read κατὰ τοῦτον, that is, *according to Panodôrus*), Ὅπερ οὐ συνάδει τῇ ἐκκλησιαστικῇ παραδόσει ὡς πρὸς (that is in English, "*as concerning*") τὸ μγ' ἔτος Αὐγούστου Καίσαρος ἡνίκα ὁ Κύριος ἡμῶν ἐσαρκώθη. Μόνα γὰρ ἀπὸ τῆς αὐτῆς καθαιρέσεως καὶ ὑποταγῆς Αἰγύπτου, μγ' ἔτη λέγεται βεβασιλευκέναι παρὰ τοῖς μαθηματικοῖς ὁ Αὔγουστος (because they had nothing to do with Augustus and his reign before the fall of the Lagidæ, and anywhere but in Alexandria). Ὅπερ εἰ δῶμεν ἀληθεύειν, εὐρεθήσεται κατὰ τὸ ἐφʹ ἔτος τοῦ κόσμου τελευτήσας ὁ Αὔγουστος. Τὸ δ' αὐτὸ ἰ ἴσται τῆς τοῦ σωτῆρος ἡλικίας. Ἀλλʹ ὅτι μὲν (Here insert from pp. 305, A, B, 319, B, ἰβασίλευσε ἔτη νϛʹ, a length of reign which from the sequel appears to have been admitted by Panodôrus) ἔστι πρόδηλον. Ὅτι δὲ κατὰ τὸν Αὐγούστου Καίσαρος θάνατον ἰὲ ἰγγὺς ἦγεν ἔτος ὁ Κύριος, καὶ κατὰ τὸ ιέ ἔτος Τιβερίου Καίσαρος ὡσεὶ ἐτῶν ἦν λʹ, ὡς τὰ λόγια, καὶ τοῦτο προφανές. Ἔσται ἄρα ὁ μὲν Αὐγούστου Καίσαρος θάνατος μεταξὺ τοῦ ἐφιδʹ κοσμικοῦ ἔτους· καὶ τὸ ἐφιέ· ἡ δὲ ἀρχὴ τῆς ὅλης βασιλείας αὐτοῦ τῷ ευνή. Πανόδωρος δὲ τῇ μαθηματικῇ ἐξακολουθῶν ἐκδόσει, τὴν μὲν ἀρχὴν τῆς Αὐγούστου βασιλείας τῷ ευνά ἔτει τοῦ κόσμου ἐστοιχείωσε, τὸ δὲ τέλος τῷ ἐφϛʹ· τὴν δὲ σωτήριον γένησιν τῷ ευλγʹ, οὐ καλῶς διανοησάμενος.

Thus it appears Panodôrus had placed the Lord's nativity, agreeably to the vulgar reckoning, at 5493 years (age of the world at the Nativity) *less* 5169 years of the world (elapsed at the commencement of the era of Philip), *that is*, at the 324th year current of the era of Philip. Likewise he placed the first of the 56 years that he as well as our Syncellus assigned to the whole reign of Augustus, at the 5451st year of the World, or (5451 − 5169 =) the 282d year of Philip, beginning 6 A.M. 3d Sept. B.C. 43; while the Syncellus placed the same first regnal year of Augustus seven years later, at the 5458th year of the World, or 5458 − 5169 = the 289th year of Philip; which last began with the 3d of Sept. B.C. 36. Both writers, by their giving Augustus a reign of 56 years, are found to have reckoned his reign, as some historians did (see Clinton, *F. H.*, A.D. 14, citing Eutropius vii. 8, and Auctor Dial. de Or. cap. 17), to have begun with his first consulship, 19th August B.C. 43. Both Panodôrus and the Syncellus placed the Nativity in the 43d year of Augustus: but this 43d year, according to Panodôrus, began 19th August B.C. 43 − 42 = 1; whereas according to the Syncellus it began (35 years and 135 days B.C. + 6 years and 220 days after Christ =) 19th Aug. A.D. 6.

The same difference between the years of Christ according to the vulgar era of the Nativity and those of the more erroneous reckoning of Georgius Syncellus naturally continues. For instance, the second and last year of the *last* emperor in his Table, Carus, the predecessor of Diocletian, is, according to the Syncellus, the year of the World 5776, the year of Christ (5776 − 5500 =) 276, and the year of Philip (5776 − 5169 =) 607. The last date agrees with that given by the Canon of Reigns subsequent to Alexander's in Dodwell's Appendix. But this year of Philip began with the 14th of June A.D. 283. Compare Clinton's *F. R.* as to the reign of Carus.

We will give one other instance. The third year of Antoninus Aurelius (Elegabalus), according to our Syncellus, p. 357, Paris ed., was the year of Adam 5712, of the Nativity (5712 − 5500 =) 212, of Philip (5712 − 5169 =) 543. But this year of Philip, which is confirmed by the Canon of Reigns subsequent to Alexander's printed in Dodwell's Appendix, began at 6 A.M. 30th June A.D. 219; for Elegabalus's first year by Egyptian reckoning had ended six hours later in A.D. 218, when his actual reign was but 23 days old. Now Africanus also speaks of this emperor's third year; but he means the third year reckoned from Elegabalus's accession to the throne on the 8th of June A.D. 218, describing it as the year of the consuls Gratus and Seleucus, *i.e.* A.D. 221, in which it certainly expired. The same year is made by Africanus the year of the World 5723; and it appears that nearly six centuries before our Syncellus's labours Africanus had placed our Lord's nativity in the year of the World 5501; therefore his year of the World 5723 is his 223d of the manhood of our Lord.

Now, following Luke iii. 1, 23, but omitting the Passover indicated by John vi. 4, he placed the crucifixion in the 31st year of the manhood, and in the 5531st year of the World; also in the 16th year of the reign of Tiberius Cæsar, that is, at Passover A.D. 30. Therefore his year of the Nativity and year 5501 of the World will coincide with our year B.C. 1; his year of the Manhood 223 will coincide with our A.D. 222; and in placing here the consulship of Gratus and Seleucus he places it a year too late. See Georg. Syncellus, pp. 212, 323, 324, 325, 326 of the Paris edition; and Clinton's *F. R.*, A.D. 221; also A.D. 30, where, observing on Africanus's date of the crucifixion (which, besides the particulars already cited, has also this, *the second year of the 202d Olympiad*), Clinton says, "The Passover of the 16th of Tiberius is in the spring of A.D. 30, a little before the close of the *first* year of Olympiad 202." We only add, that Africanus made the consulate of Gratus and Seleucus to coincide with the (year of the) 250th Olympiad, otherwise denominated the first year of the 250th Olympiad; the truth being, that the six months of the consulate following midsummer coincided with the first six months of the Olympic year alleged, which is treated by Africanus as if it was a Julian year of Rome, beginning with the Kalends of January A.D. 221.

It appears, then, that it is not to our A.D. 802, but to A.D. 809, that, according to Georgius Syncellus, the Canon of Reigns in Ptolemy's *Manual Tables of Astronomy* was continued; and the discussion seems to have shown that in Georgius's difference with Panodôrus (to whom we should be glad to know the extent of his obligations) he may be considered in the wrong.

We have remarked above, that if the Syncellus supposed the first year of Philip to be the year of Adam 5170, he should have placed the nativity of our Lord (as Panodôrus did on the same supposition) in the year of Adam 5493. Accordingly, in the last days of the Græco-Roman empire at Constantinople, the year of our Lord's nativity being then held to be nine years later in the era of the first Adam and of the World than the Syncellus's date, and (9+7 =) 16 years later than the year assigned by Panodôrus, that is to say, the Nativity being placed in the year of the World beginning with September 5509 (as the Greeks compute it still), the first year of Philip was concluded to be one coinciding (nearly) with the year of the World 5186 ; the 16th, namely, from and after the year assumed alike by Panodōrus and by Georgius Syncellus. See a calculation subjoined to the Abbé Halma's edition in 4to—derived from MSS. 2394 and 2390 of the now Imperial Library of Paris, 1819—of the two Canons,—the Khaldæan, of *Reigns before Alexander's, with Alexander's own ;* and the Egyptian, of *Reigns, Macedonian and Roman, subsequent to Alexander's.* The latter is prolonged to the end of the fifth year of Constantine Palæologus and the taking of Constantinople by the Turks ; and towards the end of it, on a slight inspection, appeared to differ much in expression from the corresponding table in Dodwell's edition. The calculation we refer to is taken from the above-mentioned MS. 2394. It is an exposition made in the reign of Antoninus Palæologus or Antoninus the Monk, who reigned, according to the Table, the 45 Egyptian years from 1608 to 1652 of the era of Philip. The expounder is described as ὁ μέγας λογοθέτης ὁ μετοχίτης—*the High Chancellor* (see Gibbon, *Dec. and Fall*, chap. 53, sect. Officers of the Palace, etc.), who had proposed to make a calculation of the stars in his own time. He begins by deducting from 6791 years complete, since the creation of man, 5185 years complete since that epoch, before the era of Philip, which era he asserts to have begun in the year of the World 5186. In the end he concludes that the sixth day of October, the second month of the year of the World 6792, was the first day of Thoth, the first month of the Egyptian year of Philip 1608.

If October was the second month of the year of the World 6792, September was the first month of the year, and the year was that of the modern Greeks. It may have been to assimilate the Julian year of Constantinople to the Egypto-Julian year of the successive eras of Augustus and Diocletian at Alexandria, the year of the Greeks of that city, that the Latin September was adopted for the commencement of the Indiction year, in the time of Constantine the Great, and of the year of the era of the creation. We suppose that the same day was the first of September both at Rome and at Constantinople. But in three years out of four, the day which at Rome was the first of September was at Alexandria the fourth of a month which the Greeks called by the Egyptian name Thoth, though Latin strangers appear to have called it September.

Thus the year which the Arabian astronomer Albategni found still in use in Syria, and which he employed to measure the Seleucidan era, —a year beginning with the month called in the proper language of the country *Eilul*,—was neither the original Syrian year, whether lunar or Julian, nor yet the Khaldæan year of Seleucus. It was the Græco-Roman year of the government which his conquering countrymen, the followers of Mahomed, had subverted. It was the year used in his time, it would appear, as now by the Greeks at Constantinople. Moreover, it began and ended never more than three whole days, and in the first year of every four-year period but *two* whole days, after the Greek year of Alexandria.

The difference between 6791 and 5185 Julian years of Constantinople since the supposed epoch of man's creation is 1606 like years. But 1606 Julian years are equal to $\frac{1606}{4}$ days more than as many years of Philip, and therefore to $(401\frac{1}{2} - 365\frac{1}{4} =) 36\frac{1}{4}$ days more than 1607 years of Philip. Therefore the New-year's day of the year of Philip 1608 will begin at $36\frac{1}{4}$ days after the point at which began the year of the World 6792, that is, midnight between August 31 and 1st September. It will begin at $36\frac{1}{4}$ days (less the 30 days of September =) $6\frac{1}{4}$ days of October. And of what year of our Lord, we may learn in two ways, as follows:

1. Add the 1606 Julian years of Constantinople (between the end of the year of the World 5185 and the end of the year of the World 6791) to the 31st of August B.C. 324, the end of the year of Constantinople after which, on the expiration of $72\frac{1}{2}$ days (that is, at $11\frac{1}{2}$ November), the era of Philip began, according to our table in Section A. So added on, these years end with 31st August A.D. 1283; for 323 years and 122 days (from September 1 to December 31) before Christ, deducted from 1606 years, leave after Christ 1282 years and 243 days, ending with 31st August A.D. 1283. But we have seen that the year of Philip 1608 began $36\frac{1}{4}$ days afterwards; therefore it began $6\frac{1}{4}$ October A.D. 1283.

2. Another way of finding the year of our Lord is this. From the year of Constantinople 6791, which was completed with the August preceding the point in October where the year of Philip 1608 began, deduct 5508 years of Constantinople, completed, according to the Greeks, when on the 1st of September the year of our Lord's nativity began. The remainder is 1283 Greek years completed with August; therefore the point at $6\frac{1}{4}$ days of the following October, or of the second month of the year of the World 6792, is at $6\frac{1}{4}$ October A.D. 1283.

The other MS. of the Paris Library from which the Abbé Halma derived his Tables of Reigns, the MS. 2390, supplied him with annotations or scholia which we have found to be all derived from Georgius Syncellus, though he is not named. Among them occurs a good part of the passage we have cited, to correct it, from pp. 326, 327 of the Paris edition of Syncellus's *Chronographia*. For $εἷς μοναχὸς ἱστορικός$ we find $οὕτως μοναχὸς$, which may suggest $εἷς ἂν μοναχὸς$. Our correction, 'Ἐπεὶ γὰρ τὸ πρῶτον for 'Ἐπὶ γὰρ τὸ πρῶτον, is perhaps confirmed by the fact that in MS. 2390 a new notice begins here, thus: Δεῖ εἰδέναι ὅτι τὸ πρῶτον, κ.τ.λ. Next, the passage we have bracketed from ἀρχὴν to Αὐγούστου μηνός (proposing at the same time ἀρχῇ or ἀρχῇ for ἀρχήν) occurs without variation. Moreover, presently after, for ὁμολογουμένως ἐστί we find ὁμολογουμένης (sic) ἐπί. Further on we have τοὺς inserted as we proposed; we have, as in MS. B, No. 1764, of Syncellus, ἐπισυνάγεται for συνάγεται. Lastly, after the numeral ͵αψδ', the scholium ends thus: ἅτινα συναριθμούμενα μετὰ τοῦ ερό ἔτους ἔτη γίνονται ͵αυξδ' ἀπὸ 'Αδὰμ ἕως καθαιρέσεως Κλεοπάτρας, where perhaps the annotator thought to correct as well as to explain his author. But the first unit of both sums are the same years.

E

INSTEAD of the plural form, "Manual Tables of Astronomy," we find the title of Ptolemy's work expressed in the singular, thus: πρόχειρος κανών. For example, in Dodwell's Appendix to the *Dissertationes Cyprianicæ* we have a treatise wherein the Emperor Herakleius gives a method for finding the coincidence of month-days and week-days, and also in what years the *Bisextum* fell. According to the Egyptian method of registration he reigned from the first of Thoth of the year of Philip 934 to the last *epagomené* of the year of Philip 964, that is, from six hours A.M. the 24th of March A.D. 610 to mid-day 16th March A.D. 641. He begins his explanation thus: 'Εν τῷ προχείρῳ κανόνι τοῦ Πτολεμαίου μετὰ τοὺς κανόνας τῶν ἀπλανῶν ἀστέρων ἔγκειται κανόνια δι' ὧν δύναταί τις γνῶναι τὴν ἑκάστου μηνὸς ἡμέραν εἰς ποίαν ἡμέραν τῆς ἑβδομάδος καταντᾷ. Suidas also uses the singular form to designate this work of Ptolemy's. A commentary upon it in a list of Theon's works he entitles, Εἰς τὸν Πτολεμαίου πρόχειρον κανόνα: and in enumerating Ptolemy's works he gives us Κανὼν πρόχειρος, pp. 1174, D, and 3158, D, cited in Clinton's *F. R.* vol. ii. pp. 313 and 283.

But a better acquaintance with this work is to be had than that which we have gleaned from Geo. Syncellus from the fragment of Theon's Commentary printed by Dodwell, from the Emperor Herakleius, and from Suidas. Professor De Morgan, of University College, London, in Smith's *Dict. of Gr. and Roman Biography*, art. THEON, tells us that Kuster, speaking of an emendation of the text of Suidas, said that Theon wrote a commentary on the Canon of Ptolemy, which Canon existed in manuscript in the Imperial Library. Accordingly, Delambre found a manuscript in the Royal Library at Paris, which he has described (*Hist. Ast. Anc.* vol. ii. p. 616) under the head of Θέωνος 'Αλεξανδρέως κανόνες πρόχειροι, *Tables Manuelles de Théon d'Alexandrie*. This work was afterwards published by Halma, but under the title *Commentaire de Théon . . . sur les tables manuelles astronomiques de Ptolémée*, in three parts, Paris 1822, 1823, 1825, 4to. Having only very recently seen this last work (continues Mr. De Morgan), we have only as recently known that there is a distinct work of Ptolemy himself, the κανόνες πρόχειροι. Ptolemy's part is addressed to Syrus; Theon's to his son Epiphanius. The contents are Prolegomena, Tables of latitude and longitude, and a collection of Astronomical Tables somewhat more extensive than that in the (Magna) Syntaxis. The Prolegomena are separately headed: one set is given to Ptolemy, another to Theon. But the Tables themselves are headed, Πτολεμαίου Θέωνος καὶ 'Υπατίας πρόχειροι κανόνες. Dodwell had previously printed a fragment of the Prolegomena in his *Dissertationes Cyprianicæ*, Oxford 1684, 8vo. So far Mr. De Morgan.

Thus instructed, we inquired for the Abbé Halma's *Commentaire de Théon*, etc., at the Royal Library at Brussels; but of the three parts, 4to, above-mentioned, were informed that the Library possessed the second only. It is entitled a collection of Astronomical Tables, Πτολεμαίου καὶ Θέωνος πρόχειροι κανόνες, and is dated *de l'imprimerie de A. Bobée Rue de Tablettière, Paris,* 1823.

At pp. 112–119, in Greek and French on opposite pages, we have a Table in five parts (for so, on examination, we thought we might describe it), entitled Ἐποχαι των πεντε αστερων, *Positions of the Five Stars*, and divided into 12 columns.

The first part, as we think, will be a table of 12 columns, whereof the respective titles are—1. Εἰκοσιπενταετηρίδες; 2. Καρδια Λεωνος (the star Regulus); 3. Κρονου· κεντρον επικυκλου; 4. του αυτου αστερος; 5. Διος· κεντρον επικυκλου; 6. του αυτου αστερος; 7. Αρεος· κεντρον επικυκλου; 8. του αυτου αστερος; 9. Αφροδιτης· κεντρον επικυκλου; 10. του αυτου αστερος; 11. 'Ερμου· κεντρον επικυκλου; 12. του αυτου αστερος. We have some recollection of this first part of the *Tables of Positions* having a title of its own, εικοσιπενταετηριδες των πεντε αστερων—*Twenty-five-year periods of the five stars.*

The second part, as we suppose, will be a table of 12 columns, having its first column headed with the title ἔτη ἁπλᾶ, *single years*. The headings of the other columns are the same respectively as those of the corresponding columns in the first part. This second part has its general title, ἔτη ἁπλᾶ τῶν πεντε αστερων, *single years of the five stars*. Of this, the title of the first column, ἔτη ἁπλᾶ, is obviously an abbreviation only. .

The third part will be a table of 12 columns, having for the title of its first column, Μηνες Αιγυπτ., *Egypt. Months*. The remaining columns have the same titles respectively as the last eleven columns of the previous tables. The whole table has for a general title Μηνες Αιγυπτιων των πεντε αστερων, whereof the title of the first column is obviously an abbreviation only.

The fourth part will be a table of 12 columns, having its first column headed 'Ημεραι, and the others headed respectively as the last eleven columns in the preceding tables. A general title of this part is 'Ημερων Αιγυπτιων αριθμοι των πεντε αστερων, *Numbers of Egyptian days of the five stars*. The title of the first column signifies the same in one word.

The fifth part will be a table of 12 columns, headed respectively as before, all but the first, the title of which is 'Ωραι, *Hours;* being an abbreviation of the general title of the whole part, 'Ωρων απο μεσημβριας αριθμοι των πεντε αστερων, *Numbers of Hours counted from midday of the five stars.*

In the first of these, the *Five-and-twenty-year Table*, the first column, or column of twenty-fives, consists of 60 numbers in as many successive lines, beginning with 1, increasing progressively by 25 at a time, and ending with 1476. On a line with these 60 numbers respectively, in the other parallel columns, seem to be noted the positions at the several times of Regulus in respect of the autumn equinoctial point, and of Saturn, Jupiter, Mars, Venus, Mercury (perhaps in longitude and latitude) in respect of Regulus. The eleven columns have also a 61st line, whereon are noted (*distances*) additional. The reader, it is hoped, may derive some information from this account, though, as it comes from one wholly ignorant of astronomy, it may present very obvious blunders to him for correction.

In the second part, or *Single-year Table*, we have in the first column, headed *Single Years*, a series of numbers of years below 25, from 1 in the top line to 24 in the bottom line. Corresponding severally with these, in the other columns, are distances of Regulus and of the five planets of the same description as those of the previous table. These other eleven columns have also a line of additional distances, as in the former table, making a 25th line.

In the third part, or *Egyptian Month Table*, we have in the first column, headed *Egyptian Months*, 13 names on successive lines from top to bottom; for the five supplementary days at the end of the twelvemonth are considered as a 13th month. These names are Thoth, Phaōphi, Athyr, Khoiak, Tybi, Mekhir, Phamenōth, Pharmuthi, Pakhōn, Pagni, Epiphi, Mesōri, Epagomenæ. Opposite these 13 in the other columns are distances such as we have already noticed; and at bottom those columns have a 14th line of additional distances.

In the fourth part, or *Day Table*, the first column, headed *Days*, presents the numbers of the month-days from 1 to 30. The other columns, on as many lines, exhibit corresponding distances of Regulus and the five planets such as we have described already, and also additional distances on a 31st line at bottom.

In the fifth part, or *Hour Table*, the first column, headed *Hours*, presents the numbers of the hours from 1 to 24 after mid-day. The other columns exhibit distances such as those already described, and on a 25th line additional distances, as at the bottom of the corresponding columns of previous tables.

These five parts seem to be called by Theon κανονια, their titles κιφαλαια, and the 12 columns of each, σελιδια, in his example of the use of the *Table of Reigns in the era of Philip*, for reducing a date of one of the Alexandrian eras to the fivefold description of the same in a *Table of the five planets during a cycle of* 1476 *years of Philip*. This example we cited above in Section C.

The Table of Kings in one of Dodwell's collated copies, which he calls 1 *Voss.*, ends with Phokas, the predecessor of the Emperor Herakleius, and with the year of Philip 933 ; that is to say, at 23¼

March A.D. 610. We have also seen that the table in Geo. Syncellus's hands (ending perhaps with the predecessor of Niképhorus) enabled him to calculate the (year of the World 6302 − 5169 =) year of Philip 1133, which was the 8th (and last but one) year of the Emperor Niképhorus. Another copy collated by Dodwell, *Voss.* 2, ends with the year of Philip 1136 and the reign of Mikhael Rankabæus, to whom the Canon, after its manner, the Egyptian, gives the whole year in which Niképhorus died and the son of Niképhorus was succeeded by Mikhael Rankabæus. Another copy, *Savil.* 2, ends with Basileius the Macedonian and the year of Philip 1209; adding the name only of the next emperor, Leon. Still Dodwell had a copy which enabled him to continue his Table of Reigns subsequent to Alexander's, down to that of the first Turkish emperor, whom it miscalls the Emir Amurath or Murad—ὁ ἀμηρᾶς Ὀμυράτης. But the numbers seem hopelessly corrupt. In the Manual Tables also, we learn from Mr. De Morgan that the Table of Kings is carried down to the fall of the eastern empire, with the heading Πτολεμαίου Θίωνος, κ.τ.λ. But he may allude to Halma's two canons, mentioned above, p. 828, not to the work published in 1822–1825. Mr. De Morgan refers us, in conclusion, to a very full dissertation on the Table of Reigns in an anonymous work entitled, *Observationes in Theonis Fastos Græcos priores.* Amsterdam, 1735, 4to. Dodwell ascribes to Theon the earliest of the Greek consular Fasti given us by him.

F.

WE have lately been led to mention twice (in the cases of Mikhael Rankabæus and of Elegabalus) the Egyptian rule respecting the registration of reigns, according to which the whole year of Egypt in which a king came to the throne is counted to him as his first; so that every reign begins and ends earlier by Ptolemy's Canon than it did in fact. In the case of the Greek and Roman reigns contained in the Table of Reigns that followed Alexander's,—a document which, in opposition to the Khaldæan Canon or the Table of Reigns at Babylon, might be styled the Canon of Reigns at Alexandria,—to prove the fact must be generally easy, because of the abundance of authentic historical testimony respecting those reigns. Thus, having first shown, from the consent of our Syncellus and of Dodwell's copy of the later Canon, that the 541st year of Philip was counted, according to Egyptian registration, the first of Elegabalus; and next (by deducting from 540 Egypt years the 323 Julian years and 49¼ days that the era had been running before our vulgar era of the Nativity), having shown that the 541st year began at six hours before noon of 30th June A.D. 217; we proceed to prove from Dio Cassius, lxxviii. 13, 14, 31; Index lxxix. and lxxix. 8 (quoted by Clinton, *Fast. Rom.*), that in fact Elegabalus was proclaimed emperor the 16th of May under the consuls Severus Macrinus Augustus and Adventus, that is, A.D. 218. Whence it follows, that of the year 541 of Philip, the first of Elegabalus by the Canon, Elegabalus in fact reigned but the last 46 days. Nay, if we count his reign, as we did before with Clinton, from the day of Macrinus's death, which was the 8th of June, the year counted his first in Egypt ended on only the 23d day current after the death of his predecessor; so that the reign of that predecessor, Severus Macrinus, though it had continued in fact for the first 342 days of the year 541, was reckoned in the registration of years in Egypt to have expired with the year of Philip 540.

But we will take some examples from the earlier table, the Canon of Reigns at Babylon, according to that Egyptian view of its years which (as well as the Khaldæan view) has been exhibited in Section A of this article, in our Table of Regnal Years at Babylon from the first of Nabonassar to the first of Seleucus Nicator.

1. Let us take first the reign of the second Artaxerxes, which follows next after the reign of the second Darius.

Diodorus tells us (xiii. 104, 108) that this Darius (Nothus) died a little after that the Lacedæmonians had granted peace to the Athenians, and the Athenians had given up their city in the arkhonship of Alexias; being the fourth year of the 93d Olympiad, as may be seen on comparing of xiii. 68, 76, 80 and xiv. 3, 12, 17, 19, 35; and therefore ending about midsummer B.C. $(776 - 93 \times 4 \text{ years} =) 404$. Justin, too, tells us, vi. 8, that Darius died in the same year in which Athens capitulated, saying, *Insignis hic annus et expugnatione Athenarum et morte Darii regis Persarum et exsilio Dionysii Siciliæ tyranni fuit.* That the year was that of the arkhon Alexias, and the fourth of the 93d Olympiad, appears moreover from the testimony of Xenophon, *Hellenic.* ii. 1, § 10; ii. 3, § 1, compared with the previous narrative in *Hellenic.* i. 2, § 1; i. 3, § 1; i. 6, § 1. Xenophon also shows us that the celebration of the Olympic games about three months after the surrender of Athens was the 94th, and consequently that the year that had then just expired was the fourth year of the 93d Olympiad, as we have said, because this Olympic year, in the first month of which, a little after midsummer, the games took place, and in which at the close of the summer Lysander returned to Lacedæmon from the capture of Samos, is made by him to be *the year of the Ephor Eudikus*. Now the year of Eudikus at Sparta was the fifth ephor-year counted from that of Euarkhippus, which according to Xenophon was the year of the 93d Olympic festival. This reasoning is confirmed by the list of 29 ephors that held office at Sparta during the Peloponnesian war, the last of whom was Eudikus. Xen. *Hell.* ii. 3, § 10. Observe that though Xenophon calls the space $28\frac{1}{2}$ years, the 29 ephors give but $27\frac{1}{2}$ years even to the capture of Samos, and only 27 years to that of Athens, which is the estimate of Diodorus, xiii. 107. The year of the first of these ephors, Ainesias, expired shortly after the outbreak of the war, and the year of the 28th ephor, Arkhytas, did not expire till shortly after Lysander found himself in possession of Athens. That it was in the spring before the close of the arkhonship and Olympic year in B.C. 404 when Athens surrendered, we know from Plutarch, who, in his *Lysander*, chap. 15, relates that this event happened on the 16th of Múnykhion (the 10th Attic month). See Clinton, *F. H.* vol. ii., Appendix, *On the Attic Months*.

But if Athens capitulated early in April B.C. 404, the king of the Persians and Medes, Okhus Darius Nothus, according to Diodorus in the passage above indicated, died shortly afterwards, in the same arkhonship and Olympic year, that is, before midsummer. But whether or not before midsummer, it is enough for us if, as Diodorus says, "a little after the peace died Darius the king of Asia, after a reign of 19 years." And the same number of years is given the king in Ptolemy's (Khaldæan) Canon of kings, Assyrian and Mede, at Babylon; as the reader may see by looking back to our table, where it is embodied in the first three columns. He will also see that these 19 years make up 343 of Nabonassar; which (being taken for Egyptian years of 365 days apiece invariably, and the series as beginning with the first of Thoth in B.C. 747, that is, at mid-day the 26th of February in that year) expired at six hours after noon the 2d of December B.C. 405. So that the year, in which the demise of the crown from the second Darius to the second Artaxerxes actually happened, was by the Egyptian method of registering reigns counted to the successor as the first of his reign. And it is to exemplify the Egyptian method that we cite the case. But the reader may further observe from our table, that the same 19 years of the second Darius and 343 years of Nabonassar did not terminate, by the Khaldæan account, till the end of the month Tisri B.C. 404; for the years of Nabonassar and his successors at Babylon were reckoned to begin with the month Markhesvan, in the series of Julian years the first of which was the year B.C. 747; and the year of Nabonassar in which a king first seated himself on the throne was counted not to that king himself (in this case Artaxerxes Mnemon), but to his predecessor (in this case Darius Nothus). Thus, though the death of Nothus and Mnemon's succession actually happened, say, in the month of May of the year B.C. 404, yet by Egyptian registration the reign of Mnemon technically began with that civil year of Egypt in which the reign of Nothus expired, while by the method of the Khaldæan registrars it began with the civil year of Babylon which succeeded the year of the death of Nothus.

2. To exemplify the Egyptian method, let us take a second case, in which the evidence of the Canon of Reigns at Babylon (prefixed to the Canon of Reigns at Alexandria subsequent to that of the city's founder) may be compared with the testimony of Greek historians. It is the transmission of the crown to Darius just now mentioned from his father, the first Artaxerxes, who, with his private name prefixed on

the authority of Josephus and his Greek epithet subjoined, is Cyrus Artaxerxes Makrokheir.

As to this king's first successor,—named like his grandfather Xerxes, and according to Ktesias the legitimate heir of the throne, being the only son of Artaxerxes by his queen Damaspia, while Sekudianus or Sogdianus and Okhus, with fifteen others, were sons of concubines,—he died, according to Diodorus, in the Athenian year of the arkhon Isarkhus, and in the year of the 89th celebration of the Olympic games by the people of Elis. That is to say, Xerxes the Second died in the course of a twelvemonth which began about midsummer of B.C. 776 − 88 × 4 years, or of the year B.C. 424. Diodorus, moreover, tells of him, "*He had reigned a year, or, as some write, two months*, when he was succeeded by his brother Sogdianus, who reigned seven months, and was slain by Darius, who reigned 19 years." See Diodor. xii. 65 for the year, and xii. 71 for the incidents; and observe that the death of Sogdianus seems referred by the historian to the same year as that of Xerxes. The death of the father of both, Artaxerxes the First, had been thus recorded by Diodorus in the year of the previous arkhon beginning midsummer B.C. 425: "In the time of the arkhon at Athens Stratocles . . . died Artaxerxes king of the Persians, after a rule of 40 years; and he was succeeded by Xerxes, who reigned one year." See Diod. xii. 60, 64. That the reign of Artaxerxes lasted 40 years Diodorus had stated already, xi. 69. As to the date of the demise of the crown at his death to Xerxes, Clinton cites Thucydides, iv. 50; relating how in the winter (after October B.C. 425) the Athenians learnt at Ephesus what the historian observes actually happened about that time, that King Artaxerxes, son of Xerxes, was recently dead. Hence it appears that the reign of Artaxerxes by the Babylonian reckoning ended with the next following Tisri in B.C. 424; and thus, if the reign was, as measured by Diodorus, a length of 40 years, Thucydides agrees with our table, which shows that by the Babylonian account the 41st year ended with Tisri in B.C. 423. Clinton also cites from Thuc. viii. 58 the date of the third treaty between the Lacedæmonians and Tissaphernes, *the 13th year of Darius's reign, and the year of the ephor Alexippidas in Lacedæmon*, to show that the first year of Darius Nothus was reputed by those who drew up the instrument to have been already current in February B.C. 423, as indeed at the date of the treaty it was held in Egypt also; though at Babylon, as our table shows, the year of Darius current in February B.C. 411 was reckoned but the 12th. Note that the year of the ephor Alexippidas at Lacedæmon was the year of the 92d Olympic festival which began about midsummer B.C. 412. For Alexippidas is the 21st of the 29 ephors of the Peloponnesian war enumerated by Xenophon (*Hellenic*. ii. 3, § 9), the 25th of whom, Euarkhippus, was ephor in the year of the 93d Olympic festival (*Hellenic*. i. 2, § 1), while the 29th, Eudikus, was ephor in the year of the next Olympic festival:

Hellenic. ii. 3, § 1. Perhaps that date in the treaty with Tissaphernes, the 13th year of *Darius's reign*, is the regnal year of the king *according to the reckoning of his Greek subjects* on the Ægæan coast; and if so, it may probably have been nearly the same as the Olympic year which corresponded with the ephor-year of Alexippidas, and, as we have said, began about midsummer B.C. 412. In this case, the first of Darius will be the year beginning at midsummer B.C. 424. And this Greek year is the one to which, as we have shown, Diodorus assigns the death of Xerxes, the only legitimate son and heir of Artaxerxes; and assigns also, apparently, the death wherewith his murderer, the illegitimate Sogdianus, was afterwards punished by the other illegitimate Okhus, who assumed Darius for his regal name.

As to the duration of the two reigns of Xerxes and Sogdianus, which intervened between those of the first Artaxerxes and the second Darius, we have to say, that of the two accounts preserved by Diodorus, the one that the historian does not himself follow is the account given by Africanus and Eusebius as that of Manetho; to wit, that Xerxes reigned two months and Sogdianus seven. See Geo. Sync. p. 76, A and D, Paris ed. It also agrees with Ktesias's account. But even the epitomè of Ktesias in the Bibliotheca of Photius, cod. 72, §§ 44–49, relates with some detail the story of these two brief reigns. It tells us that on the 45th day from the death of Artaxerxes, the new king Xerxes, after drinking largely at a certain feast, was murdered in his sleep in the palace by Sekudianus (Sogdianus) and certain accomplices, in the number of whom was one of the principal eunuchs. Again, it relates how, after a reign of six months and fifteen days, that is, eight complete months since the death of Artaxerxes, Sekudianus was taken and cast into "*the ashes*" by Okhus, another son of a concubine of his father's, whom the father had made satrap of Baktria. In this post of power, after many times failing in the promises he always made to obey summonses, and present himself as required before Sekudianus, a servant in the presence of his lord, the satrap surrounded himself with numerous forces. Some of the greatest dignitaries of the empire revolted to him, and set "the *kitaris* of kingdom" on his head. He received the regal name *Dareius*, or, as it is written by Ktesias, *Dareiaius*, the monumental *Darayavush*. A treaty sanctioned by oaths was made between the kings, but Sekudianus was the party outwitted. He was entrapped and put to death, and Okhus Darius reigned *alone*. So Ktesias says expressly; thereby giving us, perhaps, his warrant to place the date of Darius's assumed and recognised royalty at less than six months and a half interval, if not immediately, after the death of his brother Xerxes. But the short reign of 45 days given to Xerxes, according to Ktesias, or two months, according to Manetho and an authority cited by Diodorus, seems incompatible with the dates given by Thucydides, Diodorus, and the Canon of Reigns at Babylon.

However, to return to Diodorus. If not only Xerxes, but Sogdianus also, met his death in the year of the arkhon Isarkhus and of the 89th Olympic festival, that is, between the two midsummers of the years 424 and 423 B.C., Sogdianus must have been put to death more than the six months and a half that he reigned after midsummer B.C. 424. Consequently Okhus (who was already king, and named Darius) must have been left *alone* in the royal dignity after (we do not say at *how late* a point after) the commencement of the year B.C. 423. But according to the Canon of Reigns at Babylon (as the reader may see in our table given above in Section A), the reign of this Darius—called Nothus as being the son of a concubine, not of the queen—began with the year of Nabonassar 325. Now (considered after Ptolemy's manner as an Egyptian year of a series which began with the first of Thoth, or at mid-day the 26th of February in the year 747 B.C.) this year began with the end of 324 Julian years *less* 81 *days* from that date, or, as our table has it, at mid-day the 7th of December B.C. 424.

Thus, if we have rightly interpreted Diodorus, as placing the death of Sogdianus no less than that of Xerxes (although seven months later) in the year between the midsummers of the Julian years B.C. 424 and 423, it appears that the Canon of Babylonian Reigns, according to Ptolemy's or the Egyptian use of it, gives for his first regnal year to Darius the Second, that year of Egypt in the course of which, by Diodorus's account, his accession happened. Now this, in the present case, as the like in the former example of the second Artaxerxes, who may be styled in full Arsakes Artaxerxes Mnemon, is just what we proposed to show.

The conclusion is also attested by the Canon according to the proper Khaldæan construction of it. For, according to the Khaldæan use of the expression, 41 *years of Artaxerxes the First, making up* 324 *years of Nabonassar*, the first regnal New-year's day of the king placed next after that Artaxerxes in the Canon, namely, Darius the Second, was the 1st day of Markhesvan (say the 1st of November) in the year B.C. 423; and, according to the Khaldæan view of the matter, that king's accession happened, as we have already concluded, at some date in the immediately preceding twelvemonth.

We might leave the case here: and yet we add a few words. We have shown that, by Diodorus's account, it was in the arkhon year of Athens beginning at midsummer B.C. 425 when, after a reign of 40 years, Artaxerxes the First expired, and his son Xerxes the Second succeeded. Omitting the two short reigns of this Xerxes and of Sogdianus, his half-brother, which intervened (the first rightfully, the latter by iniquity) between Artaxerxes and Darius the Second,—indeed, treating the interval like the reign of the Magian between Cambyses and Darius son of Hystaspes,—the Canon of Reigns at Babylon gives to Artaxerxes alone 41 years, instead of dividing them, 40 to Artaxerxes and one to Xerxes the Second, or 40 to Artaxerxes, and one partly to Xerxes the Second and partly to Sogdianus. Of this total, the last year, or year of Nabonassar 324—beginning (by the Egyptian measurement of every year, and Egyptian assignment of each first regnal year) at six hours in the afternoon of the 7th day of December B.C. 425, and being the year in the winter whereof, as was shown from Thucydides, King Artaxerxes died—may be regarded as the year assigned to Xerxes the Second by the authorities Diodorus preferred to follow. But if we believe that Xerxes the Second reigned no more than two months, the rule of the Khaldæan registration of reigns (which makes the first year of each reign begin with the New-year's day that followed next after the king's actual accession) may be thought to have excluded him from the Tables of Regnal Years at Babylon, as he is, in fact, excluded in Ptolemy's Khaldæan Canon. For *he* at least (if not his successor Sogdianus also) must be supposed already dead when the Markhesvan next after his father's death arrived, even though there should be reason to suspect the first news premature, that the Athenians received of Artaxerxes' death at Ephesus, in the winter of B.C. 425-424; and that an intimation of this is given by Thucydides, when he adds, that the king *did* die about that time.

That Xerxes the Second reigned no more than two months, is confirmed by Ktesias. This author, however, is by no means remarkable for accuracy in his details; for example, he makes Artaxerxes die after having reigned 42 years. If, then, the eight months assigned by Ktesias to the united reigns of Xerxes and Sogdianus, or the nine months reckoned by Manetho, or at least Africanus and some writers known to Diodorus, be supposed not to have begun till the year of Babylon in which Artaxerxes died had expired with Tisri B.C. 424, then the fact exhibited in our table, that Darius Nothus's reign, as registered at Babylon, began with Markhesvan B.C. 423, would be the natural consequence. The supposition means, that instead of reigning but 45 days in all, and being carried into Persis for burial by the same mules that his father's body had been committed to, *because they had refused to travel till they had received the son's body also*, Xerxes, in fact, survived the 1st of Markhesvan that followed next after his father's death for the space of five-and-forty days, so that technically his reign lasted so long by the Khaldæan account. If this were really the case, Sekudianus would be excluded from the Babylonian registers of reigns by the mere fact that no New-year's day had arrived at Babylon during his occupation of the throne; Xerxes would have a year's reign beginning with the 45 days that he survived after the commencement of the new year; and, finally, Okhus, now Darius's, reign would begin, as it does in our Canon of Reigns at Babylon, according to the Khaldæan calculation, with Markhesvan in B.C. 423.

We conclude, to the same purpose as before, with a testimony of

Greek history omitted in our former argument. By relating, xii. 71, xiii. 108, that Okhus Darius Nothus died not more than 10 weeks before midsummer B.C. 404, after a reign of 19 years, Diodorus makes this reign to have begun a little before midsummer B.C. 423, that is, either at or even before the death of Sogdianus in that year of the arkhon Isarkhus wherein we have already found our historian placing the death of Xerxes, if not that of Sogdianus also. Therefore, compared with the Egyptian and Khaldæan Tables of Reigns, Assyrian and Mede, at Babylon (the former of which exhibits the second Darius's reign of 19 years as beginning at mid-day the 7th of December B.C. 424, and the latter with the 1st of Markhesvan B.C. 423), this conclusion from Diodorus, that his accession took place shortly before midsummer B.C. 423, no less than the testimonies already cited, exemplifies two propositions. It exemplifies, as we intended, the proposition, *that the Egyptians counted for a king's first regnal year the civil year of their nation in which he began to reign, making his second year commence with the first day of Thoth next after his accession.* But it also exemplifies our other proposition, *that with the Khaldæans the first regnal year of a king did not begin till the arrival of the 1st of Markesvan, or New-year's day, next after his actual taking possession of the throne.*

3. As another example, we will now take the case of the year in which Alexander the Macedonian conqueror of Asia died, and in his stead his half-brother Aridæus received, along with the regal name of their father Philip, the title and diadem of king. According to Ptolemy's Khaldæan Canon, that is to say, his Table of Reigns, Assyrian and Mede, at Babylon, the first year of Aridæus's reign was the 425th of Nabonassar; for the last regnal year of Alexander was the 424th, not only according to what we call Theon's copy of the Canon, but, secondly, according to the copy which Georgius Syncellus borrowed from the mathematicians of his time to compare with the Church Canon of Reigns; and also, thirdly, according to the repeated testimonies of Ptolemy in the Almagest or Greater Syntaxis, and of Theon in his commentary on Ptolemy's work. Now the year which followed this, and was counted the first of Philip Aridæus, the 425th year of Nabonassar, if considered as by Egyptian mathematicians to begin 424 times 365 days after mid-day the 26th of February, or the commencement of Thoth in B.C. 747, began, as our table has it, at mid-day the 12th of November B.C. 324. But the same 425th year of Nabonassar, as it appears to have been regarded by the Khaldæans, began with the 425th Markhesvan, counted from the one in B.C. 747; that is to say, began with the Markhesvan of our year B.C. 323. So much for the first year of Philip Aridæus and 425th of Nabonassar, according to the Egyptian and Khaldæan views of the Canon respectively.

But Philip Aridæus's actual accession to the throne of Asia, and the real commencement of his reign, was at a point between these two technical commencements; for Alexander died in the summer of B.C. 323, or about six months after the Egyptian and before the Khaldæan New-year's day of the 425th year of Nabonassar. If so, it appears, in a fresh example, that by Egyptian registrars of reigns the civil year in course of which a king came into possession of the throne was counted his first regnal year. This is what we undertook to show; but it appears withal that the Khaldæan registrars give the year of the demise of the throne to him who was in possession at the beginning of the year.

To establish the date of Alexander's death, just alleged, we refer the reader first to Arrian, *Exp. Alex.* vii. 28; to Diodorus, xvii. 103, 107; to Josephus (alleging unanimous testimony), *cont. Apion.* i. 22. All agree that Alexander died in the year of the 114th Olympic festival, or between the midsummers of the years 324 and 323 B.C. The first two add that it was the year of the Athenian arkhon Hegesias or Agesias. Thus, having obtained the year of death according to the Greeks, we have to find the time of year. That Alexander died at nearly the end of the year, or not long before midsummer B.C. 323, is intimated by Diodorus's assigning the next events in his narrative to the arkhonship of Kephisodorus. See Diod. xviii. 1-3, etc. But a like conclusion is more surely drawn from the attested length of Alexander's reign and life. He reigned 12 years and 7 months according to Diodorus, xvii. 117, or 12 years and 8 months according to Aristobulus; in Arrian, *Exp. Alex.* vii. 28. Further, Aristobulus asserts that of the 33d year of his age Alexander had attained at his death those eight months which he reigned over and above 12 years. Now these 12 years and 8 months began at the death of his father Philip, in the year of the 111th Olympic festival, or between the midsummers of the years 336 and 335 B.C.; according to Diodorus, xvi. 91, and Eratosthenes, *ap. Clement. Strom.* i. p. 336, c. Eratosthenes counted 35 years from the second of the 102d Olympiad, which was the year of the battle at Leuktra, to the death of Philip, and 12 years thence to the decease of Alexander; the 35 years excluding the year of Leuktra, and the 12 years excluding the year of the death of Philip. See Clinton, *Fast. Hell.* vol. ii. Therefore Alexander died eight months later in the year beginning midsummer B.C. 324 than the date of his father Philip's death in the year beginning midsummer B.C. 336; or (as the same may be expressed) eight months later in the arkhonship of Hegesias than the day of the year at which Philip died, in the arkhonship of Pythodorus (Diod. xvi. 91) or Pythodemus (Arrian, *Exp. Alex.* i. 1), who was the 13th arkhon if one counts backward and begins with Hegesias, the arkhon of the year of Alexander's death. All the arkhons who at Athens gave name to the 12 years preceding that of Hegesias are recited by Dionysius of Halicarnassus, *de Dinarcho*, § 9; and for each of them we have other evidence. See Clinton, as before.

Again, a similar conclusion arises from Alexander's age at his death, which, as we have seen, according to Aristobulus, was 32 years and 8 months. For news of Alexander's birth, it is said, came to Philip just after he had captured Potidæa, at the same time as news of a victory gained by Parmenion over the Illyrians, and news that *his horse had won at the Olympic games*. See Plutarch, *Vit. Alexand.* cap. 3. Plutarch dates Alexander's birth more particularly by placing it on the 6th of Hecatombæon, the first month of the Attic year, beginning about midsummer; a month which, he adds, the Macedonians call Lous. This Hecatombæon would be the first month of the arkhonship of Elpines, and the year of Athens corresponding with that of the 106th Olympic festival; that is, with a twelvemonth which began about midsummer B.C. 356. See Diod. xvi. 15. See, too, the list of arkhons given by Dionysius, *de Dinarcho*, § 9; whence it appears that Elpines was the first of a series of arkhons, the last of whom, named Phrynikhus, was the immediate predecessor of Pythodemus (so Dionysius as well as Arrian, already referred to, writes the name of the arkhon), in whose year Alexander, being 20 years old, came to his father's throne.

It appears, then, that the Olympic festival (namely, the 106th) which marks the birth of Alexander was the eighth festival before and exclusively of the one at the beginning of the year in which he died, namely, the 114th celebration of the games. If, therefore, he lived, as Aristobulus attested, 32 years and 8 months, he must have lived for at least the first eight months of the Olympic and the Attic year in which he died, which began about midsummer B.C. 324; and thus his death might be presumed to have happened about the 1st of March B.C. 323. And this would serve to show, as we desire, that the Egyptian year regarded as his successor Aridæus Philip's first year, was in fact the year in which Alexander died and Aridæus came to the throne.

But Alexander died later than the 1st of March in the year B.C. 323. The odd eight months of Aristobulus over and above the 12 years' reign and 32 years' life of Alexander seem to be, not eight months of the Olympic or Attic, but eight months of the Macedonian year, which began at a later point of the Julian year than did the Olympic,—at the autumn equinox, rather than at midsummer. For the same Aristobulus dated Alexander's death on the 30th of Dæsius, though the exacter date, we presume, was the one cited from the Royal Ephemerides, the 28th of Dæsius. See Plutarch, *Vit. Alexand.* capp. 75, 76. Now Dæsius was the eighth month of the Macedonian year, and coincided in part with the 11th Attic month Thargelion, as the 10th Macedonian month Lous coincided in part with the first Attic month Hecatombæon. For Alexander, who, according to Plutarch, *Vit. Alex.* cap. 3, was born on the 6th of Hecatombæon, was born in Lous; and dying on the 28th of Dæsius, according to the Royal

Ephemerides, is said by Ælian to have died on the 6th of Thargelion. See Ælian, *Var. Hist.* ii. 25; and after Clinton compare Plutarch, *Vit. Alex.* cap. 16; *Vit. Camilli,* cap. 19. Josephus as well as Plutarch makes the Macedonian Lous correspond with the Athenian Hecatombæon. But the same Lous he makes also to correspond with the Jewish (and Assyrian) fifth month Abba or Ab, *Antiq.* iv. 4, § 7, quoted by Clinton, *F. H.* vol. iii., Appendix, chap. 4, *Macedonian Months.* Consistently with this correspondence between Abba, Lous, and Hecatombæon, and also with the correspondence he indicates, *Antiq.* viii. 3, § 1, between the seventh Macedonian month Artemisius and the second Jewish month Iyar, Josephus undoubtedly considered the eighth Macedonian month Dæsius, when he names it in his *History of the Jewish War* as the correspondent of the third Jewish month Sivan. Afterwards, when the Syro-Macedonian year of Antiokh was made a Julian year like the year of Rome, Dæsius is treated by Suidas and others as identical with June, and Lous with August. See Clinton, as before.

If, then, Alexander died on the 28th of the Macedonian month Dæsius, in the year which began with the moon of the Olympic festival in B.C. 324, he may be supposed to have died in June, that is, not long before the close of that twelvemonth and the arkhonship of Hegesias in B.C. 323. And thus it is again proved, as we proposed, that though the civil year of Babylon in which he died was given to his reign as the concluding year of it by the Khaldæan account, yet the civil year of Egypt marked by his death, according to the custom of the annals of that country, was counted as the first year of the reign of his successor Philip Aridæus. And this Egyptian year, as we have seen, was the first of a new and important era, the reigns of which were recorded in a Canon annexed to Ptolemy's Astronomical Table of 1476 Egyptian years, beginning with the first of Aridæus, at mid-day of the 12th of November B.C. 324.

Before we proceed with our proper subject, we here take the opportunity of making some observations, suggested by what has now been adduced, concerning the date of the death of Alexander the Great. Clinton remarks, that, if Alexander died, as the Royal Ephemerides testified, at the end of Dæsius, the eighth Macedonian month, or, as Ælian says, on the 6th of Thargelion, the 11th Attic month,—having also been born, as Plutarch, already quoted, affirms, on the 6th of Hecatombæon, the first Attic month, and in Lous, the 10th Macedonian month,—he must have lived ten months of his 33d year, rather than eight, as stated by Aristobulus. The account for which Arrian appears to quote Aristobulus is this, that Alexander lived 32 years and 8 months, having reigned of that space the last 12 years and 8 months. This seems to us to involve the use of a technical birth-day, as well as of a technical commencement of the regnal year. The latter fact of the two, that the regnal New-year's day was technically identified with the New-year's day of the civil calendar, the 1st of Dius, is plain from the fact, attested by Aristobulus and the Royal Ephemerides, that the eight months of the 33d regnal year were the first eight months of the Macedonian civil year. And that the 1st of Dius was not Alexander's real birth-day, appears from the testimony of Plutarch, that he was born in Lous, that is, the tenth month of the year, or third before New-year's day; and further, that the news of his birth reached Philip along with news of the king's horse having won a race at the Olympic games. But Aristobulus, whether by an old custom of Macedonia, or by one borrowed from Asia, seems to count the years of Alexander's life *from the New-year's day next after his birth*, and his regnal years from the New-year's day either next before or next after the death of Philip. We cannot tell which, till we know whether Philip died before or after the 1st of Dius B.C. 336. If, indeed, Philip's assassination could be shown to have happened on the 1st of Dius, it might be concluded that Alexander's regnal years coincided by a mere chance with the civil years of Macedonia. On the banks of the Orontes and of the Tigris, the day of the same new moon was New-year's day to the Macedonians and the Khaldæans; though by the former it was termed the 1st of Dius, and by the latter (not, indeed, in the ancient Akkad, but in the popular Aramaic dialect) the 1st of Markhesvan. Whether, under the Akhæmenian kings of the Persians and Medes, the New-year's day was not regarded as the king's birth-day, is a question suggested above, p. 139, and note (*a*).

Perhaps the day of Alexander's death is recoverable. The romance of Alexander in Latin, by Julius Valerius (printed at the bottom of the pages of the Pseudo-Callisthenes, along with the Arrian edited for F. Didot by C. Müller), ends with these words: *Obitus autem ejusdem etiam nunc Alexandriæ sacratissimum habent.* This assertion, so credible in itself, leads us to pay some attention to the dates given by the Pseudo-Callisthenes. Of the three Paris MSS. used by C. Müller, the most ancient, No. 1711, which he calls *Codex A*, ends with the following mutilated sentence: ἐγεννήθη μὲν οὖν Τυβίου τῇ νεομηνίᾳ, ἀνατολῆς οὔσης. ἐτελεύτησε δὲ Φαρμούθι τετράδι, δυσίας. . . . If we assign the corresponding dates of the Julian Calendar of Rome according to the Comparative Table used by Geo. Syncellus (a copy of whose work Dindorf's *Codex A* is part of the same manuscript volume, No. 1711), we must suppose the Pseudo-Callisthenes to refer to the Egypto-Julian year of Alexandria, which was first introduced at that city in the 295th year of Philip Aridæus. Then, according to Geo. Syncell. p. 8, B, the 1st of Tybi is the 27th of December; and according to Georg. Syncell. p. 7, A, the 4th of Pharmuthi is the 30th of March. We shall obtain the same results if we take the 29th of August for the first of the Alexandrian Thoth (as it was, except in the first year of each four-year period), and if we know that Tybi was the fifth and Pharmuthi the eighth months of the Egypto-Julian no less than the proper Egyptian year. The dates of *Codex A* have evidently been interpreted, though not accurately, according to the Egypto-Julian Calendar in use at Alexandria, either by Nectarius the monk of Otranto in Calabria, whose pen in A.D. 1469 executed C. Müller's *Codex B* (Paris MS. No. 1685), or else by a previous scribe. For that MS. exhibits the passage thus: ἐγεννήθη μὲν ὁ Ἀλέξανδρος μηνὸς Ἰαννουαρίου νεομηνίᾳ ἀνατολῆς οὔσης τοῦ ἡλίου. ἐτελεύτησε δὲ μηνὸς Ἀπριλλίου νεομηνίᾳ δύσεως οὔσης τοῦ ἡλίου. Taking the Alexandrian first month, Thoth, roughly for the Roman September, with which it nearly coincided, Nectarius regarded the fifth month, Tybi, as January, and the eighth month, Pharmúthi, as April.

But Alexander certainly was not born in December or January, nor did he die in March or April. If, however, neglecting the birth-day, which we know no reason for believing to have been always noted at Alexandria, we confine ourselves to the anniversary of his death; and believing that this was indeed, by old tradition, the fourth day of Pharmúthi, we shall refer it rather to the proper Egyptian year used at Alexandria under the Ptolemies, than to the Egypto-Julian year of that city used in the eras of Augustus and Diocletianus. Now, the year of Nabonassar 425, in which, as a year of Egypt, Alexander died, certainly began (as our table in Section A has it) at mid-day 12th November B.C. 324. Therefore the 4th day of the eighth month, Pharmúthi, or the 214th day of the year, began at *mid-day 13th June B.C.* 323. And this is sufficiently near to our former conclusion, that the Macedonian month, on the 28th of which he died, corresponded with June. But whatever was the day of Alexander's death in the summer of B.C. 323, the season of his death, compared with the position of the first year of Aridæus Philip, the year of Nabonassar according to the Egyptians 425, proves, as we have concluded already, that with the Egyptians the first regnal year of a king is the year of his succession to the throne.

4. It is not necessary to vindicate this proposition by taking a fourth example from Ptolemy's earlier or Khaldæan Canon of Reigns. But the different methods of regnal registration in use with the Egyptians and the Khaldæans will help us to understand and appreciate the different views taken and transmitted of the time when Codomannus son of Arsames, the third Darius of the Akhæmenian dynasty, was succeeded by Alexander, and when the Persian rule was superseded in Asia by the Macedonian.

The Khaldæan Canon, or Ptolemy's Canon of Reigns at Babylon, assigns a space of 12 years to the two reigns taken together of Darius and Alexander. This space extends, extremes included, from the 413th to the 424th year of Nabonassar, as our table shows. But the year of the twelve which was Alexander's first at Babylon is a point disputed. According to the copies of the Canon from which the editions of Petavius and Dodwell are given, and which we supposed to be derived from Theon, Alexander's reign at Babylon lasted eight years, and began with the year of Nabonassar 417; whereas it lasted six years only, and began with the year of Nabonassar 419, according to a copy of the Khaldæan Canon transmitted to us by Geo. Syncellus from the mathematicians and astronomers of his day. See Geo. Sync. p. 208, C, Paris ed. And in this different division of the 12 years, the Syncellus's Mathematical Canon is joined by his Church or Ecclesiastical Canon afterwards given; which last document he seems himself to follow, p. 256, B, Paris ed., when he gives six years to Darius's reign.

Following as the preferable authority the first-named version of the Canon of Reigns at Babylon, namely, that of Petavius and Dodwell, our Table of Reigns in Section A of this article makes Alexander begin to reign at Babylon with the 417th year of Nabonassar, that is, according to the Egyptian view of that year, with the 1st day of Thoth, at noon, the 14th of November B.C. 332, or, according to the Khaldæan view, with the 1st day of Markhesvan B.C. 331. Whether any genuine Khaldæan record ever, like our Syncellus's copy of Ptolemy's Canon of Reigns at Babylon, made the 419th year of Nabonassar the first of Alexander's reign, shall be discussed, but not immediately.

For, first, we observe, that the 417th year of Nabonassar was made Alexander's first on the throne of Asia by both Egyptians and Khaldæans, on the good and very apparent ground that the battle at Gaugamela, in the province of which Arbela was the capital, put Alexander in possession of the kingdom; so that, far from being able to meet him again in the field, Darius could not, and probably did not attempt to prevent his lieutenants from surrendering Babylon and Susa; could not aid the satrap of Persis either in the defence of his frontier or in the fight which he made for the capital, Parsa or Persepolis; and himself abandoned Agbatana and Media, whither he at first had fled, on the conqueror's approach in the following summer. The Egyptians could also allege that earlier in the same year of their annals in which the battle of Arbela was fought, they had surrendered to the Macedonian, and their Greek capital Alexandria had been founded. And at Babylon it was probably alleged with truth, that Alexander had arrived from his great victory, in the Assyrian province of which Arbela then was the capital, before the first day of the ensuing Markhesvan, when their new year began. Thus the Egyptians could reckon the year, after their manner, the first of the Macedonian dominion; while, on the other hand, the Khaldæans, after their rule, could make it the last of the supremacy of the Persians; and yet both Egyptians and Khaldæans (by help of the difference between the points whence they counted the years of Nabonassar, as well as in the length of their respective civil years) were able to register the 417th year of Nabonassar as the first regnal year of the Macedonian conqueror. To establish it, then, by a new exemplification, here, that the Egyptians made a rule to count for each king's first regnal year that civil year of theirs in which he came to the throne, it needs but to show by sufficient historical testimony that the battle of Arbela was fought in the course of that Egyptian year of which the first of Thoth began at noon the 14th of November B.C. 332, and of which the fifth and last supplementary day after the 12th month Mesori ended at six hours before noon the 12th of November B.C. 331.

Having left Memphis, the capital of Egypt, at the first appearance of spring, Alexander made some stay in Phœnicé, at Tyre, and then began his up-country expedition. He reached Thapsacus (where two bridges of boats for the passing of the Euphrates only waited his arrival and the flight of the enemy's cavalry to be joined on to the further bank) in Hecatombæon, the first month of a new year and arkhon at Athens, Aristophanes. See Arrian, *Exp. Alex.* iii. 6, 7. It was about July (see Clinton on the Attic Months, in the Appendix to the second volume of the *Fasti Hellenici*), and a year had now elapsed since the capture of Tyre, which Alexander accomplished in the month Hecatombæon of the arkhon *Anikétus* (called by Dionysius, *de Dinarcho*, *Niketes*, and by Diodorus Nikératus). See Arrian, *Exp. Alex.* ii. 24. Now the year of this last-named arkhon was that of the 112th Olympiad; that is, of the Olympic celebration which followed midsummer B.C. $(776 - 111 \times 4 \text{ years} =)$ 332. See Diod. xvii. 40. Thus it appears Alexander reached the Euphrates about July B.C. 331. Again, the moon was almost entirely eclipsed whilst he was resting his army after the unobstructed passage of the Tigris; and Aristander the soothsayer prophesied that within the same month the battle would be fought, and Alexander would be victorious. Arrian, *Exp. Alex.* iii. 7, § 6. And so it happened. This Arrian testifies. But he places the battle in Pyanepsion, the fourth month of the arkhon Aristophanes: *Exp. Alex.* iii. 15, § 7. Whereas Plutarch, *Vit. Alex.* cap. 31, relates that the eclipse happened in the third month Boedromion, about the beginning of the Mysteries at Athens, and that it was the 11th night from the eclipse that preceded the battle. Now the Great or Eleusinian Mysteries lasted the nine days from the 15th to the 23d of Boedromion; a fact for which Clinton sends us to Corsini, *Fast. Attic.* tom. ii. p. 378, and to Meursius there referred to. And from the 15th night of Boedromion, the 11th night would be the 25th if we count in the extremes, or the 26th night of Boedromion if we exclude the night from which the numbering begins. But Plutarch elsewhere, *Vit. Camill.* cap. 19, dates the defeat of the Persians at Arbela on the 26th of Boedromion. Clinton at first thought to reconcile these statements of Plutarch with the testimony before adduced of Arrian; but a closer examination of the Metonic Cycle led him to abandon Arrian, and give his assent to Plutarch. He found that in B.C. 331 the new moon of Boedromion would be earlier than the first day of the month by 1 day, 5 hours, 35 minutes, and 53 seconds; so that the full moon when the eclipse happened would fall on the 14th of Boedromion, or 13 days, 12 hours, 46 minutes, and 8 seconds after the beginning of Boedromion : so that the battle, if it was fought 11 or 12 days afterwards, would fall within the month, as Arrian's account of Aristander's prediction requires, and also at about the day of the month reported by Plutarch. See Clinton on the Attic Months, *F. H.* vol. ii., Appendix, chap. 19. We may say, then, that Alexander gained his victory within the third moon after midsummer B.C. 331. Before the battle, in an address to his assembled officers, Alexander had told them that it was not for Cœlé-Syria, or Phœnicé, or Egypt that they now were going to fight, but for the mastery over all Asia : Arrian, *Exp. Alex.* iii. 9, § 6. When the battle ended as it did, Plutarch tells us, *Vit. Alex.* cap. 34, that the dominion of the Persians was thought to be utterly destroyed, and Alexander, having been proclaimed king of Asia, sacrificed magnificently to the gods, and made presents to his friends of riches and households and commands.

We have good authority, then, to say that his victory in the province of Arbela made Alexander king of Asia instead of Darius, and that the battle was fought in September, or about the 26th day of the third moon from midsummer B.C. 331. Now, as our Table of Reigns in Section A, and observations since made, evince, the event thus dated falls within the limits of the 417th year of Nabonassar, as placed by the Egyptians ; and precedes by not less than five weeks, it may be supposed, the commencement of the Khaldæan year of the same number. So that in this first regnal year of Alexander at Babylon we have another example not only of the Khaldæan rule to count the years of a new king from the New-year's day next after his accession, but of the Egyptian practice, for the proof of which alone we have cited this and the previous examples. The reader, we presume, has not forgotten that this practice was to count a king's regnal years from that first day of Thoth which next preceded his accession, so that the first of Thoth which came next after was the beginning of his second regnal year.

We now take up a question which we deferred till we should have justified the 417th year of Nabonassar as an authentic Egyptian and Khaldæan date for the first regnal year of Alexander the Great on the throne of Asia. This question is, How it came to pass that the copy of the Khaldæan Canon, obtained, from astronomical practitioners of his time, by Geo. Syncellus, made the first regnal year of Alexander the Great to be, not the 417th, but the 419th year of Nabonassar? It was certainly neither a Khaldæan nor an Egyptian view of Alexander's reign that led to this decision. Considered as a Khaldæan year, the 419th of Nabonassar, being one of a series of lunar years which was made equal in parcels of years to a like number of solar years by intercalation of moons, began 418 years after the 1st of Markhesvan B.C. 747 ; that is, it began with the 1st of Markhesvan B.C. 329, and, if assigned by Khaldæan annalists to Alexander the Great as his first regnal year at Babylon, must, by their rule in like cases, have followed immediately after a year in which the demise of the crown was held to have taken place. But no event in Alexander's career involving such demise can be pointed out between the last day of Tisri B.C. 330 and the 1st day of Markhesvan B.C. 329. Again, considered as an Egyptian year, the 419th of Nabonassar began after the lapse of 418 times 365 days from mid-day of February the 26th, B.C. 747; that is, it began with the 14th of November B.C. 330, and if assigned by Egyptian annalists to Alexander the Great as the first year of his reign, it must have been marked, like every other first regnal year of Egyptian registration, by some event which might be looked upon by the Egyptians as involving a change of persons upon the throne. Now, after what we have already said, it is scarcely more than a repetition of it to observe, that no such event can be pointed out in Alexander's history during the year which began with the 14th of November in the year 330 B.C.

We showed above that what we call Theon's copy of Ptolemy's Khaldæan Canon, in making the 417th year of Nabonassar to be Alexander's first, followed the belief that it was the battle at Gaugamela, in the province of Arbela, that transferred the throne of Asia from Darius the Third to the Macedonian. But though this was the sounder view of the case, there was another, of a conventional sort, which might naturally obtain some favour. The death of Darius happened about nine months after his defeat in the province of Arbela, and might be looked upon as the termination of his reign. Arrian tells us that Darius was assassinated by Bessus satrap of Baktria, after having been for some time Bessus's prisoner, during the flight from Media towards Baktria in the month Hecatombæon, the first of the year and arkhonship at Athens of Aristophon. See Arrian, *Exp. Alex.* iii. 22, § 2. Aristophon is the third arkhon of the 112th Olympiad (Diod. xvii. 40, 49, 62); and he therefore came into office about midsummer B.C. 330.

The year, therefore, which had not been current for a whole month, when Darius met his death—that of the arkhon Aristophon, or the third of the 112th Olympiad—was by some Greek annalists made the first year of Alexander's reign over Asia. In like manner we have seen reason, above this, for believing that the year which began about midsummer B.C. 424 was by the Greeks of Asia counted the first of Darius Nothus; because that year was still current, though near its close, when this monarch came to his throne. So, too, we have seen the Hebrew prophets Haggai and Zechariah apparently counting the reign of Darius son of Hystaspes from Nisan B.C. 521, though it was not till the Markhesvan of that year that he slew the Magian usurper, and Cambyses, though dispossessed, was not yet dead in Nisan.

They were Greeks, then, who dated Alexander's reign in Asia to begin with the Greek year in the first month of which Darius died. It is of these that our Syncellus says, p. 261, A, Paris ed., *They count the first year of the kingdom of the Greeks from the seventh year of Alexander* (as king of the Macedonians) ; *for Greeks and Macedonians are the same.* And though he afterwards confounds this seventh year in which Darius was slain by Bessus with Alexander's fifth year, the year in which Alexandria was founded and the defeat of Darius at Arbela achieved, he is correct in adding here, *From the seventh year of Alexander to the 22d of Kleopatra are 300 years.* That our Syncellus's copy of the Khaldæan Canon, whether or not altered since, had come originally or by transcription from Alexandria, seems intimated by its title, which may be translated thus: *The years from Nabonassarus (who is also Salmanasar) king of the Khaldæans unto the death of Alexander the Founder (according to the Astronomical Canon).* But what seems peculiarly to stamp this seventh year of Alexander's Macedonian reign (called in the Syncellus's Astronomical Canon the 419th year of Nabonassar) as a Greek epoch, is the fact that the series of Calippic periods begins with the year of the arkhon Aristophou in B.C. 330; as passages of Ptolemy's Great Syntaxis are employed by Clinton to prove. Take for instance Ptol. vii. 3, pp. 169, 170. The date of an observation made by Timokharis is *the sixth day before the end of the (fourth Attic) month Pyanepsion in the 48th year of the first Six-and-seventy-year Period of Calippus, and the 7th day of Thoth in the year of Nabonassar* 466. Hence it appears that at the time of the observation the Attic year was $29\frac{1}{2} \times 3 + 25\frac{1}{2} = 113\frac{1}{2}$ days old when the Egyptian year was but seven days old; and that the Egyptian year corresponding with the first year of the first Calippic period was their year of Nabonassar (466 — 47 =) 419. But this year began on the 14th of November, whereas the year of the arkhon Aristophon began about midsummer in B.C. 330 ; so that, as Clinton observes, if the 419th year of Nabonassar (or seventh year of Alexander as king of the Macedonians) be made parallel with the first year of the first Calippic period, the thing is done, because the two years coincide in the greatest part of their duration. It is to be observed that, as a Khaldæan year, the 419th of Nabonassar has no correspondence with the first year of the series of Calippic periods ; for the Khaldæan 419th of Nabonassar began with Markhesvan B.C. 329. It was therefore not by Khaldæan annalists that the 419th year of Nabonassar was made the first year of the reign of Alexander at Babylon. But the Egyptian 419th of Nabonassar was certainly the Egyptian year which most nearly corresponded with the first year of the first Calippic period, the year of the arkhon Aristophon, when Darius died, and Alexander was by some regarded as having succeeded to his throne. This correspondence would naturally be pointed out by Greeks of Alexandria ; though it by no means follows that they were Greeks of Alexandria who first fixed upon the year of the arkhon Aristophon as the first year of Alexander's reign in Asia.

G

THE practice followed in the Annals of Egypt, regarding first regnal years, has now been sufficiently established. But we have been led to mention the series of those Six-and-seventy-year Periods of the astronomer Calippus which superseded among the Greeks the Nineteen-year Periods of Meton; the first Calippic period beginning with the eighth year of the sixth Metonic Period, the year at Athens of the arkhon Aristophon. And this introduces us to another topic connected with that sequel to Ptolemy's Khaldæan Canon, the Canon of Years of Philip, or of Reigns subsequent to Alexander's, of which we have already spoken in Sections C, D, and E.

From midsummer B.C. 330 four Calippic periods carry us down to midsummer B.C. (330 − 304=) 26. A little later in this Roman year the Egyptian year ended which, for the most part of it, had corresponded with the last year of the fourth Calippic period; that is, the year of Nabonassar (418 + 304 =) 722. This Egyptian year ended 722 Julian years all but 722 quarters of a day later than 25½ February B.C. 747; that is, it ended with the 29th of August B.C. 26. But at Alexandria this year was the fourth of a new era; and, being the closing year of the first τετραετηρις or Four-year Period in that era, besides the usual five days supplementary after Mesori, the 12th month, had received a sixth *epagomené*. This intercalation, according to the then ruling estimate of the length of the solar year, restored the Alexandrian year with which the next Four-year Period commenced, in that Greek capital, on the morrow, to exactly the same position in respect of the solstices and equinoxes as had been occupied by the first year of the era. The new practice thus begun was continued at Alexandria; and henceforth the Calippic period seems to have been there disused.

But, if this was so, the first day of the second Four-year Period, or fifth year of the new era at Alexandria, should have been the 30th of August by the Roman Calendar, corresponding as it did with the first day of the Thoth of the Egyptian 723d year of Nabonassar. Yet this correspondence was not uniform; for we find that the first day of the Alexandrian, or, as we have termed it, the Egypto-Julian year, was the 30th of August in the Roman Calendar for the first year, and the 29th of August for the other three years of the intercalary period.

We propose, then, an inquiry concerning the year and era of Alexandria. We begin with the important testimony of Dion Cassius, which we were introduced to by Clinton's use of it in *F. H.* vol. ii., Appendix, chap. 19.

In an enumeration of the honours it was resolved to offer to the Cæsar (afterwards surnamed Augustus) when the news reached Rome that Alexandria was taken, in the year B.C. 30, Dion, li. 19, includes a decree, that *the day of the capture should be a good day; and for the years to come it should be the point at which the numbering of them should begin: τὴν ἡμέραν ἐν ᾗ ἡ Ἀλεξάνδρεια ἑάλω ἀγάθην εἶναι καὶ ἐς τὰ ἔπειτα ἔτη ἀρχὴν τῆς ἀπαριθμήσεως αὐτῶν νομίζεσθαι.* The decree thus described seems to have established the day of the capture as the one with which, in time to come, every new year, of the series afterwards called in Egypt *years of Augustus*, was to begin. A result of the enactment would be, that henceforth the year at Alexandria would be *fixed*; and this result was obtained by adding, as we have said, a sixth *epagomené*, or day supplementary, at the end of every period of four years: for thus at Alexandria was applied a doctrine concerning the length of the solar year, which, since the reformation of the Calendar by Julius Cæsar, had been professedly followed for the last sixteen years at Rome. Thus it was expected that every succeeding New-year's day at Alexandria would fall on the same day of the Roman Calendar as that of the capture of the city. And this would have happened if the 1461st day had been intercalated in the course of the same consulship and Julian year of Rome at the Imperial City and at Alexandria.

Before we add anything on this head, we interpose two observations. First, we would illustrate Dion's meaning, in the passage above cited, by his previous words concerning the day in B.C. 31 which was ordained to be the first of the *era of Actium*. In li. 1, he writes, *τοιαύτη τις ἡ ναυμαχία αὐτῶν τῇ δευτέρᾳ τοῦ Σεπτεμβρίου ἐγένετο· τοῦτο δὲ οὐκ ἄλλως εἶπον, . . . ἀλλ᾽ ὅτι τότε πρῶτον ὁ Καῖσαρ τὸ κράτος πᾶν μόνος ἔσχεν, ὥστε καὶ τὴν ἀπαρίθμησιν τῶν τῆς μοναρχίας αὐτοῦ ἐτῶν ἀπ᾽ ἐκείνης τῆς ἡμέρας ἀκριβοῦσθαι.* Observe, that if the new year was to begin to be numbered on a certain day, the series of days in that year would also begin with that day. Secondly, we would remark, that at Rome also there was afterwards instituted a series of years called *anni Augustani*, or *anni Augustorum*. But of these the first was the Roman year B.C. 27; when, as Censorinus, *de Die Natali*, cited by Clinton, tells us, *cap.* 21, the surname Augustus was given to the Cæsar by a decree of the 16th before the Calends of February. But the Egyptian years of Augustus were counted from the end of Cleopatra's reign; that is, as we say, if pure Egyptian years according to the Egyptian method of registration, from the 1st day of Thoth next before her death; if years of Alexandria, from the day before, or the yesterday of that New-year's day, both days being to Egyptians and Alexandrians respectively, the commencement of the reign of the Romans in the person of the conqueror, afterwards named Augustus. Hence the year when Censorinus wrote,—that is, the consulship of Ulpius and Pontianus (A.D. 238),—was A.D. 238+B.C. 27 = (as he says) the 265th Augustan year at Rome; while the year at Alexandria, still current during the first two-thirds of the same year, and ending with the 28th of August, was (A.D. $237\frac{2}{3}$ + $29\frac{1}{3}$ B.C. —), as he says, the 267th of Augustus in that capital. See Censorinus, *de Die Natali*, *cap.* 21, cited by Clinton.

If we now seek the day of the Roman Calendar when the Alexandrian years of Augustus began, we shall find that it should have been counted the 30th, though it was called the 29th, of August; and consequently the first of Thoth that year, being the morrow, was the 31st, though counted as the 30th. It will be seen, too, how this difference of a day, between the common reckoning and a better, came to exist.

That the 29th of August, or fourth before the Calends of September, was the day intended by the decree of the Roman senate and people, may be sufficiently demonstrated by the following testimonies. The latest in time is that of Georgius Syncellus. We have already cited from him a passage, pp. 326, 327 of Goar's Paris edition, where the day of the Roman Calendar which answered (in three years out of four) to the Alexandrian first of Thoth is declared; though the passage in this case seems to be interpolated. For two other places where the correspondence between the Alexandrian and the Roman Calendars is given, we refer the reader to pp. 7 and 312 of the same edition marked in Dindorf's margin. Of these we will cite the former only. The Syncellus, having apparently before him a comparative table of the three calendars, is setting forth the correspondence of a certain Julian year of the Hebrews, first with that of the Romans, and secondly with that of Alexandria. Having begun with Nisan, and being now arrived at Elul, he writes, Ἕκτος μὴν Ἐλλοῦ, ἡμερῶν τριάκοντα μιᾶς, ἀπὸ τὰς κγ΄ τοῦ Αὐγούστου ἕως τὰς κβ΄ τοῦ Σεπτεμβρίου. This was the place of the Jewish Elul in the Roman Calendar. By the by, τὰς for τῶν, which here occurs twice, is certainly not the Syncellus's own. It is probably due to a transcriber of our chronographer's work, who has put into words of his own the figures of a tabular statement which he found in his original; constructing ἀπὸ and ἕως, as in modern Greek, with accusatives. What we cite next, showing the place of the same Elul in the Alexandrian Calendar, is confused, and also somewhat corrupt in the reading: ἀπὸ τὰς λ΄ τοῦ Μεσορὶ [καὶ αἱ ἐπαγόμεναι] ἕως τὰς κί τοῦ Θώθ. [ἀπὸ τὰς κδ΄ τοῦ Αὐγούστου ἕως τὰς κή. Ἡ γὰρ ἀρχὴ τοῦ Θὼθ ἀπὸ τὰς κθ΄ Αὐγούστου ἐστὶ ἐπιπινθήμερος λ΄ Αὐγούστου ἐπὶ δὲ ἐξημέρου τριάκοντα μία Αὐγούστου.] The two portions of this which we have bracketed are plainly to be taken together, and to be placed after the words ἕως τὰς κί τοῦ Θώθ,—that is, after a statement of the position of Elul as a Julian month in the Alexandrian or Egypto-Julian Calendar, corresponding with the author's notices respecting the places of the other Hebrew months. The whole appears to have been a marginal note or parenthesis, either in a document used by our Syncellus, or rather in an older copy of the Syncellus's chronography than the now surviving transcripts, or at least than *Codex A*, Paris, No. 1711; for the better *Codex B* (Paris, No. 1764) begins only with p. 95, line 13 of Dindorf's ed., ending with p. 646, line 7 of the same, and wanting several leaves in the middle.

But observe that this intruded matter is itself to be divided into two parts. Of these the former, which seems to end with the word ἐστί, contains more expressly the testimony for the sake of which we cite the Syncellus's volume here. The latter looks like a correction of the preceding observation. It would be more correctly written thus: 'Ἐπὶ πενθημέρου λ' Αὐγούστου· ἐπὶ δὲ ἐξημέρου λά Αὐγούστου. Possibly the would-be corrector has substituted this for the words ἐπὶ πενθημέρου ἐπὶ δὲ ἐξημέρου λ', which may have completed the previous sentence as it was originally written, and which would state the truth if we might render ἐπὶ π. and ἐπὶ ἐ. respectively, "*after* a five-day supplement," and "*after* a six-day supplement;" and not "*in the year of* a five-day, and *in the year of* a six-day, supplement." So to translate would require a dative instead of a genitive after ἐπί. But the genitive may be defended on the ground that the scholiast had in view, not the Alexandrian, but the Roman year, in which at Alexandria the supplementary days were five or six. These days, as it will incidentally appear below, were regarded by the Greeks of Alexandria as a month, in ordinary years called μὴν πενθήμερος, in years of intercalation μὴν ἐξήμερος. Hence they also termed the first of these days νουμηνία. But the question as to the accuracy of the second scholiast's correction in the passage now quoted, we defer. At present we cite the passage for the sake of the original statement, or, as perhaps we should rather call it, *the first scholium*, stating that *the Thoth of Alexandria began with the Roman 29th of August*.

Further, to show that it was this day the Romans had in view when they ordered the day of their taking of Alexandria to be the commencement of a new era in Egypt, we now refer the reader to the tract of the Emperor Heraclius, printed in the Appendix to the *Dissertationes Cyprianicæ* of Dodwell, where we are taught how to convert days of the Roman into the corresponding days of the Alexandrian month. Here, besides the explanation that (unlike the Roman months, seven of which have 31 days, one 28 days, and four 30 days apiece) the twelve Alexandrian months consist every one alike of 30 days, it is noted that the September of the Alexandrians, by them called Thoth, and counted the first month of the twelve, begins three whole days before the Roman September, along with the 29th of the Roman August. As to the time when this testimony was given, observe that the Emperor Phocas was slain, and Heraclius crowned in his place, on the 4th of October A.D. 610: see Clinton, *Fast. Rom.* vol. ii. p. 160.

Next we append a proof, that so early as A.D. 146, no less than, as we have seen, in the seventh and tenth centuries after the Incarnation, the Roman 29th of August was the Alexandrian first of Thoth. This proof was first extracted by Scaliger from a marble (Gruter, p. 214). As given from Corsini by Clinton, *F. H.* vol. ii., Appendix, chap. 19, the words of the marble are these: τῷ [τῇ] πρὸ ά νωνῶν Μαΐων ἥ ἐστιν κατὰ 'Αλεξανδρεῖς Παχὼν ιά, Σέξτῳ 'Ερυκίῳ Κλάρῳ β', Γναίῳ Κλαυδίῳ Σιβήρῳ κωσ. Now the *first before the Nones of May* is the 6th of May: see the art. *Calendarium*, by Professor T. H. Key, in Smith's *Dict. of Gr. and Rom. Antiquities*; or *The Roman Calendar*, in Sir Harris Nicolas's *Chronology of History*. Again, the consulship of Sextus Erycius Clarus, the second time, and Cnæus Claudius Severus, was the year of our Lord 146: see Clinton's *F. R.* Thirdly, *Pakhon* is the ninth month both of the moving Egyptian year and of the fixed year of Alexandria: see for the first, Sir J. G. Wilkinson in Rawlinson's *Herodotus*, vol. ii. p. 283; and for the latter, Geo. Syncellus, pp. 7, 8 of Goar's Paris edition. Therefore, reckoned from the 29th of August, the 6th of May is the 251st day of the Julian Calendar of Rome, as of our own also; for 3 + 30 + 31 + 30 + 31 + 31 + 28 + 31 + 30 + 6 = 251. And so is the 11th of Pakhon the 251st day from the first of Thoth; for 30 × 8 + 11 = 251. Therefore the Alexandrian year began with the 29th of the Roman month Sextilis, that is, August, A.D. 146. Wherefore also this is concluded to have been the day of the Roman Calendar whereon, in the year B.C. 30 or U.C. 724, Alexandria was taken by the Romans under C. Cæsar Octaviauus, then for the fourth time consul, and having for his colleague M. Licinius Crassus. This day was the epoch whence the years of a new era, those of Augustus, were ordered to begin at Alexandria.

Thus the first year of Augustus, by Alexandrian reckoning, did not exactly coincide with the first of Augustus by the Egyptian computation of Ptolemy. By Dodwell's edition of the Table of Reigns used for the calculations of Claudius Ptolemy's Manual Tables of Astronomy, —that is, the Table of Reigns subsequent to Alexander's,—we perceive that the Egyptian first year of Augustus was identical with the 295th year of the era of Philip Aridæus. (This era, be it observed by the way, had been in use under the Lagidæ, of whom Cleopatra was the last, from the time of Ptolemy son of Lagus, the first of that Greek dynasty; for coins of Paphos and Kitium in Cyprus bearing the likeness and legend of a Ptolemæus exhibit the 39th and 49th years of the era. See Vaillant's *Hist. Ptolemæorum*, cited by Clinton, *F. H.* vol. iii., Appendix, chap. On the *Kings of Egypt*.)

Now, being the 425th year of Nabonassar (as we have proved already, and as is shown in our Table of the Years of Kings of Babylon from the first of Nabonassar to the first of Seleucus Nicator, in Section A), the first year of Philip Aridæus began, according to the Egyptian calculation of Claudius Ptolemy, at noon 12th November B.C. 324, that is, on the expiration of 424 years of 365 days apiece since noon the 26th of February B.C. 747, or from a first of Thoth with which, according to Egyptian rule, the first year of Nabonassar king of Babylon began. Therefore the 295th year of Philip Aridæus, or, as we have stated, the first year of the Roman dominion and of the reign in Egypt of Augustus, began, according to the native Egyptian mode of reckoning, after the lapse of 294 Egyptian years, or 294 Julian years all but 294 quarters of a day, from the beginning of the first of Philip Aridæus by the same reckoning. That is, the first of Augustus, by their computation, began at midnight with the Roman civil day the 31st of August B.C. 30. Thus there seems to be the difference of two whole civil days of Rome between the Alexandrian and the native Egyptian commencement of the first year of Augustus: according to the Egyptians, it began with the Roman 31st of August; according to the Alexandrian Greeks, with the Roman 29th of August. In reality we shall see there was but half this difference, that is, there was but the difference of a single Roman day between the two accounts; the rest of the apparent difference, that is, one day, being an error in the Roman Calendar of the year B.C. 30.

Theon tells us that the Egyptian first of Thoth coincided exactly with the Alexandrian day so called in the fifth year of Augustus. In the fragment printed by Dodwell of Theon's Commentary on Ptolemy's Manual Tables of Astronomy, we have instructions how (as a preliminary to astronomical calculations by the Manual Tables) to reduce any given Greek date of Alexandria to the corresponding point of the register of Egyptian time in the Manual Tables. And here our Alexandrian professor writes thus : γέγονε δὲ ἡ εἰρημένη διὰ ανξ' (1460) ἐτῶν ἀποκαταστασις, ἀπό τινος ἀρχῆς χρόνου (Note, B.C. 26 + 1460 = 1486), τῷ πέμπτῳ ἔτει Αὐγούστου βασιλείας· ὡς ἐκ τούτου πάλιν τοῦ χρόνου τὴν ἀρχὴν εἰληφέναι τοὺς Αἰγυπτίους προλαμβάνειν καθ' ἕκαστον ἐνιαυτὸν τῷ τετάρτῳ μέρει τῆς ἡμέρας. Nor is there any doubt as to the position intended, either of the first or of the fifth year of Augustus. For in the sequel it is argued from the Canon of Reigns subsequent to Alexander's, that from the beginning of the first of these, the reign of Philip Aridæus, to the beginning of Diocletian's, were 607 Egyptian years ; and from the beginning of Augustus to the beginning of Diocletian, a total of 313. Therefore the first of Augustus was the 295th, and the fifth of Augustus the 299th, year of Philip Aridæus. Of these two, it has already been shown that the former year begins in the middle of the night between the 30th and the 31st of August, that is, with the Roman day called *Pridie Calendas Septembris*, of the Julian year B.C. 30. The latter year of the two will begin four Julian years all but 24 hours, that is, 1460 days earlier, or at midnight between the 29th and the 30th of August, along with the Roman day called *Antediem tertium Calend. Septemb.* in the Julian year B.C. 26.

Now, this beginning of the Egyptian year of Philip Aridæus 299, and of Augustus five (that is, this 30th day of August B.C. 26), Theon, as we have seen, assures us, coincided exactly with the beginning, or first of Thoth, of the Alexandrian fifth year of Augustus. Therefore, according to Theon, the civil day of the Roman Calendar with which the Alexandrian first of Thoth coincided in B.C. 26, was the 30th of August ; whereas we have found it attested, *first* in a document followed by Geo. Syncellus, *secondly* in a special treatise by the Emperor Heraclius, and *thirdly* on a marble of the consuls of the year of our Lord 146, that the Alexandrian 1st of Thoth was the Roman 29th of August. To explain this difference of a day, we offer the following observations. In the year B.C. 46, by intercalations amounting in all to 96 days, Julius Cæsar, as *Pontifex Maximus*, had restored the Roman civil year to something like its old position in relation to the seasons of the solar year; and in order to keep it continually in the restored position, having increased its days to 365, he had ordered for the future *one day besides* to be intercalated every four years *before the Sixth of the Calends of March*, that is, at the point in the old Calendar where the month used to be intercalated when it was sought to readjust the months of the then lunar year to their former seasons in the solar year. The day was henceforth to be here intercalated (in the last of) every four such years as Julius Cæsar then constituted, and as have descended to ourselves from the Romans; because, according to the common Egyptian computation (long before followed by Calippus, as then by Sosigenes and other Greeks), the length of the solar year was 365 days and 6 hours, that is, was the quarter of one day greater than the length of the Egyptian civil year. But the great dictator did not live to superintend the execution of his edict as to intercalation, even on the first occasion. He was assassinated on the Ides of March in the year B.C. 44—a year called by Censorinus (*De die natali, cap.* 22) "THE SECOND JULIAN YEAR," when the consuls were, himself a fifth time, and Mark Antony the first time. The pontiffs, thus left, without an infallible head, to their own interpretation of the edict, and mistaking the year designated as the fourth year, though probably understanding the term in a more usual sense, had intercalated a day before the sixth of the Calends of March five times, instead of four times, before the capture of Alexandria by the dictator's adopted son C. Cæsar Octavianus, and the deaths of Antony and Cleopatra in B.C. 30. The five days intercalated being days during which the year as it were stood still, during which the progress of the numbering of ordinary month-days was suspended, the pontiffs had thus diminished the number of each month-day of the Calendar more by one unit than Julius Cæsar intended since their fifth intercalation. The edict had pointed out every fourth year for a year of intercalation; and they had not regarded these fourth years as the last of so many τετρα-ετηρίδες, *distinct periods of four times* 365 *days*, but in the count of the four years had included the year of previous intercalation as the first of the four. They commenced their reckoning from *and with* the year B.C. 46, in the course of which Julius Cæsar had put in 96 days, instead of from *and after* that year. Hence they intercalated a day (*bisextum*, as it was called) in February B.C. 43; then, counting another four years from and *with*, instead of from and *after*, this year 43, they intercalated a *bisextum* in February B.C. 40. Altogether.

between the year B.C. 46, when Julius Cæsar made the great intercalation of 96 days, and the year B.C. 30, when Alexandria was taken by the Cæsar Octavianus, afterwards Augustus, they had intercalated in the years B.C. 43, 40, 37, 34, and 31, whereas they should have intercalated four times only, in what Censorinus would have designated *the 4th, 8th, 12th, and 16th Julian years*, being the years B.C. 42, 38, 34, and 30. Accordingly, the day of the taking of Alexandria, which should have ranked in the Calendar as *antediem iii. Calend. Septemb.*, that is, the 30th of Sextilis, afterwards August, was there numbered *antediem iv. Calend. Septemb.*, that is, the 29th of August. The number of the day had been put back one further than the rule of the Calendar required. Wherefore also the morrow of the capture, which happened to be the 1st of Thoth, the Egyptian New-year's day, stood as the 30th of August in the pontifical Calendar, though, if Julius Cæsar had been alive, it would have been named the 31st. So much for the error of the pontifical Calendar at Rome in the year B.C. 30, whereby the day of the capture of Alexandria and the following Egyptian New-year's day stood as the 29th and 30th, instead of the 30th and 31st, of August respectively.

But in B.C. 26, when the Roman, or, as it was afterwards termed, the Augustan, reign had lasted in Egypt 1460 days, or four whole years of the country,—that is, on the expiration of the year of Philip Aridæus 298,—the ensuing New-year's day, the 1st of the Thoth of the fifth year of Augustus and 299th of Philip, had receded 24 hours in the Calendar, or, in other words, had arrived 24 hours sooner, in the circle of the Julian year. In this year, therefore, the 1st of Thoth by the native Egyptian reckoning coincided with the anniversary of the Roman conquest, the New-year's day of the Egypto-Julian Calendar, that had been adopted at Alexandria after the conquest. By the pontifical Roman Calendar, the one as well as the other was the fourth day before the Calends of September, that is, the 29th of August; though, had the intercalations been made at Rome according to Julius Cæsar's meaning, the day would have been the 30th of August, or third before the Calends of September.

For though, in the course of the last four years, the number of each month-day in the Roman Calendar, through the yet ruling misconstruction of the plan of it, had again been put back or diminished *by one*,—since an undue intercalation in February B.C. 28,—the number of the 1st day of Thoth in the Roman Calendar had been restored to where it stood before, by the intercalating at Alexandria of a sixth supplementary day at the end of the year which completed the first Four-year Period of the new era and the Egypto-Julian Calendar. So in B.C. 26, the native or true Egyptian 1st of Thoth coincided with the Alexandrian 1st of Thoth in that Roman day which was counted the 29th, but would have been the 30th, of August in a rightly-kept Roman Calendar.

They of Alexandria, to whom the care was confided of the new Egypto-Julian Calendar (for the first day of which this 29th, that should have been the 30th, of August in B.C. 30 had been fixed upon by the senate and people of Rome), understood the principle of the Julian year better than the Roman pontiffs. The civil year in actual use consisted already of 365 days,—a duration, as it was supposed, just six hours less than that of a solar year; so that to compensate its gain upon the solar year, at every revolution, in the speediest possible manner, and to fix it in relation to the equinoxes and solstices, they merely added (as we have said already) another, that is a sixth, supplementary day at the end of the 12th Egyptian month Mesori of every period of four full ordinary years, making their total of days 1461 instead of 1460. This day made the last year of the four to consist of 366 days; and it seems to have been duly intercalated at the end of the 4th, 8th, 12th, 16th, 20th, 24th, 28th, 32d Angustan years of Alexandria, and so on without any irregularity (through the successive times of Claudius Ptolemy, of his commentator Theon, and of the Emperor Heraclius), down to the days of Georgius Syncellus. Thus their day was intercalated six months later indeed, but in the same Roman year in which Julius Cæsar had intended the Roman day to be intercalated, that is to say, in the years B.C. 26, 22, 18, 14, 10, 6, 2; A.D. 3, 7, and so on. Had the Roman pontiffs made the prescribed intercalation in the intended years from and after B.C. 46, the Alexandrian New-year's day, or first of the Thoth of the Egypto-Julian year, would always have coincided with the same day of the Roman Calendar. And that day would have been the 30th of August. For though the intercalation of a day at Rome just before the sixth of the Calends of March, making a second such sixth or doubling that day in the February, by retarding the count of the following days in the Roman Calendar, would, for six months after, have advanced the relative position of the several Alexandrian month-days, making them to be one day earlier or higher than they would have been in the Roman Calendar, yet afterwards, in August, the intercalation of a day at Alexandria at the end of the usual five days' supplement that followed the 12th month Mesori, and closed the year, would have restored the old correspondence between Alexandrian day and Roman day for the next three years and six months. For the day being a pause, and for the purpose of intercalation regarded as a sixth supplementary day of the old year, instead of the new-year's first of Thoth, and the count of the month-days being thus suspended for one day in the Alexandrian, while it was being continued in the Roman Calendar, the position of the first day of Thoth on the morrow, and of every Alexandrian month-day afterwards, would have been again lowered by a day, and brought back to the correspondence with the Roman Calendar which would have existed if there had been no intercalation made either at Rome or at Alexandria.

But, in fact, the Alexandrian 1st of Thoth, though in three years out of four it coincided with the 29th of the Roman August, *did*, in the years of Rome when a sixth supplementary day was counted at the end of the Alexandrian year, coincide with the 30th of August. We prove the assertion thus: In prescribing how to find a given Roman day in the nomenclature and numeration of the Alexandrian Calendar, and (as to a date in an ordinary Roman year) having informed us that the September of the Alexandrians, which they themselves called Thoth, began three (whole) days before the Roman September,—namely, with the 29th of August,—the Emperor Heraclius (in a tract already cited, and given us by Dodwell in the Appendix to his *Dissertationes Cyprianicæ*) next proceeds to the case of a date in the *Bisextum* or Bissextile year of Rome. He tells us that in the year of Rome preceding the Bisextum,—that is, says he, when the Alexandrians *get their full*, receiving the one day wanted to make up their complement of 1461 days in four years,—in that year (and *that only*), after their August, which with them is called Mesori, instead of the five-day month, they make up one of six days; so that the September, which they call Thoth, begins but two full days before the Roman September, with the 30th of the Roman August. The emperor's words are these: ὅτι δὲ δίσεξτόν ἐστιν, ἐν τῷ πρὸ τοῦ δισέξτου ἐνιαυτῷ, τουτέστιν ὅτι πληρωθῶσι οἱ 'Αλεξανδρεῖς, ἐκείνῳ τῷ ἐνιαυτῷ καὶ μόνῳ, μετὰ τὸν Αὔγουστον, τὸν λεγόμενον παρ' αὐτοῖς Μεσωρί, ἀντὶ τοῦ πενθημέρου μηνός, ἐξήμερον ἀποτελοῦσιν.

Thus it appears, that even after the error of the pontiffs at Rome had been discovered, and intercalation had been suspended long enough to recover, or nearly to recover, the position which had been overstepped, the intercalation was not resumed in the several Julian years at first intended, but in the February of the years next to them respectively; being the February next after an intercalation duly made at Alexandria.

It was not till after they had made twelve years bissextile instead of nine in the first 36 Julian years, according to Macrobius (*Saturnal.* i. 14, quoted by Clinton, *F. H. Tables*, B.C. 45), that the error was discovered. We have seen already that the first day alike of the Alexandrian and of the native Egyptian Thoth in B.C. 26 was by the Roman Calendar a 29th of August that should have been the 30th. In the following Julian year, B.C. 25, an intercalation by the pontiffs at Rome put back the Alexandrian New-year's day to the 28th of August; and here it remained till the year 19 B.C.; for the intercalation at Rome in B.C. 22 was balanced in its effect by that at Alexandria six months afterwards, in the same year. In B.C. 19, however, through an intercalation at Rome, the first of Thoth at Alexandria came to be the 27th of August in the Roman Calendar. An intercalation the next year, B.C. 18, at Alexandria brought it on again to the 28th, where it continued to stand in the year B.C. 17. But the year after, in B.C. 16, through an intercalation at Rome, the Alexandrian New-year's day fell back again to the 27th of August in the Roman nomenclature of days; and there it stood also in B.C. 15. But in B.C. 14 an intercalation at Alexandria restored its place to the 28th. Again, in B.C. 13, the march of the Roman days having been retarded by an intercalation in February, the Alexandrian first of Thoth arrived comparatively earlier, and coincided with the day numbered in the Roman Calendar the 27th of August. There it remained till the year B.C. 6; for in B.C. 10 two intercalations—one at Rome, the other at Alexandria—producing equal results in opposite directions, caused no change of correspondence between the days of the two calendars after the last intercalation had undone the effect of the first.

It was after the intercalation made at Rome in B.C. 10 that the erroneous interpretation of Julius Cæsar's edict was discovered, that had been followed for six-and-thirty years by the pontiffs. Perhaps it had been noticed in the August of that year, and had been loudly complained of, that for the last 16 years the Alexandrian first of Thoth had never fallen on the 29th (which should have been described as the 30th) of August, according to the decree of B.C. 30; but had coincided nine times with the 28th, and seven times with the 27th, day of that month.

Inquiry must have proved that the fault did not lie with those who managed the Calendar at Alexandria, but with the pontiffs at Rome. The conqueror of Alexandria then put forth an edict, that 12 years should pass without intercalation at Rome,—*annos duodecim sine interkalari die transigi*, as Macrobius says,—thereby, as it was calculated, making those years as much shorter than the like number of solar years, as the previous 36 years of the Calendar had been made longer than the solar years with which they had been supposed to coincide. Afterwards intercalation was to be resumed at the intervals really intended by the edict of Julius Cæsar; or, as Macrobius says, *post hoc unum diem secundum ordinationem Cæsaris quinto quoque incipiente anno interkalari jussit.*

Accordingly, one would have expected that when 36 + 12 = 48 Julian years, and therewith 12 four-year periods from the epoch of Julius Cæsar's reformation of the Calendar, had gone by, along with the year of our Lord by vulgar computation 3, a thirteenth four-year period would have begun with A.D. 4, and the intercalation of one day in four years before the sixth of the Calends of March would have been made in the years of our Lord 7, 11, 15, being the Julian years 52, 56, 60, and so on; that is, in the same years wherein intercalation was actually made at Alexandria.

But this, it seems, was not done. The Julian years 49, 53, 57, 61, and so on, being the years of our Lord, as vulgarly computed, 4, 8, 12, 16, and so forth, were made the bissextile years: the first *fifth year* (according to the new designation of the year of intercalation employed by Cæsar Augustus, *quinto quoque anno*) being found by beginning to count, not with the Julian year 48 or year 3 of our Lord, the last of the 12 years which Augustus would seem to have ordered to be let go by without intercalation, but with the year before our vulgar era,— the year in which the pontiffs, according to their interpretation of the terms of Julius Cæsar's edict, would have intercalated a day for the third time since the date of Augustus's edict suspending intercalation, and for the fifteenth time since the reformation of the Calendar in B.C. 46.

We will establish what has now been asserted as to the years which were made bissextile at Rome, when intercalation was resumed, by such proof as we have to give. That intercalation was not again put into practice at Rome, as we should have expected, in the Julian year 52, or seventh year of Christ by the vulgar computation, appears, *first*, from the fact that this is not a bissextile year by the present rule, which yet we ourselves can show to have been the one followed so early as the year of Christ 140, by means of the *Greek Consular Fasti*, printed in Dodwell's Appendix to his *Dissertationes Cyprianicæ*. By this rule leap year, or the bissextile year, is the last of a sum of years of Christ of the vulgar era divisible without a remainder by four. But that the year 7 of Christ was not bissextile, appears also from the fact that it was the year of Rome in which the intercalary day was inserted at Alexandria. For if the first intercalation there was made in August B.C. 26, as Theon testifies, then in August A.D. 7 the like must have been done for the *ninth* time. Now the Emperor Heraclius, as above quoted, shows us that intercalation was made at Alexandria in the year of the Roman Calendar before the bissextile year of Rome. Therefore, as we desired to prove, the year *Seven* of our era was not a bissextile year. Nor, again, was the bissextile year *Eight* of our era the first year that was made bissextile at Rome after the expiration of the period during which, by the order of Augustus, intercalation was suspended; because, if it had been such first bissextile year since B.C. 10, the Alexandrian first of Thoth which occurred in the previous year of our era *Seven*, and which followed the ninth intercalation of a 1461st day since the commencement of the era, the day of the capture of Alexandria by Augustus, would have been thereby carried on or delayed to the 31st of August, four whole days later than where it stood, as we have seen, in B.C. 10, when intercalation was interrupted at Rome for three turns to come. This effect would have been produced by the three intercalations made at Alexandria in B.C. 6, B.C. 2, and A.D. 3, while it is admitted no compensating delays in the count of time were made at Rome, added to the one made at Alexandria in A.D. 7; if (which we deny) intercalation was not renewed at Rome till A.D. 8, and therefore the delay created by the intercalation at Alexandria in A.D. 7 was uncompensated. And with the 31st of August in the Roman Calendar the Alexandrian

first of Thoth would have continued to correspond in *the year following an intercalation*, that is, in the first year of every four-year period
to come, after the one ending thus in A.D. 7; while in the last three
years of every such future period it would have been the 30th of
August. This, indeed, seems to be asserted as the real fact of the
matter by the *second scholiast*, as we call the penman of the second
marginal observation in a passage above quoted from Geo. Syncellus.
But the Emperor Heraclius attests that in every year of Rome in which
the Alexandrians had six instead of the usual five supplementary days
after their 12th month Mesori, the first of Thoth following was the
Roman 30th of August; though in other years of Rome it was a day
earlier, the 29th of August. Apparently, then, it follows, that after
the interruption that took place under the edict of Augustus, the first
fresh intercalation was made by doubling the sixth day before the
Calends of March in A.D. 4. For in the previous year of Rome, A.D.
3, there had a third intercalation been duly made at Alexandria; while
to remedy past mistakes no intercalation had been allowed at Rome
since the year B.C. 10, when intercalation had been made both at
Rome and at Alexandria. And these three intercalations had brought
on the new year's first of Thoth from August the 27th, where, as we
have shown, it stood in B.C. 10, to August the 30th, where it stood
in A.D. 3. And here, Heraclius tells us, it always stood in his time
after an Alexandrian intercalation; that is, in the year of Rome preceding the Roman bissextile year. Therefore the year 4 of Christ was
bissextile; and the first bissextile year after Augustus's suspension of
intercalation at Rome. The same fourth year of our era is also proved
to have been bissextile by our present rule (the antiquity of which we
have already contributed to show), because it is the last year of a sum
of years of our era divisible without a remainder by four. It was undoubtedly fixed upon as the first of the new series of bissextile years
because it was the *fifth year* current from the year B.C. 1, when, for
the third time since the intercalation in B.C. 10, a day, according to
the pontifical interpretation of the term *fourth year* in Julius Cæsar's
edict, should have been, but in obedience to the edict of Augustus had
not been, intercalated.

It would seem, then, that the edict of Augustus was construed to
order three omissions of the intercalary day *at times of pontifical intercalation*, that is, in the *fourth year*, which, by the counting of the
pontiffs, included the year of last intercalation, and happened thrice
in the space from B.C. 10 to B.C. 1; namely, in the years B.C. 7, 4,
and 1. For it would be consistent with this construction to order
that the next bissextile year, after the times omitted, should be the
year of the consuls Sextus Ælius Catus and C. Sentius Saturninus, the
49th Julian year by the computation of Censorinus, and the fourth
year of the Christian era. For intercalation, when resumed, was by
the edict of Augustus to take place *every fifth year*, by which expres-

sion the pontiffs would understand what the *fourth year* of the former edict had been intended to convey. Now, the fourth year of our era is the fifth year counted from and with the first year before our era. So, too, the next bissextile year, being the Julian 53d and the 8th of our era, is the fifth year counted from and with the year of the previous intercalation. Thenceforward, in short, from bissextile year to bissextile year, extremes included, the space was five years.

We have cited the expression of a scholiast upon the chronography of Geo. Syncellus, which seems to assert that after an ordinary Alexandrian year, the next year's first of Thoth was the Roman 30th of August; but that after the last year of an Alexandrian τετραετηρις, *four-year period*, it was the 31st of August. It has also been observed that this would really have been the state of the correspondence between the calendars of Rome and Alexandria, if, after the temporary suspension ordered by Augustus of Julius Cæsar's edict in respect of intercalation, the first bissextile year of the new series had been the Roman year counted by us as the eighth of our Lord, and by Censorinus as the 53d Julian year. But, as evidence of the actual usage, the scholiast's assertion is not only contradictory to that of a previous annotator on the Syncellus's chronography, and to the view of the Syncellus himself, it is also overruled by the testimonies we have cited of the Emperor Heraclius, and of the ancient marble adduced by Scaliger. All agree that the first day of the Alexandrian Thoth was (in three years out of every four) the 29th of August by the Roman Calendar.

The scholiast's assertion seems to proceed upon no evidence of calendars that were, or had been, in use with Romans or with disciples of Alexandrian schools; nor yet upon a belief that the eighth year of our era was the first Roman year since the 10th before our era that was made bissextile. It was probably founded on an observation, which we have ourselves justified by the evidence of Theon, that in the year B.C. 26, when the Alexandrian first of Thoth coincided exactly with the Egyptian, this day was properly the 30th of August, and the morrow properly the 31st, though, by the mistake of the pontiffs, these days stood in the Roman Calendar as the 29th and 30th respectively. The day also in the year 30 B.C., of which the Alexandrian first of Thoth was ordained to be the anniversary, had in like manner been marked with a number too low by one, when the news came that Cæsar Octavianus had entered Alexandria as conqueror on the 29th of August. · If, since the Calends of January B.C. 45, the first day of what Censorinus teaches us to call the first Julian year, the edict of Julius Cæsar concerning bissextile years had been acted on according to its true intention, the day when Cæsar Octavianus took possession of Alexandria would have been, according to the Roman Calendar, the 30th of Sextilis, the month afterwards called August. But the pontiffs (as we have cited sufficient ancient testimony to prove), by having made five years instead of four bissextile, had reduced the number of days counted as month-days since the first day of the first Julian year by one more than the edict really required. At the date of Octavianus's entry into Alexandria, one day, that had been unduly reckoned a duplicate of the sixth before the Calends of March, had to be added to the number of every day in the Roman Calendar if one would have exhibited them according to the intention of Julius Cæsar.

This error in the numerical designation of the Roman days had grown from *one* to as many as *three too few* when it was discovered, or at least brought into public notice, after the pontifical intercalation, whereby the year B.C. 10, or 36th Julian year, was made bissextile. But it would have been completely retrieved, if, under the edict of Augustus then issued, intercalation had been suspended as long as mere regard for the original intention of Julius Cæsar would have dictated, and if no year before the Seventh of our era, or 52d Julian year, had been again made bissextile. Had this been done, eight intercalations of a day at Alexandria against seven intercalations at Rome would have taken place before that year arrived, and since the Augustan era of Alexandria began in B.C. 30. The one intercalation made at Alexandria more than at Rome would have compensated the error that already existed in the Roman Calendar in August B.C. 30, and which, as we have explained, was owing to the pontiffs having made five years bissextile instead of four since B.C. 46. The day when the era of Augustus at Alexandria commenced had thus been made to correspond with the 29th instead of the 30th of August ; and if, under the edict of Augustus, by which the pontifical error was amended, and the practice for the future prescribed, the first bissextile year of the new series had been the seventh instead of the fourth of our era, the Alexandrian first day of Thoth—the 33d anniversary—would have been retarded by one day, and brought to the 30th of August, the true Julian day of the capture of the city by Augustus. And with this day of the Roman Calendar the Alexandrian New-year's day would have continually corresponded afterwards, unaffected by future intercalations, because the one at Rome making it a day earlier, and the one at Alexandria making it a day later in the Roman Calendar, would have thenceforth happened in the course of the same Alexandrian as well as Roman year.

But in this case, the act of the senate at Rome in B.C. 30, by which it was ordered that the fourth before the Calends of September, or, as we say, the 29th of August, should be the New-year's day at Alexandria, would never more have been literally obeyed. Perhaps it was to prevent this contradiction, and to preserve the due yearly commemoration of a day marked as a good and happy one in the Calendar, that a fresh intercalation, though arithmetically premature, was made at Rome, as we have proved, in A.D. 4 ; the result of which was, that the fourth before the Calends of September became the Alexandrian 1st of Thoth in three years out of every four.

To help ourselves through the foregoing argument, we did what some reader may find useful for the same purpose. We wrote down in a column the numbers denoting the successive years from B.C. 46, when Julius Cæsar first restored the position of the Roman year by intercalating 96 days, to A.D. 7; and then marked off on one side the years in which a day should have been intercalated to retard the march of the New Civil Year, according to his intention, for the future, distinguishing among them the years in which a like intercalation at the end of the Alexandrian year was actually made; for these, as it happened, were likewise years of Rome that should have been bissextile. We then marked off, on the other side of the column of 53 years, those years which were actually made bissextile by the pontiffs at Rome, together with those which would have been so made according to the same rule, had not Augustus interposed, after the pontiffs had made the year B.C. 10 bissextile, with an edict forbidding intercalation for three turns to come, and directing that the bissextile year afterwards should be always the fifth year, counted from and with the year that was (or would have been) the last bissextile year. On this side of the column also we took care to distinguish, in the series thus brought out, the years that would have been from the years that were made bissextile. To do this aright, it was only necessary to be provided with the above-cited testimony of Macrobius concerning the error of the pontiffs, and the remedy ordered by Augustus in respect of the Roman Calendar. And, as to the years of Rome in which the march of the Alexandrian year was retarded by the intercalation of a sixth *epagomené*, before it became complete, we had only to make use of the testimony of Theon, establishing the fact that such addition of a day was made at the end of the fourth year of Augustus at Alexandria, that is, in B.C. 26. This testimony is implied in a passage we have quoted, where Theon states the result, the exact coincidence of the Alexandrian with the native Egyptian New-year's day on the morrow of the intercalation, the first day of the fifth year of Augustus.

The series first obtained, of years which should have been bissextile at Rome, and years which, moreover, were marked by an intercalation at Alexandria, consists of the years B.C. 42, 38, 34, 30, 26, 22, 18, 14, 10, 6, 2, and A.D. 3 and 7. The years of the other series are B.C. 43, 40, 37, 34, 31, 28, 25, 22, 19, 16, 13, 10, 7, 4, 1,—the last three being those which the pontiffs would have made bissextile, had not their procedure been interdicted by Augustus. Nothing more was required for our purpose, except knowing that Augustus became master of Alexandria in August B.C. 30, and that the anniversary of the conquest in B.C. 26 was also the first day of the Egyptian 299th year of Philip Aridæus.

The difference of a day between mathematicians and Roman annalists in the date of the capture of Alexandria, is now accounted for. It is traced to a mismanagement of the Julian Calendar at Rome for six-and-thirty years, which it cost another twelve years to remedy. But when we had completed this solution, we found that the same source of the difference was long ago conjectured by the famous Scaliger. Georgius Syncellus's first editor, Goar, refers upon the subject to Scaliger, *De emendatione temporum*, lib. iv., and *Isag. Canon.* xxxi. 12, also to Petavius, *De doct. temp.* lib. x. cap. 71. According to Dodwell's oft-cited Appendix (*Prolegomena*, § 8), Scaliger, not having the aid of the fragment of Theon which Dodwell in that Appendix first gave to the world, supposed that the first day of Thoth in the year of Philip Aridæus 295 (the first of the native Egyptian years of Augustus) was the day of the taking of Alexandria with which the series of Alexandrian or Egypto-Julian years began. On this supposition, the difference between the pontifical Calendar and the true Julian time would have been *two days*; for the first of Thoth in B.C. 30 coincided with the 31st of August by the true time, and Alexandria was taken on the 29th of August by the pontifical reckoning. It is now certain, from the testimony of Theon, that the New-year's day of the vague Egyptian year did not coincide with that of the Egypto-Julian year of Alexandria till on the arrival of the fifth year of Augustus in Egypt. Theon's date is τῷ πέμπτῳ ἔτει Αὐγούστου; and this must be held to explain his other expression of the same, μετὰ ἓ ἔτη τῆς ἀρχῆς τοῦ (read τῆς) Αὐγούστου βασιλείας. Accordingly (he adds), *from this date the Egyptians had taken their beginning to get again ahead* (of the solar year supposed to measure 365¼ days) *by the fourth part of a day every year*: ὡς ἐκ τούτου πάλιν τοῦ χρόνου τὴν ἀρχὴν εἰληφέναι τοὺς Αἰγυπτίους προλαμβάνειν καθ ἕκαστον ἐνιαυτὸν τῷ τετάρτῳ μέρει τῆς ἡμέρας. Here are words from which it may certainly be concluded (though Dodwell appears to find fault with Petavius for having so concluded), that before the fifth anniversary of the day when Augustus took Alexandria and began there his reign in fact, there had been a day intercalated in the Alexandrian reckoning of years. It may also be presumed that, according to the same rule which was followed afterwards, this day was put into the Calendar at the end of the fourth year, making the fourth year to contain 366 instead of 365 days, and the whole four years 1461 instead of 1460 days. Secondly, it may safely be concluded that the first day of this fourth-year period, the day of the entry of Cæsar Octavianus into Alexandria, was but one day behind the Egyptian first of Thoth; that is, was the last of the five ἐπαγόμεναι or supplementary days of the year of Philip Aridæus 294. How it came to pass that the day of the capture was counted among the Romans the 29th of August, while the first day of the Thoth of the year of Philip 295 is calculated to have been the 31st of August, we have shown. Prideaux, in his *Connection of the Old and New Testaments*, vol. iv. pp. 301-303, does not mention Scaliger, but follows him in supposing that the day which began the Alexandrian era of Augustus was the first day of the civil year of Egypt, counted as the 295th of Philip Aridæus, which day should have stood as the 31st of August in the Roman Calendar. And as the day of the taking of Alexandria was certainly counted the 29th of August in that Calendar, the erroneous supposition leads him to believe that the error in the Calendar of the pontiffs amounted to two days in B.C. 30.

The fact, however, attested by Theon is, that the day of the capture of Alexandria did not coincide with the Egyptian first of Thoth till the 299th year of Philip arrived in B.C. 26; whence we conclude that a sixth supplementary day had been added to the fourth year of Augustus at Alexandria. This conclusion seems to be confirmed by the direct testimony of a no contemptible authority, discernible though contained in a confused statement of Georgius Syncellus's. The passage is referred to by Dodwell, but simply to reject its evidence as to what was the year of Alexandria that first was supplemented by a 366th day; just as he denies our conclusion from the words of Theon, which is the conclusion of Petavius. For the whole passage, which deserves much attention, see Syncell., Paris ed., pp. 312, 313. But the portion we speak of is this: κατὰ δὲ Πανόδωρον κβ΄ ἔτος ἦν Αὐγούστου (that is, it was so *when the Egyptian year began at the same point of time with the Alexandrian*) διὰ τὸ τοὺς πολλοὺς κατὰ τὸ ις΄ ἔτος τῆς Αὐγούστου βασιλείας τὴν Ἀλεξανδρείας ἅλωσιν ἱστορεῖν, καὶ τοὺς τούτου χρόνους τῆς βασιλείας ἐντεῦθεν λογίζεσθαι· μιᾶ ἦν ἀρξαμένην ἔτει ἑ Αὐγούστου τεθῆναι τὴν τετραετηρικὴν ἡμέραν· καὶ μέχρι τοῦ νῦν οὕτω καθ᾽ Ἕλληνας ἤτοι Ἀλεξανδρεῖς ψηφίζεσθαι τοὺς ἀστρονομικοὺς κανόνας ἐν ταῖς ἐκλείψεσι τῶν δύο Φωστήρων, κ.τ.λ. Hence it appears that the Egyptian chronographer Panodorus, whom we have already had occasion to introduce, living in the reign of the Emperor Arcadius, pleaded general consent that the intercalary day at the end of four years, or 1460 days, was first added at Alexandria in the fifth year of the reign of Augustus, reckoned from the taking of Alexandria. Here we may understand the fifth Roman year, counting the year 30 B.C., when Alexandria was taken, for the first year; and the year 26 B.C., when the first intercalation in the Alexandrian era was made, for the fifth year. And thus our conclusion from Theon will be confirmed. As to the other alleged point of general agreement, that Alexandria was taken in the 16th year of the (prior) reign of Augustus, it may be observed, that though the year 30 B.C. was not the 16th of Augustus's power, even reckoned, as by many it was, from the Ides of March B.C. 44, it was, however, what Censorinus teaches us to call *the* 16*th Julian year*, or 16th year of the new Roman Calendar, which came first into use on the 1st of January B.C. 45, after the restoration of the months to their seasons in the preceding year.

But our Syncellus appears to confound the Alexandrian intercalation with the Roman,—the addition of a sixth supplementary day to the

year of Alexandria in the August of the Roman year B.C. 26, with the insertion of a second sixth before the Calends of March, or a second 24th of February, improperly made by the managers of the Roman Calendar in the year B.C. 25. Two passages may be pointed out :—
1. The first is at p. 312, B, of the Paris, or p. 590 of the Bonn edition, the beginning of the same paragraph from which the citation of Panodorus has just been quoted. Here, though by and by at the end of the same page of the Paris edition he places the ἀποκατάστασις or restitution in position of the Egyptian first day of Thoth in the 5471st year of the World and 15th of Augustus (at Rome),—agreeably, as it seems, with the supposition above noted of Scaliger,—he affirms that in the 5472d year of the World, and the sixth year from the taking of Alexandria, coinciding with the 15th of Augustus (which he seems to reckon from the Ides of March B.C. 44), "*the Bisextum, as it is called, was put forth by Augustus Cæsar and the scientific men of that time.*"
2. The second place we point to is to be found at p. 309, A, of the Paris ed., and is part of an abstract from Africanus. The two parentheses, however, we have ourselves inserted to fill up manifest gaps in the expression of our author's meaning : the first is our own suggestion; for the second we have followed the example of others. Ἡν Ὀλυμπιὰς ρπθ. (Ἡ τετραετηρικὴ ἡμέρα προετίθη ὑπὸ Αὐγούστου Καίσαρος) ἥτις πρὸ ςʹ Καλανδῶν Μαρτίων, κατὰ Ἀντιοχεῖς κδʹ (ἔτει) ἤχθη· διʹ ἧς ἐπὶ τῶν ἰδίων ὅρων ἔστη ὁ ἐνιαυτός. The 189th Olympic festival, opening the year at midsummer B.C. 24, is put for the Roman year B.C. 24. But as the fourth year of the 187th Olympiad (called also the 5472d of the World) shortly before, on the same authority as it would seem of Africanus, had been assigned, instead of the third year of the same, as the year of the capture of Alexandria, this year of the 189th Olympiad, or rather this year B.C. 24, should here, by a like error, designate the year B.C. 25 for the Roman bissextile year. Again, since (as the reader may find it demonstrated by Clinton) the era of Antioch began (with the month Dius) in autumn B.C. 49, it follows that the 24th year of that era here given by Africanus, began with Dius in B.C. 26 that is, later in that year of Rome than the introduction of a sixth supplementary day to fill up the previous four-year period at Alexandria, and than the commencement of the fifth Egypto-Julian year of Augustus in that city, which happened at the same moment as the commencement of the native Egyptian 299th year of Philip Aridæus. Thus the Roman intercalation erroneously made in February B.C. 25, appears to be substituted by our Syncellus for the famous first Alexandrian intercalation in August B.C. 26.

H

To what has been said on the Canon of Reigns subsequent to Alexander's,—the Table of Years of Reign beginning with the first of Philip

Aridæus, as reckoned by the Egyptians, at noon the 12th of Nov. B.C. 324, and inserted down to his own time by Claudius Ptolemy in his *Manual Canons of Astronomy*,—we add an epitomé of the same to show how it branches off from the series of years which we have given above, in Section A, of reigns at Babylon from the first year of Nabonassar to the first of Seleucus Nicator. Our epitomé, however, is carried down only to the last year of the Emperor Phocas, the predecessor of Heraclius on the Roman throne.

Kings.	Years of Reign.	Totals.		End of each Total, calculated from 11½ Nov. B.C. 324 and 25¼ Feb. B.C. 747.
		Years of Philip.	Years of Nabonassar.	
Philip Aridæus, . . .	1	1	425	11¼ Nov. B.C. 323
Ptolemy son of Lagus, first as lieutenant, afterwards as king (besides the last two years of his life, which are counted to his son, then his partner on the throne of Egypt), reigned . .	38	39	463	1¾ Nov. B.C. 285
Nine other Lagidæ from Ptolemy Philadelphus to Cleopatra, . . .	255	294	718	30 Aug. B.C. 30
Twenty-six Roman sovereigns, from Augustus to Diocletian's predecessor Carus, .	313	607	1031	12¾ June A.D. 284
Twenty others, from Diocletian to Phocas, the predecessor of Heraclius, ...	326	933	1357	23¼ Mar. A.D. 610

On this Table it is to be observed, that the numbers of years in the second column assigned to Aridæus Philip, and to Ptolemy son of Lagus, respectively, that is 1 + 38 years, are a corrected distribution of the total. These thirty-nine years, in the Canon of Reigns published by Petavius and Dodwell, are assigned thus:

(*At Babylon*), Reign of Philip Aridæus,   7 years. Total, 7 years of Philip.
   „   „   another Alexander, 12 years.   „ 19 years of Philip.
(*In Egypt*),   „ Ptolemæus son of Lagus, 20 years.   „ 39 years of Philip.

We have here a corruption, due to critics less unscrupulous or more skilful than those who produced the Church Canon out of Ptolemy's

Khaldæan Canon, inasmuch as they respected totals while they meddled with particulars. Just such critics, however, were they who produced Georgius Syncellus's copy of the Khaldæan Canon; where the total number of years of Nabonassar that had elapsed before the reign of Cyrus is respected, and yet, in order to assign 1 + 1 + 17 additional years to the three reigns intervening between Nebukhadrezzar's and that of Cyrus, just so many, or 11 + 8 years, are taken away from the two predecessors of Nebukhadrezzar's father Nabopolassar.

Philip Aridæus was murdered by Olympias, mother of Alexander the Great, in the year of Demogenes, the fourth arkhon of the 115th Olympiad at Athens, after a reign of six years and four months. So says Diodorus, xix. 2, 11. For the Olympic year, see Porphyry of Tyre, both in the Greek and in Mai's Armenian version (translated) of Eusebius: *Fragm. Historic. Græc.* vol. iii. p. 697. See also the comparison of Diodorus's arkhons with those of Dionysius, *de Dinarcho*, instituted by Clinton, in *F. H.* vol. ii., *Introduction*, pp. xiii. xiv. Omitting fractions, Justin says, xiv. 5, Aridæus had reigned six years. His reign is measured *from the death of Alexander*, near the end of the arkhon Hegesias, say 13th June B.C. 323, to his own death after Demogenes became arkhon at Athens in B.C. 317. The arkhons officiating during this interval were Hegesias (the first arkhon of the 114th Olympiad), Kephisodorus, Philokles, Arkhippus, Neækhmus, Apollodorus, Arkhippus, Demogenes, and the duration of Philip Aridæus's reign estimated from them is six whole years and two fragments of a year. Diodorus, however, xviii. 2, places the (actual) succession of Philip Aridæus, not under Hegesias, but under the following arkhon Kephisodorus.

The seven years given to the reign of Philip Aridæus by the corrupter of Ptolemy's *Table of Reigns subsequent to Alexander's* commence with the year of Egypt in the course of which Alexander died, that is, the year of Nabonassar, according to the Egyptians, 425, at mid-day 12th Nov. B.C. 324. But they were not distinct from and followed by the 12 years assigned by the same would-be amender to *another Alexander*. This Alexander was a posthumous son of the conqueror by Roxana, who was eight months gone in her pregnancy when her royal consort died: see Justin, xiii. 2. He was murdered along with his mother by order of Cassander in the year when Simonides was arkhon at Athens, after the peace was concluded between Cassander, Ptolemy, and Lysimakhus on the one side, and Antigonus on the other: see Diod. xix. 105.

We have already given the series of eight arkhons from Hegesias, under whom Alexander the Conqueror died in June B.C. 323, to Demogenes, under whom Philip Aridæus was murdered. Between the last of this series and Simonides, under whom Roxana and her son Alexander met the fate of Aridæus, these five arkhons intervened:

Demokleides, Praxibulus, Nikodôrus, Theophrastus, and Polemon. This last gave place to Simonides at midsummer B.C. 311. Thus 12 whole years had elapsed since Alexander's death at that of Roxana's son Alexander, besides the fragment of Hegesias's arkhonship that was unexpired at Alexander's death, and the portion of the arkhonship of Simonides that preceded the assassination of the boy. But for seven years the young Alexander, who was born not only after his father's death, but apparently after the arkhonship of Hegesias was ended, was but joint inheritor with his uncle Aridæus of his father's throne. By the Egyptian annals, the year of his father's death and of his own birth, the 425th of Nabonassar, beginning at noon 12th Nov. B.C. 324, would be the first of his reign; and the year of Nabonassar 437, beginning mid-day 9th Nov. B.C. 312, being the year of his death, would be treated as the first of his successor. As we have intimated, he was associated with his uncle Aridæus in the kingship as soon as he was born. See Arrian, *Success.* (*ap. Photiam, cod.* 92), § 9; Dexippus, *ap. Phot. cod.* 82, in the *Fragm. Hist. Græc.* vol. iii. pp. 667, 668; Porphyry of Tyre, *ap. Georg. Syncell.*, ed. Paris, pp. 264, 265, and ap. Euseb. *Chron. Armen.*, ed. Mai, p. 171, given in *Fragm. Hist. Græc.* vol. iii. pp. 693, 694, 697. Compare Justin, xiii. 2–4, 6. We conclude, then, that seven years were assigned on the monuments to the joint reign of Philip Aridæus and the young Alexander, and five years more—being the eighth and four following years of his reign—to the young Alexander alone. At *Semenood*, the ancient Sebennytus, there remain (Sir J. G. Wilkinson tells us) a few sculptured stones, on one of which are the name and figure of the god *Sem, Gem,* or *Semnouti* (whence the Coptic name of the city Gemnouti). He was the same as Moui, "son of The Sun," regarded by Sir J. G. W. as the Splendour or Force of the Sun, and compared by the Greeks, as they did Khons also, the third member of the Theban Triad, with their own *Herakles.* The Semenood sculptures are of the time of Alexander, son of Alexander the Great, who was nominally sovereign; Ptolemy son of Lagus being, as we have seen, the autocratic or plenipotential governor of Egypt. See Sir J. G. W.'s notes on *Herod.* ii. 43, 166, in Rawlinson's *Herodotus.*

Our own distribution of the 39 years that begin the series in the Table of Reigns subsequent to Alexander's, whereby the first year is given to Philip Aridæus at Babylon, and the following 38 to Ptolemy son of Lagus in Egypt, rests upon the authority of Porphyry of Tyre, preserved by Eusebius. See the *Fragm. Historic. Græc.* vol. iii. p. 719: compare Clinton, *F. H.*, vol. ii. *Tables, B.C.* 306; vol. iii., Appendix, chap. 5, *Kings of Egypt.*

We must not conclude this article without observations on the commencement of Seleucus's reign, and the era of the Seleucidæ. The same Porphyry of Tyre whom we cited from Eusebius just now, writes thus of Seleucus (according to Angelo Mai's interpretation of the

Armenian version of Eusebius, p. 183): " *Seleucus enjoyed the kingdom for 32 years, from the first year of the 117th Olympiad to the fourth year of the 124th Olympiad,—his life having been prolonged to the 75th year, when he perished by the treachery of a familiar of his own, Ptolemy Keraunus;*" see *Fragm. Hist. Græc.*, vol. iii. p. 707. The year of the 117th Olympiad began midsummer B.C. (776 − 116 × 4, or 464, =) 312. How this year came to be fixed upon as the first of Seleucus's reign in Registers of Olympic years, we shall soon see. But one might have expected his first regnal year to be considered the one in which he is related to have done no less than Ptolemy, Lysimakhus, and Cassander, when, with or without the diadem, they assumed or accepted the title of king, lest they should own an inferiority to their antagonist Antigonus. For after the great sea-fight off Salamis in Cyprus, Ptolemy having there been defeated by Demetrius son of Antigonus, and having lost Cyprus in consequence, Antigonus accepted, and permitted Demetrius to accept, the title and diadem of king. This happened in the year of Anaxicrates, the second arkhon of the 118th Olympic period, B.C. 307-6: see Diod. xx. 38, 45, 53. But we have other authority for asserting that what Seleucus began at that time to do was to use in intercourse with Greeks a title which (or rather, we must say, the equivalent of which) he had already assumed in all his dealings with barbarians, that is to say, Asiatic dependents or Asiatic potentates. See Plutarch, *vit. Demetrii*, cap. 18.

This preliminary objection being removed, we now ask about the year which began at midsummer B.C. 312 with the 117th celebration of the Olympic games, why was it made by Porphyry of Tyre and his authorities the first regnal year of Seleucus? The reason that justified them is soon discovered on examining the history of that year in Diodorus, xix. 77, 80-86, 90-91, 92-100. In that year Seleucus returned from Egypt, repossessed himself of his satrapy of Babylonia, and added to it Susiana and Media. It is on account of these achievements that, in after years at least, the year was counted Seleucus's first. Since the distribution of provinces made at Triparadeisus in Upper Syria by Antipater and the Macedonians (see Diod. xviii. 39, and for the date, Clinton, *F. H.* vol. ii., Tables, B.C. 321), he had been satrap of Babylonia for more than the four years stated by Diodorus (xix. 91), and his government was become highly acceptable, when in the second year of the 116th Olympiad, the year of the arkhon Praxibulus, beginning at midsummer B.C. 315 (see Diod. xix. 55, 17), after the defeat and death of Eumenes, and the consequent establishment of Antigonus's authority in Media, Persis, and Susiana, this *general of the king's army,*—for so he had been created by the same authority which made Seleucus satrap of Babylonia,—visited Babylon. Seleucus had strenuously resisted Eumenes and aided Antigonus, and he now received the victorious general with splendid gifts, and found hospitable reception for his whole army: but he was

treated as a dependent; an account of the revenue of his province
was demanded; and perceiving his life to be threatened, he fled from
Babylon with a party of 50 horsemen, and, escaping pursuit, found a
refuge in Egypt with Ptolemy son of Lagus. Here, by his account
of Antigonus's behaviour since he had overthrown the confederacy
headed by Eumenes, not only to those who, like Peukestes, the Macedonian satrap of Persis, had supported Eumenes, but to Python, the
satrap of Media, and to himself, as well as in respect of the royal
treasury at Susa, he alarmed Ptolemy for his lordship of Egypt and
Cyrene, and pretensions upon Lower Syria; Cassander for his lordship of Macedonia, and pretensions upon Greece and parts of Asia
Minor; and Lysimakhus for his government of Thrace. They were
induced to unite in demanding of Antigonus, who pretended to act
for Roxana and her boy Alexander as general-in-chief and regent,
though they were actually in the hands of Cassander, the restoration
of Babylonia to Seleucus, the surrender of Hellespontian Phrygia to
Lysimakhus, of Cappadocia and Lycia to Cassander, and of Syria to
Ptolemy, as well as a share to each of the royal treasures of which he
had possessed himself. Their demands were rejected, and war followed. In B.C. 312, after the third summer had been spent, so far
as Ptolemy was concerned, in the putting down of a revolt at Cyréné
by his general Agis, and in an expedition led by the satrap himself,
in which he crushed all remaining opposition in the states of the
island of Cyprus, and then made successful descents upon the coasts
of Upper Syria and Cilicia, distracting the forces of Antigonus, he
returned to Alexandria, and was induced by Seleucus to invade Syria,
of which Antigonus, since the war began, had gained complete possession by the capture of Tyre, Joppa, and Gaza, and where his
forces, commanded in his absence by his son, the youthful Demetrius,
were now distributed in winter quarters. However, on his arrival at
Old Gaza, Ptolemy found Demetrius with forces assembled ready to
resist. A battle ensued, in which Ptolemy and Seleucus gained a
great victory. Demetrius fled first to Ashdod, and afterwards to
Tripolis. Ptolemy took Gaza at once; then partly by force, partly
by persuasion, recovered all the fenced places of Lower Syria, Sidon
and Tyre included. Seleucus also, eager to improve the opportunity
afforded by the absence of Antigonus in Phrygia, and by the successes
of Ptolemy in Syria, was satisfied with the slender force of no more
than 800 foot-soldiers and 200 horse, spared him by Ptolemy, and set
forth to recover Babylon. At Karrhæ in Mesopotamia he obliged the
Macedonian settlers to accompany him. When he had crossed the
Babylonian border, he was met by the inhabitants in crowds, offering
him service; and one of Antigonus's officers, named Polyarkhus (captain, perhaps, of the first fort at Babylon, the possession of which is
otherwise unaccounted for), joined him with more than a thousand
soldiers; while those who kept faith with Antigonus, seeing the

general inclination of the people towards Seleucus, fled all together to the fort at Babylon of which Diphilus was keeper, where the children and friends of Seleucus had been lodged in arrest ever since Seleucus himself went off from Babylon. That satrap now laid siege to the place, and took it; and thus, having recovered his government, began buying up horses and levying men for his service. Hearing that Antigonus's general Nicanor, with an army of more than 10,000 foot and about 7000 horse, assembled out of Media, Persis, and the parts adjoining, was coming down against him, he at once set forth to meet him, at the head of only 3000 foot and 400 horse. He crossed the Tigris at the place where Nicanor in a few days would reach the river from the east, concealed his men in covert afforded by neighbouring marsh-lands, and waited there. Nicanor, when he arrived on the Tigris, finding no enemy, encamped negligently at a king's stage-house which stood there; πρός τινι βασιλικῷ σταθμῷ. In the night Seleucus fell suddenly on the ill-guarded camp, and the Persians (or perhaps, more properly, those of the Hari river province: see Diod. xix. 48) engaging him, lost Evagoras, their satrap, and other leaders. Whereupon the greater part of Nicanor's people, partly in panic, partly out of old disaffection to Antigonus, went over to Seleucus; and Nicanor, distrusting those who remained, fled over the desert with his friends. And so Seleucus, now master of a considerable force, and behaving courteously to everybody, soon won Susiana and Media, and some of the parts adjoining. Nor did the change of fortune which befell in his absence—obliging Ptolemy to evacuate Syria, and enabling Demetrius to make an inroad into Babylonia—seriously affect his position. For Patrocles, whom he had left in command, though too weak to fight with Demetrius, caused the inhabitants to abandon Babylon, and take refuge in the desert or across the Tigris in Susiana, while, himself, he kept hovering from one strong position to another in the neighbourhood of the invaders; and though, of two fortresses in the city of Babylon, Demetrius stormed one and blockaded the other, the time allowed him by his father being spent, he was obliged to return into Syria to Antigonus, leaving only one-third of his forces behind him to prosecute the siege. Of this siege we hear no more. Whether the fortress yielded, or continued to defy the besiegers, without reinforcements these cannot have been able to face Seleucus on his return from beyond the Tigris.

It is plain, then, that the year of the 117th Olympic festival was made by Porphyry of Tyre the first regnal year of Seleucus, because in that year, during the winter which followed the defeat of Demetrius at Gaza, Seleucus recovered Babylonia and conquered Susiana and Media; thereby laying the foundation of an empire which he afterwards greatly enlarged, and which he held, as he had gained it, by the sword, not under a commission from Alexander son of Roxana, or any one acting in his name, whether Antigonus or Cassander.

But the commencement of Seleucus's reign is also the epoch of the Seleucidan era; and this was not at midsummer B.C. 312, when the Olympic year began, but in the autumn of B.C. 312, and of the first year of the 117th Olympiad. So much is proved by irrefragable evidence. We refer the reader to *seven proofs* recited minutely by Clinton in the *Fasti Hellenici*, after Norisius, in the work entitled, *Annus et Epochæ Syro-Macedonum* (4to, Lips. 1696). These proofs are derived (1) from the testimony of the Persian astronomer Moghul Ulug-Beg; (2) from a coin of Hadrian struck at Tripolis; (3) from three coins of Elagabalus struck at the same place; (4) from a coin of Caracalla struck at Emisôn-colonia; (5) from a coin of Augustus struck at Damascus; (6) from the history of the Council of Nice; and (7) from the testimony of an Arabian astronomer of the ninth century, Albategni. See Clinton, *F. H.* vol. iii., Appendix, chap. 4, "Macedonian Months."

Thus, although the epoch, or first starting-point, of the Seleucidan era stood in the autumn alike of B.C. 312 and of the first year of the 117th Olympiad, yet it was to Seleucus's successful operations during the following winter that he owed his first possession of the throne in Babylonia and adjoining provinces. His kingship, then, is antedated (being counted from a point in the autumn which preceded the actual acquisition of it), and for a reason perfectly analogous to that which caused Porphyry of Tyre, or his authorities, who dated by Olympiads, to count Seleucus's reign from midsummer B.C. 312; namely, that at Babylon (as we have shown above, p. 435) the year by which reigns were measured in the Annals began in autumn; as did the old Hebrew year, afterwards the civil year of the Jews, which (as we have argued, p. 749), under the kings of the House of David, was also the regnal year at Jerusalem. However, the year at Babylon seems to have begun with the eighth month of the Mosaic and Assyrian year, that is, with Markhesvan; whereas the Jewish civil year began with the seventh month Tisri.

The latter, under the name of *the former Tishrin*, was likewise the first month of the Syro-Julian year, followed in calculations of Seleucidan years by the Arab writer Alfergani, and the Moghul grandson of Timur, the learned Ulug-Beg, who, reigning at Samarcand, observed the stars and wrote Persian about A.D. 1430. This is shown by the account which they give of the Syrian months. The first is Tishrin *el-ewel*, and has 31 days; the second, Tishrin *el-akher*, has 30 days; the third, Kanun *el-ewel*, 31 days; the fourth, Kanun *el-akher*, 31 days; the fifth, Shebat, 28 days, and in bissextile years 29 days; the sixth, Adar, 31 days; the seventh, Nisan, 30 days; the eighth, Ayar, 31 days; the ninth, Haziran, 30 days; the tenth, Tamuz, 31 days; the eleventh, Ab, 31 days; the twelfth, Eilul, 30 days. For these names in the Syriac character we are referred to *Beveregii Instit. Chron.*, App. p. 256, ed Traj. ad Rhenum, 1734, 8vo. This twelvemonth Alfergani distinguishes as *Syrian*, from another beginning with Kanun *el-akher*, which he calls *er-rum*, Roman or Greek, and which, in fact, is the Julian year of Old Rome beginning with the 1st of January. But the Syrian twelvemonth above given, beginning with the 1st day of October, is the original Syro-Julian year. Traces of the existence of the old Roman Julian year in Syria existed in the time of Mesudi (in the ninth century); for, in an extract published by Desguignes, vol. i., of *Notes et extraits*, he says that the Syrians— *those of Antioch in particular* (which, observe, had its special era, and was the seat of the Roman administration in the province)—celebrated the *coulands* (calends) the 1st of Kanun *el-akher* (that is, the 1st of January) by bonfires which they lighted during the night. Observe that the Roman civil day began at midnight. See translations from the German of Ideler in the Abbé Halma's *Chronologie de Ptolemée, partie 3me de l'imprimerie de Bobée*, Paris 1819, 4to.

The reader will observe that the epoch *Mid-day the 9th of November B.C. 312*, the commencement of *the Egyptian year of Philip*, that would have been reckoned Seleucus's first in Egypt, though given in our "Table of the Reigns from Nabonassar to Seleucus by both Egyptian and Khaldæan reckoning" (see above, Section A of this article), does not appear to have been anywhere used as the epoch of the Seleucidan era. For in Egypt the era of Philip (Aridæus), not that of Seleucus, was the one employed. It may be observed, that if we distinguish *two* Alexanders, the son of Roxana as well as the great conqueror his father, the era of Syria, no less than the Egyptian era, may have been rightly called the era after Alexander.

At Babylon, we suppose the epoch of the Seleucidan era to have been, as our table has it, the first day of the latter Tishrin, or Tishrin *el-akher*, or Markhesvan, in B.C. 311; that is, the New-year's day of the 437th Khaldæan year of Nabonassar. For we have adduced reason to believe that Markhesvan was the first month of the old Khaldæan year; and Josephus identifies Markhesvan with *Dius*, the first month of the Macedonian twelve, *Ant.* xii. 7, § 6: to show the significance of which, we will here cite Pausanias Damascenus's work *On Antioch*, quoted by Malalas, p. 198, ed. Bonn (in *Fragm. Hist. Græc.* vol. iv. p. 469), for the assertion that Seleucus applied the Macedonian names to the Syrian months: ἐκέλευσι δὲ ὁ αὐτὸς καὶ τοὺς μῆνας τῆς Συρίας κατὰ Μακεδόνας καλεῖσθαι.

It was natural that the Macedonians should call the lunar months of the Syrian and Khaldæan Calendars by the old familiar names, rather than by the Aramaic or the Akkad denominations, as the Romans are found to have called the Egypto-Julian months of Alexandria, from Thoth to Mesori, by the names of the nearly corresponding Julian months of their own Calendar from September to August. For this fact, see the double names prefixed to each month in Ptolemy's Almanac or Calendar of the year, entitled Φάσεις ἀπλανῶν καὶ ἐπισημασίαι, which is included in Halma's volume above referred to, *Chronologie de Ptolemée*, Paris 1819.

We are not able to pronounce what cities or populations of Syria owned the year which is employed in the measurement of the Seleucidan era by Ulug-Beg, Alfergani, and Abulfaraj. It was, as we have seen, a year *coinciding exactly with the Jewish civil year* (Jos. *Ant*. i. 3, § 3), for it began with the lunar month identified by Josephus, *Ant*. viii. 4, § 1, with the Macedonian 12th month Hyperberetæus, namely, the Tisri of the Jews, that is, the former Tishrin, or *Tishrin el-ewel*, of the Syrians. The year thus commencing is spoken of by Hieronymus, *ad Ezek*. i. 1, where he writes, *In quarto mense qui apud nos vocatur Januarius, et est in anni primus exordio. Apud Orientales enim populos . . . October erat primus mensis et Januarius quartus*. Again, *ad Zechar*. i. 7, he affirms, *Est* (*Shebat*) *in acerrimo tempore hiemis, qui ab Ægyptiis Mechir, a Macedonibus Peritius, a Romanis Februarius appellatur*. Norisius infers that before Hieronymus's time this had been the year in use at Antioch. Clinton disputes the conclusion, *F. H.* vol. iii., App. chap. 4, in the section upon Hyperberetæus.

Later is found a Syro-Julian year, beginning with *Eilul*. Now Eilul, as a Hebrew no less than a Syrian lunar month, was identified by Josephus with the 11th Macedonian month Gorpiæus; which last, again, after the introduction of a Syro-Julian year, is identified with the Roman September by Evagrius and the Alexandrian Chronicle. See Clinton, as before, on the Macedonian months. Norisius proves from Evagrius, whose Ecclesiastical History was written in A.D. 593 or 594, that this Syro-Julian year was in use at Antioch in the sixth century. But the years of a cycle equal to three of the ancient *lustra*, and called *Indictions* from the emperor's annual *Indictio*, or ἐπινέμησις, that is, imposition or assessment of taxes, began in the eastern empire of Rome, like the years of the *Era of the World* at Constantinople, with the first day of September, as the Russian year did, and the modern Greek year does still. Therefore the Syro-Julian year now before us, which began with Eilul, or Gorpiæus or September, may be regarded as the civil year of the new Rome, Constantinople, which was employed in the financial administration of the Syrian province. Being thus the last form of the Roman year that had been in use before the conquest of Syria by the Arabs, it was used for the measurement of the Seleucidan era by Albategni or Albatani, the first Arab astronomer who dates by years of Seleucus. He not only is said to name Eilul before the other Syriac months in his 32d chapter, On the Movements of the Stars (whereof a Latin translation, with notes, appeared at Nuremburg in 8vo, 1537), but a computation of his in the 27th chapter is appealed to by Ideler in the Abbé Halma's version as proof that Eilul was the first month of his *year of Dsi-karnein*, "the two-horned." So Albategni and others call Seleucus, who adopted a variety of an old Assyrian head-dress in his statues, as Appian attests, *De rebus Syriac.* cap. 57, and on his coins (of which one is represented in the art. SELEUCUS in Smith's *Dict. of Gr. and Rom. Biography*). For Albategni's Seleucidan year, see too Clinton (citing Norisius) in the *F. H.* vol. iii., where he treats of the Seleucidan era in the chapter of the Appendix on Macedonian Months. According to Ideler, Albategni wrote at a city of Syria called *Rahk*, which, if the same as *Rakkah* in the general map accompanying Mr. Layard's *Nineveh and Babylon*, is on the left bank of the Euphrates, some five miles south of the 36th degree of north latitude, and in about 39 deg. 10 min. longitude east of Greenwich, that is, 9 deg. 20 min. longitude east of Alexandria, and therefore 37 min. and 20 seconds of time forwarder than Alexandria. Clinton, desirous of accounting for a difference of 39 minutes in the statements of Albategni concerning the date of his own observation and the time that elapsed since an observation of Ptolemy's, conjectures that the Arab took his observation at a place 9 degrees and 45 minutes east of Alexandria. The date of the observation, which was of the autumn equinox, as given by Norisius, p. 226, is *Anno ab obitu Alexandri* 1206, *Dylkarnaim* 1194, *die* 19o *mensis Elul* (that is, of September), *Pachon* (the ninth Egyptian month) 8vo, 4 hor. 45 min. *ante ortum diei, sive* 1 hor. 15 min. *à mediâ nocte*. Of the two dates, the Egyptian of the era of Philip, which commenced 11½ November B.C. 324, is a day which began at noon 19th September, called by Albategni *Eilul*, A.D. 882. On this day the 1194th year of Dylkarnaim, according to Albategni, was already current. If we go back 1193 Julian years complete, we arrive at noon the 19th of September B.C. 312, when the era of Seleucus was as many days old as the 1194th year of that era was at noon 19th September A.D. 882. That is to say, the first year of the era by Albategni's reckoning was already current at that time. Therefore, if the era certainly began in B.C. 312, it began, according to Albategni's form of the year, not with October, but with September, called by the Syrians Eilul.

But this later Syro-Julian year, beginning with Eilul, and the earlier one preferred by subsequent calculators, which began with *Tishrin el-ewel*, or October, were both of them still in use in the time of Gregory Bar Hebræus, a Monophysite doctor called Abulfaraj, in the 13th century of our era. He is cited by Ideler as saying (*Dynast. Hist.*) that "in one way they begin the year with the month Tishrin of the Syrians; in the other, with the month *Eilul of the Greeks*." As both months are equally Syrian, the meaning seems to be, that the year in Syrian style began with the former Tishrin, that is, *Tishrin el-ewel*, but according to the style of Constantinople with Eilul. Accordingly, the same Abulfaraj ap. Norisium, *De Epoch. Syro-Maced.* p. 228, cited by Clinton, writes, *Si æræ Seleucidarum cujus initium est Tisrin prior mensem unum addiderimus prodibunt nobis anni integri et menses anni fracti cujus initium est Elul; quæ est epocha quâ utuntur Romani nostro tem-*

pore. By *Romans*, he means the subjects of the empire seated at Constantinople. He distinguishes, therefore, the Seleucidan years of the manner of the Romans, that is, of the Greeks of Constantinople (who were Romans to the Saracens, as the provincials of Gaul were Romans to the Franks)—a year which began with September—from the proper Seleucidan year of Syria, which ended with Eilul and began with Tishrin el-ewel. Ideler (as translated by Halma) quotes Abulfaraj's *Chronicle of Syria*, where the author dates his writing of it on the 10th of Eilul in the 1587th year of Seleucus; and translates this date into the 10th of September in the year of the World 6785, according to the Greek era of the Creation, whereof the 5509th year begins with the 1st of September B.C. 1; and consequently the 10th of September in the year of the World 6785 is 10th September A.D. 1276. Hence it appears, as we might have expected from Abulfaraj's words in the former citation, that, according to his own reckoning, Eilul, or September, was not the first month, but the last of the Seleucidan year. For 10th September A.D. 1276 is the 21st day before the end of the Seleucidan year 1587, if the year be counted from the 1st of October, or the *former Tishrin*, B.C. 312; whereas it is the 10th day after the commencement of the Seleucidan year 1588, if the days of the Seleucidan years be counted from the 1st of September or Eilul B.C. 312. And here we see an exemplification of his rule for reducing Syrian years of Seleucus to Seleucidan years of the Roman or Constantinopolitan type. If to the 10th of September in the Syrian year of Seleucus 1587, that is, if to 1586 Syrian years and 345 days, we prefix the 30 days of the month Eilul by which the Roman year precedes the Syrian, we obtain the Roman date of 1587 years and 10 days, or the 10th of September in the Roman year of Seleucus 1588.

Thus, besides the Babylonian year beginning with the lunar month Markhesvan, or latter Tishrin or Dius, we have three Julian forms of the Syrian year used in the measurement of the Seleucidan era. Of these three, the first, beginning with the former Tishrin, or the Jewish Tisri, or the Syro-Macedonian Hyperberetæus, or the Latin October, may be regarded as the proper Syrian year, being the Julian form first substituted for the original lunar year. The second, beginning with the latter Kanun, that is, Tebeth, Audynæus, or January, is but the Julian year of Old Rome, beginning with the Calends of January, and having Syrian month-names instead of the Latin. The third, beginning with Eilul, that is, Gorpiæus or September, is the Julian year of Constantinople, which measured the 15 year cycle of Indictions and the Greek era of the Creation; being apparently in its origin an assimilation of the Roman year in respect of commencement to the Egypto-Julian year of the successive eras of Augustus and Diocletian, used by the Greeks of Alexandria, and beginning with the 30th of August in the first year of every τετραετηρις, but with the 29th of August in the other three years.

According to their custom, the existence of which we have already established (see pp. 441-2), and the result whereof, before the era of Seleucus, is exhibited by our table in Section A of this article, the Khaldæans did not count the regnal years of Seleucus to begin till the next New-year's day arrived after his actual coming into possession of the kingly power; for the whole year in which any transfer of kingly power took place they always counted (as did also the annalists of Jerusalem under the sons of David) to the predecessor. In the case before us the predecessor was Alexander son of Roxana, whose satrap at Babylon, Seleucus, had at first been appointed when Antipater had superseded Perdiccas in the regency or protectorate of the empire. Thus when Seleucus, after Antigonus's defeat and death at Ipsus in Phrygia, besides other acquisitions, added to his Babylonian kingdom the region of Upper Syria,—while, with such Greeks as Porphyry of Tyre, and with the native race in Syria, his reign was counted from the beginning of the year in which he conquered Babylon, whether the Olympic year beginning at midsummer, or the Syrian year beginning about the autumn equinox, in the year B.C. 312,—at Babylon, however, the original seat of his kingship, the annalists dated it from the commencement of the Khaldæan year in B.C. 311, with the month Markhesvan, which the Macedonians had learnt to call by the name of their own first month Dius.

It is not certain, however, and to us it seems hardly probable, that Alexander son of Roxana was dead so early as on the 1st day of Markhesvan in the year of Simonides, the second arkhon of the 117th Olympiad. Nevertheless, we learn from Diodorus, xix. 105, that a peace was agreed to in the year of Simonides between Antigonus and the confederated satraps Cassander, Ptolemy, and Lysimakhus, Seleucus being apparently left to shift for himself. By this convention all Asia was conceded to Antigonus, and Cassander was to be commander-in-chief of Europe till Alexander son of Roxana came to age. Ever since, in pretended retribution for the death of Philip Aridæus and his wife Eurydice, the boy's grand-dam Olympias had been overthrown and put to death by Cassander, while Antigonus was carrying on the war against Eumenes, Alexander and Roxana his mother had been kept in close and no respectful custody at Amphipolis by Cassander, into whose hands they had fallen. He had been meditating their death (Diod. xix. 52), and was now released from his war with Antigonus. His prisoners were left to his discretion: he saw the young Alexander growing (for the 12th year of his age expired about August B.C. 311): throughout Macedonia the propriety was suggested, and began to be discussed, of the boy's being brought out of his confinement and invested with the kingly attributes of his ancestors. Thus quickened, Cassander gave orders to a creature of his own, whom he had invested with the custody-in-chief of Roxana and her son, to slay them both, hide the bodies, and tell no one what had been done. The order was executed: Cassander, Lysimakhus, and Ptolemy, nay, Antigonus too, were delivered from responsibility to a superior termed by themselves the king; and henceforth all held what they had got as their own.

The fact that at Babylon the new moon of Markhesvan, called by the Macedonians Dius, in our year B.C. 311, was the epoch of the reign of Seleucus and his descendants, we might have concluded, and we did conclude, as soon as we discovered the ancient custom of the Khaldæans as to the registering of the year in which any transfer of the crown was accomplished. But the same follows also from a precious testimony to the effect that *the Khaldæan era* (which is but the era of Seleucus as calculated by the Khaldæans) began a year later than the Seleucidan era according to the Syrians.

From three passages of Ptolemy's Μεγαλη Συνταξις, or Almagest, pp. 232, 269, quoted by others, and by Clinton in the oft-cited chapter on Macedonian Months, under Dius, it appears that the 67th, 75th, and 82d years of the Khaldæans corresponded with the 68th, 76th, and 83d years respectively of the commonly known Seleucidan era.

1. For the 5th day of the second month Apellæus, or about the 35th day of the year in the 67th year κατὰ Χαλδαίους (that is, *as reckoned by the Khaldæans*), is said to correspond with the 27th day of Thoth in the 504th year of Nabonassar κατ' Αἰγυπτίους, by Egyptian reckoning. Therefore this 504th Egyptian year of Nabonassar began about (35 − 27 =) 8 whole days later than the Khaldæan 67th year; also it began 503 quarters of a day less than 503 Julian years after 25½ February B.C. 747, that is, 125¾ days before 25½ February B.C. 244. Therefore it began 22¾ October B.C. 245, and the Khaldæan year 67 began with the 1st day of Markhesvan, or Dius, at about 14¾ October B.C. 245, while the year 1 began with Dius B.C. 311.

But the Egyptian year in which Seleucus began to reign in Babylon was their 437th of Nabonassar, commencing at 8½ November B.C. 312, according to our table in Section A. Take away, then, the previous 436 years of Nabonassar from the 503 years and 27 days of Nabonassar that ended with 66 years and 35 days of the Khaldæans. What remains is 67 years and 27 days of the Seleucidan era as it would have been counted in Egypt, from 8½ November B.C. 312, ending, as before, with 66 years and 35 days of the Khaldæan era at Babylon. But this Khaldæan quantity—66 years 35 days—translated into time of the Syrian era of Seleucus, beginning in the autumn of the same year B.C. 312, will be about 30 days more, that is, 67 years and 65 days, because the Khaldæan year began a month later than the Syrian, with Markhesvan or Tishrin el-akher, instead of Tisri or Tishrin el-ewel. The difference of epochs between the Syrian era of Seleucus and the Khaldæan era is therefore a year and a month, and the 67th Khaldæan year begins a month later than the 68th year of Seleucus according to the Syrians.

2. Again, Ptolemy attests that the 14th of (the first month) Dius of the 75th year κατὰ Χαλδαίους, was the 9th of Thoth in the 512th year of Nabonassar κατ' Αἰγυπτίους; so that the 1st of Thoth was the 6th of Dius. From the end of 436 Nab. Ægypt., that is, of the year before the first of Seleucus according to the Egyptian annals, to the beginning of 512 Nab. Ægypt., is 75 complete years. But 436 Nab. Ægypt. ended 8½ November B.C. 312, and therefore the morrow was later in the year than the new moon of the former Tishrin or the Jewish Tisri B.C. 312, the epoch of the Seleucidan era of the Syrians. Thus it was the 76th year of the Syrian era of the Seleucidæ when it was but the 75th of the Khaldæans; so that if the Seleucidan era of the Syrians began (1 Tisri) B.C. 312, that of the Khaldæans began (1 Markhesvan) B.C. 311.

3. Lastly, Ptolemy affirms that the 5th day of (the sixth month) Xanthicus of the Khaldæan year 82 coincided with the 12th or 14th (for both readings are given) of Tybi (the fifth month) in the 519th year of Nabonassar κατ' Αἰγυπτίους. Deduct 81 completed Khaldæan from 518 completed Egyptian years of Nabonassar. The remainder is 437 Egyptian years of Nabonassar complete at the epoch of the Khaldæan era. But we have seen that about a month later than the Syrian epoch of the Seleucidan era, only 436 Egyptian years of Nabonassar were accomplished. Therefore the Khaldæan era began more than a year later than the Syrian era of Seleucus, that is, later in B.C. 311 than the Seleucidan era of Syria began in B.C. 312.

This difference between the epochs of the Seleucidan era according to the Syrians and according to the Khaldæans, might explain, and yet it may not be the true cause of, a presumed error in the Alexandrian Chronicle remarked by Scaliger and Norisius, and by Clinton in the discussion of the Seleucidan era, introduced after that on the era of Antioch as a sequel to the subject of Hyperberatæus, the last of the 12 Macedonian months (*F. H.* vol. iii., Appendix, chap. 4). The entry is this: ὑπ. Βινκομάλου καὶ Ὁπιλίωνος. Ἐπὶ τούτων τῶν ὑπάτων ἐτελεύτησεν ἡ δέσποινα Πουλχερία· Ἐπὶ τῶν προειρημένων ὑπάτων Βινκομάλου καὶ Ὁπιλίωνος, . . . μηνὶ Περιτίῳ ποὸ ιβ΄ καλανδῶν Μαρτίων, ἔτους Συρομακεδόνων ψξγ΄, Ἀντιοχέων φά, ηὑρέθη, κ.τ.λ. The consulate is that of U.C. 1206, A.D. 453. The date of Antioch, says Clinton, is correct. For the era of Antioch commenced in the autumn of U.C. 705 (B.C. 49); and U.C. 705 + 500 = 1205 will give autumn U.C. 1205, A.D. 452, for the beginning of the 501st year, which was therefore current in the February following. But if the 763d year of Seleucus began in autumn U.C. 1205, A.D. 452, the epoch of the era must have been at the same season in B.C. 311, U.C. 443, not in U.C. 442, B.C. 312. Scaliger therefore corrects the date to ψξδ΄.

APPENDIX NO. IV.

At the bottom of page 115 we closed Note (*i*) with the promise of an etymological discourse *on the names Tyrrheni, Prisci, Volsci, and Etrusci*. We think it better, however, now, not to lengthen our Appendix with matter so remote from the subject of the present work, and so intimately connected with early Roman history, a great theme which we have not studied, though it has been unfolded by writers— chiefly of Germany—eminent for ability, learning, and research. However, as in the course of our work we have been led to emendations of the text of several passages in Greek authors, we will add to the number one offered in the essay which itself we suppress, and relating to a text confessedly in need of cure. The passage is Strabo v. 4, § 3, where, having said that the plain of Campania is surrounded by *the mountains of the Saunitæ* (or Samnites) *and those of the Oski*, the geographer proceeds thus : Ἀντίοχος μὲν οὖν φησι, τὴν χώραν ταύτην Ὀπικοὺς οἰκῆσαι· τούτους δὲ καὶ Αὔσονας καλεῖσθαι. Πολύβιος δὲ ἐμφαίνει δύο ἔθνη νομίζων ταῦτα. Ὀπικοὺς γάρ, φησι, καὶ Αὔσονας, οἰκεῖν τὴν χώραν ταύτην περὶ τὸν Κρατῆρα. Ἄλλοι δὲ λέγουσιν, οἰκούντων Ὀπικῶν πρότερον καὶ Αὐσόνων, οἱ δ' ἐκείνους κατασχεῖν ὕστερον Ὄσκων τι ἔθνος· τούτους δ' ὑπὸ Κυμαίων, ἐκείνους δ' ὑπὸ Τυῤῥηνῶν ἐκπεσεῖν. Here, for οἱ δ' ἐκείνους, Thomas Tyrwhitt, our grandfather's elder brother, proposed to read μετ' ἐκείνους, and Kramer has proposed σὺν ἐκείνοις ; but we read Σιδικίνους, which, written in the uncial character, and with its initial of this form, C, might easily pass into ΟΙΔΕΚΕΙΝΟΥC, not being perceived by the transcriber to be a proper name. But we, on the contrary, observed that the evidently corrupt οἱ δ' ἐκείνους must occupy the place of an ethnic proper name ; whereupon a previous passage was remembered which furnished the ethnic name required. This previous passage is Strabo v. 3, § 9, where the cities are enumerated on the *Via Latina*, between the point on the *Via Appia*, near Rome, whence that road started, and Casilinum, a place 19 stades or 2½ Roman miles short of Capua, where the Via Latina rejoined the great highway. The enumeration includes these words : Κάσινον, καὶ αὕτη πόλις ἀξιόλογος ὑστάτη τῶν Λατίνων (note that the extended Latin territory in Strabo's time bordered on Campania). Τὸ γὰρ Τέανον, τὸ καλούμενον Σιδικῖνον, ἐφεξῆς κείμενον ἐκ τοῦ ἐπιθέτου δηλοῦται διότι τῶν Σιδικίνων ἐστίν. Οὗτοι δὲ Ὄσκοι, Καμπανῶν ἔθνος ἐκλελοιπός· ὥστε λέγοιτ' ἂν τῆς Καμπανίας καὶ αὕτη, μεγίστη οὖσα τῶν ἐπὶ τῇ Λατίνῃ πόλεων.

But, besides adding this emendation to others offered in preceding pages to the reader,—since we have already, p. 114, note, hazarded the conjecture that the name by which, according to Dionysius of Halicarnassus (*Antiq. Rom.* i. 30), the people of Etruria, after a certain leader of theirs, called themselves, *Rasena*, was akin to that of the Mæonian

Cabalians of Asia Minor, *Lasonians*,—it may here be added, that, in the article suppressed, we have explained the Greek appellation of the same Italian people, *Tyrrheni*, by the Roman Tarquinii, and the *Prisci* of Roman history by the *Pelasgi* of the Greeks. To the first of these explanations we were led, by observing that *Turchina* (*i.e.* Turkina), the modern name of the site of the ancient city Tarquinii, would, in the present provincial speech of Tuscany, take an aspirate instead of the guttural, and be pronounced *Turhina*, as *casa*, for example, is pronounced *hasa*. That Tyrrheni should be written also *Tyrseni* by the earlier Greeks, involves only a common substitution of sibilant for aspirate, such as we see in the equivalent Latin and Greek numerals *sex* and ἕξ, *septem* and ἑπτά. And as to the vowel of the second syllable, which is *long e*, η, in the Greek word, and *i* in the Roman, observe that the same difference of pronunciation still exists between Italian and vulgar Roman speech. Thus *sera, vero, moneta*, are in Roman pronunciation *sira, viro, monita*. Add that *Bolsena*, not *Bolsina* (which last recalls *Felsina*, the name of the old Etruscan city beyond the Apennines now called Bologna), is the present name of the city, on the south of the mountains, termed by old Roman authors *Volsinii* and *Volsinium*. Thus it would appear that the name by which the Greeks had from the remotest times designated the people of Etruria, belonged properly to the people of the Etruscan city Tarkena or Tarkina (otherwise called Tyrrhena and Tyrsena), the Tarquinii of Roman writers,—the founder of which, as of the rest of the 12 cities of Etruria, was said to be one Tarkôn or Tarchon. The chief from whom the native ethnic name Rasena is said to have been derived, would by analogy be Rasôn, which may be regarded as identical with Lasôn ; but Dionysius seems to assert that the name of the leader and of the people was the same, Rasena.

The identification of *Prisci* with *Pelasgi*, if admitted, will lead to important conclusions. Thus the famous Roman king Lucius Tarquinius Priscus will be referred to the Pelasgian population of Tarquinii, which was in a subject condition. The same *cognomen* Priscus, found as early as B.C. 495 (that is, before the death of Tarquinius Superbus) in the *gens Servilia* (one of the Alban houses transplanted to Rome), may have been applicable to many (nay, to all) the families of that *gens;* just as the surname *Sabinus Regillensis*, first bestowed in B.C. 505, afterwards was among the Claudii at Rome. The surname Priscus is also found in the *gens Numicia*, in the person of Titus Numicius Priscus, consul B.C. 467. In both houses it may be taken to have indicated the claim to descent from the *Prisci Latini*, the old Pelasgians of Latium.

APPENDIX NO. V.

At the end of the Table of Darius's Twenty Satrapies in Asia and Africa (p. 170) we promised *Notes upon the Table* here. But the subject belongs but incidentally to our work; to elucidate it properly would be out of place here,—requiring, too, more time and labour than we are able to bestow. Moreover, many points have been illustrated in previous notes as well as in our text.

CORRECTIONS, ADDITIONS, ETC.

P. 10, *last Line.*—Add to the note (*e*), "See below, p. 604."
P. 19, *Line* 10.—For, "And theirs that," read, "Of all that."
P. 21.—To what has here been said it may be added, that Thucydides, a contemporary of the fifth and sixth Akhæmenian kings,—that is, of Artaxerxes Makrokheir and Darius Nothus, the son and the grandson of Xerxes,—uses the designation "Persians and Medes" in his account of the temporary overthrow of the authority of Artaxerxes in Egypt by Inarôs the Libyan: Thucyd. iv. 104. Further, a passage of Arrian (*Exp. Alex.* vi. 29, § 3) affords an important confirmation of the fact, that Persians and Medes was the style of the nation of the Great King under the Akhæmenian dynasty; because undoubtedly Arrian drew the very language he employs from a well-informed writer of those who treated on the overthrow of the last Akhæmenian King of kings, and the substitution of a Macedonian supremacy in Asia. We refer to a passage which relates how Atropates, satrap of Media, after the return of Alexander from India, brought before his Macedonian sovereign at Pasargadæ a Mede named Baryaxes, charged with having assumed an upright *kidaris*, and called himself *King of the Persians and Medes.*

The term *Susa and Ekbatana*, used by Æschylus and Xenophon, as we have seen, is also used by Demosthenes in the 4th Philippic, § 9, where he wonders at one who is afraid of τὸν ἐν Σούσοις καὶ ἐν Ἐκβατάνοις, much as the state had been indebted to him once, and in spite of late rejected overtures; while the same person uses quite a different style of one close at the door, so growing in the midst of Greece, such a robber of the Greeks as Philip.

P. 35, *Lines* 6, 7.—Instead of, "So Josephus relates, and so we might have concluded for our ourselves," read, "So we conclude." Our error is retracted, Appendix i. Sect. C.

P. 48.—To Note (*k*) it may be added, That "as to the epoch after which Judæan or Jew became the general name of the subjects of the Mosaic law,—whether Israelites (of whatever tribe), or men of foreign stocks grafted into Israel by circumcision,—our conclusion is confirmed by Josephus, who writes in *Antiq.* xi. 5, § 7: Καὶ οἱ Ἰουδαῖοι πρὸς τὸ ἔργον (τὴν τῶν τειχῶν οἰκοδομὴν) παρισκευάζοντο. Ἐκλήθησαν δὲ τὸ ὄνομα, ἐξ ἧς ἡμέρας ἀνέβησαν ἐκ Βαβυλῶνος, ἀπὸ τῆς 'Ιούδα φυλῆς· ἧς πρώτης ἐλθούσης εἰς ἐκείνους τοὺς τόπους, αὐτοί τε καὶ ἡ χώρα τῆς προσηγορίας αὐτῆς μετέλαβον.

P. 51, Line 27.—Omit the sentence, "These conclusions," etc.

P. 53, Lines 5, 6.—For, "Admitting Josephus's testimony in explanation, we must conclude," read, "Hebrew testimony concerning the length of the captivity at Babylon, combined with other facts of Hebrew and Khaldæan chronology, has already led us to conclude."

P. 55, Lines 10, 11, 12, 13.—For, "if, as in Egypt the royal annals appear to have had it, and as is done in Ptolemy's Babylonian Canon, we include the remainder of that eighth Egyptian year," read, "if, as at Babylon the royal annals appear to have had it, we include the remainder of the eighth year."

P. 55, Line 38.—In Note (d), instead of the last three words, "Egyptian contemporary monuments," read, "contemporary monuments, we had thought Egyptian, but which we are now satisfied were, in part at least, Babylonian."

P. 61, Line 23.—For the sentence, "This assertion was casually confirmed to Mr. Layard by a Nestorian," etc. etc., read, "But from the precise testimony of the author of *The Nestorians and their Ritual*, we conclude that Mr. Layard had misunderstood his informant, when he wrote that a certain Nestorian or Khaldæan ecclesiastic had reported having seen an early manuscript among his people in which Amadiyah was so named."

P. 61, Line 38.—At the end of Note (i) add, "p. 161; and *The Nestorians and their Rituals*, by the Rev. Geo. Percy Badger, vol. i. p. 202."

P. 65, Note (m).—The word *Meseq* is in this note once or twice misprinted *Mescq*. But the note requires more important correction. Thus:

Line 30 (or 1 of Note m).—For, "there are two forms," read, "there are three forms."

Line 33 (or 4 of Note m).—For, "the other though," read, "another though."

Line 36 (or 7 of Note m).—After "Dwelling of Meseq?" insert, "for *Dar* signifies *dwelling* or *country* in Arabic; and districts of Africa, according to Sir J. G. Wilkinson in G. R.'s *Herodotus*, vol. ii. p. 180, are so called in old Egyptian inscriptions of Amunoph III. at Soleb, as at the present day. The third form of the name is *Doommeseq*, 2 Kings xvi. 10; and this may be equivalent to *Dor-meseq*, 'generation of Meseq.'"

P. 67, Line 7.—For "Egyptian," since the information about the Babylonian Calendar, I would read "Khaldæan."

P. 68, Line 32.—For, "confirms Herodotus giving," read "gives."

P. 68, Lines 34, 35.—Omit "apparently apportioning his eight months as Herodotus did; for it."

P. 68, Line 36.—Subjoin to the note, " But to reason on these years of Nabonassar correctly, they must be restored from the Egyptian to their own old Khaldæan shape and respective positions. See the Table in Appendix No. III., Section A."

P. 73, Lines 11, 12.—Omit " that is, B.C. 522."

P. 73, Line 13.—For " B.C. 526," etc. (to the end of the paragraph), read, " at latest in E.N. 222, which began, according to Ptolemy and the Egyptians, (at six hours before noon) 2d January B.C. 526; but according to the Khaldæans, as we shall show hereafter, with the month Markhesvan (which probably began in October) of the same year."

P. 73, Line 33.—For "tenth" read "fourteenth."

P. 79, Lines 13, 14.—For, " we, after the old Latin masters of the West, have learnt to call Greeks," read, " we have learnt from the Latins (what Egypt also, it seems, might have taught us) to call Greeks."

P. 79, Line 41 (the last of Note (f)).—To this note add, " That the Egyptians gave a name like that used by the Latins to the *Yavan* or *Hellenes* (a name not unknown among themselves), is proved by the Rosetta Stone Inscription, ed. M. A. Uhlemann, Lips. 1853, line 14 of the Hieratic, where '*n Graiks*, ' of Greeks,' is deciphered as the correspondent of ἱλληνικοῖς in the 54th line of the Greek text, as given by Letronne in his edition of the Greek, *Fragm. Hist. Græc.* vol. i."

P. 84, Line 22.—For " Buktrians" read " Baktrians."

P. 87, Lines 10-25.—For the three sentences, beginning " The eighth year," and ending " Asiatic Society," read thus : " Now the epoch of these events is autumn in the year B.C. 598. For they happened in the end of the Jewish civil year called the 11th of Jehoiakim and 8th of Nebukhadrezzar ; and this corresponded with the Khaldæan civil year called the 149th of Nabonassar, beginning with Tisri and ending with Elul, while the Khaldæan year began and ended a month later. Now we know that the first 149 Khaldæan years of Nabonassar ended with Tisri B.C. 598, because we know that they began with Markhesvan B.C. 747. But that the 11th year of Jehoiakim did correspond with the 149th Khaldæan year of Nabonassar is evident ; for it was the 123d of a series of civil years of Judah, the first whereof was the sixth of Hezekiah, and corresponded with the 27th Khaldæan year of Nabonassar. It was the 123d year, for 11 years of Jehoiakim, and 31 previous years of Josiah, and 2 previous years of Amon, and 55 previous years of Manasseh, and the last 24 of the previous 29 years of Hezekiah, amount to 123. And the sixth of Hezekiah, the first year of the 123, corresponded with the 27th Khaldæan year of Nabonassar, which was the first year of Merodakh Baladan or Mardokempadus king of Babylon, because it was the year according to the annals of Judah in which Samaria was taken ; while according to the Assyrian annals the first year of Merodakh Baladan was also the first year of Sargon king of Assyria, and this, again, was the year wherein Samaria was taken by the Assyrians.

"That the regnal years of the kings of Judah and Babylon were respectively civil Jewish and civil Khaldæan years; that the Khaldæan year began with Markhesvan; that the first regnal year of a king of Judah and a king of Babylon was the year after the one in which he took possession of the throne; and what the relation was of the Khaldæan years of Nabonassar to the well-known Egyptian years into which they were converted for the purpose of Ptolemy's astronomical calculations,—will be shown upon occasion hereafter. But we would here add the remark, that in Judah Nebukhadrezzar was counted king two years before he was so registered in Babylon. One proof is, that his first year, according to Jeremiah, was the fourth year of Jehoiakim, which corresponded with the 142d Khaldæan year of Nabonassar, being the 116th of the series of years of Judah which began with the aforesaid sixth of Hezekiah; whereas, according to the Khaldæan Canon, the first regnal year of Nebukhadrezzar was the 144th of Nabonassar. Another proof of the same fact is this, that according to the holy writers of Judah, the length of time from the beginning of Nebukhadrezzar's reign to the end of that of Darius the Mede was 70 years; whereas, according to the Khaldæan Canon, the same space appears to measure only 68 years; namely, 43 of Nebukhadrezzar, 2 of Evil Merodakh, 4 of Neriglissar, 17 of Nabonedus, and the first two years of the nine ascribed to Cyrus, though he reigned but the last seven of them."

P. 88, Line 24.—For, "at the end of B.C. 519," read, "in B.C. 518."

P. 89, Line 4.—For, "522, and again towards the close of B.C. 519," read, "521, and again in 519 or earlier."

P. 89, Line 5.—For "snso" print "sons."

Table of Descents, facing p. 91.—1. Under KINGS OF BABYLON, Line 4, omit "(by Khaldæan reckoning)."—2. Under PERSIAN KINGS, Line 1, for "Akhœmenes" read "Akhæmenes."

P. 93, Line 19.—For "nine" read "thirteen."

P. 109, last Line, P. 110, Line 2.—For, "It may be that Marathon saw Miltiades victorious before midsummer B.C. 490," read, "According to Plutarch, *Camill.* cap. 19, Miltiades conquered at Marathon on the 6th of Boedromion, the third Attic month (about September B.C. 490)."

P. 110, Lines 26, 27.—Instead of, "or in about the fourth month of the tenth year after the victory of the Athenians at Marathon; and so," read, "that is, in about the fourth month of the tenth Olympic year (if we begin the series at midsummer B.C. 490, with the year in which the Athenians fought at Marathon); or, in about the second month of the tenth year, if we count from the sixth of Boedromion, the date of the battle in B.C. 490. And so."

P. 111, Lines 5, 6.—For, "places at the commencement of the 75th Olympic period," read, "uses to mark the epoch of the invasion."

P. 109, *Lines* 16, 17; *P.* 110, *Line* 29; *P.* 111, *Line* 14.—The spring of B.C. 480 (the date of Xerxes' setting forth from Sardis for the Hellespont) would have been in the middle of the fifth year of Xerxes by Khaldæan tables, though it must have stood in the middle of his sixth year according to the Egyptian account which we have in Ptolemy's Canon. Our Table in Section A of Art. 3 in our Appendix will show that the year counted by the Khaldæan registrars the last of Darius's 36 was the one which ended with Tisri B.C. 485, being the year of his death. Herodotus, however, clearly takes the year of Darius's demise of the crown, whether Egyptian, Olympic, or what not, to have been the first year of the reign of Xerxes.

P. 113, *Line* 39.—After " Crœsus," add, " and by a like correction remove the ancient difficulty found in Ephorus's making the Χάλυβες an inland people of Asia Minor. See Strabo, xiv. 5, § 24."

P. 115, *Lines* 37-40.—The reader will see that the promised etymological notes have been reduced to explanations of the names Tyrrheni and Prisci, with an emendation of Strabo.

P. 124, *Line* 14.—From " But it may be well" to the end of the note, we would cancel all in another edition; being now assured, from information received after this sheet was printed, that Herodotus's allotment of the eight months' reign of the Magian (whereby he gives the first seven months to complete the eighth year of Cambyses, but gives the eighth and last month to commence the first year of Darius) was a matter of Khaldæan testimony, and that the regnal year at Babylon began with Markhesvan of the Assyrians and Jews, or Bágayádish of the Persians, a month nearly corresponding with the Julian November. Moreover, we find that the Khaldæans made the first year of a reign begin with the first of Markhesvan next after the demise of the crown by the last king. Accordingly, though the pretended Smerdis, that is, Gaumáta the Magian (who had assumed, it seems, the regal name Artakhshatra or Artaxerxes), was still on the throne during the first ten days of the Markhesvan which followed Cambyses' death,—yet, he being rejected from the annals as an usurper, the Khaldæan year beginning with that Markhesvan (Oct.-Nov. B.C. 521) was counted at Babylon the first regnal year of Darius son of Hystaspes. When the Khaldæan Canon of Reigns from Nabonassar to Alexander was prefixed (by Ptolemy say) to the Egyptian Canon of Reigns subsequent to Alexander's, beginning with the Egyptian year marked by Alexander's death, and assigned by Egyptian annalists to Philip Aridæus as his first, all the Khaldæan years were made Egyptian. Hence Darius was made to begin his reign about ten months earlier than by the Khaldæan reckoning. See Appendix, Art. 3, Section A.

P. 139, *Note* (*c*).—Subjoin to this note: " As to the festivity of the occasion among the Perso-Median Aryans, it may be remarked that Strabo, xv. 1, § 69, reports: λέγεται δὲ καὶ ταῦτα παρὰ τῶν

συγγραφίων, ὅτι ... Ἰνδοὶ ... ὅταν Βασιλεὺς λούσῃ τὴν τρίχα μεγά-
λην ἑορτὴν ἄγουσι, καὶ μεγάλα δῶρα πέμπουσι, τὸν ἑαυτοῦ πλοῦτον
ἕκαστος ἐπιδεικνύμενος κατὰ ἄμιλλαν. He adds, § 71 (apparently from
Kleitarkhus) : Ἰνδοὺς κομᾶν καὶ πωγωνοτρέφειν πάντας, ἀναπλεκομένους
δὲ μετροῦσθαι τὰς κόμας.

P. 143, Line 31.—To the note (b), "Herod. iii. 15," subjoin:
"The rule at the present day of the conduct of the Chinese government to the vassal princes of different ranks in Mongolia is similar. In his *Souvenirs d'un voyage dans la Tartarie, le Thibet, et la Chine pendent les années* 1844, 1845, *et* 1846, tome 1, pp. 285, 286, M. Huc tells us, 'Bien que les souverains Mongols se croient tenus d'aller tous les ans se prosterner devant le *fils du ciel*, *maître de la terre* ils sontiennent cependant que *le Grand Khan* n'a pas le droit de détrôner les familles régnantes dans les principantés tartares. Il peut casser le roi pour des causes graves ; mais il est obligé de mettre à la place un de ses enfants. La souveraineté appartient, disent-ils, à telle famille ; ce droit est inamissible, et c'est un crime de prétendre l'en déposséder.'

"The claims of reigning families seem to have been recognised, before the Persian supremacy, by the Assyrians and Babylonians, and also by the Egyptians. For the two last, we might cite the conduct of Nebukhadrezzar and Nekho in Judah. Perhaps Jehu, who is called *Son of Omri* in the Assyrian inscriptions which record the presents he sent to the king of Assyria, by whom Hazael king of Damascus was invaded, had given himself that title, knowing that, as a usurper of the throne of Samaria, he would be odious to the Great King of Assyria. The claim of a royal family, however, must have been always liable to be set aside, just as it is now in Mongolia by the Great Khan, the Emperor of China: 'Dont la volonté toute puissante est au-dessus de toutes les lois et de tous les usages. Dans la pratique *l'Empereur a le droit de faire tout ce qu'il fait* et ce droit ne lui est contesté par personne.'"

P. 144, Note (f).—To this note it may be added: "But another Apis city within reach of Nile water is given, on what authority we know not, in Wyld's Map, entitled *Isthmus of Suez and Lower Egypt, with the proposed Canals*. In this map, on the south shore of the Lake Mareotis is placed not only Mareia or Marea, identified with the modern *El Khreit*, where there are ruins, and a well of good water ; but also, about 14 miles away towards the Delta, *Apis*, identified with the modern *El Kasheet*, where, however, neither well nor ruins are marked.

"From Herod. ii. 30, it appears that before the Persian conquest the Pharaohs maintained a garrison at Marea, making that place the headquarters against the Libyans of a considerable division of Egyptian troops."

P. 144, Line 34, *or* 17 *of Note* (f).—After the words "into the lake" insert this sentence: "For he writes, ἐλθὼν δὲ ἐς Κάνωβον καὶ

κατὰ τὴν λίμνην τὴν Μαρίαν περιπλεύσας ἀποβαίνει ὅπου νῦν 'Αλεξάν-
δρεια πόλις ᾤκισται 'Αλεξάνδρου ἐπώνυμος. *Exp. Alex.* iii. 1, § 4. But
Alexander could hardly have had a motive for landing at the back of
the site from the lake, rather than in front of it from the sea."

P. 149, *Note* (o).—Add to this note the following : " As to the
impaling of Inaros on three stakes, we may adduce in illustration
Plutarch's *Vita Artaxerxis* (Mnemonis), cap. 17, § 2, where we read
that Arsikas, whose name when he came to the throne had been
changed to Artoxerxes, and who was surnamed Mnēmon, was engaged by his mother Parysatis at a game of *cubes*, Κυβοι, in which
each player staked a eunuch, to be selected by the winner. Parysatis
contrived to win, and chose Masabates, whom the king had employed
to cut off the head and hand of his brother Cyrus's corpse, at or after
the battle of Cunaxa. Parysatis then put her prize into the hands of
those who were over the punishments, and commanded them to skin
him alive, and then fix up the body athwart by three stakes, and
stretch out the skin apart with pegs: ἐκδεῖραι ζῶντα καὶ τὸ μὲν
σῶμα πλάγιον διὰ τριῶν σταυρῶν ἀναπῆξαι, τὸ δὲ δέρμα χωρὶς διαπατ-
ταλεῦσαι.

P. 151, *Line* 26 (or 23 of note).—For, " B.C. 458 will be the year
which next ensued after," read, " B.C. 459 will be the year of the
going forth of."

P. 151, *Lines* 29, 30 (or 26, 27 of note).—For, " Moreover the previous year, wherein the order went forth, will be that Jewish civil
year," read, " Now this first of the 490 Jewish civil years will be that
very year."

P. 151, *Lines* 34, 35 (or 31, 32 of note).—Omit the parenthesis,
" according to the Egyptian reckoning and that of Ptolemy's Canon."

P. 151, *Line* 36 (or 33 of note).—After " B.C. 459," add to the
sentence this : "according to the Egyptian reckoning ; or, as we shall
see below, on the 1st of Markhesvan B.C. 458 according to the Chaldæans, but on the 1st of Nisan B.C. 458 according to the Judæo-
Assyrian tables of years, followed not only by Haggai, Zechariah, and
the author of Esther, but, as we believe, by Ezra also."

We would also add these further observations :—Prideaux makes
the 490 years end with our Lord's crucifixion, an event which he also
places on the 14th of Nisan A.D. 33 ; and he supposes the period to
have begun with the setting forth of Ezra from Babylon on the 1st of
Nisan B.C. 458. The interval is about a fortnight more than 490
years, and might be reduced to 12 days by supposing it to have begun
with the departure from the river Ahava : Ezra viii. 31. But the
Messiah's death is fixed by the prophecy, not at the end of the seventy
weeks of years, but in the middle of the seventieth week, that is, in
the 487th year of the period. For the prophecy declares, first, that
the Messiah shall be cut off after 62 weeks, a subdivision of the 70
which follows a former group of seven weeks ; that is to say, the pro-

phecy declares, first, that the Messiah is to be cut off in the 70th week of years. Secondly, it is foretold, that in the middle of that week (during which He shall also confirm the covenant with many) the Messiah shall cause the sacrifice and oblation to cease. Now the Gospel declares, that by the sacrifice of himself the Messiah, being the true Priest typified by Aaron and his successors, caused the Mosaic sacrifices and priesthood, as to their virtue and obligation, to cease. We must therefore conclude that our Lord, the Messiah, Jesus's crucifixion, according to the prophecy, happened in the 487th year of the period. But the Lord's death, according to St. Paul's Epistle to the Galatians, happened not less than 16 years before that visit of St. Paul's to Jerusalem, during which, according to St. Luke's Acts of the Apostles, shortly after Passover, Herod Agrippa king of Judah died. See Gal. i. 18, ii. 1; Acts xi. 29, 30, xii. 1, 4–6, 19–25. But the testimonies of Josephus enable Clinton to place the death of Herod Agrippa in the summer of A.D. 44. (See that year in Clinton's *Fasti Romani.*) Now, the Jewish civil year which ended with the month Elul A.D. 44 is the sixteenth of a series beginning with the month Tisri A.D. 28. In accordance, therefore, with the testimony of St. Paul in the passages referred to of his Epistle to the Galatians, we place our Lord's crucifixion in the Nisan of A.D. 29.

We may add, that thus the crucifixion is found to have happened at the 33d Passover of a series commencing with the one that followed the death of the first Herod in B.C. 4. (For this date of Herod's death, later than an eclipse of the moon on the 13th of March, see that year in Clinton's *Fasti Hellenici*, vol. 3.) In other words, the crucifixion happened 32 full years after the death of that Herod who hoped to slay our Lord by destroying all the infants of Bethlehem "from two years old and under"—ἀπὸ διετοῦς καὶ κατωτέρω, Matt. ii. 16; or, as we understand it, born during the previous and since the commencement of the then current Jewish civil year. We suppose, then, that at Herod's death our Lord was in the first at least, but perhaps in the second, Jewish civil year since his birth. Perhaps his conception by the Virgin Mother happened in the civil year which ended with Elul, and his birth in that which began with Tisri, B.C. 5. The Passover of the crucifixion is the third distinctly marked in our Lord's course after He had received the baptism of John. See St. John ii. 13, vi. 4, and xii. 1. And it seems to be of the time of his receiving that baptism that St. Luke says He was about 30 years old (ὡσεὶ ἐτῶν τριάκοντα, Luke iii. 23). He says that Jesus was as it were 30 years old *at his beginning*, ἀρχόμενος; and this beginning is to be explained both by the previous context, in which his baptism is related, and also by Mark i. 1, where the beginning of the gospel—ἡ ἀρχὴ τοῦ εὐαγγελίου—of Jesus Christ Son of God is plainly John's ministry, and the baptism of the Lord Jesus by him. But the most precise proof of St. Luke's meaning in Luke iii. 23 is found in Acts i. 22. If the baptism happened after the 1st of Tisri A.D. 26, and commencement of the Baptizer's second year, we might suppose the 30 years to be years of the Civil Calendar completed on that day.

As to the going forth of the commandment to restore and build Jerusalem, in consequence whereof the street was to be built again and the wall in troublous times, Dan. ix. 25, the notification of this resolve of the king's appears to be regarded by Ezra as the most recent of the mercies by which, since the nation had lost its freedom, God had mitigated their condition. Confessing to God upon his knees, with his face toward the sanctuary and his hands stretched out, in the ninth month of the year in which he came to Jerusalem, Khisleu, B.C. 458, he mentions this particular last. He says, "Our God hath not forsaken us in our bondage, but hath extended mercy to us in the sight of the kings of Persia, to give us a reviving, to set up the house of our God, and to repair the desolations thereof, and to give us a wall in Judah and Jerusalem." See Ezra ix. 9. The repairing of the desolations of the house of God here spoken of may have been recent, and not included in that setting up of the house which had been accomplished nearly 60 years before; for since Ezra's arrival, the commissions which he carried for them having been delivered to the king's lieutenants and to the governors west of the Euphrates, *they furthered the people*, it is said, *and the house of God:* Ezra viii. 36. But the king's commission, giving to the people a wall in Judah and Jerusalem, and which Prideaux also makes the commencement of the 490 years, though he places it at 1st Nisan B.C. 458, instead of, as we do, before 1st Tisri B.C. 459,—that is, in the year which ended with Elul B.C 459,—is considered by that learned person to have reference to a *moral* defence. He takes "wall" metaphorically. But that a royal order to fortify Jerusalem had been issued since the completion of the house of God in the time of Darius, and perhaps very long since, we may safely infer from the lamentation of Nehemiah in the 20th year of this reign, B.C. 444-3, at the news that the people in the province of Judah were in great affliction and reproach, and that the wall of Jerusalem also was broken down, and the gates thereof burned with fire: Neh. i. 3. Nehemiah certainly was not so deeply affected by the old story of what the Chaldæans had done 140 years before.

P. 155, *Line* 27.—For "golden poniard," read "poniard."

P. 156, *Line* 18 (*i.e.* line 8 of note).—After "too unlike to Greek," insert this sentence: "For the language on the remains of Etruscan art is often (*i.e.*, apparently, when it is Tyrrheno-Pelasgian) very closely akin to Greek; as in the well-known legend, *Mi Kalairu fuios*, εἰμί (or query ἐγώ) Καλαίρου Φυιός, in Lanzi's *Epitafi scelti*, No. 191." So G. R. in his Herodotus, vol. iii. p. 545.

P. 156, *Line* 40.—To the note (*c*) ("Herod. vii. 113"), add the following: "Perhaps the many ceremonies attendant on the passage of the Strymon by Xerxes were due to the fact, that it was the boundary between the Thracians and races that spoke languages akin to Greek. G. R. observes in his Herodotus, vol. iii. pp. 542, 543, that Æschylus makes Pelasgus king of Argos rule over all Greece, from the Peloponnese on the south to the river Strymon in the north: Supplices, 245–257."

P. 157, *Lines* 13, 14 (or 2 and 3 of Note (*f*)).—For, "We think George Rawlinson's version, *set it on fire* (in his note . . .), inconsistent," read, "The version, *set it on fire* (in a note of G. R.'s on Herod. vii. 114), is a misrepresentation of the sense of the Greek verb in the Middle Voice, and carries a sense inconsistent."

P. 157, *Line* 18 (or 7 of Note (*f*)).—Instead of, "Following, then, the common meaning of ἅπτεσθαι," read, "Therefore, for the difference between ἅψαι πῦρ and ἅψασθαί τινος, referring the reader to St. Luke xxii. 51, 55."

P. 160, *Lines 5 and* 10.—Transpose "not a few of the learned" from line 5 to line 10, placing the words before "have been pleased to."

P. 170, *last Line*.—Cancel this note and the Apology No. 5 of Appendix.

P. 172, *Line* 11.—After "1013½ Eubœan talents of silver," add to the paragraph the following: "Such is the difference, according to Herodotus's statement, of the proportion between Babylonian and Eubœan talents. But a more exact account of the matter is derived from a writer followed by Ælian, *Var. Hist.* i. 22. According to him, the Babylonian talent really weighed 72 Eubœan minæ, or one-fifth more than a Eubœan talent; so that instead of six Babylonian talents being equal to seven Eubœan (as Herodotus leads us to conclude), five Babylonian equalled six Eubœan talents. Now, according to this proportion, the 7600 Babylonian talents of yearly silver tribute (which we have obtained by adding together the tributes of 19 non-Europæan and silver-paying satrapies, as stated in detail by Herodotus) will be equal to 9120 Eubœan talents,—falling short of the 9880 Eubœan talents, Herodotus's total silver tribute, by 760 Eubœan talents only. And this smaller difference may, more probably than the other, be taken to represent the king's tribute from the islands and countries of his dominion in Europe. And if the other Herodotean reading, 9540 for 9880, be preferred for the total of silver, the difference is further reduced to 420 Eubœan talents."

P. 172, *Lines* 18–21.—As to the assertion, "However," etc. . . ., what is the authority? Is not the reverse the better authenticated state of the case?

P. 173, *Line* 13.—The passage of Megasthenes is quoted from Abydenus by Eusebius, *Pr. Ev.* ix. p. 456 D, and *Chron. Arm.* p. 27, ed. Mai. In the former quotation only does Eusebius name Abydenus's authority. See *Fragm. Historic. Græcorum*, tom. ii. p. 417.

P. 174, *Line* 24.—For, "to somewhat more than 1000," read, "to 760, or perhaps only 420."

P. 174, *last Line.*—To the note (c), which forms this line, add this: "It is confirmed by the Persian monarch's grant to Themistocles (cited by George Rawlinson from Thucyd. i. 138),—a grant of the revenue not only of the inland city Magnesia, but of the sea-side Myus (comp. Thucyd. iii. 19, Herod. i. 142, Pherecydes, cited by Strabo, xiv. 1, § 3), and also Lampsacus.

"On the other hand, in Thucyd. viii. 5, 6, not only have we both Pharnabazus and Tissaphernes anxious for Peloponnesian aid to free the Greek sea-towns from the Athenians because of the tribute which they desired to recover, but, more than this, we read that Tissaphernes had been dunned by the king's treasury for the tribute due from the Greek cities of his government, although, because of the Athenians, he had been unable to recover it. Perhaps Herodotus's statement concerning the tributes in his day was to be taken with the understanding of the qualifying clause, "so far as they are still paid;" and we may suppose that for so much of their land as was insufficiently protected by the naval power of Athens, or was exposed to the ravage of the satrap's troops, the cities still paid the tribute assessed upon them."

P. 175, *last Line.*—Omit " and gold."

P. 179, *Line* 28.—For, " B.C. 515," read, " B.C. 514."

P. 179, *Line* 31.—For, " B.C. 511," read, " B.C. 510 ; or from the 23d of Sivan· in the 12th year of Darius, according to the Assyrian and Jewish registers."

P. 186, *Lines* 7, 8.—For, " in the beginning of," read, " in about November of."

P. 186, *Line* 12.—For, " at the beginning of," read, " at the accession of Darius in."

P. 187, *Lines* 36, 37.—For, " to which the command of the fleet on the same occasion was entrusted," read, " to which the admiral on the same occasion belonged."

P. 211, *Line* 3.—The name *Hien Fung* ought perhaps to be written *Tien Fung;* for we have found Mr. T. T. Meadows writing it *Teen-fung*, and saying that Teen-fung's father, the Emperor Taou-kwang, died 25th February 1850.

P. 215, *Lines* 12, 13.—For " which," read, " Now this."

P. 215, *Lines* 20, 21.—Instead of "which the analogy of other like-spelt names in the Perso-Aryan inscriptions proves to be," read, " For the analogy of other like-spelt names in the Perso-Aryan inscriptions proves '*Uwaj* to be."

P. 223 (*Title of Part* 2).—In a revision of this work, the view taken may be modified so as to allow for " Darius surnamed Khshurush," the substitution of " Khshurush surnamed Darius."

P. 226, *Line* 6.—Note: The capture of Babylon took place apparently in *Sivan* B.C. 516, when Darius's sixth year was some six months old by the Egyptian reckoning, and in its third month by the

Assyrian and Jewish reckoning. But the fifth year was still current by the Khaldæan account.

P. 227, Line 37.—After "brother," add to the paragraph: "In Plutarch's *Vit. Alexandri*, cap. 22, § 3, we read of Ada, whom Alexander made *his mother*, and appointed queen of Caria. And Strabo (xvi. 4, § 21), speaking of the Nabathæan king of Petra, says: 'He has a deputy (ἐπίτροπον), one of the Companions who is called *brother*.' Strabo particularly mentions King Obodas's deputy Syllæus, who, for his treacherous conduct when he acted as Ælius Gallus's guide in the expedition from Egypt into Arabia, was beheaded at Rome. *Ibid.* §§ 23, 24. The king's kinsmen, συγγενεῖς, in the army with which the last Darius met Alexander in Cilicia, formed, according to Curtius, a body of 15,000 men. [When Plutarch calls this Darius's Statira τὴν βασιλέως γυναῖκα καὶ ἀδελφήν, *Vit. Alex.* cap. 30, § 2, and τὴν τεθνεῶσαν ἀδελφήν καὶ γυναῖκα, *ibid.* § 4, does he not intimate a natural, not titular, relationship?]"

P. 229, Line 7.—For "five" read "six."

P. 229, Line 9.—For, "or the first six years," read, "and also."

P. 230, Lines 1, 2.—For, "Our own confidence in the conclusions at which, by the help of Herodotus, we had arrived as to the true position," read, "Our confidence in the first conclusions at which we arrived as to the position."

P. 230, Lines 11-16.—For the concluding sentence of the section beginning "When these," read, "And as to the Behistun citations from the Calendar used by the Persians during their supremacy in Asia (or at least in the days of Khshurush Darius), we were contented to hope that all remaining difficulties would be removed when those Assyrian calendars should be perfectly deciphered and understood (*a*). But as our work proceeded, an important discovery communicated by Mr. Norris (15th Dec. 1864),—being the Semitic names of the months before known only by the designations in use with those the Assyrians borrowed their Calendar from,—led us to new conclusions. Both schemes will be exhibited and discussed hereafter."

P. 230, Lines 33-40.—The last two sentences of the footnote (beginning, "The reader, when he arrives") must be cancelled, in consequence of the information which has made necessary the previous corrections in this page.

P. 232, Line 23.—For, "He was perhaps his brother," read, "He may have been eldest son of that second Teispes; perhaps his nephew, possibly his brother."

P. 233, Line 19.—Add to the paragraph which ends here the following sentence: "If Cambyses, like Darius, was the ninth of a line the first of which was Akhæmenes, then Akhæmenes may have been a contemporary of Isaiah and Hezekiah."

P. 248, Line 21.—After "Curtius iii. 4, §§ 6, 7," insert, "(It is to be remembered, however, that in this passage, according to Zumptius,

Dervices (*i. e.* Derbices) is a restoration due to Hadrianus Junius; the reading of the MSS. in general, and of the early editions universally, being *idem vicies*, while one MS. has *idem vices*, and another *idem vigies*.) Thus the region where Cyrus met his death-wound, according to Ktesias, is the same in which happened his death in battle according to Alexander Polyhistor as cited by Eusebius (Euseb. *Chron. Armen.*, ed. Mai, p. 19, cited vol. ii. p. 505 of C. Müller's *Frag. Hist. Græc.*), that is, '*in planitie Daharum.*' For the Dahæ are placed on the east of the Caspian Sea, and north of a desert on the south side of which was Hyrcania, by Strabo, xi. 7, § 1; vii. 3, § 12; xi. 8, § 2. Elsewhere Strabo makes them reach to the *Okhus* river (Strabo xi. 9, § 2), which he describes as a river of Hyrkania (Strab. xi. 7, § 3), and which seems to be the *Akes* of Herod. iii. 117.

" However, in the time of Alexander the Great there appear to have been Dahæ, Δάαι, on the Tanais, that is, the Jaxartes. See Arr. *E. A.* iii. 28, §§ 8, 10. And this is the position of the Massagetæ with whom Cyrus fought according to Herodotus. Strabo's remarks on the name Dacus might lead one to identify Dahæ with Massagetæ by aid of that middle term: see Strab. vii. 3, § 12."

P. 252, *Lines* 23, 24.—Omit the words, "attested by Josephus and."

P. 256, *Line* 5.—For ἐπυθόμην read ἐπυθόμεθα.

P. 258, *Line* 18.—Omit "with four-faced or cube-shaped stones." The original is λίθου τετραπέδου. If this be rightly translated "four-faced stone," we may understand oblong stones having two ends and four sides, any one of which might form part of the face of the wall. In the Latin version, the term is translated *Saxo quadrato.*

P. 263, *Line* 23.—For "more," read, "17 miles and 380 yards."

P. 277, *Line* 1.—Omit " the beginning of."

P. 287, *Line* 33.—Add to this note the following: " In illustration of the point that, according to Arabic authors, the Nabathæans were not children of Nebaioth (Gen. xxv. 13, xxviii. 9, xxxvi. 3), but an Aramaic people, we may perhaps adduce a passage cited by Hyde, *Rel. Vet. Pers.* pp. 41, 42, from Abu Mohammed Mustapha. ' The time of Nimrod,' says this author, ' endured in *Al Sowâd* 400 years; and Al Sowâd had for its ruler after him one of his race, whose name was *Nebat the son of Köûd*, for 100 years.' Hyde says that Chaldæa or Irak is elsewhere called Nabathæa: he refers the epithet Sowâd, ' black,' to the Arab *tents of Kedar*, or black tents, for קדר is ' blackness.'"

P. 292, *last Line of Note* (m).—Add to this note the following: " Plutarch tells us, *Alex.* cap. 36, that in the palace at Susa Alexander obtained possession of 40,000 talents of *coin*, νομίσματος; and Arrian puts the treasure at as much as 50,000 talents of *money* (ἀργυρίου), *Exp. Alex.* iii. 16, § 6. But it is apparently with more accuracy that Diodorus, xvii. 66, §§ 1, 2, reports ' more than 40,000 talents of gold and silver *uncoined*, ἀσήμου, besides 9000 talents of gold *in darics.*'

Curtius writes, v. 8, '*Incredibilem ex thesauris summam pecuniæ egessit, L. millia talentûm argenti non signati formâ sed rudi pondere ;*' where, perhaps, *et* has been dropt in transcription after *egessit*. [Note.—A woodcut representing a mould for casting coins is given by Mr. James Yates, F.R.S.: Art. *Forma* in Smith's *Dict. of Gr. and Rom. Antiquities.*]"

P. 297, *Lines* 4, 5.—Instead of "for three whole years from B.C. 525 to B.C. 522," read, "from about midsummer B.C. 525 till probably the spring of B.C. 521."

P. 298, *Line* 23.—For Αἰθιόπαων read Αἰθιόπων.

P. 301, *Line* 28.—After "Hapi" add "Moou."

P. 301, *last Line*.—Instead of "be the lake discovered by Capt. Speke," read, "include the two Nyanzas, discovered by Capt. Speke and Mr. Baker—the Victoria and the Albert."

P. 324, *Lines* 3, 4, 5.—Instead of "by Egyptian reckoning, being the 226th of Nabonassar, which coincides almost exactly with the year B.C. 522 at about midsummer," substitute, "by a Khaldæan reckoning, of which we shall have more to say hereafter, about April B.C. 521."

P. 325, *Line* 14.—Instead of "B.C. 458," substitute "B.C. 459."

P. 328, *Line* 27.—For, "town and district," read, "district and mountain."

P. 328, *Lines* 29, 30, 31.—Instead of "corresponding, we think, with the 14th of the Egyptian fifth month Tobi E.N. 226 (which day was about the 14th of May B.C. 522)," substitute, "in the year B.C. 521, probably a day of March."

P. 331, *Line* 14.—Instead of "May B.C. 522," read, "March B.C. 521."

P. 331, *Lines* 22, 23, 24.—Instead of "the 9th of the Egyptian sixth month, Mekhir, or about the 8th day of June," read, "some day of April."

P. 332, *Line* 10.—For "Darius's," read, "the Aryan version of Darius's."

P. 332, *Lines* 23-34.—Instead of "he derived his information; that is," etc. (to the end of the paragraph), substitute, "his information originated. Supposing that people to be the Egyptians, we went on, at first, to take Bágayádish to be the Persian correspondent of the Egyptian month Thoth ; and this particular Bágayádish, which should have commenced Cambyses' ninth year, to be the Thoth of E. N. 227, —that is, of the year following the eighth of Cambyses in Ptolemy's Canon, and assigned as his first to the king who slew the Magian, being, according to the method of that Canon, the year already begun when Darius succeeded to the throne. But if the Magian reign terminated in Thoth E. N. 227, it terminated in January B.C. 521 ; for it is certain that the 30 days that particular Thoth was composed of, were the first 30 days of the January we have mentioned. At this rate, too, the Garmapada when the Magian began to reign, was the

June, and the Viyakhana when he proclaimed himself to be Smerdis son of Cyrus, was the May, of B.C. 522. It will be seen below why we have abandoned these conclusions, with others depending upon them; and now regard the Bágayádish that ended the Magian's reign and began that of Darius to be nearly the Julian month November, the Viyakhana when he first appeared in Persis to be nearly the March, and the Garmapada wherein he ascended the throne in Media to be nearly the month April, of the year B.C. 521."

P. 332, Line 35.—Instead of "the Egyptians," read, "whether Egyptians or Khaldæans."

P. 339, Lines 11, 12, 13.—Instead of "(perhaps the 10th of the Egyptian Thoth E. N. 227, which was also the 10th of our Roman January B.C. 521)," read, "corresponding nearly, as we shall find, with the month November of B.C. 521."

P. 340, last Line.—To the note here ending, add the following: "Referring to Sir H. C. R.'s march from Zohab to Khuzistan, detailed in the Geogr. Society's Journal, vol. x. p. 100, G. Rawlinson remarks, Herod. vol. i. p..41, note (b), that the Nissæan district may probably have been the tract of excellent pasture land which lies between Behistun and Khorram-abad, known now as the plains of Khawah and Alistar."

P. 341, Lines 22, 23.—Omit " before the era of Nabonassar."

P. 354, Lines 27, 28.—Instead of " fifth Egyptian month in the eighth year of Cambyses E. N. 226, or to May B.C. 522," read, " fifth month of the eighth year of Cambyses, according to a calendar to be produced hereafter; and also answered nearly, as we have already said, to March B.C. 521."

P. 355, Lines 11, 12.—Instead of "what would have been counted in Egypt to Cambyses," read, "what at Babylon, as we shall show, would have been counted to Cambyses."

P. 357, Line 10.—After "the lawful king," add to the paragraph so ending the following: "Moreover, after the clause in which he sums up by saying, *So much did I after, when I became king*, Darius immediately proceeds to date the season of his ensuing achievements as, *after, when I slew Gaumáta the Magian (o)*. Thus the date at which he became king was earlier in his own estimation than the date at which he slew Gaumáta."

P. 357 (bottom of).—As a footnote on the lines introduced at line 10, add, "(o) See Aryan text, col. 1, line 73; or para. 16 according to Sir H. C. R.'s division."

P. 371, Line 14.—For λεπτῶν read λεπτῶν.

P. 389, Lines 12, 13.—For, " Khonds maintain," read, " Khonds believe."

P. 394, Line 36.—To the end of Note (h) add this: "The name Asura occurs also in the preceding hymn 54, where, in stanza 4, it is said to Indra, *Thou hast hurled . . . the . . . thunderbolt against the assembled Asuras:* for the word Asuras is not printed here within brackets as a scholiast's gloss. In the text, too, of stanza 2, hymn 30 of the 6th Mandala and 4th Ashtaka, the *Asura-destroying* vigour of Indra is proclaimed. See Professor H. H. Wilson's *Rig-Veda Sanhita*, vol. i. pp. 148, 151; vol. iii. p. 443.

P. 395, *Line* 14.—For "and" read "though."

P. 395, *Lines* 31, 32.—Instead of the short sentence, "The Jaxartes is called by Herodotus, i. 201, Araxes, *Arakhshas*," read, "For notices of the Rakhshasas in the Rig-Veda hymns, see H. H. Wilson's *Rig-Veda Sanhita*, vol. i. p. 100; vol. ii. pp. 29, 30; vol. iii. pp. 41, 143, 304, 414, 419. According to a commentator on the second of these passages, they were *of a black colour.* Araxes (*Arakhsha*), a celebrated river-name, is by Herodotus, i. 201, applied to the Jaxartes. This latter name, *Yaksharta*, may have been properly the name of a region occupied by the Yakshas, and watered by the river so called. Tanais was a mere Macedonian misnomer of this river: ὃν δὴ καὶ Ἰαξάρτην ἄλλῳ ὀνόματι πρὸς τῶν ἐπιχωρίων βαρβάρων καλεῖσθαι λέγει Ἀριστόβουλος. So writes Arrian, *Exp. Alex.* iii. 30, § 7."

P. 396, *Line* 43.—Add to the note that ends here, this: "However, for Asura, as an epithet of honour, we may refer to the 7th and 10th stanzas of a hymn which stands the 30th both in the first Ashtaka and the first Mandala of the *Rig-Veda Sanhitá;* where it is applied, along with other epithets, to Suparna (the Solar Ray), and to Savitri, the same as Surya or 'the Sun.' It is there explained 'Life-giving,' from *asu*, 'vital breath,' and *ra*, 'who gives.' See Wilson, *R.-V. Sanhitá*, vol. i. p. 99, and his note on stanza 7. In the 4th stanza of the 164th hymn, we have *Asuh* rendered by Sáyana, 'breath.' See Wilson's Translation of the 2d Ashtaka, p. 127, note (*g*)."

P. 400, *Line* 39.—To the note here ending, add, "The psalm belongs to the 5th and last section of the Book of Psalms, which begins with the 107th Psalm, and is supposed to consist in great measure of psalms written after the return from Babylon. Granting this description, the unlearned reader will yet observe that the 110th Psalm, or 4th of the bundle which forms the last section of the book, is ascribed by our Lord to David, and that the difficulty of the question He proposes—'If David call the Messiah his Lord, how is the Messiah David's son?'—might have been eluded if the scribes had known the psalm to be not one of David's. It follows, that the 136th Psalm also may be far older than the captivity, though found in the last volume of the Psalter. The previous sections begin with the 1st, 42d, 73d, and 90th Psalms respectively."

P. 403, *Line* 34.—For "ensuing," read, "the current."

P. 403, *Line* 35.—For "following," read, "in B.C. 549."

P. 403, *Line* 37.—For "Assyrian" read "Khaldæan."

P. 404, *Line* 4.—For *H*, read *h*, in "His."

P. 415, *Line* 13.—Read "Pasargadæ."

P. 416, *Line* 21.—Instead of " He is the only Persian king," read, " He was not, however, as it has been erroneously affirmed."

P. 417, *Line* 2.—Add to the paragraph ending here, " The same compliment appears to have been previously paid to Cambyses."

P. 417, *Lines* 22-25.—Instead of the present commencement of the note, from " So Sir J. G.," to " Wilkinson adds," read, " The assertion had been made in Wilkinson's *Manners and Customs of the Ancient Egyptians*, vol. i. p. 199, with an appeal for confirmation to Diod. i. 25. The error is proved by the case of Cambyses, given by the same author, in Rawlinson's Herod. vol. ii. p. 390. As to Darius, however, Wilkinson here relates."

P. 419, *Line* 17.—For "twentieth" read "nineteenth."

P. 420, *Line* 2.—The sentence beginning here with the words, " But the," and completing the paragraph which ends p. 422, line 6, will require alteration if the corrections above given should be made, as desired, in a new edition of this work. The following might be substituted: " On this subject we have been enabled to mature our conclusions through a recent discovery at the British Museum, which was made known to us by the great kindness of Mr. Edwin Norris."

P. 421, *Line* 35.—To the paragraph here ending, add the following: " The great difference between the Macedonian dialect and Greek in the time of Alexander the Great appears, where Philotas, having been called upon by Alexander to plead his cause before the mustered Macedonians in the language of their fathers, excuses himself for speaking Greek, as Alexander himself had done, on the ground that there were many present who would then understand him better. See Curtius, vi. 30. But further, there would seem to have been a resemblance between this dialect and that of Phrygia; for we find a Macedonian officer, who had risen from a low rank, adding to his other charges against Philotas, *ludibrio ei fuisse rusticos homines Phrygasque et Paphlagonas appellatos, qui non erubesceret, Macedo natus, homines linguæ suæ per interpretem audire.* See Curtius, vi. 41. Two inscriptions in the Phrygian language very nearly akin to Greek are furnished us from M. Texier's *Asie Mineure*, in G. Rawlinson's Herodotus, vol. i. p. 166."

P. 421, *Line* 36.—Omit the note in this line,—the passage it is appended to, and the page it refers to, p. 230, being alike altered in this article.

P. 422, *Line* 5.—Instead of " just now adverted to," previous corrections require us to substitute, " to this second part of our work."

P. 424, *Line* 5.—After " Nabonassar," add, " used by Ptolemy."

P. 425, *Line* 8.—Instead of " in preceding pages we have," it will be proper, for the sake of harmony with former corrections, to read, " at first we."

P. 425, *Line* 10.—Omit " have."

P. 425, *Line* 14.—Omit " have."

P. 425, *Line* 17.—For " have supposed," read " supposed."

P. 425, Line 21.—Again omit "have."
P. 425, Line 26.—Omit "now."
P. 425, Line 28.—For "tends" read "tended," and omit "even."
P. 425, Line 30.—For "are" read "would be."
P. 427, Line 1.—To "B.C. 522-518," subjoin, "or B.C. 521-516."
P. 429, Line 25.—Instead of "Ant. xi. 7, § 6," read, "Ant. xi. 5, § 4; xii. 7, §§ 6, 7."
P. 429, Line 29.—Between "148" and "called" insert, "; the eight days' annual commemoration whereof, called φῶτα by Josephus, is."
P. 429, Line 39.—After "Ezra vi. 15," insert this parenthesis: "(where Josephus, Ant. xi. 4, § 7, tells us the Macedonian name of the month was Dystrus)."
P. 437, Lines 20-23.—Omit this last sentence of the paragraph (the sentence beginning "Hence," and ending "Darius"), as no longer necessary after former corrections.
P. 438, Line 37.—For the same reason, omit "now."
P. 447, Line 23.—Instead of the sentence beginning here with the word "Formerly," and ending, p. 448, line 4, with the word "distinguished," substitute the following: "However, corresponding as it does nearly with January, Anámaka corresponds also with the last pair of the six half-zodiac signs of the quarter which the year closes with in China. The first sign of this closing pair began on the 5th of January in A.D. 1844. Now, if Anámaka was considered by the Persians (what, with its moon, that last pair of the twenty-four half-zodiac signs is considered in China) the last month of the year, then it must be owned that the moon periodically intercalated in order to adjust the lunar to the solar year, would follow immediately after Anámaka, and form a second Anámaka, according to a very general practice among the ancient nations of intercalating at the end of their respective years."
P. 448, Line 5.—For, "then supposed," read, "once supposed."
P. 448, Line 12.—Omit "or."
P. 448, Line 17.—After "Yezdegherd," insert, "the last Sassanian king of the Persians on the eve of the Arab conquest, or before that conquest was completed."
P. 448, Line 21.—To the section here ending, add this: "Thus, as Anámaka has been observed to correspond in season with what is the last month of the winter and the year in China, while by its name also may be intimated a connection of it with the end of the Perso-Aryan year; so the ensuing month, Thuraváhara, corresponding nearly with our February, corresponds likewise with the first of the twelve pairs of Half-signs into which the Chinese divide the Zodiac and the Calendar year. Nay, we find the equivalent of Thuraváhara in the name of the first of those two corresponding fortnights, Lih-tchin, which is interpreted 'Opening the Spring.' In our year 1843 the Lih-tchin began with the 5th of February; and the ceremony Ying-tchin, or 'Meeting

the Spring,' outside the east gate of a city, was fixed on the 4th of February, that is, the eve of the new year and new spring's day (o). Thus we are led to expect the old Persian year (as distinguished from the Assyrian, the Khaldæan, and the Magian) to have begun with Thuravàhara and ended with Anámaka."

P. 448.—The addition above made to the here-ending sixth Section requires the following footnote : " (o) The procession went forth by the east gate of the city to a building in an open space in the suburb, where were set up figures—one, of the god of the Spring, the other, of a parti-coloured ox. The former is sometimes a young man, said to be the deified son of one of the ancient emperors of China. With the latter is in some places used a ceremony called p'ien-tchin, or 'Hastening the Spring.' The presiding officer strikes the ox with a stick, to make him begin the work of the plough, when instantly the figure is torn in pieces, and the pieces are scrambled for by the crowd. (Compare the scramble for pieces of the flesh of a human sacrifice in Orissa among the aborigines.) In some places the Ox of Spring is a huge figure of clay ; but commonly it is a rude painting on paper, pasted to a bamboo frame three feet high and five feet broad. (See Milne's *Real Life in China*, pp. 120-150. French Translation, Part 2, chap. 3.) Mr. Milne is inclined to refer the modern ceremony to a custom spoken of in the Chou-king (Shoo-king)—under the Hia dynasty 4000 years ago—as follows: *In the first month of spring a messenger of the emperor's went here and there on the roads with a wooden rattle, to announce to the country people the return of spring and its labours.* (With the Chinese ceremony of Meeting the Spring, compare the Magian Feast of the Beardless Rider.)"

P. 454, *Lines* 34, 35.—For " Ganbil" read " Gaubil."

P. 468, *Line* 12.—Instead of "years of Yezdegherd and of Nabonassar," read, " series—one of Egyptian years of the era of Nabonassar, and another of a hundred and twenty Magian years, beginning with the eighth month of the year in which the seventh month had been doubled, and ending (if the series was complete) with the seventh month of the year in which the eighth month was doubled, under Yezdegherd's auspices, and (as we suppose) in A.D. 649, or A. Sel. 960."

P. 468, *Line* 34.—For " noon," read, " the noon of."

P. 470, *Line* 2.—For " 310" read " 210."

P. 484, *Line* 4.—After " was made," for, "and Egypt," read, " and Persis, of which no less will appear hereafter ; also Egypt."

P. 491, *Line* 7.—For " (or " read " or (."

P. 494, *last Line*.—After " 12th regnal year," insert, " by the Jewish, which was also the Assyrian reckoning."

P. 519, *Line* 26.—For " Memnoneion " read " Memnoneian."

P. 531, *Line* 6.—Instead of " With," read, " On a separate and loftier couch, having a table for his single use beside it (o), and with." *The note to be as follows:* " (o) Athenæus, iv. p. 153 A., cites from

Posidonius of Apamea in Syria, Παρὰ Πάρθοις ἐν τοῖς δείπνοις ὁ βασιλεὺς (not their own king indeed, but his captive, whom he treated like a king, Demetrius Nicator king of Syria) τήν τε κλίνην, ἐφ' ἧς μόνος κατέκειτο, μετεωροτέραν τῶν ἄλλων καὶ κεχωρισμένην εἶχε· καὶ τὴν τράπεζαν μόνῳ καθάπερ ἥρωι πλήρη βαρβαρικῶν βοινημάτων παρακειμένην. Demetrius remained in captivity nearly the 10 years B.C. 138–128, in the successive Parthian reigns of Mithridates I. and Phrahates II.; and the birth of Posidonius seems to fall within the same 10 years. There is an Assyrian sculpture in the B. M. exhibiting the king on a couch quaffing from a bowl, with ladies and eunuchs before him."

P. 533, Lines 2, 3.—For, "the wives of men of other countries of low as well as high degree," read, "those who had accompanied husbands of high degree from elsewhere."

P. 533, Line 31.—Omit "Persian."

P. 533, Line 32.—After "*kether*," insert, "And that this was not an Aryan but a Shemitic word, is sufficiently apparent from the existence in Hebrew, not only of the cognate verb (in the Piel and Hithpael forms), but also of the cognate noun *kothereth* in 1 Kings vii. 16, etc., 2 Chron. iv. 12, signifying the 'capital of a pillar.' But of late the word *kitarri* has been found in Assyrian: see Nebukhadrezzar's Borsippa cylinder, col. 2, line 13, where Mr. H. F. Talbot renders it the 'top' or 'crown' of a building; see Journal R.A.S. vol. xviii. pp. 39, 47. We may confidently suppose that the kings of the Medes adopted both the name and the thing from their Assyrian predecessors in imperial majesty."

P. 536, Line 40.—To the note (*o*), which ends here, add the following: "To the mourning proclaimed by Cyrus we have also to add that ordered by Alexander the Great after the death of Hephæstion. Diodorus tells us, xvii. 114, that all who dwelt in Asia were commanded to extinguish the Fire, called by the Persians Sacred, during the funeral rites; as they had been in the habit of doing at the death of the Great King. For an example of sacrificing to Hephæstion as to a god Assessor, θεῷ παρέδρῳ, Alexander slew 10,000 victims, ἱερεῖα, of all kinds, and entertained the multitude splendidly. *Ibid.* cap. 115. One might safely estimate the multitude at not less than 10 to every beast of sacrifice, or 100,000 in all. This illustration of Darius's feast at Susa we add to the one already given, p. 529, Note (*g*)."

P. 551, Line 33.—Omit the second "given."

P. 552, Line 25.—For "yet," read, "yet, as Persis was in revolt."

P. 569, Line 28.—For, "the chapter," read, "chap. 98."

P. 598, Line 35.—For "Vidaran" read "Vidarna."

P. 598, Line 36.—For "Yatiya" read "Yutiya."

P. 604, Line 30.—To Note (*a*) add the following: "This compound term, denoting the Two-horned Aryan realm (the kingship of which is perhaps exhibited by the two-horned head-dress of Seleucus Nicator's effigy on his coins), was still used in the days of the Jewish author of the first Book of Maccabees, who lived after the Parthian empire had reached its furthest limits towards the west. He uses it in connection with the expedition of Antiochus Epiphanes into the Upper Provinces, while treating of the siege of Jerusalem by the boy Antiochus, now king, and called Eupator, about A. Sel. 150, beginning with the month *Dius* B.C. (312 – 149 =) 163. He also uses it in connection with the expedition of Demetrius Nicator against the Parthians, undertaken A. Sel. 172, which year began with Dius B.C. (312 – 171 =) 141. In 1 Macc. vi. 55, we read why the king and captains were persuaded by the Regent Lysias to grant the Jews peace under their own laws, and to return to Antioch. The news had arrived that Philip, whom Antiokhus Epiphanes when he was yet alive at Babylon had appointed his son's guardian, was returned *from Persis and Media, ἀπὸ τῆς Περσίδος καὶ Μηδείας*, and with him the forces that had accompanied the late king, and that he was seeking to get the regency into his hands. Observe, however, that the Persis and Media of the first Book of Maccabees, like the Parthian empire, extends so far west as to comprehend *Babylon*. See 1 Macc. vi. 4, 5; where observe also that the term Persis is used alone to designate the region over which, in the author's time, the Parthian sway extended. But the double term Persis and Media, in our Kbshnrush Darius's use of it, excludes Babylon. Our other passage is 1 Macc. xiv. 1–3; where we are told how 'Demetrius gathered his forces and went to Media, that [when he had accomplished certain hopes there] he might draw to him succour to subdue [his now strong antagonist in Syria] Tryphon. And Arsakes ὁ βασιλεὺς τῆς Περσίδος καὶ Μηδείας, *the king of Persis and Media*, heard that Demetrius was come to his borders; and he sent one of his governors to seize him alive: and he went and smote the camp of Demetrius, and seized him, and brought him to Arsakes; and he put him in ward.' In both the passages cited the one singular article τῆς (though in the latter passage omitted by the Alex. MS.) being prefixed to the couple of countries is significant of *a single* kingdom, formed by the union of the two countries Persis and Media."

The expedition of Demetrius Nicator marks so important a crisis in the after history of the countries our work relates to, that we may be excused for dwelling here a few moments upon it. Posidonius of Apamea in Syria (who for the period in which he lived might have been son of Demetrius), as quoted by Athenæus, iv. p. 153, A., confirms our author above cited in the important particular that Media was the country Demetrius went to; for he related that the king (Athenæus miscalls him Seleucus) having gone up to Media, and warring against Arsakes, was taken prisoner by the barbarian, and spent a long time with Arsakes, being kept the while like a king. The Jewish historian Josephus, who makes great use of the first Book of Maccabees, gives us minuter information from some other authority on the expedition of Demetrius. Previously, in *Antiq.* xiii. 5, §§ 3, 4, he had told us, that after Tryphon had defeated Demetrius in battle, and had won the city of Antioch and the elephants, Demetrius retired into Cilicia (leaving, however, his queen Cleopatra, with her children, in the fortress of Seleucia, the port at the mouth of the Orontes, where Aeskhrion was his governor, as it would appear from Jos. *Antiq*. xiii. 7, § 1, and the extracts from Diodorus published in *Fr. Hist. Græc.* vol. ii. pp. xix. xx.). Afterwards, having detailed the successes of Jonathan, the high priest of the Jews, against Demetrius's commanders in Southern Syria, our author proceeds to relate, *Antiq*. xiii. 5, § 11, that Demetrius went across and arrived in Mesopotamia, purposing to occupy that and Babylon (query, *Babylonia*,—elsewhere coupled with Mesopotamia, as *e.g. Antiq*. xii. 3, § 4); and after he should have become possessed of the Upper Satrapies, thence to derive the resources of his whole kingly estate (or, query, the whole resources of his kingship), ἐντεῦθεν ποιεῖσθαι τὰς ὕλης (query ὅλας: comp. τὰς ὅλας ἀφορμάς, G. Sync., Dind. ed., p. 56, line 9) τῆς βασιλείας ἀφορμάς. For the Greeks and Macedonians that dwelt there were continually sending embassies to him; promising that if he would come to them, they would give themselves up to him, and help to overpower Arsakes king of the Parthians. Encouraged by these hopes, he set forth to them ; having decided (if he subdued the Parthian, and got him a power) to fight Tryphon, and expel him from Syria. And they in the province having received him heartily, he gathered a power, warred against Arsakes, and having lost all his army, was himself taken alive. So Josephus. We had before learnt that Media was the intended field of war; and here it is intimated that the Parthians were not yet masters of Mesopotamia and Babylonia. Now, Trogus Pompeius, in Justin xli. 6, assigns to the reign of the Arsakes with whom Demetrius contended, namely, Mithridates the First, a war between the Parthians and the Medes, the conquest of Media, and afterwards of the king of the Elymæans, and the extension of the Parthian frontier to the Euphrates. Demetrius, then, would seem to have interfered before the conquest of Media was fully achieved, or before the cities had thoroughly acquiesced in the new domination. And his captivity may have been quickly followed by that extension of the Parthian dominion to the Euphrates which is ascribed to his Parthian conqueror. According to Trogus Pompeius (in Justin xxxvi. 1), he undertook the Parthian war to retrieve his credit in Syria, and with no unwillingness on the part of the eastern nations, who (though they seem to have become independent of the Syrian kings) were more inclined (now that they were invaded or threatened by the Parthians) to return to their Macedonian masters than to submit to new and more oppressive masters. And so (continues Justin), assisted by Persian, Elymæan, and Bactrian succours, Demetrius routed the Parthians in many engagements. At last, however, deceived by a pretence of peace, he is taken. He is led through the gaze of the cities and exhibited to the populations that had revolted, in ridicule of their preference. Sent afterwards into Hyrcania, he is treated bountifully, and in the style of his former fortune. For the sequel, see Justin xxxviii. 9, 1. That Demetrius obtained Persian, Elymæan, and Bactrian reinforcements for his war with the Parthians, is consistent with the fact before inferred, that Media was the scene of conflict; also with the statement, that the conquest of the Elymæans by the Parthians was not accomplished till after that of the Medes. It would further appear that the Medes, or some of them, had been previously conquered by the Parthians, and revolted to Demetrius upon his arrival in the country. We know not whether the conquest of Babylonia followed or preceded that of Susiana or Elymais. Orosius, v. 4, is cited, saying, " Mithridates victo Demetrio *præfecto* Babyloniam urbem finesque ejus universos victor invasit." Porphyry of Tyre, in the *Chronicon* of Eusebius (see Mai's translation of the Armenian version), also in Syncell., p. 292, C., describes Demetrius as marching to Babylon and the upper provinces against Arsakes. We have heard Josephus describing Demetrius as having crossed (apparently from Cilicia) into Mesopotamia, intending to occupy that and Babylon. It would appear from an expression of Diodorus (*Excerpta* xxv., in the Preface to the second volume of the *Fragm. Historic. Græcorum*, p. xix.), that after Demetrius's captivity one of the satraps and generals of royal race, against whom the usurper Tryphon was still in warfare, was the satrap in charge of Mesopotamia, Dionysius the Mede. Hence it is a probable conclusion, that at least part of Mesopotamia was already belonging to Demetrius when he set forth on his Parthian war.

We know that the last Akhæmenian king of kings, Darius Codomannus, is called in the opening of the First Book of Maccabees "king of the Persians and Medes." We have cited the same author calling the Arsakes Mithridates the Second (perhaps prematurely), king of Persis and Media; and we may perhaps conclude not only that the title was given to the Parthian monarchs in that author's time, but that they claimed the title as a part of the conquest.

P. 605, *Line* 3.—For " Akbad" read " Akkad."

P. 605, *Line* 35.—Add to the note this: " Strabo's Khalybonitis has been generally identified with the district of the modern Aleppo which the Arabs call *Haleb.* Its wine has been supposed to be spoken of by Ezekiel, xxvii. 18, in the wine of Helbon supplied to Tyre from Damascus. But whatever the situation may be of the district intended by Strabo, the Helbon of Ezekiel seems to have been discovered by Mr. J. L. Porter at a modern village, the name of which in Arabic is exactly the Hebrew Helbon. It stands ten or twelve miles N.W. of Damascus, high up in Antilebanon, in a wild glen, the bottom and sides of which are covered with terraced vineyards, as the country surrounding it is also rich in vines and fig-trees. See Mr. Porter's Art. HELBON in Smith's *Bible Dictionary*, where he refers to the *Journal of Sacred Literature*, July 1853, p. 260, to his work entitled

Five Years in Damascus, ii. pp. 230 sq., and his *Handbook for Syria and Palestine*, pp. 495, 496. Geo. Rawlinson, in Art. DAMASCUS, refers to *Journ. Geo. Soc.* vol. xxvi. p. 44.

P. 617, Line 29, *note.*—For, "καίτοιγε and καίτοι, Acts xvii. 27, Lach. and Tisch.," read, " καί γε, aud so the Vat. MS."

P. 618, Line 38.—Read "Akhaia."

P. 625, Line 22.—Note that the 70th year of mournful commemoration spoken of in the paragraph here ended, belongs to a period of which a particular year is called by Ezekiel *the 14th year after that the city* (Jerusalem) *was smitten.*

P. 635, Line 32.—After "p. 328" place a full stop and cancel the remainder of the note, which will be unnecessary if the corrections in p. 328 of lines 27 and 29-31 have been made as above directed.

P. 652, Line 42.—For, "adjoined the," read, "contained the park or."

P. 664, Line 37.—After the words, "writing of his own time," insert this parenthesis: "(when the Parthian dominion had further wasted the older capital, Diod. xxxiv. frag. 21, where Euhemerus is the Himerus of Justin xlii. 1, called by Posidonius, *ap. Athen.* x. p. 466, B., tyrant both of the Babylonians and of the people of Seleukeia)."

P. 665, Lines 6, 12.—There was such a measure in Egypt: see Herod. ii. 168.

P. 668, Lines 13-19.—Place a full stop after "two miles," and then instead of "so that," etc., to the end of the paragraph, read thus: " Indeed we strongly suspect the Babylonian unit of road measure to have been shorter than the coss of Hindustan. The *half-kasbu* of the Bellino cylinder, which we may regard as the Babylonian parasang (see p. 657, note), may have been six *neri* or one *sarus* of cubits; that is, may have been 60 times the *sossus* or *sús*, that is, the 'Sixty' of cubits mentioned in the Michaux Inscription (see p. 665, note). These cubits, in number 3600, should be the *half hus*, or half cubits, that are opposed to *big hus*, or big cubits, in the Assyrian inscriptions, as ordinary Egyptian cubits differ from the double cubit of the 18th dynasty found at Karnak (see pp. 658-9, note). One *sarus of big hus*, that is, 3600 double cubits, should be the *big kasbu*,—an Assyrian parasang the double of the parasang of Babylon, and analogous to the Assyrian talent, which, as Mr. Edwin Norris has discovered, weighed double the Babylonian talent, or 164 pounds English, instead of 82. And this Assyrian kasbu being just 300 yards short of 2¼ English miles, will be identified with the parasang or skhoenus of the Perso-Median and Parthian empires, known to us from the Greeks. But at 20¼ inches each, the 3600 *half hus* (or cubits equal to the ordinary cubits of Egypt, but longer by one-eighth than Greek cubits) give us for the *half* or *small* kasbu, which we call the parasang of Babylon, in English measure, 2050 yards exactly. [It was perhaps the double of this, and not of the big kasbu of Assyria, that we should recognise in the Skhoenus which Herodotus found in Egypt, and describes to have been twice as long as the parasang (see p. 489, note), though he supposed it to be double the ordinary parasang of the Persian empire, and was led thereby to erroneous conclusions.] We have already suggested that the Greek description of the length and breadth of Babylon, 120 stades by 60, may, at their usual rate of 30 stades to the parasang, be understood to mean 4 parasangs by 2; and then, supposing these parasangs to have measured 2½ English miles apiece, we found the length of the walls, and the measure of the area they contained, to be still too great for credit. But we now propose to consider the walls of Babylon as a rectangle of 4672 *smaller kasbus*; that is, of 8200 by 4100 yards; so that the four sides measured 24,600 yards, or 40 yards only less than 14 miles; and thus in length they exceeded the circuit of the walls of Rome by more than a mile."

P. 678, *Note* (*e*).—To this note may be added the following: "Thucydides tells us, that after the 18 months' siege by the Persians of the Nile-island Prosopitis,—whither the Athenians had retired,— and after its capture, through a diversion of the stream from the channel where the fleet of the Athenians lay, there were but few of the Athenians and allies, compared with those that had perished, who made their way across Libya, and reached Cyréné in safety. According to Diodorus, xi. 79, it was a treaty with the Persian generals that permitted the Greeks thus to retire from Egypt. And this seems a different treaty from the one spoken of by Ktesias, concerning the surrender of Inaros and 6000 Greeks, who were besieged together in a city called Byblus, whether this city was situated in the island Prosopitis or not."

P. 684, *Line* 25.—After, "Of the two gates," insert, "if they were not nearly opposite to one another on different sides of the northern angle of the city."

P. 694, *Line* 31.—For, "formed originally of," read, "covered originally with."

P. 694, *Lines* 38–46.—Instead of the lines beginning, "Of these measurements," we would close the note thus: "In order to reduce these English measurements to those of Nabonedus, we observe, first, that it has been seen (p. 656, note) the Assyrians had a measure of 60 *tibki*, palms or handbreadths, equal to 10 *hu-ammas* or cubits, and the sixth part of a 100-*gar*, that is, a 100-foot or 60-cubit measure. Now, if we suppose the first of the above-given three measurements to express this *vas* or 60-*tibki* measure, we get 60 *tibki* or handbreadths of 3⅛ English inches; a *gar* or foot of (3⅛ × 4 =) 12½ inches; and a *hu-amma* or cubit of 1⅞ *gar*, or 19 English inches exactly—perhaps the very cubit which Herodotus spoke of as three fingerbreadths less than a royal cubit. The bricks of this part of the building are described as 13 inches square and 3 inches thick (see p. 658, note). Perhaps 13 inches should be 12½ inches, and 3 inches, perhaps, 3⅛ inches; but in a wall, 60 such bricks high, the interstices filled with cement might amount to 60 sixths of an inch.

"The second of the measurements above mentioned, 198 English feet length of the entire building, at the above obtained rate of $3\frac{1}{4}$ inches to the handbreadth, gives 750 handbreadths, or $12\frac{1}{2}$ vas (10-cubit rods), or 125 cubits, with but one inch to spare.

"The third dimension, 133 English feet breadth of the entire building, at the same rate of $3\frac{1}{4}$ inches to the handbreadth, gives 504 handbreadths, or 84 cubits, or $8\frac{2}{5}$ ras exactly.

"These results seem to show that the handbreadth, the foot, the cubit, the rod here used by Nabonedus, measured $3\frac{1}{4}$ inches, $12\frac{3}{4}$ inches, 19 inches, and $16\frac{3}{4}$ feet (English) respectively. As to the very early gar or foot measure, indicated by the side of the early square bricks, that is, $11\frac{1}{4}$ inches (see p. 658, note), observe that it bears to the 19-inch cubit nearly the same proportion as the *gar* to the *hu* in the Michaux Inscription; for $\frac{3}{5}$ths of 19 inches are $11\frac{2}{5}$ inches."

P. 702, *Line* 12.—To close the sentence, add these words: "or to the poorer classes of all races, such as petty traders and artisans."

P. 857, *Line* 5.—For "96" read "90."

INDEX.

ABRAHAM: His journey described by Nicolaus Damascenus, 66 note. His appellation and description of God, 398.

Abu-Shareyn: Ruin of a Khaldæan temple there, having four corners pointing to the several cardinal points, and ascended from the south-east side, compared with the Muqeyer Ruin, 694 note.

Abussefeh-Nabeh: A position suitable for an army in ancient times defending Egypt against invasion from Syria, 284.

Acanthus, town: Hero-worship here given at his grave to the Akhæmenian Artakhæes, 159.

Accad language: Old Babylonian language, 426.

Actus, or "Drove:" A Roman measure of four feet in breadth and 120 in length, being properly a *Drove*, as they say in Dorsetshire, or *lane* between two lots of land 120 feet square—the correspondent of the Greek *Plethrum* and the Assyrian Sixty-cubit or Hundred-foot measure, 663 note.

— *quadratus*: A Roman square measure of 120 feet length both ways, 682 note. The half of the rectangle called *Jugus* or *Jugerum*, 663 note, 682 note.

Adam: New-year's day of the modern Persians the anniversary of his creation, 139 note.

Adrapanan: A royal seat in the country near the city Agbatana, as old as Antigonus's victory over Eumenes, now perhaps Artaman, 569 and note.

Adukanish: An Aryan month, the place of which is not determined by the Behistun inscription, 446-7. Probably the *Tasritu* or Tisri of Assyria, Table B, opposite to page 431; 561, 526, 556.

Adyrmakhidæ: Libyans dependent upon Egypt, 143, 291.

Aesepus river: Flows beside Memnon's barrow, 515, 517 note.

Aeschylus: His date, 18. Puts Susa for the capital of Persis, 19. Intimates the precedence of the Persians over the Medes, 19, 21. Also that the Kissians ranked next after the Medes, 21.

Afarti, or Afardi: Name given to Susiana in the Kissian inscriptions instead of Elam the Assyrian, and 'Uwaja or Khoja, the Aryan appellation. Supposed by Mr. E. Norris identical with the name Mardi or Amardi, 474.

Afarti-fa: People of Afardi, 510 note, 515 note. Also called Affarti, 123 note.

Affghans: Their name *Pushtun*, or *Puhtan*, etymologically connected with that of the Paktyes of Herodotus, 642 note.

Afrinaghân: A Magian festival on the five supplementary days of the year, for gladdening departed souls, 189 note.

Agbatana (the Median), 43 note. Burial-place of Parthian kings, 16. Its image of Anaitis set up by Artaxerxes II., 65. Written in Aryan *Hagamatana*, 23, 57. Now Hamadan, *ibid.*, 408. No city so named in Sargon's inscriptions, 62. Residence of Cambyses the conqueror of Egypt, 329 note; apparently of his father and of Darius the Mede before him, 243, 244. Distance thereof from Babylon, 438-9 note. By Ezra called *Akhmetha*, 560 note. Account of, 565-9.

— of Syria, 56-59. Etymology of the appellation, *ibid.* and notes. Perhaps at Damascus, 62-65.

— the Atropatenian: Gazaka so

914

Agbatana—
 called in the third century of our era, 61. Unknown to Polybius as to previous Greek writers, 566 note.
— in Persis, near Pasargadæ, 62.
— on Mount Carmel, 326.
Ahasuerus (Akhshurush or Khshurush), Esther's: Who he was according to Josephus and the Septuagint, 2, 93. According to Joseph Scaliger, 3, 94, 95. According to Ussher, 4, 94, 96. According to Eusebius, 94. A Perso-Median king, 8, 18, 22, 49. Finally discovered, 161-175.
— the Mede (Daniel's): Apparently Astyages, 15, 34, 162 notes. Mentioned in Tobit, 54, 75 note.
— (in Ezra): Median name of Cambyses, 54, 76, 162, 325 note.
Airyanem vaejo: The country of the Aryans, whence the Persians emigrated originally, according to Zend writings, 14.
Aká, or Akka: Ptolemais, Acre, 65 note.
Akhæmenes (Hakhámanish), 11, 201, 232-3, 327, 336.
— brother of Xerxes, satrap of Egypt, 145. Slain at Papremis, *ibid.* Ktesias's erroneous description of him, 145-6 note.
Akhashoerosh, or Akhashuerush (Ahasuerus): The word ill-pointed, 218. How pronounced by Hellenist translators, 219. Without vowel points becomes Akhshurush, 219.
Akhshiresh, son of Sakhbon: A Magian, 219 note.
Akhshurush: Hebrew pronunciation of Khshurush, 219. The question why this name never appears in Darius's inscriptions, 531-33 note. Written in one place without the two *vaus,* 533 note.
Alarodians: People of Ararat, 170.
Alexander the Great, 79. His visit to the tomb of Cyrus, 257. Orders the restoration of the temple of Bel at Babylon, 688, 689 and note. Trajan's visit to the room where he died, 665 note.
— son of the former by Rokhshana, murdered by Cassander, 440 and note.
— and Philip, 530 note. (Perhaps Alexander son of Roxana and

Alexander—
 Philip Aridæus, "the kings' whose letters or warrant Eumenes bore, empowering him to draw upon the treasury at Susa. Diodorus, xix. 15, sect. 5.)
Alexandria: Its situation, 142 note.
— (in Aria or Hariva): Road from, to Ortospana in the Paropamisadan land, passed through Ariana (*i. e.* Aria) rather than Baktria, 641 note.
Alkides, of Kaunus, kills Zopyrus son of Megabyzus, and is executed as a felon by Amestris, 154.
Alor, or Aror: A Hindu capital near Bakkar in Sindh, taken by Mohammed Casim, 156 note.
Alyattes, king of Lydia, 27, 34, 548-9.
Amadiyah in Kurdistan once called Agbatana, 61, 888.
Amasis, king of the 26th Egyptian dynasty, 36 note, 39, 43, 45, 53, 295-6, 549. Successor of Apries, 282, 283. Buried in the court of the temple of Neith at Sais, 295. His mummy abused and burnt, *ibid.* How had he offended? *ibid.* Had once been master of the Cypriots who followed Cambyses against him, 300 note.
— or Amosis, of a former dynasty. Through the severity of his dealings towards vagrants and depredators, loses Egypt to Aktisanes the Ethiopian, 289 note. Apparently the same as Ames or Amôs, first king of the 18th dynasty, *ibid. See* Ames.
— A Persian of the Maraphian tribe: Trusted with a command by Aryandes, satrap of Egypt,— probably son of an Egyptian woman, 187 note.
Ameinias (brother of Aeschylus) at Salamis, 199 note.
Amenti: The region of good departed spirits in the west, where Osiris reigned, 309 note, 315.
Ames, or Amôs, first king of the 18th Egyptian dynasty, by aid of Ethiopians, took Avaris and completed the expulsion of the shepherds, 289 note.
Amestris, queen of Xerxes, 3, 4 note, 96. An obstacle to such orders as those of Esther's Ahasuerus in the sixth year of his reign,

Amestris—
129; and to identifying him with Xerxes, 130. Her children, Darius Hystaspes, Artaxerxes, Amytis, Rhodogúné, 131. Daughter not of Onophas, but Otanes, 132. Cannot be Esther, 133. Nor Vashti, 133-5. All we know of her, 136-42.

Amma: The Assyrian as well as Hebrew term rendered *cubit*, otherwise called Hu, 657 note, 665.

Ammon, temple of, in Libya, 144 note. On the expedition supposed to have been directed thither by Cambyses, 303-4. At a spot now called Siwah, 304.

— son of: A title given to a Pharaoh long before the time of Alexander the Great, 511 note.

Amorges, king of the Sacæ or Sakas, 33 note, 43 note, 70 note, 246. *See* Amyrgian, Humawarga.

Amphipolis: Town built by the Athenians at *Nine Roads*, on the east bank of the Strymon above Eion, 158.

Amún, or Ammon: The god of Egyptian Thebes, confounded with Kneph, but not like Kneph, and like the Libyan Amún ordinarily exhibited as ram-headed, 318 note. The name compared with that of the Susian deity Umman, 511 note.

Amyité, sister of Astyages, 74. The name perhaps identical with that of Cyrus's Median wife, *ibid.* Miscalled daughter of Astyages by Alexander Polyhistor, 75 note.

Amyntas (king of the Macedonians): His son Alexander, and daughter Gygæa, wife of Bubares, a Persian, 187.

— son of Bubares by Gygæa, daughter of Amyntas king of the Macedonians, 187.

Amyrgians, or Amyrgian Sakas, or Humawargá, 246, 247 note.

Amyrtæus of Herodotus and Thucydides, king in the marshes of Egypt, partner in the revolt of Inarôs king of the Libyans, 143, 147, 150.

— of Ktesias: A misnomer apparently for Psammenitus son of Amasis, 73, 148 note.

— of Manetho: Not the Amyrtæus

Amyrtæus—
of Herodotus and Thucydides, 74 note, 792-5.

Amytis (the former): Median wife of the Great Cyrus. Mother of Cambyses and Smerdis, 69-74, 131. Name perhaps the same as that of Nebukhadrezzar's wife, the daughter of Cyaxares I., 74. Her former husband, her sons by him and by Cyrus, 247-50. Curses Cambyses, and dies, 54, 70. Seems to have been left by Cyrus Lady of the Derbiká and the Barkanians, her sons Spitakes and Megabernes being her satraps, 247-8 note.

— (the younger): Daughter of Xerxes, 131. Wife of Megabyzus, 152. Her light carriage in her husband's lifetime and after his death, 152, 153. Her intimacy with Apollonides, and death, *ibid.* A benefactor of the Athenians, 153 note.

Ana (or Anu): A Babylonian god. His epithet *khi*. Female forms Anata, Anuta, Anakhita, 363 note.

Anacreon, 551 note.

Anadatus (partner of a temple at Zela with Anaitis and Omanes): The same as the Anédótus of Berosus, 64 note, 371 note. *See* Anédótus.

Anaitis (Anahid, Anakhita): Her worship propagated by Artaxerxes Mnemon, 63, 64 note. Her name written also Tanais, *ibid.*; and Tanaitis, 362 note. Confounded by Herodotus with Mithra, *ibid.* and 364 note. Her temple at Zela, 371-2 note; and at Agbatana, 376. In Cappadocia her idol had for partners of its altar in the same temple Omanes and Anadatus, and was served by Magian priests, 371 note. Her sanctuary part of the royal mansion or palace at Agbatana, 567. *See* Anakhita.

Anakhita: A Babylonian goddess much worshipped by Artaxerxes Mnemon, 361. Apparently the same as the Assyrian Aphrodité miscalled by Herodotus Mitra, 364. Images of her and of Mithra, or Mitra, set up by Artaxerxes Mnemon, 362 note.

Anakhita—
Seems to have been called by Berosus Aphrodite Tanais or Aphrodité Anaitis, *ibid.* The name in a Kissian inscription written *Anam-Tanata*, in the Aryan counterpart *Anahata*, in the Assyrian *Anakhita*, 362-3 note. Etymology of Anakhita proposed by the author, *ibid.* As wife of Anu, she may have been more like the Egyptian Isis wife of Osiris than the Hindu Bhaváni, 388 note; or than the Khond Earth-goddess *Tari Pennu*, 387-8. *See* Anata, Anaitis, Tanais.

Anámaka (*i.e.* Nameless): The Aryan correspondent of the month Thabitu or Tebeth of the Assyrians, Table B, facing p. 431. Not necessarily the intercalary month (though intercalation, when needed, may have been made by doubling this month), 447. (Probably the last month of the Aryan year. *See Additions and Corrections* on 447.)

Anaphas, son of Otanes, 187.
— king or satrap of Cappadocia, perhaps descended by females from Otanes, 187.

Andromeda, 234-5 note. Deliverance of Jonah changed by Greeks into that of Andromeda near Joppa, *ibid.*

Anédótus: Described by Berosus as the second of seven semi-dæmons, or demigods, half fish half man, who instructed the first, the third, the sixth, and the seventh antediluvian generations in Khaldæa, 371 note. The first syllable alone of his name (signifying *god*) the prefix of any name of a god in Assyrian cuneiform inscriptions, 373-4 and note.

Angel-princes, 78, 79, 119.

Annals: Hebrew, confirm and are confirmed by those of Babylon, 446.

Antediluvians: Their kings, and their half fish half human teachers, 371-2 note.

Antigonus: His march into Media from Susiana, 557-8.

Antioch (the Margian): Now *Merv-al-Rud*, built by Antiokhus Sotér son of Seleucus Nicator, 618-19 note.

Antiokhus Sotér: Son and successor of Seleucus Nicator, 614 note.
— Epiphanes, 405 note.

Aparytæ: A people of the Paktyan-land, 641, 644 note.

Apis (god): The sacred bull at Memphis, 311; mortally wounded by Cambyses, 56, 306; slaughtered and served at table by Okhus (Artaxerxes III.), 320. Burial-place near Memphis, 306-7. At an Apis funeral Osiris lamented, 307. The title *Osor-Apis*, 307 note, 308 note. The name Apis given also to the Mendesian he-goat, *ibid.* An image of Osiris and Osiris himself, metempsychosis or miraculous conception of, 308. The principal colour of it black, 309. Other marks, 309 note. His house (the *Apieium*) at Memphis, 309 note. Represented on mummy-cases bearing away a red-palled corpse, 309 note.

— city, of Egyptian Libya, 143, 144 notes. Ammon's oracle concerning Mareia and Apis, 144 note.

Apobatana: A corrupt reading in Isidore of Kharax, 59.

Apollo, 36 note.

Apollonides of Côs (a physician belonging to Artaxerxes I.): Given up to the king's mother, who, to avenge her daughter Amytis, puts him to chastisement and to death, 153.

Apries (Pharaoh-Hophra), 40 note, 45, 90. Buried in the temple of Neith at Sais, 295.

'Arab and 'Eber: Perhaps the same word, 281 note.

Arabia: That of Xenophon was the fifth of the 20 Herodotæan satrapies; "the land of the Hebrews;" the Arabia of Darius's lists of provinces, sometimes including, sometimes excluding, the maritime parts of Philistia and Phœnicé, 282 note. The name as extensive in Herodotus's notice of Sennacherib, "king of the Arabs and Assyrians," 281 note.

Arabian, The (who aided Cambyses B.C. 525), 280, 287, 289 note.

Arakadrish: A mountain in Parsa-land, or Fars, 328, 635.

Arakha: An Armenian, the second

Arakha—
that called himself Nebukhadrezzar, son of Nabunita, and made himself king of Babylon, 604. Perhaps a Khaldæan of Armenia, 605. Taken, 677. Executed, 679.
Arakhotia, or Hara'uwatiah, 636. Had Gedrosia united to it under Sibyrtius, 637.
Aram, Language of: Its wide extension, 430-31. Cognate with the language of the Assyrian inscriptions, 430, 431 note.
Ararat: Country of the Alarodians, 170.
Araxes, Arakhsha river: Etymology of the name, 219 note.
Arbaces and Belesys of Ktesias: Misnomers, 74 note.
Arbela, 476 note. Arbira, Arbil town, 376 and note, 577.
Arbelitis: A name of the Assyrian province, 577.
Ardshir, the last acknowledged predecessor of Yezdegherd III., the son of Shahriyar (with whom the Sassanian dynasty expired in Persia), died A.D. 633, p. 469 note.
Areimanius (the Evil Principle of Persian theology): Identified by Greeks with their Hades, 337 note. Parent of the evil sort of "Born Gods," *ibid.* Evidently the "Underground God" propitiated with human sacrifices by Amestris, and the God of Lies mentioned in the Behistun inscription, 337 note. Like to Darkness, 367 note. The Earth-god, as Auramazdá is the Sky-god, 367 note, 385, 386. Called *Darugadira* (i. e. κακοδαιμων), 384 note. Not by Zoroaster called *God*, as Auramazdá was, but *Dæmon*, 386. (If the Vaidik Aryaman), not originally regarded as an Evil Power, like the post-Vaidik Shiva, one of whose names, *Bhav*, is interpreted "Earth," 386 note, 388 note. (*See* Lies, God of.)
Aria. *See* Hariva.
Ariabignes, commanded the division to which Artemisia belonged at Salamis; perished in the fight, 199 note.
Ariamenes, or Arimenes: The eldest of the family of Darius Hystaspes' son, according to Plutarch, 190 note, 193, 196. Seems to have

Ariamenes—
been sent away from the seat of the kingdom before his father's death, 196-99. How he died at Salamis, 199.
Ariana, The, of Strabo: Its extent, 14 note.
Ariaspes: An ethnic as well as individual's name, 183 note. But *see* Arimaspi.
Aridæus (Philip), 440. Different beginnings of his first regnal year according to the Egyptians and the Khaldæans, 470.
Arii: An appellation of the Medes, 13.
Arimaspi: A Mongolian people beyond the Issédones, 643 note. Also a people on the Etymander river, called by Cyrus his *Benefactors*, whose country seems to be called by Isidore Sakastané, *ibid.* Arimaspi a preferable reading to Ariaspæ, *ibid.*
Arina, or Arna: Lycian name of the town called by Greeks Xanthus, 155 note. The name a sign that the Termilæ were a Pelasgian race, 156 note.
Aristobulus: Quoted by Strabo and Arrian on the Tomb of Cyrus, 258-261.
Arius, or Hari river, giving name to the country Aria or Hariva, is swallowed up at last by the sand of the desert, 617 note.
Armenia, subject to Astyages, rebelled against his son, and reduced by Cyrus, 36 note. This country, and those extending from it to the Euxine Sea, including the territory of the northern Khaldæans, should be the *seventh* instead of the latter part of the *thirteenth* satrapy of Herodotus's list, 170. That it belonged to the Medes before the wars of Cyrus, indicated by the Behistun inscription, 482 note. Did not prefer Frawartish to Darius, 491. Of the various races that inhabited it, the situation of those called Armenians by the Greeks and Persians, 492, 508. Intercourse with Babylon, 604.
Arsakes: The former name of Artaxerxes II., 19.
— (Santrokes) king of the Parthians, 467 note.

71

918

Arsakidæ (Parthian kings): Their coins dated with the years of the Seleucidan era, 470 note.
Arshâda: A fort in Arakhotia, 638.
Artabanus (Darius Hystaspes' son's surviving brother), arbiter of the succession, according to Plutarch, 193-4 note. A conjecture concerning him, 226, 227 note. The name of like meaning with the old Chinese official designation Taipao, *ibid.*
(*Artabanus*): Another of the name, called Artapanus son of Artasyras the Hyrkanian, murders Xerxes; charges Darius, eldest son of Xerxes, with the crime, and, by authority of the youngest son, puts him to death; places that son as Artaxerxes I. on the throne, 141. Perhaps was endowed with Baktria, the satrapy of the second son, 141 note, 142, 152.
Artabazanes: According to Herodotus, the eldest son of Darius Hystaspes' son by his first wife, 190, 193.
Artabazus: Carried off his division safe from Platæa, 121. Was joined with Megabyzus in the commission against Inarôs, 146. After the recovery of Egypt, resists the fresh Athenian invasion of Cyprus along with the same Megabyzus, and the two negotiate a peace with them after the death of Cimon, 149-50.
Artæa: Country of the Artæi, *i.e.* Persians, 514 note, 13.
Artæi: An appellation of the Persians, 13, 514 note. Its etymological meaning, *ibid.*
Artakhshasthra: Was there such an older Aryan form of Artakhshatra, 80 note.
Artakhshatra: Name how pronounced by different nations, 76 and note, 80.
Artamenes (of Trogus Pompeius) seems to be Plutarch's Ariamenes, eldest of Darius Hystaspes' son's family, 193, 194, 190 note.
Artaphernes: Darius Hystaspes' son's surviving brother, arbiter of the succession, according to Trogus, 194 and note. Substituted by Aeschylus and Ktesias for Intaphernes, that is, Vindafrana, 226.

Artasyras, the Hyrcanian: A great officer in Cambyses' household service, 70, 72, 335, 337 note. Ruler of the Hyrcanians under the Khaldæan kingdom, the first who revolted to Cyrus, 250 note.
Artavardiya: Commands for Darius in Persis against the pretended Smerdis Vahyasdáta, 634. Gains victories at Rakhá and Parga, 635.
Artaxerxes I. (Artakhshatra): At first named Kurush or Cyrus, 2, 80, 94, 403. Called Makrokheir, 81, 131. The protector of Ezra and Nehemiah, 80, 93. Called "king of Babylon" by Nehemiah, 77. Not the Ahasuerus of Esther, 81. Placed by Artabanus on the throne of Xerxes, 141. His war with revolted Baktria, *ibid.* note, 142. His measures on the revolt of Inarôs, 146.
— II. (Arsakes Artaxerxes Mnemon), 19, 20, 32 note, 58, 63, 93 note. Born before his father became king, 191-2. Puts his son Darius to death, 376. Introduces images of Anakhita and Mithra into a building erected by the first Darius at Susa, 377; besides setting up the former in his other residences at Babylon and Agbatana, 351-2 note, 376. His initiation or consecration as king at Pasargadæ, 413. In an inscription employs the regal names only of himself and his ancestors in all the cases where the private names are known to us, 533 note.
— III. (Okhus Artaxerxes), 12, 65 note, 73, 76 note, 93. (*See* Okhus.) Invokes the protection of Mithra, as well as that of Auramazdá, 378. Like Artaxerxes II., in an inscription employs only the regal names of himself and his ancestors in all cases where their private names are known to us, 532 note.
Artaxerxes (*Artakhshasta*): Regal name assumed by the first Pseudo Smerdis, the Magian Gaumáta, 55, 76, 325 note, 333.
Artaynta daughter of Masistes, 132, 134-35, 137-40.
Artemisia, at Salamis, 199 note.
Artemisium: The first position at which the Greeks resisted the advance of Xerxes' fleet, 119, 120.

Artystoné, 4 note, 185. Though styled "daughter of Cyrus," seems to have been a daughter of Gobryas, 186, 187. The image of her in gold made by Darius's order, 228, 697 note.

Arvad, or Arad, island: Now Ruad. Perhaps the Arpad of Holy Writ, in the Septuagint Arpad, Arfat, and Arfath, 420 note.

Aryans, The, and their god: Intimation of their high esteem with the Kissians, and of their being undervalued by the Assyrians, 13 note. Their language that of Darius Hystaspes' son, called Aryan by him, 13; and sister to Sanskrit, *ibid*.

Aryandes: Satrap of Egypt under Cambyses and Darius I., 55, 187, 324, 494. His silver coinage, and expedition on behalf of Pheretima against Barca, 493 note, 140 note.

Asagarta, Asagartiyas, country and people, 570. *See* Sagartia and Sagartians.

Aspamitres: The accomplice of Artabanus in the murder of Xerxes, 142. His execution, 152.

Assessment: Of allies of Athens by Aristides, 75. In the time of Pericles, *ibid*. One made on the motion of Alcibiades, *ibid*. Changed for a duty on exports and imports, *ibid*.

Asshur, city: The modern *Kileh Shergat*, 520 note.

Asshurbanipal, king of Assyria, 25. Important calendar on a slab of his reign, 420.

Assyria (Proper) subdued by Cyrus, 35. Indication that Assyria Proper had belonged to the empire of Babylon before the Medes were commanded by Cyrus, 482-3 note. One of the provinces that disowned Darius Hystaspes' son while he was at Babylon, 508. Its lands probably devolved to the Median owners on the conquest by the Medes and Persians under Cyrus, 577. King of, a title sometimes given by the Jews to the Persian successor to the power of Assyria, 409 note, 705. The same title assumed perhaps in some parts by the Khaldæan heir of the same, *ibid*. note.

Astaboras, river, 299 note, 301 note, 309 note.

Astapus and Astasobas: Which of them the Blue, and which the White Nile, 301 note, 309-10 note.

Astyages: Etymology of the name, 14, 15. Written by Ktesias, *Astyigas*, 33 note. The king, 17, 34. His reign, 29. Dethroned five years before Crœsus, 35. Called Ahasuerus, Akhshurush, or Khshurush, in Daniel and in Tobit, 54. Seems to have commanded his father's forces when Nineveh was taken, 75 note, 162 note. His great-grandchildren, 88. His presumed vassalage to Babylon, 237. When dethroned, resided among the Barkanians, according to Ktesias; or the Hyrkanians, according to Justin, 248 note. Why dethroned, 577.

Asuras: Enemies of the Hindo-Aryan *Devas*, 394; but themselves apparently esteemed *Devas* by the ancestors of the Medo-Persian Aryans, 394-5. Perhaps corrupted into Assyrians in Ktesias's story of the war of Ninus with Zoroaster, 395 note. Their marriage by purchase condemned by the laws of Manu, 394 and note. How far different from Mongol marriage, 395 note.

Atarbekhis, that is, Athor town, in Prosopitis of Lower Egypt, 147 and note.

Atchidu: A district of Assyria, 508.

Atesh, 58 note. Otherwise deciphered Tusu or Tush, 67 note.

Athens: Comparative cost to her subjects of her government and the Persian, 174, 896. People of Athens succeed the Spartans in the conduct of the Persian war, 174. The Acropolis there, the original *Polis* or city, 509.

Athor (Egyptian Aphrodité): Sacred cow of, at Momemphis, 307 note. Cows in general sacred to her; Isis confounded with her by Herodotus, as Amún or Ammon was with Kneph, 318 and note.

Athos (Isthmus of): Cut through by Xerxes, 109.

Atossa: Wife of Darius I., 4 note, 5, 7. Though not named in Photius's epitomé, seems to have been mentioned by Ktesias as "daughter of Cyrus" and Darius's

Atossa—
queen, 131. Herodotus's account of, 184. No crimes of hers related, 195. Her behaviour on Darius's death in the question of the succession, 194. Others of this name descendants of Esther's, 183 note.

Atrina: The first rival of Darius in Susiana, 475. A native of the country, but called by an Aryan name, *ibid*. His revolt ended perhaps in the midst of the operations against Naditabel, 579, 580 note. His capture rather than Gaumata's overthrow to be excluded from Darius's nineteen victories, 580 note.

Atropaténé, province, 60; now Adherbaiján, 61.

Auramazdá: The god of the Aryans; the Creator; opposed to the Evil God, or God of Lies, 12, 158, 360. Identified by Darius son of Hystaspes with Jehovah, 178. His worship threatened by the accession of the Magian to the Perso-Median throne, 327. Heaven or Sky-god, 367 note, 368. Figure of (in Darius's sculptures), derived from the Assyrians, 373-4. Written by Greeks *Oromasdes*, and identified with their *Zeus*, 337 note, 366 note. The Good Dæmon and Good Principle, *ibid*. Parent of the good sort of *Born Gods*, *ibid*. The Most Great God, 351 note. Intimate connection of, with Mithra, 360. Answers to the Good God of the Khonds, *Boora Pennu* or *Bella Pennu*, "Light-God" or "Sun-God," 375. Etymological signification of the appellation, 391-3. Persian worship of, misconceived by the Greeks, 397.

Autiyara: A district of Armenia, 509.

Aztecs: Their weeks, months, and years, 341 note. Ethnic origin of their science, *ibid*.

Azurbáyaján (or Adherbaiján): Name of a province of modern Persia, 61. Its etymology, 58 note.

BABEL, mound: Why flat-topped? 691. Rich and Porter's accounts of, 693 note.

Babylon, 88, 122, 134. A place in the neighbourhood of, set apart for the Persian worship, 381. Title, king of, given by Jews to Cyrus and his Akhæmenian successors, 409 note, 705 note. Ktesias and Kleitarkhus's difference in the measure of its circumference explained, 453. Its first revolt under Naditabel crushed by Darius, 474-8. Value of the city to Darius in the early part of his reign, as the centre of his civil and military operations, when first Media revolted, and other kingdoms followed the example, 479, 480, 483. How taken by Cyrus, 648. Again revolts from Darius under Arakha, an Armenian, 596, 604. Not less strong when besieged by Darius than when by Cyrus, 614. Walls of, by whom built, 609, 610-11 note. One circuit of walls demolished and two remaining in the time of Herodotus, 610-14, 611 note, 612 note, 681, 682. The outermost circuit composed of sun-dried bricks, 682, 610 note. This circuit demolished, 611 note, 681-2. Its two *breadths* or *quarters*, divided by the Euphrates, identified with the inner and outer cities of Berosus, 609 note. The eastern division being the inner and original city, *ibid*. The outer remaining wall (described by Herodotus) probably *cased* only with burnt brick, 612 note. How constructed at top, 631 note, 654, 682. The gradual destruction of the two walls spoken of by Herodotus after the Macedonian conquest, *ibid*. A road behind (two plethrums broad) separated them from the houses of the city, 663 note. Reservoirs of water within, 650 note. The two palaces on opposite sides of the river, 652-3 note, 655 note. A tunnel between them, 653 note. Genuine native account of height of walls, 651, 653, 656. What this is in English measure, 657-9. The thickness of the wall, and height of the towers upon the wall, 654, 663 note. The brazen-plated gates of the city removed by Darius, 654 and note. The city quadrilateral, as stated by Hero-

Babylon—
dotus, but not equilateral, 660. The length regarded by Ktesias as twice the breadth, 661-2 and note. Regarded by the Greeks as the Assyrian capital, 662. Occupied by houses for a distance of 70 stades, but in other parts ploughed and sowed, according to the author followed by Curtius (probably Kleitarkhus), 663. Not the city, but only the two fortresses, defensible in B.C. 312, p. 664 note. Its river-side walls, 663 note. Its two palaces, probably the two citadels, garrisoned for Seleucus by Patrocles, and attacked by Demetrius son of Antigonus, 664 note. Described by Strabo as now for the most part waste, and smaller than Seleukeia on the Tigris, 664 note. Its condition when visited by the Roman Emperor Trajan, 665 note. Ktesias's measurement of the circumference of the walls may be diminished by various suppositions: first, by supposing the 120 by 60 stades to be as many measures of 100 cubits, or indeed of 100 *gar*, or 60 cubits only, the Babylonian *plethrum*, 665-6. Again, by taking the 360 stades to merely interpret 12 Babylonian correspondents of the *Parasang*, like the Hindu *coss*, 667-8. (The correspondents of the parasang perhaps *half kasbus*, and equal each to a *sarus* of ordinary *hus* or *ammas* (cubits), that is, 3600 cubits of 20½ inches, or 2050 English yards. Thus Babylon will have been represented as four saruses long by two saruses broad, or 40 yards short of 14 miles in circuit. See *Additions and Corrections* on page 668, lines 13-19 in the Appendix.) Gates, of Semiramis, of the Ninians, of the Khaldæans, with the Belidan and Kissian gates, 670, 683. Outermost of Babylon's three circumvallations destroyed, not by Cyrus, but by Darius, 681. The remaining circuits of wall dismantled by taking away the gates, and throwing down the parapets, and housing at top for men and stores, 682. The four corners of the fortified quadri-

Babylon—
lateral area pointed perhaps to the cardinal points, 684 note. This fact apparently intimated by Aristobulus, 689-90 note. Disregard of female chastity at Babylon, 702 and note.
Babylon of the N. T., 665 note.
Badaké, on the Eulæus, 558. Identified with the Madakta of Assyrian inscriptions, 559 note. Perhaps represented by *Patak*, a town south of the mountains, on an affluent of the *Kerkhah*, 559 note.
Bagas: The *Devas* of the Hindus, so called by the Persians, 395.
Bagæus, son of Artontes, destroys Oroites, 554-5.
Bagapates: A chief eunuch in Cambyses' service, 70, 89, 335 note, 337.
Bâgayâdish: A month with which Darius's reign commenced, at first conjectured to be the correspondent of the Egyptian Thoth, which began with January B.C. 521, afterwards found to correspond with the Jewish Markhesvan, 424 (and Table A), 427 *et seq.*, and Table B.
Bagistané, and the Bagistan Mountain (Behistun), 339 note. The works at, popularly ascribed to Semiramis, 340.
Baktrians, with Amyrgian Sacas attached to them in the same division of infantry, 112; with Caspians attached in the same division of cavalry, 116; the said Caspians and Sacas occupying together the same revenue division of territory, 171. Masistes, satrap of Baktria, proposed to raise a revolt of the Baktrians and Sacas, 140.
Banquets: Great enterprises discussed at, by the Persians and other nations, 99 note.
Baptana: A place in Kampadéné; the name in Isidore corrupt. Perhaps Bagistana or Bagapatana, 59-60 note.
Baptism, Christian, 72 note.
Barca: Sends its surrender to Cambyses, 291, 297. Punished by Pheretima, mother of Arcesilaus king of Cyréné, 140 note.
Bardiya: The Persian form of the

Bardiya—
(Median) name Smerdis, 66, 328 *et passim*. The relation of Bardiya (or Mardus) to Smerdis, like that of Gaumáta to Gaumashta, and of Hydaspes and Vidaspá to Hystaspes and Vishtaspá, 329 note.
Baréné : Near Agbatana, 36 note, 43 note.
Barkanians, The, 33 note, 248. Name apparently the same as *Varkana* and Paricanians, which see.
Barsiné espoused by Alexander the Great, 538 note.
Baruch : A mistake of the Pseudo-Baruch, 503 note.
Beeves intended for sacrifice, why in Egypt not to have a single black hair ? 309 note.
Beheading, common, 587 note.
Behistun, or Bisitun : Rock inscription at, 6. In Aryan, Kissian, and Assyrian, 12 note, *et passim*. Importance of assigning its months to the right seasons of the year, 229. The Bagistané of Diodorus, 340. The sculptured tablet there exhibits the order of the risings, while the inscription relates the successive dates of defeat, 479, 483, 484 note.
Bel of Niffer (God of the city, the Semitic name of which is Nipur, Nopher, or Niffer) : The third of the thirteen (or the second of the twelve) great gods ; often identified with the Bel of Babylon, that is, Merodakh, 607 note. Called for convenience Bel Nimrod, 683 note.
Bel Merodakh : The Bel of Babylon, 124. Tenth of the thirteen (or ninth of the twelve) chief gods, 607 note. Seems a deification of the king Belus, who was said to have erected the first walls of Babylon, *ibid*. Sometimes identified with the Bel of Nipur, 684 note. Great idol of, 685 and note. *See* Belus the King.
Belesys and Arbaces of Ktesias : Misnomers, 74 note.
Belidan gate of Babylon : Whether so named because men went forth thereby to the city of Bel Nimrod, now Niffer, or because it belonged to the same quarter as the temple of Bel Merodakh at Babylon, 683-4 note.

Belshazzar king of the Khaldæans succeeded by Darius son of Khshurush (Ahasuerus), of the seed of the Medes, 8, 16, 31. Son Nitokris, 37, 38, 40. Slain at the capture of Babylon, 53, 88. His regnal years given in Ptolemy's Canon to Nabonadius (Nabonedus), *ibid*. Might have left children, 88. Son of Labynetus or Nabonedus's wife Nitokris, and named in cuneiform *Bel-sharussur*, 649 note.
Belus, the Creator : His work in creation communicated to men by Oannes, 372 note. By the Greeks called *Zeus;* by the Armenians *Aramastes*(Auramazdá), *ibid*. Perhaps the Bel of Niffer, confounded with the Bel of Babylon, 606, 607 note.
Belus the Primæval, or Of the Beginning : His tomb at Babylon, according to Ktesias, broken into by Xerxes, 606 note. Meaning of his name *Belithan*, *ibid*. Regarded as Nebukhadrezzar's ancestor, 632 note. *See* Belus the king.
Belus the king : Built the original walls of Babylon, 610 note. His palace (still standing at the Macedonian conquest) is probably represented by the Mound Amrâm, 610-11 note. *See* Belus the Olden and Bel Merodakh.
Belus, father of Kepheus, king of the Kephénes, an Ethiopian people, afterwards called Persians (as the Britons were afterwards *mis-called* English), 234 note.
Belus, Temple of : An oblong, not an equilateral parallelogram, as supposed by Herodotus, 661 and note. Description of it and its idols, 685-8 and notes. Its destruction falsely ascribed to Xerxes, 688. Why this wonder of Babylon is unnoticed by Kleitarkhus's follower, Curtius, 688 note, 695 note. Its fallen tower ordered by Alexander to be restored, 688-9 ; against the inclination of the Khaldæans, 689-90. Its condition then probably worse than that in which Nebukhadrezzar found the Temple of Nebo at Borsippa, 690. Existing result of Alexander's labour in clearing away the ruins, 691. Corners of

Belus, Temple of—
the quadrilateral pile pointed E.
W. N. S., 693 and note. The
tower or *Ziggurrat* of, described
by Herodotus while yet standing,
661, 693 ; by Strabo also, but not
on the authority of eye-witnesses,
692-3 note. Diodorus's tale of
three idols of gold at top rejected,
695. The fall of (at least the uppermost
stages of) the tower may
have happened before the time of
Ktesias, 695 note.
Belus, Tomb or Temple of, at Babylon,
8 note, 88, 258 note, 259
note, 606 note, 607 note, 622.
The four corners probably looked
to the cardinal points of the horizon,
184 note.
Bendamir : River in Fars of 113
farsakhs, course from west to
east, falling into the salt lake
Bakhtegan. The olden name of
this river, *Kúr* or *Kur*, 263 note.
Benhadad, 58 note.
Beni Israel : Mahrattas so called,
180, 181 note.
Berosus : Demolition of the ontermost
of the three ramparts of
Babylon erroneously ascribed by
him to Cyrus, 613-14.
Bessus : Took the new name of
Artaxerxes when he declared himself
king after Darius Codomannus's
death, 197 note.
Bhav and Bhaváni : Hindu male
and female earth-gods, Shiva and
Kali, 338 note.
Bible history: Confidence in, justified
by new-found Assyrian testimony,
51.
Birthday of king of Persia, 139.
Feast thereon called *Tukta*, i.e.
"Perfect" (or perhaps "perfected"),
139.
Bisitun or Behistun, 9, 225. *See*
Behistun.
Bit Saggat, or Beth Shagathu, at
Babylon and elsewhere : Meaning
and derivation of the term, 686
note.
Boges : Persian governor of Eion,
besieged by Cimon son of Miltiades,
155.
Boora-Pennu ("Light-god") : The
Good God the Creator, according
to the Khonds of Orissa, 387.
By one sect held the victor of
evil, 388.

Borsippa, Nabonedus's surrender of,
53, 88. Temple of Nebo at, now
called Birs Nimrúd, 88. Its
ruined condition when Nebukhadrezzar
set about the repair
of it, 690. The angles, not the
sides, of the Birs Nimrúd mound
look to the cardinal points, 693
note.
Brahma, 397.
Bricks: Babylonian, 652 note, 658
note.
Bryges : The parent stock (called
Thracian) of the Phrygians of
Asia Minor, 420 note. Geographical
position of, *ibid*. Perhaps a
Paionian people, *ibid*.
Bubares a Persian : Names his son
Amyntas after Amyntas, his wife
Gygæa's father, 187.
Bubastis, 164 note. *Pibeseth* or
Pi-basth, 188 note, 291.
Budii of Media, 414 note.
Budini, 415 note.
Burning alive: No profanation of
fire, 155, 159.
Burying alive: A Persian punishment,
not a profanation of earth,
145, 158-9. Burying up to the
neck, 158, 159. What god
thereby propitiated, *ibid*.
Byblus, city of Egypt, where Inarôs
after his defeat was besieged,
along with 6000 Greeks, by Megabyzus
the Persian, 148-49.
Byzek, Bihizek, and Bihterek, 466-
67 note.

CABALIANS (in Asia Minor) : Of two
descriptions, (1) the Maionian
called Lasonians (a colony of
whom may have been the Lydian
settlers in Etruria); (2) the Cabalians
Proper, 113-15 note, 170,
542 note. Said to be Solymi, as
the Milyæ also are described to
be by Herodotus, 115 note, 542
note.
— (of Libya), a tribe settled in
the midst of the Auskhisæ, 144
note.
Cabeiri, The : Had a shrine at Memphis
; were related to Phthah, as
the Cabeiri of Lemnos to Hephæstus,
323, 324 note. Their images
thrown into the fire by Cambyses,
323.
Cadusians, the, 251 note.

Calah, called by Xenophon Larissa, 35. Taken by Cyrus the Great, 238.
Calendar, Perso-Babylonian, 5, 6. Græco-Magian, 465-9 note.
Call of the Gentiles, Date of, 150 note, 893-5.
Calynda: A state bordering on Kaunus, 154 note.
Cambyses (Kabujiya), 11. Son of Cyrus, 32, 33 note, 35, 43, 54, 65, 71, 73, 80. His death and burial, 71-2. Called by Ezra Akhshurush, 76, 188, 191.
Canal of Sesostris, Nekho, Darius I., and the Ptolemies, from the Nile to the Red Sea, 163 note. Its breadth, 164 note. Point where it issued from the Nile, according to Herodotus and Sir J. G. Wilkinson. Canal from Phakussa perhaps to the Lake Ballah; also from the Lake Ballah to the "Bitter Lakes," ibid.
Candacé (Kandaké): Every king of Ethiopia's mother so called, 299 note. At Meroë the queen-mother her son's superior in the kingdom, ibid.
Candys, a sort of tunic, 260.
Canon (Ptolemy's): According to Theon, and according to Georgius the Syncellus, two versions, 30 note. Theon's copy confided in by scholars, 51, 52 note. The Khaldæan and the Hebrew chronology corroborate one another, 50. Omits Darius the Mede, as previously Belshazzar and Laborosoarkhod; also subsequently Gaumáta the Magian, and others, 53. Its Egyptian rule for registration of a first regnal year, 102, 111 note.
Canopic Nile, 143, 144 note.
Capada, Campada, Campadéné: A district of Media, 488, 557.
Cappadocia: That it belonged to the Medes before the wars of Cyrus, indicated by the Behistun inscription, 482 note.
Captivity, Egyptian, lasting 40 years, 53 note.
Carmania: Given to the conquered Nabonedus, 44 note. Ten districts of, 274. Originally an appendage of Persia, 636.
Carmanians, query Barkanians, i.e. Hyrkanians, part of the portion of Smerdis son of Cyrus, 69, 247-8

Carmanians— note, 250. The same as the Persian Germanians of Herodotus, 274.
Carthage: Menaced by Cambyses, 297, 300.
Casian Mount, Station at: One march from Pelusium towards Gaza, 288. Considered by Herodotus as the frontier of Egypt and Syria, 290 note.
Caspapúra, rather than Caspatyrus, or even Castapyrus, the place on the Indus in the Paktyan land whence Skylax started, 639, 640 note.
Caspeirians (for Caspians): A conjecture of Reizius, 117 note.
Caspians: A nation settled in two different quarters, 116 and notes. In the 11th and 15th satrapies of Herodotus's list (having the Sakas joined with them in the latter satrapy), 170, 247 note. The conjectural substitution of Caspeirians for Caspians in the second instance, disapproved, 117 note. Here the Caspians seem connected with Caspapára, 116.
Caspian Gates, 562 and note. Boundary of Media there crossed by one leaving whether for Parthia or Hyrcania, 563 note.
Caspian Sea: In one place misnamed by Polybius the Euxine, in another called the Hyrcanian Sea, 566 note.
Cassandané: Wife of Cyrus, 131, 133 note, 536 note. See Kassandané.
Castólua, Plain of, 541 note.
Catabathmus: A ridge dividing Egyptian from Cyrenian Libya, 143.
Chaldæans of the North: Neighbours of the Armenians, 492. (Probably included in the same satrapy with them, 170.)
Charioteer: Stood, or sat, in the chariot beside the king, 379 (and note), 382. No human driver took that place, during a procession, in Auramazda's car, ibid.
Chedorlaomer king of Elam, 522 note.
China, Emperor and Empire of, compared with the Perso-Median monarch and his dominions, 209, 211. Theory of the Chinese mon-

China—
 arch's place and duty upon earth, 402-3. Emperors of, called themselves by a petty name, while others spoke of them by a name of state, or regal name, 531-2 note.
Chitratakhma : Darius's Sagartian rival, 570-8. Why his overthrow is not dated, 578-9.
Cilicia : Its willing co-operation against Babylon, how said to have been rewarded by Cyrus, 541 note. Aléian plain in, more than once the rendezvous of naval expeditions against Greece, 590 note.
Cimon, son of Miltiades, 150, 153, 292 note.
Coin, Use of, by the Persian kings, 292.
Coincidence, Supposed points of, between the story of Esther and that of Xerxes, 98. The first examined, 99-105. The second, 105-127.
Colkhians, 115. Planted rather by an Assyrian than by an Egyptian conqueror, 165 note. Their quinquennial present to the Great King, 173. Perhaps included among those who, according to Megasthenes, were planted on the Pontus Euxinus by Nebukhadrezzar, ibid.
Colossæ, in Great Phrygia, 544 note.
Combapheus, eunuch of the king of Egypt, 72, 285-6.
Cometes (apparently the same as Gaumáta) : Name assigned by Trogus to a Magian (called by Herodotus Patizeithes), who placed a brother of his on the throne of Cambyses, 350-51 note.
Commemoration (of destruction of the Temple, and of Gedaliah's death). When the 70 years of, began ? 625. When they began and ended ? 645-6. When the last three sevens of them ended ? 503 note. What regnal years of successive kings completed the number, 646 note.
Corpses : How treated by ancient Magians and modern Zoroastrians, 159. How by the Persians under the Akhæmenian kings, ibid.
Cos, The Temple at, of Æsculapius, 153.
Coss : Hindu itinerary measure, 668 and note.
Councils (Persian) convened by Cam-

Councils—
 byses, and Darius I., and Xerxes, Character of, 101.
Coxe, Mr. W. H., of the British Museum : His discovery of an Assyrian Calendar in which the old Babylonian (initials of ?) month-names are accompanied by those of Assyria, 425.
Crœsus, 35, 36, 482 note, 548. His kingdom, compared with the satrapy of Oroites, 542.
Crucifixion, The, Date of, 150 note. See *Corrections and Additions* on page 151.
— Assyrian and Persian method of, 551, 564-5, 576, 628, 635, 679 and note, 714.
Cubit : Substituted for *foot* by early transcribers of Kleitarkhus's testimony as to height of wall of Babylon, 654-5 and note. *Fathom* in like manner substituted for the Cubit of Ktesias's original account of the same height, 656.
— (The Royal, of Babylon) exceeded the Greek or also the ordinary Babylonian cubit of six hand-breadths by three finger-breadths, or ⅛th of the said smaller cubit, 652, 657 note ; and was equal to the Egyptian cubit, 658 note.
— (A smaller Babylonian) consisted of six hand-breadths, each measuring 3⅛th English inches. See *Additions and Corrections* on page 694, lines 38-46.
— (The Egyptian) : Its length in English measure, 658 note ; consisted of 28 fingers, or 7 hands, i. e. palm-breadths, ibid. An Egyptian *double-cubit* corresponding with the *big Hu* of Assyrian inscriptions, 659 note.
Curds, or Koords, The, 416 note. *See* Kyrtii.
Curses and blessings, Conditional and Unconditional, 70, 71 note, 336 note.
Curtius (Quintus) : On the days of the Persian (i. e. Magian) year, 454. On the length and height of the walls of Babylon, 453-4 note.
Cush, and Cushites. *See* Kush and Ethiopians.
Cyaxares I., son of Phraortes, 11, 74. His reign examined, 26-28. Never master of Elam, 27.
— II. (son of Astyages), 7, 33 note,

72

Cyaxares II.—
238. His reign of 22 years examined, 29, 31. Remained at home while Cyrus conducted his wars abroad, 37. *See* Darius the Mede.
Cyprus: Co-operated willingly against Babylon, and was accordingly rewarded by Cyrus, 541 note.
Cyréné, 147, 140 note, 144 note, 167, 170. Submission of, to Cambyses, 291, 297.
Cyrus (Kurush), 2, 5, 7, 8, 11, 15, 17, 29, 31, 33 note. His Median wife, 32, 33 note. Subdues Assyria Proper, 35. Tomb of, at Murghâb (*i.e.* the ancient Pasargadæ), 257-61 ; compared, in one respect, with the temple of Nebo (Birs Nimrud) by Sir H. C. Rawlinson, 8 note ; guarded by Magi, 62, 258-60. Inference thence respecting the Bel of Babylon and Nebo of Borsippa, 8 note. Overthrows Crœsus, 36. Takes Babylon, 43. Succeeds to the throne the third year after, 51. May have restored their captives to Elam and to Egypt, as well as to Judah, 45. Reigns seven years, 53, 252. His name, 201, 215. Ancestors of his, of the same name, 232. His first war (in Persis) was not perhaps with the Medes, but the Babylonians, 238, 250 note. Acquainted with the name Jehovah, and with what had been written of himself by Isaiah, 402, 241. Restored the vessels brought from the temple of God at Jerusalem, 242. His last campaign and death, 246. Ktesias's account reconcilable with that of Xenophon, 251, 252. His age at death, 251 note. His seventh and last visit to Persia, 252-4. Tomb of, described by Sir William Ouseley, 262 note. Onesicritus's notion of the tomb, 692. The same year, his first as king of Persia and as king of Babylon, 409 note. Called a Persian Mule, 632. Both his sons and he born of Median mothers, 486. The lower race, or classes, in Persia, how indebted to him, 512. How he surprised Babylon, 648. Result of the position that Ezra considered Cyrus's

Cyrus—
first regnal year to begin with Nisan B.C. 536, p. 705. Result of the supposition that Ezra did not consider Cyrus's first regnal year to begin with Nisan, as Haggai, Zechariah, and the author of Esther would have done ; but with Markhesvan B.C. 536, as Nehemiah might have done, 706.
— (The Younger), younger brother of Artaxerxes II., 19, 20, 33 note, 191, 195, 296, 414, 541 note, 542 note, 545, 546.
Cyzicus, 546 note.

DADÁRSHISH the Armenian, 490-4, 508.
Dadárshish the Persian, satrap of Baktria, 543 note. Subdues the revolt in Margiané, 616.
Dadubya, father of the Megabyzus who helped Darius, 608. Whether the name be not the Persian original of the Greek Zopyrus, 608 note.
Damascus, now *Damask*, 65 and note. In Hebrew Scripture *Dammeseq*, *Darmáseq*, and *Darmeseq*, *ibid.* Etymology of the name suggested, *ibid. Damashki*, the royal city in Tusu or Tush (otherwise Atesh land), 67 note. Its population carried off by Tiglath-Pileser, *ibid.* Seems to have been the capital of Syria under the Persians, 326.
Daniel (the prophet): Two Greek versions of, 4. Indicates the original superiority of the Medes over the Persians, 8. His vision of the two-horned ram, 16. His Darius the Mede the last Medo-Persian king, 7. What was told him of the fourth successor of Cyrus fulfilled in Xerxes, 118. The plot of Darius the Mede's ministers against him, 239-40. By the term satraps of Nebukhadrezzar's, attests that king's Aryan dominion, 278, 279. Terms by which he describes Jehovah to the king, 401, 405. As an *interpreter* of Jeremiah's prophecies, how far right and how far overhasty in conclusion (made B.C. 538-7), p. 503 note. Set right by a revelation to himself, *ibid.*
Daphnæ (Tahpanhes) of Egypt, 56.

Daphnæ—
Otherwise Daphnas, Taphnas, or Taphanhes, 285 notes. Now Tel-Defeineh, 284.
Dárayavush (Darius), 3 note, 5, 77. The name indicates royal Median descent no less than Akshurush or Khshurush, 533 note.
Darius I. (son of Hystaspes), 12. How his name degenerated to Gushtasp, Hydaspes, and Darius Hystaspes, 3 note. His titles, 17. Famous in Biblical and Greek history, 77. Tomb of, at Nakhsh-i-Rustam, 12. Said to have removed the Magi from Pasargadæ, 63. A temple built by him at Susa, 63 note. His Scythian expedition, 82 note. Like Esther, of the same generation as the great-grandchildren of Astyages, 89, 162. The husband of Esther, 161-65. More direct proof, 165-75. His death certainly happened in the Egyptian year, E.N. 263, which began with 22d Dec. B.C. 486, and was by Egyptian registration the first of Xerxes, 111 note. The first Asiatic sovereign who ruled from India to Ethiopia, 162. Compared with Sesostris, 162, 163. Completes to the Red Sea the canal made first by Sesostris, and again by Nekho, 163 note. The voyage of exploration executed by his order from Kaspapúra on the Upper Indus to Egypt, 163 note ut alibi. Nicknamed the Huckster, 167. His 20 satrapies in Asia and Africa, with their tributes, 167, 173. The tribute paid him from his European acquisitions, 170, 171. (Compare Additions and Corrections on 173.) Two characteristics of Darius's, besides the extent of his dominion, ascribed to Esther's Ahasuerus, 173, 174. Believed to be Esther's Ahasuerus by the compiler of Esdras, á, 177, 178. He identified Auramazdá with Jehovah, 178. Table of his wives and children, facing p. 178. His title to the throne, 184, 185. His last act, 193. Styled "Son of the Sun," like a native king in Egypt, 204. His ovals on the large temple in the Great Oasis, ibid. His pedigree on the father's

Darius I.—
side, 231. Born about the third year after Confucius, and seventh before the Buddhist era, 237. His mother perhaps a daughter of Darius the Mede, 281. Serves in the body-guard of Cambyses at Memphis, 282. Dream of Cyrus father of Cambyses concerning him, 322. Probably escorted the corpse of Cambyses to Pasargadæ, 326 and note. The first Akhæmenian king that resided principally at Susa, 329 note. The six who helped him against the Magian, how named, 335, 338, 343. Claimed to be king before he slew the Magian, 353-7. Worship of Auramasdá, before a sacred fire, sculptured on his tomb, 373. First publicly recognised and proclaimed king probably at Agbatana, 408-9. Reverses the acts of Gaumáta, 410, 411. Forces the passage of the Tigris, and defeats the Babylonian Naditabel, 477. Defeats Naditabel at Zazána on the Euphrates, 477-8. His headquarters then for some considerable time at Babylon, 478. Despatches Hydarnes into Southwest Media, 588-90; Dadárshish into Armenia, 490. His policy in respect of national worships, 416. His regnal years in Judah, 496-7. His 187 days' stay at Susa in B.C. 519 (not incompatible with the Behistun inscription), why unnoticed there, 526. The business of his stay, why untouched in the book Esther, 528. The question raised whether Akhshurush was not rather his private than his regal name, 531, 532 and notes. His punishment of Vashti considered, 539. Despatches Bagæus to kill or capture Oroites, 554. Crosses the mountains into Media, 537-8, 561. Defeats, captures, and at Agbatana impales Frawartish the Mede, 561-64. Sends Takhmaspáda the Mede against the Sagartians, 574. From Rhagá sends Persian succour to his father in Parthia, 586. Causes the Sagartian chief to be impaled at Arbela, 586, 579. Sends Otanes to Sardis, and orders him to put Syloson in possession

Darius I.—
of Samos, 588. Sends to his satrap in Baktria to act against the Margiana, 616. His final order concerning the temple at Jerusalem, 627-8. Sends Vindafrá the Mede to smite Babylon, 630-31. Sends Artavardiya against the new pretended Smerdis in Persia, 634-35. His first regnal year according to Assyrian and Jewish reckoning, 645 note. The same, by the Khaldæan account, 646 note. How he dealt with Babylon after its capture by Vindafrá, 679, 681 ; how, with the temple of Bel Merodakh, 685, 686. Makes Esther his queen, 710. To him is to be ascribed (not to Cyrus) the occupation of Babylon by a numerous Persian force, 696.
— II. (Okhus Darius Nothus): Called Okhus before his accession, 64 note, 93, 94, 201, 542 note.
— III. (Codomannus), 49, 65 note. Son of Arsames, 75, 77.
— (eldest son of Xerxes): His age in the seventh year of his father's reign, 132, 137. Accused of his father's murder, and put to death, 141.
— (son of Artaxerxes II.): His quarrel with his father, and death, 376.
— (the Mede), 7, 8, 15, 22. His reign of 20 years at Agbatana, and two years as king also of Babylon, 29, 40-3, 237. Not Esther's Ahasuerus, 30, 33, 37. Josephus's account of him, 31. King supreme, not a viceroy placed by Cyrus at Babylon, 40, 45, and notes. Cannot be Astyages, ibid. His regnal years in Ptolemy's canon given to Cyrus, 53. Had a Greater than Cyrus to help him, 79. Add 485.
Darugadiva, or Darauga-diva (Kakodæmon) : Epithet apparently of Areimanius, as the Evil Being was called by the ancient Persians, 384 note, 385 note.
Daskyleium : Seat of the satraps Mitrobates and Pharnabazus, 543. Ravaged and burnt by Agesilaus, 544-5 note.
Daskylitis : Lake formed by the

Daskylitis—
now *Lufer Su* river, which discharges its waters into the old Rhyndacus, and thereby into the Propontis, 545 note.
Dates of Darius's successes: Why sometimes omitted in the Behistun inscription, 578-9.
Daughter of Cyrus: Title of the crowned wife of Cambyses the Magian, and Darius Hystaspes' son, 184 *et seq.* Applied not only to Atossa, but to Artystoné wife of Darius, 185.
Deiokes, king of the Medes before Phraortes, 25. His building posterior to Sargon's invasion, 62.
Demetrius son of Antigonus: Defeated at Gaza, recovers Syria, marches against Petra of the Nabathæans, and invades Babylonia, 440 and note. Captures and pillages one of the fortresses within the city Babylon, 664 note.
Démokédés, the physician, 83; from Crotona, 550, 551, 556, 581. His adventures as a servant of Darius misplaced by Herodotus, 594.
Derbikes, the, 33 note. Derbiká or Derbikæ, subdued by Cyrus, 246, 247. They and the Barkanians adjoining nations, 248 note (the Barkanians being the Hyrcanians, who dwelt to the south of the Derbikes, *ibid.*). The *Dariwika*, "Wasps," of the Vendidad, 248 note. Their worship of Earth, and other customs, *ibid.*
Derketo, 214.
Diadem (as worn on the Persian king's *kidaris* or tiara): Described by Curtius, 167 note. Worn by the numerous class called "king's kinsmen," 198 note. On the forehead of the king's *diadema* or head-band, a figure of the Sun, 202 note, 198 note.
Didrachma of Alexandria, worth an ordinary *tetra-drachma*, and accordingly sometimes used in the Septuagint to express a *shekel*, 687 note.
Difference (arithmetical), Cause of, in Herodotus between the total of his particulars of payment in silver to the royal Persian Treasury, and the total reported by himself, 171.
Dispersion, Jewish, 48.

Domitian (Emperor and Pontiff) banished St. John to Patmos, 78.
Doriscus, 112, 113.
Durgá, or Kali, or Bhaváni: Wife of the Hindu Evil Deity Shiva, 388 note, 390.
Duru city (that is, Dor, Josh. xvii. 11), 234 note.
Dynasties (26th and 27th of Manetho), 107; (28th, 29th, and 30th), 773-804.

EARTH: Whether undefiled, according to the Magi, by the consigning of living bodies thereto, 158, 159. Modern Zoroastrian angel of, 158. Sacrifice to, by Xenophon's Cyrus, 367 note, 382. (Apparently as the habitation or vehicle of Areimanius, the Evil Spirit, 367 note, 383, 386.) Propitiation of, compared with the worship of the Earth goddess by the Khonds, *ibid.* Perhaps Kissian rather than Aryan, *ibid.*
Earth goddess, worshipped by the Derbikes, 248 note. Of the Skyths, wife of their greatest god Papæus, 367 note. Compare the *Herthum* of the Angli and other ancient Germans, *ibid.* In the Rig Veda, *Earth Mother* is opposed to *Heaven Father*, *ibid.* The Earth goddess of the Greeks and Romans, *ibid.* The evil goddess of the Khonds (See *Tari-Pennu*), 386.
'Eber and 'Arab: Perhaps the same name, 281 note.
Ecbatana, 62. See Agbatana.
Eclipse of the sun, B.C. 603, p. 26 note; B.C. 557, p. 35, 238.
Egypt: Conquered by the Persians under Cambyses, 54, 107. Rejected Darius at the beginning, 484; but seems to have been brought to submission by its satrap, 495. Having revolted the year before that of Darius's death, was subdued again by Xerxes, 102, 103. Revolt of, in the reign of the son of Xerxes, 143-50. Independent under Artaxerxes Mnemon, and during part of Okhus's reign, 73, 93.
Egyptians: Made no mention of Nebukhadrezzar in the story of Apries; nor of any Assyrian invaders but the defeated Sennacherib, 103. Supposed (but too hastily) to have been Herodotus's informants concerning Cambyses, Darius, and Xerxes, 107.
Eion: On the east bank of the Strymon, 155, 158.
Eilethyias, in Egypt: Old Coptic and modern Arabic names of, 297 note.
Elam, or Kissia, 22, 23, 25. Probably allied with Nabopolassar king of Babylon, 27. Crushed by Nebukhadrezzar, 28 note, 41. The Elymæans and Kissians united in war against the Babylonians and Susians, 28 note. The "Bow of Elam," *ibid.* When conquered by Cyrus, 42, 43. See Afardi or Afarti, Khoja, and Susiana.
Elam and Media: Isaiah's prophecy of, xxi. 2-9; when fulfilled, 24 note.
Elephantiné: An island in the Nile, 56, 302. Home of Manetho's 2d and 5th dynasties, 311 note.
El-Guisr, the plateau of, the passage by which Jacob entered Egypt, 285.
El-Khargeh (of the Great Oasis): Its distance in hours and in marches from Egyptian Thebes, 489-90 note. Occupied by Cambyses, 304.
Elumat (rather than Eluti): An Assyrian name no less than Elam, equivalent to the Aryan *Khoja* and the Kissian *Afardi*, that is, Susiana, 510 note.
Emendations:—Of Æschylus, Persæ 532, p. 19; of the place-names *Baptana* and *Apobatana* in Isidore's *Mansiones Parthicæ*, 59-60 note; of the account of the Pasargadas in *Marcianus Heracleota*, 62 note; of Herod. vii. 76, p. 113 note; of the name *Khalybes*, in Herod. i. 28, and in Ephorus, ap. Strab. xiv. 5, § 24, *ibid.*; of the name Orthokorubantii in Herod. iii. 92, p. 170; of the word *felicitate* in Justin ii. 10, p. 194; of the epithet *Persic* in Arrian, *Exp. Alex.* iii. 25, § 3, countenanced however by Diod. xix. 14, § 5, p. 197; of a name in Quintus Curtius, iii. 4, § 5, p. 249 note; of Arrian, *Exp. Alex.* vi. 29, § 9, p. 260 note; of Herod. ii. 42, p. 317 note; of Athenæus, xiv. 639 C, 342 note; of Plutarch, *Vit. Alex.*

Emendations—
cap. 30, § 2, p. 366 note; of Strabo, vii. frag. 41, p. 420 note ; of Josephus, *Antiq.* i. 3, § 3, p. 429 note; of Diodorus, ii. 7, § 3, p. 453 note; of Diodor. ii. 22, § 3, p. 519 note ; of Herod. i. 98, near the end, 569 note; of Strabo, xi. 10, § 1, completing Carl Muller's restoration, 617 note; of Strabo, xv. 2, § 7, where, however, if adopted, *Ariané* must be understood of the *Hariva territory*, 641 note ; of Herod. i. 191, p. 649 note; of Josephus, *Antiq.* iii. 6, § 7, p. 688 note; of Arrian, *Exp. Alex.* vii. 17, p.690; of Henry Dodwell's Fragment of Theon's Commentary on Ptolemy's Canon, 818, 819; of Geo. Syncell. p. 207 A, p. 204 C, pp. 326-327, p. 7 ed. Paris, 819, 820, 825, 853-4; of Strabo, v. 4, § 3, p. 884; Quint. Curtius, v. 8, p. 900.

Ephraim, 47.

Epidaurus, Mother city of Côs: Had been occupied by the Carians before the "Return of the Heracleidæ," 153. Temple of Æsculapius there, *ibid.*

Erdavirâf Náma: How old a book, 3 note.

Esarhaddon : His colony in the country of which Samaria had been the capital (the Samaritans), 245.

Esdras, *ε*: Consequence of this book's omission of Ezra iv. 6, p. 76 note, 81 note.

Esfendarmad: Zoroastrian angel of Earth, 158.

Esfitamán, Sfitamán, or Espintamán: Father of Zoroaster, 3 note. (Spitamenes.)

Esfintamad : The third of the Angel Sisters presiding over the five supplementary days of the Magian year, 189 note.

Esther : Identified by Joseph Scaliger and others with Amestris, 3. Of the same generation as the great-grandchildren of the great Nebukhadrezzar and of Astyages; also as Psammenitus, 87, 90, 91. Why not mentioned in the book Ezra, 94 note. *Liberally* identified with Amestris, 96. Her story ill appreciated, 97. The supposition of Scaliger, Eichhorn, Milman examined, that she entered on her preparation for

Esther—
Xerxes' bed not later than the month Tebeth next after the battle of Salamis, 129. Cannot be Amestris, 133, 136. Proved to be Atossa, the queen consort of Darius son of Hystaspes, 178 *et seq.* Esther the private name of Atossa in her own family and people, 180. Supposed by Gesenius to be a name given her by the Persian, equivalent to *Sitareh*, that is, "Star," 180 note. Like Zerubbabel, a Babylonian name, *ibid. ;* and related to Ishtar as Mordecai to Merodakh, 180 note, 182, 699. Though a favourite name among the Jews, not given to daughters among the Mahratta Beni Israel, *ibid.* Born at Babylon, but carried by her cousin Mordecai to Susa, 700. Her marriage erroneously placed in the month Adar by the Septuagint and Josephus, 711 note.

— (The Book) : An internal proof that it was written before the time of Nehemiah, 456 and note.

Ethiopians (both Asiatic and African), 297, 298, and notes. Asiatic Ethiopians well known to the ancestors of the Homeric Greeks, 299, 300 notes. Straight-haired, 113. The African *Macrobii*, 298 note. Their bows, 299 note. Power of queen-mothers among them, *ibid.* The Macrobii identified by Herodotus with the Ethiopians of Meroë, 300. Woolly-haired above Egypt, 82 and note. Served under Xerxes, 84, 95, 113. Their triennial present to the Great King, 173, 305.

Etymander river, 643 note.

Eulæus river : According to Diodorus, the most westerly of the three rivers of Susiana,—Pasitigris, Coprates, and Eulæus, 558 note; thus answering to the Khoaspes of Strabo in one passage, *ibid.* By other authors, the Pasitigris, or more easterly of the three rivers, is called Eulæus, 558-9 note.

Eumenes : Resists Antigonus first on the Pasitigris, afterwards on the Parætakenian frontier of Persis, 530 note, 558. Taken and starved to death, 562 note.

Euphrates: Breadth of, in Babylon, 664 note, 668.

Evil Merodakh, 29, 39 and note, 40 note. During his reign the people of Persis appear to have revolted under Cyrus, 238. His regnal years began, by Babylonian account, with Markheavan B.C. 561, p. 441. After his father's death he released Jeconiah before the end of the year, that is, when his first regnal year had not yet begun, 441.

Ezra, 17. When he was sent to Jerusalem, the restoration of the walls had been also ordered by the king, 150 note. His commission, 403. His account of the completion of Zerubbabel's temple, 703-4. Whether the regnal years he mentions began with Nisan or Markheavan, 705-6. (That they began with Nisan, evinced in the case of the seventh of Artaxerxes, see *Additions and Corrections* on p. 151.)

FARS: Meaning of the name, 236 note. *See* Parsa.

Farsakh (Parasang) of Sir W. Ouseley, of Herodotus, and of the Arab geographers, appealed to by Capt. Felix Jones, I.N., 262-3 note. *See Parasang, Kasbu, Skhœne.*

Faruâb, or Paruâb: The stream that runs by Murghâb and Mader-i-Suleiman, and that falls into the Bendamir, 263 note. Its course 18 *farsakhs, ibid.*

Feasts: A season for consultation among many nations, 528 and note.

Ferrardaghân: Five sisters—Ahunavad, Ashtuvad, Esfintamad (which name see), Vahukhshater, and Vahishtûshiyush, who, according to Magian doctrine, spin, weave, and sew, making garments (when the Creator of the universe so ordains) for souls that are stript of their bodies. They preside over the five supplementary days of the year, 189 note.

Fire, Persian, *i.e.* Magian, Worship of, 156. Profanation of, 157 note. The worship connected with that of the Sun, 368. (Like Agni by the Hindus) invoked by the Persians as a mediator, 370, 373, 375. The worship a corruption of the divine institution of the sacrifice of animals by fire, 370. Practised in Cappadocia not only in the fire-temples, but in the temple courts of Anaitis and Omanes, 371 note. Portable grates of sacred fire, 383 note. What Strabo calls sacrifice to, 384.

Fire and Water: Images of gods to the Persians, 362 note, 368 note.

Fire-burners (Pyræthi): Magi so called in Cappadocia, 371.

Fire-temples (Pyrætheia), and the daily service of, by the Magi, 371 note.

Forbes, Alexander Kinloch (in Memoriam), 69 note.

— Rev. G. H., of Burntisland: A suggestion of his to the author, 503 note.

Fráda: Darius's antagonist in Margiané, 616, 620. May have saved his life in the defeat and butchery of his people, 621.

Frankincense: Arab tribute of, 173.

Frawartish: Darius's Median rival, 483. His cause maintained in Armenia and Parthia, 484. His name the same as that of the second king of the Medes, 487 note. Defeated, taken, and impaled, 561-4.

Free training grounds in Persis: Whether at other places (*e.g.* among the Maraphii and Maspii as well as at Pasargadæ)—a question connected with this other, Whether the 12 tribes mentioned by Xenophon were hereditary or arbitrary divisions, 270.

GABÆ in Gabiané, 249 note.

Gadára: Gandára (the Gandaræ of Hecatæus, and Gandarii of Herodotus), 82 note, 83, 85 note, 641. They and their town Kashtapúra or Kaspapúra, part of the empire won by Darius from the Magian usurper, 84 note, 640 note. Their country, Paropamisus, 84 note, 639, 640 note. May have possessed the valley of the Kôphên river, as well as that of the Khoaspa, 85 note. Called a Hindu people by Hecatæus, 640 note. Perhaps in-

Gadára—
tended by Arrian's *Hindus of the hither side the Indus*, and conquered by Alexander between Bactra and the Indus, 85 note. Not Paktyans Proper, though they lived in Paktyanland, 642 note.
Gadutava, or Kanduvata: A district of Arakhotia, 638.
Gandaridæ of Diodorus, 85 note.
Gandaris of Strabo in the Panjáb, 85 note.
Gandaritis of Strabo: Traversed by a Khoaspes, a tributary of the Kôphên river, 84, 85 note.
Gar: Three-fifths of a *hu* (or Babylonian cubit), apparently the Babylonian foot, 656 note, 658 note, 665-6 note. Its length in English measure, 657-8 note. A *hundred* Gar the correspondent of the Greek *plethrum* and Roman *actus* or *half-juger*, 666 note, 663 note. (2.) *Another* Gar, 12⅜ English inches (the two-thirds of *another* cubit, three fingers shorter than the Royal cubit), used at Mugheir under Nabonedus. (3.) A *still shorter* Gar of the oldest Khaldæan times, measuring 11¼ inches, the three-fifths of the common short cubit of 19 inches. See *Additions and Corrections* on p. 694, lines 38-46.
Garmapada: First month of the stage of heat, 447.
Gate: Attendance at king's or satrap's, 712-3 note.
Gather son of Aram, 395 note.
Gaugamela (village near which Alexander defeated Darius Codomannus in the province of Arbela): Its situation, 577.
Ganmáta the Magian, 10, 66, 88. Perhaps *Gomashtah* in modern Persian, 69, 329, 351 note. *Gumatta* is to *Gumashta* as the Sanskrit *ritta*, "gotten," to the Zend *vista*, 329. The name preserved in the Cometes of Trogus, 350 note. Two phases of his usurpation, 354-5. His acts regarded after his death as of no validity, 410.
Gaza or Kadytis, 286.
Gazaka, or Ganzaka: The capital of Atropaténé, sometimes styled *the second Agbatana*, 61. Not walled, 60 note.
Gedaliah: Murdered in the last

Gedaliah—
month of the Khaldæan year that was reckoned the 19th regnal year of Nebukhadrezzar by the Jews, but his 17th by registers at Babylon, 624-5.
Gedrosia: United to Arakhotia under the satrap Sibyrtius, 637. Its capital Púra, 637 note.
Georgius Syncellus. *See* Syncellus.
Germanians or Carmanians, 636, 637 note.
Germans, Ancient: Analogy between their religion and that of the ancient Persians, 358-9, 362 note. Their horses brought with them from the steppes of Tartary and Russia, 359 note.
Gerrha, on the Persian Gulf: Its ancient trade, 288 note.
— on the Mediterranean, 288 note. Now *Tel Gerreh*, 284 note.
Geshem or Gashmu, the Arabian; that is, the Nabathæan, 280.
Getæ, on the Danube, 342 note.
Gháva the blacksmith and Dahhak the king, story of, alluded to, 268 note.
Gimirri: An Assyrian name for a people in Thrace called Saká and Sakka in Persian and Kissian. Query, *Kimmerii*, 82 note, 246 note.
Gobryas: His daughter Darius's wife, the Vashti of Scripture, seems to be the wife named "Artystóné daughter of Cyrus," 186.
— son of Darius by Artystóné, 186-7.
— (son of Mardonius), one of Darius's six fellow-conspirators, probably the same as Gobryas who was sister's husband to Darius, and father of the Mardonius who fell at Platæa, 277. Possibly the same as Herodotus's Gobryas, who was wife's father to Darius, 277-8. If a different person, not the son, but perhaps the nephew of the other, 278.
— Wife's father, according to Xenophon, of Hystaspes the father of Darius, supposed to be the person more correctly described by Herodotus as wife's father to Darius, 277-9.
Gojesta (the Devil of the Zoroastrian Book Sad-der): The same called in the Behistun inscription

Gojesta—
God of lies, 268 note. The name one of many applied by Persian writers to the devil, 269 note.
Gold, the Hindu, 85 note. In what shape hoarded by the Persian kings, 292.
Gudrush or Gundrush in Media, 82 note.
Gushtasp = Vishtaspa, *i.e.* Hystaspes, 3 note.
Gyndes: River on the road to Babylon from Media, 56 note.

HADASHAH, a Samaritan female name, 189 note.
Hadassah : Identity of the name with Atossa noticed by Usher, 4 note. Esther's court name, 180, 182, 183, 199. Written *Edesa* by Georgius Syncellus, 184 note.
Haggai the prophet, 496 *et seq.*
Hakhâmanish (Akhæmenes), 10, 11, 55, 103, 184, 231.
Hall, Professor Fitz-Edward, 218 note.
Halys, river, 35-6.
Hamadan, 23, 50, 60.
Haman, 34, 50, 166, 185.
Hamath, Khámath, afterwards Epiphania, now *Hamah*, 57.
Handbreadths (*Tibki*): Heights reckoned in, by the Assyrians, 656, 694, 651 note. Those of Herodotus, whereof four made an ordinary foot and six an ordinary cubit, 657 note. Those of Egypt measuring four fingers each, and whereof seven made a cubit, 658 note. Those of 3¼ inches in the Temple of the Moon at Mugheir. See *Additions and Corrections* on p. 694, lines 38-46.
Hapi-Môou (name of the Nile-god): If Hapi intimates *blackness*, " Black Water," 310 note; or " Blue Water," as perhaps *Nil* also indicates, *ibid*. The Black Water, as well as the Black Bull Apis, connected with Osiris, 311 note.
Hariva: The country watered by the Hari or Arius, and inhabited by the Arii, 615. Its three cities Artakoana, the original chief town ; Kandak (called from a Macedonian founder *Akæa*); and Alexandreia (now Herat), built

Hariva—
by Alexander the Great, 118 note, 641 note. Hariva had Thatagush or the Satagydas on the east, 641 note.
Head-washing of the Persian monarch, and of the Scythians, 139.
Heaven, Son of (that is, Son of God), a title of the Emperor of China, 209.
— (Father) of the Rig-Veda, 367 note. Among the Persians Heaven = Auramazdá, *ibid*. Exhibited the ubiquity of Auramazdá, 365. Seems intended by the Circle in the sculptured emblem of Auramazdá, 374 note. Among the Jews, "Heaven" or "Heavens" = The God of the Heavens, *i.e.* Jehovah, 405 and note, 406. So, too, among the Chinese, Heaven = The Supreme Being, 407.
Hecatompylos: Seat of royalty in Parthia, 562 note.
Hephæstion: His funeral pile at Babylon, 611 note.
Hephæstus (called by the Latins Vulcan): Cast down from Heaven into Lemnos, 323. Recognised by the Greeks in the Phthah of Memphis, *ibid.* note. Entertained in Lemnos by the Sinties, *ibid.*
Hermotybians : One section (the Calasirians being the other) of the warrior caste in Egypt, 145, 147.
Herodotus: Confounds the husband and the son of Queen Nitocris, 37 and note. Supposes (probably incorrectly) Susa to have been the chief residence of Cyrus, Cambyses, and the Magian, 156. Misapplies the name Mithra, 64 note, 364 note. His confusion of the 7th and 13th satrapies of his list, making what should have been the *seventh* to be the latter part of the *thirteenth*, and what should have been the latter part of the 13th to be the 7th of his list,—an error connected with the fact that in the original document the 13th was the satrapy that in his order should have been the seventh, 169, 170, 640 note. His error in supposing Cyrus the immediate successor of Astyages proved by a record of Cyrus's at Agbatana, 244. Preferred accounts by which Cyrus was depreciated, 251. His

Herodotus—
knowledge, displayed in the Thalia, of the Ethiopians that Cambyses wished to conquer, and of the Medes in the reign of Darius I., supplemented in the Euterpé and the Clio, 301, 302. His testimony that the Magian Pseudo-Smerdis was slain in the eighth month, leads to correct conclusions as to the order of the Persian months Bágayádish, Atriyádiya, Anámaka, Thuraváhara, Viyakhana, Garmapada, and Thaigarchish, 421-3. By making the month Bágayádish the first month of the first of Darius's 36 regnal years, suggests the inquiry, What was the civil year he had in view? 423, 432, 433, 435. Supposed the Magian usurpation of the throne of Cambyses made in the interest of the Medes, 485 note. Herodotus blended *two* revolts of Babylon into one under Darius I., and ascribed the character of the Median revolt under Frawartish to the Magian usurpation, 595. His observation as to the final letter of Persian names, 598 note. Misunderstood what he was told of the height of the Wall of Babylon, being unable to judge by the eye, 651 note. The knowledge he possessed, when he wrote the Thalia, of the state in which Darius I. left Babylon, supplemented in the Clio, 612 note. Mistaken in supposing both Babylon and the temple of Belus to be equal-sided as well as four-sided parallelograms, 660-61. Misunderstood his story of the 20th month of the siege of Babylon, 626, 676-7. Certainly mistaken when he gives to the first stage or story of the *Ziggurrat* or tower of the Bel temple at Babylon, the height given by Strabo to the whole pile, *one stade*, 693 note.

Herthum, Earth-goddess of the Angli, 367 note.

Hesperidæ, 144 note.

Hestia: By this name of the Greek Hearth-goddess (the Roman Vesta), Xenophon means the Sacred Home Fire of the Persians, 351-2 note.

Hezekiah, sixth year of, 50, 51.

Hiddekel or Tigris, 78, 79 note.

Hidush, Sintus, Indi (or Hindus): Men of Hind or Sindh, 81 note. Not in the Behistun, but added in Darius's subsequent lists of his provinces, 83; and forming the 20th satrapy, 170. Account of the exploration, subjugation, and tribute imposed upon them, 83, 84 note. Situation of, 639 note. Served under Xerxes against Greece, 83 note. The Indians in the several contingents of the Baktrian and Arakhotian satraps at Arbela, 85 note. Darius's India re-annexed by Alexander the Great, 437 note.

Hillah, town, 664 note, 666 note.

Hind, Homa, and *Harequaiti,* for Sindh, Soma, and Saraswati, 214.

History (Ancient Persian): Disregard of truth in the compilation and reciting of, 272.

Homa (in Zend) or Soma (in Sanskrit), the Moon-god, 364 note, 394.

Horses sacred to the Persian Sungod, 358-9. Their neighings oracular among the Germans, 358-9. Eaten by the Persians, 383 note. Sacrificed to the Sungod by the Massagetæ, 359; as well as by the Persians, 359, 381, 382. Of Nisæa, 339 note, 379.

Horus: Last king of the 18th Egyptian dynasty, 164 note.

Hu: Proved by the late Dr. Hincks equivalent to the Hebrew, Aramaic, and Assyrian *amma* or cubit, 657 note, 655 note. A *big Hu* and a *little* or *Demy Hu* equal to 41 inches and 20½ inches respectively, *ibid.* For ancient Egyptian double cubit measures, see 659 note. (A *smaller cubit* of 19 inches. See *Additions and Corrections* on p. 694, lines 38-46.)

Huiyama, or Uhyama, in Armenia, 493.

Humawargá (Amyrgii): These and the Tigrakhudá, two nations of Sakas (besides the Sakas of Europe, who seem to be Thracians), enumerated by Darius I., 247 note.

Huresh, or Hurush: The natural Perso-Aryan form of the Sanscrit Suresh (which see), 214.

Husband: A sun to his wife, that

Husband—
should receive her homage in the place of Mithra, 220.
Hydarnes, 488. *See* Vidarna.
Hydaspes: Corrupted from Hystaspes, 3 note. Or a dialectic variety of Hystaspes, whereof there are other analogous instances, 329 note.
Hyksôs (of Avaris in Egypt): These invaders, whether their name be connected etymologically with the names Shus and Avar of Susiana, 522 note. Whether connected by a certain 13 years found in the history of Chedorlaomer king of Elam, and a like period in Manetho's history of Egypt, *ibid.*
Hymns of the Rig-Veda, 411-12 note.
Hyrkanians, 112. In Aryan *Varkana*, 249. Probably intended by the Parikanii of the 10th satrapy, 248. Regarded as the equals of the Persians and Medes, 250, 583. Had precedence over the Parthians, their fellow-provincials, 582. Xenophon's account of them and their service to Cyrus, 583. Their name interpreted by Sir H. C. R. "wolves," *ibid.* note.
Hystaspes (Vishtaspa): Father of Darius, 77. The name corrupted to Hydaspes, and by modern Persians to Gushtasp, 3 note. Survived Cyrus many years, 89. His wife not the daughter of Gobryas, but perhaps of Darius the Mede, 276-80. Presided probably at the funeral of Cambyses in Persia, 327. Crushed the Parthian revolt from his son, 585-87.
— (son of Xerxes), 131. Satrap of Baktria at the time of his father's murder, 141.

IENYSUS: The waterless tract between this and the Casian Promontory, 286, 288. A vestige perhaps of the name in the present *Khán-Yunas*, 290 note.
Ikhthyophagi (of Elephantiné): How employed by Cambyses, 302. Fish-eating clans (in Babylonia), 302 note.
Il, or El (that is, God), 205-6 note. Semitic equivalent of old Babylonian Re or Ra, *ibid. Daughters*

Il—
of, Arab equivalent of the old Egyptian *daughter of Ra*, 206.
Iloarudamus (Evil-Merodakh), 39 note.
Imanish: The regal name assumed by Darius's second antagonist in Susiana, 510 and note. Perhaps akin to *Umman*, a god whose "eldest son," a king of Susa in Sennacherib's time was called, 511.
Inarôs (son of Psammetikhus, and king of the Libyans at Mareia): His revolt from Artaxerxes I., 142, 143. Probably descended from the Egyptian dynasty overthrown by Cambyses, 143. Maintained his revolt for six years, 144. How supported by the Athenians, 145. His end, 148.
Indi, or Hindus. *See* Hidush.
Indra, 397.
Indra and Agni: Ride together in a car, which seems to be the Sun, 365 and note.
Indus, river, 83.
Intaphernes: One of the six, 186. Usher's fancy about him, 4 note. Miscalled Artaphrenes and Ataphernes by Æschylus and Ktesias, 226 note. His end, 347.
Isfendarmad (a Magian month), 139 note. *See* Esfendarmad (Zoroastrian angel of Earth), 158.
Ishtar (whence Esther): The Assyrian Venus, 180 note, 182, 699.
Isis (Egyptian goddess), 319, 318 note.
Issidu (so-called in Assyrian): The Aryan Machchiyas or fish-eaters of the Tomb List; apparently the Issedones of Herodotus, 83 note, 415 note.
Itinerary (Antonine), 284 note.
Izabates: A chief eunuch in Cambyses' service, 70, 89, 326 note, 327, 335 note.

JAXARTES (or Yaksharta), the Sir or Sihon river, 219 note, 395 note. How it came to be called Tanais, 566 note.
Jeconiah (Jehoiakin) king of Judah: Carried to Babylon, 86-7. Contemporary of Psammis or Psammetikhus II., 90. Released from his prison in Adar B.C. 561 by

Jeconiah—
Evil-Merodakh, 441. Years of his captivity connumerary with the regnal years of Zedekiah, 442 note. Days of his reign, *ibid.*
Jehoahaz (son of Josiah): His three months' reign, 443 note.
Jehoiakim (son of Josiah) king of Judah, 35, 87, 441 note. His corpse not buried, 296 note. His regnal years, and those of Zedekiah, a continuous series of the same sort, 442 note.
JEHOVAH: Reserve of the Jews as to this name of God, 398.
Jelaleddin, Sultan: His fixed years related to the proper Magian year, as the Alexandrian to the proper Egyptian year, 456. Commencement of, 457 note.
Jeroboam: Reign of, 47. Seems to have made the civil year of Israel begin with Markhesvan instead of Tisri, 434.
Jews: Exaggerate the time taken in the rebuilding of the temple, 17. When it was, the name came to be applied to men of all the tribes of Israel, 46, 47. When they began to withhold the name Jehovah from the knowledge of strangers, 398. Permitted by Cyrus, many returned from Babylon to Jerusalem to rebuild the temple, 241-5. Resume under Darius the work that had been suspended, 495-507.
Joakim son of Zerubbabel, 178.
John, St., the apostle, 1, 78.
Jonah, 399, 234-5 note.
Josephus the historian: On Esther's Ahasuerus, 2. Asserts that Artaxerxes I. was named Kurush, 2. Mistakes the patron of Ezra and Nehemiah for Xerxes, *ibid.* note. Rightly identifies the Darius under whom Ezra places the completion of Zerubbabel's temple with the father of Xerxes, 5. His error concerning Elam son of Shem, 24 note. Follows not Ezra, but Esdras, 81 note, 177. Not the Hebrew Esther, but some paraphrase, 166. Follows the Septuagint or Vernacular Targums rather than the original text of the canonical books of Holy Hebrew Scripture, 106 note. Why, having ignored the person of the Lord

Josephus—
Jesus in his *Jewish War*, he names Him in his *Antiquities*, 179. Like the Septuagint book Esther, knows not the name Hadassah, 181. Supposes erroneously that the name Meroé was due to Cambyses, 298 note, 301. Contradicted by the book Esther, and also by the state of Babylon before the time when Esther was taken to the house of women at Susa, in the statement that Mordecai and Esther were then living in Babylon, 527 note.
Josiah: His regnal years form a continuous series with those of Jehoiakim and Zedekiah, 442-3 note.
Judah: Political growth of the tribe in Israel, 47.
Judith, The book, Anachronism in, 18.
Jugus or *Jugerum:* The Roman measures of length and surface so called, 663 note, 682 note. (As the Roman *actus*, signifying a measure of length, corresponded with the Assyrian *Sús* (or sixty) of *half-Hus* (or *small cubits*), so the Roman *Jugerum* seems to correspond with an Assyrian Sús of *big Hus*, equal to Egyptian double cubits, and to be the sixtieth part of the Assyrian *big Kasbu*. See Kasbu.)

KADYTIS (Gaza), 286.
Kampadéné: Province of Lower Media, 59 note, 62. *See* Capada.
Kandak: The town in Aria so named by Isidore identified with the Akæa of Strabo, 618 note.
Kanduvata or Kadutava: District in Arakhotia, 638.
Kapishkanish: Fort in Arakhotia, 638.
Karæ kómæ, or *Karôn kómæ:* A place on the right bank of the Tigris, at the same distance from Babylon as (afterwards) Seleukeia, and where there was a passage of the river, 558 note.
Karda (whence a sort of men, Kardakes): Meaning of this Persian word, 413.
Kardukhians, 21, 251 note.

Karka or Karsa: Whether Kolkhians? 83 note.
Kasbu: An Assyrian measure of distance; the big and the little or half kasbu, 657 note. The *little kasbu* may have been 60 Babylonian *plethra*, or 60 sús of cubits, *i.e.* a *sarus* of cubits, or (at 20¼ inches to the cubit) 2050 English yards; while the well-known *parasang* of the period of Persian supremacy may have been the *big kasbu*, a sarus or 3600 of double cubits or *big hus*. See *Additions and Corrections* on page 668, lines 13 to 19.
Kaspapúra, or Kastapura (not Kaspatyrus): A town of the Gandáræ in the Paktyan region, 83-4 note, 116, 117 note. Probably on the Indus near Peshawar, 85 note, 163 note.
Kassandané: A Persian wife of Cyrus, not the mother of Cambyses, 74. *See* Cassandané.
Kaunus city, 154. The people described themselves as originally from Crete (being perhaps Termilæ, like the intruders in the land afterwards Lycia), 154 note.
Kephénes (Ethiopians of the East): The people of Kepheus, son of Belus and father of Andromeda, 234 note, 513. Migration of, from Khaldæa to Khogé; under Perses colonize the Artæan land, *ibid.*, 234 note. Left their former country to the Khaldæans, 513, 514 note.
Kepheus king of the Ethiopian Kephénes, 234, 235 note, 513.
Kerkhah river: Its upward course probably followed nearly by Darius I. (as afterwards by Antigonus) in marching from Susiana into Media, 557-8. The Eulæus of Diodorus, *ibid.* note. A branch or canal once carried a part of its waters to the Karún, while the remainder, as now, ran to the Shat-el-Arab, but by a course nearer to Susa, 560 note.
Kerkúk: Sends wine to Baghdad, 604 note, 66.
Khairémon: A Greek pretender to knowledge of Egyptian history and science, 452 note.
Khalybes in Herod. i. 28 (and Ephorus quoted in Strabo, xiv. 5,

Khalybes—
§ 24): Perhaps a misnomer of Kabalians, 113 note. *See* Cabalians.
Kharax (Spasini), 66-7 note.
Kharitimides the Athenian, 146. Slain, 148.
Khartummim, "Magicians:" Etymology of the term, 41 note.
Khawona of Diodorus, between Bagistané and Agbatana: Perhaps the "royal residence" where Gaumata was slain at Sikthakotish, 340. The name perhaps the same as the old Persian *awahanam* and the modern Persian *khána*, 340.
Khebar river in Khaldæa, 78.
Khedorlaomer, 24 note.
Khem (Ham), god of Kabti, 110 note. Worshipped at Khemmis (Panopolis) in Upper Egypt, 307 note.
Khoaspes, river of Susiana: Its course made by Strabo in one place more westerly than the rivers Koprates and Pasitigris, so as to answer to the Eulæus of Diodorus, 558 note. But before confounded with the Pasitigris, *ibid.*
— A tributary of the Kóphén river, 85 note.
Khodaidaya or 'Uwadaidaya, town in Persis, 635.
Khogé (whither the Kephenes emigrated), 513, 234 note. The name perhaps identical with the name *Khoja*, *ibid.* Although Salmasius proposed to read *Khokhé*, signifying a place also called *Kokhé*, 514 note. Considered by Hellanicus a part of Artæa, *ibid.*
Khoja, '*Uwaja* (now Khuzistan), 417. Perhaps Khogé of Hellanicus, 234 note. The Aryan name of Susiana, 474 and note. The man of the country called by the Greeks Κίσσιος and Κίσσαιος in Aryan Khojiya or 'Uwajiya, 475 note. Sometimes has the precedence over Media, 480. *See* Susiana.
Khojas or Khossas: A Biluchi tribe, 475 note.
Khokhé or Kokhé, 514 note.
Khonds: Religion of the, 386 *et seq.* Confound the Creator and Satan with Adam and Eve respectively, 387. Two sects of, 388, 389.

Khonds—
Their human sacrifices adopted by the Hindus, 390. Their purchase of wives the practice also of the Mongolians, condemned by the laws of Manu, 394 and note.
Khosru Nushirraván, or Anushirván, king of the Persians, 467 note.
Khshatriya (Hindu of the warrior caste): Age at second birth, 266-7 note.
Khshayársha (Xerxes), 3 note, 4 note.
Khshurush: Perhaps considered by Josephus the equivalent of Akhshurush in Hebrew, and of Kurush in Persian and Greek pronunciation, 2 note, comp. 219. The etymological parent of *Khusru* or Chosroes, 220. Why did Cambyses assume the name? 325 note.
Khurush: An ancient form inferred from the modern Persian term *khur*, signifying the sun, 211-12.
Kidaris (a tiara), 197 note. The Hebrew *Kether*, 199 note. (See, too, *Corrections and Additions* on 533 note.) Perhaps properly the *band* (diadem) worn on the head or on the tiara, *ibid*. Also called by the Greeks *kitaris*, 533 and note. The "kitaris of kingdom," *ibid*.
Kikkar, Kinkàr, or, according to Gesenius, Kirkar. The Hebrew term rendered by the Greeks *Talent*, 688 note.
Kimmerians, 246 note, 240 note. *See* Gimirri.
Kir, 67 note.
Kish (now *Gerf-Hossain* in Nubia), 28 note.
— Esther's ancestor, 86. Date of his deportation, 87, 698.
Kissia or Elam (Susiana), 23. Wars of the Assyrians in, 25. The *people* considered Ethiopian (that is, Kushite) by those who placed Tithonus among them, 519-20 note. The kindred population in Persis remained true to Darius when Vahyasdáta was crowned king by the dominant Aryan race, 634. *See* Khoja.
Kissian language: That also of the most ancient population of Persis, 261. So we call the second language of the Behistun inscription, 476 note.

Kneph: An Egyptian deity confounded with Amún, 315, 316 note.
Konkobar, near Agbatana, now Kangavár, 568 note.
Koprates in Susiana: A tributary of the Pasitigris on the side of Susa. Either a branch that once connected the Eulæus with the Pasitigris, or else the modern *Disful river*, which falls into the Karún at Bend-i-kir, 557, 559 note.
Kóphén, son of Artabanus, 65 note.
— Ancient name of the Cabul river, perhaps meaning "Mountain foam," 84-5 note. This Josephus calls an *Indian* river, *ibid*.
Korylas king of Paphlagonia, 541 note.
Korys river, 289.
Kossæans or Kissians, 28 note. *See* Khoja and Kissia.
Kritalla: Xerxes left this in autumn B.C. 481, not in spring B.C. 480, p. 110-11 note, 129.
Ktesias: Perhaps referred to by Xenophon on Cyrus's Median wife, 33 note. His account of Cyrus, *ibid*. Followed by Nicolaus of Damascus, *ibid*. Unusually accurate as to the length of the Magian reign, 68, 69. His story of the Magian, 69-74. Proved by the Behistun inscription less accurate than Herodotus as to the names of *the seven*, 72. Confirmed by the same against Herodotus as to the time of the death of Smerdis, 73. Puts sons for fathers, contemporary names for ancient ones, 74 note, 132. Misdescribes Akhæmenes brother of Xerxes as Akhæmenides brother of the first Artaxerxes, and son of queen Amestris, 145-6 note. His story of Memnon the first he had to tell in connection with his list of Assyrian kings, 518 note. Misrepresents the revolt of Babylon, which happened while one of the six, Megabyzus, was governor, and while Darius son of Hystaspes was king, as a revolt while Zopyrus, son of that Megabyzus, was governor, and Xerxes, son of that Darius, was king, 605. His assertion that the wall of Babylon was 50 fathoms high inconsistent

Ktesias—
with his making the 100 foot height of the Nineveh wall, one since unparalleled, 655.
Kundrush or Kudrush in Media, the place where Frawartish was defeated, 561. To ascertain its situation important, 563.
Kur (with vowel both long and short): The modern name of rivers in Fars and Georgia called by Greek writers Κυρος (Cyrus), 211. Meaning of the name indicated by that of the Tatar river Gihon, 212 note. Analogous in its two forms to Sūrā (having both its vowels short) and Sūrā (having the first vowel long and the last short), an appellation of the sun in Sanscrit, 213. The Kur of Fars now called the Bendamir, 263 note.
Kurush (Cyrus): The former name of Artaxerxes the First, 2. Perhaps taken by Josephus for an equivalent of Khshurush, 2 note. The name meant *the Sun*, 201; being also pronounced Khurush, 211, 212 note, 213, 216. Other varieties, 214-216. May be the Persian form of Khshurush, 329 note, 531.
Kush or Kish (in Africa) represented by an *unstrung bow*, 28 note. Some of them conquered by Cambyses, 82. Both these and the eastern Cushites followed Xerxes, 113. *See* Ethiopians.
Kyrtii of Strabo: Whether a name akin to Sagartii, 416 note.

LABOROSOARKHOD, 39, 40 note.
Labynetus or Nabunita, husband of Nitokris, 649 note. *See* Nabonedus.
Labyzus: Chief eunuch of Tanaoxares or Smerdis, 70.
Lactantius: Error of, 3 note.
Larissa: Calah so called, 35.
Lasonians: A portion of the Cabalians that was descended from the Maionians or primitive population of Lydia, 113-14 note, 170. Perhaps the parent stock of those called *Rasena* by Dionysius of Halicarnassus, and it is thought *Lasne* on Etruscan monuments, *ibid.* Identified with *Lysineans*

Lasonians—
(inhabitants of Lysinöe or Lysinia), 114 note. May be those inhabitants of Cabalis mentioned by Strabo, from whom one of the four dialects of Kibyra (the *Lydian*) was derived, 115 note.
Lemnos: Its fires, ancient inhabitants, and god Hephæstus, 323 note.
Lesbos: Its relations with the Asian mainland before and after the establishment of the Medo-Persian supremacy, 547-8 and note.
Liars (supposed): Punished by Cambyses, 306.
"*Liberals,*" 70. In criticism, 96. Surrender whatever makes against them, 105. All for Haman and the Amalekites, 136-7. Instinctively hate Israel and sympathize with his enemies, 160.
Libyans west of Egypt: Surrender to Cambyses, 291.
Lies, God of: Perhaps an object of Magian worship, 158. The Gojesta and Devil of the Zoroastrian book Sad-der, 268 note. *See* Areimanius.
Lih-tchun, commencing spring of the Chinese year, 509 note.
Liturgy, the Magian, 459-60.
Lucky days and hours, 462-4 note.
Lycians, originally Termilæ from Crete, who settled in the territory of the Solymi, 118, 154. The Lycian language Indo-Germanic, *ibid.*
Lydians, subdued by the Medes under Cyrus, 238-9.
Lysinöe or Lysinia: Its situation, 114, 115 note. Perhaps marked by a village still called *Allahsún* or *Allaysoon*, 115 note. *See* Lasonians.

MADA (Medus), 14 note. *See* Madai.
Madai (in Aryan *Mada*), ancestor of the Medes, 9.
Mader-i-Suleimán (on the road from Istakhr to Ispahan): Extensive ruins of, a farsakh and a half short of Murgháb, and near to which is the tomb of Cyrus, 261 note. Taken by Sir W. Ouseley for the ruins of a city, 262 note.
Mæander river, 544 note. Magnesia on the, 550 note.

Mæandrius: Secretary and successor of Polycrates at Samos, 550. Deposits Polycrates's hall furniture in the temple of Hera, 552 note, 592 note. His conduct when Darius's lieutenant came to install Syloson at Samos, 590-1.

Mæotis lake: Apparently an ancient misnomer of the lake now called Aral, if that existed in Polybius's author's time, 566.

Magi, The, at Pasargadæ, 63. Guard the tomb of Cyrus, 62, 258-9. Interpret prodigies to Cambyses, 71. Idolatrous Magi in Cappadocia spoken of by Strabo; their idols called Persian, but really Kissian and Babylonian, 371 note. Under name of *Magas* recognised as a caste of Brahmans, 414-15. Medes, but not Aryan Medes, 414 note. Their influence as a caste of priests in Persis, before the overthrow of the Akhæmenian dynasty, 415. Under the Parthians supersede the royal Persian clan at Pasargadæ, *ibid*. And by Strabo are counted a tribe in Persia, *ibid*. note. Probably belonged to either the Elamite or Kushite population of Susiana, 448. Their different prayers for the 365 days of their year, 459-60. That they were not an Aryan tribe, intimated perhaps by Xenophon, 460 note. Why they objected to such a method of intercalation as that of the Egyptian year, first made by the Greeks of Alexandria B.C. 26, and introduced into the Magian year by Sultan Melek Shah Jelaleddin A.D. 1079, p. 462 and 462-3 note. On the Magian intercalation and the Græco-Magian Calendar, 465-9 note, 470.

Magidu: Assyrian correspondent of Megiddo (Josh. xvii. 4), 234 note.

Mago-phonia: The Persian commemorative festival, 338-9.

Mahadeva: Epithet of the malignant Siva in the Puranas, 395.

Manatsuah: Assyrian correspondent of the name Manasseh (M'nashsheh), 234 note.

Mandané, 31.

Maraphii and Maspii, the second and third of the three leading Persian tribes, 274, 276. Compare 187 note.

Marathon (Battle at), fought the 6th of Boedromion, the third Athenian month B.C. 490, p. 122 note. Interval between this and the battle at Salamis, 109-10 note.

Marble, The Parian, 36 note.

Marching, Alexander's rate of, 562.

Mardghiran: A Magian festival, 139 note.

Mardokempadus: See Merodakh Baladan; his first regnal year by the Khaldæan account, 443-4. Connumerary with the first of Sargon king of Assyria, *ibid*. note.

Mareia: The seat apparently of the deputy king of the Adyrmakhidæ or Libyans dependent upon Egypt, 142-144 note.

— The fresh water lake Mareotis, 142-144 note. Filled from the Nile, 144 note, 290 note.

Margiané (*Margush*): Its vines, 616 note. Treated by Strabo as a province united to Aria or Hariva, 616-17 note. Now *Merv*, 615. A dependency of the Baktrian satrapy; its revolt, 480, 616-19. Watered by the Margus river, now Murgh-âb, 615.

Markazana: An Aryan month, the position of which is not determined by the Behistun inscription, 446-7. Probably the Sivannu or Sivan of Assyria; see table B opposite page 431. That is, the eighth month of the Khaldæan year, which began with Markhesvan, 590, 677-8.

Markhesvan or Khesvan: The only Jewish month-name not found in the list of Assyrian month-names, where its place is taken by the designation *eighth month*, 425, 427-29 note, 429 note. Why numbered and not named in the Assyrian Calendar, 447.

Marmaridæ: Libyans of Cyrenaica, 143 and note. Comprised apparently by the Gilligammæ, the Asbystæ, and (including Cabalians) the Auskisæ, 144 note.

Marriage: Among the Persians a duty of the young man, 269-70 and note, 279. As among the high-caste Hindus, 267 note, 270 note. The Asura marriage (condemned by Manu) practised by Mongols and Khonds, 394.

Martiya (Darius's second rival in

Martiya—
Susiana): Proclaims himself king by the name of *Immanis*, 510. A Persian, but of Kephénian, that is, Kissian, rather than Aryan blood, 512-13, 515. Whether the name of his father and of his domicile in Fars do not betray a Kissian origin, 516-21. Slain by those who had owned him their chief, 522, 525. Why is his death not dated ? 578-9.

Marus or Maru'a, in Campadéné, 488, 470-1 note, 56.

Masistes: Younger brother of Xerxes, 132, 134, 135. Present during the disaster at Mycalé, 137.

Massagetæ, The: Their queen Tomyris and her son Spargapeises, 246, 249 note. Sacrifice horses to their only god, the sun, 359 note. An etymology of the name proposed, 360 note.

Measures of length: Greek, 657 note. Certain Roman ones, 663 note. Assyrian, Babylonian, Egyptian, 556-8 note, 665-6 note.

Medes: Called Arii, 13. Called Aryans by Armenian writers, 14. Termed Aj-dahak, "the biting snake," in the Zendavesta, 15. Their tribes, 414 note. Their country extended by Xenophon westward to the Tigris, 20, 281-2 note. Their position in the Behistun List of Nations explained, 481 note, 482 note. Their revolt from Darius under Frawartiah justified, 485-87.

— and Persians: Significance of the term used by Daniel, 8. Both nations of Aryan race, 4.

Megabazus: The general who conquered Thrace for Darius proved by a new argument to be a different person from the Megabyzus who helped to slay the Magian, 609 note.

Megabernes, 33 note.

Megabyzus (in Aryan Bagabukhsha): Father of Zopyrus, son of Daduhya, and one of the six, 608. Five generations of his family enumerated, 608-9 note. Governor of Babylon, and slain when the city was won by the second pretended son of Nabunita, 605-8, 672, 680.

— son of Zopyrus, and one of

Megabyzus—
Xerxes' generals-in-chief, 606 note. Re-conquers Egypt for Artaxerxes son of Xerxes, his wife's brother, 146, 148, 673-4. Resists the fresh Athenian invasion of Cyprus, and makes peace, he and Artabazus, 150. His revolt from Artaxerxes, 149-50, 674. Reconciled, exiled, forgiven, and at his death lamented, 151. Husband of Amytis, Xerxes' daughter, complains of her to her father; listens to but reveals the scheme of Artapanus against her brother king Artaxerxes; desperately wounded in fight with the sons of Artapanus, but cured by Apollonides, a physician of the king's, 452-3.

Megasthenes: Envoy of Seleucus's satrap of Arakhotia to Chandragupta, the great Hindu monarch, 632 note.

Melek Taôos: Appellation by which the Yezedees signify Satan, 385.

Memnon: Polygnotus's picture of, described by Pausanias, 515 note. By the painter's contemporaries the hero was supposed to have come from Susa, *ibid.* By later Greeks brought from above Egypt, *ibid.* His statue at Thebes not assigned to him by the Egyptians, 516 note. Son of Priam's brother Tithonus by the goddess of the Morn, *ibid.* Why Hellenicus may have made his mother, not Morn, but Day, *ibid.* The epic poet Arktinus's account of him gleaned from Proclus, and from the Posthomerica of Quintus Smyrnæus, 517. Pindar's account of him, *ibid.* His mother a Kissian according to Æskhylus, 518 note. His story as told by Ktesias, 518-19 note. The old palace or king's fortress at Susa, that was called Memnon's, replaced under the Persian supremacy, 519 note. *Where* the hero was buried, according to Simonides, 520 note.

Memphis, city, 54, 55, 104. A third part of it, called the White Fortress, besieged by the Athenians, 145. Taken by Cambyses, 291.

Memucan: His sentence in the matter of Vashti, 535. The tact displayed in it, 537.

Mendes: The sacred he-goat at, 307 note, 311 note, 316 note. Perhaps Osiris with the attributes of Khem (Ham); the mourning at its death being, it would seem, mystically a mourning for Osiris; reason for believing that, like the bull at Memphis, it was called Apis, 307 note, 317 note.

Mendesian Nile-mouth, 147 note, 148.

Merodakh Baladan: Antagonist of Sargon and Sennacherib, 25. His son and grandson, *ibid*. The Mardokempadus of Ptolemy's Canon, 51. Expelled by Sargon from Babylon, 52 note.

Meroë, city and country, 298-9 note. Written *Meru* or *Merua* in hieroglyphic, 299 note. Its kings *first priests of Ammon*; succeeded by their consorts before their sons, who were *second priests of Ammon*, *ibid*. Soldiery that fled from Psammetikhus, where planted in Ethiopia, 301 note. Table of the sun a daily public entertainment at Meroé, 302. The prison there, the fetters of which were of gold, *ibid*. The dead enclosed in pillars of glass, *ibid*. Meaning of the unstrung bow sent thence to Cambyses, 303.

Merv Shah Jân: Near which Yezdegherd was killed, 406 note. More than 100 miles lower down the water than Merv-al-Rud, 619 note.

Mesanæans, The, 66-7 note.

Meshech, son of Japhet, 66 note.
— son of Aram, 66 note. Called Mésés, father of the Mesanæans, by Josephus, *ibid*.

Mespila: Opposite the modern Mosul, 20.

Metiskhus, son of Miltiades: His story, 513. Query, How would the edict on Vashti's case have affected him? 536 note.

Michaux's inscription, 665 note.

Mihr or Mithra: A Zoroastrian Izad, 214 note.

Milyans: Anciently called Solymi, 114, 154, 170. Their language supposed to be Semitic, 156 note.

Mithra, the sun-god, 63 note. In the Rig-Veda of the Hindus, *Mitra*, 364 note. For this name Xenophon substitutes the Greek

Mithra—
term signifying *the sun*, as for Auramazda he substitutes the name of the chief Greek god, 351-2 note. Connection between the sun-god Mithra and the sky-god Auramazda, 360, 365-66. Distinct from Auramazdá, 361, 363-4. Strabo first attests this to be the name of the sun-god, 364 note. Name misapplied by Herodotus, *ibid*. Hymns to Homa and Mithra in the Zendavesta, *ibid*. Perhaps regarded as the charioteer of Auramazda, 365. Named the Mediator, 366. As such analogous to the Agni of the Vedas, 367. More prominent under the second and third Artaxerxes than under the first Darius and Xerxes, 377-8, 387. A wife's substitute for, 539 note. Daily salutation of, 540 note.

Mitra, worn by the Kissians, 198 note.

Mitrobates, satrap at Daskyleium, slain by Oroites, 553.

Mnevis: The sacred bull of On, 311 note. Represented Osiris, 307 note. Its title Osor-Mnevis, 307-8 note.

Months: Order and season of the Persian and the proper Babylonian months established by aid of the Assyrian correspondents, 421, 431. Conclusion from Herodotus, as to the order of them, verified by the ordinary Babylonian Calendars, 422. Synonymous and connumerary, the Assyrian and Mosaic months were also contemporary, 435.

Month-names: *Assyrian*, 427, and in Tables A and B facing page 431. Adopted by the Jews, 426, 430. *Aryan*, 427, and Tables A, B, as before. *Jewish*, attested, so far as they occur, from the Bible, Josephus, and the books Maccabees, 428-9. *Syrian* and *Macedonian*, 430 note. *Magian*, 459. The Aryan form of the Magian names not anterior to the reform of Magianism attributed to Darius son of Hystaspes, 457-8. *Persian* (of a new calendar ascribed to Yezdegherd, the last of the Sassanians), 472.

Mordecai, 34, 88, 90, 166, 179, 185,

Mordecai—
527 note, 698. The interpretation, Esther ii. 5, 6, which would make, not Kish, but Mordecai, the fellow-captive of Jeconiah, refuted, 699 note. Born at Babylon, but migrated to Susa, 700. Takes a seat at the king's gate, 712.
Mugheir (Muqeyer): Cylinders of Nabonedus found at, 38. Mentioning his son Bel-shar-ussur, 649 note, 653 note, 658 note, 661, 694 note. The angles, not the sides of the big ruin at, face the four cardinal points, 693, 694 note.
Mu'j, The book, 189 note.
Mu'jizât, The book, 235 note.
Mula, a Babylonian deity, 683 note.
Murghâb (about 15 farsakhs from Persepolis on the road to Ispahan): The ancient Pasargadæ; tomb of Cyrus near extensive ruins called Mader-i-Suleiman, about 1½ farsakh on the Persepolis side of Murghâb, 261 note.
Musulman and "Oriental" not synonymous, 538 note.
Mycalé: Destruction of the Persian fleet ashore at, 121. On the 3d of Boedromion, the third Attic month, Sept. B.C. 479, p. 122.
Mygdonians: Called Thracian; perhaps akin to the Homeric Phrygians, 421 note.
Mylitta: The goddess so called by Herodotus, 364-5 note.
Myriad: A division of cavalry or infantry, not necessarily consisting of so many as 10,000 men, 112, 117. Xerxes's army measured by means of an enclosure, which admitted one myriad at a time, 118. The myriads of the proper Persian army as many as the Persian tribes, 273. The 12 myriads of Persians represented apparently by 12 *khiliads* of foot and 12 khiliads of horse, in attendance upon Xerxes, 380 note.
Mysians, 113, 170. Their invasion of Europe, 240 note, 420 note.

N (the letter): Elided by the Persians, but not by Kissians or Assyrians of Babylon, 81-2 note, 519-20, 560 note.
Nabathæans: Conquered Edom after the destruction of Jerusalem by

Nabathæans—
the Khaldæans, 280 note, 286. Not Ishmaelite, but Aramaic, 287 note. Number of the Nabathæans of Petra at about B.C. 312; their cisterns underground in the desert, 288-9 note.
Nabo-imduk, another name of Nabonid or Nabunita (having perhaps the same significance in the Accad as the other in Assyrian), 38 note.
Nabonadius, form given in Ptolemy's Canon of the name Nabonedus, 37.
Nabonedus (Labynetus, Nabonadius, Nabunita), king of Babylon, 36-39 and note, 40, 53, 88. Two pretenders to the throne of Babylon successively assume the name of Nebukhadrezzar son of Nabunit, 88, 90, 476, 604. Might be believed the father of a grown-up son when the first pretender appeared, 476. His coalition with Amasis and Crœsus, 549. His buildings at Babylon, 610 note, 612-13 note. Called by Abydenus Nabannidokhus or Namanédokhus, 610 note. His works ascribed by Herodotus to his queen Nitokris, 613 note.' Perhaps the builder of that outermost circumvallation of Babylon which Darius son of Hystaspes destroyed, 613 note, 614 note. Builder perhaps of the wall of Media described by Xenophon, *ibid*.
Nabonassar, Years of: Difference as to the commencement of these regnal years in the Egyptian and the Babylonian computations, 439, 440, 441, and Appendix, Art. 3.
Nabopolassar, king of Babylon, assisted by Cyaxares son of Phraortes the Mede, 27. Polyhistor's story of his negotiation with the "satrap of Media," derived from Berosus, 75 note. Died in the year that ended with Tisri B.C. 604, p. 646 note.
Nabunita, Nabunit, Nabonid, 36, 38. *See* Nabonedus.
Naditabel, Darius's first rival in Babylonia, 476-8.
Nakhsh-i-Rustam: Darius Hystaspes' sons' tomb at, 12, 83, 229, 348 note, 373. (Add 745.)
Names (Regal) assumed on accession to the throne by modern Chinese,

Names—
as by the old Perso-Median monarchs, 210-11.
Namirri: Assyrian appellation applied to the Sakas of Asia, while *Gimirri* appears to be applied to the Sakas of Europe (Thracians), 82 note. Whether, however, Namirri should be deciphered Gimirri, *ibid.*, 246 note, 280 note.
Nana or Nanæa (a Babylonian deity): Perhaps the same as the Anæa of Strabo, 364-5 note.
Nations (names of the) that went *with Xerxes* against Greece, 112-117. The 36th name concluded to be *Non-Mœonian Cabdlians*, 113-115 note.
— forming the empire of Cambyses son of Cyrus, 417-18.
— that revolted while Darius was at Babylon, 480.
— List of the tributary, at Persepolis, 480. The tomb-list at Nakhsh-i-Rustam, 481.
Nearkhus, 84.
Nebo son of Merodakh: His temple at Borsippa (Birs Nimrúd), 8 note, 88.
Nebukhadrezzar, 27-29, 36 note, 38, 46, 75 note, 86. His eighth regnal year in Hebrew reckoning the 11th of Jehoiakim king of Judah, 87. Generation of his great-grandchildren, 87, 88. The holy vessels taken by him from the temple at Jerusalem, 242-3. Wars with Nekho the grandfather, and Hophra or Apries the grandson, 90. Close of his reign, 399-400. His satraps (mentioned by Daniel) lieutenants of Aryan provinces, or Aryans beneficed in non-Aryan parts of his empire, 278, 279. Commencement of his regnal years by Jewish reckoning (before his father's death), 441, 445, 625, 646 note. By that of the Khaldæans, *ibid.* His victory over Nekho at Karkhemish before his father's death, *ibid.* The actual beginning of his reign at Babylon, 445 note. His buildings there, 609 and note, 610 note.
— and Cyrus: Their dealings with the temple at Jerusalem, 506.
Nehemiah: Additions to book of, 49, 77. Sent to repair the *recently* broken walls of Jerusalem, 150,

Nehemiah—
404. Regnal year employed by, 435. Inference from his using the month-names Khisleu, Nisan, and Elul, without adding the number of the place of each in the twelvemonth, like the author of Esther, 436.
Neith, goddess, 294. A "tomb" of Osiris behind her sanctuary at Sais within the holy precinct, 294 note. There being other so-called tombs of Osiris elsewhere, 308. In the same precinct, the tombs of Amasis, as well as those of Apries and his predecessors of the 26th dynasty, 295.
Nekho (I.), Asshur-bani-pal's deputy at Memphis and Sais, 25. (*See* Appendix, Art. 1.)
— II. (Pharaoh), 90. His canal to the Red Sea, and circumnavigation of Africa, 163 note. Defeated at Karkhemish in the fourth year of Jehoiakim, 445.
Nergel-shar-uzur: The same as Neriglissar, 39 note.
Neriglissar, 29, 38 note, 39 note.
Nerus (number, measure): Ten times the Sús or Sôssos of Babylon, 665 note.
Nicephorus, Archbishop of Constantinople, 94 note.
Nicolaus Damascenus, 33 note, 66-7 note.
Niffer, anciently Nipur: Semitic name of the city of the *second* of the Babylonian twelve gods, whose Accad name appears to be as yet unknown, 683 note.
Nile, 286 note. The Blue River and the White, 301 note. Meaning, antiquity, and ethnic origin of the appellation, 310 note. Whether a *twofold* Nile is indicated by the monuments, *ibid.*
Nimrod son of Cush, 299 note.
Nin, deity, 683 note.
Nine Roads: A spot on the east bank of the Strymon, whence the river was crossed in the country of the Edonian Thracians, and where Amphipolis was afterwards built, 158.
Nineveh or Ninus, taken, 26, 27. Pretended height, length, and thickness of its walls, 655. Sennacherib's palace at, 656. Ktesias's purely imaginary account of

Nineveh—
the city walls, based on the shape and dimensions (with which he was familiar) of Babylon the Assyrian capital of his own time, 662. Ktesias's 150 by 90 stades circuit of Nineveh, perhaps a version of 5 by 3 *parasangs* or hours of march, 667-8. Probable deportation of citizens to Babylon after capture of Nineveh, 683-4.

Nineteen battles gained by Darius, 602 note.

Ninians (or Ninevites), Gate of the (at Babylon), 670, 683. Seems to be Nebukhadrezzar's *Gate of Nin*, 683 note.

Nirikassolassarus: That is, Neriglissar, 39 note.

Nisæa (Nisaya) of Media: Its great horse-breeding establishment visited by Alexander on his way to Agbatana from Opis on the Tigris, after having passed Bagistané, 339 note. The place where Alexander stayed in the district, a seven days' march from Agbatana, 340 note.

— on the Okhus or Akes river in (or bordering on) Hyrkania, 340 note.

Nitêtis, daughter of Apries, 90.

Nitokris, wife of Nabonedus, 36, 37, 38, 42, 88, 90. Perhaps the same as Nitêtis daughter of Apries, 40 note, 90. Her burial-place, 683.

Norris, Mr. Edwin: Valuable information received from, 6. In one of the ordinary Assyrian calendars (containing the monograms or *initials* of the old Babylonian month-names, without interpretation), 230; and subsequently, in an account of a newly-discovered calendar, wherein these names have their Assyrian correspondents annexed, 425, 426 and note. (*See*, after the Appendix, *Additions and Corrections*.) His Kissian version of the Behistun inscription, and other contributions to the R. A. S.'s Journal, *passim*.

Nu (for *Nuva* or *Numa-ki*) explained to mean Elam, 510 note. Equivalent to Khoja and Afardi, *ibid*.

Nus: Hieroglyphic name of a town once situated on the left bank of the Nile, opposite the rock necropolis at Beni-Hassan, 305 note.

Nysa (above Egypt): Sacred to Dionysos, that is, Osiris, 305 and note.

OANNES and his successors the instructors of antediluvian men, 371-2 note.

Oasis, the Greater (now *Wah El-Khargeh*): Of old an image of Osiris's realm of spirits in the west, being called "Isle of the Blessed," 304. (Can el-Khargeh be connected with Kargh, a Zend or Perso-Aryan form of Swarg, "Heaven," in Sanskrit? *See* G. R.'s Herod. vol. i. p. 348.)

Okhus (whose regal name was Artaxerxes III.): Calls himself Artakhshatra (Artaxerxes) in his only known inscription, 532 note. In the same calls his father Arsakes and grandfather Okhus by their regal names Artaxerxes and Darius only, *ibid*. Calls the son of Hystaspes, not Khshurush, but Darius, *ibid*. *See* Artaxerxes III.

— River, the Akes of Herodotus, 340 note.

Olympic games, 119.

Omanes: Probably a Kissian, but called by Strabo a Persian deity, 24 note. Sharer with Anadatus in the temple of Anaitis at Zela, 64 note, 371 note. His image carried in procession, 371 note. Perhaps the deity of Susa named Umman, 511. Taken for the Khomæus Apollo worshipped at Khumana or Humania, 511 note.

Omens, anc. Persian, 337, 350, 351, 357; anc. German, 358.

On, surnamed Rabek or Heliopolis, 147 note, 291.

Onesicritus: His account of the tomb of Cyrus and its bilingual inscription, 259 note, 262 note, 692 note.

Onophas (or Anaphas), son of Otanes and brother of Amestris, mistaken for his father by Ktesias, 132.

Opis, on the river Physkus, 20. Near its confluence with the Tigris, 339 note. Opposite this city, on the right bank of the Tigris, the Median wall or cross wall of Semiramis seems to have begun, 614 note.

Oroites: His story, 540-56.

Oromasdes, Oromazes, 376, 385,

Oromasdes—
386. The Power of good and God, and of all sensible objects most like to Light, 367 note. *See* Auramazdá.
Orontes: A Persian, 534 note, 543.
— Mountain (now called Elwend), 566.
Oropasta: Name given by Trogus to the Magian Smerdis of Herodotus, the Sphendadates of Ktesias, the Gaumáta of the Behistun inscription, 351 note.
Orotal and Alilat: Deities invoked by the Arabians or Nabathæans in treaty-making, 287 note.
Orthokyrbasians of the 10th satrapy, 170.
Ortospana: In the land of the Paropamisadas, 641 note.
Osiris: His character derived from primeval revelation, 207. Why diversely regarded as son of Saturn and son of the Sun, *ibid.* Receives the acquitted dead in Amenti, 214, 296, 304. His lesser and greater mysteries, 294 note. Red-haired men said to have been sacrificed of old at one of his tombs, 297 note. Identified by Greeks with their Dionysos, 305. Represented by Apis, Mnevis, and other sacred animals of Egypt; perhaps also by the he-goat of Mendes; Phallic figures of his filled with grain, and buried; by many identified, like Khem, with the Greek Pan, 307 note. Figured as a man with a bull's head, and called Apis Osiris, 308 note. Herodotus' religious silence on the mystery of the death of Osiris, and connection with Apis, 308 note. Tomb of, in the precinct of the sanctuary of Neith at Sais, and other tombs in other places, 308 note. His figures black or green, 309 note. His name by some interpreted *many-eyed*, 315. His death lamented in those of Apis, of the Mendesian goat, and of a ram annually sacrificed at Thebes, 317 note.
Ostrakiné: Half-way station between Rhinokorura and Mount Casius, now *Ras Straki;* why so called, 288 note.
Otanes, 132, 133: Helped Darius against the Magian; commanded

Otanes—
the forces that put Syloson in possession of Samos, 136, 588-93. Also commanded the Persian division of the army of Xerxes, *ibid.* Father of Phaidima detects the Magian's imposture, 335, 337, 343, 346. His name, 588 and note. In what capacity he was sent down by Darius to the Ægæan sea, 589. His service against the Magian exaggerated among the Greeks, 674.

Paionians: Called themselves a colony of Teucri, 420 note. Part of the nation transplanted into Phrygia by Darius Hystaspes' son, *ibid.*
Paktyan land, 83-4 note, 170. The Paropamisadan province divided into Thatagush on the west, and Gandára on the east, 639. In some respects a "Scythian" country, 640 note.
Paktyes, or Paktyan people: The name perhaps connected etymologically with the Kissian text of the Behistun inscription signifying *Helper to me;* and the nation perhaps of the same stock as the Kissian, and the original population of Persis, 116 note, 643 note. The Paktyes proper were perhaps the Satagydas (Thatagush) and Aparytas, 641 note. The name Paktyes exists in that given to themselves by the Affghans, 642 note. Whether Cyrus' benefactors the Arimaspi on the river Etymandrus were Paktyans, 643 note.
Panticapæum, or *Kertch,* 341 note.
Paphlagonians: Having co-operated heartily against Babylon, were left free from the residence of a Persian satrap, 541 note.
Paprêmis, city of Egypt, 145, and one of the Nomes of the Hermotybian warriors, *ibid.* The Persians and Egyptians slain there in the defeat of Akhæmenes by Inarôs; why left unburied, 159 note.
Paradise, Zoroastrian notion of, 270 note.
Parasang, usually reckoned equivalent to 30, sometimes to 25 stades, 577-8 note, 619 note. Herodotus' 450 from Sardis to Susa, suppos-

Parasang—
ing the march to pass by Issus and Mosul, calculated by Rennell equivalent to 2½ geogr. miles apiece, 581 note. See Farsakh, Kasbu, Skhœne.
Parétakéné: A second name given by Isidore to his Sakastané, 644 note.
Paretakanians, Parætakæ, or Baréticani: Whether a distinct nation from the Medes, 249 note. This name (not Barcani) the true reading in Q. Curtius, iii. 4, § 5, p. 249 note.
Parga (mountain town in Persis): Perhaps the modern *Fahraj*, 635 and note.
Parikanians, 113. One set perhaps the Hyrkanians in the 10th; another in Herodotus' 17th satrapy, 170, 248. The two appear as Hyrkanians and Parikanians under Xerxes, 248 note.
Parmenion takes Damascus, 65 note.
Parmises, 33 note.
Paropamisadas of Eratosthenes: Occupy partly the Satagydan country, partly the Gandarian, 642 note. They are the people of Herodotus' Paktyan land, *ibid.*
Paropamisus, 85 note. The name confined to the country of the Gandáræ by the Assyrian version of the Behistun inscription, but extended so as to include Thatagush by Strabo, 639, 641 note.
Parsa (Perses), ancestor or founder of the Persians, 9, 234 note. By some made son of Mada, 14. See *Perses.*
Parsa, land (Persis, now Fars), 233 note.
Parsá (Persæ): That is, not only the people, but their capital Persepolis, 64 note, 233, 263 note.
Parthians: Their supremacy beyond the Euphrates, 471 note. Their Greek coins, how dated, 470 note. Their Tartar origin, and signification of the name, 584 note. Along with the Hyrcanians, take Frawartish's part against Darius, and are subdued by the king's father, 584-7.
Parthia and Hyrcania, united as one government, 563 note, 582.
Partmim: A designation applied to great men of Judah by Daniel,

Partmim—
and to great men among the subjects of Ahasuerus by the book Esther, 528-9 note. The word supposed to be Aryan, and akin to the Greek πρῶτοι, *ibid.*
Partsu: Assyrian term for Perses, Persis, or Persæ, 233-4 note.
Parysatis: Wife of Darius II., 84, 191-2, 195, 201. Conversed with Ktesias, 211. Intercedes for her son Cyrus with his elder brother, 414.
Pasargadá, or Pasargadæ, now *Murgháb*, 7; or *Mader-i-Suleiman*, near Murgháb, 261. Magian occupation of, 62 and note, 72. Persian capital in time of Cyrus, 253, 254, 276. Royal park at, 258. Its ruins, or those of the royal mansion there, now called Mader-i-Suleiman, 261-2 note. Etymology, and various forms of the name, 264 note. Cambyses there buried, 326. Idol temple at, where each new Persian king was inaugurated, 413. Ultimately a Magian town, 415.
Pasargadas, The tribe: First of the ten hereditary Persian tribes, emigrate to the Carmanian coast, 62 note, 274.
Pasht, the goddess of Bubastis or Pi-basht, 188.
Pasitigris, river, 530 note. The *Karún* river of Khuzistan, 158-60 note. Reached on the fourth march from Susa for Persis, 559 note.
Passover: First that was celebrated in the temple rebuilt by Zerubbabel, 704-5.
Patigrabana: A town of Parthia, 587.
Patiskhorii: A Persian clan, 415-6 note.
Patizeithes: A Magian, 55, 68. His employment that of a modern *Gomashtah*, 65, 329-30. His part given by Trogus to Cometes (Gaumáta), 350-51 note.
Patrocles (Seleucus' lieutenant): His measures of defence when Babylonia was invaded by Demetrius, 664 note.
Patumos, Pithom: The name of a place near where the Red Sea canal issued from the Nile, 164 note.
Pausiris, son and successor of Amyr-

Pausiris—
tæus, "king in the marshes" of Egypt, 143.
Pelusium, 283-4, 288, 290 note, 291.
Persepolis, 64 note, 253-4 note. About 40 miles from Pasargadæ, and the work of the kings descended from Hystaspes, 263. Called Parsá, i.e. Persæ, ibid. Darius' list of provinces there, 229. Now *Istakhr*, 261 note. Perhaps founded by Darius son of Hystaspes, 263.
Perses, son of Perseus by Andromeda, daughter of Képheus king of the Ethiopian Képhénes, 234-5 note. Arab and modern Persian stories of, 235-6 note.
Perseus son of Danaé, 234.
Persis: Extended application of the name in later times, 24 note. Ten districts of, 274. Its liberties, 344-5. Its tribes by Herodotus' account and by Strabo's, 415-6 note. By a *first* extension of the term includes Susiana, 519 note. The country rejects Darius for a new pretender to the character of Smerdis son of Cyrus, 524. See Parsa land.
Persis and Media: The united kingdom of, 604 and note. Compare *Additions and Corrections* on page 604, note (a).
Persians: Of old called Artæans, 13. Derive themselves in the Vendidad, from the *Airyanem vaejo*, 14. Twelve tribes of, perhaps not differenced by descent or proper native district, 273-5. The ten hereditary tribes of Herodotus seem to correspond with the ten districts or departments of Persis mentioned by Marcianus Heracleota, 274, 636-7 note. The twelve represented apparently in Xerxes' army in the king's own division, and the contingents of the three leading tribes particularly distinguishable, 380 note. At what season did their civil year begin, 106 note. Free from tribute, 172. Delivered from vassalage, not to the Medes, but to Babylon by the great Cyrus, 483 note.
Persians and Medes: Significance of this style used in Esther and the Behistun inscription, 8-10. When

Persians and Medes—
this style was adopted, 15. The nations a united kingdom, 10, 11. Alike of Aryan race, 14.
Petra of the Nabathæans, 440 note.
Peukestes: At Persepolis feasts the army commanded by Eumenes, 530 note.
Phœdimé: Daughter of Otanes, 335.
Phakússa, below Bubastis: A canal from this ran perhaps into the lake *Ballah-el-Mamleh*, 164 note.
Phanes: Deserts to, and advises Cambyses, 285-6.
Pharnabazus, son of Pharnakes: Satrap by inheritance at Daskyleium, 541 note, 544 and notes. Territories subject to him, ibid. Others of his family in the time of Alexander the Great, 545 note.
Pharnakes: A name occurring more than once among the ancestors of Pharnabazus, 544 note. (Compare the name Pharnúkhus, 541 note.)
Pharaoh, (according to rabbinical punctuation): more properly *Phrah*, i.e. *Pi-Ré*, Coptic for "The Sun," 202-3. Written by the Assyrians *Pi-rhu*, ibid.
Pharos, island: Considered Libyan, 142, 143-9 note, 144 note.
Pheraulas: A Persian plebeian. His education, 275 note.
Pheretima: Her vengeance on the citizens of Barca, 140 note.
Phraortes, or Frawartish, son of Deiokes king of the Medes, 25, 233-4. Not master of Susa, 26.
Phrygians: The people from whom the Greeks named the greater part of the country and people named Sparda and Sparta-fa in Aryan and Kissian, 420 note. Spoken of by Homer as a people of Asia Minor, ibid. Believed by the Macedonians of the fifth century B.C. to be a branch of the Thracian Bryges, ibid. Apparently connected with the Mygdonians of Thrace, 421 note. On the resemblance of their language to the Macedonian and Paphlagonian, see *Additions and Corrections* on 421 note.
Phthah, or Pthah, 323 note. Temple of, at Memphis, 163. The god named by the Greeks Hephæstus,

Phthah—
  ibid. His image laughed at by Cambyses, 323.
Physcus, river, 20.
Pishya' uwádá, or Pishiyakhodá: A district of Parsa or Fars country, 328, 635.
Platæa: The Persians defeated at, 121. On the 3d of Boedromion (third Attic month, about September B.C. 479), 122.
Plynus: Bay and harbour of Egyptian Libya, 143, 144 note.
Polycrates (tyrant of Samos), 321, 544. His story, 547-551.
Poniard, the Persian, called *Akinakes*, 535-6 note.
Pontus, Euxinus: The right hand side of this sea, 173.
Prexaspes: Employed by Cambyses to slay Smerdis, 335. Publishes the fact, and casts himself headlong from a tower-top, 336.
Prideaux, Dean: Confutes the opinion that Darius Nothus was king when Zerubbabel's temple was completed, 6 note.
Prosopitis (in the Nile Delta): A tract surrounded on all sides by branches of the river, 147. One of the six Nomes where the Hermotybian division of the warrior caste had its lands, *ibid.* At the apex of the Delta, between the Canopic Nile-mouth and the Thermuthiac branch of the Sebennyte Nile-mouth, 147 note.
Provinces possessed by Cambyses, Behistun list of the, 417, 418.
Psammenitus, 54, 74 note, 148 note. Of the same generation as Esther and Darius, invaded, overthrown, and put to death, 283-294. His six months' reign explained and assigned to its place, 292-3.
Psammis, or Psametik II., 90.
Ptolemy son of Lagus, 651.
Ptah. *See* Phthah.
Purim, the feast: Authenticates the story of Esther, 96.
Putiyá and Kushiyá: In Darius' tomb-list, 83 note, 414 note.

Rá or Ré: Egyptian name of the sun or sun-god, 204-5. *Son* and *Daughter of*, titles of gods and goddesses, male and female sovereigns, *ibid.* Other gods take Rá

Rá or Ré—
  as a second name, *ibid.* Equivalent at Babylon to the Assyrian Il, or El, *ibid.* Among the present Bechuanas of South Africa, Rá signifies *father*, *ibid.* This perhaps the original signification in the land of Ham, in which case the name should have been applied especially to the Creator, 206, 207. Why Rá disputed with Seb among the Egyptians the paternity of the children of Seb, 207.
Ragá (in Greek, Rhaga and Rhagæ): A district as well as a city of Media, 561-2, 586 note. The city (now ruins near Teheran, called Rey, 562) in Isidore's time the greatest in Media, *ibid.* note.
Rakshasas and Yakshas: Conjecture as to the locality of these non-Aryan tribes, 395 note.
Ram: The two-horned Aryan, 16, 41, 240.
Rameses I. (father of Sethi), 163 note, 165 note.
Rameses II.: Son of Sethi, associated with his father on the throne, 165 note. *See* Sesostris.
Raphia: The beginning of Syria, 290 note.
Rawlinson, Sir H. C. (cited *passim*): His criticism of Assyrian documents concluding that Samaria was taken in the first year of Sargon king of Assyria, 52 note. His opinion that Gazaka in Atropaténé was the most ancient Agbatana, 61.
Reeds (layers of): How used in ancient Babylonian building, 653 note, 651-2 note, 653.
Regnal Year: What civil year was counted a king's first by the Egyptians, 102. What by the Assyrians and the annalists of the house of David, 442. By the Jews Mosaic years counted for the regnal years of their Persian masters, and their civil year for the regnal year of their own ancient kings, 104, 87. *See* Years.
Religion, Patriarchal: A type recognised by it of the Son of man, the Redeemer, 269, 270 note.
— Aryan and Magian: A compromise between these two perhaps effected in the reign of Darius son of Hystaspes, 411, 412.

Religion, conservative policy of Darius regarding, 416.
Revelation, Primæval, 221. Its great subject, 207.
Rezin or Arasên taken and slain by Tiglath-pileser, 67 note.
Rhaga: Its distance in miles and by Alexander's marches from Agbatana, 490 note. *See* Ragá.
Rhaká: A town in Persis, 635.
Rhakôtis: An old coast-guard station, afterwards a quarter of the Greek capital of Egypt, 142 note.
Rhinocolura or Rhinocorura (on the ancient border between Egypt and Syria): The *Nakhal Mitsrayim*, or River of Egypt, 288 note, Now *El Arish*, 289 note. Diodorus' and Strabo's legendary etymology of the name, *ibid.* Another suggested, *ibid.* A port whence the Nabathæans of Petra shipped for the West the goods they received by caravan from the Red Sea and the Persian Gulf, *ibid.*
Rhodoguné: Daughter of Xerxes, 131, 152.
Riblah, in the land of Hamath, 91.
Rivers, Magian propitiation of, 155 note, 156.
Rokhshana (Roxana): Own sister and wife of Cambyses, 71, 184.

SABÆANS: Children of Sabas, son of Cush, 298 note.
Sabas son of Cush, 298 note.
Sabathéni: People of Sabathas, son of Khusôs (Cush), *called by the Greeks Astabori*, 298 note.
Sacrifice (Animals of): Their typical character known to Moses, though not declared in the law, 315, 316.
Deified by the Egyptians, 319, 370-71.
— Fire of, deified by Hindus and Magians, 319, 370-71.
— A typical accompaniment of prayer, 320 note.
Sadder (Hyde's Epitomé of the Book), 3 note, 189 note, 220 note, 235 note, 267 note, 268 note, 269 note, 270 note.
Sagartia (Asagarta), 481. Argument to show that it was anciently an appendage of Media, 574, 572. Situation of, 572.
Sagartians: Persian in language, but Paktyan in equipment, 115.

Sagartians—
Perhaps in blood partly Paktyan, 116 note. Perhaps called Kyrtii by Strabo, 416 note. Called in Aryan Asagartiyas, 570; and their country Asagarta, *ibid.* note.
Sah (Dynasty in Surashtra in the two centuries before our era): Styled Satraps, 619 note.
Sais: Visited by Cambyses, 294.
Sakæa: A feast at Babylon, 342 note.
Sakas (Amyrgian): In Aryan Hamawargá, 247 note. Joined with the Baktrians, under the same commander, in the army of Xerxes, 112. Apparently an appendage to the satrapy of Baktria, 140. At first enemies, afterwards allies, of the great Cyrus, 246.
— (Tigrakhudá), 247 note.
— (Xenophon's): Apparently Parthians, 583.
— (in Europe): Thracians, 82-3 note, 246 note, 581-2.
Sakastané: Country so called by Isidore of Kharax, 643 note.
Sakuka, The Saka, the only one of Darius's foes in the sculptured tablet at Behistun not called a liar, 484-5 note.
Salamis, Sea-fight at, 18, 120. Date of the battle, 122.
Samaria, Fall of, 47, 50, 51-2 note, 334, 444.
Samaritans: Their account of themselves to Zerubbabel, 245. Complain to Cambyses son of Cyrus against the Jews, 324-5. Petition, and receive a favourable answer from, the Magian, 333.
Samos: Darius's first acquisition in the West, 174. Under and before Polycrates, 547-52. How taken and handed to Sylosôn by Otanes, 590-92. Its condition at the end of Darius's reign, 593.
Sanskrit and Zend sister languages, descended from an older Aryan, 216 note.
Sarangas: People of Zaranga, 571.
Sardis: Taken by Cyrus, 36. Receives an image of Anaitis, 63.
Sardô (Sardinia): Speculation as to the name, 420 note. Its population in part Tyrrhenian, *ibid.* Projects of the Greeks of Asia as to emigration thither, *ibid.*
Sargon king of Assyria, 47, 50, 51-2

951

Sargon—
note. Invaded Media before the date of Deiokes's building, 62. Perhaps did not advance beyond Campadéné, *ibid.* Mentions the Yavan of Cyprus, 79 note. His regnal years connumerary with those of Merodakh Baladan of Babylon, 444 note.
Sarpedon, at the head of the Termilæ, driven by Minos from Crete to the land of the Solymi, 154 note.
Sarsamas : Satrap of Egypt, 148.
Sarus (Six times the Nérus and sixty times the Sóssus of Babylon) : Applied to measurement of space, 665 note. See *Additions and Corrections* on page 668.
Sassanians (Persian dynasty) : Accession of, 471 note. Overthrow of, 459.
Satan, 370, 384. Why worshipped by the Yezedees, 385.
Satagydians, Gandarians, Dadikas, and Aparytas, ought to be subjoined to "the Paktyan land," and so, form the 13th satrapy on Herodotus's list, instead of giving up that situation to "Armenia and the countries thence as far as the Euxine," and standing in the stead of these in the seventh Herodotean satrapy, 170. In Aryan *Thatagush*, Situation of, 639, 641 note. Seem to have been Paktyans proper, *ibid.*
Satrap, lord, king : The terms distinguished, 247-8 note. On the original form and etymology of the word Satrap, 619 note.
Satrapies, List of Darius's twenty, exhibiting the order adopted by Herodotus, and also that of the original document, 170. Compare 167, 169.
Satrapy : Error of Herodotus corrected as to the 7th and 13th satrapies of his list, 170.
Saturn (Kronos) : Most properly *Il*, that is, "God," according to the Hamites of Khaldæa, 206.
Saul king of Israel : His arms and body, how treated by the Philistines, 680 note.
Savitri and his Car (in the Rig-Veda), 265 note.
Saxons, *i.e. Long-knives*, 556 note. (Anglo-Saxons) Long hair of the, 564 note.

Scaliger, Joseph : His identification of Esther and Ahasuerus, 3. His notion concerning the identity of the Darius of Ezra confuted by Prideaux, 6 note.
Scythians (of the once Kimmerian land) : Their reign of 22 years in the Assyrian empire, 26 and note. Serve Alyattes six years against Cyaxares (I.) king of the Medes, 27. Their country invaded by Darius son of Hystaspes, 82 note. Their name Skyths in Aryan, Kissian, and Assyrian, 82, 83 note. Mode of purifying themselves after a funeral, 139. Sacrifice horses, 359. Concubines and servants buried with deceased kings of, 341 note. Fresh immolations of men and horses on the first return of the day of death, 342 note. Their scornful presents to Darius, *ibid.* Appear to have been Indo-Germanic, 583 note.
Seb, The Egyptian Saturn : His wife Netpe, his children Osiris, Aroeris, Seth (Typhon), Isis, Nephthys, 204, 205, 207.
Sebennytic branch of the Nile, 147 note.
Seleucia on the Tigris, 488 and note, 514 note. At the very distance from Babylon where stood, on the right bank, the Karæ, or Karôn, villages, 558, 689. Walled, probably by Seleucus, with burnt brick taken from the old walls of Babylon, 612 note. Described by Strabo as greater (bigger) than Babylon, 664 note.
Seleucidæ (Coins of the) : The first coin extant that bears a date, one of Antiokhus the Great, 461 note.
Seleucidan Era (of the Khaldæans) : How it came to begin a year after that of the Greeks, 439 and Appendix Art. 3.
— Of the Greeks, 457 note, 468, 469. Began on the expiration of 12 years from the death of Alexander, or rather of the Egyptian era of Philip Aridæus, 457 note, 466-8. The Magian intercalation-period of 1440 years (whereof 960 had elapsed at some point in the reign of the last Sassanian king) probably began with this era, 470.
Seleucus : His first regnal year by Babylonian reckoning, the civil

Seleucus—
year next after the one in which he won the throne, 440 and Appendix Art. 3. Surnamed Nicanor, or Nikator, 567 note. Storms a citadel at Babylon where friends of Antigonus had taken refuge, 664 note. Builder of Seleucia on the Tigris, 689.
Self-immolation, 155-6 note.
Selli and Helli (whence perhaps Hellénes, if Agrianes may be referred to Agrioi), 215.
Semiramis (Sammuramit), 183 note. According to Ktesias and his school, author at Babylon of all the works of Nitokris and her consort, also (except the Hanging Gardens) of those of Nebukhadrezzar and his predecessors, 613 note. Also of the Wall of Media, ibid. Herodotus's sober account of her, ibid. Gate of, at Babylon, perhaps identical with the "Gate of Mula," 683 note.
Sennacherib: His regnal years, 442.
Seraiah (the priest): Parallel descents from him and from Kish, 91.
Serbonid Lake: The part west of the Mons Casius, perhaps alone so called by Herodotus, 290 note, 489 note. Once perhaps received water from the Nile, ibid. Frequented of old by the hippopotamus, ibid.
Sesosis: Perhaps signifies "Son of Sethi" (who was Rameses II.), 164 note. See Sesostris.
Sesostris of Herodotus, or Sesosis of Diodorus, compared with Darius son of Hystaspes, 162, 163, 164. Proved to be Ramses Mi-Amun son of Sethi, and grandson of Rameses or Ramases, the first king of the 19th Egyptian dynasty, 163 note. His canal from the Nile to the Red Sea, supposed by Herodotus to have been begun by Nekho, ibid. His war-fleet on the Red Sea, 164 note. The Shoaly Sea, to which his naval expeditions reached, perhaps the head of the Persian Gulf, ibid. Sesostris for Sesosis or Sesothis, the mispronunciation of Persian informants, ibid. Extraordinary length of his reign alluded to by Darius Hystaspes' son, 163, 165 note.

Sesostris—
How the story originated that he conquered the Scythians and Thracians, ibid.
Seventy Years: Four periods of, laid down by the prophets, 706 note.
— of Babylonian supremacy foretold in xxv. 11, 12 of Jeremiah, 503 note, 706 note. (Whether the punishment of the king of Babylon was foretold of three kings, 503-4 note.)
— of Captivity of Jews at Babylon: How connected with the 70 years' supremacy of Babylon, 241. When the captivity began and ended, 441 note, 445, 503 note, 706 note; foretold xxix. 10 of Jeremiah, 503 note.
— of divine indignation against Jerusalem and the cities of Judah, 502, 504. Spoken of by an Intercessor with Jehovah in Zechariah's hearing, ibid.
(Seventy years) of commemoration by fast of the fifth and seventh months, beginning Markhesvan B.C. 587, p. 625, 645-6 and note, 706 note. The commemoration suddenly stopped in the 71st year, 678.
Sfendermad. See Isfendermad.
Sŭtamân and Esfitamân (or Spintamân and Espintamân), father of Zoroaster, 3 note.
Shahpoor (or Sapor): Titles assumed by, 208.
Sheba (Gr. Saba), Queen of: Whence came she to Solomon? 298 note. In her time the king of Egypt subordinate to Ethiopia, 299 note.
Sheikh Adi, 385.
Shekel (of the law): Worth a tetradrachm; the half of it, or bekah, worth a didrachm; the quarter worth a drachma of Athens, 687 note.
— Of the Rabbins, worth but two drachmas, 687 note.
Sheshak: Babylon so called, 645 note.
Sheshbazzar: The official name of Zerubbabel, 180 note, 242, 506 and note.
Sheth or Seth: The Egyptian name of Typhon, 321 note. Meaning of the name, 341.

Shinar, kingdom, 522 note.
Shita, or Khita, of Egypt monuments identified with the Khatti of the Assyrians and the Hittites of Holy Scripture; confounded by the Egyptians with the Skyths of Herodotus's time, 165 note.
Shiva and Durgá of the Hindus, 390, 386 note, 388 note. Meaning of Shiva as a Sanskrit appellative, 391.
Shiyátish: Meaning of the word, 396 note.
Shudra, caste: Sprung from the Creator's foot, 266 note. Etymology of the name, 217.
Shushan, that is, Susa, 23, 24 note.
Shuster (on the Karûn): Why so called, 557 note.
Sibilants: Derived through palatals from gutturals, 216 note.
Sibyrtius: His satrapy, 637.
Sikthakôtish (in Nisæa of Media): The place where Gaumáta was slain, 339. Situate apparently between Bisitun (Bagistané) and Hamadan (Agbatana); as was Khawona of Diodorus, 340. The *didá* or fort at, also an *awahanam* (query, "royal residence"), *ibid.* See *Khavona.*
Simonides (the poet): In his time the Kissian land not yet generally recognised as Memnon's birthplace, 520 note.
Sinties of Lesbos and Sinti of Thrace, 323 note.
Sirbis, river of Lycia, by the Greeks called Xanthus, 156 note (query, whether the name may not be allied to the Gr. ἕρπω and Lat. *serpere*, whence *serpens* and ἕρπις; correspondents, according to Liddell and Scott, of the Sanskrit *Sarpa*).
Skhœne or *Parasang*, 488-9 note. A skhœne of Egypt equal to two parasangs, *ibid.* See *Parasang* and *Kasbu.*
Skylax (the Karyandian): His voyage from Kaspapura on the Indus to the mouth of the Nile canal in Egypt, 83, 84 and note, 117 note, 163 note, 639 note.
Smerdis son of Cyrus: Slain by his brother Cambyses five years before the Magian proclaimed himself king, 56, 70, 73. Twice personated after death, 89. How en-

Smerdis—
dowed by his father's last will, 250.
— The Magian pretender, 55, 57, 66. Length of his reign, according to Ktesias, 68. His story from Herodotus and the Behistun inscription, 328-340. *See* Sphendadates and Gaumáta.
— The Persian pretender to the name. *See* Vahyasdáta.
Solymi, afterwards Milyes, ancient inhabitants of Lycia, 114, 154 note. Supposed to be of Semitic tongue, 156 note.
Soma, the moon-god. *See* Homa.
Sorush or Surush: His function, according to Zoroastrians, on the bridge of Paradise, 214 note. Otherwise, in function no less than in name, he answers to the younger Horus of the Egyptians, *ibid.*
Sosigenes: Employed in reforming the Roman calendar, 451 note.
Sothis, or dog-star: The Heliacal rising of, 452 note, 464 note.
Sparda, Sparta-pa, or Saparda: The name in Aryan, Kissian, and Assyrian, for which the Greeks substituted Sardis, 419 note. Sparta of the Peloponnesus, perhaps a name derived from the same people, *ibid.* Whether the same race may not have given name to Sardinia, 420 note.
Sphendadates (equivalent to Zend *Spentadâta*): Ktesias's appellation of the Magian Gaumáta, 68, 70. Very like the son of Cyrus, 70. Assumes for his regal name Artaxerxes, 68. *See* Gaumáta.
Spitakes and Megabernes, sons of Spitamas, 33 note, 247.
Spitamas: Former husband of Amytis wife of Cyrus, 33 note, 247.
Stasandrus: Made satrap of Aria and Drangéné on the promotion of Stasanor, 617-18 note. Superseded after the defeat of Eumenes, 618 note.
Stasanor (satrap of Baktriané and Sogdiané under Antipater and Antigonus): The name felicitously restored to the text of Strabo by Carl Muller, 617 note.
Strymon, river, 155, 156, 157.
Sun, The: Type of the King of kings, 201, 202, 366 note. Signified by the royal title in Egypt

Sun—
(*see* Pharaoh), 202-3. Sole god of the Massagetæ, according to Herodotus, 359 note; and of the Persians, according to Trogus Pompeius, *ibid*. Image of the Sun or the disk of the Sun beamed above the tent of Darius III., 361 note. With the Persians an image not of the Great God, but of a Mediator with Him, 369. *See* Mithra.
— Son of the: Title of every king of Egypt, 203; and of every king of Ethiopia, 299 note; as of each Inca of Peru, *ibid*.
— Daughter of the: Applied in Egypt to a female sovereign, 204. A title also of goddesses, as Nephthys, who was really supposed to be daughter of Seb, 204-5. The Arab equivalent, "daughter of God," 206.
Suphis (two brothers successively kings at Memphis) received from the dynasty at Elephantiné stone for the great pyramid, 311 note.
Suresh or Suresha (lord of the Sun): Title of the Hindu god Indra, 213. A softened form of Khshurush, 189 note. Perhaps the same word as Syrus, the name of Semiramis's father, and the latter element of the name Artasyras the Hyrkanian, 213, 214. Apparently identical with the Zoroastrian angel Sûrush or Sôrush, 214.
Surush, the Magian angel of the 17th of the month, 189 note.
Surya (the Sun-god) and his car, 366.
Sus, or Soss, "Sixty:" A measure of space, as well as time, in Babylonia, 665-6 note. Equal to 100 *gar* or Babylonian feet, *ibid*. And correspondent of the Greek *plethrum* and Roman *actus* of 120 feet, 663 note, 666 note. Seems to have been turned into a stade by Ktesias in his account of the bridge at Babylon, *ibid*. Also by Berosus in his account of Khshisuthrus's ark, *ibid*. That is, to have been regarded as the 30th part of a parasang or *big kasbu*. See *Additions and Corrections* on page 668, lines 13-19.
Susa (capital of Elam), called the mother city or the capital of the Persians, and even of Persis, 24

Susa—
note. Seems to have been Nebukhadrezzar's in his war with the Elymæans and Kossæans, 28 note. Never belonged to the Medes, Phraortes, Cyaxares I., and Astyages, 25, 27, 29, 40, 41, 42. Made the Perso-Median capital by Darius I., 253. Itself and its palace called Memnonian in Herodotus's time, 515 note. Its old palace had been replaced in Ktesias' time, 519 note. A Greek etymology of the name, and modern description of its neighbourhood, 522 note. Situation of, 556-7. The modern name Shush has a signification that belongs also to the word *Khush*, 557. Its distance from Sardis, 581.
Susa and Ecbatana: A Greek designation of the Perso-Median kingdom, 19, 20.
Susia: A place in Areia or Hariva, 197 note.
Susiana: First revolt there against Darius I., 474-5. Various populations of, 474 note. Its three different names in the trilingual inscriptions of Darius, *ibid*. To one of its peoples belonged the second language of the Behistun inscription, 474-5 note. Its intimate connection with Persis indicated to have been like that of Armenia with Media, 483 note. Older series of its kings, with the language and character of their records, 521 note. Probably equal in power and arts to the Khaldæans of the Lower Euphrates, *ibid*.
Syennesis king of Cilicia, 541 note. His supply of money through his wife to Cyrus the younger explained, *ibid*.
Syloson, brother of Polycrates, 321. An exile, 549. Sues for his brother's inheritance, 587-8. Obtains it, 592. Assisted by Otanes to re-people Samos, 592.
Syncellus (Georgius the): Lumps into one Astyages, Nabonedus (or Nabonadius), Darius son of Ahasuerus, of the seed of the Medes, and Esther's Ahasuerus, 30.
Syrians, the White, of Cappadocia, 371 note, 113, 170, 520 note, 542 and note.

TABÆ : In Parætakéné, 249 note.
Table, Comparative, of Descents, facing 91. Of Darius's 20 satrapies, 170. Of his wives and children, facing 178. Of corresponding months, Assyrian, Old Babylonian, and Aryan, 427. Of Behistun dates, on the supposition that the eighth regnal month of Gaumáta corresponded with the Egyptian month Thoth (A), facing page 431. On the supposition that this month was the Assyrian Markhesvan (B), *ibid*. Remark on Table B, 446.
Takhmaspáda, the Mede : Commanded for Darius against the Sagartians, 574, 584 note.
Talents, Eubœan and Babylonian, 171, 172 (see *Corrections and Additions*), 687 note. The Eubœan the same as the Old Attic, the Babylonian as the Æginetan, *ibid*. Weight of the Babylonian but half that of the Assyrian talent, viz. 82 pounds, and its manahs but half of the Assyrian manahs, 688 note. Understood by Josephus to signify the *kikkar* of Exod. xxv. 39, *ibid*. The new Attic talent, how it stood to the Aeginetan or Babylonian, *ibid*.
Tanais and Tanaitis (a goddess) : In Kissian Tanata, 362 note. The initial perhaps a feminine article, *ibid. See* Anata, Anakhita, Anaitis.
Tanais : A Macedonian misnomer of the Jaxartes river, 566 note.
Tanaoxares (Smerdis), 32, 67. His story, 69–70, 88.
Tanaoxarkes, 33 note, 67, 69.
Tarva or Tarrahuva : A town in Yutiyá, or Ihutiyas, a district of Persis, 598.
Tari, Pennu : The earth goddess of the Khonds, 386-8 note. Her name Tari perhaps identical with Kali, wife of the Hindu god Shiva, 388 note. In quality of earth goddess corresponds with the Hindu Bhaváni wife Bhav or Shiva, *ibid*. Communicates with men in the form of a woman, Umbally Bylee, 388-9. Requires human sacrifices, 390.
Tatnai : Darius's governor in Syria, 505, 506, 628. Various Greek forms of the name, 505 note.

Te and Wang : Difference between these Chinese titles, 407.
Tebeth : The 10th Jewish and Assyrian month corresponding with the Syro-Macedonian Audynæus, 429 note. Its season according to the calendar used in the times of Philo and Josephus ; also in the Judæo-Julian calendar (preserved by Geo. Syncellus), 709-10 note. The fast on the 10th of, 503-4.
Teen-tse and "younger brother of Jesus Christ :" Intended difference between, 407.
Teispes (in Perso-Aryan *Chishpish*) : Two ancestors of Darius so called, blended into one person in the Behistun inscription, 231, 232.
Tel Defeineh : The ancient Takhpankhas, or Daphnas, as the position of an army guarding against an invasion of Egypt from Syria, 285.
Temple at Jerusalem : Might have been mistaken as reasonably as the sky by such as Strabo for the Object of Jewish worship, 407. The rebuilding of, by Zerubbabel ended in Adar B.C. 515, p. 704. Dedication of, *ibid*. Error of the Jews as to the time taken in rebuilding, shared apparently by Josephus, 703 note. How deferred to by early Christian chronologers, *ibid*.
Teucri : Along with the Mysians said to have invaded Europe before the Trojan war, 420 note.
Teutamus : Ktesias's 20th king of Assyria, who sent aid under Memnon to king Priam, 518 note. Possibly an Egyptian Thothmes, 520 note.
Texts of Scripture : Concerning Elam and Media, Isa. xxi. 2, p. 24. Concerning the Bow of Elam, Jer. xlix. 34, p. 28 note. The seventy weeks before the call of the Gentiles, Dan. ix. 24-27, pp. 150-51 note. Call of the Gentiles, when and how made, Gal. i. 18-21, Acts ix. 26-30, xi. 25, 26, xxii. 17-21, xv. 7-9, xi. 16, x. 47, xi. 17, x. 48, xi. 12, x. 23, *ibid*. Correlation of Water and Holy Spirit, Acts x. 47, *ibid*. Satraps under Nebukhadrezzar, Dan. iii. 2, 3, 27, p. 278. The Arabian, Neh. ii. 19, p. 280 note. The 3d, not 11th, of Jehoiakim referred to, 2 Chron. xxxvi.

Texts of Scripture—
6, 7, p. 290 note. Zech. i. 1-6,
Hagg. ii. 15, 18, p. 500 note.
Dan. x. 13, p. 503 note. Zech. vii.
5, pp. 503, 640, notes. Ezra iv.
8, 9, 17, 23, p. 534 note. Zech.
vii. 2, pp. 622 note, 706 note. 1
Pet. v. 13, 2 John 1, 13, p. 666
note. Esther ii. 5, 6, pp. 698-9
note. Zech. i. 12, p. 766 note.
Dan. x. 1-4, pp. 706-8 note. Gal.
i. 18, ii. 1, p. 894. Luke iii. 23,
ibid. Ezra ix. 9, Neh. i. 3, p. 895.
Thannyras, son and successor of
Inarôs king of the Libyans, 143.
Thatagush or country of the Sattagydas: Situation of, 639.
Thermopylæ (pass of) held against
Xerxes by the Greeks, but lost,
119, 120.
Thuraváhara: An Aryan month,
the correspondent of the Assyrian
Sabatu, or Shebat. Table B,
facing p. 431. Probable meaning
of the name, 448. Answers to
the first month of the Chinese
year, 509. Probably the first of
the Aryan twelve, its first fortnight answering to the Lih-tchun
or "Opening Spring" of China.
Additions and Corrections on p.
448. See Lih-tchun.
Thracians: Seem intended by the
Sakas beyond the Bosporus of the
Aryan and Kissian tomb-list, and
by the Gimirri of the Assyrian,
83 note.
Tiara (also Kidaris): "The Upright,"
ὀρθή, or directa, and the Folded
one, projecting towards the forehead, ἐπτυγμένη καὶ προβάλλουσα ἐς
τὸ μέτωπον, involuta et in frontem
demissa, also the reflexa, 196, 197
note, 198 note.
Tibki: Assyrian measure of a palm,
656 and note. See Handbreadths.
Tigra: A fort in Armenia, 493.
Tigris, river, 20.
Tiridates I., of Armenia, 61.
Tissaphernes, 20, 414, 541-2 note,
544 note, 545, 546 and note.
Tithonus, 516, 518 note.
Titles of the kings of Persia, 17.
Tosh: Monumental Egyptian name
equivalent to Coptic Ethosh or
Ethaush, 28 note.
Traders among the Aryans of Persis
and of Hind, 265-6 note.
Trajan: Visits Babylon, and burns

Trajan—
an oblation to Alexander in the
room where the conqueror was
said to have expired, 665 note.
Tributes substituted for gifts to the
Persian king by Darius (I.), 167.
Levied in Europe, 171-7. Not ex-
cessive, 175.
Troizén, anciently Poseidonia:
Mother-city of Halicarnassus, 153
note. Naval station of the Greek
reserve fleet, while the advance
squadron lay at Artemisium to
oppose the fleet of Xerxes, 120.
Tusu, or Tush: Otherwise deciphered
Atesh, the land of Damascus, 67
note.
Tutzis (in Nubia) of the Romans:
How called in Coptic, and now, 28
note.
Twenty-one (or three weeks of)
years: Two such periods of obstruction to the granting of Daniel's prayer for Jerusalem, the
latter beginning two years after
the former, 706-8 note.
Typhon (Seth or Sheth): Brother of
Osiris, 321 note. Hid in the Serbonid Lake, 290 note. Incarna-
tions of, 307 note. His birthday
the third supplementary day (Epagomené), unlucky, 341 note.
Typhonian: Human sacrifices so
called that were annually burnt
alive at Eilethyiaspolis in Egypt,
297 note. The epithet more ex-
tensively applied, 317, 319.
Tyre, 236.
Tyre and Sidon, 10.
Tyrrhenian rocks on the coast of
Egyptian Libya, 144 note.

ULAI river, 41, 42. See Eulæus.
Umman: A deity of Susa in the
time of Sennacherib, perhaps the
Omanes of Strabo, 511. The name
identified with the Egyptian Amún,
ibid.
Usher, or Ussher, Archbishop: His
identification of Esther's Ahasuerus embraced and established, 4,
177. Of Esther and Vashti rejected, ibid. His fancy about the
Artaxerxes of Ezra vi. 14, ibid.
note.

VAHYASDÁTA: Darius's rival in Per-

Vahyasdáta—
sis, 599, 601, 602. His pretensions incompatible with those of Frawartish in Media, if not with the claims of others elsewhere, 603. Conquered by Darius's general Artavardiya, and impaled, 635. Had invaded Arakhotia by a lieutenant with considerable success, 636, 637.

Vaidik theology, 393 note.

Varéné : Perhaps = Baréné, 36 note.

Varkaná: The Hyrcanians, 248, 249, 584 note.

Vas: An Assyrian measure = 60 handbreadths = 10 cubits = ⅙th of the Sús or Sóssus, that is, of the 60 cubit measure, 656 note.

Vashti, 4 note, 34, 97, 130. The same as that daughter of Gobryas who bore Darius three sons before he became king, 186, 187. The same, too, as Artystóné, 187, 533; the one or the other being the name conferred on coronation along with the title *Daughter of Cyrus*, 188. Her disgrace, 533-39.

Vaumisa : His acts on behalf of Darius in Armenia, 508-9.

Vendidad, The book, 14.

Vibanus, satrap of Arakhotia, 503 note. See Vivana.

Vidafrá (Vindafrá) : In the Kissian inscription Vintaparna. A Mede the lieutenant by whom Darius took Babylon, 187 note, 630, 634, 672. Extraordinary compliment of Darius to, 672, 677. That the name is abbreviated from Vidafraná shown by an analogous example, 673 note.

Vidafraná, or Intaphernes, 186, 226 note, 673.

Vidarna, or Hydarnes, defeats the Medes in Campadéné, 488, 557.

Vidaspa, or Hydaspes : As the name of the Jelum river in the Panjáb, a misnomer for Vitasta, the true Sanskrit name, 330 note.

Vintaparna : The Kissian form of Vidafrá and Vidafraná. *See* those names.

Vishnu : The Hindu deity. Whether the name be cognate with the Perso-Aryan *Vashna*, 391 note.

Vishtaspa, *i.e.* Hystaspes, 3 note, 5. Vidaspa a dialectic variety of, 329 note. His residence in Parthia;

Vishtaspa—
the province revolts, and he subdues it, 585-7.

Vispanzatish: A town in Parthia, 586.

Vivána, satrap of Arakhotia : Invaded from Persis, 636. His successes, 638. Their date, 641-644.

Vritra : The foe of the god Indra, 397 note.

WALLS *of Jerusalem* restored by Artaxerxes at the time of Ezra's mission ; broken down apparently in the war between Megabyzus satrap of Syria and the king's forces under the satrap of Babylonia ; restored under the king's commission, by Nehemiah, 150. *Of Babylon*, height and length of, 652-668 ; also *Additions and Corrections* on p. 668.

Water : Magian worship of running, 156, 157. How defiled, 156 note, 157.

Week, *Five-day*, 34 note. A natural rather than (as the seven-day week) an arbitrary division of time, 342 note. Used by the Magi, 455.

— *Seven-day :* A divine institution, 342.

Weeks, *Of years*, 10 + 3 + 8 + 70 + 82 + 180 from 1 Tisri B.C. 606 to last day of Elul A.D. 1866, 708.

Weeks, *Seventy*, of years, 150, 151 note (as corrected in *Additions and Corrections*), 708 note.

Wives, Chief, and concubines, of Persian monarchs, 130. Zoroastrian precepts concerning, 539-40, and note.

Winds : Adored by the Persians, 368 ; as also (under the name of Maruts) by the Vaidik Hindus, 384. Connection of, with the sacred fire (Agni), *ibid.*

Women : Their freedom among the old Persians conjectured, 538 note. Accompanied their husbands to feasts, *ibid.* Manu's maxims concerning, 540 note See *Wives*.

Works, of Superhuman Power and Words of Superhuman Knowledge essential to communications of God's, with men, 158 note.

World : Dominion of the, claimed formerly by the Persian kings, as now, and of old, by the Emperor of China, 209-10.

Writs, or Letters Royal: Their form, 555 note.

XANTHUS: *Town* in Lycia, so called by Greeks, but Arna or Arina by the natives, 155 note. *River* of Lycia which gave the Greek name to the town upon it, 155 note. Its ancient name *Sirbis*, whether rightly or not, supposed to signify Xanthus (*i.e. yellow*) in the language of the Solymi or Milyes, 155, 156 note.

Xenophon: His use of the term "Susa and Agbatana," 20, 21, 253. His account of Cyaxares son of Astyages, historical, 32. His Cyropædia, how far historical, 254, 256. Correctly or incorrectly ascribes burnt-offerings (in the worship of Auramazdâ, Mithra, and others) to Cyrus and succeeding Akhæmenian kings, 352 note.

Xerxes, *the name*, in Persian *Khshayarsha*, 77. Found by Gesenius in *Ahasuerus*, 3 note, and substituted for Ahasuerus by the old Greek translator of Daniel, 4. Compared by Gesenius with the modern *Shêr-Shah*, "Lion-King," 77 note. His inscriptions near Hamadan at Persepolis, and at Van, 12 note. Defeated at Salamis, 18. Not Esther's husband, 95, 96, 97, 135. His adulterous amours, 98. His first seven regnal years according to Herodotus, 107 *et seq*. Seems already arrived in Egypt on the 9th January B.C. 484, p. 110 note. Subdued the revolt there in the second year of his reign, 102, 108. His invasion of Europe in his sixth year and spring of B.C. 480, pp. 109-120. Order of the march of his own division out of Sardis, 378-80. Leaving Mardonius to continue the war, retires from Athens to Sardis, autumn B.C. 480, p. 121. After nearly a year's stay at Sardis, sets off on his return thence about September B.C. 479, p. 122. Seems to have wintered at Babylon, *ibid*. Spent at Sardis the Tebeth of his seventh regnal year according to the Egyptian reckoning, *ibid*. Plundered Bel-Merodakh's temple at Babylon of a

Xerxes—
golden image, not of a god, but of a man, 134, 686. Murdered in his bed, 141, 142. At the Hellespont, 112, 155 note. At Doriskus, 112-119. At the Strymon, 156. At Acanthus on the Athos Canal, 159. Loses his father's European dominions, 174. His succession to Darius disputed by one, if not two, of his half-brothers, 190-194. Said to have broken into the tomb of Belus at Babylon, 692. Falsely reported, in the time of Alexander the Great, to have demolished the tomb or temple tower of Belus, 688, 692 notes.

YAKSHAS and Rakshasas of Sanskrit books: Whether dwellers on Yakhsharta, the Jaxartes of later writers, and the Arakhsha of Herodotus, 395 note.

Yavan: Ionians, *i.e.* Hellénes or Greeks, 41, 79, 258 note. Son of Japhet, 79 note. The Yavanu or Yuna, apparently conquered by Darius son of Hystaspes beyond the Bosporus, 82-83 note. The *Yunâ takabarâ* seem to include the Macedonians, 267 note.

Year, *Babylonian*, beginning with the 8th Assyrian and Mosaic month, that is, with the second month of the old Hebrew year, 434. Seems to have been identical with one introduced into Israel by Jeroboam, *ibid*. The regnal year used by Nehemiah, 435, and by Herodotus in respect of Cambyses and Darius son of Hystaspes, *ibid*. *The Assyrian*, 427. The regnal year used in the book Esther, 435. *The Magian* probably that used at Susa, 448-9. Described, 450. Perhaps of antediluvian origin, 454. Analogous to the Egyptian, 463 note. A month intercalated in, once in 120 years between the times of the Seleucidan Antiokhus the Great and the Sassanian Yezdegherd, 456 note, 458 note, 461-2. At one time the Egyptian month Thoth and Persian Degh-month began together, 467 note. *The Egyptian*, 451-2 note. Analogous to the Magian, 463 note. Egyptian *square year* adopted for the Roman

Year—
civil year by Julius Cæsar, 452 note. The Chinese, Passage of the Shoo-king concerning, 454-5 note.
Yezdegherd: The last of the Sassanian kings of Persia, 456 note, 459. Years of the era of, 457 note. In his reign the eighth intercalation of one month in an 120th Magian year, 461, 464. Two eras of Yezdegherd, one ordinarily recognised (which began with the month Fervardin 15½ June A.D. 632, or 447 years and 18 days of Yezdegherd before the era of Jelaleddin), 457 note; the other era now discernible (which seems to have begun with the month Fervardin A.D. 633. See 468-9 note). The king did not take his seat on the throne till after November A.D. 634, ibid.
Yezedees: Why they worship the Evil One and neglect Him who is Good, who is from the Light, 385.
Yu, or Hu: Name of the Assyrian sky-god; an element in the name of a king; the grandson of the one who received presents from Jehu king of Israel, 184 note.
Yuná: Persian form of the word Iones, or Ionians. See Yavan.
Yutiya, or Ihutiyas: A district in Persis, 598.

ZAGROS, MOUNT, 488.
Zaranga, Sarranka, Zaraka, province, 417, 418, 571. Also called Drangæ, 617 note. Drangéné, 618 note. See, too, 641 note, 643 note.
Zariaspa: Capital of Baktria, 643 note.
Zazána: By Babylon, on the Euphrates, 477.
Zechariah the prophet, 496, etc.
Zedekiah of Judah, 87.
Zela in Pontus: A temple here of Anaitis, Omanes, and Anadatus, 64 note, 371 note.

Zeratusht, or Zerdusht, son of Esfintaman, i.e. Zoroaster, 3 note, 58 note, 268 note.
Zerubbabel lays the foundation of the house of God, 244-5. Rejects the proffered co-operation of the Samaritans, 245. Resumes the building in the reign of Darius, 498. See Sheshbazzar and Zorobabel.
Zeus: A deity of theirs found by the Greeks in the Perso-Median Auramazda, 337 note, 351-2 note, 379. Also variously in Osiris, Amún, and Noum or Kneph of Egyptian mythology, 119, 203 note. Compare 317-18 note. Identified also with the Khaldæan Belus the Creator, 372 note. Father of Perseus by Danae, 234 note. Threw down Hephæstus into Lemnos, 323.
Ziggarrat, or Tower, of Khaldæan Temples, 652 note.
Zirbanit wife of Bel Merodakh, or the Zeus Belus of Babylon, 363 note.
Zodiac, Chinese fortnightly divisions of the, 509 note.
Zopyrus I. son of Megabyzus I., 608 note. Helped to recover Babylon, whereof afterwards he was made Darius's satrap, 669-696.
Zopyrus II. son of Megabyzus II., and nephew of the first Artaxerxes, 153, 154, 609 note, 673.
Zoroaster, 3 note. Whether the Baktrian antagonist of Ninus was or was not so named by Ktesias, 395 note.
Zorobabel, or Zerubbabel, the Babylonian name of a prince of the captive Jews in Babylon, whose official name was Sheshbazzar, 180 note. Along with Joshua the priest, renews the out-door services of God at Jerusalem, 243. See Sheshbazzar, Zerubbabel.
Zuza in Armenia, 490. A royal or viceregal residence there, 490-91 note.

T H E   E N D.